Complete Book of the American Musical Theater

COMPLETE BOOK OF THE
American Musical Theater
BY DAVID EWEN

Theater lovers and music fanciers will revel in this magnificent treasury of the American musical stage — recalling enchanted moments from over 300 productions in one lavish jubilee album.

David Ewen opens this superb guide with an exciting introduction, hitting the highlights of the changing musical theater in America. Brilliantly noted are nineteenth-century satirical burlesques...the rowdy, uninhibited horseplay of such revues as *Hellzapoppin'*... brash, breezy extravaganzas, and comic operas ...and finally the dramatic, subtle, and sophisticated works of Leonard Bernstein, Rodgers and Hammerstein, Loewe and Lerner.

From 1866 to the smash hits of today, this unique volume features plots, songs, and production history; priceless photographs from shows old and new; stars, composers, and librettists. Alphabetically arranged and cross-indexed for ready reference, the information is presented clearly and compactly.

The main section covers both major and minor productions by composer and lyricist, by year, by performance, and by song titles. A brief biography of each composer or lyricist (from George Abbott to Vincent Youmans) is followed by a chronological listing of his work. Complete details of each production are given, including opening date and number of performances, names of producer, director, choreographer, cast, as well as synopses of plots, names of leading songs, performers, skits, and—where significant —quotes from reviews.

Valuable supplementary sections furnish chronological listings of musical productions and even lesser productions by composers not discussed in the main section. Here, too, is an alphabetical listing of the outstanding songs of the American musical theater, the productions in which they were introduced, and the stars who introduced them.

Spanning over 300 musical comedies and musical plays, the COMPLETE BOOK OF THE AMERICAN MUSICAL THEATER blends a wealth of information with nostalgic reminiscence and sets a new landmark in the literature of the American stage.

COMPLETE BOOK OF THE

AMERICAN MUSICAL THEATER

BY DAVID EWEN

A GUIDE TO MORE THAN 300 PRODUCTIONS

OF THE AMERICAN MUSICAL THEATER

FROM *THE BLACK CROOK* (1866) TO THE PRESENT,

WITH PLOT, PRODUCTION HISTORY, STARS,

SONGS, COMPOSERS, LIBRETTISTS, AND LYRICISTS

illustrated with photographs

HENRY HOLT AND COMPANY, NEW YORK

TO DICK RODGERS—

whose forty years in the American musical

theater is such a salient part of its

history

PREFACE

This is the first reference book to gather together in one volume all the information a theatergoer might wish to have about the American musical theater, past and present: plots, production histories, stars, songs, composers, and writers. Here will be found a discussion of over 300 American musical productions by more than 100 composers. All the veins of the American musical theater have been tapped: extravaganzas, spectacles, and burlesques; operettas and comic operas; revues, both the lavish kind and the intimate variety; musical comedies and musical plays. Material about musicals not only of a bygone era but even of the recent past is not readily accessible, except to those ready to wade laboriously through clipping files in libraries. This volume hopes to fill this hiatus in the literature on the American stage by providing material succinctly and compactly.

The book has a dual purpose: to satisfy curiosity in regard to productions of the past about which much still is said but little remembered, and to revive in theatergoers memories of enchanted evenings.

In the main body of the book will be found the biographies of forty-seven leading stage composers—presented alphabetically from Richard Adler to Vincent Youmans, and embracing all the giant musical figures of the American theater. Each biography is followed by a chronological guide to that composer's most significant and representative musicals. (In Appendix I, more than fifty additional musical productions by other composers are discussed; an alphabetical listing of these composers appears at the head of the appendix.)

Biographies of the most important librettists and lyricists of the American theater also will be found in the main body of the book, some appearing as individual sketches in proper alphabetical sequence—for example, George Abbott, Guy Bolton, Oscar Hammerstein II, or P. G. Wodehouse. Cross-references at the conclusion of each biography indicate the composers and the productions with which these writers have been associated.

In cases where a librettist or lyricist is almost completely identified with a single composer, his biography is included with that of the composer with whom he has worked. Lorenz Hart, for instance, is discussed with Richard Rodgers; Alan Jay Lerner with Frederick Loewe; Bert Kalmar with Harry Ruby; Ira Gershwin with his brother George.

In the selection of more than 300 musicals for analysis either in the main body of the book or in Appendix I, the author was guided by the following considerations:

1. Only the work of American composers is considered. However, the term "American" is used in its broadest possible connotation: anyone born in this country; anyone naturalized as a citizen; and anyone who has established permanent residence here and has used Broadway, rather than a foreign theater, as the point of origin of his work. Significant foreign musicals, imported to the Broadway stage, are considered only if an American composer has served as a collaborator or if the music of an American composer has been interpolated into the score. All other foreign importations, however significant—plays such as *Floradora* or the more recent *The Girl Friend*, the comic operas of Gilbert and Sullivan, or the opéras bouffes of Offenbach—must be ignored.

2. Since this volume is devoted to the popular musical theater, opera —even the operas of Gian-Carlo Menotti, many of which originated in the Broadway theater rather than the opera house—cannot come within its scope. A few exceptions, however, have to be made. Marc Blitzstein's *The Cradle Will Rock* and *Regina* are sometimes designated as operas; but they are discussed in this book because, in the opinion of this author, they are essentially Broadway musical plays in the same way that Leonard Bernstein's *West Side Story* or Frank Loesser's *The Most Happy Fella* are musical plays. George Gershwin's *Porgy and Bess* is also included, not only because all his life Gershwin belonged to the popular musical theater, but also because *Porgy and Bess* has roots so deeply embedded in that theater that its omission from this book would have created a serious gap.

3. All major box-office successes have been included, a major box-office

success being any production with a consecutive run of more than 500 performances.

For the sake of clarification, it should, however, be pointed out that the number of consecutive performances enjoyed by any single production is not always an accurate barometer of its success. A quarter of a century ago, when production costs were low and competition keen, a run of two hundred or so performances often represented a solid hit; today, such a run indicates a dismal failure. Going even further back in time, a play may have had an initial run of only fifty or so performances on Broadway; but in subsequent returns through the years it may have lived to achieve as many as 1000 performances.

4. This book, however, does not completely ignore the failures. From time to time there have appeared on Broadway musicals that for one reason or another were failures when first given and were rarely, if ever, revived. Yet some of these plays have such historic or dramatic or musical interest that they are still remembered and spoken of. Since a knowledgeable theatergoer might reasonably wish to refer to such plays, they have been included. In this category belong Vincent Youmans' *Rainbow*, Frederick Loewe's *Paint Your Wagon*, Kurt Weill's *Johnny Johnson*, Marc Blitzstein's *Regina*, and Leonard Bernstein's *Candide*, among others.

As has already been mentioned, Appendix I discusses significant musical productions by composers other than those considered in the main body of the book.

Appendix II presents a chronological table of all musicals discussed in the book—a bird's-eye view of our changing musical theater through the years.

Appendix III lists some of the outstanding songs of our musical theater.

For permission to quote a few paragraphs from their publications, the author wishes to express his indebtedness to Simon and Schuster and Theatre Arts Books. These publications are: *Bring on the Girls*, by Guy Bolton and P. G. Wodehouse, and *The Jerome Kern Song Book*, edited by Oscar Hammerstein II (both published by Simon and Schuster); and *Musical Comedy in America* by Cecil Smith. The quotation from Cecil Smith's *Musical Comedy in America*, copyright 1950 by Cecil Smith, is reprinted by permission of Theatre Arts Books, publishers of the volume.

The author also wishes to acknowledge gratefully the cooperation of the Drama Room of the New York Public Library which placed all its facilities—including its imposing clipping files—at his disposal.

D. E.

CONTENTS

Preface *vii*

Introduction: Our Changing Musical Theater *xxi*

The American Musical Theater

Appendixes

ILLUSTRATIONS

Dennis King and Mary Ellis sing the title song in *Rose Marie* (1924)

Florrie Millership, Janet Velie, James Marlow, and Georgia Caine in *Mary* (1920)

Joseph Cawthorn, Donald Brian, and Julia Sanderson in Jerome Kern's first Broadway success, *The Girl From Utah* (1914)

Ernest Truex and Alice Dovey in the "Princess Theatre Show," *Very Good, Eddie* (1915)

Dorothy Walters, Eva Puck, and Gladys Miller in *Irene* (1919)

Philip Loeb, Sterling Holloway, and Romney Brent as the Three Musketeers in the *Garrick Gaieties* (1925)

William Gaxton as *A Connecticut Yankee* in King Arthur's Court (1927)

Charles Winninger, Howard Marsh, Norma Terris, and Edna May Oliver in a scene from *Show Boat* (1927)

THE FOLLOWING ILLUSTRATIONS FACE PAGE   *228*

Eddie Cantor makes *Whoopee* (1928)

Victor Moore as Vice-President Throttlebottom and William Gaxton as President Wintergreen in the first musical to win the Pulitzer Prize, *Of Thee I Sing* (1931)

Ethel Waters starts a "Heat Wave" in *As Thousands Cheer* (1933)

Fred and Adele Astaire in *The Band Wagon* (1931), their last appearance as a team

Fred Allen in his first Broadway success, *The Little Show* (1929)

There's *Music in the Air* in the little Bavarian town of Edendorff (1932)

Monty Woolley and Ray Bolger in *On Your Toes* (1936)

Mitzi Green and two young men in *Babes in Arms* (1937)

Gene Kelly is "Bewitched, Bothered, and Bewildered" by Vivienne Segal in *Pal Joey* (1940)

Fay Templeton, Tamara, Bob Hope, and George Murphy in *Roberta* (1933)

Todd Duncan and Ann Brown in *Porgy and Bess* (1935)

Todd Duncan, Ethel Waters, and Rex Ingram in *Cabin in the Sky* (1940)

Luther Saxon and Muriel Smith in *Carmen Jones* (1943)

Oklahoma! (1943)

INTRODUCTION

OUR CHANGING MUSICAL THEATER

Since *The Black Crook* (1866) was the first American musical production in which there could be detected some of the ritual that the American musical theater would subsequently pursue, it is often singled out as our first musical comedy. But musical productions of other varieties had existed in this country long before *The Black Crook*. What is generally conceded to be the first musical performance on our stage took place during the Colonial period: *Flora*, a ballad opera, given in a courtroom in Charleston, South Carolina, on February 8, 1735. The English ballad opera subsequently became almost as popular in the Colonies as it was in the mother country. Through its interpolation of popular songs (to which new lyrics were adapted) within the context of a spoken play, the ballad opera was the first suggestion, however faint, of musical comedy.

Other kinds of musical-stage performances besides the ballad opera became popular in this country after the Revolution. Early in the 1800's a native theatrical product, designated as "burlesque," sprang to popularity. The burlesque of this period should not be confused with that of a later era. Its emphasis in the early 1800's was not on sex but on parody and caricature. The first such successful performance came in 1828 with a burlesque on *Hamlet* by John Poole. After that, burlesques of other famous plays, and of performers, became standard operating procedure on the New York stage. Perhaps the best of these was *La Mosquita* (1838), in which William Mitchell satirized the celebrated Viennese dancer, Fanny Elssler.

Burlesque left its mark on the American stage for years to come. Travesties like *Evangeline* (1874) and *Adonis* (1884) were burlesques in the style and format crystallized a half-century earlier. The extravaganzas of Weber and Fields, the burlesques of Harrigan and Hart, and outstanding productions like Charley Hoyt's *A Trip to Chinatown* (1891) were all legitimate offspring of early burlesque. Even in a much later era the influence of caricature could be detected: in the rowdy and uninhibited horseplay of Olsen and Johnson in their revues *Hellzapoppin'* and *Sons O' Fun* in 1938 and 1940; and in the more subtle take-offs on current plays and performers found both in lush and intimate revues after 1910.[1]

Burlesque could also be found in the minstrel show, which blossomed on the American stage just before the Civil War to become another significant genre of our musical theater. The minstrel show, as finally crystallized by Ed Christy, was in a three-part format, the last being a burlesque on all previous activity. The first part of the traditional minstrel show was the olio, made up of variety entertainment; the second was a fantasia, or free-for-all, in which individual performers were featured in their specialties. The revue of a later era generally was a partial development and outgrowth of the first two sections of the minstrel show. The revue also profited from styles, techniques, and formats devised and perfected in the variety show, or vaudeville, which displaced the minstrel show in public favor in the latter part of the nineteenth century.

Some of the elements of ballad opera, burlesque, and the minstrel show were subsequently absorbed by the later-day musical theater. But any resemblance between these early stage plays and musical productions of a later period is, at best, remote. Such resemblance becomes somewhat less remote when we begin to consider the extravaganza, which flourished after the end of the Civil War.

A favorable climate for public acceptance of the extravaganza had been created by the so-called pantomime, which enjoyed a vogue on the New York stage several years before the extravaganza. Usually deriving its plots and characters from fairy tales or *Mother Goose*, the pantomime exploited not only song, dance, and comedy but also spectacular stage effects. The heyday of the pantomime came with such productions as *Humpty Dumpty*, which starred the foremost pantomimist of his day, George L. Fox.[2]

---

[1] For a discussion of *Evangeline*, see Appendix I—1874; *Adonis*, Appendix I—1884; Weber and Fields, John Stromberg; Harrigan and Hart, David Braham; *A Trip to Chinatown*, Appendix I—1891; *Hellzapoppin'* and *Sons O' Fun*, Sammy Fain.
[2] See Appendix I—1868.

It is but a short step from the pantomime to the extravaganza. The term "extravaganza" makes its first appearance in the American theater with *Novelty, with the Laying of the Atlantic Cable,* produced in New York in 1857 by the Ronzani troupe, a European ballet company. *Novelty* was not a success, but the extravaganza was here to stay. It was the foundation upon which the structure of our musical theater was to be erected.

The Black Crook was not only the most successful of these extravaganzas but also the most successful musical production of any genre seen in this country up to 1866. Its significance, however, rests not merely on its box-office appeal but more specifically on the fact that it was the first musical in America to indicate some of the procedures of later stage productions. In its strong emphasis on chorus girls in pink tights or diaphanous costumes, in its concern for stunning stage effects and spectacle, in its dedication to large dance sequences, *The Black Crook* created a tradition that such later showmen as Florenz Ziegfeld would carry on, that was to prosper for about a decade at the Winter Garden in plays starring Al Jolson and for about twenty years at the Hippodrome Theatre, and that was suddenly to crop up again in the middle 1930's in *Jumbo*.[3]

If extravaganza still is not musical comedy, the latter is not far off. In 1879 Nate Salsbury presented a "burlesque-extravaganza," *The Brook,* which—through the plot device of a picnic—made a first tentative effort to integrate text, comedy, song, and dance.[4] Primitive and naïve though it was, *The Brook* is so much in the over-all pattern of later musical comedies that it comes as no surprise to learn that the term "musical comedy" is used for the first time in conjunction with this play—a description by its producer.

A powerful influence was now exerted on the American musical theater: European operettas, comic operas, and opéras bouffes dominated the American stage in the 1880's and 1890's. America became enchanted with the glamour world of make-believe and the gay spirit evoked by the theater of Offenbach, Suppé, Johann Strauss II, and, most of all, by Gilbert and Sullivan. *Pinafore,* particularly, was a rage. Introduced to America at the Boston Museum on November 15, 1878, it achieved a triumph equaled by few productions of that era. In one season ninety different companies presented *Pinafore* throughout the country—five different companies running simultaneously in New York alone. There were perform-

[3] For a discussion of *The Black Crook,* see Appendix I—1866; for the Winter Garden extravaganzas starring Al Jolson, Sigmund Romberg; for Hippodrome extravaganzas, Manuel Klein; for *Jumbo,* Richard Rodgers—I. Rodgers and Hart.
[4] See Appendix I—1879.

ances by children's groups, colored groups, and religious groups. There were numerous parodies. Its catch phrases ("What, never? No, never!" and, "For he himself has said it") entered the nation's speech. A success of such proportions affected the theater of the day profoundly, and in more ways than one.

Through *Pinafore,* the musical theater acquired a large, new clientele —women and children. It must be remembered that before *Pinafore,* the stage was looked upon with suspicion by the respectable American family, glorifying as it often did females in various stages of deshabille. *The Black Crook,* for example, was violently denounced in press and pulpit as devil's brew. Consequently, women and children rarely went to the theater—that is, not until *Pinafore* proved that a stage presentation could be wholesome and refined entertainment.

Besides winning for the theater a large and formerly untapped reservoir of theatergoers, *Pinafore* was largely responsible for encouraging American librettists and composers to emulate Gilbert and Sullivan. Two of the earliest American comic operas were obvious and undisguised imitations of *The Mikado:* Willard Spencer's *The Little Tycoon*[5] and Reginald de Koven's *The Begum.*

The Little Tycoon, with its 500 performances in Philadelphia before appearing in New York, had the longest run of any American stage production up to that time. This success was decisive proof that an American-made operetta could prove as popular with audiences as a foreign importation. The inevitable result was that other American composers and writers were stirred to emulation. Thus was ushered in a golden age of American comic operas and operettas, first with Reginald de Koven's *Robin Hood,* and after that with the beloved operettas of Victor Herbert, the first great composer for the American stage. Up until about 1930 the American operetta was in its glory, and with such varied composers as Gustav Luders, Ludwig Englander, Gustave Kerker, Karl Hoschna, Rudolf Friml, and Sigmund Romberg. The era of operetta ended with Romberg; but by then the operetta had succeeded in establishing in the American theater a single package labeled "entertainment," coordinating song, dance, comedy, spectacle, burlesque, and large production numbers.

The problem was now to endow such entertainment with contemporary interest and an American identity. Most of the American-written operettas and comic operas were patterned after European models and had a decided European personality. Such a contemporary immediacy and Amer-

[5] See Appendix I—1887.

ican identity were first realized by George M. Cohan in the early 1900's, with brash, breezy, energetic musicals like *Little Johnny Jones, George Washington, Jr.,* and *Forty-five Minutes from Broadway.* Here the characterization, dialogue, situations, songs, and frequently locale were American to the very core; so were the tempo, spirit, drive, and raciness with which each play was imbued. This was something new and vital for the American stage—something soon also to be found in the work of other composers, notably A. Baldwin Sloane in *Hen Pecks* and *Summer Widowers* and Irving Berlin in *Watch Your Step.* This, at last, was American musical comedy, with some of the clichés, formulas, and stereotypes to which it would henceforth cling.

While American musical comedy was finally coming into existence, another important branch of the musical theater was beginning to flower. It was the revue. The revue, as we have already suggested briefly, was merely an extension of the fantasia section of the minstrel show (in which individual performers did their pet routines) and of the variety show, or vaudeville, entertainment that was prospering in the 1880's in show places like the Tony Pastor Music Hall. To the varied song-and-dance, comedy, and novelty features of minstrel show and vaudeville were added the stage embellishments of the extravaganza (spectacular sets and costumes, stunning stage effects, attractive females in provocative dress and poses, impressive production numbers) and the main attractions of old-time burlesque (satire, travesty, horseplay).

The revue was a conception of George W. Lederer, who rented the Casino Theatre in 1894 to present his *Passing Show.* Its success was so immediate and substantial that as early as 1895 similar revues began to sprout on the New York stage. Then in 1907 Florenz Ziegfeld produced the first of his *Follies;* in 1912 J. J. Shubert, the first of his *Passing Shows* (not to be confused with the 1894 *Passing Show* presented by Lederer); in 1919 George White, the first of his *Scandals;* in 1921 Irving Berlin, the first of his *Music Box Revues.* The lush revue was now in its heyday. It passed that heyday in the late 1940's, then seemed to lose caste completely, probably a victim of television, now providing similarly opulent entertainment on a giant scale.[6]

[6] For a discussion of *The Passing Show of 1894,* see Ludwig Englander; later *Passing Shows* produced by the Shuberts, see Louis A. Hirsch, Sigmund Romberg, and Jean Schwartz; *The Ziegfeld Follies,* see Appendix I—1907, and Irving Berlin, Louis Hirsch, and Raymond Hubbell; George White's *Scandals,* see De Sylva, Brown, and Henderson, also George Gershwin, and Richard Whiting; *The Music Box Revue,* see Irving Berlin.

With the passage of time and the accumulation of experience, production techniques grew more ambitious, stage techniques slicker, and techniques in writing music, lyrics, and dialogue more subtle and sophisticated. The revue and the musical comedy prospered in the 1920's and 1930's as more and more it began to tap the talent of creative and imaginative composers, lyricists, librettists, stage directors, scenic and costume designers, and dance directors.

But, in most instances, the revue and the musical comedy of this period adhered to a set pattern and time-tried methods. In the revue one producer tried to outdo another in extravagance of sets and costumes, complexity of stage effects, and in the display of female pulchritude, while skits, sketches, blackouts, songs, dances, and production numbers followed a consistent program. In musical comedy, too, tradition was slavishly adhered to. Plot, characters, and setting were all just a convenient hook on which to hang song, dance, and comedy. The relevancy of such routines within the text was not important; what was important was the interest of these individual routines.

Yet such arbitrary and undeviating procedures were able to yield rich results in productions filled with the magic of wonderful songs, dances, comedy, and the performances of lustrous stars—musicals like Jerome Kern's *Sally, Good News* of De Sylva, Brown, and Henderson, Cole Porter's *Anything Goes,* George Gershwin's *Oh Kay!,* or *A Connecticut Yankee* of Rodgers and Hart. And that these rigid formulas and patterns can still yield inexhaustible riches in terms of stage entertainment is proved by such more recent productions as Irving Berlin's *Annie Get Your Gun,* Cole Porter's *Kiss Me, Kate,* Frank Loesser's *Guys and Dolls,* Leonard Bernstein's *Wonderful Town,* and *The Pajama Game* by Richard Adler and Jerry Ross.

But from time to time—and increasingly so in recent years—there have been bold attempts to revolutionize the techniques and concepts of the musical theater. One such effort took place as early as the mid-1910's, when the so-called "Princess Theatre Shows" of Kern-Bolton-Wodehouse represented a reaction against the plush, elaborately designed comedies and operettas then in vogue. These little musicals helped to introduce a new note of intimacy, economy, and informality, a welcome change from the ostentation and display then current on the stage.

A reaction of a similar kind took place with the revue in the 1920's. In 1922 a modest affair called the *Grand Street Follies* was put on in downtown New York. Equipped with more talent and imagination than finances, these *Follies* had to emphasize wit, sophistication, satire, and freshness of ideas over the star system and elaborate staging. Simplicity and a lack of pretension entered the revue. Thus the "intimate" revue came into being. It flourished within the next two decades or so with productions such as *The Garrick Gaieties, The Little Shows, Pins and Needles,* and their numerous contemporaries, successors, and imitators.[7]

An even more radical departure from accepted values in the musical theater came with several writers making a conscious effort to bring to musical comedy originality of subject matter, authenticity of characterization and background, dramatic truth, and freshness of viewpoint. This was a studied effort to make of musical comedy an integrated artistic creation. These writers and composers searched for a more intimate relationship between all the elements of the musical theater. Their aim was to have each song, dance sequence, comedy routine, and production number rise naturally, perhaps inevitably, from the context of the play. Among those who progressed along these lines most boldly were Rodgers and Hart in plays such as *On Your Toes* and *Pal Joey,* Jerome Kern with *Showboat, Music in the Air,* and *The Cat and the Fiddle,* Gershwin's *Of Thee I Sing,* and Vincent Youmans' *Rainbow.*

And so, slowly, the musical play came into existence—with Rodgers and Hammerstein, Kurt Weill, and productions such as Frank Loesser's *The Most Happy Fella,* Leonard Bernstein's *West Side Story,* and *My Fair Lady* by Frederick Loewe and Alan Jay Lerner. Dramatic text, musical score, and ballet now acquired new scope and breadth and achieved a singleness of thought and spirit heretofore found only in opera and music drama. Sometimes realism, profound human values—even tragedy—were permitted to intrude into a world previously dedicated only to escapism; sometimes American folklore was accentuated.

In her autobiography Mary Garden has remarked that in her opinion native American opera of the future will probably resemble *South Pacific* and *The King and I.* Perhaps these two plays of Rodgers and Hammerstein or Kurt Weill's *Lost in the Stars* or Bernstein's *West Side Story* are not American operas in the strict sense of the term. But there can be no question that they are vital, dynamic, living theater.

The American musical has traveled a long way since *The Black Crook,* and tortuous has been the road. Today, as yesterday, its goal is entertainment. But today it is also sometimes deeply moving, unforgettable art.

[7] For a discussion of *The Grand Street Follies,* see Appendix I—1922; *The Garrick Gaieties,* Richard Rodgers—I. Rodgers and Hart; *The Little Shows,* Arthur Schwartz; *Pins and Needles,* Harold Rome.

THE AMERICAN
MUSICAL THEATER

GEORGE ABBOTT, librettist

In addition to his fruitful career as director of stage comedy, George Abbott has also distinguished himself as a librettist for musical comedies. His influence in both fields—as stage director and musical-comedy writer —has been far-reaching; many of the advanced techniques of the present-day musical stage owe their development to him. As Brooks Atkinson wrote in the New York *Times* (May 26, 1957):

> Mr. Abbott is the recognized panjandrum of the Broadway musical carnival. Give him exuberant material in the vernacular and he can put together a rousing professional entertainment. He can translate the exuberance into comedy, dancing, uproar, sentiment and revelry and exuberate the audience accordingly.

George Abbott was born in Forestville, New York, on June 25, 1889. He was educated in New York at the Kearney Military Academy and Hamburg High School; at the University of Rochester, from which he received a Bachelor of Arts degree in 1911; and at Harvard University, where in 1912 he attended the "47 Workshop," Professor George Pierce Baker's famous school of the drama.

His bow on the Broadway stage took place in 1913 when he appeared as an actor in *A Misleading Lady*. And it was as an actor that he first achieved success: in George S. Kaufman's *Dulcy* (1921), the 1923 Pulitzer

Prize drama by Hatcher Hughes, *Hell-Bent for Heaven,* and John Howard Lawson's social-conscious expressionistic play, *Processional* (1925). Meanwhile, in 1919, he branched out into stage direction, soon bringing to stage farces an infallible sense of timing—that breathless pace and exciting tempo which has since become his personal trade-mark. Among his finer productions were *Chicago* (1926), *Twentieth Century* (1932), *Boy Meets Girl* (1935), and *Room Service* and *Brother Rat* (1936). This same kind of excitement, energy, and seemingly tireless motion he brought into plays of his own writing, sometimes with the collaborative assistance of other playwrights. Some of these are among the best stage comedies of the 1920's and 1930's: *Broadway,* written with Philip Dunning; *Love 'Em and Leave 'Em,* with John V. A. Weaver (1926); and *Three Men on a Horse,* with John Cecil Holm (1935).

He made his entrance into the musical theater only after his reputation as one of the most skillful and astute technicians of stage comedy had been fully established. In 1935 Rodgers and Hart planned a musical about ballets and ballet dancers, *On Your Toes.* Their own script needed tightening and they called on Abbott for help. "George straightened out the story line and kept it straight through the turmoil and upheaval of rehearsals and out-of-town tryouts," Rodgers recalls. Abbott's name appeared in the credits (with those of Rodgers and Hart) as a collaborator on the book of *On Your Toes.*

But actually, that was not Abbott's first association with musical comedy. When Rodgers and Hart first talked with him about working on *On Your Toes,* they also suggested he get the "feel" of musical comedy by working with them on *Jumbo,* an extravaganza with Rodgers and Hart music which Billy Rose was planning for the Hippodrome. Abbott helped direct the production, which opened five months before *On Your Toes.*

After that, Abbott's association with Rodgers and Hart continued through several more musicals; in one instance he also worked with Rodgers and Hammerstein. But beyond his activity with Rodgers, Abbott has also been connected with other outstandingly successful musical productions.

See: RICHARD ADLER and JERRY ROSS (*Pajama Game, Damn Yankees*); LEONARD BERNSTEIN (*On The Town, Wonderful Town*); FRANK LOESSER (*Where's Charley?*); RODGERS and HART (*On Your Toes, The Boys from Syracuse*); RODGERS and HAMMERSTEIN (*Me and Juliet*); ARTHUR SCHWARTZ (*A Tree Grows in Brooklyn*); JULE STYNE (*High Button Shoes*); Appendix I (1941— *Best Foot Forward,* 1945—*Billion Dollar Baby,* 1957—*New Girl in Town*).

HAROLD ADAMSON, lyricist. *See* JIMMY McHUGH

RICHARD ADLER and JERRY ROSS, lyricists-composers

Richard Adler was born in New York City on August 23, 1923, the only son of the well-known pianist and teacher, Clarence Adler. Richard attended Columbia Grammar School in New York City and was graduated from the University of North Carolina, where he had studied play-writing with Paul Green. For three years during World War II he served with the Navy in the Pacific.

Though he had no musical education, could neither read music nor play the piano by ear, Adler started writing songs while holding down various jobs. One day in June, 1950, he was introduced to another young man who, like himself, wrote songs and was incapable of getting them marketed, Jerry (Jerold) Ross. They compared experiences, matched ambitions, and decided to work together.

Jerry Ross was born in New York City on March 9, 1926. As a boy he combined attendance in the city public schools with appearances in singing roles in Yiddish stage productions and a Yiddish motion picture. While attending high school he wrote his first song. He kept up his song-writing activity during a four-year academic course at New York University, where he took courses in music. After graduation he wrote songs for productions on the so-called "Borsch Circuit" in the Catskill Mountains. There he met Eddie Fisher who, in turn, introduced him to several publishers, none of whom showed any interest in Ross' songs. Nevertheless, Ross kept on composing while supporting himself with odd jobs. In 1950 he met Richard Adler and they became a team.

Theirs was a unique collaboration, since they worked together on both words and music. As they told an interviewer:

> It's impossible to say who does what and when. We've got rules. If I come in with what I think is a beautiful idea and he says, 'I don't like it,' I can scream, I can rave, but it's out. It obviates arguments. There has to be unanimity in our operation.

For a while they produced material for several singers, acts, and for the radio give-away program, "Stop the Music." They finally attracted Frank Loesser, the famous popular composer who headed his own publishing firm. Loesser placed the young pair under contract. It was not long before they justified his faith by producing their first song hit, "Rags to Riches" (1953), which sold a million copies of sheet music and records and reached the top of "Hit Parade." More hits, though of lesser stature, followed: "Teasin'," "The Newspaper Song," "Now Hear This," "You're So Much a Part of Me," and "True Love Goes On and On."

Their first assignment for Broadway came with the John Murray Anderson *Almanac*, which opened on December 10, 1953, with Hermione Gingold and Billy de Wolfe. Adler and Ross contributed four songs. George Abbott now became convinced of their talent and engaged them to write the complete score for a musical comedy he was projecting, *The Pajama Game*. That musical was a triumph in 1954. So was its successor a year later, *Damn Yankees*. Two successive smashes on Broadway and five songs on "Hit Parade" made the team of Adler and Ross one of the most important to appear in Tin Pan Alley in over a decade. Tragically, this fruitful partnership came to an abrupt end in 1955 with the death of Jerry Ross of chronic bronchiectasis.

1954 THE PAJAMA GAME, a musical comedy with book by George Abbott and Richard Bissell, based on Bissell's novel, *7½¢*. Produced by Frederick Brisson, Robert E. Griffith, and Harold S. Prince at the St. James Theatre on May 13. Directed by George Abbott and Jerome Robbins. Choreography by Bob Fosse. Cast included John Raitt, Eddie Foy, Jr., Carol Haney, and Janis Paige (1063 performances).

A great deal of new, fresh talent was gathered for this musical with which the 1953-54 theatrical season in New York came to its culmination. Adler and Ross were writing their first complete musical-comedy score. Two of the producers (Griffith and Prince), the choreographer (Bob Fosse), and one of the stars (Carol Haney) were unknowns making their Broadway bows. And besides drawing so heavily on new people, *The Pajama Game* challenged Broadway tradition on other counts. It opened in May, just before the summer months, which usually spelled disaster for any production with an as-yet-unestablished popularity. And it used for its plot the labor troubles in a manufacturing plant, something musical comedy had long scrupulously avoided.

Yet *The Pajama Game* not only weathered the summer heat of 1954 but several summer heats thereafter. It became the eighth musical in Broadway history to exceed a run of over 1000 performances. "About the best-natured musical you may have ever seen," was the way William Hawkins described it, ". . . young and funny and earthy and fast." Robert Coleman called it a "royal flush and grand slam all rolled into one."

Labor-management difficulties at the Sleep-Tite Pajama Factory in a small Midwestern town create a rift between Sid Sorokin (John Raitt), superintendent, and Babe Williams (Janis Paige) of the Union Grievance Committee. The union is demanding a pay rise of seven and a half cents an hour. To force the hand of the management the union first orders a slowdown, then a strike. By simulating interest in the bookkeeper, Gladys (Carol Haney) and taking her out for the evening to Hernando's Hideaway, Sid manages to gain access to the firm's books. He discovers that for several months past the boss had been adding to his prices the pay increases so long demanded by his workers. With this information Sid is able to bring about the boss' consent to the pay raise, and to restore peace not only to the factory but also to his own love life.

The score had two substantial hits. One was the principal love song, "Hey There," first introduced by Sid Sorokin into his dictaphone machine when he discovers he loves Babe; it then becomes a delightful one-man duet when the dictaphone plays back to him the song as he makes pointed comments. The other hit was a tango, "Hernando's Hideaway," in which Gladys informs Sid of a night spot to which she wants to be taken.

Other numbers that were strong assets to the production were "7½¢" in which the Union members, headed by Babe, compute how much their raise will mean to them over a period of time; "There Once Was a Man," a duet of Sid and Babe, and "Once a Year Day," presenting the Union members in a jubilant mood during their annual picnic.

In two amusing and show-stopping dance numbers, Carol Haney proved herself a star, though a novice on the Broadway stage. She had been a dance teacher, a dancer with Jack Cole, and for five years assistant to Gene Kelly. For several years she hung around the M.G.M. studios waiting for the "break" that never came, though she did do a short dance number with Bob Fosse in the screen adaptation of Cole Porter's *Kiss Me, Kate*. Bob Fosse remembered that dance when he was preparing the choreography for *The Pajama Game* and brought Carol to Broadway.

One of her dance numbers was a take-off on a strip tease, performed during the Union picnic festivities. The other, and the triumph of the production, was "Steam Heat." Dressed as a gamin, but in derby and black tight-fitting man's suit—and flanked by two men similarly dressed— she performs a routine accompanied by hissing and other vocal sounds. Haney also appeared in a slapstick bedroom-closet episode, "Jalousy Ballet."

Eddie Foy, Jr., provided much of the comedy. He participated in one of the score's best comedy numbers, "I'll Never Be Jealous Again," following it with a delightful soft-shoe dance. He was also the central character in the show's best farcical scene, one involving a recalcitrant zipper.

Less than six months after its long run, *The Pajama Game* was revived on Broadway—at the New York City Center on May 15, 1957.

1955   DAMN YANKEES, a musical comedy with book by Douglass Wallop and
       George Abbott, based on Wallop's novel, *The Year the Yankees Lost
       the Pennant.* Presented by Frederick Brisson, Robert E. Griffith, and
       Harold S. Prince at the 46th Street Theatre on May 5. Directed by
       George Abbott. Dances and musical numbers staged by Bob Fosse. The
       cast included Stephen Douglass, Gwen Verdon, and Ray Walston (1022
       performances).

The Faust theme is here applied to a baseball story for the first time. Joe Boyd is a middle-aged baseball fan who suffers because his favorite team, the Washington Senators, never seem able to make any progress in the pennant race. When the devil, personified by Applegate (Ray Walston), proposes that Joe trade his soul for a pennant-winning team, Joe is all too willing to accept the bargain. Joe now becomes Joe Hardy (Stephen Douglass), a member of the Senators, who carries his team to a pennant. But while achieving this miracle, Joe is homesick for his wife whom he had to abandon suddenly and mysteriously. He even rents a room in her house to be near her, unrecognized because he is again a young man. To help woo his victim from the wife, Applegate calls on a beautiful witch, Lola (Gwen Verdon). Lola looks upon this luring business as just another job, until she falls in love with Joe. The pennant is won in a crucial final series with the Yankees. Joe is now able to evade the deadline set by the devil by refusing to play in the World Series, despite Applegate's entreaties. Thus he is able to save his soul, revert to his former status as a middle-aged baseball fan, and return to his wife.

Abbott's direction was one element that helped make *Damn Yankees* a winner. The raciness and excitement he always brought to a production provided this musical with a breathless pace that proceeded unhaltingly from the first to final curtain. As Maurice Zolotow wrote in *Theatre Arts:*

> When Abbott is at his best—and he is at his best in *Damn Yankees* . . .
> there is a feeling of perpetual motion created by the adroit multiplication
> of hundreds of large and small movements. Everything is fluid. Everything
> moves. When one character has to divulge a bit of information to another,
> they do it either strolling, or jumping, or running. A show like *Damn Yankees*
> has about it the fascination of a fine Byzantine mosaic. At a distance it is a
> gaudy pageant. Regarded closely, it becomes an artfully assembled design

in which many small pieces have been fitted together by a master crafts-man.

As the siren Lola, Gwen Verdon stole the limelight with a seductive number with which she strives to win Joe, "Whatever Lola Wants," the score's most popular song. She was also seen in a striking mambo, "Who's Got the Pain?" "Heart" was a secondary song hit, a number in which the manager of the Senators, played by Russ Brown, tries to instill courage into his effete team. The play opened with an amusing chorus, "Six Months Out of Every Year," the lament of baseball players and their wives on the way in which baseball life disrupts a normal domestic ex-istence.

HAROLD ARLEN, composer

Harold Arlen was born in Buffalo, New York, on February 15, 1905. His father was a synagogue cantor, his mother a gifted amateur pianist. The chants of the synagogue, and the piano, were significant in Harold's early musical development. As a boy he sang in the synagogue choir and was given formal piano instruction by his mother. (To this day when he per-forms his own songs, which he does most effectively, he brings to them the figurations and inflections of a cantorial hymn.)

His father hoped he would become a cantor; his mother wanted him to go on the concert stage. But the boy had a mind of his own. He hoped to make a place for himself in popular music. Soon after his fifteenth year he found odd jobs playing the piano in a little Buffalo night club and on lake steamers. He soon formed his own jazz ensemble, for which he sang vocal choruses and wrote all the arrangements. The latter were so good that a New York booking agent brought the ensemble in 1927 to The Silver Slipper, a New York night club.

When Arlen first entered the Broadway theater professionally, it was as pianist and arranger rather than as composer. His first job was in the orchestra pit of one of the editions of George White's *Scandals*. After that he worked as rehearsal pianist for Vincent Youmans' musical, *Great Day,* and branched out into song-writing for the first time. While playing the accompaniment for one of Youmans' songs, Arlen improvised an accom-paniment that led the choral director of the show to advise him to put it down on paper. Arlen inveigled his friend, Ted Koehler, to write some lyrics, and the number was published as "Get Happy." It was introduced in 1930 in the *9:15 Revue,* a show that ran only seven performances and is completely forgotten. But the song became popular and is still heard. George Gershwin, who saw an out-of-town tryout of the revue, came to Arlen after the performance to tell him he thought "Get Happy" one of the best production numbers he had heard.

Largely on the strength of this song Arlen found a job as composer in Tin Pan Alley, with Remick. For about three years, up to 1933, he supplied songs for shows produced at the Harlem night spot, "The Cotton Club." Among these songs were such outstanding successes as "Between the Devil and the Deep Blue Sea," "Minnie Moocher's Wedding Day," and a classic, "Stormy Weather." The last was introduced at The Cotton Club by Duke Ellington and his orchestra, and the blues singer, Ivy Anderson. These songs are probably the only successful numbers written directly for a night club.

Random numbers by Arlen appeared in the 1930 and 1932 editions of *The Earl Carroll Vanities*. Between these two years came Arlen's first complete stage score—*You Said It*, a splash-dash musical starring Lou Holtz in which a newcomer named Lyda Roberti brought a piquant Hungarian accent and a dynamic personality to several pleasing Arlen songs, including "Sweet and Hot."

In 1934 there was *Life Begins at 8:40*, with Bert Lahr and Ray Bolger, an uneventful revue for which Arlen wrote ten numbers, none outstanding. *Hooray for What?* three years later was Arlen's first Broadway success.

Meanwhile Arlen went out to Hollywood where, in a few years' time, he wrote some of the songs by which he is best known: "It's Only a Paper Moon," "Let's Fall in Love," "Blues in the Night," "That Old Black Magic," "Happiness Is Just a Thing Called Joe," "Accentuate the Positive," and "Over the Rainbow"—the last, a song now associated with Judy Garland, which she introduced in *The Wizard of Oz* and which brought Arlen an Academy Award in 1939.

Some of Arlen's best song-writing has been done in collaboration with E. Y. Harburg, lyricist. Arlen and Harburg wrote their first song, "As Long as I Live," in 1934. In the same year they worked together on the musical numbers for *Life Begins at 8:40*. After that Harburg and Arlen collaborated on *Hooray for What?* and for such motion-picture songs as "It's Only a Paper Moon," "Over the Rainbow," and "Happiness Is Just a Thing Called Joe."

When Arlen returned to Broadway in 1944, after a seven-and-a-half-year absence, it was with his foremost box-office attraction, *Bloomer Girl* (lyrics by Harburg). Since then Arlen has alternated between Broadway and Hollywood. For Broadway he wrote the score for *St. Louis Woman,* the *House of Flowers,* and *Jamaica;* for Hollywood, songs for *A Star Is Born* (Judy Garland) and *The Country Girl* (Bing Crosby), lyrics by Ira Gershwin.

1937   HOORAY FOR WHAT? a musical comedy conceived by E. Y. Harburg, with book by Howard Lindsay and Russel Crouse. Lyrics by E. Y. Harburg. Produced by the Shuberts at the Winter Garden on December 1. Production supervised by Vincente Minnelli. Book staged by Howard Lindsay. Dances by Robert Alton. Cast included Ed Wynn, Paul Haakon, June Clyde, Vivian Vance, and Jack Whiting (200 performances).

Hooray for What? was an extravaganza built around the special talent of Ed Wynn. To it Wynn brought his varied assortment of bizarre costumes and hats, his inexhaustible repertory of screwy inventions and gadgets, his lisp, and the other equipment with which he has long been identified. He appears as "Chuckles," a horticulturist who seeks a formula for a gas to destroy insects and worms. In the search he comes upon a lethal gas that can destroy human beings and which becomes an important weapon of war. The League of Nations gets hot on its trail. "Chuckles" manages to elude both international spies and the delegates of the League of Nations; he also manages to save the world from his awesome discovery. While all this is happening, "Chuckles" gives voice to pearls of political wisdom. For example: "The trouble with Europe [and one must recall the year was 1937], is that Italy'th in Ethiopia, Japan'th in China, Ruthia'th in Thapain—and nobody's home."

Of additional value to a swiftly moving production were two ballets conceived and danced by Paul Haakon. Arlen's two best numbers were "I've Gone Romantic on You" and "Moanin' in the Mornin'."

1944   BLOOMER GIRL, a musical comedy with book by Sig Herzig and Fred Saidy based on an unproduced play by Lilith and Dan James. Lyrics by E. Y. Harburg. Produced by John C. Wilson in association with Nat Goldstone at the Shubert Theatre on October 5. Staged by E. Y. Harburg. Book directed by William Schorr. Choreography by Agnes De Mille. Cast included Celeste Holm, Joan McCracken, Margaret Douglass, and David Brooks (654 performances).

Before *Bloomer Girl* came to New York, advance publicity and rumor suggested it was another *Oklahoma!* the Rodgers and Hammerstein musical play that had taken Broadway by storm a year and a half earlier. And there were several similarities: *Bloomer Girl* was an American period piece; Celeste Holm was in a starring role; its choreography was by Agnes De Mille. But here, regrettably, the similarity ended. There was no artistic pretense about *Bloomer Girl*, nor did it tap folklore. It was a big, colorful show that made no attempt to depart from the established conventions and formulas of musical comedy.

Its setting is a small New York town—Cicero—in 1861. One of its principal characters is Dolly Bloomer (Margaret Douglass), the dynamic feminist who espoused Temperance and Women's Rights, helps escaped Negroes in the Underground, and is passionate about the practicability of women wearing bloomers instead of hoop skirts. (Her real name was not Dolly but Amelia.) The issue of bloomers versus hoop skirts becomes a crisis in Dolly's personal life. Her brother-in-law, Horatio Applegate (Matt Briggs), is a wealthy manufacturer of hoop skirts who wins five of his daughters over to his way of life by having them marry salesmen from his establishment. But his sixth daughter, Evelina (Celeste Holm), is a rebel, Dolly Bloomer's ally. By helping a Negro in the Underground, Evelina antagonizes her Southern sweetheart, Jeff Calhoun (David Brooks), who owns the slave. When Dolly lands in jail for her courageous crusading, Evelina joins her there. But in some way not altogether explained on the stage, all matters are straightened out when at the play's conclusion the Secessionists fire on Fort Sumter. Jeff Calhoun frees his slave and is reconciled with Evelina.

Arlen's score included a song in the dusky style for which he was already famous, a blues, "I Got a Song," which he had originally written for a motion picture. "I Got a Song" was sung by William Huey (a former redcap) who regularly inspired an ovation with his stirring rendition. Another Arlen number to delight audiences was Evelina's amusing ditty, "T'morra, t'morra." Other significant musical numbers were the haunting lullaby, "Evelina"; the duet of Jeff and Evelina, "Right as the Rain"; the male chorus and waltz, "Pretty as a Picture"; and the rousing "When the Boys Come Home."

The main contribution by Agnes De Mille came in the closing scene. It was a Civil War ballet, the tragedy of women waiting for their lovers or husbands to return from the war. A handsome production number was built around the song, "Sunday in Cicero Falls," and another was inspired by the auction of slaves and other parts of *Uncle Tom's Cabin*.

1946   ST. LOUIS WOMAN, a musical play with book by Arna Bontemps and Countee Cullen based on Bontemps' novel, *God Sends Sunday*. Lyrics by Johnny Mercer. Produced by Edward Gross at the Martin Beck Theatre on March 30. Staged by Rouben Mamoulian. Dances directed by Charles Walters. The all-Negro cast included Pearl Bailey, Ruby Hill, Rex Ingram, and the Nicholas Brothers (113 performances).

The authors intended to create a Negro folk play, set in the colored section of St. Louis in 1898. But somewhere in the writing the artistic direction was lost. Folk drama was often side-stepped for straight musical comedy.

The story involves the turbulent love affair of jockey Little Augie (Harold Nicholas) and his St. Louis woman, Della Green (Ruby Hill). That love leads Augie to kill his rival, Brown (Rex Ingram). The dying man utters a deathbed curse that throws a jinx on all the horses Augie henceforth rides.

As long as the story line was adhered to, the text carried conviction, particularly when the situation was emotionally charged with songs like the sexy "Legalize My Name" and "A Woman's Prerogative," both torridly sung by Pearl Bailey, or the sentimental "Come Rain or Come Shine"; or the lyrical "I Had Myself a True Love." But when the play digresses into a cakewalk routine with which the first act ends—however beautifully executed in deadpan by Enid Williams—or into a big carnival scene, it is folk drama no more. "There are moments of exciting theatrical alchemy in the production," wrote Howard Barnes, "but they are random and infrequent. . . . Unfortunately it has inspired little more than colorful tableaux, which have some vitality as nicely done picture postcards."

Apparently aware of the limitations of this production—and of its inherent strength—Arlen rewrote it entirely and renamed it *Blues Opera*. Much of the original plot was retained, and some of the original music; but the score was further enriched with songs previously written by Arlen for other productions: "Blues in the Night," "That Old Black Magic," and "Accentuate the Positive," for example. An extended twenty-five-minute sequence in pantomime was also interpolated into the first act. The entire structure was extended to make the work more of an opera than a popular musical production.

1954　HOUSE OF FLOWERS, a musical comedy with book and lyrics by Truman Capote. Produced by Saint Subber at the Alvin Theatre on December 30. Staged by Peter Brook. Dances and musical numbers directed by Herbert Ross. Cast included Pearl Bailey, Juanita Hall, and Diahann Carroll (165 performances).

Truman Capote, author of sensitive short stories, here wrote his first musical-comedy text. The setting is the West Indies, during Mardi Gras week. The House of Flowers is a bordello run by Mme Fleur (Pearl Bailey), its name derived not only from that of the proprietress but also from the fact that each of its girls was named after a flower. This house is run in competition with another one headed by Mme Tango (Juanita Hall), as a result of which it comes upon hard times. During an epidemic of mumps brought on by visiting sailors, the House of Flowers is forced to close. In an effort to retrieve her lost fortune Mme Fleur is ready to turn over her young and innocent protégé, Ottilie (Diahann Carroll) to a wealthy white ship merchant. But Ottilie is in love with Royal, a bare-foot boy from the hills (Rawn Spearman). To get him out of the way, Mme Fleur contrives to get him abducted aboard a ship, from which he manages to escape. At first he is believed to be the victim of sharks. But just as Ottilie is about to give herself up to the wealthy merchant, Royal appears, becomes the town hero, and is reunited with the girl he loves.

The rich atmospheric colors and vivid local background of the West Indies—fully exploited by Oliver Messel in his beautiful sets and costumes —provide much of the interest. But the play itself has an irresistible charm. Its more or less static tempo is accelerated by a frenetic voodoo rite, and by some exciting native dances. Such moments provide a wel-come change of pace and mood, but the over-all languorous spell remains unbroken, maintained in Capote's poetic dialogue, and in some of Arlen's songs, richly spiced with West Indian flavors. Arlen was at his best in "Two Ladies in de Shade of de Banana Tree"; "One Man Ain't Quite Enough" and "Has I Let You Know?" both dynamically projected by Mme Fleur; "I Never Has Seen Snow," sensitively sung by Ottilie; "Gladiola," the inspiration for a breath-taking dance by Dolores Harper, Carmen de Lavallade, and the ensemble; the title song; and "A Sleepin' Bee."

As Ottilie, Diahann Carroll made an impressive debut on the Broadway stage. A native of Trinidad, she had first attracted attention in this coun-try on a TV program.

1957   JAMAICA, a musical comedy with book by E. Y. Harburg and Fred Saidy. Lyrics by E. Y. Harburg. Produced by David Merrick at the Im-perial Theatre on October 31. Directed by Robert Lewis and Josephine Premice. Choreography by Jack Cole. Cast included Lena Horne, Ri-cardo Montalban, Joe Adams, Adelaide Hall, Ossie Davis, Erik Rhodes, and Josephine Premice.

As in *House of Flowers,* the Caribbean provides *Jamaica* with ample material for colorful sets, costumes, dances, production numbers, and songs. The specific locale is Pigeon Island, off Kingston, Jamaica. Savannah (Lena Horne) yearns to leave the island for the allurements of New York, about which she has heard from tourists and read in magazines. A humble fisherman, Koli (Ricardo Montalban) loves her, but she refuses to marry him unless he is willing to go off with her to New York. For a while she is beguiled by the slick, oily talk and free spending of Joe Nashua (Joe Adams), a visitor from Harlem come to the island to exploit a shark-riden pearl bed. But a hurricane reveals Koli to be a hero, when he saves the life of Savannah's little brother, Quico (Augustine Rios). Savannah is now reconciled to find happiness on the island with Koli. Her ambition to see New York has been realized only in a brief "dream" sequence, set in the Persian Room. The secondary love interest engages Cicero (Ossie Davis), whose visions of grandeur to rule the island are momentarily realized by the hurricane, and Ginger (Josephine Premice).

The plot is only incidental to its trimmings and adornments, the most arresting being the performance of Lena Horne, making her first Broadway appearance in a starring role. (The last time she was seen on the stage was long before she became a celebrity of night clubs and motion pictures—in 1939 when she was a member of the chorus in an edition of the *Blackbirds* revue.) In *Jamaica*—as in motion pictures, night clubs, and on television—Lena Horne is irresistible. "She shines," reported *Life*, "like a tigress in the night, purring and preening and pouncing into the spotlight." Walter Kerr described her as an "enchantress," adding: "She stands as lithe as a willow at the center of the stage, sucks in her breath as though she were inhaling a windstorm, and coos out the most imperturbable of mating-pigeon sounds."

The authors see to it that she is on the stage most of the time. Of the eighteen numbers in the prolix score, she is heard in five solos (one reprised), and three duets (two reprised). Some of these are Arlen's best: the sensual torch song that she sings in the "dream" sequence scene, "Take It Slow, Joe"; a glib patter song in duet with Ginger, "Ain't It the Truth?"; the ballad, "Cocoanut Sweet"; "Push the Button," Savannah's dream picture of life in New York made blissful by mechanical wonders; and the satirical "Napoleon," where she proves that most of the great men and women of the past are now merely trade names for commercial products.

Nor does the strength of Arlen's music end here. There are several other appealing numbers: a haunting lullaby, "Little Biscuit"; "Savannah," Koli's hymn to the girl he loves, which opens and closes the play; "Leave the Atom Alone," a witty treatment of a deadly serious subject; and a calypso, "Incompatibility." In the last two songs—as in "Push the Button," "Napoleon," and "Ain't It the Truth?"—"Yip" Harburg produced some of his most brilliant lyrics since *Finian's Rainbow*.

In contemplating the absence of an original plot and the wealth of music, Walter Kerr inquired: "The question is: can you make a whole show out of sheet music?" The resounding box-office success of *Jamaica* proves it can be done—provided Lena Horne is present to sing continually, and provided the production enjoys the embellishments of Oliver Smith's scenery, Miles White's costuming, Jack Cole's choreography.

HAROLD ATTERIDGE, lyricist. *See* LOUIS A. HIRSCH

IRVING BERLIN, composer-lyricist

Irving Berlin was born Israel Baline in Temun, Russia, on May 11, 1888. In 1892 a pogrom by the Cossacks drove the Baline family to America and they settled on New York City's East Side, where the father earned a meager income supervising kosher meats and serving as a cantor in the local synagogue. Irving's older brothers worked in sweatshops and sold papers in the streets.

Irving's public-school education was brief. When he was about nine, shortly after his father's death, he ran away from home to be on his own. For a while he earned pennies leading a blind singer along the Bowery and into saloons, sometimes singing with him the sentimental songs of the day. Irving soon found occasional employment as a singer in popular haunts near Chinatown, and after that as a song plugger for the publishing firm of Harry von Tilzer.

His first full-time job was as singing waiter at Pelham's Café, in 1906. It was hard work and it paid poorly, but it provided him with an opportunity to entertain audiences on a permanent basis. It also, unexpectedly, presented him with his first chance to write a song. At a competing café two waiters had written a song that was published. The proprietor of Pelham's Café wanted his own men to follow suit. Nick, the pianist, was recruited for the music. Since Irving had proved himself adept at writing parodies to current songs, he was asked to write the lyrics. Their song, "Marie from Sunny Italy" was introduced in the café and then published by Joseph W. Stern. This was Berlin's first opus, and the published copy had his name in bold letters. It was on this occasion that Irving Berlin assumed for the first time the name that he was to make famous.

When Berlin left Pelham's Café, he went uptown to Union Square (then the song Mecca of the city). For a while he worked as singing waiter at Jimmy Kelly's restaurant. All the while he kept on writing lyrics to other people's music. Then accident transformed him into a composer. He had written words for a ballad about an Italian marathon runner named Dorando, which he tried to peddle to Ted Snyder. The manager of that firm assumed that Berlin had a tune for it and offered twenty-five dollars for both the words and the music. Rather than lose the sale, Berlin hastily concocted a melody.

Success first came to him through his lyrics for "Sadie Salome Go Home" (music by Edgar Leslie), which sold over 200,000 copies, and "My Wife's Gone to the Country" (music by Ted Snyder), which had a 300,000-copy sale. Now a staff lyricist for Ted Snyder, Berlin was reaping a harvest in 1910 not only with his published songs but also with parodies that the New York *Journal* published, and with personal appearances with Ted Snyder in the Broadway musical, *Up and Down Broadway*.

He also was beginning to write his own music. In 1909 he had a hit in "That Mesmerizing Mendelssohn Tune," a ragtime version of Mendelssohn's popular "Spring Song." And it was through ragtime that he first became famous as a composer. In 1911 he wrote both music and words (a practice he would henceforth follow) for a ragtime tune that put him as a leader in Tin Pan Alley. The song was "Alexander's Ragtime Band," which Emma Carus helped to make a rage in Chicago. In a short period it sold over 1,000,000 copies of sheet music, and the whole country was rocking to its rhythm. "Alexander's Ragtime Band" made Berlin the king of ragtime; he maintained this regal position with several other outstanding ragtime numbers, including "That Mysterious Rag," "Everybody's Doing It," and "Everybody Step."

Hardly had he solidified his position as a ragtime writer when he achieved popularity in still another style of composition, the sentimental ballad. The sudden death of his bride, the former Dorothy Goetz, a victim of typhoid contracted in Cuba during their honeymoon, drove him to write "When I Lost You." This ballad joined the select company of million-copy song hits. From then on, and for the rest of his career, Berlin would pour forth some of his most beautiful and tender melodies within the ballad.

In 1914, Berlin wrote his first complete score for the Broadway stage, *Watch Your Step*. One year later another Broadway revue, *Stop, Look and Listen*, boasted fifteen Berlin numbers, including one that is a particular favorite with the composer, "I Love a Piano." In 1916 Berlin wrote six songs for the Victor Herbert operetta, *The Century Girl.*

Soon after America's entry into World War I, Berlin was called into uniform and stationed at Camp Upton. When the camp became the temporary station for troops embarking for Europe, the commanding general felt the need for a Service Center. He asked Berlin to produce and write an all-soldiers show, and Berlin complied with *Yip, Yip, Yaphank.*

After the war Berlin extended his activities to the point where he became a one-man trust of popular music. He formed his own publishing firm (after having been associated for a dozen years with Waterson, Berlin and Snyder). The opening of Irving Berlin, Inc., was celebrated throughout the country with an "Irving Berlin Week," with theaters everywhere playing his songs. From the beginning this firm was one of the most powerful in Tin Pan Alley. But besides engaging in publishing, Berlin also toured the vaudeville circuit; in partnership with Sam H. Harris he built the Music Box, a new Broadway theater on 45th Street, and he kept on writing songs for Tin Pan Alley and scores for Broadway.

In 1925, Berlin met Ellin Mackay, daughter of the Postal Telegraph tycoon, and heiress to a fortune then estimated at 30,000,000 dollars. They fell in love, but Ellin's father would not hear of marriage, and used every resource at his command to break up the affair. Nevertheless, Berlin and Ellin were secretly married on January 4, 1926. It was some years before her father became reconciled to the marriage. Out of this turbulent love affair came some of Berlin's most celebrated love ballads: "Always," "Remember," "All Alone," and others.

Berlin became a victim of the economic crisis that ravaged the country in 1929. He was left virtually penniless. To make matters even worse, he suddenly lapsed into a period of creative sterility and frustration that lasted almost two years and convinced him he was through as a composer. But in 1931 he recovered his winning stride with his score for the Broadway revue, *Face the Music.* In 1932 two old ballads—"Say It Isn't So" and "How Deep Is the Ocean?"—were successfully revived. In 1933 he enjoyed a major Broadway hit with the revue, *As Thousands Cheer.*

Once again at the top of his profession, Berlin stayed there, and his position in Tin Pan Alley and Broadway was never again threatened. His music was heard in a long succession of Broadway plays and revues, and in some of the best motion-picture musicals of the 1930's. One of his motion-picture songs, "Cheek to Cheek," won an Academy Award; another, "White Christmas," not only won an Academy Award but became a holiday classic which has sold over 20,000,000 records and about 4,000,000 copies of sheet music, figures as yet unequaled by any other American song.

During World War II, Berlin became America's musical laureate. In 1938 he wrote "God Bless America" for Kate Smith, which in the years preceding and during the war assumed almost the status of a second national anthem. (It was sung in both national conventions for President in 1940, and in 1954 it received from President Eisenhower a special gold medal.) After Pearl Harbor, Berlin enlisted his music in the war effort. He wrote songs for patriotic causes and war agencies, for the sale of war bonds, for the Red Cross, to spur arms production, for Navy Relief. His supreme war effort, however, came with the writing and production of his second all-soldier show, *This Is the Army*. Everything Berlin earned from his war songs and soldiers' show went to various war agencies and charities.

1914 WATCH YOUR STEP, a revue, with book by Harry B. Smith. Produced by Charles Dillingham at the New Amsterdam Theatre on December 8. Staged by R. H. Burnside. Cast included Irene and Vernon Castle, Charles King, Frank Tinney, and Elizabeth Brice (175 performances).

The program described the revue as "a syncopated musical show," and for it Berlin wrote a saucy ragtime tune tailor-made for the dancing Castles, "Syncopated Walk." Two other numbers from those Berlin prepared in his first Broadway score were of special interest: "Play a Simple Melody" (still remembered) and "When I Discovered You."

Vernon Castle was the star of the revue. With his wife Irene, he not only danced enchantingly the tango, polka, and fox trot, but also played the tap drums, sang a delightful satirical number about his success as a dance teacher, and filled the stage with his charm and personality. Frank Tinney appeared as a carriage caller at the opera, as a Pullman porter, and as a coat-room boy—and indulged in his famous practice of engaging the orchestra leader in the pit in informal conversation. Elizabeth Murray brought a charming brogue to the delivery of "Minstrel Parade," and Charles King and Elizabeth Brice sang the sentimental numbers. A production highlight came in the second act when the opera master, Giuseppe Verdi, appeared to protest about the irreverent manner in which his tunes were being syncopated, and was silenced into submission when he was convinced that syncopation gave his music a new "zip."

1918   YIP, YIP, YAPHANK, an all-soldiers revue with book, music, and lyrics by Irving Berlin. Produced by Irving Berlin at the Century Theatre on August 19. Cast was made up mostly of amateurs, the soldiers stationed at Camp Upton, New York (32 performances).

Ancestor of the more ambitious and epoch-making all-soldier revue of World War II, *This Is the Army*, *Yip, Yip, Yaphank* was produced to raise 35,000 dollars for a new Service Center at Camp Upton where Irving Berlin was stationed during World War I. The cast of 350 was recruited from amateurs and professionals stationed at the camp. All the material was created by Berlin himself, and the scenery was improvised from whatever materials were available.

After the opening chorus the captain appears before his men to order them to attack the enemy. The "ememy" in this case is the audience across the footlights, and the "attack" is made up of a relentless barrage of songs, skits, and dances. There followed a sometimes humorous, sometimes wistful, sometimes poignant picture of rookie life in an army camp —told in song, dance, comic routines, and large production numbers. Berlin, one of the stars, appeared in front of a pail of potatoes lamenting his fate as a K.P. Another scene, "In the Y.M.C.A.," brought up a picture of the loneliness of the average rookie. One of the highlights was a song delivered by Berlin himself. Dragged from his cot by the bugler's morning blast, he scrambled to reveille and wailed, "Oh, How I Hate to Get Up in the Morning." This song became the hit of the show, and one of the song hits of World War I. (It was recalled in Berlin's World War II army show, *This Is the Army*.) Another song hit was "Mandy," although this did not become popular until it was interpolated into the *Ziegfeld Follies* of 1919.

Yip, Yip, Yaphank also included a boxing routine by the then-lightweight champion of the world, Benny Leonard, boxing director at Camp Upton. And there was stirring drama in the finale, in which soldiers, packs on their backs, board ship for overseas duty.

After the final curtain on opening night Major General J. Franklin Bell, commanding officer of Camp Upton, rose to make a brief speech: "I have heard," he said, "that Berlin is among the foremost song writers in the world, and now I believe it." *Variety* called *Yip, Yip, Yaphank* "one of the best and most novel entertainments Broadway has produced." It played to capacity houses for four weeks, earning 83,000 dollars for the Service Center; and this sum grew to 150,000 dollars after a brief tour in Boston, Philadelphia, and Washington.

1919, 1920, 1927   *The Ziegfeld Follies*

1919 edition, produced by Florenz Ziegfeld at the New Amsterdam Theatre on June 16. Other songs by Gene Buck, Rennold Wolf, and Dave Stamper. Ballet music by Victor Herbert. Cast included Marilyn Miller, Eddie Dowling, Johnny and Ray Dooley, Eddie Cantor, Van and Schenck, John Steel, and the Fairbanks Twins (171 performances).

1920 edition, produced by Florenz Ziegfeld at the New Amsterdam Theatre on June 22. Other songs by Gene Buck, Joseph McCarthy, Harry Tierney, and Victor Herbert. Staged by Edward Royce. Cast included Fanny Brice, W. C. Fields, Van and Schenck, Ray Dooley, and John Steel (123 performances).

1927 edition, produced by Florenz Ziegfeld and Erlanger at the New Amsterdam Theatre on August 16. All songs and lyrics were by Berlin. Sketches by Harold Atteridge and Eddie Cantor. Staged by Florenz Ziegfeld, Sammy Lee, and Zeke Colvan. Cast included Eddie Cantor, Ruth Etting, the Brox Sisters, and Andrew Tombes (167 performances).

For other editions of the Ziegfeld Follies see
LOUIS A. HIRSCH; RAYMOND HUBBELL; APPENDIX I—1907.

Ziegfeld brought a greater wealth of setting and costuming to his 1919 edition of the *Follies* than he had done heretofore. His production cost hit a new high of 100,000 dollars and had such a glittering array of stars that he had to meet a weekly payroll of 20,000 dollars, a figure unparalleled at the time. The lavishness of setting was particularly evident in a harem scene which, in 1919, was considered the last word in garish display. Almost equally prolix in sets, costuming, and beautiful girls was the setting provided by Ziegfeld for one of Irving Berlin's greatest songs—written expressly for this production—"A Pretty Girl Is like a Melody."

The 1919 edition marked Marilyn Miller's last appearance in the *Follies*. She brought such glamour and fascination to Berlin's "Mandy" (lifted from *Yip Yip, Yaphank*) that the song became one of the year's big hits. The blackfaced comedian, Bert Williams, made his last appearance on any stage in this 1919 edition, and was at his hilarious best in a sharpshooting scene. Eddie Cantor sang Berlin's slightly suggestive "You'd Be Surprised" and brought down the house with his clowning in a skit entitled "At the Osteopath." Besides the songs by Berlin there was a notable number, "Tulip Time," by Dave Stamper, lyrics by Gene Buck.

In the 1920 edition Berlin's best songs were "Girl of My Dreams," "Syncopated Vamp," and "Tell Me, Little Gypsy." Other highlights were a skit involving W. C. Fields with a noisy automobile, Ray Dooley appearing as a howling infant, and Fanny Brice as a "vamp from East Broadway."

The 1927 edition broke precedent on two counts. It was the first *Follies* produced by Ziegfeld in which the entire score was written by a single man; and it was the first *Follies* with a single star, Eddie Cantor. Cantor was on the stage most of the time. He impersonated Mayor Jimmy Walker distributing keys to the city to so many celebrities that before long there were more celebrities than keys; he appeared in a sketch as the proprietor of a dogshop who tries to sell a poor sad sack of a dog nobody wants to buy. He sang two fine Berlin numbers: "You Gotta Have It" and "Learn to Sing a Love Song." Somewhere during the run of the show he managed to interpolate into the production a song not by Berlin, but one he helped catapult to success—"My Blue Heaven," by Walter Donaldson. Beyond all these strong elements the 1927 was notable in that it was the springboard from which Ruth Etting first leaped to fame as a torch singer.

1921-24   *The Music Box Revues*

> 1921 edition, book, music, and lyrics by Irving Berlin. Produced by Sam H. Harris at the Music Box Theatre on September 22. Staged by Hassard Short. Ballet by I. Tarasoff. Cast included William Collier, Sam Bernard, Joseph Santley, Ivy Sawyer, and Wilda Bennett (313 performances).
>
> 1922 edition, book, music, and lyrics by Irving Berlin. Produced by Sam H. Harris at the Music Box Theatre on October 23. Staged by Hassard Short. Dances by William Seabury. Cast included Clark and McCullough, Grace La Rue, Charlotte Greenwood, William Gaxton, John Steel, and the Fairbanks Twins (273 performances).
>
> 1923 edition, book, music, and lyrics by Irving Berlin. Produced by Sam H. Harris at the Music Box Theatre on September 22. Staged by Hassard Short. Cast included Frank Tinney, Joseph Santley, Robert Benchley, Ivy Sawyer, John Steel, and Phil Baker (273 performances).
>
> 1924 edition, book, music, and lyrics by Irving Berlin. Produced by Sam H. Harris at the Music Box Theatre on December 1. Staged by John Murray Anderson. Cast included Fanny Brice, Clark and McCullough, Oscar Shaw, Grace Moore, and the Brox Sisters (184 performances).

The annual *Music Box Revue* (of which there were four editions) combined lavishness of production with smartness and sophistication of

material. The first edition entailed a production cost of 187,613 dollars
—a figure unequaled up to then by any revue. No wonder, then, that
many skeptics along Broadway insisted that the venture was sure to ruin
both Harris and Berlin; that the new theater they had just built for the
production, the Music Box, would prove not a monument but a tomb.

> Such ravishingly beautiful tableaux, such gorgeous costumes, such a wealth
> of comedy and spectacular freshness, such a piling of Pelion on Ossa of
> everything that is decorative, dazzling, harmonious, intoxicatingly beautiful
> in the theatre—all that and more was handed out in a program that seemed
> to have no ending.

Thus wrote Arthur Hornblow in *Theatre Magazine*. The show was a box-
office smash. With a five-dollar top—once again without precedent—it
grossed 28,000 dollars the first week and over half a million during its
run.

A most effective tableau, "Dining Out," presented the girls dressed as
various courses of a gala dinner, through the demitasse. One of the best
production numbers, "The Legend of the Pearls" had a set with a dazzling
jewel effect. Comedy was found in Rene Riano's rendition of "I'm a
Dumbbell" and in a travesty on modern dances by Riano and Sam
Bernard. Berlin's score of twelve numbers included two outstanding
songs: "Everybody Step," one of his best ragtime melodies, presented by
the Brox Sisters; and the ballad, "Say It with Music," hauntingly sung by
Wilda Bennett and Paul Frawley.

The 1922 edition had other Berlin delights. "Lady of the Evening,"
a ballad, was beautifully sung by John Steel; another exciting ragtime
melody, "Pack Up Your Sins," was presented by the McCarthy Sisters in
an elaborate production number entitled "Satan's Palace"; and Grace
La Rue introduced a bit of sentimental nostalgia, "Crinoline Days." Comedy prospered with the first appearance on a major Broadway stage of
Clark and McCullough. Another comedy highlight was a take-off on
grand opera. Six opera characters appeared to the strains of the "Tri-
umphal March" from *Aïda*, then made a burlesque of several famous
operatic ensemble numbers. In this sketch Bobby Clark appeared as a
character from *Il Trovatore* and William Gaxton (also making his first
major Broadway appearance) as Siegfried. In an Oriental fantasy, "The
Porcelain Maid," Hassard Short produced one of his most dazzling spectacles.

Berlin's outstanding songs in the 1923 edition were "Climbing Up the
Scale" (a delightful tune built on the progressive steps of a major scale),

and the sentimental and tender "Waltz of Long Ago." The latter song was presented by Grace Moore, then a young and unknown singer making her first bid for stardom. She was also heard in "Orange Groves in California," an elaborate production number. Florence O'Dennishawn did a pantomime dance of a starfish in "A Fisherman's Dream," while in another elaborate spectacle a row of girls and a reflecting mirror turn out to be two rows of dancing girls.

In this edition we have the first stage appearance of Robert Benchley, in a monologue by which he will always be remembered, "The Treasurer's Report." Frank Tinney was the central character in a skit burlesquing the hunt of wild game in Africa. One of the best satirical sketches was by George S. Kaufman, "If Men played Cards as Women Do."

In the 1924 (and last) edition, Grace Moore returned to sing one of Berlin's immortal ballads, "What'll I Do?" as well as "Call of the South" and "Rock-a-bye Baby." Another immortal Berlin ballad, "All Alone" (not written for this revue but interpolated into the score), became an effective duet for Grace Moore and Oscar Shaw; at opposite ends of a dark stage, Grace Moore and Oscar Shaw sang the refrain to each other via lighted telephones. Humor and burlesque were contributed by Bobby Clark, who appeared as a hapless boxer in "The Kid's First and Last Fight," and by Fanny Brice as a befuddled Russian immigrant (singing "Don't Send Me Back to Petrograd") and as an equally confused ballet dancer. The principal dance numbers were presented by Ula Sharon and Carl Randall in "Ballet Dancers at Home" and by Tamaris and Margarita in "Tokio Blues."

1925   THE COCOANUTS, a musical comedy with book by George S. Kaufman. Produced by Sam H. Harris at the Lyric Theatre on December 8. Staged by Sammy Lee and Oscar Eagle. Cast included the Four Marx Brothers, with Frances Williams and Janet Velie (377 performances).

Fresh from *I'll Say She Is*, in which they had made their transition from vaudeville to Broadway musical comedy in 1924, the four zany Marx Brothers went through the Kaufman text and the Berlin score with the devastating impact of a bulldozer, leaving behind them only ruin and havoc. The story, such as it finally developed, had Florida for a setting, during its early real-estate boom. Henry W. Schlemmer (Groucho Marx) is in charge of a hotel and real-estate development as phony as its proprietor. (The property is only a stone's throw from the station; throw enough stones and he'll build a station.) Between rapid-fire puns and wisecracks he manages to mishandle haughty Mrs. Potter (Margaret Dumont). Silent Sam (Harpo Marx) tears up the guests' mail, steals the silver, eats telephones as if they were delicacies, and runs pell-mell after every girl in sight; somewhat incongruously he also manages to produce a sentimental tune or two on his harp. Willie the Wop (Chico Marx) contributes an Italian accent to his own brand of wisecracks and also does digital tricks on the piano keyboard. Jamison (Zeppo Marx) is the normal member of the family who speaks his lines straight, makes love to the heroine, and sings the principal love songs. By the time the brothers are finished with their shenanigans—some of them contrived spontaneously—any resemblance of dialogue and plot to the original concept of the authors is purely coincidental. The story goes that at one point during the run of the show George S. Kaufman turned with dazed amazement to a friend and said, "Say, I really think Groucho just spoke one of my lines as I wrote it."

Irving Berlin's main songs were "A Little Bungalow," "We Should Care," "Lucky Boy," and "Minstrel Days."

1932   FACE THE MUSIC, a musical comedy with book by Moss Hart. Produced by Sam H. Harris at the New Amsterdam Theatre on February 17. Staged by Hassard Short and George S. Kaufman. Dances by Albertina Rasch. Cast included Mary Boland, Andrew Tombes, and Hugh O'Connell (165 performances).

In 1932 the depression was at its height. *Face the Music* somehow succeeded in finding laughter, wit, and satire in this tragic event. Martin Van Buren Meshbesher (Hugh O'Connell) is a police sergeant who has a cache of illicit funds in a tin box. With an investigation under way he must get rid of his money in the fastest possible way. What way could be faster than an investment in a Broadway musical? He becomes the angel for a lavish production put on by Hal Reisman (Andrew Tombes), since Reisman's past association with the musical stage seemed to be a guarantee of financial failure. During out-of-town tryouts the projected Reisman show, *The Rhinestone Girl*, proves to be the kind of dud for which Reisman has become famous. When Meshbesher's fortune is wiped out—not by the show but by the investigation, which finds him guilty— he must depend upon Reisman's play to extricate him from his financial woes. *The Rhinestone Girl* is now spiced with sex situations, becomes a hit, and brings a fortune to all involved.

The book was peppered with satirical allusions to the depression and its impact on the American way of life. It shows the Roxy Theatre in New York giving four feature films to attract customers (providing also room and bath free), and all this for a dime; Wall Street tycoons eat in the Automat; Albert Einstein appears at the Palace Theatre, which now offers free lunches with its all-star shows.

The hit song, "Let's Have Another Cup o' Coffee," sung by Kay Carrington in the Automat scene, became something of a theme song for the depression years. Two other outstanding Berlin numbers were "Soft Lights and Sweet Music" (one of Berlin's enduring ballads) and "On a Roof in Manhattan."

1933   AS THOUSANDS CHEER, a topical revue with book by Moss Hart and Irving Berlin. Additional music and lyrics by Edward Heyman and Richard Myers. Produced by Sam H. Harris at the Music Box Theatre on September 30. Staged by Hassard Short. Dances by Charles Weidman. Cast included Marilyn Miller, Clifton Webb, Ethel Waters, and Helen Broderick (400 performances).

Sketches, dances, and even the curtain design, contained satirical allusions to current events. Helen Broderick stepped into the shoes of Mrs. Herbert Hoover and Aimée Semple McPherson with devastating results; in a third sketch she was seen as the Statue of Liberty in a song whose chorus began: "We'll all be in heaven when the dollar goes to hell." Clifton Webb gave an unforgettable impersonation of Gandhi and the then-ninety-four-year-old John D. Rockefeller. There were amusing comments on the change of administration in the White House and the effect of radio sponsorship on the Metropolitan Opera House.

The most important song—and it is one of Berlin's greatest—was "Easter Parade," seen in a production number for the first-act finale and sung by Marilyn Miller and Clifton Webb. This was not a new melody. Berlin had used it in 1917 for another lyric, "Smile and Show Your Dimple"; it was a failure then, and soon forgotten. Other outstanding musical numbers were "Heat Wave," torridly sung by Ethel Waters, and "Not for All the Rice in China," used in the finale.

1940   LOUISIANA PURCHASE, a musical comedy with book by Morrie Ryskind based on a story by De Sylva. Produced by Buddy de Sylva at the Imperial Theatre on May 28. Staged by Edgar MacGregor. Ballets by George Balanchine. Dances staged by Carl Randall. Cast included William Gaxton, Victor Moore, Vera Zorina, and Irene Bordoni (444 performances).

Senator Oliver P. Logansberry (Victor Moore) is sent down to New Orleans by the United State Senate to investigate the Louisiana Purchase

Company and its slick and shady lawyer, Jim Taylor (William Gaxton). It did not require much snooping for the Senator to uncover the high-handed deals taking place and the unsavory methods being employed. There was only one way to silence the troublesome Senator, and that was by involving him in scandal. The dancer, Marina van Linden (Vera Zorina) and the vivacious flirt, Mme Bordelaise (Irene Bordoni), become partners in the business of undermining the Senator's unimpeachable moral character—first by photographing him with a glamour girl on his lap, then by planting a girl in his bedroom. But the hapless Senator manages to wriggle out of their intrigues and to emerge triumphant over the crooks.

The principal song is a ballad, "It's a Lovely Day, Tomorrow," delivered by Mme Bordelaise, who also contributes an amusing defense of Latin techniques in love-making in "Latins Know How." Carol Bruce delivers two appealing numbers—the title song and a spiritual, "The Lord Done Fixed Up My Soul"; the latter becomes the preface for an elaborate dance sequence. A delightful comic number, "Sex Marches On," is given by Jim Taylor.

1942   THIS IS THE ARMY, an all-soldier revue assembled by Irving Berlin, with his own book, lyrics, and music. Additional dialogue by James McColl. Produced for the benefit of Army Emergency Relief Fund by Irving Berlin at the Broadway Theatre on July 4. Staged by Ezra Stone. Dances directed by Robert Sidney and Nelson Barclift. Cast included Ezra Stone, William Horne, Jules Oshins, and Irving Berlin (113 performances).

The idea to produce an all-soldier show—like the one he had previously given during World War I—occurred to Berlin soon after Pearl Harbor, when he recognized the acute need of American soldiers for entertainment. Army officials, faced with the grim business of transforming civilians into seasoned troops quickly, frowned on his suggestion. But he persevered until he won the grudging consent of the Pentagon.

Assigned to a small room in the barracks at Camp Upton (the same camp where he had been stationed during World War I), Berlin gained firsthand experiences of life in a modern army camp. He found material for songs, sketches, and dances on the training field, in the service club, the mess hall, the PX, and so on. Getting seasoned performers was something else again, involving as it did army red tape and the cumbersome machinery of transferring men from one unit to another. It also meant working mainly with amateurs (though there were a few professionals around); of the final cast, 60 per cent had never before appeared on any stage. "It wasn't long before I realized I had taken on more than I could handle, but it was too late," Berlin later told an interviewer. "I had the tiger by the tail and I just couldn't let go."

With the help of Dan Healy (who had trained dancers in the 1917 *Yip, Yip, Yaphank*) and Ezra Stone, a veteran of theater and radio, Berlin selected about 300 candidates for his show. Since the army insisted that this be no "goldbrick" assignment, rehearsals could take place only after regular army details had been completed. But by fits and starts, and usually late into the night, the show was gradually whipped into shape. Starring Ezra Stone, Philip Truex, Jules Oshins, and Irving Berlin (of whom only the last was a civilian), *This Is the Army* finally came to Broadway on July 4.

The revue passed from sentiment to humor, burlesque, and satire, from song and dance to large production numbers. There were rousing tributes to other branches of the service: to the Air Force in "American Eagles" and to the Navy in "How About a Cheer for the Navy?" There was humor in the opening chorus, "This Is the Army, Mr. Jones," in which a group of inductees in long underwear are being warned what their new life will be like; in the over-optimistic belief expressed by Ezra Stone, Philip Truex, and Jules Oshins in "The Army's Made a Man Out of Me"; in the delightful take-offs on Vera Zorina, Alfred Lunt and Lynn Fontanne, and Gypsy Rose Lee in the Stage Door Canteen scene. There was abundant sentiment in two beautiful ballads: "I'm Getting Tired So I Can Sleep," delivered by Stuart Churchill in the barracks scene and in "I Left My Heart at the Stage Door Canteen," sung by Earl Oxford in the Stage Door Canteen number. There were eye-filling sequences too: "What the Well-Dressed Man in Harlem Will Wear," vital with Negro song and dance; and an anti-Hitler dirge called "That Russian Winter." Finally there were poignant bits of nostalgia. One scene was dedicated entirely to veterans of *Yip, Yip, Yaphank*, all of them wearing the army uniform of that period. Berlin's song "Mandy" was revived from the 1917 army show. And the number that always stopped *This Is the Army* was "Oh, How I Hate to Get Up in the Morning," from *Yip, Yip, Yaphank*, delivered in a rasping, broken voice by Irving Berlin wearing his 1917 uniform. (The chorus that supported him included six alumni from *Yip, Yip, Yaphank*.)

This Is the Army, in short, had everything that made for effective musical theater, and the New York *Times* described it as "the best show of a generation."

So great was the demand at the box office of the Broadway Theatre that a four-week engagement had to be extended to twelve weeks. A nationwide tour followed, culminating in Hollywood, where the production was filmed. The tour then swung back East, across the ocean to England, Scotland, and Ireland. By special permission it was then dispatched to the combat areas of Europe, the Near East, and the Pacific. *This Is the Army* gave its last performance in Honolulu on October 22, 1945. It earned over 10,000,000 dollars for Army Emergency Relief and another 350,000 dollars for British relief agencies. It was seen by 2,500,000 American soldiers in all parts of the world. For this epic achievement Berlin was decorated with the Medal of Merit by General George C. Marshall.

1946 ANNIE GET YOUR GUN, a musical comedy with book by Herbert and Dorothy Fields. Produced by Rodgers and Hammerstein at the Imperial Theatre on May 16. Directed by Joshua Logan. Dances by Helen Tamiris. Cast included Ethel Merman and Ray Middleton (1147 performances).

In 1944 Rodgers and Hammerstein organized a producing firm to put on shows not necessarily of their own writing. Their second project as producers was a musical comedy based on the fabled exploits of sharpshooter Annie Oakley. They interested Jerome Kern in writing the music, but with Kern's sudden death another composer had to be found; Rodgers and Hammerstein went to the top of the profession for a replacement and engaged Irving Berlin.

This is perhaps the only time in stage history that one of America's greatest song writers was acting as producer of a musical comedy for which another all-time great was writing the score. While Rodgers never ventured into Berlin's domain by making suggestions on the kind of music needed (no more than Berlin would tell Rodgers how to run the production), this unusual association resulted in one of the richest and most varied scores Berlin ever wrote for the stage and made possible the greatest box-office success of his career.

Annie Oakley, the central character (Ethel Merman), was of course the rough-and-tumble backwoods girl who was handier with a rifle than with men. She falls in love with Frank Butler (Ray Middleton), whose preference in women is for the soft and gentle old-fashioned variety such as he glorified in his sentimental waltz, "The Girl That I Marry." This would be enough to create a barrier for them, at least for the duration of most of the play, but there is still another complication in the fact that they are business rivals. Annie is the star of Buffalo Bill's Wild West

Show, while Frank is the head of Pawnee Bill's outfit (Buffalo Bill played by William O'Neal; Pawnee Bill by George Lipton). Nevertheless their problems are happily resolved when the two outfits merge into one and Frank finally comes to realize that Annie, after all, is the girl of his heart.

Many things in the production joined to make it a "smash" (as *Variety* described it), a "bespangled carnival" (in the description of the New York *Times*), a "bull's-eye" (according to William Hawkins). There was Joshua Logan's imaginative staging, Tamiris' colorful and at times exciting choreography, with Sioux Indian dances as a high spot, Jo Mieziner's effective sets and costumes. Then there was Ethel Merman's strident, compelling, irresistible performance as Annie, one of the summits of her magnificent career in the musical theater. "Seldom is seen in the theater an offering in which everything is just as it should be," said Vernon Rice.

But as large a measure of credit for the success of the play as for any other single factor must go to Irving Berlin. Never before had he produced a score so prolix with hits and so varied in style. He was sentimental in "The Girl That I Marry"; witty and risqué in "Doin' What Comes Naturally" and "You Can't Get a Man With a Gun," both vigorously sung by Annie; rousing in another Annie Oakley song, "Sun in the Morning." The main love song, a duet of Frank and Annie, was "They Say It's Wonderful," while a second duet shared by them compared their respective talents, "Anything You Can Do." The score also included a paean since become something of an anthem for the theater, "Show Business."

1949   MISS LIBERTY, a musical comedy with book by Robert Sherwood. Produced by Irving Berlin, Robert Sherwood, and Moss Hart at the Imperial Theatre on July 15. Directed by Moss Hart. Choreography and musical numbers staged by Jerome Robbins. Cast included Eddie Albert, Mary McCarty, and Allyn McLerie (308 performances).

Robert Sherwood—three times recipient of the Pulitzer Prize for drama—here makes his first and only attempt at writing a musical-comedy book. He chose the setting of New York and Paris in 1885, and involved two great New York editors (James Gordon Bennett of the *Herald* and Joseph Pulitzer of the *World*) in a bitter rivalry for circulation. Pulitzer gains the upper hand when he helps raise money for the base of the recently acquired Statue of Liberty. During the ceremonies attending the presentation of the check by Pulitzer to the mayor of New York, Horace Miller, a *Herald* reporter (Eddie Albert), pulls a boner in his photography work and is fired. He tries to reinstate himself in Bennett's favor by going to Paris, finding the model for the Statue, and bringing her back to New York for some valuable *Herald* publicity. Bennett is overjoyed when Horace cables him from Paris that the model has been found in Monique Du Pont (Allyn McLerie). But the model proves to be a fraud. Bennett is so furious that he puts both her and Horace in jail. All ends well, however, as Horace gets a job with Pulitzer and finds that he is in love with Monique.

One of the most stirring musical episodes comes at the end, a hymn by Monique inspired by her American experiences. This is a setting to music of the poem by Emma Lazarus which is inscribed on the base of the Statue of Liberty, "Give Me Your Tired, Your Poor." A duet between Horace and Monique, "Let's Take an Old-Fashioned Walk"; a paean to Paris sung by a Parisian lamplighter, "Paris Wakes Up and Smiles"; and a duet between Horace and his original girl friend, Maisie (Mary Mc-Carty), "A Little Fish in a Big Pond," are other outstanding musical numbers.

1950   CALL ME MADAM, a musical comedy with book by Russel Crouse and Howard Lindsay. Produced by Leland Hayward at the Imperial Theatre on October 12. Staged by George Abbott. Dances and musical numbers staged by Jerome Robbins. Cast included Ethel Merman, Russell Nype, and Paul Lukas (644 performances).

A note in the program explained: "The play is laid in two mythical countries. One is called Lichtenburg, the other is the United States of America."

Lichtenburg, of course, is the little duchy of Luxembourg under a fictitious name, and the heroine, Mrs. Sally Adams (Ethel Merman), the American Ambassador to Lichtenburg, is Mrs. Perle Mesta, renowned Washington, D.C., party giver whom President Eisenhower appointed as Ambassador to Luxembourg. The play moves swiftly from Washington where Mrs. Adams, like her prototype, is a society woman famous for her parties, to Lichtenburg and back again. All the while it embroils its central characters in foreign intrigue, diplomatic red tape, international incidents, and love conflicts. For in Lichtenburg, Mrs. Adams is attracted to its Prime Minister, Cosmo Constantine (Paul Lukas), whom she tries to win over to herself by gaining for his country a Washington loan of 100,000,000 dollars. Her attempts prove unsuccessful and she is recalled to Washington. But in the end she emerges triumphant both as a woman and Ambassador. A secondary love interest engages the Ambassador's assistant, Kenneth Gibson (Russell Nype), and Princess Maria (Galina Talva).

As the American Ambassador, Ethel Merman gets entangled in the long train of her impressive gown, fluctuates between diplomatic dignity and earthy American slang, and all in all manages to create confusion and consternation with her brash personality, swagger, and lack of inhibitions. Naturally, the most important songs are assigned to her, and as is habitual with her, were projected with an irresistible vigor: "There is something about that volume of sound," reported Richard Watts, Jr., "that is indescribably soul satisfying. . . . She is one of the joys of the world."

The hit song was "You're Just in Love," a duet by the Ambassador and her assistant in a delightful two-voice counterpoint. Ethel Merman's brassy delivery was heard to good advantage in "The Hostess with the Mostes' on the Ball" and "The Best Thing for You," the latter a duet with Cosmo Constantine. A trio of Congressmen deliver a paean to Dwight D. Eisenhower, "They Like Ike," which may have had more than casual influence in carrying him into the White House. Another delightful number was a duet of Kenneth Gibson and Princess Maria, "It's a Lovely Day Today."

LEONARD BERNSTEIN, composer

Leonard Bernstein is a master of all musical trades. He is one of the world's outstanding conductors, a serious composer whose works are performed by leading musical organizations in America and Europe, a pianist, teacher, and lecturer. He is, finally, also a composer for the Broadway stage—and one of the best.

He was born in Lawrence, Massachusetts, on August 25, 1918. As a child he received from one of his relatives the gift of an upright piano, and from then on he knew he wanted to become a professional musician. While attending public school he studied the piano with Helen Coates (in later years his devoted secretary) and Heinrich Gebhard. Later on, as a student at Harvard College, he took music courses with Walter Piston and Edward Burlingame Hill. His pronounced musical gifts even then attracted attention, for one of his fellow students recalls: "His extraordinary memory and his flair for improvisation were almost legendary."

He was graduated from Harvard in 1939. Several prominent musicians, including Dimitri Mitropoulos, advised him to specialize in conducting. He entered the Curtis Institute as a conducting student of Fritz Reiner, and after that he worked under Serge Koussevitzky at the Berkshire Music Centre. Koussevitzky soon accepted Bernstein as his protégé. When Artur Rodzinski was appointed musical director of the New York Philharmonic Symphony Orchestra in 1943, Koussevitzky convinced him to take on Bernstein as an assistant, even though Bernstein had never conducted a professional orchestra.

A dramatic incident brought Bernstein forcefully to the attention of the entire music world. In November, 1943, Bruno Walter, then guest conductor of the New York Philharmonic, fell suddenly ill and was unable to appear for a Sunday afternoon performance on November 13. With hardly more than a dozen hours' notice, Bernstein was called upon to substitute. He had to conduct the orchestra without a single rehearsal, and he assumed an exacting program that included a world première. He revealed such a penetrating understanding of the music he was conducting and such a consummate technique at leading an orchestra, that the concert went off brilliantly. The following morning the New York *Times* reported the feat on its front page and commented upon it editorially. Overnight Bernstein was a celebrity.

Fortunately, his formidable talent was the insurance that subsequent appearances with orchestras—soon frequent events—were not anticlimactic. He gathered triumph after triumph in Europe as well as the United States. In 1953 he became the first American-born conductor to conduct at La Scala in Milan. In 1958 he succeeded Dimitri Mitropoulos as music director of the New York Philharmonic Symphony, the only American-born and the second youngest conductor ever to hold this post.

Being a man of remarkable energy as well as diversified gifts, he was to win triumphs in more than one field of music. While following his career as conductor he also wrote serious music. In 1942 he completed his first work for orchestra, the *Jeremiah Symphony*, which was played by virtually every major American orchestra, was recorded, and was selected by the New York Music Critics Circle as the most distinguished new American orchestral work of the season. *The Age of Anxiety*, introduced by the Boston Symphony under Koussevitzky in 1949, won the Hornblitt Prize as the best new work played that season by the orchestra, and a year later was adapted into an important ballet by Jerome Robbins. He also wrote another excellent ballet, *Fancy Free*, described by John Martin as "a rare little genre masterpiece," together with a one-act opera and various other compositions.

And as if this were not activity enough, he also taught conducting at, and later became assistant director of, the Berkshire Music Centre in

Tanglewood, besides giving courses in music at the Brandeis University. He lectured on various musical subjects from Bach to modern music, from musical comedy and jazz to Beethoven's Fifth Symphony on the television program "Omnibus," and has appeared as concert pianist in performances of concerti in which he also served as his own conductor.

He has also written in a popular vein. *On the Town* (1944), his first musical comedy, immediately established him as one of the most successful new composers on Broadway. A decade later came *Wonderful Town*, an even greater stage hit. *Candide* (1956) and *West Side Story* (1957) revealed still greater dimensions in his stage music.

1944   ON THE TOWN, a musical comedy with book and lyrics by Betty Comden and Adolph Green, based on an idea by Jerome Robbins. Produced by Oliver Smith and Paul Feigay at the Adelphi Theatre on December 28. Staged by George Abbott. Choreography by Jerome Robbins. Cast included Sono Osato, Betty Comden, Adolph Green, and Nancy Walker (463 performances).

On the Town was a musical-comedy adaptation of Bernstein's ballet, *Fancy Free*, in which three sailors on leave are in pursuit of girls. In the musical comedy the three sailors are on shore leave in New York for only twenty-four hours. Gabey (John Battles) sees a picture in the subway of "Miss Turnstiles"—who is really Ivy (Sono Osato)—and falls in love with her. His two buddies, Ozzie (Adolph Green) and Chip (Cris Alexander), help him in his search for her, and invade different parts of the city including Central Park, Carnegie Hall, a night club, the Museum of Natural History, and Coney Island. During these peregrinations Chip and Ozzie find girls of their own: Chip falls in love with Claire (Betty Comden), a female taxi driver with a lusty appetite for males; Ozzie finds an anthropolgy student, Hildy (Nancy Walker). Gabey finally finds the girl of his dreams in a music studio, taking singing lessons.

On the Town was a young people's frolic. The average age of producers, co-authors (both of whom also appeared in the cast), stars, and the composer was in the neighborhood of twenty-five. And it was the energy, breeziness, and ebullience of youth that made the show so exhilarating. "It shoves dullness off the curbstone," remarked *Time* magazine. Lewis Nichols called it one "of the freshest of musicals to come to town in a long time."

The production gave Bernstein opportunities to demonstrate his serious musical background with episodes requiring spacious orchestral design, such as the breezy opening scene, "New York, New York," the subway-ride fantasy, the ballet music for "Miss Turnstiles" and "Gabey in the Playground of the Rich." But he did not abandon the writing of good tunes by any means, producing two haunting ballads in "Lucky to Be Me" and "Lonely Town," and excellent comic songs (with sparkling lyrics) in "I Get Carried Away" and "I Can Cook Too."

1953   WONDERFUL TOWN, a musical comedy with book by Joseph Fields and Jerome Chodorov based on the play *My Sister Eileen* by Joseph Fields and Jerome Chodorov, derived from stories by Ruth McKenney. Lyrics by Betty Comden and Adolph Green. Produced by Robert Fryer at the Winter Garden on February 25. Staged by George Abbott. Dances and musical numbers staged by Donald Saddler. Cast included Rosalind Russell, Edith Adams, and George Gaynes (556 performances).

George Abbott had *Wonderful Town* ready for rehearsal when he asked Leonard Bernstein to write one or two new musical numbers to spruce up the musical score. Bernstein refused to be partial collaborator but offered to write a new full score in five weeks. He went to work with his lyricists and completed his assignment on time, even though it was the most ambitious stage music he had thus far produced, comprising fourteen numbers.

The protagonist of *Wonderful Town* is Eileen, an eager-eyed, baby-voiced innocent whose ingenuousness is a natural trap for the male animal. Her sister Ruth is more sophisticated and worldly-wise but less fortunate in winning the adulation of the opposite sex (as she laments in a hard-boiled satirical number, "One Hundred Easy Ways to Lose a Man"). They both hail from Columbus, Ohio, and they come to New York in 1935 seeking success—Eileen as an actress, Ruth as a writer. They move into a basement room in Greenwich Village formerly occupied by an apparently successful *fille de joie,* but which now rests insecurely above blasting operations for a new subway. They soon find themselves involved with a strange assortment of creatures who bring them an endless round of confusing crises and adventures—an ex-football star, a magazine editor, a newspaperman, a night-club owner, the manager of the 44th Street Walgreen's, and even some members of the Brazilian Navy. For a while the girls' dream of success appears shattered as Eileen is arrested (only to win over the police with her baby ways) and Ruth is sent on a phony newspaper assignment by a prankster. But the publicity created by Eileen's arrest brings her a coveted spot in a night-club show, while Ruth actually finds a place for herself on a newspaper. The girls from Ohio not only make good in this wonderful town but also find men of their choice.

The breathlessness of the overture, which leads to a frenetic ragtag dance by the Villagers, sets the hectic pace for the entire production (directed by George Abbott with his customary keen sense of movement and speed). The pace continues to accelerate in tempo and high-pitched nervousness until the devastating final curtain. "It roared into the Winter Garden," reported Robert Coleman, "like a hurricane."

The dynamo keeping these proceedings charged with electric energy was Rosalind Russell as Ruth. To her role she brought a seemingly inexhaustible vitality and lack of inhibitions that left audiences limp with exhaustion. She was the focal point for the play's searching caricatures of Broadway and Greenwich Village and for its stinging satires on sophisticates, sports heroes, and college intellectuals in songs like "Story Vignettes" and "Pass the Football." She threw herself all over the stage without stopping to catch her breath, as she became the central character of a feverish conga with the Brazilian Navy and of a high-voltage swing number, "Wrong Note Rag."

Edith Adams, a graduate of television, provided a welcome and refreshing contrast as Eileen. She was the pianissimo to give greater impact to Ruth's fortissimo passages. Together, Ruth and Eileen voiced their homesickness in a nostalgic little tune called "Ohio," which Bernstein really intended as a tongue-in-cheek parody of home-town songs but which was taken seriously by audiences and television and radio performers. There was, however, no mistaking the satirical intent in Bernstein's amusing take-off of Irish ballads in "My Darlin' Eileen," with which the police speak of their fondness for their prisoner, or the rowdy humor of "Story Vignettes" and "Pass the Football." Other Bernstein numbers were in a sentimental vein, the best being "A Quiet Girl," and Eileen's confession of her inmost feelings in "Never Felt This Way."

1956   CANDIDE, a musical comedy with book by Lillian Hellman based on Voltaire's satirical novel of the same name. Lyrics by Richard Wilbur. Additional lyrics by John La Touche and Dorothy Parker. Presented by Ethel Linder Reiner in association with Lester Osterman, Jr., at the Martin Beck Theatre on December 1. Staged by Tyrone Guthrie, with the assistance of Tom Brown. Cast included Max Adrian, Robert Rounseville, Barbara Cook, and Irra Pettina (73 performances).

Lillian Hellman was more or less faithful to the story of Voltaire's famous satire on optimism. Taught by Dr. Pangloss (Max Adrian) that all is for the best in this best of all possible worlds, Candide (Robert Rounseville) leaves Westphalia. Accompanied by his sweetheart, Cunegonde (Barbara

Cook) and Pangloss, he sets forth to seek out honesty and goodness. His travels carry him to Lisbon, Paris, and Buenos Aires where he confronts one major disaster after another, misery and crime, malice and greed. Cunegonde meets various sordid sexual experiences and Candide himself is cheated, beaten, and finally reduced to killing people. He returns to Westphalia sadder but wiser, no longer the idealist but a practical man ready to cultivate his own garden. He marries Cunegonde though now she is old and ugly.

It was rather to the spirit of Voltaire, than to the letter, that Lillian Hellman was not altogether true. As *Time* remarked: "Where Voltaire is ironic and bland, she is explicit and vigorous. Where he makes lightening rapier thrusts she provides body blows. Where he is diabolical, she is humanitarian." This may partially explain why *Candide* was a box-office failure, or it may have been that, as Brooks Atkinson noted, "the eighteenth-century philosophical tale is not ideal material for a theater show." But despite shortcomings of the text, *Candide* was a "distinguished musical," as Robert Coleman described it. "It towers head and shoulders above most of the song-and-dancers you'll get this or any other season. It has wry humor, mannered grace, and marvelous music."

Especially "marvelous music." Bernstein's score alone should have won for *Candide* a far longer run than it enjoyed, the best that Bernstein had thus far written for the popular theater. The scintillating overture, with its mockery and laughter, immediately sets the proper tone for everything that follows. Bernstein wrote four excellent, rich-sounding melodies in "Eldorado," "What's the Use?" Cunegonde's "Glitter and Be Gay," and Candide's "It Must Be So." The parody, satire, and wit were like rapier thrusts: "You Were Dead, You Know," "The Best of All Possible Worlds," and "I am Easily Assimilated" revealed a different and no less delightful facet of Bernstein's creativity. The spacious score further embraced duets, trios, quartets, choral numbers; a mazurka, waltz, serenade, ballad, gavotte, and tango; operatic music, music-hall ditties, folk music, jazz. "None of his previous theater music," said Brooks Atkinson, "has had the joyous variety, humor, and richness of this score."

1957 WEST SIDE STORY, a musical with book by Arthur Laurents based on a conception of Jerome Robbins. Lyrics by Stephen Sondheim. Produced by Robert E. Griffith and Harold S. Prince at the Winter Garden on September 26. Production directed and choreographed by Jerome Robbins. Cast included Carol Lawrence, Larry Kert, Chita Rivera, Art Smith, Mickey Calin, and Ken Le Roy.

West Side Story is a contemporary treatment of Shakespeare's *Romeo and Juliet*. Italy's Verona becomes present-day Manhattan. The feuding Capulets and Montagues are recreated in two teen-age gangs, the "Jets" and the "Sharks." Romeo is a city boy named Tony, Juliet is a Puerto Rican girl, Maria. The balcony scene becomes an idyl on the fire escape of a Puerto Rican tenement, and, as in Shakespeare, the love affair has a tragic ending.

The entire action takes place in two days, but within this brief period of time there is uncovered all the ugliness, bitterness, neuroticism, savagery, and turbulence in the lives of young people of the city streets; but there are also flashes of beauty and love and hope that also sometimes touch them.

The Jets are a teen-age gang of American boys determined not only to check but to destroy the growth of Puerto Rican population and influence on their block. They are opposed by a Puerto Rican gang, the Sharks. Both gangs meet at a dance in the neighborhood gym for the purpose of naming place, time, and weapons for a big "rumble" to decide which one will be dominant. Maria (Carol Lawrence), sister of the leader of the Sharks, and Tony, of the Jets, meet at the dance and fall in love. Being of rival factions, they must carry on their love secretly. In a bridal shop where Maria is employed, they improvise a mock marriage—with dress dummies as wedding attendants—pledging eternal love. But their love is doomed by the bitter hatred that separates the Jets and the Sharks. In the heat of the gang war that follows, Tony kills Maria's brother. Nevertheless, Maria is willing to elope with the boy she loves. Tony, however, is shot and killed by an avenging Shark.

This, then, is a grim musical play, vivid in realism and vital with social problems. To tell such a story the authors created a new form of musical theater in which the drama is projected not only through music but even more forcefully through the dance. From the very opening scene—when, against the bleak background of warehouse windows the two gangs drift into view in a sinister dance movement—the bitter story unfolds with what Walter Kerr described as "a catastrophic roar." The dance carries the action forward up to the shattering climax of "The Rumble," savage teen-age warfare interpreted in ballet terms. In "Cool," on the other hand, dance reveals the deceptive façade of relaxation behind which these teen-age gangsters reveal their inner frenzy, while "Somewhere" is a dream ballet that introduces a touch of softness and tenderness. In short, the theatrical substance of *West Side Story* is realized, as John Martin pointed out, not in talked plot but in moving bodies. The muscles of trained dancers are tensed and untensed and tensed again, stimulated by emotional tensions and stimulating them still further in return. These tensions are transferred automatically across the footlights and into the musculature of every spectator in the house, willy nilly. The cast acts and reacts in terms of movement, and that is the most direct medium that exists for the conveying of inner states of feeling.

The excitable music of the overture, with its mood of grim foreboding, is vivid and dramatic tone-painting. Much of Bernstein's score is similarly high-tensioned, but a great deal of it reflects lighter hues. The numbers include four lyrical episodes: Tony's hymn of love, "Maria"; Maria's charming tune, "I Feel Pretty"; Consuelo's offstage ballad, "Somewhere"; and the duet "I Have a Love." They also embrace two excellent comic songs. In "America" the Shark girls speak of the joyous life encountered by Puerto Ricans in this country, while "Gee, Officer Krupke" is a satirical commentary by several members of the Jets on the problem of juvenile delinquency.

MARC BLITZSTEIN, composer-lyricist

Marc Blitzstein, who first became popular in the 1930's with "social-conscious" musicals, was born in Philadelphia on March 2, 1905. He was a child prodigy in music who began taking piano lessons when he was three, gave concerts at five, and at seven started to study composition. After attending the Philadelphia public schools, he received a scholarship to the University of Pennsylvania, where he stayed only a single year. He then enrolled at the Curtis Institute, specializing in composition. At the same time he commuted regularly to New York to study piano with Alexender Siloti. In 1926 he went to Europe to study composition with Nadia Boulanger in Paris and Arnold Schoenberg in Berlin.

Back in the United States, Blitzstein at first supported himself by lecturing on music at women's clubs, colleges, and schools. During this period he wrote several works, which, performed in New York, Paris, and London, were so advanced in style, form, and approach and so dissonant that one critic described them as "full of Donner and Blitzstein."

The impact of the depression in the early 1930's removed him from his ivory tower. But even before this happened he had shown his light touch in a satirical one-act opera, *Triple Sec*, which had appeared in the 1930 edition of *The Garrick Gaieties*. After 1930 Blitzstein embraced the leftist movement in politics, and in his music became motivated by the mission to make it an instrument of propaganda.

This new social viewpoint first became evident in 1932 with an oratorio, *The Condemned,* inspired by the trial and execution of Sacco and Vanzetti, a political *cause célèbre* in the 1920's. For three years after that, Blitzstein wrote little. When he resumed composition he completed both text and music for a musical play that carried the social revolution to musical comedy—*The Cradle Will Rock* (1938). Politics continued to dominate his writing for several years thereafter. In 1937 he wrote *I've Got the Tune,* a musical written expressly for radio. A second stage musical, *No for an Answer,* was produced in New York on January 5, 1941. Soon after its opening the show was closed down by the Commissioner of Licenses on the grounds that the theater was not equipped for stage musicals; but it was no secret that the real reason for its closing was its radical viewpoint.

During World War II, Blitzstein served in the Army Air Force for which he completed several musical assignments. Out of uniform, he returned to professional commitments. After receiving a grant from the American Academy of Arts and Letters in 1946, he completed a "social-conscious" ballet, *The Guests,* which was introduced by the New York City Ballet in 1949. A few years later came his musical *Regina,* followed by a brilliant adaptation (text only) of Kurt Weill's *The Three Penny Opera.* The latter was a triumph in an off-Broadway production at the Theatre de Lys, on March 10, 1954, where its sustained run was the longest of any off-Broadway presentation; Lotte Lenya (Weill's widow) once again appeared in Jenny, a role she had created in Germany a quarter of a century earlier.

1938   THE CRADLE WILL ROCK, a musical drama with book, lyrics, and music by Blitzstein. Produced by Sam H. Grisman as a Mercury Theatre Production at the Windsor Theatre on January 3. Staged by Blitzstein. Cast included Howard da Silva, Will Geer, and Marc Blitzstein. Blitzstein played the musical score at the piano while providing a verbal commentary (108 performances).

With *The Cradle Will Rock,* Blitzstein emerged as one of the most provocative and exciting new writers for the musical theater in several years (whether or not one agreed with his politics). Virgil Thomson called the play "the most appealing operatic socialism since *Louise,*" and George Jean Nathan described it as a "miscegenation of a Union Square soap box with a talented juke box."

Its première was as dramatic a page as can be found in the history of the contemporary theater. As a production of the WPA Theatre (John Houseman as producer and Orson Welles, director), *The Cradle Will*

Rock reached dress rehearsal on June 15, 1937. Pressure was brought to bear on the Federal Theatre by government officials and agencies objecting to its left-wing propaganda, and the decision was finally reached in Washington to cancel the production. Notification of this cancellation reached the members of the cast just before curtain time on opening night. The audience already was beginning to file into the Maxine Elliott Theatre. While various members of the cast entertained the waiting audience, the neighborhood was scouted for some empty auditorium in which the play could be presented without the financial help of the government. The nearby Venice Theatre was available, and performers and audience were shifted there. Since all the scenery and costumes belonged to the Federal Theatre, and since there was no money to pay for an orchestra, *The Cradle Will Rock* was given in oratorio style: actors and the chorus stood on a bare stage in everyday costumes. Blitzstein performed the score at the piano and between scenes succinctly explained to the audience what was going on.

The curious and unexpected result of this makeshift arrangement was that the play gained in dramatic power. Much that previously had seemed specious and contrived was eliminated by Blitzstein's rambling and charming commentary. Even the music itself profited from the piano rendition and within these informal proceedings. Brooks Atkinson called it "the most versatile triumph of the politically insurgent theater." To the amazement of all concerned, the play was a box-office attraction. Sam Grisman now financed a regular Broadway run. Still played without scenery, costumes, or orchestra—this time by design rather than necessity—*The Cradle Will Rock* moved to the Windsor Theatre where it stayed on for four months and proved a profitable venture.

The setting is a night court; the principal action gravitates around the efforts of steel workers to create a union in Steeltown. Methods fair and foul were adopted by the powerful men of the community to frustrate these efforts. Mr. Mister (Will Geer), symbol of capitalism, who has the entire town under his thumb, compels leading members of each group and organization to join a "Liberty Committee" whose sole aim is to destroy the incipient union. The power of united workers proves more potent than wealth and influence, and the union emerges triumphant.

The Cradle Will Rock is sometimes described as an opera—a glaring euphemism. Blitzstein's music—especially numbers like "Junior's Gonna Go to Honolulu," "Croon-Spoon," or "The Nickel Under the Foot"—are popular songs for the popular stage; there is no point in assigning them a status in which they are a decided misfit. Blitzstein's rich score includes ditties, patter songs, tap dances, torch songs, parodies, blues, ballads— most of them in designs and styles completely acceptable to musical comedy. The composer's skill in making music play an active part in projecting dramatic action, however, must be noted. The music becomes commentator and protagonist. Now it points up a personal trait in one of the characters; now it makes a satirical aside; now it emphasizes the conflict. Rhythm, harmony, counterpoint, all serve the play well. But this hardly makes a political musical comedy an opera.

A decade following its première, *The Cradle Will Rock* was revived by the New York City Symphony under Leonard Bernstein. Audience and critics once again proved enthusiastic. A second attempt was made to bring it to Broadway, on December 27, 1947, with Howard da Silva, Will Geer, Muriel Smith, and Shirley Booth. But the intervening years had dulled its emotional and psychological impact. The play, with its stock characters, contrived situations, unrelieved blackness of villainy and unrelieved whiteness of those who sided with the angels, the unashamed and undisguised propaganda, completely lacked conviction, and it died an early death.

1949   REGINA, a musical drama with book, lyrics, and music by Marc Blitzstein based on Lillian Hellman's play, *The Little Foxes*. Produced by Cheryl Crawford, in association with Clinton Wilder, at the 46th Street Theatre, on October 31. Staged by Robert Lewis. Dances by Anna Sokolow. Cast included Jane Pickens, William Warfield, and Brenda Lewis (56 performances).

Lillian Hellman's vitriolic play about a decaying Southern family had been a bitter account of the way deceit, avarice, ruthlessness and hate annihilate all its members, until only a single one is left, Regina Giddens (Jane Pickens). Having destroyed all those around her, including her invalid husband, whom she refuses to help during a fatal heart attack, Regina is now in a position to control a lucrative cotton mill built up by the family. But her victory is hollow. She is lonely and afraid and hated by her own daughter.

If there is an indictment of society in this play, it is not thundered from a soapbox but lies implicit in the tragedy of a family consumed by its own vices. This is also the basic strength of Blitzstein's musical. It is a human drama on a large design; a drama underscored and emphasized through music varied in style and idiom. When a colored band appears on the stage in the party scene the music has the pulse of ragtime; and when a group of servants raise their voices in song we hear a spiritual.

There are lilting tunes, and other songs that are tortured and anguished like Birdie's "scena" in the third act. There are also some songs touched with mysticism, as in Addie's "Night Could Be the Time to Sleep." Blitzstein employed Handelian recitatives and others that resemble the *Sprechstimme* (song-speech) of Alban Berg. He presents some remarkable ensemble numbers, notably in the quartet, "Listen to the Sound of Rain." "With *Regina*," wrote Leonard Bernstein, "we have a kind of apex, a summation of what Blitzstein was trying to do. The words sing themselves, so to speak. The result is true song—a long, flexible, pragmatic, dramatic song."

Regina was effective theater when originally introduced at the 46th Street Theatre, even if it failed to attract customers. It was also effective opera when the New York City Opera Company incorporated it into its repertory on April 2, 1953. Regardless of its official genre—musical play or opera—*Regina* provides proof of how far Blitzstein can progress in the theater when he abandons the soapbox and becomes concerned with the forces motivating the lives and actions of his characters.

GUY BOLTON, librettist

One of the most prolific writers of musical-comedy books, Guy Reginald Bolton was born in Broxbourne, Hertfordshire, England, on November 23, 1887, son of a famous engineer. After being trained in France as an architect, he pursued his profession in New York, where he helped design the Soldiers and Sailors Memorial on Riverside Drive. He turned to playwriting in 1911 by collaborating with Douglas J. Wood on *The Drone,* produced that same year. He had also written some sketches for *The Smart Set.* This was the sum total of his literary experience when, in 1915, he met Jerome Kern and they decided to work together. Their first collaboration was *Ninety in the Shade* (1915), in which Clare Kummer assisted Bolton in writing the text. The second Kern-Bolton musical was *Nobody Home,* again in 1915, which helped to initiate a new genre in musical comedy known as "The Princess Theatre Shows" (*See* JEROME KERN). Afterward, Bolton collaborated with Kern in the writing of more formal musical comedies: *Leave It to Jane* and *Sally.* Bolton also wrote the motion-picture script for Kern's screen biography, *Till the Clouds Roll By.*

Bolton has produced musical-comedy texts for other famous Broadway composers besides Kern, among them being Ivan Caryll, George Gershwin, Cole Porter, and Harry Tierney.

See: GEORGE GERSHWIN (*Lady Be Good, Tip Toes, Oh, Kay!, Rosalie, Girl Crazy*); JEROME KERN (The Princess Theatre Shows; *Leave It to Jane, Sally*); BURTON LANE (*Hold On to Your Hats*); COLE PORTER (*Anything Goes*); HARRY RUBY (*The Ramblers, Five O'Clock Girl*); HARRY TIERNEY (*Rio Rita*); Appendix I (1921—*Tangerine*, 1944—*Follow the Girls*).

DAVID BRAHAM, composer

Though David Braham wrote many songs with lyricists other than Ed Harrigan, he achieved his foremost successes as a composer for the burlesques of Harrigan and Hart. He is always identified as a "Harrigan and Hart composer" in the same way that John Stromberg is a "Weber and Fields composer."

Braham was born in London in 1838, and he settled in the United States fifteen years later. While still in England he knew he wanted to become a professional musician and began to study the harp. The story goes that his failure to get his bulky instrument aboard an English stagecoach was the motivation for his changing to the violin, on which he became such an adept performer that he actually did some concert work.

Upon arriving in New York, Braham found a job as violinist in the orchestra accompanying the Pony Moore Minstrels. After that he led a military band, and played in the pit orchestras of most of the famous New York auditoriums. In the early 1870's he achieved some measure of fame with popular songs modeled after English music-hall tunes. These included special numbers for Annie Yeamans as a child star ("The Bootblack" and "The Sailing on the Lake"), for James McKee ("Over the Hill to the Poorhouse"), and for Major Tom Thumb when he appeared with P. T. Barnum.

Braham's first collaboration with Harrigan and Hart was on the song, "The Mulligan Guard," lyrics by Harrigan, in 1873. Though Braham occasionally wrote melodies to the lyrics of other writers after that, both his personal and musical history from 1873 on was inextricably associated with Harrigan and Hart—his personal history because in November, 1876, Harrigan married David's sixteen-year-old daughter, Annie; his musical because Braham's success in the Broadway theater came almost exclusively from his Harrigan and Hart scores. When Harrigan and Hart came to the parting of the ways in 1885 Braham's best days as a composer were over. But he lived on for another two decades and died on April 11, 1905.

1879-1885 *The Burlesques of Harrigan and Hart*

1879 THE MULLIGAN GUARD'S BALL, a burlesque by Ed Harrigan and Tony Hart. Lyrics by Ed Harrigan. Produced by Harrigan and Hart at the Theatre Comique, New York, on January 13. Cast included Harrigan and Hart, Annie Yeamans, John Wild, and William Gray.

On July 15, 1873, at the Academy of Music in Chicago, Ed Harrigan and Tony Hart appeared in a vaudeville sketch in which they sang "The Mulligan Guard," lyrics by Harrigan, music by David Braham. At that period there existed splinter organizations, aftermath of the Civil War, that enjoyed flaunting military uniforms. The Harrigan and Hart sketch and song reduced this practice to absurdity. Both Harrigan and Hart appeared in outlandish military costumes, and in their song they made a mockery of the pretenses that inspired men to keep on wearing uniforms.

From such an embryo came forth the series of New York burlesques, with Braham's music, that made Harrigan and Hart the toast of the city for a decade or so. In these burlesques Harrigan and Hart presented a cross-section of life in New York, particularly in the lower strata of society, embracing such racial groups as the Irish, Germans, and Negroes. Their plays represented one of the first attempts of the American musical theater to identify itself with everyday life (however much that life was satirized); to provide locales, characters, manners, speech, and racial types indigenous to New York and familiar to all New Yorkers.

The first of these full-length burlesques was *The Mulligan Guard's Ball*. It set a pattern for all future Harrigan and Hart "Mulligan" plays. The principal characters included Dan Mulligan (played by Harrigan), his wife Cordelia (Annie Yeamans, who became a star in these productions), their son Tom, their colored maid Rebecca Allup, and sundry other characters including two lovable Negroes (played by John Wild and William Gray), a German butcher, his Irish wife, the Captain of the Skidmore Guard (the Skidmores being rivals to the Mulligans), and so forth. Tony Hart usually played the leading female part.

Through Harrigan's subtle gift of characterization—both in his writing and acting—and in his remarkable attention to detail, he helped establish for the first time on the American musical stage racial characterizations. "He has really had more influence in directing the course of the contemporary stage than any fictitious personage of his time." So reported the *Illustrated American*, a journal of that period. And Isaac Goldberg wrote: "As playwright, as producer . . . and as actor, Edward Harrigan marks an important epoch in the development of the American song and dance show. His day was a great day for the Irish."

The Mulligan Guard's Ball won New York completely. A sequel was inevitable, and after that still another sequel. A whole series of Mulligan Guard plays followed, first at the Theatre Comique in New York, then at the New Theatre Comique. Among these plays were: *The Mulligan Guard's Picnic, The Mulligan Guard's Chowder, The Mulligan Guard's Christmas, The Mulligan Guard's Surprise, The Mulligan Guard's Nominee, The Mulligan Guard's Silver Wedding,* and, for a change of title, though not of characterization or content, *Cordelia's Aspirations* and *Dan's Tribulations.*

These were spoken plays with interpolations of songs and dances, usually ending up in some kind of variety entertainment. The plots carried the Mulligans to a picnic, chowder party, silver-wedding anniversary—usually simple, homey, everyday affairs for simple, homey, everyday people. Complications set in through the coincidences, accidents, and mishaps that continually dog these good people. Sometimes the incidents are somewhat beyond the pale of the daily life of simple people. In one of the plays Dan Mulligan runs for alderman and wins through the help of the Negro population. In another Cordelia makes a mess of her effort to reach high society and tries to commit suicide. She drinks from a bottle marked *Poison,* but which actually contains liquor, and yields not to death spasms but to a hilarious drunken scene.

Out of these Mulligan plays came a long chain of popular songs, all of them by Braham, which delighted the nation for a decade. Some of the most famous were: "The Babies on Our Block," "The Pitcher of Beer," "My Dad's Dinner Pail," "Maggie Murphy's Home," "Taking in the Town," "Hats Off to Me," "They Never Tell All What They Know," "When Poverty's Tears Ebb and Flow," and "Skidmore Fancy Ball."

The Mulligan series ended with *Dan's Tribulations,* produced on April 7, 1884. With that play an era in the American musical theater closed. Soon after that the New Theatre Comique burned down, and then the partnership of Harrigan and Hart corroded through bitter disagreements. After appearing in their last production together, *Investigation* (1885)— *not* a Mulligan play—they tried going separate ways. But neither Harrigan nor Hart was ever able to win for himself alone the adulation or the financial success they had enjoyed as a team.

LEW BROWN, lyricist. *See* DE SYLVA, BROWN and HENDERSON

GENE BUCK, lyricist and librettist

Edward Eugene Buck is perhaps best known through his long and rich association with Florenz Ziegfeld. He was born in Detroit on August 8, 1885, attended Detroit public schools, then in his eighteenth year found a job as bank messenger for two dollars a week. His ambition at that time lay in art rather than the theater. He took courses at the Detroit Art Academy, after which he found employment as a designer for a Detroit stationer and printer who produced all the sheet-music covers for Whitney and Warner, a major publisher in Tin Pan Alley. At that time covers were simple in design and done only in black and white. For his firm Buck originated colored poster-like covers, which soon became a rage in Tin Pan Alley. When Remick bought out Whitney and Warner, Buck was hired to design all its song covers. He created over 5000, an occupation that proved so taxing to his sight that he lost it and had to suspend all work for eight months.

After recovering from a blindness that fortunately proved to be temporary, Buck came to New York with only thirteen dollars in his pocket and no job. He was, however, known in Tin Pan Alley and before long he was back at his old occupation of designing song covers.

In 1911 he wrote his first song lyric, "Daddy Has a Sweetheart and Mother Is Her Name," music by Dave Stamper. This song and the one that followed it—"Some Boy," also to Stamper's melody—was introduced by Lillian Lorraine in her vaudeville act. She helped skyrocket both songs to a million-copy sheet-music sale.

Now a successful lyricist, Buck was sought out by Ziegfeld. In the 1912 edition of *The Ziegfeld Follies,* Buck's song "Daddy Has a Sweetheart" was interpolated, thus setting into motion an association between Buck and Ziegfeld that lasted seventeen years. In the 1913 edition of the *Follies,* Buck and Stamper had three numbers. After that, Buck provided songs and sketches for eighteen more *Follies* and for all the sixteen editions of *The Midnight Frolics,* a restaurant-night club atop the Amsterdam Theatre, which he helped to originate for Ziegfeld. Among Buck's best-known songs in the various *Follies* were: "Hello, Frisco, Hello" (Hirsch) in 1915, "Garden of My Dreams" (Hirsch) in 1918, "Tulip Time" (Stamper) in 1919, " 'Neath the South Sea Moon" (Hirsch and Stamper) in 1922, "Lovely Little Melody" (Stamper) in 1924. As Ziegfeld's right-hand man,

Buck also helped uncover many outstanding stars for the *Follies*, including Ed Wynn, Eddie Cantor, Will Rogers, and Joe Frisco.

Between 1927 and 1931 Buck became an independent producer of musical shows, but in 1931 he returned to work for Ziegfeld for the last of the *Follies* produced by Ziegfeld himself. After that, Buck confined his activities to executive duties with ASCAP, serving as its president from 1924 to 1941.

Gene Buck died in a hospital in Manhasset, Long Island, on February 24, 1957.

See: IRVING BERLIN (*The Ziegfeld Follies*); LOUIS HIRSCH (*The Ziegfeld Follies*); RAYMOND HUBBELL (*The Ziegfeld Follies*); DAVE STAMPER (*Take the Air*).

ABE BURROWS, librettist

Abe Burrows has contributed to the musical stage as a writer of texts, director, and play doctor. Born in New York City on December 18, 1910, he attended public schools in Manhattan, Brooklyn, and the Bronx. After being graduated from New Utrecht High School in 1928, he enrolled in a premedical course at the College of the City of New York, but the thought of attending sick people proved too morbid, and after two years he transferred to the New York University School of Finance to study accounting. In 1931 he found a job with a Wall Street brokerage firm, where he remained three years. Then for several years more he worked in his father's paint business and traveled as a salesman for a maple-syrup firm.

Several summers as an entertainer in the Catskill Mountains, on the Borsch Circuit, convinced him that humor was the commodity he could best sell. In 1938 he started selling sketches for radio, and in a few years' time became "top banana" in the industry through his writing chores for such leading programs as Ed Garden's "Duffy's Tavern" (with which he remained four years), the CBS Texaco Star Theatre, the Joan Davis Show, and the Ford Program.

While working in Hollywood on his radio programs, he became famous at swank, exclusive parties for his satirical songs and recitations. He startled and delighted audiences with zany songs like "The Girl with the Three Blue Eyes," "I Looked Under a Rock and I Found You," and "I'm Walking Down Memory Lane Without a Single Thing to Remember"; also with his wry commentaries on education, radio, and Boulder Dam. He subsequently recorded two albums of his songs, published the *Abe*

Burrows Song Book, appeared on many radio and television programs, and in 1948-49 was a night-club star.

One of his bosses at CBS, Hollywood, was Ernest Martin. When Martin joined up with Feuer to produce *Guys and Dolls* he asked Burrows to work with Jo Swerling in making the stage adaptation of the Damon Runyan stories. Burrows' initiation into musical comedy, then, came with a production that ran several years. A year after *Guys and Dolls* opened on Broadway, Burrows was asked to doctor the musical, *Make a Wish,* based on Ferenc Molnàr's *The Good Fairy.* This was a failure. Burrows' subsequent association with the Broadway musical stage was in the direction of the revue, *Two on the Aisle;* in writing the books of Cole Porter's *Can-Can* and *Silk Stockings;* and in directing the Ethel Merman musical, *Happy Hunting.*

See: FRANK LOESSER (*Guys and Dolls*); COLE PORTER (*Can-Can, Silk Stockings*); JULE STYNE (*Two on the Aisle*).

SAMMY CAHN, lyricist. *See* JULE STYNE

IVAN CARYLL, composer

Ivan Caryll, born Felix Tilken, was one of the most successful composers of operettas in the 1910's. He was born in Liége, Belgium, in 1861. A comprehensive training in music at the Liége Conservatory and in Paris included such notable teachers as Eugène Ysaÿe and Camille Saint-Saëns. For a brief period Caryll tried writing music for the French stage. He then went on to London to become conductor of The Gaiety, a theater devoted to musical productions. After trying his hand at writing functional music for the stage, he began adapting French operettas for the English theater. *La Cigale,* starring Lillian Russell, was the first show to introduce his name to the American public (1891).

The first operetta with his own music was *Little Christopher Columbus,* a London success in 1893, and well received in New York a year later when it was presented with additional music by Gustave Kerker. For the next seventeen years Caryll kept on writing music for the London stage, frequently in collaboration with Lionel Monckton. Several of these plays were imported to America, some with the original English casts, some in American adaptations. The first to achieve outstanding success was *The Girl from Paris,* produced in 1897 with an English cast. *The Runaway Girl,* in 1898, was an even greater hit, its score including such lilting numbers as "The Soldiers in the Park" and "Oh, How I Love Society." Later

Caryll musicals to originate in London and achieve success in New York were: *The Girl from Kay's* (1903) in which Sam Bernard portrayed the part of Mr. Hoggenheimer for the first time, and in which Mary Nash made her first professional stage appearance; *The Earl and the Girl* (1905), of special interest to American music since it was a showcase for Jerome Kern's first song heard on the Broadway stage, "How'd You Like to Spoon with Me?"; in *The Orchid* (1907) in which Eddie Foy achieved his first success.

In 1911 Caryll settled in the United States. From then on America was his permanent home, and he became a citizen. We learn from *Bring on the Girls* (by P. G. Wodehouse and Guy Bolton):

> Upon first arriving in New York, he did not actually charter a private liner, but took most of Deck C on whichever was the best boat crossing, and on arriving settled down with his five children, his wife Maud, and a cohort of nurses, tutors, governesses, valets, and lady's maids in a vast suite at the Hotel Knickerbocker. Then, instead of calling on the managers like the rest of the *canaille*, he would send word to them that he was, so to speak, in residence, ready to receive them and consider offers. And they came, trotting like rabbits. . . . What happened was that Felix would say he had found a wonderful play in Paris which would make an ideal musical, and being an impulsive sort of a fellow who had taken a sudden fancy to the manager whom he had selected to be the goat, was prepared to let him have this and to write the score for the customary composer's royalty of 3 per cent. No need for you to read the thing, my dear boy—it was, he assured his dear boy, superb, and he had the contracts here, all ready to sign. . . . And what Felix in the rush and bustle of the conversation had completely forgotten to mention was that, as he had bought the French authors out for a few thousand francs before leaving Paris and was the sole owner of the property, the entire 7 per cent (which he had previously demanded for the French writers as royalty) would be added to his personal take-home pay.

His most important operettas now had their point of origin in New York and thus belong to the American rather than English repertory. The most important were *The Pink Lady* (1911), *Oh! Oh! Delphine* (1912), and *Chin-Chin* (1914). But there was also a long list of other operettas which, through the years, found a responsive audience. In *Jack O'Lantern* (1917), written for its star Fred Stone, Rags Ragland made one of his rare excursions out of burlesque into musical comedy. This score had two numbers that became popular: "Wait Till the Cows Come Home" and "Come and Have a Swing With Me." In 1918 two of Caryll's operettas boasted lyrics by P. G. Wodehouse: *The Girl Behind the Gun* and *The Canary*. In the former can be found two more popular Caryll songs,

"There's a Light In Your Eyes" and "There's Life in the Old Dog." Caryll's last operetta, *Tip Top,* was produced on October 5, 1920.

He died in New York on November 28, 1921. The New York *Herald* noted in its obituary:

> Caryll's music combined freshness and lightness with careful workmanship, a knowledge of his medium that is uncommon among musical-comedy composers today, and that enabled him to turn out musical hits of enduring merit.

1911　THE PINK LADY, an operetta with book and lyrics by C. M. S. McLellan (Harry Morton), adapted from *Le Satyre,* a French farce by Georges Berr and Marcel Guillemaud. Produced by Klaw and Erlanger at the New Amsterdam Theatre on March 13. Staged by Herbert Gresham. Musical numbers staged by Julian Mitchell. Cast included Hazel Dawn, William Elliott, Alma Francis, and Alice Dovey (312 performances).

The Pink Lady not only shattered the existing attendance record for the New Amsterdam Theatre but also enjoyed a triumphant tour equaled by few other musicals of that period. "Everyone should see *The Pink Lady,*" wrote Earl Derr Biggers. Philip Hale reported that "here we have . . . an amusing book, pleasing music, a rare combination. Here we have a musical comedy that does not depend upon the antics of an acrobatic comedian, or the independent display of brazen-faced show girls." It was because of the success of this show that pink became the prevailing style in women's clothes in 1911.

The plot was of modest proportions. Lucien (William Elliott) takes his onetime girl friend Claudine, the "Pink Lady" (Hazel Dawn), to a restaurant. When by chance they meet Lucien's current fiancée, Angele (Alice Dovey), he introduces Claudine as Mme Dondidier, wife of a furniture dealer. The ensuing entanglements take up the rest of the evening, but as one critic pointed out "the fun develops logically out of the situations."

Some of the interest stemmed from the effective scenery, particularly the settings for the forest of Compiègne, a furniture shop on the Rue Ste.-Honoré, the Ball of Nymphs and Satyrs. But most of the interest rested in the infectious score, the highlight being a sentimental waltz, "My Beautiful Lady," sung by the Pink Lady as she seems to be playing her own accompaniment on the violin. In the "Kiss Waltz," the Pink Lady tries teaching a male the art of kissing. A breezy comic song, "Donny Did, Donny Don't" usually stopped the show—presented by the cast as it filed down a sweeping double stairway. Another pleasing number was a duet, "By the Saskatchewan."

1912   OH! OH! DELPHINE, an operetta with book and lyrics by C. M. S. Mc-
Lellan (Harry Morton) based on *Villa Primrose*, a French farce by
Georges Berr and Marcel Guillemaud. Produced by Klaw and Erlanger
at the Knickerbocker Theatre on September 30. Staged by Herbert
Gresham. Cast included Octavia Broske, Frank McIntyre, Frank Doane,
and Grace Edmond (248 performances).

Oh! Oh! Delphine reveals its French origin by being a frothy sex comedy.
Alphonse Bouchette (Frank McIntyre) and Victor Jolibeau (Scott
Welsh) decide to bring a new filip to their lives by exchanging wives.
Thus Simone Bouchette (Stella Hoban) marries Victor, and Delphine
Jolibeau (Grace Edmond) becomes Alphonse's wife. Victor's rich uncle
would disinherit his nephew if he ever knew of this arrangement. Consequently when uncle and nephew cross paths, Victor must convince
Delphine to come back and live with him as wife, even though they are
divorced. The problems and situations that crop up as a result of this
arrangement provide most of the humor of the play; other amusing
episodes are contributed by Frank Doane as a lady-killing colonel, and
Octavia Broske as a Persian-carpet salesman. By the time the uncle and
nephew separate, Victor and Delphine are convinced they are, after all,
made for each other; and Alphonse and Simone must console each other.

The principal musical numbers were the title song, a duet by Delphine
and Alphonse, and the charming "Venus Waltz," sung by Octavia Broske
dressed in flimsy Turkish dress. Alphonse delivers two comic numbers,
"Why Shouldn't You Tell Me That?" and "Everything's at Home Except
Your Wife," the latter a decided favorite with audiences.

1914   CHIN-CHIN, a musical fantasy, with book by Anne Caldwell and R. H.
Burnside. Lyrics by Anne Caldwell and James O'Dea. Produced by
Charles Dillingham at the Globe Theatre on October 20. Staged by
R. H. Burnside. The cast included David Montgomery, Fred Stone,
Helen Falconer, and Douglas Stevenson (295 performances).

This Oriental extravaganza was a modernization of the Aladdin story
that ranged from musical comedy to broad burlesque. As the advertisements took pains to publicize, the fantasy was filled with "caravans of
pretty girls; carloads of novelties; tingling-jingling numbers; gorgeous
costumes; wonderful scenes; startling situations; quaint Toy bazaar;
teddy bear dances . . . and so on."

Two Chinamen, Chin Hop Lo (David Montgomery) and Chin Hop Hi
(Fred Stone), search for the precious lamp of Aladdin. They come to the
toy bazaar of Abanazar where they find a rich American who wants to

buy Aladdin's lamp for his daughter Violet (Helen Falconer). Abanazar (Charles T. Aldrich) knows that the precious lamp is owned by a poor widow who does not know its value, and he contrives to defraud her of it. But two Chinese manikins in his store come to life, and they assist the shop's clerk (whose name also happens to be Aladdin) to frustrate the swindle. Violet then falls in love with the clerk.

As Chin Hop Hi, Fred Stone is given ample opportunity to demonstrate his versatility. He assumes the roles of a ventriloquist, lady horseback rider, eccentric dancer, and "Paderiski" who deserts a mechanical piano to dance with Violet.

The hit song was Aladdin's "Good-bye, Girls, I'm Through" (lyrics by John Golden). Aladdin also delivers several other attractive numbers: "Violet," "The Mulberry Tree," and "Love Moon," the last two being duets with Violet. During the run of the play an English song was interpolated, soon to become a favorite of World War I: "It's a Long, Long Way to Tipperary" by Harry Williams and Jack Judge.

GEORGE M. COHAN, composer-lyricist-librettist

The son of veteran vaudevillians, George Michael Cohan was born in Providence, Rhode Island, on July 3, 1878. He was only an infant when he made his first stage appearance, carried on as a human prop for his father's vaudeville sketch. When he was nine, George made a more official stage bow, billed as "Master Georgie" in a sketch starring his parents in Haverstraw, New York. In 1888 the act was further extended to include still another Cohan, George's sister, Josephine. "The Four Cohans" soon became headliners across the country, and as time passed it was George Michael who was its spark plug. He was not only the principal performer, but also business manager and the writer of most of the songs and dialogue. By the time the century closed, the act boasted still a fifth Cohan in the person of the singing comedienne, Ethel Levey, who became George M. Cohan's wife in the summer of 1899.

In 1901 Cohan expanded one of his vaudeville sketches into a full-length musical comedy, *The Governor's Son,* produced at the Savoy Theatre in New York on February 25, 1901, starring the five Cohans. Cohan's debut on the musical-comedy stage was not particularly auspicious, since the play lasted only thirty-two performances. In 1903 Cohan made a second attempt at expanding a vaudeville sketch into a Broadway musical comedy, and once again met failure.

Then in 1904 Cohan entered into a producing partnership with Sam

H. Harris. Their first venture was a completely new George M. Cohan musical, *Little Johnny Jones*. As was often to be his practice in the future, Cohan not only helped produce the play and wrote book, lyrics, and music, but he also starred in it. At first *Little Johnny Jones* did not do well in New York, since the critics were hostile, but after a successful out-of-town tour, it returned to New York to establish itself as a hit.

For the next decade the firm of Cohan and Harris—and sometimes other producers—put on musicals by Cohan in which he often starred. Generally they were the cream of the season's crop. In 1906 there were *Forty-Five Minutes from Broadway* and *George Washington, Jr.*, two of Cohan's best musicals. After that came *The Talk of the Town* (1907), *The Yankee Princess* (1908), *The Man Who Owns Broadway* (1910), *The Little Millionaire* (1911), and *Hello Broadway* (1914).

Everything about Cohan was personalized. He injected a new note of brashness and informality into the American stage. As a performer he wore a straw hat or a derby slightly cocked over one eye, and in his hand he held a bamboo cane. He sang out of the corner of his mouth with a peculiar nasal twang; he danced with a unique halting kangaroo step. He had his own way of gesturing—with an eloquent forefinger. The way he strutted up and down the stage—often with an American flag draped around him—was singularly Cohanesque; so was the way he could create a bond between himself and his audiences with informal, at times slangy, salutations or little speeches or homey monologues.

As a writer of musical-comedy texts and songs he also introduced a fresh, new manner. The plays, like their author, were jaunty, swiftly paced, vivacious. As Heywood Broun once wrote, Cohan became "a symbol of brash violence in theatrical entertainment, a disciple of perpetual motion." Cohan was not equally gifted in all the departments in which he functioned. He himself once confessed his limitations by saying: "As a composer I could never find use for over four or five notes in any musical number . . . and as a playwright, most of my plays have been presented in two acts for the simple reason that I couldn't think of an idea for the third act." He also once remarked, "I can write better plays than any living dancer, and dance better than any living playwright." He had his limitations, and for all his bravado and self-assurance he recognized them. But he knew the theater and his audience, and he was a superb showman. He might frequently be "a vulgar, cheap, blatant, ill-mannered, flashily dressed, insolent smart Alec," as James S. Metcalf described him in *Life* magazine at the time, but he did succeed in bringing into the musical theater a new exuberance, a healthy vitality, a contagious excitement.

Up to 1919 Cohan continued to dominate the Broadway theater as producer, writer, composer, and actor. Several of his nonmusical plays were also outstanding hits, particularly *Get-Rich-Quick Wallingford* (1910), *Broadway Jones* (1912), and *Seven Keys to Baldpate* (1913). In 1917 he wrote the song destined to become one of America's foremost war hymns, "Over There," inspired by America's entry into World War I. By 1919 he was at the height of his fame and power—one of the richest and most influential figures in the American theater.

But in 1920 he began to lose interest in the theater. One reason was his bitterness in losing a major battle with the Actors Equity Association, which in 1919 had called a strike to compel theater managers to recognize it as a bargaining representative for its members. Cohan lined up against Equity and expected all his actor-friends to do likewise. Their alliance with Equity appeared to him as personal betrayal. The complete victory of Actors Equity represented a personal defeat to Cohan, and he became a tired and bitter man. He withdrew his membership from both the Friars and Lambs Clubs; he refused to speak any longer to many who had been his lifelong friends; he dissolved the prosperous firm of Cohan and Harris.

But he did not withdraw completely from the stage, though at one point he threatened to do so. He continued writing and appearing in plays, both musicals and nonmusicals. Two nonmusicals were minor successes: *The Tavern* (1920) and *The Song and Dance Man* (1923). Most of the others were failures. "I guess people don't understand me no more," he remarked, "and I don't understand them."

What Cohan was suffering from was not merely the aftermath of his defeat by Equity, with its shattering blow to his ego. No less poignant to him was his discovery that the theater had been moving so rapidly forward that it was leaving him behind. Both on the musical and the nonmusical stage there had emerged writers with creative imagination, subtlety of wit, technical mastery, and inventiveness of ideas. Their best work was mature, slick, sophisticated. Cohan's plays and Cohan's songs— compared to theirs—seemed old-fashioned, and many of the audiences no longer responded to them. An unhappy episode in Hollywood in 1932, where Cohan went to star in the Rodgers and Hart screen musical *The Phantom President* and where he was continually ignored and slighted, accentuated for him his loss of caste in the theater.

Yet he was not forgotten, nor was he a man without honors. In the 1930's he was starred in two Broadway plays: Eugene O'Neill's homespun American comedy, *Ah, Wildnerness!*, and the Rodgers and Hart musical satire, *I'd Rather Be Right,* in which he was cast as President Franklin D. Roosevelt. Both performances were acclaimed, and there were even some to consider him one of the foremost actors of the American stage. In May, 1940, by a special act of Congress, he received from President Roosevelt a special gold medal. And in 1942 his rich career in the theater was brilliantly dramatized on the screen in *Yankee Doodle Dandy*, with James Cagney playing Cohan.

Cohan was gradually recovering from an abdominal operation in 1942 when he insisted that his nurse allow him to tour Broadway in a taxi. Accompanied by the nurse, he cruised around Union Square, then up to Times Square and through its side streets. He stopped off for a few minutes at the Hollywood Theatre to catch a scene from *Yankee Doodle Dandy*. It was almost as if he were reviewing for the last time the highlights of his career.

A few months later—on October 5, 1942—he died. "A beloved figure is lost to our national life," wired President Roosevelt. Mayor La Guardia said: "He put the symbols of American life into American music." And Gene Buck hailed him as "the greatest single figure the American theater has produced."

1904   LITTLE JOHNNY JONES, a musical comedy, with book, lyrics, and music by George M. Cohan. Produced by Sam H. Harris at the Liberty Theatre on November 7. Staged by George M. Cohan. Cast included George M. Cohan, Ethel Levey, Jerry and Helen Cohan, and Donald Brian (52 performances).

During a visit to England seeing the sights, Cohan decided he must write a musical comedy using two locales that had impressed him. One was the pier at Southampton; the other, the court of Cecil Hotel in London. Back in America, he heard about Tod Sloan, an American jockey who had ridden in the Derby for the King of England in 1903. Cohan put two and one together and in short order came up with his first original musical comedy, *Little Johnny Jones.*

Johnny Jones (George M. Cohan) comes to London to ride in the Derby. There he meets and antagonizes Anthony Anstey (Jerry Cohan), an American gambler who has made a fortune running Chinese gambling houses in San Francisco. When Johnny loses the Derby race, he is pursued to Southampton by angry mobs who accuse him of being crooked and having thrown the race. A detective who poses throughout the play as a drunkard and who is merely called "The Unknown," proves Johnny's innocence at the same time that he uncovers Anstey's role in destroying Johnny's reputation and his iniquitous activities in San Francisco's China-town. Now fully cleared, Johnny is able to win back the love of his estranged sweetheart, Goldie Gates (Ethel Levey).

Johnny Jones was Cohan's first starring vehicle, and he rose to the occasion by underplaying his part and by abandoning many of the little tricks and the absurd costume that up to now had been his trade-mark. With his first breezy entrance song, "Yankee Doodle Boy," the "new Cohan" won the hearts of his audience completely; and he solidified that affection with his equally vivacious rendition of another Cohan classic, "Give My Regards to Broadway," and his delivery of a sentimental sermon in verse, "Life's a Funny Proposition After All." Of the remaining numbers in the Cohan score the best were "Good-Bye, Flo," sung by Ethel Levey, and an amusing ditty presented by six coachmen, "Op in My 'Ansom."

1906   FORTY-FIVE MINUTES FROM BROADWAY, a musical comedy with book, lyrics, and music by George M. Cohan. Produced by Klaw and Erlanger at the New Amsterdam Theatre on January 1. Cast included Fay Templeton, Victor Moore, and Donald Brian (90 performances).

The setting is New Rochelle, a New York suburb "forty-five minutes from Broadway." A local miserly millionaire has died and no will has been found. It had been assumed that his wealth would go to his housemaid, Mary Jane Jenkins (Fay Templeton), but due to the absence of a will the fortune passes to the dead man's only living relative, Tom Bennett (Donald Brian). Tom arrives in New Rochelle to claim his legacy, accompanied by his showgirl sweetheart, Flora Dora Dean (Lois Ewell), her nagging mother, Mrs. David Dean (Julia Ralph), and his secretary Kid Burns, former loafer and horse player (Victor Moore). Because of Kid Burns' bad manners and outspoken behavior, Tom gets into a fight with his sweetheart and her mother at a party at the Castleon mansion. Meanwhile, Kid Burns falls in love with the housemaid, Mary Jane. In an old suit of clothes Kid Burns finds the dead man's will in which the fortune goes to Mary Jane. When Kid Burns refuses to marry an heiress, Mary Jane destroys the document.

On the morning of the première of *Forty-Five Minutes from Broadway*, the New Rochelle Chamber of Commerce called an emergency session to pass several resolutions regarding this musical: (1) to institute a boycott; (2) to send out press releases denouncing the play as libelous to their community and its inhabitants. The Chamber of Commerce objected particularly to the title song which said that the town did not have a single café and which spoke of the males as having "whiskers like hay." After the show opened, the commotion in New Rochelle died down as the town came to realize that the play was succeeding in making New Rochelle famous.

Most of the critics did not like Cohan's new musical. The editor of *Theatre* reflected the prevailing opinion when he called it "rubbish" and added, "Mr. Cohan had little art" and intended only "to catch the unthinking crowd." But like *Little Johnny Jones,* the new musical, despite a comparatively short Broadway run, was a triumph on its road tour and returned to Broadway as a major success.

For Fay Templeton, the starring female role marked her first appearance in a so-called "clean play"—for twenty years before this she had been a burlesque star. She was a hit; and so was Victor Moore in the first of his many Broadway triumphs as a comedian, after many years in vaudeville and stock companies.

The best songs from the score are still remembered, including the title song, "Mary's a Grand Old Name," and "So Long, Mary."

1906   GEORGE WASHINGTON, JR., a musical comedy with book, lyrics, and music by George M. Cohan. Produced by Sam H. Harris at the Herald Square Theatre on February 12. Staged by George M. Cohan. Cast included the Four Cohans and Ethel Levey (81 performances).

Described as "an American play," *George Washington, Jr.,* had for its central theme the rivalry of two Senators in Washington, D.C.: James Belgrave (Jerry J. Cohan) from Rhode Island, and William Hopkins (Eugene O'Rourke) from the South. When Senator Hopkins makes a determined effort to expose corruption in the Senate, Belgrave decides to go off to England to buy his way into British society by inducing his son, George (George M. Cohan) to marry Lord Rothburt's daughter. But George is in love with Senator Hopkins' lovely niece, Dolly Johnson (Ethel Levey). Disgusted by his father's Anglophile tendencies, young George becomes a super-patriot and assumes the name of the first President of the United States. As it turns out, the lord and his "daughter" are frauds, hired by Senator Hopkins to get the goods on his rival. This fact is uncovered by young George, who sets his father wise. Senator Belgrave now becomes an intense patriot. Since Senator Hopkins is in love with

Belgrave's widowed sister, he is ready to forget his hostility and at the same time give his blessings to George and Dolly.

The pace of the play is so swift, the dialogue so amusing, and the songs so effective that the editor of *Theatre*—who had recently referred to *Forty-Five Minutes from Broadway* as "rubbish"—said that there was "plenty that is genuinely and legitimately diverting" and called the play "mighty good entertainment."

The outstanding song in *George Washington, Jr.*, is "You're a Grand Old Flag," in which Cohan institutes a routine for which he became famous and which he would repeat in many later plays—draping an American flag around his body and running up and down the stage singing the praises of flag and country. Strange to recall, a scandal followed the first performance of this song in the play. The idea for the song first occurred to Cohan when a G.A.R. veteran told him he had been a color-bearer during Pickett's charge at Gettysburg; pointing to the American flag, the old man said, "she's a grand old *rag*." In writing his song Cohan kept the expression "grand old rag." One day after opening night, several patriotic societies arose to denounce Cohan for insulting the American flag by referring to it as a rag. (Cohan insisted that this protest had been instigated by a New York drama critic who had been denied seats for his show.) When Cohan changed "rag" to "flag" all was forgiven, and the furor died down.

Two other songs became popular in 1906: Dolly Johnson's "I Was Born in Virginia" and "You Can Have Broadway." A high spot of the production was Cohan's delivery of some homey philosophy in a verse-monologue entitled "If Washington Should Come to Life."

1911   THE LITTLE MILLIONAIRE, a musical comedy with book, lyrics, and music by George M. Cohan. Produced by Cohan and Harris at the Cohan Theatre on September 25, 1911. Staged by George M. Cohan. Cast included George M. Cohan, Jerry Cohan, Helen Cohan, and Lila Rhodes (192 performances).

The late Mrs. Spooner has left a will specifying that her fortune can be shared by her husband and son only if they get married. Since Robert Spooner, the son (George M. Cohan) loves Goldie Gray (Lila Rhodes) the demands of the will present no problem to him. However his friend Bill Costigan (Tom Lewis) is sure that Goldie is interested only in Robert's fortune, and does everything he can to break up the love affair. In this he is unsuccessful, since Goldie loves Robert for himself alone.

To fulfill the requirements of the will, the father—Henry Spooner (Jerry Cohan)—courts and wins Goldie's aunt, Mrs. Prescott (Helen Cohan).

A pattern already established by Cohan in his musicals was here rigidly followed. The play was filled with sentimental recitations, topical songs and ballads, flag numbers, and eccentric dances. One of the leading song hits was a comedy number, "We Do All the Dirty Work"; other popular musical items included "Oh, You Wonderful Girl," "Musical Moon," and "Barnum Had the Right Idea."

1914   HELLO BROADWAY, a musical comedy with book, lyrics, and music by George M. Cohan. Produced by Cohan and Harris at the Astor Theatre on December 25. Cast included George M. Cohan, William Collier, Louise Dresser, and Lawrence Wheat (123 performances).

Cohan described *Hello Broadway* as "a crazy quilt patched and threaded together." It was a burlesque in the style of those made famous by Weber and Fields in which Cohan plays the part of George Babbitt, the millionaire son of a Jersey City soap manufacturer, who returns to America from China in the company of his friend, Bill Shaverham (William Collier). The plot, however, was incidental to its satirical trimmings. Many of the current plays were burlesqued broadly. Cohan did a take-off of Leo Dietrichstein; Louise Dresser, of Mrs. Patrick Campbell as she had appeared in Shaw's *Pygmalion;* William Collier, of Pauline Frederick. Cohan's best songs were "I Wanted to Come to Broadway," "That Old-Fashioned Cakewalk," and for one of his famous flag routines, "My Flag."

BETTY COMDEN and ADOLPH GREEN, lyricists-librettists

In the writing of musical-comedy books and song lyrics, Betty Comden and Adolph Green have functioned as a single creative organism. It consequently should afford little surprise to find that their biographies coincide in many details. They were both born in New York City, and in the same year, 1915—Betty on May 3, Adolph on December 2. Both attended New York University; both were active as members of the Washington Square Players, a period in which their friendship ripened. In the 1930's Comden and Green appeared in a night-club act, for which they wrote all their own songs and dialogue. During this period they called themselves "The Revuers," and one of the members of the group was Judy Holliday. But success did not come to Comden and Green until 1944 when they wrote book and lyrics for Leonard Bernstein's *On the Town.*

The spontaneity and vitality of their writing was by no means the least of the factors in the substantial success enjoyed by this musical. Now recognized among the most important new writers for the musical stage, Comden and Green found numerous assignments awaiting them both in Hollywood and on Broadway.

See: LEONARD BERNSTEIN (*On the Town, Wonderful Town*); JULE STYNE (*Two on the Aisle, Bells Are Ringing*).

J. FRED COOTS, composer

Pat Boone's revival in 1957 of the song "Love Letters in the Sand" was a nostalgic reminder that J. Fred Coots was once a leader in Tin Pan Alley. He was also a leader in writing musical-comedy scores. He was born in Brooklyn, New York, on May 2, 1897. His mother, an excellent pianist, hoped he would become a concert pianist, and Fred was early given instruction. But he had other ambitions. After his academic education ended in the Brooklyn Public schools (he was only sixteen), he tried to emulate a successful uncle by making his way in the world of finance. His first job was in the banking house of the Farmers Loan and Trust Company in Wall Street. One year later Coots found a new goal. A song-plugger playing some Tin Pan Alley tunes in a music shop stimulated him to become a popular composer. He gave up his banking job and became a stock boy and pianist in the McKinley Music Company, a small Tin Pan Alley firm.

His first song came in 1917, inspired by the efforts of Henry Ford to send a peace ship to war-torn Europe and thus bring World War I to a conclusion. Called "Mister Ford You've Got the Right Idea," it was published and earned for its proud composer a royalty of five dollars. Encouraged by the sight of his name on printed sheet music, Coots now became prolific, completing a number of songs that were heard in vaudeville theaters.

At the Friars Club, of which he was now a member, Coots gained access to Eddie Dowling, then planning a Broadway musical. Somehow Coots managed to convince Dowling to gamble on him as the composer of the score. The results were happy for both Dowling and Coots, for the show was *Sally, Irene and Mary* (1922), one of the biggest stage hits of the period.

Now an esteemed composer, Coots was contracted by the Shuberts as staff composer. For nine years he wrote songs for many important Shubert musicals and revues. During this period he also wrote special numbers for night clubs and the movies, appeared as a headliner in vaudeville, and wrote a few independent songs that were outstanding successes, including "I Still Get a Thrill Thinking of You" (1930), "Love Letters in the Sand" (1931), "Santa Claus Is Coming To Town" (1934), and "You Go to My Head" (1938). However, long before 1938, Coots' career on the Broadway stage ended, and to round out the circle of his activity on Broadway, it ended as it had begun, with a major hit, *Sons O' Guns* (1929).

1922   SALLY, IRENE AND MARY, a musical comedy with book by Eddie Dowling and Cyrus Wood. Lyrics by Raymond Klages. Produced by the Shuberts at the Casino Theatre on September 4. Staged by Frank Smithson. Cast included Eddie Dowling, Jean Brown, Kitty Flynn, and Edna Morn (312 performances).

Three young ladies are living in a New York tenement. They are: Sally (Jean Brown), Irene (Kitty Flynn), and Mary (Edna Morn). Winning the admiration and affection of an important theatrical producer, the three girls manage in a year's time to become stage stars. Mary's hometown boy friend, Jimmie Dugan (Eddie Dowling) purchases a Ford and comes to the big city in pursuit of his girl. He finds that she and her friends are moving in high social circles in which he is highly uncomfortable. But he finally succeeds in reawakening Mary's interest in him and his basic virtues.

Three songs were of particular appeal: "I Wonder Why," "Something in Here," and "Time Will Tell."

1924-25   *Artists and Models*

1924 edition, a revue with book by Harry Wagstaff Gribble. Lyrics by Sam Coslow and Clifford Grey. Additional music by Sigmund Romberg. Produced by the Shuberts at the Winter Garden on October 15. Staged by J. J. Shubert. Cast included Trini, Frank Gaby, and Mabel Wither (261 performances).

1925 edition, a revue with book by Harold Atteridge and Harry Wagstaff Gribble. Lyrics by Clifford Grey. Additional music by Alfred Goodman and Maurice Rubens. Produced by the Shuberts at the Winter Garden on June 24. Staged by J. Shubert. Cast included the Gertrude Hoffman Girls, Lulu McConnell, Billy B. Van, and Phil Baker (411 performances).

On August 20, 1923, the Shuberts introduced a new annual revue at the Winter Garden. Called *Artists and Models*, it presented the males of the chorus dressed as artists, and the undraped girls as their models. The first edition had book and lyrics by Harold Atteridge, music by Al Goodman and Jean Schwartz, and a cast headed by Frank Fay and Grace Hamilton. This show was evolved from a revue originally staged by the Illustrators Society of New York to which several eminent artists and cartoonists contributed—among them, James Montgomery Flagg, Rube Goldberg, H. T. Webster, and Harry Hirschfield.

In the 1924 edition, local color was injected with numbers like "Off to Greenwich Village" and "What a Village Girl Should Know"; there was spectacle in "Mediterranean Nights," and ear-caressing songs in "Who's the Lucky Fellow?" and "I Love to Dance When I Hear a March," both by Coots.

The best spectacles in the 1925 edition, enhanced by the presence of undraped females, included "Oriental Memories" and "The Magic Garden of Love," while the most pleasing Coots songs were "Follow Your Stars" and "Take a Little Baby Home with You."

1926   A NIGHT IN PARIS, a revue with book and dialogue by Harold Atteridge. Lyrics by Clifford Grey and McElbert Moore. Additional music by Maurice Rubens. Produced by the Shuberts at the Casino de Paris on January 5. Staged by J. C. Huffman. Cast included Jack Osterman, Jack Pearl, and Norma Terris (335 performances).

A Night in Paris opened the reconstructed Casino de Paris atop the Century Theatre. While the emphasis was on beautiful sets and costumes and huge production numbers—of the last, one of the best being "In Chinatown, In Frisco"—there was also considerable comedy in the capable hands of the suave Jack Osterman and in the rowdy burlesque humor of Jack Pearl. Even satire was well represented, principally in burlesques on two stage plays recently successful on Broadway, Noel Coward's *Vortex* and Michael Arlen's *The Green Hat*. Nostalgia for Paris was expressed in a song called "Paris," effectively rendered by Yvonne George.

1929   SONS O' GUNS, a musical comedy with book by Fred Thompson and Jack Donahue. Lyrics by Arthur Swanstrom and Benny Davis. Produced by Connolly and Swanstrom at the Imperial Theatre on November 26. Staged by Bobby Connelly. Ballets by Albertina Rasch. Cast included Jack Donahue, Lily Damita, and William Frawley (295 performances).

Sons O' Guns had an army background and threw nostalgic glances back to the days of World War I. Jimmy Canfield (Jack Donahue) is a wealthy, happy-go-lucky, irresponsible young man who has to go to war. In camp he finds that his former valet, Hobson (William Frawley) is his top sergeant. Jimmy's unhappy adventures at the hands of his onetime employee, who takes full advantage of his august military position, and his tribulations with a vivacious French girl, Yvonne (Lily Damita), provide the basic materials for much of the comedy. Aggravating Jimmy's complications is the further fact that he is falsely accused of being a spy. He manages to clear himself and even to become a hero —particularly to Yvonne.

A vivacious tune, "Cross Your Fingers," was the leading song in the score. Additional musical interest was provided by "May I Say I Love You," "Sentimental Melody," and "It's You I Love."

RUSSEL CROUSE and HOWARD LINDSAY, librettists

The play-writing team of Crouse and Lindsay made stage history with their adaptation of *Life with Father,* which enjoyed the longest run of any Broadway play. *Life with Father* was their first nonmusical play. Before that they had written a number of texts for musical comedies.

Russel Crouse was born in Findlay, Ohio, on February 20, 1893. After receiving his education in Toledo public schools, he found a job in his seventeenth year as reporter for the Cincinnati *Commercial Tribune.* Other newspaper jobs followed, including one as sports writer for the Kansas City (Missouri) *Star* for five years, and as political reporter for the Cincinnati *Post* for one year. During World War I he served in the navy as yeoman second class. After the war he settled in New York, working successively in the newsrooms of the city's leading papers. The apex of his newspaper career was a daily humor column in the New York *Evening Post* between 1924 and 1929.

The theater soon became a new and broader avenue of activity. In 1928 he turned actor by playing the part of a newspaperman in Ward Morehouse's *Gentlemen of the Press.* In 1931, in collaboration with Morrie Ryskind and Oscar Hammerstein II, he wrote his first musical-comedy text, *The Gang's All Here,* music by Lewis Gensler. *The Gang's All Here* folded up after only twenty-three performances. Two years after that, Crouse collaborated with Corey Ford on *Hold Your Horses,* a musical starring Joe Cook that accumulated only eighty-eight performances.

Between 1932 and 1937 Crouse was press agent for the New York Theatre Guild. One year after assuming this post he worked with Howard Lindsay for the first time. They adapted a text by Guy Bolton and P. G.

Wodehouse into the Cole Porter musical, *Anything Goes,* a smash box-office hit. Russel Crouse had won his first laurels in the theater, and at the same time he had found a writing partner in Lindsay.

Before becoming Crouse's collaborator, Howard Lindsay had achieved success in the theater as actor and director, besides being a writer. He was born in Waterford, New York, on March 29, 1889. When he was thirteen, his family moved to Boston where Howard attended the Boston Latin School and Harvard College on a scholarship. He was heading toward a career as minister when he came upon a catalogue of the American Academy of Dramatic Arts. Interest in the theater thus awakened, Lindsay enrolled at the academy and stayed there six months. In 1909 he acted in a road show, *Polly of the Circus.* For a few years after that he performed in vaudeville, burlesque, and in silent films; and for five years, from 1913 on, he was a member of the Margaret Anglin company. After a hiatus during World War I—when he served in France with the 76th Division and for a few months produced soldier shows—Lindsay acted in and helped direct a major Broadway hit, *Dulcy,* by George F. Kaufman and Marc Connelly (1921). After that he was active as actor and director, both on and off Broadway. He was director of the Skowhegan Playhouse when he met Dorothy Stickney, a young actress there; they were married on August 13, 1927. Lindsay also distinguished himself as playwright by collaborating on several Broadway stage hits including *She Loves Me Not, By Your Leave,* and *A Slight Case of Murder.*

In 1936 Crouse and Lindsay wrote two more musical-comedy texts, Cole Porter's *Red, Hot and Blue* (with Ethel Merman and Jimmy Durante) and Harold Arlen's *Hooray for What?* In 1937 Crouse abandoned press-agenting and went out to Hollywood to work on the screen plays of several important motion-picture musicals, including *The Great Victor Herbert. Life with Father* brought Crouse back to Howard Lindsay and to Broadway. Subsequently, Crouse and Lindsay wrote the 1946 Pulitzer Prize play, *State of the Union,* together with several other successful stage plays and librettos for musical comedies.

See: HAROLD ARLEN (*Hooray for What?*); IRVING BERLIN (*Call Me Madam*); COLE PORTER (*Anything Goes*); Appendix I (1956—*Happy Hunting*).

REGINALD DE KOVEN, composer

The comic operas of Reginald de Koven may be strangers today, but in their time they were popular, and their composer was generally regarded as one of the leading writers of operetta music in the era immediately preceding Victor Herbert.

Reginald de Koven was born in Middletown, Connecticut, on April 3, 1859, son of a clergyman. When he was thirteen, the family moved to England where Reginald received his academic training. In 1879 he received his degree from St. John's College at Oxford. By this time he had arrived at the decision to make serious music his life work. He consequently went to Germany for intensive training in piano, harmony, and counterpoint. His studies ended in Paris under Léo Delibes.

He returned to the United States in 1882, settling in Chicago. For a while he earned his living as a bank teller, and after that in the office of a stock-brokerage house. His marriage to Anna Farwell, daughter of a successful dry-goods merchant, brought him affluence. For a while he worked in his father-in-law's establishment. When an investment in Texas real estate, made for him by his father-in-law, brought him wealth, he abandoned business permanently and returned to music.

During a visit to Minneapolis, De Koven met Harry B. Smith, a young writer who had written librettos and lyrics for two unsuccessful operettas. They decided to collaborate. For De Koven this partnership was to carry him into the popular theater; for Smith it meant his first contact with success.

In their first comic opera, De Koven and Smith tried to imitate Gilbert and Sullivan's *The Mikado*. Their comic opera, *The Begum*, had for its setting India, where the reigning princess (the Begum) is permitted as many husbands as she desires; when she tires of one of them, a general, she creates a war to get rid of him. Starring De Wolf Hopper, Digby Bell, and Jefferson de Angelis, *The Begum* was introduced in Philadelphia on November 17, 1888; four days later it appeared at the Fifth Avenue Theatre in New York, where it was a failure.

Their next effort, *Don Quixote* (1889), was also a failure. But then came their crowning success—*Robin Hood* (1890). After that a string of comic operas unfolded, some of them successes enjoying several revivals, but all now forgotten. Besides *Rob Roy* and *The Highwayman,* the team of De Koven and Smith wrote *The Knickerbockers* (1892), *The Little Duchess* (1901), *Maid Marian* (1902), and *The Golden Butterfly* (1908), among others.

While working for the popular theater, De Koven did not abandon serious music. He wrote two operas, both introduced by the Metropolitan Opera: *The Canterbury Pilgrims* (1917) and *Rip Van Winkle* (1920).

Over a period of many years De Koven also served as music critic and symphony conductor.

De Koven died on January 16, 1920, in New York City. His mansion at 1025 Park Avenue was converted by his widow into a memorial, with his bedroom and studio left precisely as they had been when he was alive. In the late 1940's, however, the house was demolished to make way for an apartment building.

1890   ROBIN HOOD, a comic opera, with book and lyrics by Harry B. Smith. Produced by The Bostonians at the Chicago Opera House on June 9, 1890, and at the Standard Theatre, New York, on September 28, 1891. Cast included Eugene Cowles, George Frothingham, Edwin Hoff, Jessie Bartlett Davis, and Caroline Hamilton.

Robin Hood was the most successful comic opera written in this country before Victor Herbert; and it is the only pre-Victor Herbert operetta that is sometimes revived. The story, to be sure, is based on the exploits of Robin Hood during the reign of Richard I of England. Deprived of his lands and earldom, Robin Hood (Edwin Hoff) becomes an outlaw and gathers about him a loyal band of outlaws. They appear, and are warmly welcomed, at the Nottingham market place where a gay fair is taking place. There Robin Hood learns that his enemy, the Sheriff of Nottingham, is planning to marry his ward, Guy of Gisborne (Peter Lang), to Maid Marian (Marie Stone). When Robin Hood sees Maid Marian he decides to frustrate these plans. Robin Hood and his men are followed into their forest by the Sheriff and are defeated. Guy seizes Maid Marian and is about to compel her to marry him when Robin Hood—now the recipient of a royal pardon and the return of his lands—arrives to save her.

If *Robin Hood* is remembered today—and occasionally revived—it is mainly due to a single song; a song with which its composer is most often identified; a song which has become a permanent fixture at American weddings. The song is "Oh, Promise Me." In the opera it appears in the third act, just before the threatened wedding of Maid Marian and Guy, and it is sung by Alan-a-Dale, portrayed by Jessie Bartlett Davis. It is interesting to note that the song was not originally intended for the comic opera. Isidore Witmark tells the story in his autobiography, *From Ragtime to Swingtime:*

It was not a part of the original score; and the lyric had been written not by Harry B. Smith but by Clement Scott, the English critic. The song had been published independently. It had been found that *Robin Hood* needed another song; De Koven for some reason did not relish composing a new tune, so he brought this old one to rehearsal. He could not interest any of the singers in the song! Finally, it was offered to Jessie Bartlett Davis, the contralto, playing the role of Alan-a-Dale. Miss Davis, annoyed because she had not been offered the song at first, hummed it over, then disdained it. Something in the melody, however, remained. She found herself singing it an octave lower. MacDonald (the producer) happened to pass her dressing room; all who heard Jessie sing will understand why he stopped. He could not contain himself until the song was finished. "Jessie!" he cried, bursting into her room, "if you ever sing that song as you're singing it now, on the low octave, it will make your reputation." She sang it, and the prophecy came true.

While "Oh, Promise Me" has thrown into obscurity the other musical numbers of the opera, a few are not without merit. The best are the "Brown October Ale," "The Amourer's Song," and "The Tailor's Song," the last of which had a delightful background of humming voices.

1894   ROB ROY, a comic opera, with book and lyrics by Harry B. Smith. Produced by Fred C. Whitney at the Herald Square Theatre on October 29. Staged by Max Freeman. Cast included William Pruette, Lizzie Machnicol, Juliette Cordon, and Joseph Herbert (168 performances).

The setting is Perth, Scotland, during the uprisings attending the attempt to restore the Stuarts to the throne of England. Rob Roy (William Pruette) is a Highland chief secretly married to Janet (Juliette Cordon), daughter of the Mayor of Perth. Rob Roy's men pledge allegiance to the cause of Prince Charles Edward Stuart, "the young pretender" to the English throne (Barron Berthald), but the Mayor of Perth, always an opportunist, betrays the Prince for a reward. One of the Prince's adherents, Flora MacDonald (Lizzie Machnicol), disguises herself as the "pretender" and is imprisoned, but is saved from death by the Prince. Flora is once again captured, and in an attempt to save her life, the Prince surrenders himself. The Highlanders, however, are able to obstruct the advance of the English troops until the Prince and Flora can effect their escape to France.

No single number stands out as prominently in this score as "Oh, Promise Me" does in *Robin Hood*. But the music for *Rob Roy* is more consistently notable. Of special interest is Janet's haunting ballad, "My Home Is Where the Heather Blooms"; the rousing song of Rob Roy and his men, "Come, Lads of the Highlands"; Flora's tender love song, "Dearest Heart of My Heart"; "Rustic Song," a duet of Rob Roy and Janet; and the "Lay of the Cavalier," by the Prince and his men.

1897   THE HIGHWAYMAN, a comic opera, with book and lyrics by Harry B. Smith. Produced by Andrew A. McCormick at the Broadway Theatre on December 13. Staged by Max Freeman. Dances arranged by Carl Marwig. Cast included Jerome Sykes, Joseph O'Mara, and Hilda Clarke (144 performances).

The Highwayman is one of De Koven's best scores and, all things considered, one of his best comic operas. The character of Foxy Quiller—performed in the original production by Jerome Sykes—was so well delineated that the term "foxy quiller" entered the argot of the period to describe a shrewd and conniving fellow.

The plot is set in England where Dick Fitzgerald (Joseph O'Mara), soldier of fortune, has come to ruin at the hands of the gambler, Hawkhurst. He is forced to become "Captain Scarlet," a highwayman who is the terror of the countryside. He is eventually pardoned, but his pardon papers fall into the hands of his arch-enemy. These papers are rescued through a bold and ingenious maneuver by Lady Constance (Hilda Clarke) who, disguised as Captain Scarlet, holds up the stagecoach in which the papers are concealed.

A consistently tuneful score includes such delights as the duet of Dick and Constance, "Do You Remember, Love?" Constance's "Moonlight Song," the "Gypsy Song" of Quiller and his men, and the robust "Highwayman Song" of Dick and his followers.

DE SYLVA, BROWN, and HENDERSON,
librettist, lyricist, and composer

The song-writing team of De Sylva, Brown, and Henderson introduced a welcome tonic into the musical theater of the 1920's. In contrast to the escapist and unreal world in which most of the musical comedies of that period moved, those of De Sylva, Brown, and Henderson were concerned with everyday themes of everyday life—modern Americana generously spiced with the salt and pepper of comedy and satire.

Ray Henderson was the composer. Buddy de Sylva and Lew Brown collaborated on the lyrics. But the three men worked together so intimately and harmoniously that they represent a single entity. The musician often contributed ideas and approaches to the lyricists, and vice-versa. As long as they functioned as a single unity they were fruitful contributors to the theater.

Buddy de Sylva was the base of the triangle on which the other two rested. He was born George Gard de Sylva in New York City on January 27, 1895. His father had toured the vaudeville circuit until his marriage, when he abandoned the stage for law. Buddy was only a child when he made his stage bow at the Los Angeles Grand Opera House; he was such a success in a song-and-dance routine that a vaudeville tour was planned for him on the Keith circuit. This attempt to exploit a child prodigy was frustrated by Buddy's grandfather, and a more normal development followed in California's public schools, and after that at the University of Southern California.

In his freshman year De Sylva helped produce a college show. During the same period he played the ukelele in a Hawaiian band and started writing song lyrics. A few of the last came to the attention of Al Jolson, who set them to music and interpolated them in *Sinbad* at the Winter Garden. De Sylva's first royalty check from Tin Pan Alley—the sum of 16,000 dollars—lured him to New York City to pursue more actively a career as song writer. Engaged by the publishing house of Remick, he went on to work with Arthur Jackson, also a lyricist, in writing lyrics for George Gershwin's first musical comedy, *La, La, Lucille*. During the next few years De Sylva became an ace lyricist who wrote for Jerome Kern, Victor Herbert, Gershwin, and Jolson, among others, and who produced such outstanding song hits as "Look for the Silver Lining" (Kern), "A Kiss in the Dark" (Herbert), "Somebody Loves Me" (Gershwin), and "April Showers" (Louis Silvers).

Until 1925 De Sylva wrote lyrics to Gershwin's music for George White's *Scandals*. When Gershwin withdrew to advance his own career in the musical-comedy field, he was replaced at the *Scandals* by the song-writing team of De Sylva, Brown, and Henderson.

Lew Brown was also a lyricist. By the time he joined up with De Sylva and Henderson he had become successful for ballads like "I May Be Gone for a Long, Long Time" and "I Used to Love You." He was born in Odessa, Russia, on December 10, 1893. As a boy he settled in New York City. While working as a lifeguard on Rockaway Beach he amused himself by writing parodies of popular songs. This activity stimulated a latent desire to write songs. He now abruptly terminated his academic education, which had taken place at De Witt Clinton High School in New York, to invade Tin Pan Alley. He found a place for himself with the veteran composer-publisher, Albert von Tilzer. In 1912 Brown wrote lyrics for five Tilzer songs, one of which was outstandingly popular "I'm the Lonesomest Gal in Town." For the next two years he kept on writing words to Albert von Tilzer's music, collaborating on the popular World War I ballad, "I May Be Gone for a Long, Long Time," and "Oh, by Jingo" and "I Used to Love You." Then, in 1922, Lew Brown produced lyrics for "Georgette," a song introduced in *The Greenwich Village Follies of 1922*. Its music was by a young man named Ray Henderson.

Ray Henderson had been trained as a serious musician. Born in Buffalo, New York, on December 1, 1896, he was the son of a mother who was an excellent pianist and who gave him his first music instruction before he could read or write. As a boy, Ray played the organ and sang in the choir of the local Episcopal church. He also started writing serious music. Showing unusual musical aptitude, he was then enrolled in the Chicago Conservatory of Music for intensive training. But even before he had entered the conservatory he began to drift toward popular music by playing the piano in jazz bands. While attending the conservatory he received a regular income by performing popular tunes on the piano at parties and by occasionally appearing in vaudeville in an act that included an Irish tenor and a Jewish comedian.

Once out of the conservatory, he abandoned serious music. His first job was as song plugger for the firm of Leo Feist in Tin Pan Alley. After a few weeks there he became arranger and staff pianist for Fred Fisher. His next job was with Shapiro-Bernstein where his talent impressed Louis Bernstein, who found a post for Henderson with various vaudevillians. He was also instrumental in getting Ray Henderson to work with Lew Brown, a lyricist who had already proved himself. The first two songs by Brown and Henderson (published by Shapiro-Bernstein) were "Humming" and "Georgette," both of them hits.

Now sometimes with Brown, now sometimes with other lyricists, Ray Henderson wrote songs that became leaders in Tin Pan Alley: "Alabamy Bound" and "Five Foot Two, Eyes of Blue," for example. His status in the Alley was sufficiently impressive to warrant George White to recruit him to write music for the *Scandals*, succeeding George Gershwin; Lew Brown and De Sylva were provided as the lyricists. De Sylva, Brown, and Henderson wrote songs for the *Scandals* of 1925, 1926, and 1928. And it was there that their first song successes were born.

While working for George White, De Sylva, Brown, and Henderson were able to work on several musical comedies, some of them major box-office attractions. Their first musical was *Good News* (1927), a hit. *Manhattan Mary*, starring Ed Wynn, came three weeks after *Good News*, but it proved to be merely a hiatus between two triumphs. *Hold Everything* (1928) was another box-office bonanza, and was followed by *Follow Through* (1929) and *Flying High* (1930).

The end of the decade also brought about the end of this fruitful collaboration. De Sylva went to Hollywood to work as producer, first for Fox, then for 20th Century-Fox. (Before this, however, the team of De Sylva, Brown, and Henderson had contributed some excellent songs for the screen: "Sonny Boy" and "There's a Rainbow 'Round My Shoulder" for Al Jolson's *Sonny,* and the score for the Janet Gaynor-Charles Farrell musical, *Sunny Side Up.*) Somewhere and somehow, in the midst of his frenetic activities in Hollywood, De Sylva found time to return to Broadway to produce several musical shows, and to write some musical-comedy texts. In 1932 he helped produce and write *Take a Chance* (*see* RICHARD E. WHITING). After that he had three box-office triumphs in succession: *Du Barry Was a Lady, Panama Hattie,* and *Louisiana Purchase;* for the first two of these he also helped to write the books (*see* COLE PORTER). De Sylva died in Hollywood on July 11, 1950, still a giant figure on Broadway and in Hollywood.

Divorced from De Sylva, the team of Brown and Henderson kept on writing songs for the Broadway stage. None of these productions had the vigor or originality that enlivened the shows they had previously written with De Sylva. Their failure to hit a winning stride led them to break up partnership temporarily. Lew Brown went out to Hollywood as a producer. He died in New York City on February 5, 1958. Henderson worked with other lyricists on songs for various Broadway and Hollywood productions. His Broadway plays included George White's *Scandals* of 1931 and 1935 and *The Ziegfeld Follies* of 1943, the last of which achieved the longest run of any edition of the *Follies* (*see* Appendix I—1907, *Ziegfeld Follies*).

It was the screen that helped recall the heyday of De Sylva, Brown, and Henderson in 1956, when it presented *The Best Things in Life Are Free,* a biography of the song-writing trio and a cavalcade of their most popular songs.

1925-28   The George White's *Scandals*

> **1925 edition,** a revue with book by George White and William K. Wells. Presented by George White at the Apollo Theatre on June 22. Staged by George White. Cast included Tom Patricola, Helen Morgan, Harry Fox, and the McCarthy Sisters (171 performances).

1926 edition, a revue with book by George White and William K. Wells. Presented by George White at the Apollo Theatre on June 14. Staged by George White. Cast included Ann Pennington, Frances Williams, Willie and Eugene Howard, Tom Patricola, and the Fairbanks Twins (424 performances).

1928 edition, a revue with book by George White and William K. Wells. Produced by George White at the Apollo Theatre on July 2. Staged by George White. Cast included Willie and Eugene Howard, Harry Richman, Tom Patricola, Frances Williams, and Ann Pennington (230 performances).

For other editions of the Scandals, *see* GEORGE GERSHWIN *and* RICHARD WHITING.

In replacing George Gershwin as composer for the *Scandals*, De Sylva, Brown, and Henderson did not make an auspicious debut. Their score for the 1925 edition (their first) was mostly second-rate, with the possible exceptions of "I Want a Lovable Baby," "Lovely Lady," and "What a World This Would Be" which, while pleasant, were without particular significance.

For that matter, the entire edition lacked distinction, as more than one critic pointed out. There was a pleasing parade of beautiful girls dressed in various furs; a presentation of a melodrama by a Southern stock company with the same emphasis on the dance that many Broadway productions gave in the 1925 era; and an amusing take-off on Irving Berlin (enacted by Gordon Dooley) who sang "All Alone" while a bevy of beautiful girls swarmed all around him. The contributions made by the stars were less impressive.

But in 1926 the *Scandals* presented one of its best editions—and in consequence it had the longest run of any of the *Scandals*. De Sylva, Brown, and Henderson created a remarkable score that had four bull's-eye hits: "The Birth of the Blues," "Black Bottom," "The Girl Is You," and "Lucky Day." "The Birth of the Blues" was used for a lavish production number that appeared as a first-act finale, and which was appropriately climaxed by an interpolation of parts of Gershwin's *Rhapsody in Blue*. "Black Bottom" became the inspiration for a demoniac dance by Ann Pennington, and was responsible for a new dance craze that swept the country. "The Girl Is You" was a sentimental number for Harry Richman in his first significant Broadway appearance.

The 1926 *Scandals* deserves attention for reasons other than its songs. An opening-night ticket for a seat in the first ten rows cost the unprecedented sum of fifty-five dollars. To justify such extravagance, George White gave an opulent production. Besides "The Birth of the Blues," the revue had a remarkable production number in "Triumph of Woman." The cream of the comedy included Willie Howard as a feuding Southern mountaineer, and a Western Union skit burlesquing the recent marriage of Irving Berlin and Ellin Mackay.

There was no edition of the *Scandals* in 1927. In 1928 it once again boasted a score by De Sylva, Brown, and Henderson. This time, as in 1925, the musical pickings were comparatively slim. About the only song worthy of special notice was a sweet, nostalgic number called "An Old-Fashioned Girl."

1927   GOOD NEWS, a musical comedy with book by Laurence Schwab and Buddy de Sylva. Lyrics by De Sylva and Brown. Music by Henderson. Produced by Schwab and Mandel at the 46th Street Theatre on September 6. Staged by Edgar MacGregor. Cast included John Price Jones, Mary Lawlor, Zelma O'Neal, Inez Courtney, and Gus Shy (551 performances).

Tait College is a school where football holds a position of greater importance than the curriculum, the kind of a place that has a college attached to the football stadium. Tom Marlowe (John Price Jones) is captain of the football team. He can play in the season's big game with Colton College only because Constance Lane (Mary Lawlor) has coached him in astronomy well enough for him to pass the exams. During the all-important game he is saved by Bobby Randall (Gus Shy) from making a fumble, and the game is won by Tait. Marlowe, still a hero, can now proceed to the more important business of winning Constance, whom he has loved for a long time.

The audience was made conscious of the college spirit even before the curtain went up. The ushers were dressed in college jerseys, and before the opening bar of the overture the men in the orchestra sounded off with several loud "rah rahs." Robust tunes in the college spirit helped maintain this rah-rah atmosphere throughout the production, which Brooks Atkinson described as "a constantly fast entertainment with furious dancing and catchy tunes played to the last trombone squeal." The best songs included two, so magnetically projected by a freshman girl, Flo, that Zelma O'Neal, who played the role, became a star: "Varsity Drag" and "Good News." The main love song was "The Best Things in Life Are Free," a duet by Connie and Tom, who also presented "Lucky in Love." A girl chorus gave a rousing presentation of "The Girls of Pi Beta Phi."

1928   HOLD EVERYTHING, a musical comedy with book by Buddy de Sylva and John McGowan. Lyrics by De Sylva and Brown. Music by Henderson. Produced by Aarons and Freedley at the Broadhurst Theatre on October 10. Dances staged by Jack Haskell and Sam Rose. Cast included Bert Lahr, Jack Whiting, Ona Munson, and Victor Moore (413 performances).

Though Bert Lahr, after half a lifetime in burlesque and vaudeville, had made his Broadway debut one year earlier in Harry Delmar's *Revels of 1927*, his career as a star of the Broadway musical-comedy stage began in *Hold Everything* where he appeared as Gink Schiner, a badly mauled pugilist. His boisterous, rough-and-ready comedy (punctuated by exclamations of "gang, gang, gang"), grimaces and clowning—and a hilarious sparring routine in the dressing room of the boxing champ—inspired rapturous reports from the critics. "He had me rocking," said Gilbert W. Gabriel. St. John Ervine, then guest critic for the New York *World*, wrote:

> His resourcefulness is astonishing. He seems never at a loss for a way of making fun. If he cannot think of a facial expression he uses a ludicrous utterance, or a floppy gesture, or the funniest of all, falls silent. . . . This man is funny.

Hold Everything spoofs the prizefight game and "clean sportsmanship." Sonny Jim Brooks (Jack Whiting), the welterweight champion, and Sue Burke (Ona Munson) are in love. But the society girl, Norine Lloyd (Betty Compton), is also after Sonny. Enraged by her jealousy, Sue refuses to have anything to do with Sonny. The champ is so downcast he has lost all interest in the forthcoming welterweight championship match. Sue rallies Sonny by convincing him she still loves him, and arouses him to fight his best match by telling him his opponent had insulted her.

The big song hit was presented by Sonny Jim Brooks: "You're the Cream in My Coffee." Another outstanding number, "Don't Hold Everything," was sung by Alice Boulden, who appeared in the role of Betty Dunn.

1929   FOLLOW THROUGH, a musical comedy with book by Laurence Schwab and Buddy de Sylva. Lyrics by De Sylva and Brown. Music by Henderson. Produced by Schwab and Mandel at the 46th Street Theatre on January 9. Staged by Edgar MacGregor and Donald Oenslager. Cast included Jack Haley, Zelma O'Neal, John Barker, and Eleanor Powell (403 performances).

The program described *Follow Through* as a "musical slice of country life." The plot revolved mainly around a golf match in a country club—

between Ruth Van Horn (Madeline Cameron) and Lora Moore (Irene Delroy). The latter, daughter of a golf pro, wins not only the match but also the love of the golf champ, Jerry Downs (John Barker).

Jack Haley appears as Jack Martin, the psychopathic son of a chain-store magnate, afraid of women but relentlessly pursued by Angie Howard (Zelma O'Neal). Martin and his friend, J. C. Effingham (John Sheehan) cavort about in the country club. One of their best comedy scenes is a burlesque of a golf game. ("The trouble with your game," Martin tells Effingham, "is that you stand too close to the ball—*after* you've hit it.") Another hilarious scene involved them in a ladies' shower room, which they had invaded, disguised as plumbers.

For Eleanor Powell, *Follow Through* represented her first Broadway success. From childhood on, she had been appearing in vaudeville. And one year earlier, on January 29, 1928, she made her first Broadway appearance—in a minor part in *The Opportunists* at the Casino de Paris. *Follow Through* provided her with an opportunity to win a Broadway audience with her singing, dancing, and personal charm—and she won it completely.

Zelma O'Neal, risen to stardom in *Good News*, had a big musical number in "I Want to Be Bad"; and with Jack Haley she sang the show's hit song, "Button Up Your Overcoat." They also presented the duet, "I Could Give Up Anything But You," while the main love song, "You Are My Lucky Star," was assigned to John Barker.

1930 FLYING HIGH, a musical comedy with book by Buddy de Sylva and John McGowan. Lyrics by De Sylva and Brown. Music by Henderson. Produced by George White at the Apollo Theatre on March 3. Staged by Edward Clark Lilley. Dances staged by Bobby Connelly. Cast included Oscar Shaw, Bert Lahr, Grace Brinkley, and Kate Smith (357 performances).

This was the last of the De Sylva, Brown, and Henderson musicals for Broadway; and largely because of Bert Lahr's inimitable clowning it was one of their best. The principal male characters are mail airplane pilots. The hero, Tod Addison (Oscar Shaw), engages in a transcontinental race, which he wins from a hated rival; at the same time he captures the hand and heart of Eileen Cassidy (Grace Brinkley), whom he first met when his plane landed on the roof of her New York apartment house. Rusty Krause (Bert Lahr) is a comic pilot who steals the plane of Tod's rival. Not knowing how to get it down on ground again, Rusty breaks an all-time record for keeping a plane in the air—and himself becomes something of a hero.

Lahr's best scene was in a doctor's office where he had come for a physical examination. He also had a fine comedy song number in "Mrs. Krause's Blue-Eyed Baby Boy." Rusty's girl friend, Pansy Sparks (Kate Smith), scored decisively with her only song, "Red Hot Chicago." Other winning songs were: "Thank Your Father" and "Happy Landing," both sung by Tod; also "Good for You, Bad for Me" and "Wasn't It Beautiful While It Lasted?"

VERNON DUKE, composer

Vernon Duke was born as Vladimir Dukelsky on October 10, 1903, in Pskov, northern Russia. His father, a direct descendant of the kings of Georgia in the Caucasus, planned to make his son a diplomat, and saw to it that the boy began the study of languages early. But the child was propelled to music. He was seven when he started music study, eight when he completed a ballet in fourteen acts. His father disregarded this activity and enrolled him in the Naval Academy in Kiev, but his mother interceded for him and finally gained the father's permission for Vladimir—or Vernon as we shall henceforth call him—to enter the Kiev Conservatory. There he studied with Glière until he was fifteen.

During the Revolution Vernon fled with his mother and brother to Odessa, and from there they made their way to Constantinople where Duke supported himself by arranging concerts for a club for refugees run by the Y.M.C.A. His first major work was completed at this time, a ballet, *A Syrian Tale*, and its score became his first publication.

At the club he came across several copies of sheet music of American popular songs. One was George Gershwin's "Swanee." From that moment on he not only became a dedicated Gershwin fan but was stimulated to write popular songs of his own. The craving to produce such songs remained unsatisfied until after his arrival in the United States in 1921. Through the concert singer, Eva Gauthier (who had recently sung some of his songs in New York), he was introduced to Gershwin, already a power on Broadway and in Tin Pan Alley. Duke played for Gershwin some of his esoteric piano sonatas. "There's no heart in it," Gershwin told him and urged him to try writing "real popular tunes, and don't be scared about going low-brow." Gershwin was generous with advice, help, and encouragement; he was also responsible for Duke's adopting an Americanized name, which from then on he would use for his popular productions. Sixteen years later Duke repaid at least partly the debt he owed Gershwin by completing Gershwin's score for *The Goldwyn Follies*, left unfinished by Gershwin's last fatal illness.

While making tentative efforts at writing popular tunes, Duke supported himself by taking on any job that brought a fee. He wrote musical accompaniments for a magician's act; for a week he conducted an orchestra in a 14th Street burlesque house; he played a piano in a 42nd Street restaurant; he created music for a night-club show. All the while he kept on writing serious musical works, but he felt he was on a treadmill and he finally decided to jump off by escaping to Europe and furthering his career as a serious composer. This was in 1924. In Paris he met Sergei Diaghilev, director of the Ballet Russe, who commissioned the young composer to write music for a new ballet, *Zephyr et Flore*. The ballet was introduced by the Diaghilev troupe in Monte Carlo in 1925, and was soon afterward performed in Paris, London, Berlin, and Barcelona.

In Paris, Duke met Serge Koussevitzky. Just recently appointed music director of the Boston Symphony Orchestra, Koussevitzky was also owner and director of a Paris music-publishing establishment. He accepted some of Duke's works for publication and subsequently became one of Duke's most ardent champions. In 1929 Koussevitzky introduced Duke's First Symphony in Boston. During the next few years other major works by Duke were introduced by the Boston Symphony; in a ten-year period Koussevitzky performed more than six times as many compositions by Duke than all the other American conductors combined.

After his stay in Paris in 1925, Duke proceeded to London, where he made his first professional contact with the stage. Charles Cochran, outstanding producer of musicals, engaged him to write music for a show that never materialized. But another project had happier results. *Yvonne*, a musical to which Duke contributed six numbers, was produced in 1926. *Yvonne* did fairly well at the box office until Noel Coward destroyed it by describing it as "Yvonne the terrible." Soon after *Yvonne* was produced, Duke wrote his first complete stage score, for an Edgar Wallace thriller, *The Yellow Mask*, which had a London run of seven months.

Duke was back in the United States in 1929. For a while he worked in a movie theater in Long Island playing the piano for silent-screen performances. During this time he started storming the citadels of Broadway with songs. In 1930 he sold two to the third edition of *The Garrick Gaieties*: "I'm Only Human After All" (lyrics by Ira Gershwin and E. Y. Harburg), "Too Too Divine," and "Shavian Shivers" (lyrics to both by

Harburg). Other songs appeared in various revues; of particular interest were "Talkative Toes" in *Three's a Crowd* (1930), "Muchacha" in *Shoot the Works* (1931); and "Let Me Match My Private Life with Yours" in *Americana* (1932).

Success came in 1932 with his first full Broadway score, for the revue *Walk a Little Faster*. In 1934 and 1936 Duke wrote a few numbers for *The Ziegfeld Follies* editions of those years, including such fine songs as "What Is There to Say?" and "I Can't Get Started With You." A musical comedy with a score entirely his did not appear on Broadway until eight years after *Walk a Little Faster—Cabin in the Sky*, one of the ornaments of the musical theater of the 1940's.

In 1941 came *Banjo Eyes*, starring Eddie Cantor, a box-office success. After that came a string of failures, including *Sadie Thompson* (1944), an unhappy adaptation of Somerset Maugham's *Rain*, and two revues. The first of these revues was *Two's Company* (1952) in which Bette Davis made a heroic effort to sing and play comedy, an effort that never quite came off; the other was an unimpressive and unimaginative thing called *The Littlest Revue* (1956).

1932   WALK A LITTLE FASTER, a revue with sketches by S. J. Perelman and Robert MacGunigle. Lyrics by E. Y. Harburg. Presented by Courtney Burr at the St. James Theatre on December 7. Dances by Albertina Rasch. Staged by Monty Woolley. Cast included Beatrice Lillie, Clark and McCullough, and Evelyn Hoey (119 performances).

Walk a Little Faster was Vernon Duke's first complete score for the Broadway theater. It was a moderate success and deserves to be remembered if only because it was the showcase for what to this day is Duke's most popular song, "April in Paris." Writing that song was almost an afterthought, and it was interpolated into the revue after it had gone into rehearsal. One day, during the rehearsal period, Duke and some of his collaborators discussed the necessity of including a romantic number. During the course of the conversation Dorothy Parker happened to remark wistfully, "Oh, to be in Paris now that April's here." This served as a cue to Duke for the romantic song he needed, and Harburg quickly provided a lyric. The song was introduced into the revue during Boston tryouts, in a scene re-creating the Left Bank, the setting by Boris Aronson; it was sung by Evelyn Hoey. H. T. Parker, renowned Boston drama and music critic, singled out the song for special praise. " 'April in Paris,' " he wrote, "is worthy, in place and kind, of that city in spring. There's a catch in the throat from it—if one has too many memories." But, strange to say, the song was a failure when the show hit New York. One reason may have been that, a victim of laryngitis, Evelyn Hoey sang it in almost a whisper. Most of the critics ignored the song entirely, while Robert Garland considered it an "unnecessary item." This neglect infuriated the Boston writer, Isaac Goldberg, who wrote to Duke: " 'April in Paris' is one of the finest musical compositions that ever graced an American production. If I had my way, I'd make the study of it compulsory in all harmony courses." But in time the song caught on, particularly after it was sung in night clubs and on records by Marian Chase, the blues singer.

"April in Paris" was the best song in the Duke score, but there were other numbers worthy of mention. One was a touching tribute to Manhattan, "Loneliest Isle"; "Off Again, on Again," "Speaking of Love," and "Where Have We Met Before?" were others.

Beatrice Lillie was the stand-out performer in the revue. She appeared as a 1906 college girl, as a belle of the Yukon, as a radio songstress, and as a French *diseuse* who provides commentary on the songs she sings. Her comedy was supplemented by that of Clark and McCullough, who appeared in their familiar outfits and equipment; one of the best sketches in the revue was a take-off on a then-recent musical, *Flying Colors*, in which Bobby Clark appeared as Clifton Webb and Beatrice Lillie as Tamara Geva.

1940   CABIN IN THE SKY, a musical fantasy with book by Lynn Root. Lyrics by John La Touche. Produced by Albert Lewis in conjunction with Aaron Freedley at the Martin Beck Theatre on October 25. Staged by George Balanchine. Cast included Ethel Waters, Todd Duncan, Rex Ingram, and Katherine Dunham (156 performances).

Cabin in the Sky is one of the most poignant and sensitive portraits of Negro life and psychology presented by the Broadway musical theater in the 1940's. The story has the simplicity and at times the ingenuousness of folklore. A tug of war ensues between Lucifer, Jr. (Rex Ingram), and the Lawd's General (Todd Duncan) for the poor soul of a humble Negro, Little Joe (Dooley Wilson). Little Joe, though well meaning, simply cannot keep out of trouble. Petunia (Ethel Waters) tries to help Joe win the battle for the forces of Good; and there are the the primitive and lustful wiles of Georgia Brown (Katherine Dunham) to weaken Little Joe's resistance to Evil and arouse his flesh. Joe shoots Petunia in a dance hall, but Petunia is all-forgiving and makes it possible for Joe to slip into Heaven.

The folk character of the play was rarely permitted to degenerate into vaudeville humor, gawdy spectacle, or outright caricature. Every element in the production maintained the quiet dignity and integrity of the Lynn Root play, particularly the simple and earthy lyrics of John La Touche, the choreography of George Balanchine, and the exciting dancing of Katherine Dunham, who was making her first appearance on the Broadway musical-comedy stage.

Duke's music tapped a creative vein hitherto reserved for his more serious efforts for the concert stage. Songs like "Taking a Chance on Love" (which George Jean Nathan considered the best musical-comedy song of the year), "Cabin in the Sky," "Honey in the Honeycomb," and "Love Me Tomorrow" have the overtones of Negro folk songs.

1941   BANJO EYES, a musical comedy with book by Joe Quinllan and Izzy Elinson based on the Broadway stage comedy, *Three Men on a Horse*, by John Cecil Holm and George Abbott. Lyrics by John La Touche and Harold Adamson. Produced by Albert Lewis at the Hollywood Theatre on December 25. Directed by Hassard Short. Dances by Charles Walters. Cast included Eddie Cantor, Lionel Stander, June Clyde, Audrey Christie, and the De Marcos (126 performances).

The musical adaptation of *Three Men on a Horse* digresses from the original stage play. In the play Erwin Trowbridge is a meek, mild-mannered writer of greeting-card verses who has a unique gift for doping out horses on paper. After a fight with his wife, he goes off to the nearest bar, gets drunk for the first time in his life, and then becomes involved with gamblers who take full advantage of his rare gift for picking horses. But Erwin can pick winners only so long as he does not profit from his choices. Since he has been compelled to take a percentage of the gamblers' winnings, he can figure winners no more. He extricates himself from the clutches of the gamblers, returns to his wife and to his former placid and uneventful existence as a writer of greeting-card poems.

In the musical Erwin (Eddie Cantor) gets his horse information in a dream, which leads him to the racing stables where he talks to the horses and finds out from them who will be the winner.

Corn is generously introduced to provide the musical with audience appeal. There is, for example, a hackneyed horse routine—long a staple of vaudeville and burlesque—in which the horse is played by two actors, one the head, the other, the tail. Also, since Pearl Harbor had been a recent disaster when *Banjo Eyes* opened and America was deep in war, an army-drill scene was interpolated to inject a timely martial note; this scene culminated in one of the first stirring songs of World War II, "We Did It Before, We'll Do It Again" (not by Vernon Duke but by Charles Tobias and Cliff Friend).

Eddie Cantor gave an impressive rendition of this war song. But the song that stopped the show regularly was a humorous item, "We're Having a Baby," its risqué lines and provocative innuendoes accentuated by Eddie's rolling eyes and clapping hands. Cantor had another amusing song hit, "Who Started the Rhumba?" which he sang to a race horse. The closest thing to a love ballad was "Haven't a Nickel to My Name," danced to by the De Marcos.

Banjo Eyes was much more successful than its run of 126 performances might suggest. *Billboard* reported that there was not a single dissenting vote among the critics about its entertainment value, and audiences were also enthusiastic. The show played to capacity houses during its run. When it closed it was not for lack of customers but because Cantor had to undergo a serious operation. The show had been tailor-made for his special talents, and he dominated it so completely that a substitute for him was impossible.

LUDWIG ENGLANDER, composer

The fame of Ludwig Englander has been so completely eclipsed—and that eclipse began even while he was still alive and working—that very little information about him has survived. When he died, only a few lines of obituary reminded theatergoers that he had once written some lovable operetta scores. Since his death he has been forgotten so completely that not even the standard reference books mention him. The meager biographical facts are these: He was born in Vienna in 1859, received his academic education at the university there, and had some musical training from Jacques Offenbach. In 1882 he came to New York, where he became the conductor of the Thalia Theatre. His first musical, *The Princess Consort*, was a failure. In 1894 he became known through *The Passing Show*, and in the next dozen years or so his reputation was established with several prominent productions, among them *The Rounders* (1899), *The Casino Girl* (1900), *Belle of Bohemia* (1900), *The Strollers* (1901), *A Madcap Princess*, based on Charles Major's novel *When Knighthood Was in Flower* (1904), and *Miss Innocence* (1908). By the time he died—at his home in Far Rockaway, New York, on September 13, 1914—he had written the music for thirty-five operettas. He was a skilled craftsman in writing facile melodies that had the lilt, pulse, and charm of Vienna. But his range was small, and his storehouse of melodic ideas not too well stocked. His last few operettas were failures; the last one, *Mlle. Moselle* (1914) ran only nine performances. And by the time he died there were not many to recall that a decade earlier he had been a major musical figure on Broadway.

1894   THE PASSING SHOW, a revue with book and lyrics by Sydney Rosenberg. Produced at the Casino Theatre on May 12. Cast included Jeff de Angelis, Adele Ritchie, Johnny Henshaw, and Paul Arthur.

The Passing Show created a new genus in the American musical theater —the revue; consequently it was the forerunner of *The Ziegfeld Follies,* George White's *Scandals* and all the other elaborate or intimate revues that brightened the Broadway theater for over half a century. (This 1894 production should not be confused with the annual editions of *The Passing Show,* which the Shuberts presented at the Winter Garden from 1912 on, and which are discussed in the sections devoted to LOUIS A. HIRSCH, SIGMUND ROMBERG, and JEAN SCHWARTZ.)

Like later revues, the 1894 *Passing Show* was a conglomeration of many things: burlesque, vaudeville, extravaganza; comedy, satire, song, dance, female pulchritude. It boasted comedy in skits, and routines by the Tamale Brothers; acrobatics in stunts by the Amazons; comedy in imitations of popular actors of the day and satires of current plays; female pulchritude in a series of "living pictures"; spectacle in a sumptuously mounted "divertissement" on *L'Enfant prodigue;* dances by Lucy Daly, who contributed a novel plantation dance with a group of young colored men.

1900   THE CASINO GIRL, an operetta, with book and lyrics by Harry B. Smith. Additional music by Marion Cook, Harry T. MacConnell, and Arthur Nevin. Produced by George V. Lederer at the Casino Theatre on March 19. Cast included Virginia Earle, Albert Hart, Sam Bernard, Mabelle Gilman, and Lotta Faust (91 performances).

The Casino Theatre in New York was for many years the home of musical comedies and operettas, and on its stage passed some of the theater's most beautiful show girls in the era preceding Florenz Ziegfeld. It was inevitable, then, that a Casino Theatre production be built around the personality of these girls. She is Laura Lee (Mabelle Gilman), who is loved by Percy (Virginia Earle), seventh son of the Earl of Doughmore. Because of Percy's infatuation, his father sends him off to faraway Egypt.

But Laura grows weary of night life in New York and herself goes off to Cairo to open a millinery shop there. She meets Percy again, falls in love with him, and they finally marry. But before that happens they go through various adventures. Laura must elude the clutches of the Khedive (Sam Bernard) who wants her for his harem, and Percy must extricate himself from the grip of two slick crooks, Fromage and Potage.

The plot was enlivened by sparkling performances; by Sam Bernard who brought an amusingly incongruous Dutch accent to the character of the Khedive; by Virginia Earle, vivacious in her impersonation of the male character of Percy and who (as one critic noted) "sang and danced like a dream"; by the malapropisms of a minor character played by Carrie E. Perkins. Englander's best songs included an Oriental-type number, "Slave Dealer's Song"; the title song; "Mam'selle"; and a nostalgic tribute, "New York." But the hit song of the show came from another pen, that of John H. Flynn: "Sweet Annie Moore," whose lyrics (also by Flynn) contained an amusing succession of puns.

1900   BELLE OF BOHEMIA, operetta with book and lyrics by Harry B. Smith. Additional music by T. MacConnell. Presented by George W. Lederer on September 24. Staged by George Lederer. Ballets arranged by Aurelia Coccia. Cast included Sam Bernard, Irene Bentley, Virginia Earle, and Trixie Friganza (55 performances).

Belle of Bohemia is a comedy of errors. Adolph Klotz, a Coney Island photographer (Sam Bernard), and Rudolph Dinkelhauser, a wealthy brewer (Dick Bernard), look alike. While bathing in Coney Island they are mistaken for each other. When Dinkelhauser is arrested for indiscretions committed by Klotz while drunk, Klotz is taken home by Dinkelhauser's wife and valet who believe he has gone crazy because he insists he is a photographer. At the Dinkelhauser villa in Newport, a fraudulent lawyer is trying to swindle Dinkelhauser of his fortune and confuses Klotz with the man he is trying to swindle. Klotz saves Dinkelhauser's fortune.

"He Was a Married Man," sung by Adolph Klotz, "When Shall I Find Him?" introduced by Klotz' wife, played by Virginia Earle, and "Plain Kelly McGuire" were the principal musical numbers. As a first-act finale the sextet from Donizetti's *Lucia di Lammermoor* was satirized.

1901   THE STROLLERS, an operetta with book and lyrics by Harry B. Smith based on *Die Landesstreicher* by L. Kremm and C. Lindau. Produced by George W. Lederer at the Knickerbocker Theatre on June 24. Staged by Messrs. Nixon and Zimmerman. Cast included Francis Wilson, Irene Bentley, Harry Gilfoil, and Eddie Foy (70 performances).

The word "strollers" is a euphemism for "tramps." The tramps in this operetta are August Lump (Francis Wilson) and his wife Bertha (Irene Bentley). When, in a small Austrian town, they find a thousand-mark note and try to cash it, they are arrested as suspicious characters. They manage to escape and stay free when a Prince (Henry Gilfoil) and his girl friend are mistaken for them and are herded into prison. Meanwhile, the strollers go through varied adventures in different towns and in high society. They attend a swank garden party and elude detection through the assumption of numerous disguises.

At one of the society parties they manage to crash, the strollers witness an elaborate spectacle, "The Ballet of the Fans," the production highlight of the play; and during their incarceration they are attended by a drunken jailer (Edwin Fay) who contributes some of the big comic moments. Otherwise the play was most notable for the following numbers by Englander: "Gossip Chorus"; Bertha's "A Lesson in Flirtation"; and a song that courses throughout the play, a duet of Lump and Bertha, "Strollers We."

1905 THE RICH MR. HOGGENHEIMER, a musical comedy with book and lyrics by Harry B. Smith. Additional songs by Jerome Kern and others. Produced by Charles Frohman at Wallack's Theatre on October 22. Staged by Ben Teal. Cast included Sam Bernard, Marion Garson, and Georgia Caine (187 performances).

In 1903 a musical comedy by Ivan Caryll called *The Girl from Kay's* was imported from London and presented on Broadway with Sam Bernard in the role of a rich, overbearing Jew named Mr. Hoggenheimer. Bernard's success in that part led him to appear as Mr. Hoggenheimer in several subsequent Broadway musicals. *The Rich Mr. Hoggenheimer* was not only his greatest triumph in a Hoggenheimer role but also in any role up to 1913 when he joined Alexander Carr to star in the nonmusical, *Potash and Perlmutter*.

Mr. Hoggenheimer (Sam Bernard) of London learns that his son Guy (Edwin Nicander), while visiting the United States, was planning to marry Amy Leigh (Marion Garson), a poor, untitled American girl. Hoggenheimer decides to make a secret trip to America to prevent his son from making such an undesirable match. Since he is a friend of the actress, Flora Fair (Georgia Caine), and since she is aboard the same ship as he, Hoggenheimer's wife is convinced that the only reason he is going to America is for a love escapade. She follows him and catches up with him at a charity bazaar in Great Neck where Hoggenheimer is toasting Flora. When Hoggenheimer arranges for Flora to marry the man she actually loves—Percy Vere (Percy Ames)—Mrs. Hoggenheimer becomes aware of his innocence. Meanwhile Hoggenheimer has become reconciled to Guy's forthcoming marriage to Amy.

As Flora Fair, Georgia Caine completely won over her audiences, particularly when she gave her charming rendition of songs like "Don't You Want a Paper, Dearie?" and "This World Is a Toy Shop." But the hit song of the play, the love duet of Guy and Amy, "Any Old Time at All," was not by Englander but by Jean Schwartz, to William Jerome's lyrics. Another interpolation in the Englander score was one of Jerome Kern's earliest songs, "Bagpipe Serenade," sung by Flora Fair and a bevy of young girls dressed in fetching Scottish kilts.

SAMMY FAIN, composer and IRVING KAHAL, lyricist

Sammy Fain was born in New York City on June 17, 1902, the nephew of the celebrated comedians, Willie and Eugene Howard. In his boyhood his family moved to the Sullivan County section of New York State where the boy attended public schools, taught himself to play the piano, and started writing popular songs which he faithfully dispatched by mail to Tin Pan Alley without encouraging results. After completing high school Fain decided to return to New York City and make a more energetic and determined effort at promoting his career in popular music. He found a job as staff pianist for the Jack Mills publishing house, then toured the vaudeville circuit with Artie Dunn and finally made a name for himself as a radio entertainer.

His first professional song came in 1925, "Nobody Knows What a Red-Headed Mama Can Do," (lyrics by Irving Mills and Al Dubin). In 1927 Fain met and teamed up with a gifted lyricist, Irving Kahal, with whom he established a seventeen-year partnership. Kahal was born in Houtzdale, Pennsylvania, on March 5, 1903, was educated in public schools in Connecticut and New York City, and at sixteen attended Cooper Union art school on a scholarship. By the time Fain met him, Kahal had already toured with the Gus Edwards Minstrels as a singer, and had written some song lyrics.

The first song by Fain and Kahal was a winner, "Let a Smile Be Your Umbrella." From then on—and up to the time of Kahal's death, in New York City, on February 7, 1942—they produced a long string of song hits, some for the Broadway stage, most of them for Hollywood where they had worked since 1930. Their best motion-picture songs were: "You Brought a New Kind of Love to Me" (made famous by Maurice Chevalier), "By a Waterfall," and "I'll Be Seeing You." Other outstanding songs by Fain for the screen were to words by other lyricists. The lyricist for "That Old Feeling" was Lew Brown, while with Paul Francis Webster Fain wrote two songs that won Academy Awards: "Secret Love" in 1953 and "Love Is a Many-Splendored Thing" in 1955.

Fain's first endeavors for the Broadway stage were in collaboration with Kahal: a single song, "Satan's Holiday" in *Manhattan Mary* (1927); the entire score for a revue, *Everybody's Welcome* (1931).

Fain's greatest Broadway successes came with the two riot-filled extravaganzas of Olsen and Johnson: *Hellzapoppin'* (1938) and *Sons O' Fun* (1941). Other musicals and revues with Fain's songs included the following: *Right This Way* (1938), which had "I Can Dream, Can't I?" and whose cast included Joe E. Lewis and Tamara; *Boys and Girls Together* (1939), a revue starring Ed Wynn; *Toplitsky of Notre Dame* (1946); and *Flahooley* (1951). The lyrics for *Toplitsky* were by Jack Barnett; those for *Flahooley* by E. Y. Harburg.

1938 HELLZAPOPPIN', a free-for-all vaudeville revue, with book mostly by Olsen and Johnson. Additional songs by Charles Tobias and Earl Robinson. Produced by Olsen and Johnson at the 46th Street Theatre on September 22. Staged by Edward Dowling. Cast included Olsen and Johnson, Barto and Mann, Hal Sherman, the Radio Rogues, Bettymae and Beverly Crane, and the Charioteers (1404 performances).

The program described *Hellzapoppin'* as a "screamlined revue designed for laughing." Except for the "audience participation" number at the end of the show, the program tried to follow the accepted pattern of the formal revue. There were skits (on English detectives, cabinet meetings of foreign powers, Wall Street, maternity wards); songs ("It's Time to Say Aloha," for example, beautifully sung by Bettymae and Beverly Crane, and "Strolling Through the Park"); parody and satire (the Radio Rogues gave travesties of celebrities like Walter Winchell, Kate Smith, and Rudy Vallee). What the program did not suggest—and what made this show one of the most successful in Broadway history, with the longest run of any Broadway play up to that time—was the endless parade of improvisations, scatterbrained stunts, unexpected bits of tomfoolery, and schoolboy pranks. These made a shambles of the formal program and sometimes turned the theater into bedlam.

The revue began in an unorthodox manner, with a motion-picture newsreel showing President Roosevelt, Mayor La Guardia, Mussolini, and Hitler—with unexpected sounds and sentiments coming out of their mouths. (Hitler was made to speak with a Yiddish accent.) Then Olsen and Johnson appeared in an outlandish automobile, and from then on the surprises descended on the audience with profusion. A woman kept running down the aisles calling for "Oscar." A ticket scalper hounded some in the audience to sell them seats for other shows. A lady suddenly left her seat to announce she was going to the lady's room. A stuffed gorilla dragged a lady from her box seat, and a gentleman Godiva rode a horse in the balcony. A cyclist performed on a bicycle with square wheels. The theater suddenly grew black, and through a loud-speaker came the warning that the audience would be afflicted with snakes and spiders—as it was pelted with puffed rice.

The cast included midgets, barkers, clowns, even pigeons. Balloons burst, autos exploded, guns popped. The breath-taking sequence of incongruous events and slapstick created a momentum that was irresistible and made some of the critics—the most vocal being Walter Winchell— say this was the funniest show they had ever seen.

1941   SONS O' FUN, a vaudeville revue, with book by Olsen and Johnson and Hal Block. Lyrics by Jack Yellen and Irving Kahal. Additional songs by Will Irwin. Produced by the Shuberts at the Winter Garden on December 1. Staged by Edward Dowling. Dances by Robert Alton. Cast included Olsen and Johnson, Carmen Miranda, Ella Logan, and Frank Libuse (742 performances).

Madcap improvisations and interpolations made *Sons O' Fun* as riotously funny—and almost as successful—as *Hellzapoppin'*. When the audience entered it was warned by a policeman not to smoke—but he himself was puffing on a huge lighted cigar. Frank Libuse conducted some of the patrons to their seats—the wrong ones. Other patrons had to reach their seats in the boxes on ladders. During the performance members of the audience were invited on the stage where they jumped hurdles, and where women's skirts were blown over their heads. Chorus girls came down to the audience to dance in the aisles with celebrities. During the intermission an Indian family in full regalia created havoc in the lobby.

And so it went—from the unexpected to the absurd. The woman who had been running down the aisles in *Hellzapoppin'* calling for "Oscar" was still looking for her man. A stork flying overhead neatly deposited a child in a lady's lap. A fellow atop a telegraph pole was listening to the radio. When Chic Johnson appeared on the stage dressed in panties, a man rose haughtily in his seat in the audience and proceeded to undress as a protest; and so did his wife.

Amid all these shenanigans there was a show—a revue hewn along more traditional lines. Ella Logan sang "Happy in Love," one of three outstanding songs; the other two were "Why?" and "Cross Your Fingers." Rosario and Antonio performed exciting Spanish dances, and Carmen Miranda went through her frenetic South American ways. The skits included burlesques on *Panama Hattie* and *Charlie's Aunt,* a farcical army-training sketch with Joe Besser, and another with Chic Johnson spending a "quiet night in the country."

HERBERT and **DOROTHY FIELDS**, librettists, lyricist

JOSEPH FIELDS, librettist

Herbert Fields was born with theater blood in his veins. His father was Lew Fields, erstwhile partner in the famous team of Weber and Fields which for many years starred in Broadway extravaganzas (*see* JOHN STROMBERG). After the breakup of this partnership, Lew Fields embarked on a new career as a producer of, and frequently star of, Broadway musicals; as a producer he was responsible for lifting young Richard Rodgers to the rank of professional composer.

Herbert Fields was born in New York City on July 26, 1897. He was educated in New York City schools and at Columbia College. When first he entered the theater, it was as an actor and not as a writer. He had a pleasing stage presence, a nice voice, and a gift for dialect; all these qualities led his father to cast him in minor roles.

The idea of his turning from actor to writer was born with his friends Lorenz Hart and Richard Rodgers. Hart and Fields had known each other from boyhood. They used to play on the city streets in Harlem, where both lived at the time; during the summer of 1910 they produced shows at a boys' camp. Fields' first meeting with Rodgers, however, did not take place until 1919 when the latter came to Lew Fields' summer place in Far Rockaway, New York, to play some of his songs. When Lew Fields accepted the Rodgers and Hart song, "Any Old Place with You" for *A Lonely Romeo,* the paths of Rodgers and Herbert Fields crossed again, for Herbert played a small role in that show.

One evening, at Larry Hart's home on 119th Street, Rodgers and Hart suggested to Herbert Fields that he try writing musical-comedy texts.

The three of them went to work on a musical, *Winkle Town,* which nobody wanted to produce. Under a pseudonym the three men then wrote a comedy about Tin Pan Alley (with several interpolated songs) called *The Melody Man.* Lew Fields produced and starred in it in 1924, but it was a failure. Rodgers, Hart, and Fields also worked together on some amateur musical productions.

They achieved their first musical-comedy success in 1925 with *Dearest Enemy,* for which Herbert Fields wrote the text, and Rodgers and Hart the songs. For the next half-dozen years, the team of Rodgers, Hart, and Fields wrote a succession of musicals, some of which were outstanding successes. Herbert Fields' courage in the selection of unusual subjects for musical-comedy treatment, his complete sympathy with the unusual approaches and procedures of his partners, made him one of the most important musical-comedy writers of the 1920's. But during this period he worked with other composers as well, notably Vincent Youmans and Cole Porter.

After Herbert Fields parted company with Rodgers and Hart, he continued to write musical-comedy texts for other composers, the most important of whom was Cole Porter. It was for the Cole Porter musical, *Let's Face It* (1941), that the brother-and-sister writing partnership was launched; but by then Dorothy Fields, like Herbert, had already won acceptance as a writer for the musical stage.

Dorothy, youngest of the Fields children, was born in Allenhurst, New Jersey, on July 15, 1905. She attended and later taught dramatic arts at the Benjamin School for Girls in New York, where she appeared in amateur musical productions written for the school by the then-still-unknown Rodgers and Hart. She also wrote smart verses for the magazines and tried writing song lyrics. Although she made little headway in the latter, she was able to induce Jimmy McHugh, the composer, to write music for her lyrics. Their first collaboration was a box-office smash, an all-Negro revue, *Blackbirds of 1928.* With that revue Jimmy McHugh and Dorothy Fields became a song-writing team that for many years contributed notable scores to the Broadway musical stage and the Hollywood screen, and many outstanding song hits.

It was only after Dorothy Fields and Jimmy McHugh ended their partnership that she joined her brother Herbert in writing text and lyrics for musical comedies—not only for those by Cole Porter but also by Irving Berlin and Sigmund Romberg.

Herbert Fields died of a heart attack in New York City on March 24, 1958.

For Herbert Fields *see:* COLE PORTER (*Fifty Million Frenchmen, Du Barry Was a Lady, Panama Hattie*); RICHARD RODGERS (*The Garrick Gaieties,* 1926, *Dearest Enemy, The Girl Friend, Peggy-Ann, A Connecticut Yankee, Present Arms, America's Sweetheart*); VINCENT YOUMANS (*Hit the Deck*).

For Dorothy Fields *see:* JIMMY MCHUGH (*Blackbirds of 1928*); ARTHUR SCHWARTZ (*A Tree Grows in Brooklyn*).

For Herbert and Dorothy Fields *see:* IRVING BERLIN (*Annie Get Your Gun*); COLE PORTER (*Let's Face It, Something for the Boys, Mexican Hayride*); JIMMY MCHUGH (*Hello Daddy*); SIGMUND ROMBERG (*Up In Central Park*); ARTHUR SCHWARTZ (*By the Beautiful Sea*).

Joseph Fields is the oldest of the Fields children, born in New York City on February 21, 1885. He is best known as a playwright in the nonmusical field, having had a hand in such redoubtable successes as *My Sister Eileen* and *Junior Miss,* among many others. For the musical stage he helped write the text for Sigmund Romberg's *The Girl in Pink Tights* and Jule Styne's *Gentlemen Prefer Blondes.*

GEORGE FORREST, composer. *See* ROBERT WRIGHT and GEORGE FORREST

RUDOLF FRIML, composer

Rudolf Friml was in his heyday in the 1910's and 1920's, when the American operetta was still subservient to European methods and styles. Friml could only function successfully within those formulas and conventions set by the Continental operetta. As he told a newspaper interviewer in the middle 1930's, "When I write music for the theater, I like books with charm to them. And charm suggests the old things—the finest things that were done long ago. I like a full-blooded libretto with luscious melody, rousing choruses, and romantic passions." A contemporary setting, an American background, modern raciness of style and tempo, sophistication—all these were incapable of stimulating him. Once, analyzing the newer kind of American musicals springing into vogue in the 1930's and 1940's, he remarked, "No romance, no glamour, and no heroes. I can't write music unless there are romance, glamour and heroes." And since the kind of operetta he preferred writing had become passé after the 1930's, Friml has ceased to be a dominating figure in the musical theater.

But what he had produced before 1930 had won for him the right to join the foremost stage composers of that period. The traditions in which he functioned best might die, but the music he wrote conforming to those traditions survives.

He was born in Prague on December 7, 1879, the son of an impoverished baker who loved music passionately and who could play the zither and accordion. Rudolf showed unusual musical ability from childhood on. He was only ten when his "Barcarolle for Piano" was published. Friends and relatives pooled contributions into a fund sending him to the Prague Conservatory, then directed by Antonin Dvořák. Friml, aged fourteen, took entrance examinations and was put into the third year, thus enabling him to complete a six-year course in three years.

Soon after being graduated from the Conservatory, Friml was engaged by Jan Kubelik (a violin virtuoso who had been his fellow student at the conservatory) to appear with him in joint recitals throughout Europe. Friml toured with Kubelik for about ten years. Since in that time Kubelik had become one of Europe's most celebrated violinists, the assignment of appearing with him placed Friml among Europe's most successful pianists.

Daniel Frohman, the American producer, signed Kubelik for an American tour in 1901. Friml had not been engaged, but when Kubelik's accompanist fell ill, the violinist prevailed on Friml to tour with him. After a second American tour with Kubelik in 1906, Friml decided to remain in America for good and to pursue there his own career as pianist and composer. He had already made his American debut as solo pianist at a performance in Carnegie Hall in 1904. In the fall of 1906 Friml appeared as soloist with the New York Symphony Society in a performance of his own Piano Concerto in B-flat major. After that he was heard in recitals, and as soloist with important orchestras. He also wrote a good deal of music —mostly songs, piano pieces, and short instrumental pieces. They revealed a good technique and a pleasing lyricism rather than genuine creative power.

He was, then, an industrious, competent, but not particularly brilliant composer when chance brought him into the Broadway theater. Victor Herbert had planned an operetta for Emma Trentini to follow his own *Naughty Marietta*. During the run of *Naughty Marietta*, however, Herbert and Trentini became involved in a bitter feud and refused to communicate with each other. Herbert bowed out as the composer for the singer's new operetta, and a new composer had to be found. Rudolph Schirmer and Max Dreyfus, two perceptive publishers, suggested the then-unknown name of Rudolf Friml, since both felt that Friml had the talent to write well for voices and for the stage. Arthur Hammerstein, the producer, followed their advice and contracted Friml. Thus Friml put both feet into the theater with a triumphant production—for the play for which he was asked to write the music was *The Firefly* (1912).

With *The Firefly* outstandingly successful, Friml no longer had a dearth of assignments. When the book did not stand in the way of his gracious, charming lyricism, he created shows that were acclaimed, among them some of the best-loved operettas and musical comedies of the American stage. Among the lesser Friml successes, but those with attractive scores, were *Katinka* (1915), *You're in Love* (1917), and *Tumble Inn* (1919).

But by 1930 Friml's day as a successful stage composer was over. The musical theater had changed radically, and Friml's musicals had not changed with it. Like Victor Herbert before him, Friml found himself outdated. An operetta with a Hawaiian setting, *Luana* (1930), was a failure; so was *Anina* (1934). After 1934 Friml's main center of activity was Hollywood.

1912   THE FIREFLY, an operetta, with book and lyrics by Otto Hauerbach (Harbach). Produced by Arthur Hammerstein at the Lyric Theatre on December 2. Staged by Frederic G. Latham. Cast included Emma Trentini, Roy Atwell, and Audrey Maple (120 performances).

The Firefly was written for the prima donna, Emma Trentini, who had previously scored on Broadway with Victor Herbert's *Naughty Marietta*. In *The Firefly* she appears as Nina, a little Italian street singer who has won the interest of Jack Travers (Roy Atwell). When Jack is invited as a guest of Mrs. Vandare on a yachting trip to Bermuda, Nina is disguised as a boy called Tony, and gets employment on the ship. She becomes such a favorite that Mrs. Vandare decides to give her permanent employment. Complications enter when Tony is accused of being a notorious pickpocket sought by the police. She is cleared and is adopted by Jack's valet, Pietro. Two years later Mrs. Vandare gives a garden party during which a famous prima donna performs. She is none other than Nina. Jack now realizes he is in love with her and loses no time in winning her.

The most important songs were, of course, assigned to Emma Trentini's large voice, and to Mme Trentini must go much of the credit for making them immediate successes. These songs were "Giannina Mia," "Love Is Like a Firefly," "The Dawn of Love," and "When a Maid Comes Knocking at Your Heart." Another fine number was the duet, "Sympathy."

1913   HIGH-JINKS, a musical comedy with book by Otto Harbach and Leo Dietrichstein. Produced by Arthur Hammerstein at the Lyric Theatre on December 10. Staged by Fred Smithson. Cast included Elizabeth Murray, Tom Lewis, and Ignatti Martinetti (213 performances).

It was the incidentals to the plot, rather than the plot itself, that made *High-Jinks* so attractive. These incidentals included fascinating cartwheel dances by Emilie Lea (in the role of Chi-Chi); the song "All Aboard for Dixie," magnetically sung by Elizabeth Murray; a hilarious after-dinner speech in the last act delivered by Tom Lewis in the part of J. J. Jeffreys (not the boxing champ but an American who is continually being mistaken for him); and Ignatti Martinetti's amusing caricature of a jealous Frenchman. The story, such as it is, concerns the effect a certain perfume has in making people feel gay and irresponsible; under its influence a doctor, at a French bathing resort, passes off another lady as his wife with amusingly risqué consequences.

The casting had two points of interest. One was Elaine Hammerstein, daughter of Arthur, who was here making her stage debut and who made a profound impression with "When Sammy Sang the *Marseillaise.*" The other was Mana Zucca, seen in a minor role. Mana Zucca had been a child-prodigy pianist; in subsequent years she would make her mark as a serious composer. The main song was "Something Seems Tingle-Ingling."

1918   SOMETIME, an operetta with book and lyrics by Rida Johnson Young. Produced by Arthur Hammerstein at the Shubert Theatre on October 4. Cast included Francine Larrimore, Ed Wynn, and Mae West (283 performances).

The play opens in the dressing room of a famous stage star, Enid Vaughn (Francine Larrimore), who for five years has been separated from the man she loves, Henry. A flashback carries us back five years, explaining the cause of the separation. Finding her lover in a compromising position with a vampire, Mayme Dean (Mae West), Enid refuses to see him any longer or allow him to explain. But in a return to the opening scene, five years later, Mayme Dean confesses to Enid that she had planned to compromise Henry and that he had been innocent of any wrongdoing. The sentimental play then ends with the long-delayed reconciliation.

As Mayme Dean, Mae West—a graduate from vaudeville—made her first successful appearance on the Broadway stage; but her greatest successes would come in later years, first on the stage, then in the movies. Francine Larrimore, onetime child star, who one year earlier had appeared in *Fair and Warmer,* was now a star—and in her first musical-comedy role. Mildred La Gue, in a minor part, was acclaimed for a striking Argentine dance; and the three best songs from Friml's score were "Sometime," "Keep on Smiling," and "The Tune You Can't Forget."

1924   ROSE MARIE, musical play, with book and lyrics by Otto Harbach and Oscar Hammerstein II. Music by Friml, in collaboration with Herbert Stothart. Produced by Arthur Hammerstein at the Imperial Theatre on September 2. Staged by Paul Dickey. Dances arranged by David Bennett. Cast included Dennis King, Mary Ellis, William Kent, and Arthur Deagon (557 performances).

The Canadian Rockies is the background for *Rose Marie,* with the redoubtable Canadian Mounted Police among the characters. Rose Marie La Flamme (Mary Ellis) is in love with Jim Kenyon (Dennis King). When Jim is falsely accused of murder, Rose Marie stands ready to save her lover's life by giving herself up to Edward Hawley (Frank Greene). The Canadian Mounted Police, headed by Sergeant Malone (Arthur Deagon), get into the act. Jim is vindicated; the police get their man; so does Rose Marie. "Its plot," reported the New York *Telegram,* "clings together sufficiently to sustain interest." But in the New York *Tribune,* Charles Belmont-Davis went further to call the production:

A bon-voyage basket of musical shows. . . . There is drama and melodrama, musical comedy, grand opera, and opera comique. . . . A beautiful . . . composite photograph of a three-ring circus . . . [with] the most entrancing music it has long been our privilege to hear.

Besides its run of one year and four months at the Imperial Theatre, *Rose Marie* had four companies on the road and enjoyed a successful revival on Broadway in 1926.

Mary Ellis, formerly of the Metropolitan Opera Company, here made her bow on the Broadway stage. "She establishes herself," said Arthur Hornblow in *Theatre,* "as the peer of any musical-show star in the country."

A program note had this to say about the Friml score: "The musical numbers of this play are such an integral part of the action that we do not think we should list them as separate episodes." Nevertheless, several numbers did stand out prominently. Two are among Friml's best songs: the duet of Jim and Rose Marie, "Indian Love Call," and the title song, also a duet. Other ear-catching melodies included "Totem Tom-Tom," Rose Marie's ballad, "The Door of My Dreams," and several attractive instrumental passages, among them an Empire March and Gavotte, and the Bridal Procession.

1925   THE VAGABOND KING, a musical play with book and lyrics by Brian Hooker and W. H. Post, based on J. H. McCarthy's romance *If I Were King*. Produced by Russell Janney at the Casino Theatre on September 21. Staged by Max Figman. Cast included Dennis King and Carolyn Thomson (511 performances).

The central character of this romantic play is François Villon, the fifteenth-century French vagabond-poet, played by Dennis King in one of his most celebrated roles. Louis XI makes him king for a day in order to humble the pride of beautiful Katherine de Vaucelles (Carolyn Thomson). In that one day Villon must make love to her. The day proves eventful for Villon: He not only makes love to Katherine but also manages to save Paris and the French throne from the Burgundians. In the battle with the Burgundians, Villon is rescued by his peasant sweetheart, Huguette (Jane Carroll), who gives up her own life to save his. Villon finds consolation at court in Lady Anne, who becomes his wife by royal decree.

The picaresque character of the play is admirably reflected in the rousing chorus of Villon's followers, "Song of the Vagabonds," about which Alexander Woollcott said, "It cut loose magnificently." Other songs were in a more lyric vein, the best being "Only a Rose," "Love Me Tonight," "Some Day," and "Waltz Huguette."

1928   THE THREE MUSKETEERS, an operetta, with book by William Anthony McGuire, based on the romance of the same name by Alexander Dumas. Lyrics by Clifford Grey and P. G. Wodehouse. Produced by Florenz Ziegfeld at the Lyric Theatre on March 13. Staged by William Anthony McGuire. Cast included Dennis King, Vivienne Segal, Lester Allen, and Harriet Hoctor (318 performances).

In this musical adaptation of the famous Dumas romance, D'Artagnan (Dennis King) comes to Paris, where he becomes friendly with the king's guards and falls in love with Constance Bonacieux (Vivienne Segal). He then joins the musketeers Athos, Porthos, and Aramis. He proceeds to London to recover the queen's jewels, which had come into the possession of the Duke of Buckingham. Swordplay and the heroics of D'Artagnan and his musketeers glamorize this mission and bring it to a successful resolution. D'Artagnan, now back in Paris, is able to avert a major scandal at the king's sumptuous ball.

An opulent score included a stirring choral number, "All for One, One for All," and the equally virile "With Red Wine" and "March of the Musketeers." In a more sentimental vein were "Heart of Mine," "Queen of My Heart," and "Ma Belle."

GEORGE GERSHWIN, composer and IRA GERSHWIN, lyricist

George Gershwin wrote music for over twenty major Broadway musicals and contributed songs to about another dozen. Only three of these productions sounded a new note for the American stage: *Strike Up the Band, Of Thee I Sing*, and the opera, *Porgy and Bess*. All other Gershwin musicals were traditional in aim and technique, faithful to the well-tried patterns of the period. The best of the Gershwin musicals were outstanding, however, because Gershwin was an outstanding composer.

He was born in Brooklyn, New York, on September 26, 1898. There was little in his boyhood to suggest that here were the makings of a musician. He liked to play the games of the streets with his friends, and showed little interest in books, music, or the theater.

A few scattered musical experiences stirred something deep within him. One was hearing Rubinstein's "Melody in F" in a penny arcade when he was six. Another was listening to some real jazz music outside a Harlem night club when he was seven. A third was a violin performance by a schoolmate at a public-school assembly. It was this schoolmate who first helped to introduce him to good music—a boy named Maxie Rosenzweig, who later in life became famous as a violin virtuoso under the name of Max Rosen. Maxie would play the violin for George and talk to him about the great composers. Stimulated, George tried writing a melody of his own, which he proudly exhibited to his friend. Maxie told him firmly, "You'd better forget about music, George. You haven't the talent to be a composer."

When George was twelve, a piano entered his home and he started taking lessons. A significant influence came into his life when he began studying with Charles Hambitzer in 1912. Hambitzer was a remarkable musician who had the capacity to excite in his pupils the wonder of great music. Through Hambitzer, Gershwin came to know for the first time the music of many classical composers, and even of such moderns as Debussy and Ravel.

Though Gershwin now came to cherish the classics, he knew even then that if he was to make his way in music it would have to be in the popular field. He loved ragtime, Irving Berlin, the songs of Tin Pan Alley. And, amazing to remark, he felt strongly that American popular music could become an important art—if the composer brought to it the same background and equipment he did to the writing of a symphony or opera. Again and again Gershwin tried to convince Hambitzer of the validity of such convictions. "The boy is a genius without a doubt," Hambitzer wrote to his sister. "He wants to go in for this modern stuff, jazz and what not. But I'm not going to let him for a while. I'll see that he gets a firm foundation in the standard music first." To get that firm foundation, Hambitzer encouraged Gershwin to study theory, harmony, and instrumentation with Edward Kilenyi.

When Gershwin was fifteen, he found a job in Tin Pan Alley as song plugger and staff pianist for Remick. He now started writing popular songs. "When You Want 'Em You Can't Get 'Em" was the first to be published, the publisher being Harry von Tilzer. "The Making of a Girl" became his first song sung on the Broadway stage, in *The Passing Show of 1916*, which opened at the Winter Garden on June 22 with a score by Sigmund Romberg.

Gershwin soon felt constricted by his work at Remick's and decided to find something else. After trying several other jobs (none more satisfying) he got the break he was looking for. Max Dreyfus, head of the powerful publishing house of Harms, became interested in him and offered him thirty-five dollars a week just to write songs and submit them to him. Gershwin had no other set duties and no set hours.

Through Dreyfus' influence, Gershwin received an assignment in 1918 to write the score for a revue, *Half-Past Eight*. The revue opened and closed in Syracuse, New York, and Gershwin never received the 1500 dollars promised him. But other associations with the musical stage proved happier. Nora Bayes sang his "Some Wonderful Sort of Someone" and "The Real American Folk Song" in *Ladies First;* "You-oo Just You" was interpolated into *Hitchy Koo of 1918;* and in 1919 Al Jolson brought "Swanee" into his Winter Garden production, *Sinbad,* and made it such a hit that it sold 2,000,000 phonograph records and a million copies of sheet music. Then on May 26, 1919, came Gershwin's first score for a Broadway musical comedy, *La, La, Lucille.*

By 1920 Gershwin was sufficiently well known to corner a desirable assignment—writing the music for George White's *Scandals*. He wrote all the music for five editions, through 1924, and in that time became one of Broadway's most highly esteemed composers. In 1922 Beryl Rubinstein, a concert pianist, told a startled newspaper interviewer that in his opinion Gershwin "has the spark of musical genius. . . . When we speak of Ameri-

The Grotto of Stalacta spectacle from *The Black Crook* (1866)

THE BIRTH OF EXTRAVAGANZA

Culver Service

Harrigan and Hart (1879)

Culver Service

Weber and Fields in a characteristic scene (1898)

Scene from *The Prince of Pilsen* (1903)

Fred Stone (interpreter) and Dave Montgomery (tourist) arrive at *The Red Mill* (1906)

Sam Bernard (Mr. Hoggenheimer) bids adieu to Georgia Caine (Flora Fair) in *The Rich Mr. Hoggenheimer* (1905)

George M. Cohan and Fay Templeton in *Forty-five Minutes from Broadway* (1906)

Fanny Brice (*center*) and four bathing belles (1910)

THE HEYDAY OF *The Ziegfeld Follies*

Leon Errol, Will West, and Ed Wynn (about 1914)

"Every little movement has a meaning all its own," in *Madame Sherry* (1910)

Hazel Dawn sings "My Beautiful Lady," the
sentimental waltz hit from *The Pink Lady* (1911)

Emma Trentini (*2d from left*) in *The Firefly* (1912). (The young
man at the extreme right is Sammy Lee, later famous as a dance
director for musical comedies)

Al Jolson bids his "Toot, Toot, Tootsie, Good-bye," in *Bombo* (1921)

Marilyn Miller and Leon Errol in *Sally* (1920)

Dennis King and Mary Ellis sing the title song in
Rose Marie (1924)

Florrie Millership, Janet Velie, James Marlow, and
Georgia Caine in *Mary* (1920)

Joseph Cawthorn, Donald Brian, and Julia Sanderson in Jerome Kern's first Broadway success, *The Girl From Utah* (1914)

Ernest Truex and Alice Dovey in the "Princess Theatre Show," *Very Good, Eddie* (1915)

Dorothy Walters, Eva Puck, and Gladys Miller in *Irene* (1919)

Culver Service

ilip Loeb, Sterling Holloway, and Romney Brent
the Three Musketeers in the *Garrick Gaieties*
25)

Vandamm Studio

William Gaxton as *A Connecticut Yankee* in King
Arthur's Court (1927)

Charles Winninger, Howard Marsh, Norma Terris, and Edna May Oliver
in a scene from *Show Boat* (1927)

can composers, George Gershwin's name will be prominent on our list."
Eva Gauthier, a concert singer, regarded Gershwin's popular songs so
significant that she sang a few of them in a recital of serious vocal music
in Aeolian Hall, New York (Gershwin was her accompanist), an event
expansively described by Carl van Vechten as "one of the most important
. . . in musical history." Indeed, Gershwin was soon destined to make
musical history—with the *Rhapsody in Blue,* his first symphonic work,
which Paul Whiteman and his orchestra introduced at Aeolian Hall on
February 12, 1924. This was the first of several large works for orchestra
in the jazz idiom that made Gershwin one of the outstanding American
composers of the time. These works included the Concerto in F, for piano
and orchestra; the tone poem, *An American in Paris;* the *Second Rhapsody; Cuban Overture;* the five piano preludes; and the *Variations on
I Got Rhythm,* for piano and orchestra.

Gershwin now became a Colossus bestriding the world of music (as
Isaac Goldberg once described him), one foot in Carnegie Hall, the
other in Tin Pan Alley. After leaving the *Scandals,* Gershwin returned
to the musical-comedy field with his first musical-comedy success, *Lady
Be Good* (1924).

Lady Be Good was the first musical for which George's brother, Ira,
provided all the lyrics. From this time on they would work together harmoniously, producing a long string of imperishable songs and successful
musical comedies.

Ira Gershwin was born in New York City on December 6, 1896. While
attending Townsend Harris Hall he wrote, edited, and illustrated (and
distributed privately) a one-page newspaper. At the College of the City
of New York, he wrote a literary column for the college newspaper and
contributed sketches and verses to one of its magazines. But Ira was no
scholar. He failed several courses and for a while it appeared that (as
he later explained) "the only possible way, seemingly, of getting a diploma was to remain long enough to earn one by squatter's rights." He
never did get that diploma. He had to transfer to night college, and
during the day worked as cashier for a Turkish bath partly owned by his
father. While holding down this job he sold a little humorous paragraph
to *The Smart Set* in 1917. It paid only one dollar, but it gave Ira the
satisfaction of being a professional writer. After that, Ira sold some more
humorous pieces and verses to various newspapers and magazines, receiving hardly more than a pittance for his efforts. In 1918 he tried his
hand at song lyrics for the first time. He kept on writing lyrics—assuming the pseudonym of Arthur Francis, in order not to capitalize on his

brother's growing fame in the theater—while working at various jobs, including one as cashier for the Colonel Lagg Empire Show (a traveling circus) and another as vaudeville reviewer for *The Clipper*. George provided music for some of Ira's lyrics, their first collaboration being "The Real American Folk Song" which Nora Bayes sang in *Ladies First*.

Ira first achieved success as a lyricist for the stage with Vincent Youmans in *Two Little Girls in Blue,* successfully produced in 1921. Early in 1924 he wrote lyrics for *Be Yourself,* music by Lewis Gensler and Milton Schwarzwald; it was on this occasion that he used his own name professionally for the first time. Later the same year, when he teamed up officially with his brother George for *Lady Be Good,* he still used his own name. The brothers remained collaborators, one of the major words-and-music teams in the theater of the 1920's and 1930's.

After *Lady Be Good,* George and Ira Gershwin were often represented on Broadway with musical comedies that were excellent box-office attractions. The most important of these are discussed in the pages that follow. Others—failures in varying degrees—included *Tell Me More* (1925), *Treasure Girl* (1928), and *Pardon My English* (1933).

Gershwin's last production on Broadway was also his most ambitious, the opera *Porgy and Bess* (1935), in which he finally succeeded in elevating musical comedy to a folk art. After that he devoted himself to writing music for motion pictures. He had worked for Hollywood in 1931 when he wrote the music for *Delicious,* starring Janet Gaynor and Charles Farrell. He returned to Hollywood in 1936, planted his roots there permanently, and created music for several important musicals. The last of these, *The Goldwyn Follies,* he left unfinished, and his music was completed by Vernon Duke.

George Gershwin died at the Cedars of Lebanon Hospital in Los Angeles on July 11, 1937, following an operation on the brain; he had been suffering from a cystic tumor on the right temporal lobe of the brain. Memorial concerts and radio broadcasts expressed the shocked reaction of the entire country to the sudden death of a beloved composer.

In 1945 Gershwin's screen biography, *Rhapsody in Blue* (with Robert Alda playing the composer), paid tribute to his genius with a presentation of his greatest songs and concert works. In 1951 another motion picture—inspired by and named after his tone poem, *An American in Paris*—was chosen as the Academy Award winner, the best picture of the year (the fourth time a musical was thus honored). And between 1952 and 1955, an entire world paid tribute to Gershwin's genius when *Porgy and Bess* toured Europe, the Near East, the Soviet Union, smaller countries behind the Iron Curtain, South America, Mexico, and other distant points.

After George Gershwin's death, Ira Gershwin wrote lyrics to Kurt Weill's music for several Broadway productions, the most significant being *Lady in the Dark*. He also wrote lyrics to music by Jerome Kern, Harold Arlen, and several other composers of notable screen musicals.

1919   LA, LA, LUCILLE, a musical comedy with book by Fred Jackson. Lyrics by Arthur Jackson. Additional lyrics by Buddy de Sylva. Produced by Alex A. Aarons at the Henry Miller Theatre on May 26. Staged by Herbert Gresham and Julian Alfred. Cast included Jack Hazard and Janet Velie (104 performances).

The significance of *La, La, Lucille* rests in the fact that it was George Gershwin's first musical-comedy score. It was a bedroom farce set in a Philadelphia hotel. John Smith, a dentist (Jack Hazzard), can inherit a fortune from his aunt, but only if he is willing to divorce his wife, Lucille (Janet Velie), a former chorus girl. A shrewd lawyer advises him to divorce his wife, take over the inheritance, then remarry her. To gain that divorce John Smith goes to a Philadelphia hotel to be compromised by a woman selected for him by Lucille—the hotel scrubwoman. It so happens that at that very time the hotel was crowded with no less than thirty-eight John Smiths. One of these is a honeymoon couple, whose suite adjoins that of our hero and his corespondent. The difficulties and embarrassments that result from the problem of mistaken identities provide the musical with much of its merriment.

La, La, Lucille marked the bow of young Alex A. Aarons as a Broadway producer. It was he who selected Gershwin for the musical score (though wiser and more experienced men advised him to consider Victor Herbert), because he was delighted with the fresh and original approaches he found in Gershwin's songs. A few years later, in partnership with Vinton Freedley, Aarons would produce most of Gershwin's leading Broadway successes.

Gershwin wrote twelve numbers for *La, La, Lucille*. The best was the principal love song, "Nobody but You"; a secondary hit was a vital rhythmic number called "Tee-Oodle-Um-Bum-Bo."

1920-24   George White's *Scandals*

1920 edition, revue with book by Andy Rice and George White. Lyrics by Arthur Jackson. Produced by George White at the Globe Theatre on

June 7. Cast included Ann Pennington, Lou Holtz, George White, Lester Allen, and George (Doctor) Rockwell (318 performances).

1921 edition, a revue with book by Bugs Baer and George White. Lyrics by Arthur Jackson. Produced by George White at the Liberty Theatre on July 11. Cast included Ann Pennington, George White, Charles King, Lou Holtz, and Lester Allen (97 performances).

1922 edition, a revue with book by George White, W. C. Fields, and Andy Rice. Lyrics by E. Ray Goetz and Buddy de Sylva. Produced by George White at the Globe Theatre on August 28. Staged by George White. Cast included W. C. Fields, Jack McGowan, Lester Allen, and Paul Whiteman and his orchestra (88 performances).

1923 edition, a revue with book by George White and William K. Wells. Lyrics by E. Ray Goetz, Buddy de Sylva, and Ballard MacDonald. Produced by George White at the Globe Theatre on June 18. Staged by George White. Cast included Johnny Dooley, Winnie Lightner, Tom Patricola, and Lester Allen (168 performances).

1924 edition, a revue with book by George White and William K. Wells. Lyrics by Buddy de Sylva. Produced by George White at the Apollo Theatre on June 30. Staged by George White. Cast included Tom Patricola, Winnie Lightner, Will Mahoney, and Lester Allen (192 performances).

For other editions of George White's Scandals *see* DE SYLVA, BROWN *and* HENDERSON, *and* RICHARD WHITING.

When George Gershwin started writing music for George White's *Scandals*, the revue was only one year old (*see* RICHARD WHITING).

For his second edition George White engaged as his composer the then-young and comparatively inexperienced Gershwin, paying him at first fifty dollars a week for the job. Gershwin remained with the *Scandals* five years, and during this period he developed to maturity as a song composer and gave repeated hints of his future direction as a serious composer.

The 1920 edition showed marked progress over the earlier one, both in text and music. Comedy was strengthened through the interpolation of satire: one sketch mocked Prohibition, its setting an airship three miles up in the air; another jeered at profiteering landlords; others spoofed political conventions and the grim Russian drama. Nevertheless it was the dancing of Ann Pennington, the "shimmy queen"—and a graduate from *The Ziegfeld Follies*—that was the high point of the production. (Ann Pennington had also dominated the 1919 edition.) Gershwin wrote seven numbers, the best being "Scandal Walk" and "On My Mind the Whole Night Long."

In 1921 Gershwin had six songs, among them "South Sea Isles" and "I Love You." The 1922 edition—with twelve Gershwin numbers—had "I'll Build a Stairway to Paradise," in which the composer revealed for the first time his bent for original approaches and techniques. This song had originated as "New Step Everyday," lyrics by Ira Gershwin. When Buddy de Sylva read the lyric, he suggested to Ira that he write another, using one of its lines as the title. He helped Ira write that lyric, and with George's music it was brought into the *Scandals*. White provided a lavish setting: a huge white stairway with dancers dressed in black, walking up and down as the song was sung.

Besides his more formal songs, Gershwin also contributed to this edition a one-act Negro opera, the first testimony of his subsequent evolution as a serious composer. Originally it was called *Blue Monday*, text by Buddy de Sylva, and a cast including Richard Bold, Lester Allen, Jack McGowan, and Coletta Ryan. The setting was a basement on Lenox Avenue in New York's Harlem. Vi is loved by both Joe and Tom. When Joe leaves New York to visit his sick mother, Tom convinces Vi he has really gone off for a rendezvous with a girl. When Joe returns, Vi shoots him but discovers her error just before he dies.

Gershwin's score was his first attempt to write in a design larger than the song. The opera contained a few good individual numbers: "Blue Monday Blues," "Has Anybody Seen My Joe?" and the spiritual, "I'm Going to See My Mother." But the score was not a coherent entity. Inchoate and immature though it was, however, *Blue Monday* was the embryo out of which Gershwin's opera, *Porgy and Bess*, emerged a decade later. *Blue Monday* appeared only once in the *Scandals*, on opening night. It was removed the following day because White felt that it depressed the audience. However, since then—and under its new title, *135th Street*—it has been revived several times, including once over television on the "Omnibus" program.

The 1923 edition of the *Scandals* had a *Folies Bergère* curtain of living nudes, perhaps its most interesting feature. Gershwin had twelve songs but none of distinction. But for 1924 he produced one of the songs by which he will always be remembered—"Somebody Loves Me," fetchingly sung by Winnie Lightner. This edition also had a delightful social-drama sketch in which not a single word was spoken—but which consisted merely of the sound "ah."

1924   LADY BE GOOD, a musical comedy with book by Guy Bolton and Fred
Thompson. Produced by Aarons and Freedley at the Liberty Theatre
on December 1. Cast included Fred and Adele Astaire, Cliff Edwards
and Walter Catlett (184 performances).

When Gershwin left the *Scandals* in 1924, after a five-year stint, to advance his own career in musical comedy, he joined up again with Alex A.
Aarons, who had produced *La, La, Lucille* in 1919. Aarons was now a
producing partner of Vinton Freedley; for the next half-dozen years
Aarons and Freedley would present several outstanding Gershwin
musicals.

When the producing firm of Aarons and Freedley was first organized,
it was with the intent of putting on a smart musical starring Fred and
Adele Astaire. Aarons approached Fred Astaire with the suggestion of
engaging George Gershwin to write the music. While Astaire recognized
and appreciated Gershwin's talent, he was skeptical about the composer's
ability to produce commercial tunes. But Aarons knew Gershwin's worth
and was able to convince Astaire to accept him.

The musical, finally called *Lady Be Good,* cast Fred and Adele Astaire
as Dick and Susie Trevor, a brother-and-sister dance team. They lose
their money, are unable to get engagements, and are reduced to entertaining at private parties and at the homes of friends. A rich girl in love
with Dick, but for whom he has little interest, brings about the eviction
of the Trevors from their apartment. One of the best scenes in the play
follows this eviction early in the first act. The Trevors, homeless and
broke, find their furniture in the street. Susie tries to bring a homey atmosphere to her new setting by arranging her furniture neatly around
the corner lamp post and hanging a sign on it reading, "God Bless Our
Home." The Trevors then try to find an answer to their financial problem
by having Dick tie up with the rich girl. Susie, however, contrives to
rescue her brother from this undesirable marriage by plotting with a
shady lawyer, J. Watterson Watkins (Walter Catlett), to impersonate
a Mexican widow for the purpose of gaining an inheritance. The scheme
falls apart. But even though the Trevors are unable to put their hands
on this fortune, they are able to arrive at a happy resolution of their
problems.

Lady Be Good was Gershwin's first musical-comedy hit. His score was,
as the *Sun* described it, "brisk, inventive, gay, and nervous." The best
song was the title number, sung by J. Watterson Watkins. Another favorite was "Fascinating Rhythm," remarkable for its rhythmic dexterity

and beautifully sung and danced to by the Trevors. "So Am I," also presented by the Trevors, was another musical asset.

The score would also have boasted one of Gershwin's song classics—if it had been allowed to remain in the score. "The Man I Love" was written for *Lady Be Good,* was tried out in the opening scene by Adele Astaire when the show opened in Philadelphia, and was found wanting. Vinton Freedley said that it was too static and convinced Gershwin to drop it from the production.

1925 TIP TOES, a musical comedy with book by Guy Bolton and Fred Thompson. Produced by Aarons and Freedley at the Liberty Theatre on December 28. Cast included Queenie Smith, Allen Kearns, Robert Halliday, Andrew Tombes, and Jeanette MacDonald in a minor role (194 performances).

Though *Tip Toes* had less of a run than several other Gershwin musicals produced by Aarons and Freedley, it was nevertheless a huge box-office success and earned more money for the producers than did other productions with longer runs. Queenie Smith played the heroine—Tip Toes Kaye, a young and attractive dancer. She is brought to Miami by two conniving brothers, Al and Hen (Andrew Tombes and Harry Watson, Jr.), fitted out in style, and put on the marriage market. She succeeds in winning the heart of wealthy Steve Burton (Allen Kearns) and is able to convince him she loves him for himself alone and not for his money.

The Gershwin score was studded with gems: "That Certain Feeling," a duet of Tip-Toes and Steve; "Sweet and Low-Down"; and Tip-Toes' haunting refrain, "Looking for a Boy." Gershwin's music was certainly the strong point of the show, as Alexander Woollcott pointed out. *"Tip Toes,"* he wrote, "was a Gershwin evening, so sweet and sassy are the melodies he has poured out . . . so fresh and unstinted the gay, young blood of his invention."

1925 A SONG OF THE FLAME, an operetta, with book and lyrics by Otto Harbach and Oscar Hammerstein II. Music written in collaboration with Herbert Stothart. Presented by Arthur Hammerstein at the 44th Street Theatre on December 30. Book staged by Frank Reicher. Dances and ensemble pictures arranged by Jack Haskell. Cast included Tessa Kosta, Guy Robertson, Dorothy MacKaye, and Hugh Cameron (194 performances).

A Song of the Flame was a "romantic opera" with a Russian setting. A peasant uprising takes place under the leadership of Anuita (Tessa

Kosta), a rebel of noble birth who came to be known as "The Flame." She falls in love with Prince Volodya (Guy Robertson). Each succeeds in modifying the other's political beliefs, and they end up together in Paris.

Colorful sets and costumes, big scenes, songs with a pseudo-Russian identity, frenetic folk dances, and poignant choral music were combined in a lavish spectacle that did not always come off successfully. As Percy Hammond wrote: "There were mobs, riots, balls, and carnivals, both in Paris and Moscow. Picture trod on picture as fast as they came . . . yet . . . the play lacked what used to be known as 'that something.' " Brooks Atkinson called it a "romantic spectacle," but complained that "the size of the production makes the opera generally heavy."

Gershwin's share of the score included two numbers with a recognizable Slavic personality: the title song, presented by Anuita and the Russian Art Choir; and the main love song, "The Cossack's Love Song" (also known as "Don't Forget Me"), a duet of Anuita and Volodya.

1926 OH KAY!, a musical comedy with book by Guy Bolton and P. G. Wodehouse. Produced by Aarons and Freedley at the Imperial Theatre on November 8. Staged by John Harwood and Sammy Lee. Cast included Gertrude Lawrence, Victor Moore, Oscar Shaw, and Harland Dixon (256 performances).

Aarons and Freedley discussed with Gertrude Lawrence the possibility of starring her in her first Broadway musical comedy. (She had previously made her Broadway debut in 1924 as one of the stars in the visiting *Charlot's Revue* from London, but she had never appeared in an American production.) She told them she was considering a similar offer from Florenz Ziegfeld. Only when Aarons revealed he was planning to engage George Gershwin for the music did she decide to hitch her wagon to his star.

In the Bolton and Wodehouse text, Gertrude Lawrence appeared as Kay, sister of an English Duke (Gerald Oliver Smith), come to the United States on their yacht. Impoverished by the recent war (World War I), they use their yacht for rum-running and store their illicit liquor in a deserted house on the beach at Southampton, Long Island. The house is owned by a socialite, Jimmy Winter (Oscar Shaw). Shorty McGee (Victor Moore) assumes a job as butler in order to keep watch over the liquor. Jimmy recognizes Kay as a girl who had once saved his life. He helps throw the police off her trail and falls in love with her.

To cast Gertrude Lawrence as Kay was a happy event for Broadway. Kay was the first of several unforgettable performances she would contribute to our theater. But no less felicitous was placing Victor Moore in the role of hapless Shorty McGee, the pseudo-butler. Since he achieved in this part one of the triumphs of his long and active career in the theater, it is amusing to note that at first the producers thought he was miscast. When the play tried out in Philadelphia, Vinton Freedley planned paying Victor Moore 10,000 dollars to step out of the play and allow Johnny Dooley to take over the part. As it turned out, Victor Moore brought down the house in Philadelphia, and he remained in the cast. A large measure of the play's success was due to his poignant characterization, his unique gift of blending humor with wistfulness—with his sad face and high-pitched, broken voice.

Oh Kay! was one of Gershwin's best scores—a veritable storehouse of musical riches which Brooks Atkinson described as "a marvel of its kind." The love song, "Someone to Watch Over Me," introduced by Kay, is a Gershwin classic. Kay also presented "Do, Do, Do." In a more rhythmic vein was "Clap Yo' Hands," while the title song, "Maybe," and "Fidgety Feet" were other distinguished numbers.

1927   FUNNY FACE, a musical comedy with book by Paul Gerard Smith and Fred Thompson. Produced by Aarons and Freedley at the Alvin Theatre on November 22. Cast included Fred and Adele Astaire, Victor Moore, and Allen Kearns (244 performances).

Funny Face opened a new theater—the Alvin on 52nd Street, owned by Aarons and Freedley. The theater almost had an inauspicious beginning, for in its out-of-town tryouts, *Funny Face* gave the appearance of being a failure. A drastic revision was called for. Robert Benchley, who had been one of the original authors of the text, withdrew. He was replaced by Paul Gerard Smith who helped Fred Thompson rewrite the play completely. In the revision a large part was built for Victor Moore as the blundering thug, Herbert, whose hobby was to take pictures of comets. The revised material was introduced in Wilmington, Delaware, where *Funny Face* became an immediate hit.

The plot remained a routine affair. Jimmy Reeve (Fred Astaire) is the guardian of Frankie (Adele Astaire). He insists upon keeping her pearls in a safe. Frankie gets her boy friend, Peter (Allen Kearns), to try to procure the pearls for her; at the same time the two comic thugs—Dugsie Gibbs (William Kent) and Herbert (Victor Moore)—are also hot on the trail of this treasure. Inevitably, Frankie gets both her man and the pearls.

The two thugs contributed to the play most of its comedy. In one scene, while on the job of stealing the pearls, they get drunk, with hilarious consequences; in another scene Herbert is about to be shot by his crony, Dugsie, a development that he accepts with almost amazing stoicism.

The major number in the Gershwin score was the love song " 'S Wonderful," a duet between Frankie and Peter. "Let's Kiss and Make Up" was also a distinctive song. A third one, "The Babbitt and the Bromide" (introduced by Frankie), is largely outstanding for some of the wittiest lyrics of Ira Gershwin's career, good enough to become the only song lyrics included in Louis Kronenberg's *An Anthology of Light Verse*.

1928   ROSALIE, an operetta with book by Guy Bolton and William Anthony McGuire. Lyrics by Ira Gershwin and P. G. Wodehouse. Additional songs by Sigmund Romberg. Produced by Florenz Ziegfeld at the Ziegfeld Theatre on January 10. Staged by Florenz Ziegfeld, Seymour Felix, and William A. McGuire. Cast included Marilyn Miller, Bobbe Arnst, Frank Morgan, and Jack Donahue (335 performances).

Gershwin wrote music for two Ziegfeld productions. *Rosalie* was the first. Sigmund Romberg had originally been signed to do the music. But Ziegfeld demanded the full score in three weeks, a deadline Romberg could not meet; Romberg suggested to Ziegfeld that George Gershwin be recruited for half the score. As it turned out, Romberg wrote eight numbers and Gershwin seven. Gershwin's best songs were "How Long Has This Been Going On?" and "Oh Gee, Oh Joy."

Rosalie was a typical operetta in that it involved a princess from a mythical kingdom. She is Rosalie of Romanza (Marilyn Miller) who falls in love with an American lieutenant from West Point, Richard Fay (Jack Donahue). When the royal family of Romanza visits the United States, Richard becomes the leader of its color guard and thus can pursue his love affair; and when Rosalie's father, King Cyril (Frank Morgan), is forced to abdicate, Richard can seek Rosalie's hand in marriage.

1929   SHOW GIRL, a musical comedy with book by William Anthony McGuire based on J. P. McEvoy's novel of the same name. Additional songs by Jimmy Durante. Additional lyrics by Gus Kahn. Produced by Florenz Ziegfeld at the Ziegfeld Theatre on July 2. Staged by Florenz Ziegfeld, Bobby Connelly, and Albertina Rasch. Cast included Ruby Keeler, Clayton, Jackson, and Durante, Joseph MacCauley, Harriet Hoctor, and Duke Ellington (111 performances).

Show Girl was Gershwin's second job for Ziegfeld. The text traced the history of Dixie Dugan (Ruby Keeler) in her rise to stardom on the musical stage. Ziegfeld himself becomes involved in her career. Dixie crashes an interview with him, wins him over completely, and becomes the star of the *Follies*. En route to fame Dixie becomes involved in several love affairs.

Dixie sang and danced to the leading musical number in the Gershwin score, "Liza" (a song to which Gershwin himself was always partial). During the first few nights of the run of *Show Girl*, Dixie found an unexpected and unpaid-for collaborator in the performance of "Liza" in Ruby Keeler's husband, Al Jolson, who ran up and down the aisle singing the song with and to his wife. "So Are You" was another outstanding Gershwin song, and the Gershwin tone poem, *An American in Paris* (it had been introduced at Carnegie Hall by the New York Philharmonic Symphony under Walter Damrosch) was used as background music for a stunning ballet danced by Harriet Hoctor and the Albertina Rasch girls.

Jimmy Durante, appearing as a property man, interpolated three songs, which he had formerly featured in night clubs and which are still a part of his permanent song repertory: "So I Ups to Him," "I Can Do Without Broadway," and "Who Will Be with You When I'm Far Away?" (none of them, to be sure, by the Gershwins).

Despite the winning performances of Jimmy Durante and Ruby Keeler, the spectacular production by Ziegfeld, and two outstanding Gershwin songs, *Show Girl* was a box-office failure. It was too slow-moving to be dramatically effective, and the plot, such as it was, was crushed under the weight of Ziegfeld's massive production numbers. Gershwin had to threaten a lawsuit before he could collect the royalties Ziegfeld owed him—money that Ziegfeld had lost not only in the ill-fated production but also in the stock-market crash.

1929   STRIKE UP THE BAND, a musical play with book by George S. Kaufman and Morrie Ryskind. Produced by Edgar Selwyn at the Times Square Theatre on January 14. Staged by Alexander Leftwich. Dances by George Hale. Cast included Clark and McCullough, Blanche Ring, and Anne Draper (191 performances).

Strike Up the Band was one of the most original and provocative musical satires to reach the Broadway stage in the early 1930's. It took a long time to jell. It originated in 1927 with a book by George S. Kaufman, and with Jimmie Savo and Vivian Hart as stars. But when the show was tried out in Philadelphia it was found lacking in popular appeal and was abandoned. But in 1929 the author decided to return to it, and enlisted

Morrie Ryskind to rework the Kaufman text and make it more commercial. With Clark and McCullough now selected as stars, *Strike Up the Band* was once again tried out of town—this time successfully. It was now brought to Broadway where the critics acclaimed it for its adult intelligence, bite, and sting. "Here," wrote William Bolitho, "is a bitter . . . satirical attack on war, genuine propaganda at times, sung and danced on Broadway."

Strike Up the Band was meant to be a lampoon on war. It was that, and much more too. It heaped ridicule on American big business, international relations, secret diplomacy, international treaties, Babbitry. Horace J. Fletcher (Dudley Clements) is an American manufacturer of chocolates who resents Washington, D.C., because it refuses to raise the tariff on chocolates. A sleeping pill administered by his physician induces strange dreams in which Horace sees himself as General of the American Army in a war against Switzerland over the issue of chocolate. When the enemy's secret call to arms (a yodel) is uncovered, the American troops are able to rout the Swiss. Fletcher remains a hero only until the American newspapers reveal a scandal: Fletcher has been using only Grade B milk for his confections.

Up to 1930, Gershwin had produced music only for formal musical comedies. Now he was inspired by an unusual text—and by the incisive, biting lyrics of Ira Gershwin—to create a score that had mockery and malice, which caught every subtle nuance of the play and the characters. The now-celebrated title song deflated military pomp and circumstance, while a delightful little march called "Entrance of the Swiss Army" was also a tongue-in-cheek commentary on a bogus army. There was more spacious writing (a hint of Gershwin's later powers at producing stage music) in the brilliant finale where the chorus reviews all that has occurred, in a series of sprightly lyrics, while the music itself is a recollection of some previously heard melodies.

There were some prominent songs. "Soon" (introduced by Margaret Schilling) is one of Gershwin's most moving ballads; this song was built from an eight-bar sequence previously used for the first act finale of the first version of the play. "I've Got a Crush On You" had actually been written for an earlier musical (*Treasure Girl*) but had been deleted from that production; it now became a hit. Gershwin's famous song, "The Man I Love," omitted from *Lady Be Good* in 1924, was once again tried out in the first version of *Strike Up the Band,* once again was found wanting, and once again had to be abandoned.

1930 GIRL CRAZY, a musical comedy with book by Guy Bolton and John
McGowan. Produced by Aarons and Freedley at the Alvin Theatre on
October 14. Staged by Alexander Leftwich. Dances staged by George
Hale. Cast included Ethel Merman, Ginger Rogers, Allen Kearns, and
Willie Howard (272 performances).

The plot was not one calculated to bring distinction to the musical stage.
Danny Churchill (Allen Kearns) is a Park Avenue playboy. As a cure
for his dilatory ways, he is sent by his father to Custerville, Arizona, a
town with few temptations and no women. Danny makes the trip in the
taxi of Gieber Goldfarb (Willie Howard). It does not take him long to
transform Custerville into a fleshpot. He opens a dude ranch studded with
Broadway chorus girls and equipped with a gambling room. He manages
to get into all kinds of trouble, but then sees the error of his ways when
he falls in love with the town postmistress, Molly Gray (Ginger Rogers).

What lifted the play to significance was the earthy, shattering performance of Ethel Merman. In the role of Kate Fothergill, wife of the man
who runs the gambling room, she made her Broadway stage debut and
was immediately lifted to the summit of her profession.

A former stenographer named Ethel Zimmerman, who had appeared
in small night clubs, at parties and weddings, Merman came to the
attention of Vinton Freedley during an appearance at the Brooklyn Paramount Theatre. Freedley, in turn, introduced her to Gershwin, who auditioned her at his apartment and forthwith engaged her for *Girl Crazy*.
She did not have looks by Broadway standards; her voice was not the
kind that caresses and woos an audience. Yet when she appeared for
the first time on that stage, dressed in a tight black satin skirt, slit to the
knee, and a low-cut red blouse, and threw her brassy tones across the
footlights in "Sam and Delilah"—filling the entire theater with the dynamism of an irresistible personality—the effect of singer on audience
was cyclonic. As one unidentified critic said: "She has the magnificent
vitality of a steam calliope in red and gold loping down a circus midway
playing the 'Entry of the Gladiators.'"

"Sam and Delilah," a parody of the Frankie and Johnny type of ballad,
was one of three numbers introduced by Merman in *Girl Crazy*. The other
two Gershwin gems are also inevitably associated with her. In "I Got
Rhythm" she electrified the theater by holding a high C for sixteen bars
while the orchestra proceeded with the melody; the second was a sophisticated ditty called "Boy, What Love Has Done to Me."

There were other treasures in this score. "Embraceable You"—this was

Molly Gray's big song, the role in which Ginger Rogers was making her Broadway debut—is one of Gershwin's most beautiful love songs. "But Not for Me," also presented by Molly, is a poignant ballad. (Strange to say, Willie Howard used the latter song to set forth his talent at imitating famous performers of the day, such as Rudy Vallee and Maurice Chevalier.) And "Bidin' My Time," sung by a quartet of rubes who drift in and out during scene changes, is a satire on hillbilly tunes.

The orchestra that played in the pit for *Girl Crazy* deserves at least a footnote in the history of jazz—for its members included Benny Goodman, Glenn Miller, Red Nichols, and Gene Krupa.

1931   OF THEE I SING, a musical comedy with book by Morrie Ryskind and George S. Kaufman. Presented by Sam H. Harris at the Music Box Theatre on December 26. Staged by George S. Kaufman. Dances staged by Chester Hale. Cast included William Gaxton, Victor Moore, Lois Moran, Grace Brinkley, June O'Dea, and George Murphy (441 performances).

Of Thee I Sing made stage history by becoming the first musical comedy to win the Pulitzer Prize for drama. The citation read: "This award may seem unusual, but the play is unusual. . . . Its effect on the stage promises to be considerable, because musical plays are always popular and by injecting satire and point into them, a very large public is reached."

The citation was right on both counts. The play was "unusual" in that it avoided the trite boy-meets-girl theme so prevalent on the musical stage at the time; in that it side-stepped the stilted trappings of formal musical comedy; in that through dialogue, lyrics, and music it introduced a devastating wit and needlepointed satire into musical comedy while considering the political scene in Washington, D.C. And its "effect on the stage" *did* prove considerable—it encouraged other and later musical-comedy writers to adopt unusual subjects and to treat them in a fresh and unorthodox manner.

In the year 1931, Washington, D.C., was a stuffy place filled with sometimes dull, sometimes self-righteous politicians and a musty legislature that failed to cope with the grim realities of a major economic depression. The times were ripe for dissection by a satirical scalpel. Kaufman, Ryskind, and the Gershwins handled that scalpel with the skill and sensitivity of a master surgeon.

The main thread of the story was a presidential campaign. In the smoke-filled hotel room the political bosses agree to run Wintergreen for President, with Throttlebottom as his running mate. Wintergreen (William Gaxton) is a brash fellow, while Throttlebottom (Victor Moore) is a mild, meek little man with a sad face and broken voice. The nomination in the bag, a five-minute political torchlight parade sets the campaign into full swing. The illuminated signs read: "A Vote for Wintergreen is a Vote for Wintergreen," and "Even Your Dog Loves Wintergreen," while the music, "Wintergreen for President," carries sly references to such old chestnuts as "Hail, Hail, the Gang's All Here," "A Hot Time in the Old Town Tonight," "Tammany," and "The Stars and Stripes Forever"; there are even melodic references to Jews and the Irish, for Wintergreen loves them equally.

The campaign issue is "Love," and for this reason a beauty contest is conducted in Atlantic City to determine who will be "Miss White House," the First Lady of the Land. Diana Devereaux (Grace Brinkley) is the lucky winner—and on the platform of "Love" Wintergreen is swept into office. But Wintergreen does not follow the program set for him. He falls in love with Mary Turner (Lois Moran) because she "can really make corn muffins," and marries her instead of Diana. When it is discovered that Diana is the illegitimate daughter of an illegitimate son of an illegitimate nephew of Napoleon, international complications set in. Wintergreen is about to be impeached when the news breaks that Mary is about to become a mother. No expectant President has ever been impeached, and Wintergreen must be no exception. The situation is straightened out with Throttlebottom assuming the duty of a Vice-President to serve for the President when the latter is unable to fulfill his appointed task: Throttlebottom takes Diana as his own wife, and none too reluctantly.

The writers contribute most of their acid in the detailed working out of the main plot. Many different aspects of our political life are reduced to absurdity: the showmanship of political campaigns (the political rally is combined with a wrestling match); hagglings in the Senate (it ponders the problem of providing an overdue pension to Jenny, Paul Revere's horse); cerebrations of the Supreme Court (which must decide the sex of the President's expected children, for Mary has twins); the anonymity of the Vice-President (he cannot gain access to the White House except by joining a conducted tour, and he is unable to join the Public Library because he cannot provide two references).

Stimulated by his text, Ira Gershwin produced some of his most brilliant lyrics, which had an almost Gilbertian virtuosity to them. George Gershwin prepared a spacious score, which included two hit songs, "Of Thee I Sing," introduced by Wintergreen and Diana Devereaux, and "Love Is Sweeping the Country." There were extended sequences combining melodies with recitatives, solo numbers with choruses. Innumerable subtle details translated into musical terms nuances of the text. The mock pomp of the Senate is pointed up with the "vamp till ready" chords that usher in the scene; the recitatives are a tongue-in-cheek take-off on grand opera. The music laughs gaily at maternity with a sentimental Viennese-type waltz ("I'm About to Be a Mother"), at France and the French ("*Garçon, s'il vous plaît,*" the lyrics in gibberish French), at political campaigns ("Wintergreen for President").

No wonder, then, that the critics raved. George Jean Nathan called it a "landmark in American satirical musical comedy"; H. T. Parker of Boston considered it "one of the drollest musical operettas of all time"; Brooks Atkinson thought it was "funnier than the government, and not nearly so dangerous."

Besides winning the Pulitzer Prize, *Of Thee I Sing* broke a second precedent. It became the first musical-comedy text to be published in book form. Other earned distinctions included the longest run of any Gershwin musical on Broadway, with a second company on tour (the only Gershwin musical ever to have two simultaneous productions). The national company included Oscar Shaw, Donald Meek, and Harriet Lake —the last now better known as Ann Sothern.

An attempt to revive *Of Thee I Sing* twenty years later—at the Ziegfeld Theatre on May 5, 1952, with Jack Carson and Paul Hartmann—proved a failure. A startling innovation in 1931, *Of Thee I Sing* had had so many imitators since then that, in 1952, it provided neither shock nor surprise; it is also possible that after four terms of the Roosevelt Administration and a world war, a satire on Washington and politics no longer held appeal for the general public.

1933   LET 'EM EAT CAKE, a musical comedy with book by Morrie Ryskind and George S. Kaufman. Produced by Sam H. Harris at the Imperial Theatre on October 21. Staged by George S. Kaufman. Dances and ensembles by Van Grona and Ned McGurn. Cast included William Gaxton, Victor Moore, Philip Loeb, and Lois Moran (90 performances).

Let 'Em Eat Cake tried to duplicate the success of *Of Thee I Sing* by calling on the same producer, writers, and stars and narrating the further adventures of Wintergreen and Throttlebottom. They run for re-election and are defeated. Wintergreen then becomes head of a revolutionary movement to overthrow the government, abetted by the Union Square rabble-rouser, Kruger (Philip Loeb). The revolution proves successful, and a dictatorship of the proletariat is set up. A critical international dispute arises, the settlement of which requires a baseball game between nine members of the Supreme Court and nine foreign representatives of the League of Nations. Throttlebottom, officiating as umpire, makes an unhappy decision that almost brings him doom at the guillotine, imported for this unhappy event from France. Mary Wintergreen's quick thinking saves his life, and when the republic is restored, he even becomes President.

Like so many sequels, *Let 'Em Eat Cake* was a failure, but an interesting one. It had moments in which the wit and satire sparkled no less brilliantly than in *Of Thee I Sing:* the opening scene; the Union League scene; "Comes the Revolution"; "Union Square." And it had an outstanding Gershwin song in "Mine," introduced by Wintergreen, in which delightful use is made of an aside by the chorus sung contrapuntally to the main melody.

But the play as a whole touched on too many unsavory subjects to be consistently amusing—a left-wing revolution, dictatorship in America with a blue-shirt army gaining control, the threatened death of a principal at the guillotine. As Brooks Atkinson noted: "Their [the writers'] hatred had triumphed over their sense of humor."

1935   PORGY AND BESS, an opera with libretto by Du Bose Heyward based on the play, *Porgy*, by Dorothy and Du Bose Heyward. Lyrics by Du Bose Heyward and Ira Gershwin. Produced by the Theatre Guild at the Alvin Theatre on October 10. Directed by Rouben Mamoulian. Cast included Todd Duncan, Anne Brown, John W. Bubbles, J. Rosamond Johnson, and the Eva Jessye Choir. Alexander Smallens conductor (124 performances).

Since *Porgy and Bess* is an opera (by any definition at all), it would hardly seem to require a place among Broadway musical comedies, revues, and plays. Yet its composer came from the Broadway musical stage, and the artistic roots of *Porgy and Bess* were deeply embedded in the soil of that stage; moreover, it was on the Broadway stage—and not in an opera house—that *Porgy and Bess* was first given. Actually *Porgy and Bess,* while an opera, is musical comedy lifted to the status of a powerful and moving native art; and the arbitrary fact that it has recitatives in place of spoken dialogue should not exclude it from consideration in any panorama of the American musical theater.

The idea of writing *Porgy and Bess* came to Gershwin several years before he actually sat down to work—when he first read Du Bose Heyward's novel, *Porgy*, and wrote to the author expressing his enthusiasm.

Then and there he and Du Bose Heyward decided to collaborate on an opera based upon the novel, but pressing commitments compelled both men to postpone the project continually; for one thing, Du Bose Heyward was busy working with his wife on a play adaptation of the novel for the Theatre Guild.

Then, one day in 1933, Heyward informed Gershwin that the Theatre Guild was interested in adapting the Dorothy and Du Bose Heyward play, *Porgy,* into a Jerome Kern musical comedy starring Al Jolson. "I want you to tell me if you're really going to write our opera," Heyward told him. "If you are, I'm going to turn the Guild down definitely." Gershwin promised Du Bose Heyward to begin work immediately—and he did.

It took Gershwin about twenty months to write and orchestrate the opera. Some of that time was spent in South Carolina where Gershwin steeped himself in the life and folk music of the Negroes there, and acquired a firsthand acquaintance with the locale of his opera. The actual date of completion appears at the end of the manuscript—September 2, 1935—but Gershwin continued to revise and edit, up to the time that the cast was being assembled by the Theatre Guild and first rehearsals began.

The cast was mostly Negro, and the principals were all new to the stage. Todd Duncan, Porgy, was a teacher of music at Howard University in Washington, D.C. Anne Brown, Bess, was a then-unknown young singer without much professional experience. Both auditioned for Gershwin (together with many others); Gershwin recognized their talent and accepted them; both, then, may well be said to have been Gershwin's discoveries. For that matter, so was John W. Bubbles, Sportin' Life, even though he had previously had a long career in vaudeville. Bubbles could not read a note of music and seemed completely incapable of mastering his role. Yet Gershwin was convinced he was the ideal Sportin' Life, and exerted infinite patience in training him in the intricate score (at times the rhythm of a song had to be tapped out for Bubbles before he could understand it). The effort expended by Gershwin on Bubbles brought rich reward, for his performance was one of the shining lights of the production.

The setting of *Porgy and Bess* is a Negro tenement, Catfish Row, in Charleston, South Carolina. As the curtain rises, a crap game is taking place in one corner of the court, while in another part a few people are dancing. Clara (Abbie Mitchell) is sitting in a third corner, lulling her baby to sleep with one of the most beautiful and popular songs from the entire opera, "Summertime." When the child fails to fall asleep, Clara's husband, Jake (Edward Matthews), seizes the child and sings to it a ditty of his own, "A Woman Is a Sometime Thing." As the heat and the fever of the gamblers rise in the crap game, a quarrel erupts between Robbins (Henry Davis) and Crown (Warren Coleman), in which the former gets killed. Crown goes into hiding, leaving behind his girl friend, Bess, who is now being enticed by Sportin' Life (John Bubbles) to go off with him to New York. Bess, however, prefers the protection of the cripple, Porgy, who loves her selflessly and devotedly.

The scene shifts to Robbins' room where the mourners are lamenting Robbins' death, and neighbors drop in to put coins in the saucer for burial money. The widow, Serena (Ruby Elzy), distraught with grief, gives voice to her tragedy in "My Man's Gone Now," and the religious atmosphere is heightened with Bess' spiritual, "Oh, the Train Is at the Station."

The second act returns to Catfish Row. Bess is happy with her new life with Porgy and has come to love him. Porgy speaks of his newfound joy in an exultant refrain, "I Got Plenty of Nuttin'," while the lovers exchange tender sentiments in the duet, "Bess, You Is My Woman Now." Since the people of Catfish Row are about to leave for a lodge picnic on Kittiwah Island, Porgy insists that Bess go along with them.

The lodge picnic on Kittiwah Island is a gay affair, marked by riotous singing and dancing. Sportin' Life entertains his friends with a recital of his cynical philosophy, "It Ain't Necessarily So." When the picnic is over and the merrymakers proceed back to the boat, Crown—who has been in hiding on the island—accosts Bess, breaks down her resistance, and drags her off into the woods.

A few days later, in Catfish Row, the fishermen are off to sea. While they are gone, Bess returns, sick and feverish, to be gently nursed by a forgiving and solicitous Porgy. In "I Loves You, Porgy," they repeat their avowal of love. Suddenly hurricane bells sound an ominous warning. The hurricane sweeps across the skies, and the woman folk huddle in Serena's room to pray for the safe return of their husbands. Suddenly Crown bursts in, searching for Bess. He injects a mocking, sacrilegious note into the terrified atmosphere by singing "A Red-Headed Woman Makes a Choochoo Jump Its Track." From her seat at the window, Clara sees her husband, Jake, fall out of his boat. Crown taunts Porgy for being a cripple and unable to give any help to anyone. Then Crown runs out into the storm to save Jake. When he returns to Catfish Row for Bess, he is murdered by Porgy.

Porgy is taken to prison for questioning. Sportin' Life arrives to tempt Bess to go off with him to New York in "There's a Boat That's Leavin' Soon for New York." When she spurns him, he uses a package of "happy dust" to break down her resistance.

Now back from prison, and free since no one will provide any testimony against him, Porgy searches for Bess. When he learns she has gone off to New York with Sportin' Life, he steps into his goat cart to follow her, chanting "Oh, Lawd, I'm on My Way to a Heavenly Land."

When *Porgy and Bess* tried out in Boston it was received rapturously by audience and critics. But there was mixed reaction in New York two weeks later, with most music critics bringing in negative reports. When, therefore, the opera closed after only 124 performances—and piled up a considerable deficit—it seemed that American opera had once again chalked up a failure. Gershwin, who never wavered in his conviction that he had produced an important work, did not live to see his faith justified.

A revival in New York on January 22, 1942 (almost five years after Gershwin's death), marked the beginning of the resuscitation of the opera. It proved so successful that it stayed on eight months and achieved the longest run up to then of any revival in New York stage history. The music critics now reversed themselves by unequivocally calling it a masterwork—"a beautiful piece of music and a deeply moving play for the lyric theater," as Virgil Thomson said of it. A decade later the triumph of *Porgy and Bess* was complete. In a production by Blevins Davis and Robert Breen, an American-Negro company toured for several years through Europe, the Near East, the Soviet Union, smaller countries behind the Iron Curtain, South America, and Mexico—to arouse unparalleled excitement and enthusiasm wherever the opera was given. One Viennese critic said that no new foreign opera had been so well received in Vienna since the Austrian première of *Cavalleria Rusticana* in 1902. The *Daily Herald* of London announced in a headline that "it was worth waiting 17 years for *Porgy*." An Israeli newspaper described the performance of the opera in Tel-Aviv as "an artistic event of first-class importance." When *Porgy and Bess* came to the historic La Scala opera house in Milan (the first time an opera by an American-born composer was performed there), *L'Unita* placed the work "among the masterworks of the lyric theater." The whole world now came to realize how monumental was *Porgy and Bess*.

Porgy and Bess is a folk opera, an epic of the Negro people told with humanity and compassion. Gershwin made extended use of musical materials basic to the Negro. His recitatives were modeled after Negro speech; his songs and choral numbers were derived from the folk and religious music of the Negro and the street cries of vendors in Charleston. So completely did Gershwin assimilate all the elements of Negro song and dance into his own writing that, without quoting a single melody, he produced authentic Negro folk music.

As this writer said in his biography of George Gershwin, *A Journey to Greatness:*

> *Porgy and Bess* was Gershwin's inevitable achievement . . . for it represents, at last, the meeting point for the two divergent paths he had all his life been pursuing—those of serious and popular music. The serious music is found at its best in the musically distinguished tone-speech, in the powerful antiphonal choruses, in the expressive dissonances and chromaticisms, in the brilliant orchestration, in the effective atmospheric writing, in the skillful use of counterpoint in the duets and particularly in the last-scene trio. The popular composer emerges in the jazz background of several choruses, like that in "Woman to Lady"; in the two songs of Sportin' Life, "It Ain't Necessarily So" and "There's a Boat That's Leavin' Soon for New York"; and in Crown's blues ditty, "A Red-Headed Woman Makes a Choochoo Jump Its Track." Yet there is no feeling of contradiction, no sense of incongruity, in this mingling of the serious and the popular, for the popular is as basic to Gershwin's design as the serious, with its own specific artistic function.

JAY GORNEY, composer

Jay Gorney was born in Bialystok, Russia, on December 12, 1896. Like the Irving Berlins, the Gorney family fled from Russia during a pogrom. They came to the United States in 1906 and made a home in Detroit. There Jay started studying the piano when he was ten, and at twelve he founded and led the Cass Technical High School Orchestra. Later on, while attending the University of Michigan, he created a student jazz band of his own which performed at college dances.

Despite his activity in music, he did not plan a musical career. He attended law school, but the war in 1917 interrupted his studies. Gorney enlisted in the United States Navy where, at one period, he led one of John Philip Sousa's bands at the Great Lakes Training Station. After the war he completed his law course, passed the bar exams, and started a practice in Detroit. He practiced law for only one year. In 1923 he landed one of his songs, "I've Been Wanting You," in a Broadway musical, *The Dancing Girl.* A year later his songs were placed in three other Broadway productions: *The Greenwich Village Follies of 1924, Top Hole,* and

Vogues of 1924. In 1927 Gorney contributed several songs to the intimate revue, *Merry Go 'Round,* and in 1929 to the *Sketch Book.*

In 1929 Gorney made a trip to Hollywood to write music for Paramount. He returned to Hollywood in 1933 to work at the Fox Studios, where he remained several years; there he was credited with helping to discover Shirley Temple for whom he found a starring role in her first major picture, *Stand Up and Cheer.* In Hollywood, Gorney wrote such successful songs as "Ah, But Is It Love?" "You're My Thrill," "Baby, Take a Bow," and "I Found a Dream."

His work in Hollywood did not keep him from contributing more songs to various Broadway musical productions in the 1930's—notably to *The Earl Carroll Vanities* in 1929 and 1930; the last of *The Ziegfeld Follies* produced by Ziegfeld himself (1931); and such intimate revues as *Shoot the Works* (1931) and *Americana* (1932). For the last-named production he wrote a smash hit (lyrics by Harburg) to a song that became something of the leitmotiv, or lament, of the Great Depression: "Brother, Can You Spare a Dime?" His greatest success on the Broadway stage came with a topical revue, *Meet the People,* which originated in Hollywood in 1939, before coming to New York for a long run.

In 1942 and 1943 Gorney was a producer for Columbia Pictures. During World War II he was active with the Hollywood Writers Mobilization Committee, creating songs and sketches for radio programs sponsored by the armed forces. Two of his later Broadway musicals were failures: *Heaven on Earth* (1948) and *Touch and Go* (1949).

1929   SKETCH BOOK, a revue with book by Eddie Cantor. Lyrics by E. Y. Harburg. Additional songs and lyrics by other writers. Produced by Earl Carroll at the Earl Carroll Theatre on July 1. Staged by Earl Carroll, Edgar MacGregor, and Leroy Prinz. Cast included Will Mahoney, William Demarest, Patsy Kelly, and George Givot (400 performances).

Earl Carroll produced only two editions of the *Sketch Book.* The first was in 1929; the second came six years later. The best parts of the 1929 *Sketch Book* were those written by Eddie Cantor. There was a filmed sequence in which Earl Carroll negotiates with Cantor for the writing of this material; when Cantor explains how generous Ziegfeld had been to him (showing Carroll a gold watch presented him by Ziegfeld) Carroll proves equally generous: He gives Cantor a grandfather's clock. The opening scene was called "Legs, Legs, Legs": The curtain is only partially raised to reveal a row of shapely legs, to which a chorus of female voices sing a hymn of praise; but when the curtain rises, the legs are attached to phonographs. The best comedy sketch was a bathroom scene in which Patsy Kelly (who here revealed for the first time her extraordinary gifts at comedy) takes a bath while Will Mahoney, her husband, is shaving. A plumber comes in to fix a leak. "My wife is taking a bath," Mahoney shouts. "So what," inquires the plumber, "didn't I take off my hat?" He proceeds to work on the pipes with no further concern. Before Patsy can finish her bath, the room becomes crowded with policemen; with supreme nonchalance Patsy emerges from the tub to serve them tea.

Gorney's best songs were: "Like Me Less, Love Me More" and "Kinda Cute." Harry and Charles Tobias, in collaboration with Vincent Rose, contributed two other fine numbers: "Song of the Moonbeams" and "Fascinating You."

1930 THE EARL CARROLL VANITIES, a revue with book and lyrics by Ted Koehler and E. Y. Harburg. Dialogue by Eddie Welch and Eugene Conrad. Additional songs by Harold Arlen, Burton Lane, and others. Produced by Earl Carroll at the New Amsterdam Theatre on July 1. Staged by Earl Carroll, Priestly Morrison, and Leroy Prinz. Cast included Jimmy Savo, Jack Benny, Patsy Kelly, and Dorothy Britton (215 performances).

Earl Carroll produced his first edition of the *Vanities* at his own theater on July 5, 1923. Book, lyrics, and music were by Carroll himself; cast included Joe Cook, Dorothy Knapp, and Peggy Hopkins Joyce. From the beginning Carroll made the *Vanities* an extravagant showcase for sets and costumes. As one critic remarked: "One lavish scene is succeeded by another with such prodigality that one is given to wondering idly just how much money Mr. Carroll may have sunk in the venture." The revue continued to appear annually until 1932 (except for 1929, when Carroll instead put on the *Sketch Book*) and was revived for a single edition in 1940 with a cast of Hollywood starlets. Most of the scores for the *Vanities* comprised songs by numerous composers and lyricists. Those who wrote either the bulk or the complete score for the various editions were Earl Carroll (1923 and 1924), Charles Gaskill (1925), Morris Hamilton (1926), and Jay Gorney (1930). Among the stars who appeared in the various editions were: W. C. Fields, Sophie Tucker, Julius Tannen, Ted Healey, Will Mahoney, Ray Dooley, Lillian Roth, Jimmy Savo, Patsy Kelly, Milton Berle, Moran and Mack, Helen Broderick, Joe Frisco, Joe Cook, Dorothy Knapp, and Yvette Rugel.

Though the 1930 edition placed as much emphasis on spectacle and production numbers as did earlier productions (in 1930 there was a breath-taking undersea ballet), comedy was not slighted. Jimmy Savo contributed his Chaplinesque pantomime, Jack Benny his droll and suave delivery of wisecracks; among the skits was a travesty on Prohibition.

The 1930 *Vanities* made front-page news when it ran afoul of the law for being "obscene." The main culprits seemed to be Faith Bacon, who performed a provocative fan dance; and Jimmy Savo who appeared in a skit as a department-store window-dresser required to remove certain items of feminine clothing from a dummy.

Gorney's score included "I Came to Life" and "One Love." Other notable numbers came from Harold Arlen ("The March of Time") and Burton Lane ("It's Great to Be in Love").

1940   MEET THE PEOPLE, an intimate revue with book by Henry Myers. Sketches by Edward Eliscu, Milt Gross, and others. Additional music by George Bassman. Produced by the Hollywood Alliance at the Mansfield Theatre on December 25. Staged by Danny Dare. Cast included June Haver, Jan Clayton, Jack Gilford, Betty Garrett, Nanette Fabray, and Joey Faye (160 performances).

Meet the People originated in Hollywood on December 25, 1939, at a modest outlay of 3600 dollars. It was a "topical revue," so refreshing in its originality and so brash in its satire that it stayed on in California for about a year, passing through three editions. It then came for a short run to Chicago and, a little over a year after its birth in California, reached Broadway.

Its incisive social viewpoints, sardonic commentaries on the political scene, and its devastating attacks on current foibles were a delight. "Let's Steal a Tune from Offenbach" laughed gaily at the prevailing Tin Pan Alley practice of stealing melodies from the classics. "It's the Same Old South" was a barbed commentary on Southern bigotry. "Union Label" pointed up social consciousness, and "The Bill of Rights" and "Senate in Session" were gay asides on the facts of life of the political scene. Torch songs were satirized in a flat, dead-pan rendition by Marion Colby.

Besides being a source of not-so-innocent merriment, *Meet the People* proved to be the incubator for future stars for the Broadway stage. The most important of these were Nanette Fabray (still passing under her original name of Nanette Fabares), June Haver, Jan Clayton, Betty Garrett, and Jack Gilford—all unknowns when the revue first hit Broadway.

Besides numbers already mentioned, Gorney's sprightly score included three pleasing items: "A Fellow and a Girl," "The Stars Remain," and "No Lookin' Back."

ADOLPH GREEN, librettist and lyricist. *See* BETTY COMDEN and ADOLPH GREEN

OSCAR HAMMERSTEIN II, librettist and lyricist

Oscar Hammerstein II was born in New York City on July 12, 1895, to a family of distinguished theater people. His grandfather (after whom he was named) was the celebrated opera impresario who built the Manhattan Opera House in 1906 where for several seasons he produced such brilliant performances that he shaped opera history in this country; he was finally bought out for a million dollars by the competitive Metropolitan Opera. The lyricist's father, William, was the manager of the leading vaudeville theater in New York, the Victoria on 42nd Street. Uncle Arthur Hammerstein was a successful Broadway producer.

Though the youngest of the Hammersteins loved the theater and wanted to follow the family tradition by engaging in it professionally, he was directed to law. When he was seventeen he entered Columbia College where his classmates included several later famous in the theater—Lorenz Hart, Howard Dietz, Morrie Ryskind, among others. At Columbia he appeared in and wrote several skits and lyrics for the annual Columbia Varsity Show. In 1917 he passed on to the law school and while attending there served as process server for a New York law firm. When he asked his employer for a raise and was turned down, he decided to abandon law for a job in the theater. His Uncle Arthur hired him as assistant stage manager and general factotum for a Broadway musical, *You're in Love*.

During the year he worked backstage for *You're in Love*, he wrote a song lyric that was interpolated into one of the shows put on by his uncle. His debut as lyricist passed unnoticed, and with good reason: this was no lion's roar. The lyric began: "Make yourselves at home, 'neath our spacious dome, do just as you please." After that, Oscar Hammerstein completed a four-act tragedy of small-town girls, which opened and closed out of town. One year more, and he wrote book and lyrics for a musical comedy produced by his uncle on January 5, 1920—*Always You*, music by Herbert Stothart. *Always You* had a short run of sixty-six performances, but a critic for the New York *Times* did point out that the "lyrics are more clever than those of the average musical comedy." A few days after the road tour of *Always You* ended, Hammerstein was once again represented on Broadway—this time with *Tickle Me*, music by Stothart, and with Otto Harbach and Frank Mandel assisting Hammerstein in the writing of book and lyrics. *Tickle Me* was Hammerstein's first success. An even more substantial success followed in *Wildflower* (1923), music by Vincent Youmans and Stothart; and in 1924 came Rudolf Friml's *Rose Marie*, a box-office triumph and now a stage classic.

In 1924 Hammerstein met Jerome Kern at Victor Herbert's funeral. They joined up as a words-and-music team, their first show, *Sunny*, coming in 1925 and starring Marilyn Miller. In 1927 they collaborated on *Showboat*, to this day one of the proudest achievements of the American musical theater. After that followed *Music in the Air* and *Sweet Adeline*. During this period Hammerstein also wrote either book or lyrics (or both) for other important Broadway composers including Sigmund Romberg, George Gershwin, and Vincent Youmans.

After enjoying major successes on Broadway and in Hollywood (including the winning of an Academy Award for the song, "The Last Time I Saw Paris," in 1938, music by Kern), Hammerstein came upon a lean period in which failure followed failure. In Hollywood, on Broadway, in London, he seemed incapable of recovering a winning stride, and even his closest friends suspected that his career was over.

Then in 1943 he teamed up with Richard Rodgers, with whom he was henceforth to work exclusively. He had known Rodgers many years. More than twenty years earlier he had written one or two lyrics to Rodgers' melodies; and he was on the Columbia Varsity committee that selected a Rodgers and Hart musical for the Varsity Show. But not until Lorenz Hart bowed out as Rodgers' collaborator in 1943 did Rodgers and Hammerstein begin to work together professionally. And their first production made stage history—for it was *Oklahoma!* From then on—with Rodgers' music—Hammerstein scaled new heights as a writer for the theater, with a series of Broadway productions that contributed to the musical stage much of the grandeur it now possesses. In addition to their stage work, they wrote the songs for the motion picture, *State Fair*, winning an Academy Award for the song "It Might As Well Be Spring" and for the television production *Cinderella*. A skillful and even significant writer when he had worked with Friml, Kern, and Youmans, Oscar Hammerstein was stimulated by Rodgers' music—and the inspiration of his friendship—to achieve new horizons as a sensitive poet and a humane dramatist.

See: GEORGE GERSHWIN (*A Song of the Flame*); RUDOLF FRIML (*Rose Marie*); JEROME KERN (*Sunny, Showboat, Sweet Adeline, Music in the Air*); RICHARD RODGERS—II. RODGERS and HAMMERSTEIN (*Oklahoma! Carousel, Allegro, South Pacific, The King and I, Me and Juliet, Pipe Dream*); SIGMUND ROMBERG (*The Desert Song, The New Moon, May Wine*); HARRY RUBY (*Good*

Boy); VINCENT YOUMANS (*Wildflower, The Rainbow*); Appendix I (1920—
Tickle Me).

1943   CARMEN JONES, a musical play, a modern Negro adaptation of George
      Bizet's opera *Carmen*, with music entirely by Bizet. Produced by Billy
      Rose at the Broadway Theatre on December 2. Staged by Hassard
      Short. Choreography by Eugene Loring. Cast included Muriel Smith
      and Muriel Rahn (alternating as Carmen), Luther Saxon and Napoleon
      Reed (alternating as Joe), Carlotta Franzell and Elton J. Warren (alter-
      nating as Cindy Lou), and Glenn Bryant (502 performances).

In the difficult years just before he began to work with Richard Rodgers,
and when successes seemed to have eluded him permanently, Oscar Hammerstein found an idea in a recording of the Bizet opera, *Carmen*. Listening to this vital, throbbing music, Hammerstein conceived the notion of
modernizing the operatic text. The months he spent on libretto and lyrics
represented a labor of love; this was the first time he was writing something for the stage without the stimulus of a signed contract. When he
finished, he let his manuscript lie on his desk for about a year, hoping
to produce the play himself. One day he happened to show his script
to Billy Rose who was so delighted with it he offered to be its producer.

The critics were unqualified in their praises. Lewis Nichols called it
"wonderful, quite wonderful"; Robert Garland said it was "a memorable
milestone in the upward and onward course of the great American show-
shop"; Robert Coleman considered it "superb . . . enchantingly beautiful . . . musically exciting and visually stirring." It stayed on Broadway
almost two years, then went on a transcontinental tour.

In bringing Bizet's opera up to date, Hammerstein transferred its locale
from early nineteenth-century Seville to a Southern town during World
War II; from a cigarette to a parachute factory. Don José of the opera
becomes Joe, a Negro corporal; Escamillo, the toreador, was transformed
into Husky Miller, a heavyweight fighter (Glenn Bryant). The seductive
Carmen Jones manages to steal Joe from Cindy Lou. Joe goes AWOL and
the lovers flee to Chicago, where Carmen soon falls in love with Husky
Miller and abandons Joe. Joe begs Carmen to return to him. When she
refuses, he kills her outside the fighting arena on the night of Husky's
championship bout.

In using Bizet's music for his text and lyrics, Hammerstein made no
additions, and only the most negligible deletions. One or two numbers
were taken out of their order in the opera; the recitatives were displaced

by spoken dialogue (as Bizet originally had intended). As Hammerstein explained in the program:

> Believing *Carmen* to be a perfect wedding of story and music, we have adhered as closely as possible to the original form. . . . The small deviations we have made were only those which seemed honestly demanded by a transference of *Carmen* to a modern American background.

In the modernized score, in which the Bizet music was used with respectful fidelity, the celebrated "Habanera" becomes "Dat's Love" (Carmen Jones); the Seguidille, "Dere's a Café on de Corner" (Carmen Jones and Joe); the Flower Song, "Dis Flower" (Joe); Micaëla's Air, "My Joe" (Cindy Lou); and the toreador song, "Stan' Up and Fight" (Husky Miller).

OTTO HARBACH, librettist

Few have been so prolific as Harbach in writing texts or musical comedies. By 1950 he had written several hundreds of them, with an aggregate of over 12,000 performances! And few have been more distinguished. A skillful craftsman who knows both the stage and its audience, Harbach has a facile pen that drips entertainment and at times enchantment.

He was born Otto Hauerbach in Salt Lake City in Utah on August 16, 1873, the fourth of eight children. His parents had emigrated to America from Denmark, then had come to Salt Lake City by foot and ox cart during the Civil War era.

Otto received a comprehensive academic education, first at the Salt Lake College Institute (a Presbyterian grade school where he was a classmate of Maude Adams), later at Knox College, in Galesburg, Illinois. All the while he supported himself by delivering newspapers and groceries and shining shoes. In 1895 he won an interstate prize for oratory and soon after became a teacher of English and public speaking at Whitman College in Walla Walla, Washington.

He came to New York in 1901, intending to work toward a doctorate at Columbia University. But when both his money and his eyesight gave out, he abandoned his studies and went to work on various jobs: as an insurance agent, a reporter on the *Evening News,* an advertising copywriter for six years with George Batton.

In 1902 he collaborated with Karl Hoschna, the composer, on *The Daughter of the Desert.* For six years they tried marketing the play (on three occasions they actually received options) but without success. They were luckier with *The Three Twins* in 1907, which not only was produced but was a hit. Harbach did not make much money from his text (all he was paid was a flat fee of a hundred dollars and a royalty of one cent a copy for the sale of sheet music), but he had finally won recognition.

For several years he continued doubling as an advertising copywriter and stage librettist. With Hoschna he wrote a few more successes, including the formidable *Madame Sherry* (1910), which finally convinced him that he could make a living entirely from his stage efforts.

He continued as Hoschna's collaborator until the composer's death in 1911. He then worked with Rudolf Friml, and after that with many other important Broadway composers, including Kern, Romberg, Gershwin, Tierney, and Youmans. In the meantime—while working with Friml in the early 1910's—he had changed the spelling of his name from Hauerbach to Harbach, having become impatient with the many combinations and permutations of the way it was being misspelled.

Harbach's creative fertility has been truly remarkable. Season after season he had two, three, and sometimes four musicals running simultaneously. In the season of 1925 he had five plays on Broadway at the same time.

See: RUDOLF FRIML (*Firefly, Rose Marie*); GEORGE GERSHWIN (*A Song of the Flame*); LOUIS A. HIRSCH (*Going Up, Mary*); KARL HOSCHNA (*The Three Twins, Madame Sherry*); JEROME KERN (*Sunny, Criss Cross, The Cat and the Fiddle, Roberta*); SIGMUND ROMBERG (*The Desert Song*); HARRY TIERNEY (*Kid Boots*); VINCENT YOUMANS (*Wildflower; No, No, Nanette*); Appendix I (1920 —*Tickle Me*).

E. Y. HARBURG, lyricist

E. Y. Harburg (better known as "Yip" Harburg) was born in New York City on April 8, 1898. He was a child of the New York City East Side slums and had to support himself through public and high school by selling newspapers and working for the city, lighting street lamps. At Townsend Harris Hall, and later at the College of the City of New York, he contributed bright verses to the school publications and to the renowned newspaper columns of F.P.A. But not until 1929, after a disastrous experience in business, when he tried running an electrical shop, did he finally decide to try earning his living by writing song lyrics. As he later told an interviewer, "I had my fill of this dreamy abstract thing called business and I decided to face reality by writing lyrics."

His first lyrics (to music by Jay Gorney) made an impression on Earl

Carroll, who commissioned both him and Gorney to write songs for *The Sketch Book* (1929). They had six songs there; and they were good enough to bring them a contract to write songs for the Paramount Pictures studios in Hollywood. Harburg also contributed lyrics to several Broadway revues, many of them of the intimate variety that came into vogue in the 1930's; among these productions were the third edition of *The Garrick Gaieties* (1930), to music by Vernon Duke; *Shoot the Works* (1931), in which columnist Heywood Broun was a genial master of ceremonies; *Americana* (1932), to music by Vernon Duke, Burton Lane, and Harold Arlen; and *Life Begins at 8:40* (1937), to music by Harold Arlen. With Gorney he also wrote songs for more ambitious revues produced by Earl Carroll and Florenz Ziegfeld. From these varied productions came several songs that established Harburg's reputation as an ace lyricist, among them the anthem of the depression, "Brother, Can You Spare a Dime?" (Gorney) and "April in Paris" (Duke).

Other triumphs came to Harburg in Hollywood where he worked mostly with Harold Arlen, and produced such songs as "Only a Paper Moon" and "Over the Rainbow," the latter winning an Academy Award.

When Harburg returned to Broadway, it was to be Arlen's collaborator in *Bloomer Girl* (1944). Three years after that he reaped an even richer harvest—and revealed himself a master of his craft—in *Finian's Rainbow*, music by Burton Lane.

See: HAROLD ARLEN (*Hooray for What?, Bloomer Girl, Jamaica*); JAY GORNEY (*The Sketch Book, The Earl Carroll Vanities of 1930*); BURTON LANE (*Hold On to Your Hats, Finian's Rainbow*); HARRY RUBY (*Good Boy*).

LORENZ HART, lyricist. *See* RICHARD RODGERS—I., RODGERS and HART

MOSS HART, librettist

To his texts for musical comedies and revues, Moss Hart has carried his incisive wit, his trenchant intelligence, his sparkling dialogue, and his impertinence of spirit that made him one of Broadway's foremost writers of nonmusical stage comedies.

He was born in New York City on October 24, 1904, and was educated in the city public schools. In 1925, while working as office boy and typist for Augustus Pitou, Broadway producer and manager, he submitted anonymously a melodrama, *The Holdup Man*. Pitou liked it well enough to try it out in Chicago, where it died stillborn. Thus ended Hart's career as a writer of melodrama, but it was some time before he was reincarnated into a creator of comedy. Meanwhile he performed various chores as dramatic director for several Jewish organizations in New York City and Newark, and as social director in resort hotels in the Catskill Mountains.

In 1930 he completed a play satirizing Hollywood which he submitted to George S. Kaufman for criticism. Kaufman recognized its merit and joined him as collaborator. After drastic rewriting the play was produced on Broadway as *Once in a Lifetime* and was a smash hit. The Hart-Kaufman collaboration flourished during the next decade or so with other sparkling Broadway comedies. The best were: *Merrily We Roll Along,* *You Can't Take It with You* (which won the Pulitzer Prize in 1937), *George Washington Slept Here,* and the unforgettable caricature of Alexander Woollcott, *The Man Who Came to Dinner.*

Hart's first effort in writing for the musical stage came in 1932 with Irving Berlin's *Face the Music.* This was followed by a succession of impressive musicals, culminating with what is Hart's best musical-comedy book, Kurt Weill's *Lady in the Dark.* Of lesser interest were his adaptation for Broadway of *The Great Waltz* (1934) and his text for Cole Porter's *Jubilee* (1935). During World War II Moss Hart wrote and helped to produce the Air Force's play, *Winged Victory.*

Hart has also won accolades for his skillful stage direction of two important musical comedies, Irving Berlin's *Miss Liberty,* and the Frederick Loewe-Alan Jay Lerner triumph, *My Fair Lady.*

See: IRVING BERLIN (*Face the Music, As Thousands Cheer*); RICHARD RODGERS —I. RODGERS AND HART (*I'd Rather Be Right*); KURT WEILL (*Lady in the Dark*); ARTHUR SCHWARTZ (*Inside U.S.A.*); Appendix I (1936—*The Show Is On*).

RAY HENDERSON, composer. *See* DE SYLVA, BROWN, and HENDERSON

VICTOR HERBERT, composer

Victor Herbert, a giant figure in American operetta, was of Irish birth—Dublin, February 1, 1859. His father died when Victor was three, and the child and his mother went to live with her father, Samuel Lover, a novelist famous for *Handy Andy,* and a dilettante who cultivated the arts. His house "The Vine," in Seven Oaks, twenty miles from London, was a gathering place for artists, writers, and musicians. In such an atmosphere of culture Herbert spent five impressionable years. It was his mother who first detected in him the signs of musical talent. Herself a competent pianist, she began giving him lessons when he was only seven. He showed such a natural aptitude for music that the grandfather insisted the boy be taken to Germany for training. Mother and son settled in Lungenargen, at Lake Constance, in 1866, where the mother met and married Dr. Carl Schmid. The family now moved to Stuttgart, Germany, where Victor studied the cello at the conservatory. Six years later he went to Baden-Baden for an additional year or so of private study with Bernhardt Cossman. After this he spent four years playing the cello in small-town orchestras and in several led by world-renowned musicians. He finally accepted a permanent post as cellist with the Stuttgart Royal Orchestra conducted by Max Seifritz. The conductor became Herbert's teacher in composition and orchestration, and under his guidance Herbert wrote several symphonic works introduced by the Stuttgart Orchestra.

Now a man-about-town, tall and strikingly handsome, Herbert was adored by women and he had a roving eye for them. But one woman above others attracted his interest. She was Theresa Förster, principal soprano of the Stuttgart Opera. He contrived to meet her and offered his services as voice coach. They fell in love and became engaged when Theresa Förster received a contract from the Metropolitan Opera in New York. Her acceptance was contingent on the engagement of her fiancé as cellist in the opera-house orchestra.

Herbert and Theresa Förster were married in Germany in the spring of 1886. Soon afterward they sailed for America, where she made her Metropolitan Opera debut on the opening night of the 1886-87 season in Karl Goldmark's *The Queen of Sheba.* The critics found much to praise in her performance. Nobody, of course, suspected that the big news that evening was the presence in the orchestra pit of a cellist named Victor Herbert. In the future the limelight would be his.

Herbert became an American and took out his papers for citizenship. He identified himself with American music in every way he could. He conducted and wrote music for American festivals. He created American music—for example, the *American Fantasia,* a spirited medley of American patriotic tunes climaxed by a Wagnerian treatment of "The Star-Spangled Banner." In 1893 he became head of one of America's native musical outfits when he succeeded Patrick Gilmore as bandmaster of the renowned 22nd Regiment Band. From 1898 to 1904 he was principal conductor of the Pittsburgh Symphony, one of America's leading orchestras. In 1904 he organized a band of his own, and in 1910 he wrote an American opera. In 1916 he became the first American composer to write an original score for a motion-picture presentation (*The Fall of a Nation*). But his greatest contribution to American music and American culture came through the scores he wrote for operettas that enlivened the American theater for more than a quarter of a century, and the best of which are still loved.

His first attempt at writing music for the stage consisted of a few numbers for a pageant planned for the Chicago World's Fair. The pageant was never produced, but Herbert's appetite for writing stage music was whetted. "I *must* write for the theater," he told his wife with finality. Consequently, he was highly receptive to a suggestion by William MacDonald, director of the Boston Light Opera Company, which had introduced De Koven's *Robin Hood,* that he write an operetta. The proposed text was a satire on people of the theater by Francis Neilsen (later a distinguished writer on politics). *Prince Ananias,* as the operetta was called, was introduced by the Bostonians at the Broadway Theatre in New York on November 20, 1894, and was a failure.

Success came early—only one year and one operetta later—and it came with *The Wizard of the Nile.* This was the first of many operettas that brought Herbert to the pinnacle of his profession.

There was much to sadden Herbert in the last decade of his life. The war in 1917 put a stigma on all things German. There never was any question of Herbert's allegiance to America or of his disavowal of Prussian militarism. But the sudden vilification of all German culture and music was hard for him to accept. When the prejudice of the times compelled Herbert to remove from his concert programs works by German composers, he complained bitterly: "What have Beethoven and Wagner to do with this war?" But he yielded to public pressure. The end of the war resolved his conflicts with his integrity, but it brought him a deprivation of another kind. Prohibition had become the law of the land, denying Herbert one of his greatest pleasures—alcohol. So keenly did Herbert miss wines and beer that for a period he seriously contemplated leaving America and re-establishing his home in Europe.

His own music also caused personal disturbances. His disappointment in the public and critical reaction to his two operas, both performed by the Metropolitan Opera, was immense; yet it is extremely doubtful if, deep within him, he was not aware of the serious shortcomings of his operas. Even his lighter music was giving him cause for concern. His greatest triumphs were behind him. He seemed incapable of recapturing the formula that had once made him unique. He felt, for example, that the finest score he wrote was for the Irish operetta, *Eileen* (1917), set in rebellion-torn Ireland. Indeed, the score does contain one of Herbert's most beautiful songs, "Thine Alone," whose sale through the years has been rivaled only by "Ah, Sweet Mystery of Life." Yet *Eileen* lasted only sixty-four performances.

His operettas continued to appear on Broadway up to the end of his life. He also wrote special music for other productions, including *The Ziegfeld Follies* between 1918 and 1923. He was still in demand, still regarded with veneration by his associates. More important, he still had his rare gift of melody, as in "Thine Alone" and "A Kiss in the Dark," the latter heard in *Orange Blossoms* in 1922. Yet it was obvious that his day was over. He had belonged to the era of the waltz, an era in which he was king, for he had the precious gift of wonderful melody, and the knowledge of harmony and orchestration to set off that melody to best advantage. His romantic, tender, sentimental music belonged to an epoch that died with World War I. In the newer, frenetic period of the fox trot and the Charleston, of ragtime and jazz, his songs sounded almost like an anachronism. "My day is over," he told a friend. "They are forgetting poor old Herbert."

Yet in spite of lengthening shadows, the last years of his life were by no means somber. To the end he retained his extraordinary zest for living, working, eating, and drinking, and for the society of friends.

He was working on some special numbers for the 1924 edition of *The Ziegfeld Follies* when, on May 26, he suffered a heart attack at the Lambs Club. He died a few hours later in his physician's office.

Within his own world, and measured by its standards, Herbert was an outstanding composer. "My idea of heaven," once said Andrew W. Carnegie, "is to be able to sit and listen to the music of Victor Herbert all I want to." The greatness of Herbert is that, today as yesterday, so many Americans everywhere feel the way Carnegie did.

Fifteen years after Herbert's death Paramount Pictures released *The Great Victor Herbert*, starring Allan Jones as the composer. The sound track boasted seventeen Herbert gems—only a fraction of his life's production—but enough to remind a later generation of how much Victor Herbert had once meant for so long a time and to so many people.

1895   THE WIZARD OF THE NILE, a comic opera, with book and lyrics by Harry B. Smith. Produced by Kirke La Shelle and Arthur F. Clark at the Casino Theatre on November 2. Cast included Frank Daniels, Dorothy Morton, and Walter Allen (105 performances).

Harry B. Smith, DeKoven's librettist, wrote an Oriental text for a new operetta which he submitted to Kirke La Shelle, manager of The Bostonians. La Shelle liked it and suggested Victor Herbert for the music. Smith objected strongly, since at the time Herbert had written only a single operetta and that had been a failure. But he finally permitted himself to be convinced by La Shelle of Herbert's potential gifts. Thus began a partnership between Smith and Herbert that was to yield a harvest of operetta productions, beginning with *The Wizard of the Nile*.

The setting was ancient Egypt, afflicted by a drought. Kibosh, a Persian magician (Frank Daniels) discovers that anybody capable of relieving the drought can win the hand of Cleopatra (Dorothy Morton). Since Kibosh knows he has an ally in the season of the year—a period in which the Nile overflows habitually—he performs an elaborate ritual calling upon the mighty river to relieve the distress. The Nile overflows—but, regrettably, much more generously than Kibosh had hoped for. Kibosh does not have the power to arrest the tide. The King (Walter Allen) condemns Kibosh to torture and death in a sealed tomb. Somehow the King as well as Kibosh are left in the tomb, but both manage to escape. The King is so delighted with his freedom that he forgives Kibosh.

The operetta and the role of Kibosh were conceived for the comedy gifts of Frank Daniels, here making his bow in operetta. It was Daniels who was responsible for bringing to the play most of its merriment. A favorite Kibosh phrase—"Am I a wiz?"—caught on outside the theater and entered the speech of the day. Daniels also helped make popular a witty topical song, "That's One Thing a Wizard Can Do."

Some of Herbert's music neatly caught the Oriental spirit and atmosphere of the play, particularly the descriptive background music and the pompous Oriental march. The most popular vocal number was a lilting waltz-quintet, "Starlight, Star Bright." Other effective numbers included "My Angeline," "Pure and White Is the Lotus," and "In Dreamland."

1897   THE SERENADE, a comic opera, with book and lyrics by Harry B. Smith. Produced by Henry Clay Barnabee and William H. MacDonald at the Knickerbocker Theatre on March 16. Stage direction by W. H. Fitzgerald. Cast included Eugene Cowles, Jessie Bartlett Davis, Henry Clay Barnabee, and Alice Neilson (79 performances).

Harry B. Smith long insisted that this play was derived from an interlude by Carlo Goldoni, but this was finally proved a hoax; no such Goldoni interlude exists. Smith's text (and it is his own) concerned Alvarado

(W. H. MacDonald) a handsome opera singer who wins the heart of Dolores (Jessie Bartlett Davis) with a beautiful serenade. For her he is ready to jilt his former sweetheart, Yvonne (Alice Nielson). Alvarado and Dolores come into the hands of the brigand chief, Romero (Eugene Cowles). The Duke of Santa Cruz (Henry Clay Barnabee) brings Dolores into a monastery to keep her from Alvarado, but Alvarado finally wins Dolores and Yvonne finds consolation with another man.

It has been said that the real hero of the play is not a character but the serenade "I Love Thee, I Adore Thee," which first appears as the second half of a duet between Alvarado and Dolores and then courses throughout the entire operetta. The serenade reappears in many different forms: as a parody on grand opera; a monk's chant; a parrot's call; a rousing song of brigands. It makes a final appearance in its original sentimental version—as love conquers all.

Though Yvonne is not the heroine of the play, Alice Neilson first became a star in that role. She had not originally been intended for the part when the operetta was first contemplated. One day, just before *The Serenade* went into rehearsal, Victor Herbert's wife heard the then-unknown Neilson at the Murray Hill Theatre and became convinced she was the actress to play Yvonne. Herbert concurred. Though Hilda Clark had been engaged for the part, Neilson was contracted, and they shared the role at alternate performances.

While the serenade was the leading vocal number in the score, there were several others that caught on: a humorous parody on the serenade, "The Singing Lesson"; a gay waltz sung by Yvonne, "Cupid and I"; "The Monk and the Maid," a lusty idyl of the pleasures of the flesh; and Alvarado's rousing postilion song, "With Cracking of Whip." Also in the score were some fine concerted and dramatic numbers, including such appealing choruses as the opening brigands' hymn and the chant of the monks, "In Our Quiet Cloister."

1898   THE FORTUNE TELLER, a comic opera book and lyrics by Harry B. Smith. Presented by L. Perley and the Alice Neilson Opera Company at Wallack's Theatre on September 26. Stage direction by Julian Mitchell. Cast included Alice Neilson, Eugene Cowles, Frank Rushworth, and Joseph Herbert (40 performances).

Having discovered Alice Neilson and established her as a star in *The Serenade,* Herbert and Smith had to create a new vehicle for her. They placed her within a Hungarian setting and cast her in the dual role of Musette, a gypsy fortuneteller, and Irma, a ballet student at the Budapest

Opera. Irma loves and is loved by Ladislas, a Hungarian Hussar (Frank Rushworth); Musette, by Sandor, a gypsy musician (Eugene Cowles). Irma, however, must elude marriage with Count Berezowsky, a Polish pianist-composer (Joseph Herbert). In this she is aided by Musette. Since the two girls look amazingly alike, they succeed in confounding their rivals and enemies. The entanglements are finally unraveled to allow the two girls to marry the men they love.

Herbert created for this operetta music rich with Hungarian atmosphere and flavor. To this day the stirring Hussar chorus of the first act, Sandor's languorous serenade, "Gypsy Love Song" (sometimes known also as "Slumber On, My Little Gypsy Sweetheart"), and Sandor's song with chorus, "Gypsy Jan," are so hot with gypsy blood and so colorful with gypsy temperament that they never fail to arouse audiences. The military march that closes the second act and the extended first-act finale are effective instrumental pieces.

1903 BABES IN TOYLAND, a musical extravaganza with book and lyrics by Glen MacDonough. Produced by Fred R. Hamlin and Julian Mitchell at the Majestic Theatre on October 13. Staged by Julian Mitchell. Cast included William Norris, George W. Denham, Mabel Barrison, and Bessie Wynn (192 performances).

It was no secret to anybody that *Babes in Toyland* was intended by its authors as an imitation of the highly successful and the then recently produced extravaganza, *The Wizard of Oz,* an effort to capitalize on its success. The setting of Oz was transferred to Toyland, a convenient way of introducing characters from fairy tales and children's story books, including Tom Thumb, Jack and Jill, Bo-Peep, Red Riding Hood, Tommy Tucker, and so forth.

The plot is a loosely knit and not often clear affair. Jane (Mabel Barrison) and Alan (William Norris) are victimized by a miserly uncle, Barnaby (George W. Denham), who plans their death. They manage to survive a shipwreck and find their way to the garden of Contrary Mary where they meet various characters from Mother Goose. From there they proceed to Toyland, dominated by a wicked Toymaker, who can bring toys to life. These living toys eventually bring about the Toymaker's doom. In the end the children are able to conquer over the evil plans of their uncle and to achieve a happy life.

This plot, however, was only an excuse to present elaborate scenes and spectacles. The production boasted a huge cast not only of principals but also of minor characters—even personified butterflies, French and

Dutch dolls, toy soldiers, and so forth. There was a breath-taking Christmas spectacle, a delightful butterfly ballet that consisted of a wordless prologue against music of symphonic breadth, and a spectacular number in the "Legend of the Castle." In short the show was a continual feast for the eye. The New York *Dramatic Mirror* reported that it was "a perfect dream of delight to the children and will recall the happy days of childhood to those who are facing the stern realities of life."

Herbert's music was full of delights, the most famous being "Toyland" and "March of the Toys," both in the second act. About the now celebrated "March of the Toys" the critic of the *Tribune* wrote in 1903: "It is a capital piece . . . with just a suggestion of the grotesque. [It] harmonizes charmingly with the scene and with the ballet which follows with its sounds from Toyland."

The score also included a delightful little choral piece, "I Can't Do the Sum," in which the children beat out the rhythm with their chalk on slates; a tender song, "Go to Sleep, Slumber Deep"; and the witty "Rock-a-bye Baby," in which Herbert parodied the style of several composers, including Sousa and Donizetti.

1904   IT HAPPENED IN NORDLAND, a comic opera with book and lyrics by Glen MacDonough. Produced by Hamlin, Mitchell and Fields at the Lew Fields Theatre on December 5. Staged by Julian Mitchell. Cast included Lew Fields, Harry Davenport, Joseph Herbert, and Marie Cahill (154 performances).

By using as its central character an American Ambassadress to the court of Nordland, *It Happened in Nordland* anticipated Irving Berlin's *Call Me Madam* by almost half a century. Katherine Peepfoogle, the Ambassadress (Marie Cahill), bears a striking resemblance to the Nordland Queen. When the Queen disappears to escape an undesirable marriage, the American Ambassadress is compelled to impersonate her in order to save the kingdom. The difficulties are straightened out when the Queen is permitted to marry the man she loves, Prince Karl (Frank O'Neill). The Ambassadress finds happiness in recovering a long-lost brother, Hubert (Lew Fields).

One of the most familiar numbers from this score is "Al Fresco," which opens the second act. Herbert published it originally as a piano piece under an assumed name to see if it could win the public without the benefit of the composer's fame. When it sold well, he decided to adapt it for the carnival scene in this musical. Immediately after the performance of the "Al Fresco" music in the second act comes the song hit of the production, an infectious waltz, "A Knot of Blue," sung by a girl's chorus. Other numbers include the sophisticated "Absinth Frappé," the spirited march "Commanderess-in-Chief," and "She's a Very Dear Friend of Mine."

Marie Cahill, star of the show, left the cast impetuously, following a bitter fight with Herbert, who objected to her frequent interpolations of songs by other composers. On April 29—when Herbert was conducting as a substitute for Max Hirschfield, who was ill—she left the stage weeping, midway in the play, complaining that Herbert had purposely interpolated two discords to disconcert her. (Herbert said the discords were the result of her singing off pitch.) When the play went on to Boston she refused to go along with the company, and her role was assumed by several other performers, including Blanche Ring and Pauline Frederick; the latter here began her career that would bring her to stardom in the theater and on the screen.

1905 MLLE. MODISTE, comic opera with book and lyrics by Henry Blossom. Produced by Charles Dillingham at the Knickerbocker Theatre on December 25. Staged by Fred G. Latham. Cast included Fritzi Scheff, William Pruette, and Walter Percival (202 performances).

The setting is Paris—in Mme Cecile's hat shop on the Rue de la Paix, where Fifi (Fritzi Scheff) is employed. She and Captain Etienne de Bouvray (Walter Percival) are in love. Since Etienne's family objects, marriage is out of the question. An American millionaire, Hiram Bent (Claude Gillingwater), becomes interested in Fifi, who has a talent for singing. He finances her studies and her career until she becomes a famous prima donna. Under her stage name of Mme Bellini, Fifi comes to sing at a charity affair at the De Bouvray castle. Her singing makes such a profound impression on Etienne's uncle that he now allows his nephew to marry Fifi.

As Fifi, Fritzi Scheff soared to the heights in the American musical theater. Previously she had enjoyed only a moderately successful career at the Metropolitan Opera. Victor Herbert recognized her possibilities in the popular theater and lured her away from the Metropolitan by offering her 1000 dollars a week to appear in an operetta he wrote expressly for her—*Babette. Babette* (1903) was a failure. But two years later, in her second Victor Herbert operetta—*Mlle. Modiste*—she was a triumph, particularly when she sang "Kiss Me Again," unquestionably the most celebrated single number in the score.

Many legends exist about the origin of that famous waltz. One has it that when Herbert first kissed Fritzi Scheff, after the première of *Babette*, she said to him, "Kiss me Again," and an idea for a waltz was born. Another legend insisted that one hot summer night, as Herbert strolled in the garden of the Grand Union Hotel in Saratoga Springs, New York, he heard a woman asking her lover to kiss her again. Such stories are manufactured, but it is no legend that Herbert did not write this melody for *Mlle. Modiste*. He had completed it in 1903 and put it aside for future use. In preparing the score for *Mlle. Modiste*, Herbert wrote a first-act number called "If I Were on the Stage," in which Fifi proves her versatility by singing various types of songs—a gavotte, a polonaise, a dreamy waltz, and so forth, each being a caricature of that type of song. For the waltz part, Herbert reached back to the melody he had written in 1903, and intended it as a parody of sentimental waltzes. The audience liked this part so well that Herbert eventually had to write a new verse for the melody and present it as a sentimental waltz.

When Herbert first went through "Kiss Me Again" for Fritzi Scheff, she did not like it, insisting the tonal register was too low for her voice. Herbert was insistent that she sing it, and she finally consented. Her success with the waltz was of such magnitude that from that time on she and the song became inextricably associated.

There are other appealing numbers in this operetta, though they have been somewhat obscured by the enormous popularity of "Kiss Me Again." One is one of the best marches Herbert ever wrote, "The Mascot of the Troop," which contains a brief quotation from the *Marseillaise;* another is a concert waltz, "The Nightingale and the Star," in which Fifi reveals her artistry; a third, an amusing piece sung by Count de Bouvray, "I Want What I Want When I Want It"; finally, "The Time, the Place and the Girl," in which Etienne speaks of his disappointment in being unable to combine all three into a single blessed unity.

1906   THE RED MILL, a comic opera with book and lyrics by Henry Blossom. Produced by Charles Dillingham at the Knickerbocker Theatre on September 24. Staged by Fred G. Latham. Cast included Fred Stone, David Montgomery, and Augusta Greenleaf (274 performances).

The success of Fred Stone and David Montgomery in *The Wizard of Oz* (1903) led Henry Blossom and Victor Herbert to fashion an operetta for their comic talent. *The Red Mill*—ambitiously designated in the program as a "musical play"—had Holland for a setting, specifically the little Dutch port of Katwyk. Two Americans are stranded penniless in the little inn, "The Sign of the Red Mill." They are Con Kidder (Fred Stone) and Kid Conner (David Montgomery). Despite all their devious efforts, they are unable to get money for their passage home. They become the allies of pretty Gretchen (Augusta Greenleaf) in her efforts to marry Captain Doris van Damm (Joseph W. Ratliff); and by the same token they become the enemies of the Governor of Zeeland (Neal McCay) who wants Gretchen for himself. When Gretchen is locked in the mill in order to be kept from her lover, Kid Conner and Con Kidder contrive to rescue her by taking her through the window and bringing her to safety on the arm of a revolving windmill. The absent bride complicates the wedding festivities arranged by the Governor. These festivities are enlivened by the intermittent appearance of our two Americans in various disguises (as Italian organ grinders, Sherlock Holmes and Dr. Watson, and so forth). When the discovery is made that Captain van Damm is heir to a large fortune, all resistance to him collapses, and the lovers are reunited.

"*The Red Mill,*" wrote one New York critic prophetically in 1906, "will grind its grist of mirth, music and melody for a long time to come." It is Herbert's music that keeps this operetta alive. When it is revived—as it is done periodically, in New York, for example, on October 16, 1945, when it amassed the impressive run of 531 performances—the book and the comedy, however revised and modernized, prove dated. But Herbert's music remains fresh and winning to the ear. One of his most beguiling songs is the ardent love duet of Gretchen and Captain Doris, "The Isle of Our Dreams," and in Gretchen's haunting refrain in the extended first-act finale, "Moonbeams," we have mood music that casts an inescapable spell. As a change of pace Herbert included in his score a delightful comedy song in "Every Day is Ladies' Day to Me," with which the Governor anticipates his delight in marrying Gretchen; and an Italian number by Conner and Kidder when they appear as Italian street musicians, "Good-a-bye, John." There has long existed the suspicion that this last song was not by Herbert at all, since a similar song was published by Remick a year before *The Red Mill* was produced (lyrics by Harry Williams, music by Egbert van Alstyne). Yet since neither Remick nor the authors issued a protest, it cannot be said with any degree of certainty that the song was plagiarized.

1910 NAUGHTY MARIETTA, a comic opera with book and lyrics by Rida Johnson Young. Produced by Oscar Hammerstein at the New York Theatre on November 7. Cast included Emma Trentini and Orville Harrold (136 performances).

In April, 1910, the first Oscar Hammerstein sold his interests in the Manhattan Opera Company to the Metropolitan Opera. One month later he decided to enter the Broadway musical theater. He contracted Victor Herbert and Rida Johnson Young to write an operetta, and for its leads Hammerstein selected two alumni from his opera house—Emma Trentini and Orville Harrold. The Manhattan Opera also contributed a few of the lesser singers, the members of the chorus, a large part of the orchestra, and the conductor.

Herbert's operetta used New Orleans of 1780 as a setting, a period when Louisiana was under Spanish rule. Marietta (Emma Trentini) is of noble birth, but she has fled from Naples and an undesirable marriage by joining a group of *casquette* girls en route to Louisiana to marry the planters there. In New Orleans she comes under the protective wing of Captain Dick Warrington (Orville Harrold), come to pursue the pirate, Bras Pique. Marietta has heard a fragmentary melody in her dreams, and she announces her willingness to marry any man who can finish it for her. Etienne Grandet (Edward Martindel), son of the Lieutenant Governor—and actually also the pirate whom Warrington is pursuing—falls in love with Marietta and almost wins her love. But he is unable to complete the melody. Since Dick Warrington can do so, he wins Marietta.

Possibly inspired by the fact that he was here working with a famous opera impresario, and with so many graduates from opera, Herbert produced his most ambitious score. Some of his songs have the spaciousness of arias, while some of the instrumental numbers have symphonic breadth. The opening scene, with interpolations of street cries, and the chorus of flower girls are two excerpts demonstrating the amplitude of Herbert's style.

Among the songs are three of Herbert's greatest: "Ah, Sweet Mystery of Life," is the melody Marietta has dreamed of, and with which Warrington wins her. Story has it that the melody originated as an instrumental number, but that Orville Harrold, aware of its commercial appeal, convinced Herbert to have words added to it. This is not true, since the song was in the operetta from the beginning of its run.

"I'm Falling in Love with Someone," sung by Warrington when he realizes he loves Marietta, is remarkable for its chromaticisms in the opening bars and in the unusual leap of a ninth in the refrain. "Italian Street Song," with which Marietta recalls Naples; the march, "Tramp, Tramp, Tramp," with which Captain Dick and his men make their first appearance; the vocal quartet, "Live for Today"; and the beautiful serenade,

" 'Neath the Southern Moon"—these are other highlights from a remarkable score.

During the run of the play Herbert and Trentini became so hostile to each other that they vowed never again to work together. Herbert was antagonized by Trentini's artistic temperament and whims, her tendency to stay away from a performance when she felt like it, and her refusal to give encores. Trentini considered Herbert a tyrant. An operetta that Herbert planned to write for Trentini as a successor to *Naughty Marietta*, therefore, had to be assigned to another composer. The composer was Rudolf Friml, and the operetta, *The Firefly*.

1913   SWEETHEARTS, a romantic operetta, with book by Harry B. Smith and Fred de Gresac. Lyrics by Robert B. Smith. Produced by Werba and Luescher at the New Amsterdam Theatre on September 8. Staged by Frederick G. Latham. Ensembles and dances by Charles S. Morgan, Jr. Cast included Christie MacDonald, Tom McNaughton, and Thomas Conkey (136 performances).

A program note explained:

The story of the opera is founded on the adventures of Princess Jeanne, daughter of King René of Naples, who reigned in the 15th century. Time has been changed to the present, the locale to the ancient city of Bruges, to which the little princess is carried for safety in time of war and is given the name of Sylvie.

Sylvie (Christine MacDonald) is a foundling, raised as a daughter by Paula, proprietress of the Laundry of White Geese. When Prince Franz of Zilania (Thomas Conkey) meets and falls in love with her, Sylvie rejects him, for she realizes she can never marry one of so high a station. The rival of Franz for Sylvie's love is Lieutenant Karl (Edwin Wilson). Sylvie is repelled by Karl's fickle nature, and when it turns out that Sylvie is really the Crown Princess of Zilania—abducted from her native land in childhood—she is all too willing to accept Prince Franz.

Herbert F. Peyser, later a noted music critic, said this of Herbert's score: "From first to last this music is utterly free from any suggestions of triviality. The abundant melodic flow is invariably marked by distinction, individuality, and a quality of superlative charm." This charm was most apparent in the duet of Franz and Sylvie, permeated with a radiant glow, "The Angelus." Also winning is Sylvie's popular waltz, "Sweethearts," a spacious two-octave melody with an intriguing rhythmic pulse. "Sweethearts" was written long before the production of the operetta itself, a sketch having been found in Herbert's notebook dated 1896. "Pretty as a Picture," in which woman's use of cosmetics is deplored, was intended by Herbert as a comedy number, but in the play it was changed into a sweet and sentimental song.

In a more ambitious vein was the effective entr'acte between acts, built from the thematic material of the opening chorus; the burlesque of religious music in "Pilgrims of Love"; and the elaborate finale made up of recitatives, choral ejaculations, orchestral interludes, and a recurrence of the main love song.

LOUIS A. HIRSCH, composer

Just how prolific Hirsch was in writing songs for the Broadway stage was forcefully underscored during World War I. There was one period then when about a dozen plays running simultaneously had one or more of his songs. How successful he was is also underscored by one of his songs, "The Love Nest," which sold millions of copies of sheet music and records and which more recently has become the theme music for Burns and Allen.

Louis Achille Hirsch was born in New York City on November 28, 1887. A musical prodigy, he managed to teach himself the piano when he was an infant. While attending New York public and high schools he studied the piano with local teachers. During his senior year at the College of the City of New York, he was taken by his parents to Europe where he attended the renowned Stern Conservatory in Berlin, a pupil of Rafael Joseffy. He was now fired with the ambition of becoming a concert pianist. But after his return to the United States, in 1906, he came to the conclusion that he had set a too-distant goal for himself, and he compromised by engaging in popular-musical activity. He found a job as staff pianist in Tin Pan Alley—first with the firm of Gus Edwards, then with Shapiro-Bernstein. He also started writing songs and making arrangements. One of his assignments was writing the music for Lew Dockstader's Minstrels. Other Hirsch songs sprouted in various Broadway musicals, including *The Gay White Way* (1907), *Miss Innocence,* starring Anna Held (1908), and *The Girl and the Wizard* (1909). His first complete musical-comedy score was for *He Came from Milwaukee* (1910); the first revue with his complete score was the *Revue of Revues* (1911), in which Gaby Deslys, mistress of King Alfonso of Spain, made a sensational American stage debut.

Success came to Hirsch in 1911 with *Vera Violetta*. In 1912, as staff composer for the Shuberts, Hirsch wrote songs for the Winter Garden production *The Whirl of Society*, starring Al Jolson, and for the first edition of *The Passing Show*.

Toward the end of 1912 Hirsch and the Shuberts parted company, his job assumed by Sigmund Romberg. Hirsch went to England where he wrote for the London stage. When World War I broke out in Europe, he managed to get boat passage home. Back in the United States, he was hired by Ziegfeld to write music for *The Ziegfeld Follies of 1915*. During the next decade Hirsch's music was heard in several editions of *The Ziegfeld Follies*, as well as in editions of *The Greenwich Village Follies*, and several musical comedies, the most successful being *Going Up* (1917) and *Mary* (1920).

Hirsch was at the height of his success when he died in New York City on May 13, 1924.

1911   VERA VIOLETTA, an extravaganza, with book by Harold Atteridge and Leonard Liebling, adapted from a German play by Leo Stein. Additional songs by Edmund Eysler and others. Produced by the Winter Garden Company at the Winter Garden on November 20. Cast included Al Jolson, Gaby Deslys, Harry Pilcer, Jose Collins, and Mae West (112 performances).

Vera Violetta was only one-half of a two-part bill presented at the Winter Garden. The other half was *Undine*, an "idyl" with music by Manuel Klein, starring Annette Kellerman.

Vera Violetta consisted primarily of "spectacular" variety entertainment. It focused the spotlight on Gaby Deslys, a sensation in the song "The Gaby Glide" (years ahead of its time in its ingenious use of ragtime rhythm and blues harmony). Other stellar attractions were the dance routines of Gaby Deslys and Harry Pilcer; Jose Collins singing the title song and "Olga from the Volga" (both by Edmund Eysler), and her interpolation of the 1890 classic, "Ta-ra-ra-bom-de-re"; and such Hirsch songs as "Come and Dance with Me" and "When You Hear Love's Hello."

But the big news of *Vera Violetta* was the first rise to stardom of a minstrel in burned cork—Al Jolson, then twenty-six. For over a decade he had been shuttling around the stages of burlesque and vaudeville theaters—singing, dancing, jesting, and slowly assimilating some of the mannerisms and gestures that would become his permanent trade-mark. First he imitated the Southern accent of one of his playmates, a Negro boy; then in a Brooklyn vaudeville theater he put on burned cork for the first time; on still another occasion he went down on one knee while singing a song. Lew Dockstader engaged him for his Minstrels in 1909 where Lee Shubert saw him and engaged him at a salary of 250 dollars a week. Al Jolson made his Broadway stage debut in 1911 in *La Belle Paree,* an extravaganza that opened the Winter Garden on March 20.

In *Vera Violetta,* Jolson sang George M. Cohan's "That Haunting Song" and Jean Schwartz' "Rum Tum Tiddle"—and had the audience in the palm of his hand. From that moment on he was a Broadway star, and one of the most brilliant. In 1912 he inaugurated his famous Sunday-evening concerts at the Winter Garden for show people. In 1913 the Shuberts gave him a bonus of 10,000 dollars to sign a seven-year contract, guaranteeing him 1000 dollars a week for a thirty-five-week period each year; and he was paid 2500 dollars a week to appear in vaudeville.

1912 THE PASSING SHOW, a revue with book by George Bronson Howard. Lyrics by Harold Atteridge. Produced by the Winter Garden Company at the Winter Garden on July 22. Dances staged by Ned Wayburn. Cast included Willie and Eugene Howard, Jobyna Howland, and Harry Fox (136 performances).

For later editions of The Passing Show see SIGMUND ROMBERG *and* JEAN SCHWARTZ.

This production should not be confused with *The Passing Show,* in 1894, with which the modern-day revue came into being (*see* LUDWIG ENGLANDER). The 1912 *Passing Show* was the first edition of a new revue put on annually by the Shuberts at the Winter Garden until 1924.

The Passing Show emphasized remarkable sets, which carried the audience from a steamship pier to a harem, from Greeley Square in New York to a hotel roof garden. En route, Adelaide and Hughes did some striking dances (particularly in the harem scene); Willie and Eugene Howard made their first step from vaudeville to the Broadway theater and Charlotte Greenwood enjoyed her first stage success; Clarence Harvey did a lively dance to the song "Handy Andy"; and such excellent songs by Hirsch as "Always Together" and "The Wedding Glide" were supplemented by an interpolated number by Irving Berlin, "The Ragtime Jockey Man."

1915-22 *The Ziegfeld Follies*

1915 edition, a revue with book and lyrics by Channing Pollock, Rennold Wolf, and Gene Buck. Additional music by Dave Stamper. Produced by Florenz Ziegfeld at the New Amsterdam Theatre on June 21. Staged by Julian Mitchell and Leon Errol. Cast included W. C. Fields, Ann

Pennington, Mae Murray, Leon Errol, Bert Williams, George White, Ed Wynn, and Ina Claire (104 performances).

1916 edition, a revue with book and lyrics by George V. Hobart and Gene Buck. Additional music by Dave Stamper and Jerome Kern. Produced by Florenz Ziegfeld at the New Amsterdam Theatre on June 12. Staged by Ned Wayburn. Cast included Ina Claire, Bert Williams, Marion Davies, Ann Pennington, Fanny Brice, and W. C. Fields (112 performances).

1918 edition, a revue with book and lyrics by Rennold Wolf and Gene Buck. Produced by Florenz Ziegfeld at the New Amsterdam Theatre on June 18. Staged by Ned Wayburn. Cast included W. C. Fields, Marilyn Miller, Eddie Cantor, Ann Pennington, the Fairbanks Twins, and Lillian Lorraine (151 performances).

1922 edition, with book and lyrics by Ring Lardner, Ralph Spence, and Gene Buck. Additional music by Dave Stamper and Victor Herbert. Produced by Florenz Ziegfeld at the New Amsterdam Theatre on June 5. Staged by Ned Wayburn. Cast included Will Rogers, Mary Eaton, Gallagher and Shean, and Olsen and Johnson (333 performances).

For other editions of The Ziegfeld Follies see IRVING BERLIN, RAYMOND HUBBELL, *and Appendix I (1907).*

By 1915 *The Ziegfeld Follies* had become one of the most lavish and glamorous spectacles on Broadway—so much so that for the opening-night performance, Diamond Jim Brady paid 750 dollars for a pair of tickets. This edition was notable for several reasons. It was the first *Follies* in which W. C. Fields appeared. Previously a comparatively obscure comedian, Fields stopped the show with a pantomime that subsequently became one of his favorite routines: a game of billiards, which the critic of the New York *Daily Mirror* described as "a screamingly funny exhibition." Fields was also seen in a skit with Ann Pennington, Leon Errol, and Bert Williams called "Hallway of the Bunkem Court Apartments."

This was also the first *Follies* for Will Rogers, to which he had come straight from his success in Karl Hoschna's operetta, *The Wall Street Girl*. On this occasion Will Rogers added a dry and penetrating monologue to his famous lariat act, a practice he would henceforth continue.

Comedy was further enriched in this edition with sketches starring Ed Wynn. He appeared as a motion-picture director and as a cabaret impresario. He gave W. C. Fields such stiff competition for laughs that at one performance Fields lost his temper and hit Wynn over the head with his billiard stick.

Joseph Urban's sets also made a distinguished contribution to the 1915 edition, particularly in the opening and closing scenes; the first was "Under the Sea"; the other in Elysium. The score had three fine songs in "Hello, Frisco, Hello," "Hold Me in Your Loving Arms," and "Marie Odile"—the last a take-off by Frances Starr on Ina Claire (recently starring on Broadway in *Marie Odile*).

In 1916, W. C. Fields (now a *Follies* favorite) gave remarkable impersonations of Teddy Roosevelt and Secretary of the Navy Josephus Daniels. Hirsch's best songs were "Beautiful Island of Girls" and "I Want That Star." Among interpolated songs was one by Jerome Kern, "Ain't It Funny What a Difference a Few Drinks Make?".

Stage history was made in the 1918 edition on two counts. It was the first time W. C. Fields spoke in his act, the result of an ad-lib that was permitted to stay in. During his famous golf pantomime a young lady continually disturbed him by passing by him provocatively and saying, "Oh, I forgot something." After one of her interruptions Fields ad-libbed: "Must've forgotten her horse." Besides this golf routine Fields appeared in a sketch with Eddie Cantor in which they became involved in a battle of half-wits in a patent-attorney office. Eddie Cantor, in still another skit, was an Air Corps recruit receiving a physical examination.

Stage history was also made in 1918 through the first *Follies* appearance of Marilyn Miller. She walked down a flight of stairs—dressed in a minstrel costume emphasizing her exquisitely shaped legs—and became the very essence of feminine allure. She was also seen as a ballet dancer, while other dancing acts included the dynamic Ann Pennington (a *Follies* staple), and some jazz numbers by Joe Frisco. Hirsch's songs included "Garden of Your Dreams," "When I'm Looking at You," and "Syncopated Tune." This score also had a few interpolated songs by Irving Berlin and a wartime topical hit in "Would You Rather Be a Colonel with an Eagle on Your Shoulder or a Private with a Chicken on Your Knee?" (words by Sidney D. Mitchell, music by Archie Gottler).

The 1922 edition had one of Hirsch's best scores, with songs like " 'Neath the South Sea Moon," "My Rambler Rose," and "Throw Me a Kiss" (in all three of which he collaborated with Stamper); and "Some Sweet Day" and "Hello, Hello, Hello." But the song that caught on most quickly, and then spread throughout the country like contagion, was a topical item by Gallagher and Shean which they themselves presented in a sprightly exchange of verses and which was entitled "Mr. Gallagher and Mr. Shean."

1917   GOING UP, a musical farce with book and lyrics by Otto Harbach based on James Montgomery's *The Aviator*. Produced by Cohan and Harris at the Liberty Theatre on December 25. Staged by Edward Royce and James Montgomery. Cast included Frank Craven, Edith Day, Ruth Donnelly, and Donald Meek (351 performances).

The main attraction of *Going Up* was the performance of Frank Craven as Robert Street, author of six best-selling books on aviation. In a summer resort in the Berkshire Mountains, he boasts of his skill at aeronautics until he is coerced into accepting a challenge in an air race with an actual aviator. His efforts to extricate himself from this disagreeable proposition provide most of the comedy of the play and give Craven many opportunities for his winning characterization. Actually, to win the girl he loves—she is Grace Douglas (Edith Day)—he must go through with the challenge, from which he emerges victorious.

The musical had an outstanding song hit in "Tickle Toe" ("Ev'rybody Ought to Know How to Do the Tickle Toe"), which was introduced by Grace in a captivating song and dance. Three other songs were also of interest: the title song, "Do It for Me," and "If You Look in Her Eyes."

1920   MARY, a musical comedy with book and lyrics by Otto Harbach and Frank Mandel. Produced by George M. Cohan at the Knickerbocker Theatre on October 18. Staged by Julian Mitchell, George M. Cohan, and Sam Forrest. Cast included Jack McGowan, James Marlowe, Janet Velie, Georgia Caine, and Charles Judels (219 performances).

Mary was the kind of sweet, sentimental, and wholesome musical comedy for which George M. Cohan was famous, even though his only association with it was as a producer. Jack Keane (Jack McGowan) hopes to rehabilitate his family fortune in Kansas by building cheap homes known as "love nests." The land which he purchases for this venture has oil. Thus Jack suddenly becomes a wealthy man. He now realizes that he is in love with simple, wholesome Mary Howells (Janet Velie) and not the seductive widow he has thus far been pursuing.

If any single element was responsible for the success of *Mary* it was neither the story nor any of the performers—but the song "Love Nest," which appeared as a recurrent leitmotif throughout the play. It is first heard as a solo by Jack, then as a duet by Jack and Mary, as a choral number, and in a variety of other guises. The title song, "Anything You Want to Do, Dear," "Everytime I Meet a Lady," and "Waiting" were other excellent numbers.

1922-23   *The Greenwich Village Follies*

1922 edition, a revue with book and lyrics by George V. Hobart, John Murray Anderson, and Irving Caesar. Produced by The Bohemians at the Shubert Theatre on September 12. Staged by John Murray Anderson. Cast included John Hazzard, Savoy and Brennan, Carl Randall, and Yvonne Georges (216 performances).

1923 edition, a revue with book and lyrics by Irving Caesar and John Murray Anderson. Additional music by Con Conrad. Produced by The Bohemians at the Winter Garden on September 20. Staged by John Murray Anderson. Cast included Tom Howard, Sam White, and Eva Puck (140 performances).

For other editions of The Greenwich Village Follies see A. BALDWIN SLOANE.

It did not take the 1922 edition long to establish its geographical identity. The overture curtain was an attractive view of Greenwich Village. Otherwise there was not much in the revue to remind audiences of the Village. The edition highlighted a beautiful ballet based on the Oscar Wilde tale, "The Nightingale and the Rose," danced by Ula Sharon and Alexander Yakeloff; broad comedy by Savoy and Brennan; a travesty on the melancholy plays of Eugene O'Neill; and an effective parody on old ballads by John Hazzard in "Goodbye to Dear Old Alaska." Yvonne Georges, an importation from Paris, sang *Mon Homme*." Hirsch's best songs were "A Kiss from a Red-Headed Miss" and "Sixty Seconds Every Minute I Dream of You." Another popular number was an interpolation, "Georgette," by Lew Brown and Ray Henderson.

Big production numbers proved to be the staple of the 1923 edition: "The Garden of Kama," a fantasy based on Laurence Hope's love lyrics of India, set to music by Amy Woodford-Finden; a Spanish fiesta; and a dream fantasy, "Barcarolle." But there was no sacrifice of comedy or nostalgia or sentiment. Eva Puck and Denman Maley presented a burlesque about a quarrelsome married couple; Tom Howard appeared in a howling skit atop a floating raft where he is slowly starving to death; and Buster West delighted audiences with his amusing eccentric dancing. Nostalgia was contributed by Daphne Pollard with several delightful English music-hall songs and sentiment by Marion Green's romantic songs. Hirsch's leading song was "Just a Bit of Heaven in Your Smile."

KARL HOSCHNA, composer

Hoschna was an outstandingly successful composer in the period just before World War I, when the American musical stage was dominated by European influences. He was Bohemian by birth—in Kuschwarda, on August 16, 1877. His musical education took place at the Vienna Conservatory on a scholarship. One of the requirements of that scholarship was the study of some band instrument, and Hoschna selected the oboe. Upon graduating with honors, Hoschna played the oboe in the Austrian Army band for several years. In 1896 he came to the United States, which from then on remained his permanent home. For two years after his arrival he played in one of Victor Herbert's orchestras.

An obsession that the vibration from the oboe's double reed might affect his mind led him to write an unusual letter to the publishing house of Witmark, asking for a job, no matter "how menial" and "at any salary you care to pay." Isidor Witmark later recalled that this letter was "so pitiful and so original that he decided to give the signer a chance." Hoschna was at first engaged as a copyist. After that he served as an arranger, and finally as Isidor Witmark's personal adviser on manuscripts and other musical matters. During this period Hoschna also started writing popular songs.

In 1902 he met and became a friend of a young advertising man, Otto Hauerbach (later Otto Harbach) who had ambitions to write for the stage. They started a partnership and in short order completed *The Daughter of the Desert*. During the next few years they rewrote this operetta several times, and on three occasions even succeeded in getting options. But always some unforeseen development blocked a production. Between 1905 and 1908 Hoschna finally did manage to put a foot into the professional theater with music for three operettas. The first was *Belle of the West* (1905), book and lyrics by Harry B. Smith. It was a failure, and so were its two successors.

In 1908 Witmark engaged Hoschna to write music for a projected operetta adaptation of a play, *Incog*. Hoschna in turn interested Witmark in hiring Harbach for the lyrics. As *The Three Twins* it reached Broadway in 1908 and established the reputations of both Hoschna and Harbach.

During the next three years Hoschna and Harbach wrote eight operettas, the crowning success of which was *Madame Sherry* (1910). Hoschna also provided music for plays by other writers, the most prominent being *Wall Street Girl* (1911).

Hoschna was not fated to enjoy his successes for a long time. He died only a year or so after the première of *Madame Sherry*—on December 23, 1911. He was only thirty-four.

1908   THE THREE TWINS, an operetta with book by Charles Dickson, adapted from a farce by R. Pancheco, *Incog.* Lyrics by Otto Hauerbach (Harbach). Produced by Joseph M. Gaites at the Herald Square Theatre on June 15. Staged by Gus Sohlke. Cast included Bessie McCoy, Clinton Crawford, and Willard Curtiss (288 performances).

One day in 1908 the actor-playwright, Charles Dickson, stepped into the office of Witmark, the music publisher. He arrived to discuss the possibility of adapting *Incog* into an operetta. Witmark thought the idea sound, and suggested as composer his arranger, Karl Hoschna. Hoschna in turn brought his friend and collaborator, Otto Harbach, into the picture. Witmark signed Harbach by paying him a flat fee of 100 dollars and a royalty of one cent a copy for the sheet-music sale; Hoschna was engaged on a royalty basis.

The operetta, named *The Three Twins*, was Hoschna's first success for the stage and the making of the team of Hoschna and Harbach. The "three twins" in the play were the brothers Harry and Dick Winters (Willard Curtiss and Joseph Kaufman) and Tom Stanhope (Clifton Crawford) who decides to disguise himself as Harry. The reason for this deception is that Tom is in love with Kate Armitage (Alice Yorke). Since his rich, dyspeptic father, General Stanhope (Joseph Allen) threatens to disinherit him if he pursues Kate, Tom finally decides to look and act like Harry Winters in carrying on his affair with Kate. What Tom does not know is that Harry has a twin brother who is half insane. In the role of Harry, Tom finds himself in all kinds of amusing complications. Finally his father is willing to let him marry the girl of his choice, and the two real twins are left in peace to pursue their own respective love affairs.

One of the salient reasons—if not *the* reason—why *The Three Twins* was a triumph was the performance of Bessie McCoy as Molly Sommers, Harry Winters' girl friend. Bessie McCoy was then only eighteen and unknown (one year earlier she had appeared in *The Echo*, music by Deems Taylor, a failure). Dressed in a cone-shaped cap and white-pompomed black velvet trouser suit—and singing her songs with a tiny pouting mouth while performing a dance step—she became a sensation, particularly in the song, "Yama-Yama Man" (lyrics not by Harbach but by Collin Davis). So completely was Bessie McCoy identified with the song that from then on, as one of Broadway's luminous stars, she was known as the "Yama-Yama Girl."

A second song hit was Kate Armitage's song, "Cuddle Up a Little Closer," sung against a setting representing the seven stages of lovers from infancy to old age.

Strange to say, neither "Cuddle Up a Little Closer" nor "Yama-Yama Man" were originally intended for *The Three Twins*. Hoschna wrote the music for the first song for a vaudeville sketch, and only much later decided to interpolate it into his operetta score. "Yama-Yama Man" was written while the operetta was already in rehearsal, and was put into the score in Chicago before the New York première.

Tom Stanhope delivered two other pleasing numbers, "Over There" and "Good Night, Sweetheart," and most of the comedy sprang from a riotous performance by W. J. McCarthy as a sanatorium doctor.

1910   MADAME SHERRY, operetta with book and lyrics by Otto Hauerbach (Harbach), adapted from George Edwardes' adaptation of a French vaudeville. Produced by Woods, Frazee and Lederer at the New Amsterdam Theatre on August 30. Staged by George W. Lederer. Cast included Ralph Herz, Lina Abarbanell, and Frances Demarest (231 performances).

Madame Sherry is one of the most famous American operettas in the era preceding World War I. Edward Sherry (Jack Gardner) tries to dupe his wealthy Uncle Theophilus (Ralph Herz) by passing off his Irish landlady, Catherine, as Madame Sherry (Elizabeth Murray). At the same time he presents Lulu (Frances Demarest) and her dancing pupils as his children. Theophilus uncovers this deception through some ingenious detective work. He forgives his nephew, who by now is in love with his charming cousin, Yvonne Sherry (Lina Abarbanell), whom he decides to marry.

Hoschna's music was described by the editor of *Theatre Magazine* as "the best native score since *Mlle. Modiste*." The hit song was a charmingly suggestive thing called "Every Little Movement." But there were other musical pleasures, among them an "Afro-American" number, "Mr. Johnson, Good Night"; the infectious waltzes "Girl of My Dreams" and "The Birth of Passion"; and a ditty that amusingly disclosed the inebriated condition of Theophilus, "I'm All Right." Ralph Herz as Theophilus and Elizabeth Murray as the Irish landlady contributed most of the comedy, while the best dancing came from Dorothy Jardonas, particularly in a solo Spanish number.

1912   WALL STREET GIRL, an operetta with book by Margaret Mayo and Edgar Selwyn. Lyrics by Hapgood Burt. Produced by Frederick McKay at the George M. Cohan Theatre on April 15. Staged by Charles Winninger and Gus Sohlke. Cast included William P. Carleton, Harry Gilfoil, Charles Winninger, Will Rogers, and Blanche Ring (56 performances).

Though *Wall Street Girl* had had a far less prosperous Broadway career than several other Hoschna operettas, it nevertheless deserves special attention for a number of reasons. In it Blanche Ring, as the heroine, gave her first winning performance in New York, and Charles Winninger, in a secondary role, scored his first stage hit. Then, too, Will Rogers stole some of the limelight with his extraordinary lariat feats, thus achieving his first major Broadway victory. (His next step, a year later, would be *The Ziegfeld Follies*.) Finally, Hoschna's score contained an outstanding number in "I Want a Regular Man," which profited from Blanche Ring's presentation.

Blanche Ring appeared as Jemina Greene, a young lady who likes men, money, and ostentatious clothes. She comes to Wall Street, there to create something of an upheaval. She meets Dexter Barton, a Westerner (William P. Carleton) who induces her—despite the advice of her well-intentioned friends—to join him in a mining investment in Goldenrod, Nevada. They hit the jackpot. Jemina becomes rich and can now indulge her passion for men and clothes. She is also able to rescue her father, James (Harry Gilfoil), from financial ruin.

RAYMOND HUBBELL, composer

While the name of Raymond Hubbell is today probably remembered only for a single song—"Poor Butterfly" (lyrics by John Golden)—he was one of Broadway's most successful composers in the early 1900's. His melodies flooded the stage of thirty-eight productions, including seven *Ziegfeld Follies* and several Hippodrome extravaganzas between 1915 and 1923.

He was born in Urbana, Ohio, on June 1, 1879, where he received his academic education in the public schools. In early manhood he went to Chicago, there to study harmony and counterpoint, to organize a dance orchestra, then to work as staff composer for the publishing house of Charles K. Harris. In 1902 he wrote the music for *Chow Chow*, an operetta given successfully that year in Chicago. Under the new title of *The Runaways*, it had a prosperous run at the Casino Theatre in New York and a five-year tour on the road.

Hubbell then proved he was no flash in the pan. Three box-office successes followed: *Fantana* (1905), *Mexicana* (1906), and *A Knight for a Day* (1907). The last of these had two of his best songs in "Life Is a See-Saw" and "Little Girl Blue." Now a leader in his field, Hubbell was eagerly sought after by major Broadway producers. His music was heard in important musical comedies, revues, and extravaganzas. His last appearance on Broadway was in 1928 with *Three Cheers*. After 1928 Hubbell went into retirement in Miami, Florida.

His most famous song, "Poor Butterfly," appeared in a Hippodrome extravaganza, *The Big Show* (1916), where it was sung by a Japanese soprano, Haru Onuki. These Hippodrome spectacles had other important Hubbell songs, two of the best being "Hello, I've Been Looking for You" in *The Big Show*, and "Melodyland" in *Cheer Up* (1917). Still other Hubbell songs were heard in various musical comedies, the most important being "What Am I Going to Do to Make You Love Me?" in *The Jolly Bachelors* (1910) and "Somebody Else" and "Look at the World and Smile" in *Yours Truly* (1927).

Hubbell died in Miami, Florida, on December 13, 1954.

1903 THE RUNAWAYS, an extravaganza with book by Addison Burkhardt. Produced by Sam S. Shubert, Nixon, and Zimmerman at the Casino Theatre on May 11. Cast included Alexander Clark, Edna Goodrich, Dorothy Dorr, Arthur Dunn, and William Gould (167 performances).

The producers made a great to-do of the fact that they had expended 75,000 dollars before the curtain went up on *The Runaways*. It was a sumptuously mounted production. Much less distinguished was the plot. General Hardtack (Alexander Clark) is an ex-waiter who rises to his high military station through political pull. At a race track he meets and is captivated by Josey May, comic-opera prima donna (Dorothy Dorr). The General, a dyspeptic, is delighted to learn from Josey that there exists an island in the South Seas where dyspepsia does not exist. When the General wins a fortune on a horse race, he decides to marry Josey and settle in that island. There he becomes king. But uneasy rests his crown: He discovers that by the law of the land he must either marry the widow of the preceding king or commit suicide. At a critical moment he and Josey are saved by American warships.

The strength of the play—apart from the sets and costumes—lay in the comedy of William Gould as a race-track tout and Al Fields as a patent-medicine faker; in a brilliant clog dance by Walter Stanton, Jr., dressed up as a giant rooster; and in several Hubbell songs, the best being "If I Were a Bright Little Star" and "A Kiss for Each Day in the Week."

1905   FANTANA, an operetta with book by Sam S. Shubert and Robert B. Smith. Lyrics by Robert B. Smith. Produced by Sam S. Shubert at the Lyric Theatre on January 14. Staged by R. H. Burnside. Cast included Jefferson de Angelis, Katie Barry, Adele Ritchie, George Beban, Eleanor Browning, and Julia Sanderson in a minor role (298 performances).

Commodore Everett (Hubert Wilke) takes his pretty daughter, Fantana (Adele Ritchie), to Japan to save her from what he regards as an undesirable marriage with a handsome Englishman. The Englishman follows her and thwarts her father's plan to marry her to a French count by producing the count's wife. Meanwhile, the Commodore has a valet, Hawkins (Jefferson de Angelis), who disguises himself as a Japanese minister, a role in which he involves both his employer and himself in endless trouble. Things become hectic, but the Commodore, Fantana, and Hawkins manage to escape retribution by fleeing Japan aboard the yacht of a Japanese Ambassador; and the valet can fall into the arms of the girl he loves.

The *tour de force* was Jefferson de Angelis' antics as valet and hokum Japanese minister—including his broad take-offs on a music leader and a strong man, and his effective rendition of two humorous ditties, "That's Art" and "What Would Mrs. Grundy Say?" Two more songs proved popular: "The Farewell Waltz" and "My Word."

The only song to survive to this day from *Fantana* was not by Hubbell but an interpolation, "Tammany," lyrics by Vincent Bryan, music by Gus Edwards. The song was written for a party held by the National Democratic Club of New York, for which Gus Edwards was master of ceremonies. On his way to the party Gus Edwards heard a hand organ in the street play some Indian songs, and the idea came to him to write a number for the party parodying an Indian song. The song went over so big that it was soon interpolated into *Fantana,* then enjoying a successful Broadway run; there it was introduced by Lee Harrison, who played a minor role. Since then "Tammany" has become an official song of New York's Tammany Society.

1911-17 *The Ziegfeld Follies*

1911 edition, revue with book and lyrics by George V. Hobart. Additional music by Maurice Levi. Produced by Florenz Ziegfeld at the Jardin de Paris on June 26. Staged by Julian Mitchell. Cast included Bessie McCoy, Leon Errol, George White, the Dolly Sisters, Bert Williams, Harry Watson, Jr., and Fanny Brice (80 performances).

1912 edition, a revue with book and lyrics by Harry B. Smith. Produced by Florenz Ziegfeld at the Moulin Rouge on October 21. Staged by Julian Mitchell. Cast included Leon Errol, Harry Watson, Jr., Bert Williams, Lillian Lorraine, and Ray Samuels (88 performances).

1913 edition, a revue with book and lyrics by George V. Hobart. Additional songs by Gene Buck and Dave Stamper. Produced by Florenz Ziegfeld at the New Amsterdam Theatre on June 16. Staged by Julian Mitchell. Cast included Ann Pennington, Leon Errol, Frank Tinney (96 performances).

1914 edition, a revue with book and lyrics by George V. Hobart. Additional lyrics by Gene Buck. Special numbers by Dave Stamper. Produced by Florenz Ziegfeld at the New Amsterdam Theatre on June 1. Staged by Florenz Ziegfeld and Leon Errol. Cast included Ed Wynn, Ann Pennington, Leon Errol, and Bert Williams (112 performances).

1917 edition, a revue with book and lyrics by George V. Hobart and Gene Buck. Additional songs by Dave Stamper and Irving Berlin. Patriotic finale by Victor Herbert. Produced by Florenz Ziegfeld at the New Amsterdam Theatre on June 12. Staged by Ned Wayburn. Cast included Will Rogers, Eddie Cantor, W. C. Fields, Bert Williams, the Fairbanks Twins, and Fanny Brice (111 performances).

For other editions of The Ziegfeld Follies *see* IRVING BERLIN, LOUIS A. HIRSCH, *and Appendix I (1907).*

Bessie McCoy, fresh from her triumphs as the "Yama-Yama Girl" in Hoschna's *The Three Twins* made her *Follies* bow in the 1911 edition. She was irresistible, particularly in the dance "Tad Daffydills" and the song "Take Care, Little Girl." Among those whose hearts she won completely was the newspaperman, Richard Harding Davis, who habitually occupied a front-row seat to watch her, and then married her in 1912.

Another eventful *Follies* debut took place in 1911, that of Leon Errol, whose rubbery legs and eccentric dancing were to be a feature of the *Follies* for several years to come. For his debut Errol appeared with Bert Williams in what has been described as one of the funniest skits to appear in the *Follies*. It was called "Upper and Lower Level" and cast Williams as a redcap for Errol's Major Waterbrush. The entire skit, except for four opening lines, was done in pantomime. Another sketch starred Arline Boley as an outraged American traveler in trouble with a United States Customs officer. She haughtily insists she is innocent of smuggling, but then is found with yards and yards of fabric under the folds of her dress.

Spectacle emerged in a beautiful poppy-field scene, in which stacks of wheat soon turned out to be dancing girls; also in a scene called "New Year's Eve on the Barbary Coast," in which an apache dance was performed by Harry Watson, Leon Errol, and Lillian Lorraine.

Besides "Take Care, Little Girl," Hubbell's most successful song was "My Beautiful Lady." The score also boasted several interpolated songs by Irving Berlin, including "Epraham" and "Woodman, Spare That Tree."

In 1912 Leon Errol and Vera Maxwell introduced a dance soon to achieve vogue—"The Seasick Dip," described as "a whirling maze." Leon Errol was also seen as a bounder in a sketch involving Bert Williams as a cabbie. "A Palace of Beauty" was an outstanding spectacle number, an eyefilling tableau of Ziegfeld beauties who paraded about to the strains of "Beautiful, Beautiful Girls." A single song lyric by Gene Buck (music by Dave Stamper), "Daddy Has a Sweetheart and Mother Is Her Name," launched Buck's long and rich association with Ziegfeld. Hubbell's best songs were "Romantic Girl" and "The Broadway Glide," but two interpolated numbers were even more popular—"Down in Dear Old New Orleans" (words by Joe Young, music by Conrad and Widden) and "Row, Row, Row" (lyrics by William Jerome and music by Jimmie V. Monaco) both presented by Lillian Lorraine.

In 1913 Ann Pennington made both her *Follies* debut and her first important appearance in the Broadway theater. She was a sensation for her exciting dancing, and also for her role in a beautiful tableau, "September Morn." For the next few years she would be the dancing star of the *Follies*. This edition was also memorable for an eccentric dance by Leon Errol satirizing the turkey trot (called "Turkish Trottishness"); for Fanny Brice's impersonation of a telephone switchboard operator; and for a closing-scene spectacle with the Panama Canal as a setting, a warship seen entering one of the locks. One of the best songs was "Isle d'Amour" (words by Earl Carroll, music by Leo Edwards), while Nat Mills won favor with "If a Table at Rector's Could Talk."

Leon Errol did another dance travesty in 1914, this time of the tango. He also appeared in a sketch where, in a dancing school, he is mistaken for the teacher, and a group of girls follow his dance steps with hilarious consequences. The best spectacle was a Fifth Avenue scene immediately after a snowstorm, with a skyscraper in the process of construction. A first-act finale assumed a martial character with the Revolutionary Army marching downhill behind George Washington. But the greatest single element in the 1914 edition was Ed Wynn, making his *Follies* debut and his first Broadway appearance after many years in vaudeville. Odette

Myrtil, subsequently a star of musical comedy and operetta, also made her New York debut.

In 1917 the most significant event was the debut of Eddie Cantor. Ziegfeld had discovered Cantor in *Canary Cottage* which played on the West Coast in 1916; and in the same year Ziegfeld presented Cantor on the Midnight Roof of the New Amsterdam where he brought down the house in Albert von Tilzer's "Oh! How She Could Yacki, Hacki, Wicki, Wacki, Woo." After that the step downstairs to the stage of the New Amsterdam was inevitable. It took place in 1917. Cantor once again was a triumph, this time with "That's the Kind of Baby for Me" (by Alfred Harrison and Jack Egan), in which he had to give a dozen encores each evening. (Victor had him make a recording of it only two days after his *Follies* première.)

Will Rogers also made his *Follies* debut in 1917; while performing his famous lariat act he proved himself a trenchant commentator on the current scene. ("Congress is so strange," he said. "A man gets up to speak and says nothing. Nobody listens. Then everybody disagrees.") Fanny Brice did one of her famous routines, a take-off on an Egyptian dancer; and a dog stole the limelight with a drunk act. One of the sketches, "Velvet Lady," introduced a new performer, making his first appearance on the New York stage; his name was Eddie Dowling.

Hubbell's songs included "Beautiful Garden of Girls," "Hello, Dearie," "Just You and Me," and "Chu Chin Chow," the last a ragtime number. Some of the interpolated numbers also proved popular. Cantor's hit song was one of these. Another was a stirring patriotic finale by Victor Herbert, "Can't You Hear Your Country Calling?" which culminated with a parade of the United States forces before President Wilson. Jerome Kern also had an interpolated song in "Because You're Just You."

1915 HIP-HIP-HOORAY, an extravaganza with book by R. H. Burnside. Lyrics by John Golden. Produced by Charles Dillingham at the Hippodrome Theatre on September 30. Staged by R. H. Burnside. Cast included Joseph Parsons, Toto, Anna May Roberts, and Harvey Griffiths (425 performances).

For earlier Hippodrome spectacles see MANUEL KLEIN.

A new regime was inaugurated at the Hippodrome, home of the spectacle in 1915. The management and musical director were changed —but not the policy of the theater to present extraordinary visual feasts. *Hip-Hip-Hooray* had an international character—with skaters from Scandinavia, a clown from Germany (Toto), acrobats from England, dancers from Italy, and a native band from Guatemala.

One spectacular scene followed another in breath-taking sequence: one depicted the rooftops of New York, with the Brooklyn Bridge in the distance; cats impersonated by dancers cavorted on the roofs. Another showed Grand Central Station, with tumblers deftly juggling baggage. A third reproduced a fashion parade on Fifth Avenue. A fourth carried the audience to Chinatown, and a fifth to St. Moritz, Switzerland, for a thrilling winter scene as background for a skaters' ballet. "Toyland" featured the wedding of Jack and Jill; a haunting song, "The Ladder of the Roses" was sung within a setting of a bower of roses. The climax was achieved with a background of the "Tower of Jewels" for a performance by Sousa and his Band, the concert ending with a potpourri of marches from various states.

WILLIAM JEROME, lyricist. *See* **JEAN SCHWARTZ**

IRVING KAHAL, lyricist. *See* **SAMMY FAIN**

GEORGE S. KAUFMAN, librettist

One of Broadway's most brilliant writers of comedy, Kaufman has left the strong impression of his wit and satire on the musical stage. He was born in Pittsburgh on November 16, 1889, and was educated in the public schools. He held down various jobs—stenographer for a coal company, surveyor for the city of Pittsburgh, a traveling salesman for a concern manufacturing shoelaces—while contributing witty pieces to the celebrated newspaper column of F.P.A. It was F.P.A. that arranged for Kaufman to run his own column, "This and That," for the Washington *Times*. Kaufman came to New York in 1914, where he wrote another humorous column—this time for the *Evening Mail* and afterward served as reporter for the *Herald* and the *Times*.

In 1918 he made his stage debut with the play, *Someone in the House*, of which he was co-author. During the next two decades virtually all of his most successful plays (with the exception of *The Butter and Egg Man*) were written collaboratively with various writers—principally Moss Hart, Marc Connelly, Edna Ferber, and Ring Lardner. The best of these plays were smash box-office hits, including *To the Ladies, Dulcy, Merton of the Movies, Beggar on Horseback, The Royal Family, June Moon, Dinner at Eight, Merrily We Roll Along, You Can't Take It with You* (which won the Pulitzer Prize), and *The Man Who Came to Dinner*.

In 1923 Kaufman, in collaboration with Marc Connelly, entered the musical theater for the first time with *Helen of Troy, New York* (*see* HARRY RUBY). A year later came *Be Yourself*, again with Connelly, but this time with music by Lewis Gensler and Milton Schwartzwald, and lyrics by Ira Gershwin. In 1925, without any assistance, Kaufman completed the book for the Four Marx Brothers jamboree, *The Cocoanuts*, music by Irving Berlin. The habit of success now assumed in the musical theater, Kaufman became associated with some of the leading musical comedies and revues of the 1930's. With Gershwin's *Of Thee I Sing* he won the Pulitzer Prize.

In still another capacity, as stage director, his gift for timing and pace was profitably felt in the musical theater—in such major productions as Irving Berlin's *Face the Music* and Frank Loesser's *Guys and Dolls*.

See: IRVING BERLIN (*The Cocoanuts*); GEORGE GERSHWIN (*Strike Up the Band, Of Thee I Sing, Let 'Em Eat Cake*); COLE PORTER (*Silk Stockings*); RICHARD RODGERS—I. RODGERS AND HART (*I'd Rather Be Right*); HARRY RUBY (*Helen of Troy, New York, Animal Crackers*); ARTHUR SCHWARTZ (*The Band Wagon*).

GUSTAVE A. KERKER, composer

A favorite on Broadway when operettas were popular, Gustave Kerker was born in Herford, Germany, on February 28, 1857. As a child of seven he started studying the cello, and at ten he came to the United States, settling in Louisville, Kentucky. He conducted several theater orchestras there and when he was twenty-two, wrote the music for his first operetta, *Cadets*, which made a four-month tour of the South. Edward E. Rice, the producer, was so impressed by this music that he arranged for Kerker to come to New York and become conductor of the Casino Theatre, then the home of outstanding musical productions. Kerker's first Broadway operetta was *The Pearl of Pekin* (1888), and success came with *Castles in the Air* (1890). His best operettas, many of them produced at the Casino Theatre, placed him among the most popular Broadway composers of that day. Even his less successful musicals yielded notable songs, such as "In Gay New York" (in the operetta of the same name), "Baby, Baby" (in *The Lady Slavey*), and "The Good Old Days" (in *The Whirl of the Town*). Kerker died in New York City on June 29, 1923.

1890   CASTLES IN THE AIR, an operetta with book by C. A. Byrne, adapted partly from Meitter's text for Offenbach's *Les Bavards* and partly from a one-act intermezzo by Cervantes, *Les Dos Habiadores.* Produced by the De Wolf Hopper Opera Bouffe Company at the Broadway Theatre on May 5. Cast included De Wolf Hopper, Della Fox, and Marion Manola (160 performances).

In *Castles in the Air,* De Wolf Hopper had his first starring role, and the show was his from beginning to end. His clowning as Judge Pilacoudre stole the thunder from all other performers, although in one instance Della Fox shared the limelight by joining him in a song duet about a pantomime game of billiards. Other delightful Kerker numbers were "What in the World Could Compare to This?" "Is It a Dream?" and the title song.

The plot involved the efforts of Bul-Bul (Marion Manola) to flee from his creditors by means of a costume furnished by Cabolastro (Thomas Q. Seabrooke). Cabolastro is willing to provide the costume free of charge if Bul-Bul is successful in bettering Cabolastro's garrulous wife in a battle of words. Bul-Bul consents and is successful. Since Bul-Bul is in love with Cabolastro's daughter, Blanche (Della Fox), the prospective father-in-law is willing to pay all of the young man's debts.

1897   THE BELLE OF NEW YORK, an operetta with book and lyrics by Hugh Morton. Produced at the Casino Theatre on September 28. Staged by George W. Lederer. Cast included Edna May and Harry Davenport (56 performances).

The Belle of New York was only a modest success in New York, but subsequently at the Shaftsbury Theatre in London it amassed the formidable run of 697 performances and became one of the best-loved operettas of that period; and its success on the road in the United States was no less impressive. The setting was New York, where Harry Bronson's escapades give his father considerable cause for alarm, particularly since the father is actively engaged in fighting vice as President of the Young Men's Rescue League. Harry finally sees the error of his ways when he falls in love with sweet and simple Violet Gray, a Salvation Army girl. As Violet, Edna May became an overnight star—after stepping suddenly into the role on the second night—and won the hearts of both New York and London with "I'm the Belle of New York" and "They All Follow Me." Another delightful song in the score was "Teach Me How to Kiss."

1902   A CHINESE HONEYMOON, a musical comedy with book and lyrics by George Dance. Additional music by Howard Talbot. Produced by the Shuberts at the Casino Theatre on June 2. Cast included Thomas Q.

Seabrooke, Adele Ritchie, William Pruette, and Annie Yeamans (376 performances).

In 1902 the Shuberts gained control of the Casino Theatre and inaugurated their regime with a major success—*A Chinese Honeymoon,* a London operetta, rewritten for the American public with many new songs by Kerker. Samuel Pineapple (Thomas Q. Seabrooke) is an English stockbroker who marries his typist and takes her off on a honeymoon to Yiang Yiang, a mythical section of China. While Mrs. Pineapple (Adele Ritchie) is herself very much of a flirt, she is intensely jealous of her husband. In Yiang Yiang, Pineapple discovers a long-lost nephew; the young man is about to marry a native princess. When Pineapple kisses her he learns to his horror that by local law he is now the legal husband of the girl. Then, to complicate matters further, Mrs. Pineapple kisses the Emperor, and by this means becomes his wife. The law must now be revised, to the complete satisfaction of all concerned.

As part of the musical score imported from London, there were two charming cockney songs, both of them delightfully presented by Katie Barry, appearing in the role of Fi-Gi, a lovelorn English slavey: "I Want to Be a Loidy" and "Twiddley Bits." But Kerker's contribution was equally notable, highlighted by "À la Girl," and the title song. "Mister Dooley" by Jean Schwartz, was a significant interpolation.

1908   THE SOCIAL WHIRL, a musical comedy with book by Charles Doty and Joseph Herbert. Lyrics by Joseph Herbert. Additional songs by E. Ray Goetz and others. Produced by the Shuberts at the Casino Theatre on April 9. Staged by R. H. Burnside. Cast included Charles J. Ross, Adele Ritchie, and Elizabeth Brice (195 performances).

A certain gadfly, identified only as "J.E.," is accused by *The Social Whirl,* a society paper, of having gone off on an auto ride with the Broadway actress, Viola Dare (Adele Ritchie) and then stopping off at a roadside inn for champagne. Since there are four gentlemen in the play whose initials are "J.E." and since three of them are married and, finally, since each uses every means to throw suspicion on the others, the complications are numerous, involving even attempted blackmail; and they are amusing. Two of the suspects are elderly gentlemen, still susceptible to the allure of feminine charm. What actually happened is that Viola took both of them in her car—but only because she wanted to persuade James Ellingham (Frederick Bond) to consent to her marriage with his son, Jack (Willard Curtiss). At the Hunt Club everything is finally explained and the suspicions that have beclouded the four men are completely dispelled.

The best musical numbers were "You're Just the Girl I'm Looking For," "Bill Simmons," "Old Man Manhattan," and a specialty number performed by Frederick Bond, "Just Kids."

JEROME KERN, composer

The later musicals of Jerome Kern are so fresh in mind as a result of revivals and screen adaptations that it is sometimes difficult to remember how early he first appeared on the Broadway scene. The year, as a matter of fact, was 1905; Victor Herbert and George M. Cohan were in their heyday—musical comedy in its infancy.

Kern was born in New York City on January 27, 1885. The Kerns were comparatively well off, the father being head of a water-sprinkling company that had the concession to water the city streets. The mother was an amateur pianist and a devoted music lover who gave Jerome his first piano lessons. When she sensed that the boy had talent she engaged a local piano teacher for more professional instruction.

When Jerome was ten, his father became head of a merchandising house in Newark, New Jersey; the family went there to live; and Jerome continued his piano lessons while completing his elementary and secondary schooling. At Newark High School he played the piano in assemblies, wrote music for the school shows. His teachers sometimes referred to him as "that musical genius" and were quietly tolerant of his comparative indifference to any subject in the curriculum outside of music.

After leaving high school Kern prevailed on his father to permit him to continue his music study. He entered the New York College of Music, where his teachers included Paolo Gallico and Alexander Lambert. He also took some private lessons in theory and harmony from Austin Pierce. Kern then wanted to go to Europe for instruction under some of its outstanding teachers, but his father preferred his going into business. It was the father's opinion that Kern had thus far not sufficiently proved himself in music to consider it a life career.

In 1902 Kern entered the father's merchandising house. One day the father sent him to the Bronx to buy two pianos. Hypnotized by the talk of a glib salesman, Kern bought not two but two hundred pianos, and with that single transaction almost ruined the merchandising business. This led the father to reconsider his earlier decision. He now gave his son his blessing to go off to Europe and continue his music study there.

Kern went to Europe in 1903. He did some studying in Germany, but mostly he traveled about absorbing musical experiences. He also tried writing some serious music, but abandoned these attempts when he recognized the sad truth that his ambition was greater than either his technique or talent. Finally he settled in London, there to find a job with Charles K. Frohman, an American producer then putting on musical shows in London. Kern was employed to write songs and musical pieces for the opening numbers of these productions, a poorly paid and insignificant assignment since London theatergoers came habitually late and never saw the opening act. But this humble position accomplished one thing for Kern. It convinced him that if he was to make his way in music it would have to be through popular music—and probably in the popular musical theater.

In London, Kern wrote several songs, one of which was called "How'd You Like to Spoon with Me?" It later appeared on the Broadway stage in *The Earl and the Girl,* produced at the Casino Theatre on November 4, 1905. Some of the lyrics to which Kern wrote melodies in London were by a young man named P. G. Wodehouse; indeed their first collaboration, a topical number called "Mr. Chamberlain," took London by storm. (In the future Wodehouse was to be not only famous as the author of humorous tales and whimsical novels, but he would also become Kern's collaborator in the writing of American musical comedies.)

By the time Kern returned to the United States in 1905 he knew that his ambition lay with popular music. Consequently he decided to work in Tin Pan Alley, and for two years he filled several menial jobs there. He worked as a song plugger, adapted the songs of other composers, wrote stock numbers of his own. One of his jobs was as salesman for the publishing house of Harms, Inc., headed by Max Dreyfus. Dreyfus, whose sensitive nostrils had an uncanny faculty for sniffing out potential talent, recognized Kern's gifts and did what he could to encourage and develop them. He published a few of Kern's early songs, found for him a job as accompanist for the vaudevillian Marie Dressler, then helped him get some assignments from Broadway.

Kern's first step into the theater was made in 1905. Five of his songs appeared in *The Rich Mr. Hoggenheimer,* score by Ludwig Englander, produced on October 22. Another song was the already-mentioned "How'd You Like to Spoon with Me?" in *The Earl and the Girl.* In 1907 Kern's songs were heard in four Broadway shows. Five more productions used his songs before he received his first major assignment. This happened in 1910, when he was called upon to revise the music of *Mr. Wix* of Wickham, in which Julian Eltinge, the famous female impersonator, made his Broadway debut. "Who is this Jerome Kern," inquired Alan Dale in the New York American in his review of Mr. Wix of Wickham, "whose music towers in an Eiffel way above the average hurdy-gurdy accompaniment of the present-day musical comedy?"

In 1911 the Shuberts engaged Kern to collaborate with Frank Tours in writing music for La Belle Paree, an extravaganza with a Parisian setting that was part of a dual bill with which the Winter Garden opened on March 20. One year later Kern wrote his first complete original score for Broadway, The Red Petticoat, a play about Nevada miners described as a "comic opera Girl of the Golden West."

In 1914 Kern made his first bid for success with several remarkable songs interpolated into The Girl from Utah, an English operetta by Rubens and Jones adapted for the American stage. One of these was "They Didn't Believe Me," which had a sheet-music sale of 2,000,000 copies. When Victor Herbert heard Kern's songs from The Girl from Utah at the office of Harms, he said: "This man will inherit my mantle."

Between 1915 and 1919 Kern collaborated first with Guy Bolton, and then with Bolton and P. G. Wodehouse, in a series of intimate musical comedies produced at the Princess Theatre that came to be known as the Princess Theatre Shows. This series was inaugurated with Nobody Home (1915), and its first outstanding hit was Very Good, Eddie (1915). For the next few years the Princess Theatre Shows helped inject a new note of informality and charm and vivacity into the American musical theater.

With lavish productions like Sally (1920), Good Morning, Dearie (1920), Stepping Stones (1923), and Sunny (1925), Kern reverted to a more traditional kind of musical theater than the Princess Theatre Show, a theater dependent on stars, sets, costuming, routines, and songs. But in 1927 he once again departed from accepted procedures when, to Oscar Hammerstein's book and lyrics, he wrote the music for Show Boat, since then become a stage classic. From 1927 on, Kern divided his energies and interests between musical productions that were new and fresh in their material and approach—musicals like The Cat and the Fiddle (1931) and Music in the Air (1932)—and the more routine and formal kind of stage entertainment represented by Sweet Adeline (1929) and Roberta (1933). Kern's last musical comedy for the Broadway stage was Very Warm for May (1939), a failure. But Very Warm for May has not been forgotten, for it was the showcase for one of Kern's song masterpieces, "All the Things You Are."

After 1939 Kern wrote exclusively for motion pictures. A song written independent of any stage or screen production—but interpolated into the motion picture, *Lady Be Good*—won the Motion Picture Academy Award in 1941. It was "The Last Time I Saw Paris," lyrics by Oscar Hammerstein, and inspired by the then-recent occupation of Paris by Nazi troops. This was the second time the Academy Award was won by Kern; the first time had been in 1936 for "The Way You Look Tonight" in *Swing Time*.

After completing the score for the motion picture *Centennial Summer* in 1945, Kern planned to return to the Broadway stage. Rodgers and Hammerstein, as producers, contracted him to write music for a new show to be put on the following season, and at the same time, a new revival of *Showboat* was being projected. Kern consequently came East. On November 5—a half-hour after auditioning singers for *Showboat*—he collapsed on Park Avenue in New York. He died six days later at Doctors Hospital. Irving Berlin who came to visit Kern on November 11 was one of the first to learn that Kern had just died. (And it was Irving Berlin who took over the assignment of writing the score for the musical Kern had been engaged to do; and who achieved with that musical—*Annie Get Your Gun*—the greatest stage triumph of his career.)

Less than three years after Kern's death his life was told in the motion picture, *Till the Clouds Roll By*, scenario by Kern's lifelong friend and collaborator, Guy Bolton. In 1949 came a second motion picture studded with Kern's songs, the biography of Marilyn Miller, *Look for the Silver Lining*.

1914 THE GIRL FROM UTAH, a musical comedy with book and lyrics by James F. Tanner. Additional music by Paul Rubens and Sydney Jones. Produced by Charles Frohman at the Knickerbocker Theatre on August 24. Staged by J. A. E. Malone. Cast included Julia Sanderson, Joseph Cawthorn, and Donald Brian (120 performances).

The Girl from Utah originated in London as an operetta with a score by Rubens and Jones, starring Ina Claire. In its transfer to the American stage it retained some of the musical numbers of the original production and interpolated several new songs by Jerome Kern. Those Kern songs were the first in which he gave indication of his future creative power, and are the reason why *The Girl from Utah* will be remembered.

Una Trance (Julia Sanderson) flees from Utah to London rather than be one of the many wives of a Mormon. The Mormon pursues her across the ocean. A taxi accident brings Una to Rumpelmeyer's tea room, where she seeks haven and meets Sandy Blair (Donald Brian), a young actor. The pursuing Mormon also comes to the tea room, and so does Trimpel, proprietor of a ham and beef shop (Joseph Cawthorn). Somehow the Mormon and Trimpel put on each other's hat and Trimpel becomes helplessly involved in difficulties as he is mistaken for the Mormon. The Mormon finally succeeds in carrying Una off to a house in Brixton. But since she leaves a trail of confetti, she is tracked down by Blair and Trimpel, who have joined forces to save her. They finally catch up with her at the Arts Ball, where all difficulties are resolved, with Una in Sandy's rooms.

The three stars each contributed his or her own special gift to make the play a lively diversion: Julia Sanderson brought her enchanting singing; Donald Brian, his vital dancing; and Cawthorn, his rich comedy, particularly when in search for Una he assumes several disguises. But it is the songs of Kern that are the most rewarding features of the production. "They Didn't Believe Me" (lyrics by Herbert Reynolds), sung by Una, was Kern's first big song hit, and to this day it is one of his gems. Equally enchanting were "You're Here and I'm Here" and "I'd Like to Wander with Alice in Wonderland," both once again sung by Una; and a little rhythmic number called "Why Don't They Dance the Polka Any More?"

1915-18   *The Princess Theatre Shows*

1915   NOBODY HOME, an intimate musical with book and lyrics by Guy Bolton and Paul Rubens. Produced by F. Ray Comstock at the Princess Theatre on April 20. Staged by J. H. Benrimo. Dances by David Bennett. Cast included Lawrence Grossmith, Adele Rowland, and Charles Judels (135 performances).

1915   VERY GOOD, EDDIE, an intimate musical with book by Philip Bartholomae and Guy Bolton based on Bartholomae's *Over Night*. Lyrics by Schuyler Green. Produced by the Marbury-Comstock Company at the Princess Theatre on December 23. Cast included Ernest Truex, Alice Dovey, Oscar Shaw, Ada Lewis, and Helen Raymond (341 performances).

1917   OH BOY!, an intimate musical with book by Guy Bolton. Lyrics by P. G. Wodehouse. Produced by William Elliott and F. Ray Comstock at the Princess Theatre on February 20. Staged by Edward Royce. Cast included Tom Powers, Anna Wheaton, Edna May Oliver, and Marion Davies (463 performances).

1918   OH LADY, LADY!, an intimate musical with book by Guy Bolton. Lyrics by P. G. Wodehouse. Produced by F. Ray Comstock and William Elliott at the Princess Theatre on February 1. Staged by Robert Milton and Edward Royce. Cast included Carl Randall, Vivienne Segal, Edward Abeles, and Florence Shirley (219 performances).

Nobody Home was the first of the Princess Theatre Shows, named after the theater in which it was housed. These shows helped to introduce a new kind of musical theater into Broadway, consisting of intimate entertainment, small casts and orchestra, economical scenery and costuming, an intimate tone, an informal manner, and a bright, sophisticated air. All this was a departure from the sumptuous entertainment then being presented by producers like Ziegfeld and the Shuberts.

The idea for a compact and intimate kind of musical show was born with Elizabeth Marbury who, in conjunction with Ray Comstock, ran the Princess Theatre in New York. The theater had only 299 seats, and it was suffering financially because there were not enough productions around able to use such a small house; the last venture there, a series of one-act plays, had been a box-office disaster. To turn defect into virtue Elizabeth Marbury thought up the idea of a miniature musical, with no more than two sets, an orchestra of about ten, eight to twelve girls in the chorus, and a smiliarly small cast of principals. Naturally, since the box-office intake was limited, she could not afford to engage famous librettists or composers for her venture. She selected Jerome Kern because Kern—with only the success of *The Girl from Utah* under his belt—was still modest in his financial expectations. And Kern suggested Bolton for the libretto. A few months earlier Bolton and Kern had collaborated on a musical, *Ninety in the Shade*, a failure. Since Bolton was still without a success to his credit he was ready to accept from Marbury a flat fee of 500 dollars.

Nobody Home was Bolton's adaptation of an English operetta by Paul Rubens. Its central character was Freddy Popple of Ippleton, England (amusingly portrayed by Lawrence Grossmith). He comes to the United States—fully equipped with the accouterments of a hunter, trapper, and fisher—to find his brother, Vernon (George Anderson), a New York society dancer. Freddy's escapades in America—and more specifically in the apartment of Tony Miller (Adele Rowland), a Winter Garden prima donna—provides much of the hilarity of the evening. And three Kern songs—"The Magic Melody," "You Know and I Know," and "Any Old Night Is a Wonderful Night"—contribute some of its charm.

Nobody Home had a pleasant run of over one hundred performances, enough to encourage Elizabeth Marbury to proceed further with this new kind of entertainment. Once again Kern and Bolton were hired. This time they achieved a major success—*Very Good, Eddie*—with which the Princess Theatre Show became a vogue in New York.

The title came from a pet phrase used by Fred Stone in one of his extravaganzas at the Globe. The story concerned two honeymoon couples about to take a trip on *The Catskill*, a Hudson River Dayline boat. One couple is Eddie Kettle (Ernest Truex) and Georgina (Helen Raymond); the other, Percy Darling (John Willard) and Elsie (Alice Dovey). The two men had been onetime acquaintances and they are delighted to see each other at the boat pier and to introduce their respective wives. Somehow the couples become separated, and Eddie sails with Percy's wife, Elsie, while Percy remains behind with Georgina. The principal action now involves Eddie and Elsie, two innocents, who—to avoid attention and comment—must put up a pretense of being husband and wife. Eventually the other couple catches up with them at the Rip Van Winkle Inn, but not before Eddie and Elsie undergo many embarrassing developments.

Everything about the production was so intimate and informal that the audience was made to feel that the performers were playing in its own living room. One unidentified critic described it as a "kitchenette production"; another referred to it as "parlor entertainment."

Kern's score now began to reveal the scope of his versatility. His personal way with a soft and sensitive melody—and an enchanting mood—was demonstrated in "Babes in the Wood," "I've Got to Dance," "Isn't It Grand to Be Married?" and "Nodding Roses." And his ability with a comic song was just as forcefully evident in "When You Wear a Thirteen Collar" which Ernest Truex as Eddie delivered with more charm and histrionic skill than voice.

Oh Boy! which followed *Very Good, Eddie* by a little over a year was an even greater hit. Guy Bolton tried to point out the qualities that set *Oh Boy!* apart from other musicals of the same period. "It was straight, consistent comedy with the addition of music. Every song and lyric contributed to the action. The humor was based on the situation, not interjected by comedians." Then Bolton went on to say that "realism and Americanism" were other distinguishing traits.

Perhaps *Oh Boy!* did not do everything Bolton said. Nevertheless it was a gay adventure. The setting was a college town, and the rah-rah spirit of college life gave the play much of its vitality. Lou Ellen (Marie Carroll), a bride, must suddenly leave her husband, Tom Powers (George Budd), to attend an ailing mother. While she is away, Tom attends a party at the local college inn. A rumpus ensues in which Jackie Sampson (Anna Wheaton) becomes involved. To save her from the police, Tom must secrete her in his apartment. The play now becomes a boudoir farce in which the young lady must go through various impersonations to give plausibility to her presence in the young man's apartment, and in which a pair of lace-trimmed blue pajamas becomes a vital piece of stage property. The sudden return of Lou Ellen does not help matters. The whole entanglement becomes unraveled when Lou Ellen's father explains that he had been Jackie's escort at the party and that Tom's involvement with the lady was entirely innocent.

Not a little of the gaiety came from the effervescent song lyrics of P. G. Wodehouse. Though Wodehouse had previously worked with Bolton and Kern, *Oh Boy!* was their first Princess Theatre Show. Both in *Oh Boy!* and in its successor, *Oh, Lady, Lady!*, the team of Bolton, Wodehouse, and Kern worked together so harmoniously that one unnamed New York drama critic was led to write:

> This is the trio of musical fame:
> Bolton and Wodehouse and Kern;
> Better than anyone else you can name.
> Bolton and Wodehouse and Kern.
> Nobody knows what on earth they've been bitten by
> All I can say is I mean to get lit an' buy
> Orchestra seats for the next one that's written by
> Bolton and Wodehouse and Kern.

Kern's score for *Oh Boy!* was outstanding for two ballads: "Till the Clouds Roll By," a song so distinguished that many years later it was used as the title of Kern's screen biography; and "An Old Fashioned Wife," in which Lou Ellen gave voice to her life's ambition. An excellent comedy number was "Nesting Time," a parody on "Apple Blossom Time"—but with Flatbush, Brooklyn, as the setting.

Oh, Lady, Lady! was set in Long Island. As a bridegroom, Willoughby Fitch (Carl Randall) is confronted at his bride's house by an old girl friend, Mollie Farringham (Vivienne Segal). He thinks she has come to make trouble for him, and contrives all kinds of situations to prove to her that he is really a bounder and a cad and unworthy of her. Actually, Mollie is not interested in him at all; she has come merely to help prepare the bride's trousseau. Further hilarity is contributed by Edward Abeles, as a reformed crook who has become the bridegroom's valet; and his fiancée, played by Florence Shirley, who has a weakness for shoplifting.

Kern's score included three lilting tunes: "Before I Met You," "You Found Me, I Found You," and the title song.

Oh, Lady, Lady! was the last of the Princess Theatre Shows in which Kern was involved. The very last was produced later in 1918: *Oh, My Dear!*, music by Louis Hirsch.

1917   LEAVE IT TO JANE, a musical comedy with book by Guy Bolton based on *The College Widow*, a play by George Ade. Lyrics by P. G. Wodehouse. Produced by William Elliott, F. Ray Comstock, and Morris Gest at the Longacre Theatre on August 28. Staged by Edward Royce. Cast included Edith Hallor, Robert G. Pitkin, Oscar Shaw, and Georgia O'Ramey (167 performances).

Among those who attended the opening-night performance of *Very Good, Eddie* was P. G. Wodehouse, then spending several years in this country as drama critic and as a writer of humorous tales for *The Saturday Evening Post*. After the première, Kern suggested to Wodehouse that they resume a collaboration, begun a decade earlier in London, by having Wodehouse write lyrics for subsequent Bolton-Kern productions. Bolton was also persuasive, with the result that on that night a new stage triumvirate was born which would dominate the Broadway musical theater for the next two years.

The first musical was *Have a Heart*, which opened on January 11, 1917. This was a slight play about a department store proprietor and his wife who impetuously go off on a second honeymoon on the eve of getting their divorce. Kern's score had a pleasing ballad in "And I'm All Alone" and a vivacious topical song in "Napoleon." But notwithstanding such assets, *Have a Heart* was a failure.

Leave It to Jane opened less than a half a year after *Have a Heart* closed. Based on George Ade's delightful comedy, it was a satire on college life in a Midwestern town. In Atwater College in Indiana, Jane (Edith Hallor) is a "college widow" who uses the wiles of a siren to keep the star halfback, Billy Bollton (Robert G. Pitkin), from going off to a rival college. Her siren's ways are sufficiently alluring to keep Billy at Atwater and to win him for Jane.

Most of the comedy was assigned to Georgia O'Ramey as Flora, a waitress. Her brusque and at times grotesque characterization provided the brightest humor of the evening, and for her Kern wrote his best comedy song, "Cleopatterer." "The Siren's Song," sung by Jane was the best of Kern's more serious efforts. Also of melodic interest were "What I'm Longing to Say," "The Sun Shines Brighter," "Just You Watch My Step," and the title song.

1920   SALLY, a musical comedy with book by Guy Bolton. Lyrics by Clifford Grey. Additional lyrics by Buddy de Sylva. Additional ballet music by Victor Herbert. Produced by Florenz Ziegfeld at the New Amsterdam Theatre on December 21. Staged by Edward Royce. Cast included Marilyn Miller, Walter Catlett, Leon Errol, and Stanley Ridges (570 performances).

Ziegfeld was planning three different musicals, one each to star Marilyn Miller, Leon Errol, and Walter Catlett. When Bolton and Kern brought him the play and score of *Sally,* Ziegfeld decided to roll the three projects into one. The Bolton text had a part for Errol—as Connie the waiter, formerly a Balkan grand duke thrown out of his country during a revolution. Its starring role was ideal for Marilyn Miller. All that remained was for Bolton to write into the play a special part for Walter Catlett, that of Otis Hooper.

As Sally, the dishwashing waif at the Elm Tree Inn, Marilyn Miller dominated the production. Through the strategy of a waiter-friend, Connie, Sally is able to invade a millionaire's Long Island estate during a garden party where she poses as a Russian dancer. Her dancing wins the hearts of everyone present and starts Sally off on a dancing career that carries her into the *Follies.* At the party she also meets and falls in love with the wealthy Blair Farquar (Irving Fisher). The love affair progresses through various vicissitudes until it ends in marriage.

Sally was one of Ziegfeld's most bountiful productions, and it had a great deal with which to woo audiences: Joseph Urban's attractive scenery and costuming; the grotesque dances of Leon Errol; the buffoonery of Walter Catlett. But the brightest attraction was Marilyn Miller. "*Sally* is Marilyn Miller—from her head to her toes," wrote Louis R. Reid in the New York *Dramatic Mirror.* "She danced divinely. . . . Her performance is one of the daintiest things of this unusual season." Even the perspective of many years was unable to dim Guy Bolton's recollection of Miller. In *Bring on the Girls,* written collaboratively with P. G. Wodehouse, Bolton recalled: "It was Marilyn who really mattered. . . . Marilyn who gave to the play a curious enchantment that no reproduction in other lands or other mediums ever captured." She brought a radiance to whatever she said and did; while merely standing on the stage she flooded it with glamour. But she was particularly unforgettable in one of the most beautiful songs Kern ever wrote, sung as a duet with Blair: "Look for the Silver Lining."

Another number was thunderously received by audiences each evening, "The Little Church Around the Corner," sung by Connie in the final scene.

The title song (shared by Blair and the chorus), "Wild Rose," and "Whippoor-will" were also outstanding.

1921   GOOD MORNING, DEARIE, a musical comedy with book and lyrics by
       Anne Caldwell. Produced by Charles Dillingham at the Globe Theatre
       on November 1. Cast included Louise Groody, Oscar Shaw, Harland
       Dixon, and Ada Lewis (265 performances).

Billy van Cortlandt (Oscar Shaw) is a wealthy young man who falls
in love with Rose-Marie (Louise Groody), who works in a costume shop.
She in turn has a boy friend, a crook known as Chesty (Harland Dixon).
In Chinatown the two rivals exchange blows without solving any problems. Later on, at a ball at the house of Billy's sister, Rose-Marie appears
in a disguise to save the family jewels from being stolen by Chesty. Rose-
Marie keeps the jewels from Chesty, a fact that helps considerably to
bring her and Billy together.

The special attractions of *Good Morning, Dearie* were Harland Dixon's
nimble dancing, a farcical performance of Mme Bompard by Ada Lewis,
and an amusing caricature of a detective by William Kent. Kern's best
serious numbers were the title song, "Blue Danube Blues," "Every Girl,"
and a Hawaiian piece that became a hit, "Ka-lu-a." "Look for the Silver
Lining" was lifted from *Sally* as a bonus. The best comedy number was
"Easy Pickin's."

1923   STEPPING STONES, a musical comedy with book by Anne Caldwell and
       R. H. Burnside. Lyrics by Anne Caldwell. Produced by Charles Dilling-
       ham at the Globe Theatre on November 6. Staged by R. H. Burnside.
       Cast included Fred Stone, Allene Stone, and Dorothy Stone, Oscar Rag-
       land, and Roy Hoyer (241 performances).

The pun in the title points up the fact that *Stepping Stones* was written
for the three performing Stones—Fred, the father; Allene, his wife; and
Dorothy, his seventeen-year-old daughter. Fred and Allene were veterans
of the musical-comedy stage, but Dorothy was here making her bow in
an important stage role. The text—hardly more than an excuse to permit
the various Stones to demonstrate their respective gifts—was a modernization of the Red Riding Hood fairy tale. Dorothy played Roughette Hood
who meets adventure with Prince Silvio (Roy Hoyer) and becomes involved with a trio of conspirators, one of whom is a villain named Otto
de Wolfe (Oscar Ragland). Allene Stone is her widowed mother. In the
end Roughette Hood is saved by a plumber, Peter Plug (Fred Stone).

The story was sufficiently elastic to enable Fred Stone to go through many of the routines for which he was famous. Always certain of doing the unexpected, he made his first entrance from the ceiling by parachute and ended the first act with tricks on a horizontal bar. However, the limelight was not his, but Dorothy's. She sang, danced, and acted enchantingly, all the while flooding the stage with the sunshine of her personality. Kern's three main songs were "Once in a Blue Moon," "In Love with Love," and "Raggedy Ann."

1925 SUNNY, a musical comedy with book and lyrics by Otto Harbach and Oscar Hammerstein II. Produced by Charles Dillingham at the New Amsterdam Theatre on September 22. Staged by Hassard Short. Dances arranged by Julian Mitchell and Dave Bennett. Cast included Marilyn Miller, Jack Donahue, Mary Hay, Clifton Webb, Joseph Cawthorn, and George Olsen and his orchestra (517 performances).

This was the first musical in which Kern teamed up with librettist-lyricist, Oscar Hammerstein II. Their job, as Hammerstein explained, was:

One of those tailor-made affairs in which [we] . . . contrived to fit a collection of important theatrical talents. Our job was to tell a story with a cast that had been assembled as if for a revue. Charles Dillingham, the producer, had signed Cliff Edwards, who sang songs and played the ukelele and was known as Ukelele Ike. His contract required that he do his specialty between ten o'clock and ten fifteen! So we had to construct our story in such a way that Ukelele Ike could come out and perform during that time and still not interfere with the continuity. In addition to Marilyn Miller, the star, there was Jack Donahue, a famous dancing comedian, and there were Clifton Webb and Mary Hay, who were a leading dance team of the time, Joseph Cawthorn, a star comedian, Esther Howard, another, Paul Frawley, the leading juvenile. In addition to the orchestra in the pit we had also to take care of George Olsen's Dance Band on the stage. Well, we put it all together and it was a hit.

Hammerstein might also have added that the writers had still another mission to perform—to duplicate the success won a few years earlier by Marilyn Miller in *Sally*. The plot—inevitably complicated, in view of all the demands it had to meet—remained essentially a showcase for Marilyn Miller, for her personal glamour, for her remarkable gifts at song and dance. She now played the part of Sunny, a horseback rider in a circus. In Southampton, England, she falls in love with an American soldier, Tom Warren (Paul Frawley). Love's path never being smooth (particularly in the musical theater), the heroine is compelled by expediency to marry the owner of the circus where she is employed. She prefers returning to America, and can do so only by remarrying Siegfried Peters (Joseph

Cawthorn) whom she had divorced some years earlier. After stowing away aboard ship, which is carrying Tom home, she and Tom are re-united.

Kern's melodious score, described by the *Herald Tribune* as "aristo-cratic," had an all-time Kern favorite in "Who?" presented as a duet by Tom and Sunny. Sunny also sang "D'ye Love Me?" while Tom introduced the title song.

1926   CRISS CROSS, a musical comedy with book and lyrics by Anne Caldwell and Otto Harbach. Presented by Charles Dillingham at the Globe Theatre on October 12. Staged by R. H. Burnside. Dances by David Bennett. Cast included Fred Stone, Allene Stone, and Dorothy Stone (206 performances).

The promise shown by Dorothy Stone in her first major stage appearance three years earlier (in *Stepping Stones*) was so completely fulfilled in *Criss Cross* that a few critics ventured the opinion that she threw her eminent father into the shade. This was by no means an easy thing to do. In *Criss Cross*, Fred Stone was at his comic best—appearing with a trick camel, Susie, and singing the droll, "I Love My Little Susie"; doing a burlesque of a harem dance; weeping profusely over the poignancy of his music as he plays a cello; serving as a member of a troupe of Algerian tumblers.

Dorothy Stone appeared as Dolly Day, an heiress compelled to attend a French academy. Plotters from Algeria hope to swindle her of her for-tune by getting her married to a scoundrel. Christoper Cross, an aviator (Fred Stone) swoops down on a trapeze and saves her. Dolly can now marry the man she really loves, Captain Carleton (Roy Hoyer).

As Dolly, Dorothy participates in the two best songs in *Criss Cross*: "You Will, Won't You?" and "In Araby with You."

1927   SHOW BOAT, a musical comedy with book and lyrics by Oscar Hammer-stein II, based on the novel of the same name by Edna Ferber. Produced by Florenz Ziegfeld at the Ziegfeld Theatre on December 27. Dances and ensembles arranged by Sammy Lee. Cast included Helen Morgan, Howard Marsh, Charles Winninger, Edna May Oliver, Jules Bledsoe, and Norma Terris (572 performances).

With *Show Boat*, the musical theater in America acquired new dimen-sions. This was musical comedy no more (though it was thus designated by its authors). This was a musical play with an artistic entity, dramatic truth, authentic characterizations, effective atmosphere, a logical story line. This, too, was a musical in which music, dance, and comedy were basic to the stage action.

When Kern first approached Edna Ferber with the plan to adapt her *Show Boat* novel into a musical, she thought he had gone mad. She could hardly envision her atmospheric story of life on a Mississippi showboat, in the closing 1800's, as a "girlie" show crammed with conventional musical-comedy attractions. Only when Kern explained he was thinking in terms of a new kind of musical theater, in which old methods would be by-passed in favor of more imaginative approaches, was she willing to assign to Kern the musical-comedy rights.

Friends of Kern insisted that this project was not commercially sound. People attending musical comedies, they argued, were concerned with diversion, not art. They tried to dissuade Kern from such a quixotic project. Only Oscar Hammerstein was quickly convinced (it took only a single telephone call to win him over). He, too, had definite ideas on the direction musical comedy should take, and a quick reading of the Ferber novel convinced him that this material could carry the musical theater toward goals he had in mind. Neither Kern nor Hammerstein allowed themselves to be discouraged by their well-intentioned colleagues and friends—and went to work with a will. "We had fallen in love with it," Hammerstein explained. "We couldn't keep our hands off it. We acted out scenes together and planned the actual direction. We sang to each other. We had ourselves swooning."

Their enthusiasm apparently infected Florenz Ziegfeld, who consented to be the producer even though *Show Boat* was not actually his meat. But there were agonizing delays. When *Show Boat* was not ready for the recently constructed Ziegfeld Theatre, Ziegfeld opened his new house with *Rio Rita;* and *Rio Rita* was so successful that *Show Boat* had to wait a full year before the Ziegfeld Theatre was again available. Then, before it was finally produced, *Show Boat* had to undergo extensive alterations and deletions. This accomplished, Florenz Ziegfeld suddenly lost heart in the whole venture and had to be won back all over again.

But despite his recalcitrance and doubts, Ziegfeld spared no expense in making his production as handsome as possible; that is the only way Ziegfeld worked. Practically an all-star cast was assembled. Joseph Urban designed nostalgic sets; John Harkrider prepared the striking costumes.

Show Boat was both an artistic and box-office triumph. It grossed about 50,000 dollars a week for almost two solid years in New York. After that it played to sold-out houses on an extended road tour. The critical acclaim was equally impressive. Robert Garland called it an "American masterpiece," and Richard Watts, Jr., described it as a "beautiful example of musical comedy." Alan Dale wrote: "*Show Boat* is going to have a wonderful sail—no storms—no adverse winds—nothing to keep it from making port—goodness knows when."

Most of the action takes place on *Cotton Blossom*, a showboat plying the waters of the Mississippi in the 1880's; some of the action transpires at the Chicago Fair Midway. Cap'n Andy (Charles Winninger), owner of the *Cotton Blossom*, is the shepherd of a flock of performers. His carefully guarded daughter, Magnolia (Norma Terris) falls in love with a river-boat gambler, Gaylord Ravenal (Howard Marsh), and runs off with him to Chicago. The vicissitudes of a gambler's life poison their marriage. Though they are still in love, and though Magnolia is pregnant, they part. After her daughter, Kim, is born, Magnolia earns her living in Chicago singing the songs she had learned on her father's showboat. Cap'n Andy hears her there, and takes her back to the *Cotton Blossom* where Gaylord Ravenal is waiting for his wife to beg her forgiveness. Magnolia and Gaylord are reconciled; and their daughter, Kim, becomes the new star of the showboat.

Long before 1927 Kern had proved himself to be one of Broadway's leading melodists. But to his score for *Show Boat* he brought a range and variety of style—and tapped veins of tenderness and compassion—he had never before demonstrated. One of the reasons *Show Boat* has become a classic is that Kern's score is a veritable cornucopia. Perhaps most famous of all the songs is Joe's immortal hymn to the Mississippi, "Ol' Man River," so remarkable in catching the personality and overtones of the Negro spiritual that it is now sometimes described as an American folk song. "Here," Hammerstein has explained, "is a song sung by a character who is a rugged and untutored philosopher. It is a song of resignation with a protest implied." When Kern first played "Ol' Man River" for Edna Ferber, "the music mounted, mounted, and I give you my word my hair stood on end, the tears came to my eyes, and I breathed like a heroine in a melodrama," she has written. "This was great music. This was music that would outlast Jerome Kern's day and mine."

Other outstanding musical numbers include the love duets of Magnolia and Ravenal, "Only Make Believe" and "Why Do I Love You?" Magnolia's poignant lament, "Can't Help Lovin' Dat Man," first heard in the play as a quintet; "Bill," still another lament, made famous by Helen Morgan's plangent performance. This last song had not been written for *Show Boat* but came from Kern's trunk. With lyrics by P. G. Wodehouse, it was originally meant for *Oh, Lady, Lady!* in 1918. But its unusual intervallic construction, together with its somber mood, made it seem out of place in a gay show, and it was removed. When Kern heard Helen Morgan sing for the first time, he realized at once that his forgotten song had found its singer, and it was not difficult for him to find a place for it in the play.

Show Boat is now a classic. It is often revived, and each return is more welcome than the last. On three different occasions it was adapted for the screen. In 1952 Oscar Hammerstein prepared a special concert version of the play, with special narrative, for performance at the Lewisohn Stadium in New York. Kern himself developed the principal music from his score into a symphonic work, *Scenario,* introduced by the Cleveland Orchestra under Artur Rodzinski in 1941. And on April 8, 1954, *Show Boat* made its first appearance in a regular opera repertory, when it was performed by the New York City Opera.

1929   SWEET ADELINE, a musical romance, with book and lyrics by Oscar Hammerstein II. Produced by Arthur Hammerstein at the Hammerstein Theatre on September 2. Book staged by Reginald Hammerstein. Dances and ensembles staged by Danny Dare. Cast included Helen Morgan, Charles Butterworth, Irene Franklin, and Robert Chisholm (234 performances).

Addie (Helen Morgan) is a singer at her father's beer garden where she falls in love with Tom Martin (Max Hoffman, Jr.), first mate of the S.S. *St. Paul.* When Tom goes off to the Spanish-American War, Addie enters the professional musical-comedy stage and becomes a star. She then falls in love with the backer of her show, James Day (Robert Chisholm).

It was a play heavy with sentiment and nostalgia; a play filled with fresh comedy (in the hands of Irene Franklin and Charles Butterworth). Most of all it was a play overflowing with heart-warming melodies. Some of them magically caught the spirit of the Gay Nineties: the folk song, " 'Twas Not So Long Ago"; the waltz-ballad, "The Sun About to Rise"; and the opening song-and-dance, "Play Us a Polka Dot." Two others, sung by Addie, were ever after associated with Helen Morgan, "Why Was I Born?" and "Here Am I."

All in all, *Sweet Adeline* was the kind of entertainment that spelled business at the box office. The critics were virtually unanimous in their praises. Robert Littell said it was "a grand and gorgeous show"; Percy Hammond called it "a gentle opera"; John Mason Brown felt it rose to "its moments of complete enjoyment." So brisk was the demand at the box office that sold-out performances became the rule. But less than two months after *Sweet Adeline* opened, the stock market crashed. Suddenly

the kind of sweetness and humor engendered by *Sweet Adeline* had lost
its appeal. *Sweet Adeline* managed to last 234 performances—placing
it in the hit class—only because the advance sale had been so heavy; but
once that advance was tapped, the play was doomed.

1931   THE CAT AND THE FIDDLE, a musical comedy with book and lyrics by
       Otto Harbach. Produced by Max Gordon at the Globe Theatre on
       October 15. Staged by José Ruben. Cast included Odette Myrtil, George
       Meader, Georges Metaxa, and Bettina Hall (395 performances).

Having broken with the past in *Showboat,* Kern was emboldened to try
once more to produce an unusual musical comedy with unorthodox materials. Harbach's setting was Brussels. There, Shirley Sheridan (Bettina
Hall), an American girl mad about popular music, falls in love with a
serious composer, a Romanian named Victor Florescu (Georges Metaxa).
Florescu is writing an opera, *The Passionate Pilgrim,* right near the studio
where Shirley absorbs herself with popular music activity. At first neither
Victor nor Shirley is tolerant of the other's musical preferences. When
a producer, Daudet, comes to Florescu's studio to listen to his opera score,
Shirley is in her room busy playing a popular song. Daudet points out
that song as the kind that could make Florescu's opera a success. By the
time Florescu's opera is performed, the two young people resolve their
aesthetic differences and fall in love.

As had been the case with *Show Boat,* old and tried routines were
avoided. *The Cat and the Fiddle* had no chorus-girl routines, no syn-
thetic comedy scenes, no set numbers, no spectacles. The story moved
easily and naturally; the characters were believable human beings; and
the music progressed gracefully out of the context. Kern's score (which
at one point was sufficiently adventurous to interpolate a fugue) had three
winners: "The Night Was Made for Love," a canzonetta that courses
throughout the play; Shirley's song, "She Didn't Say Yes"; and Victor's
serenade, "The Breeze Kissed Your Hair."

1932   MUSIC IN THE AIR, a musical comedy with book and lyrics by Oscar
       Hammerstein II. Produced by Peggy Fears at the Alvin Theatre on
       November 8. Staged by Oscar Hammerstein II and Jerome Kern. Cast
       included Walter Slezak, Katherine Carrington, Tullio Carminati, and
       Al Shean (342 performances).

The program described *Music in the Air* as a "musical adventure." This
"adventure" takes place in the little Bavarian mountain town of Edendorff, a setting and atmosphere which the Germans describe as *Gemütlich.*
Sieglinde Lessing (Katherine Carrington) and Karl Reder, the local

schoolmaster (Walter Slezak), are in love. Sieglinde's father, Dr. Walter Lessing (Al Shean), is the town music teacher, and the conductor of the Edendorff Choral Society. He has written a melody for which Karl has provided the lyrics, and he and Sieglinde walk all the way to Munich to try to get it published. In the big city they meet a stage star, Frieda Hatzfeld (Natalie Hall), and a musical-comedy librettist, Bruno Mahler (Tullio Carminati). Frieda is flirtatious with Karl, while Bruno Mahler is so attracted to Sieglinde he wants to star her in his new operetta. Sieglinde and Karl thus come to the parting of the ways. But in time Sieglinde suffers a setback on the stage, and Frieda gets tired of Karl. The disillusioned couple rediscover each other and return to Edendorff.

The picturesque background of a Bavarian mountain town provides much of the charm of the play, and this charm is enhanced by songs like "Egern on the Tegern See" and the beer-hall tunes rendered by Dr. Lessing's Chorale, which have the personality of German folk songs. There are also songs of the American variety. The best of these include the theme song, "I've Told Every Little Star," the melody for which came to Kern from listening to the song of a bird at Cape Cod; Bruno Mahler's love song, "The Song Is You"; and the ballads "And Love Was Born" and "I'm Alone."

The unorthodox techniques and procedures that characterized *Show Boat* and *The Cat and the Fiddle* also distinguish *Music in the Air*. Brooks Atkinson went so far as to declare that

at last the musical drama has been emancipated. . . . Without falling back into clichés of the trade he [Hammerstein] has written sentiment and comedy that are tender and touching . . . and it provides a perfect setting for Mr. Kern's score.

Mr. Atkinson found no reason to change his mind when *Music in the Air* was revived on Broadway on December 1, 1951 (the cast including Mitchell Gregg, Charles Winninger, Dennis King, Jane Pickens, and Lillian Murphy). "Although ours is a graceless world," Atkinson now wrote, "the lovely Kern score is still full of friendship, patience, cheerfulness, and pleasure."

1933   ROBERTA, a musical comedy with book and lyrics by Otto Harbach, based on the novel of the same name by Alice Duer Miller. Produced by Max Gordon at the New Amsterdam Theatre on November 18. Staged by Hassard Short. Dances staged by John Lonergan. Cast included Tamara, Raymond E. (Ray) Middleton, Fay Templeton, George Murphy, and Bob Hope in a minor role (295 performances).

After the bold innovations in *Show Boat, The Cat and the Fiddle,* and *Music in the Air,* Kern seemed satisfied to return to the more familiar patterns of musical comedy. *Roberta* was actually little more than an attractive showcase for a fashion parade. The story and love interest were incidental, and the humor was at best perfunctory. An all-American fullback, John Kent (Ray Middleton), jilted by his girl friend, goes to Paris to visit his Aunt Minnie, known as "Roberta," proprietress of a modiste shop (Fay Templeton). Together with its chief designer, Stephanie (Tamara), he takes over its management. Somewhere along the devious path of this plot it turns out that Stephanie is really a Russian princess.

Much of the success of *Roberta* was due to a single song—the ballad, "Smoke Gets in Your Eyes," with which Tamara created a storm in the theater each evening she sang it. It became one of Kern's greatest hits from the point of view of sheet music and record sales; it is now one of his classics. Five other important songs gave the play additional eminence: "Yesterday," "The Touch of Your Hand," "You're Devastating," "Something Had to Happen," and "Armful of Trouble."

As Roberta, Fay Templeton made her farewell appearance on the musical-comedy stage. As though in compensation, a new star rose over Broadway at the same time: Bob Hope, a bright, fresh comic in the part of Huckleberry Haine.

MANUEL KLEIN, composer

Though Manuel Klein wrote scores for several Broadway musical comedies, his name is always associated with the spectacles, or extravaganzas, that made the Hippodrome Theatre an institution for many years. He was of English birth, London, December 6, 1876, a member of a notable family in English cultural life. His brothers Herman, Charles, and Alfred, respectively, were famous as music critic, playwright, and actor. Manuel received his musical training in London. He came to the United States in the early 1900's, and in 1903 made his Broadway stage bow with *Mr. Pickwick,* the text by his brother Charles, with De Wolf Hopper as star. Through Gus Edwards he managed to get the job of music director of the Hippodrome in 1905, soon after its sensational opening, and for the next decade he not only led the orchestra there but also wrote the music for the annual presentations.

A disagreement between J. J. Shubert, then manager of the Hippodrome, and Manuel Klein brought about the latter's resignation in 1915. Shubert needed some drums and trumpets for a Winter Garden production and asked Klein to send them over; since Klein needed them for his own rehearsals he refused to do so. Klein was summarily dismissed; and Shubert, now having antagonized the whole Hippodrome company, relinquished his interest in the Hippodrome to Charles Dillingham.

Klein returned to London in 1915 where he conducted the musical productions at the Gaiety Theatre. He died in London on June 1, 1919.

1905-14 *The Hippodrome Extravaganzas*

1905 A SOCIETY CIRCUS, an extravaganza with book by Sydney Rosenfeld. Lyrics by Sydney Rosenfeld and Manuel Klein. Additional music by Gustav Luders. Produced by Thompson and Dundy on December 13. Staged by Edward P. Temple and Frederic Thompson (596 performances).

1906 PIONEER DAYS, an extravaganza with book by Carroll Fleming. Lyrics by Manuel Klein. Produced by Shubert and Anderson on November 28. Staged by Edward P. Temple (288 performances).

1907 THE AUTO RACE, an extravaganza with book and lyrics by Manuel Klein and Edward P. Temple. Produced by Shubert and Anderson on November 25. Staged by Edward P. Temple (312 performances).

1908 SPORTING DAYS, an extravaganza with book and lyrics by Manuel Klein and Edward P. Temple. Produced by Shubert and Temple on September 5. Staged by Edward P. Temple (448 performances).

1909 A TRIP TO JAPAN, an extravaganza with book by R. H. Burnside. Lyrics by Manuel Klein. Produced by the Shuberts on September 4. Staged by R. H. Burnside (447 performances).

1910 THE INTERNATIONAL CUP AND THE BALLET OF NIAGARA, extravaganza with book by R. H. Burnside. Lyrics by Manuel Klein. Produced by the Shuberts on September 3. Staged by R. H. Burnside (333 performances).

1911 AROUND THE WORLD, an extravaganza with book by Carroll Fleming. Lyrics by Manuel Klein. Produced by the Shuberts on September 2. Staged by Carroll Fleming (445 performances).

1912 UNDER MANY FLAGS, extravaganza with book by Carroll Fleming. Lyrics by Manuel Klein. Produced by the Shuberts on August 31. Staged by Carroll Fleming (445 performances).

1913 AMERICA, a spectacle "invented" by Arthur Voegtlin. Book by John P. Wilson. Lyrics by Manuel Klein. Produced by the Shuberts on August 30. Staged by William J. Wilson (360 performances).

1914   WARS OF THE WORLD, an entertainment "conceived and invented" by
Arthur Voegtlin. Lyrics by Manuel Klein. Dialogue by John P. Wilson.
Produced by the Shuberts on September 5. Staged by William J. Wilson
(229 performances).

For other Hippodrome extravaganzas see RAYMOND HUBBELL.

The Hippodrome Theatre first opened on April 12, 1905, under the
management of Thompson and Dundy, with a gala program including a
circus show, ballet, and a spectacular drama entitled *Andersonville*. The
Hippodrome Theatre was advertised as "the largest, safest, and costliest
playhouse in the world." Built at a cost of 1,750,000 dollars, it had a seat-
ing capacity of over 5,000 and boasted some of the most elaborate trappings and stage equipment of any theater anywhere. It was planned as a
home for the elaborate type of circus then popular in Europe. For the
next decade and a half the Hippodrome was unrivaled in presenting lavish
spectacles combining visual magnificence with breath-taking stage effects,
productions requiring enormous forces both on and behind the stage.

Manuel Klein became associated with the Hippodrome beginning with
its second production, *A Society Circus*, in which the lovable French
clown, Marcelline, made his debut, and which was notable for such outstanding production numbers as "Song of the Flowers" and the "Court
of Golden Fountains."

During the decade in which Klein was associated with the theater, the
Hippodrome presented stage miracles to startle, delight, and at times
baffle audiences. *Pioneer Days* (1906) opened with a spectacle involving
cowboys, Sioux Indians, Mexicans, and even the U. S. Cavalry. A circus act
presented the Powers Elephants, Herzog's Performing Stallions, the Eight
Flying Jordans, and Little Hip, the smallest elephant in the world. And
the production ended with a tank act for which, from then on, the Hippodrome became famous. Bespangled chorus girls marched down a flight
of stairs into a forty-foot-deep tank filled with water, never to reappear.
During all the years the Hippodrome flourished, the secret was never disclosed how this trick worked. But when the answer was finally revealed
it proved remarkably simple. Behind the scenes there was partly sub-
merged in water an airproof "shed," a kind of diving bell, which because
of the pressure of water from underneath retained the air originally in
it. The girls had only to hold their breath for two or three seconds, duck
under the edge of the bell, and emerge inside it above the water. Having
got their breath, they then ducked under the further edge of the bell and
walked up a second set of stairs to the safety of the backstage. A telephone

operator, sitting at his switchboard, within the bell, reported to a central office upstairs the safe arrival and departure of each girl.

The stage wonders continued during the ensuing years. In 1907 there took place a naval battle in a huge tank, and the Vanderbilt Cup Auto Race was reproduced. "The Four Seasons," featured Margaret Townsend as the "Ice Maid." During the run of this production "The Battle of Port Arthur" was added to the repertory, while "Lady Gay's Garden Party" replaced the auto race.

In 1908 *Sporting Days* presented, among other attractions, a bird ballet and an airplane battle. In *Around the World* (1909) the audience was carried off to England, Switzerland, Egypt, and the Sahara Desert amid the most unusual effects of clouds, storms, distances, and depths. In *Under Many Flags* (1912) herds of deer pounded across an Arizona scene. Additional thrills were provided by a reproduction of a tornado and an earthquake. In the opening scene of *America* (1911), American history was traced, from the discovery of the country by Columbus to a rush-hour scene at the Grand Central Station. In this production there was also seen a fire on New York's East Side, finally subdued by the Fire Department. *Wars of the World* (1914) provided a realistic picture of the French Revolution, the Civil War, the Battle of Vera Cruz, and other historic conflicts. And so it went.

Most of the music Klein wrote for these extravaganzas was functional, serving the individual and specific needs of the Hippodrome. Nevertheless—and despite the fact that the huge house was not ideal for presenting ingratiating songs—he did manage to write some numbers that retained their popularity outside the theater. One of Klein's best songs, "Moon Dear," was heard during his first association with the Hippodrome. Other Klein song hits were: "Meet Me When the Lanterns Glow" in *A Trip to Japan;* "Home Is Where the Heart Is" and "Sweetheart" in *Under Many Flags;* "In Siam" in the *Wars of the World;* and "Love Is Like a Rainbow" in the *International Cup and the Ballet of Niagara.*

While Klein's association with the Hippodrome ended after 1914, extravaganzas continued to flourish there for several years more.

BURTON LANE, composer

Burton Lane was born in New York City on February 2, 1912. His father was a successful real-estate operator. The boy early showed his aptitude for music, but the family was opposed to his studying it, feeling that it imposed too much of a strain on him. Nevertheless, while attending elementary and secondary schools in New York, and the Dwight School, Burton Lane managed to take piano lessons and receive some instruction in harmony and theory from Simon Bucharoff; while still a boy he began writing serious pieces for the piano.

In his fourteenth year Lane impressed the noted bandleader, Harold Stern, then working for J. J. Shubert. Stern arranged for Shubert to hear some of Lane's compositions. The result was that Shubert commissioned the boy to write music for a forthcoming edition of *The Greenwich Village Follies*. Stimulated by this assignment, Lane completed about forty numbers, asking Shubert to take his pick. Unfortunately Lane's debut on Broadway had to be delayed since the projected *Follies* was canceled due to the illness of one of its stars. However, Lane did manage to write some marches for the Dwight School which were published.

From 1927 to 1929 Lane was employed as pianist at Remick's. Here he acquired his apprenticeship in writing popular songs, now his main interest. George Gershwin gave him valuable criticism and encouragement. Howard Dietz, the lyricist, arranged to have two of Lane's songs appear in the Broadway revue, *Three's a Crowd* (1930): "Forget All Your Books" and "Out in the Open Air" (lyrics by Howard Dietz). In 1931 Lane's songs appeared in two more Broadway musicals: Beatrice Lillie sang "Say the Word" in the *Third Little Show*, while four Lane songs were heard in *The Earl Carroll Vanities*.

For a while, victimized by the depression, Lane was unable to place more songs in Broadway productions (though he did manage to publish two). Then, when the talkies became popular, Lane was hired by the M.G.M. Studios in Hollywood. From 1934 to 1936 he worked for various other lots, and in 1936 he became an ace composer for Paramount Pictures.

Lane returned to Broadway in 1940 with his first complete stage score— *Hold On to Your Hats*, starring Al Jolson. That play was important in Lane's career by bringing him a working partner in E. Y. Harburg, the lyricist. Lane had previously written a few melodies to Harburg's lyrics, but in *Hold On to Your Hats* he worked with Harburg on a Broadway musical for the first time. And it was with Harburg that Lane achieved his greatest Broadway success in 1947—*Finian's Rainbow*.

Indicative of Lane's serious approach to music is the fact that after he achieved his formidable success with *Finian's Rainbow* he decided to return to the study of composition. Lane is already a composer who has proved his remarkable ability; but he is also a composer who leaves the suspicion that his best work, and his greatest successes, are still to come.

1940 HOLD ON TO YOUR HATS, a musical comedy with book by Guy Bolton, Matt Brooks, and Eddie Davis. Lyrics by E. Y. Harburg. Presented by Al Jolson and George Hale at the Shubert Theatre on September 11. Staged by Edgar MacGregor. Directed by George Hale. Dances by Catherine Littlefield. Cast included Al Jolson, Martha Raye, Eunice Healey, and Jack Whiting (158 performances).

In *Hold On to Your Hats*, Al Jolson returned to the Broadway stage after an absence of almost a decade; and as it turned out it marked his last Broadway appearance as well. He was cast as a radio cowboy, the Lone Rider—a timid, gun-shy singer who allows himself to be convinced by his script-writer to go off to Sunshine Alley and try to capture the Mexican bandit, Fernando (Arnold Moss). Out West and in Mexico, the Lone Rider gets involved in madcap developments, and through a series of fortunate accidents actually manages to capture the bandit.

The play was studded with songs written with Jolson in mind and delivered by him with his customary gusto and dynamism. Among these were "Walkin' Along Mindin' My Business," "There's a Great Day Coming Mañana," and "Would You Be So Kindly." Toward the end of the evening, Jolson abandoned his role and the plot to step in front of the stage to sing a cycle of the songs he had helped to make famous; and in 1940, as in years earlier, he took complete command of his audience.

Besides the Jolson numbers there were several others of interest, including two ballads, "The World Is in My Arms" and "Don't Let It Get You Down," and two boisterous songs presented by Martha Raye, "Life Was Pie for the Pioneer" and "She Came, She Saw, She Can-Canned." Still another song found favor with audiences nightly: "Down the Dude Ranch," introduced by Jolson, Raye, and Bert Gordon, the last of whom ("The Mad Russian") contributed an amusingly incongruous Russian accent to his role of Concho, the Indian.

1944 LAFFING ROOM ONLY, an extravaganza with book by Olsen and Johnson and Eugene Conrad. Lyrics by Burton Lane and Al Dubin. Produced by the Shuberts and Olsen and Johnson at the Winter Garden on December 23. Staged by John Murray Anderson. Dances by Robert Alton. Cast included Olsen and Johnson, Betty Garrett, Frank Libuse, Mata and Hari, and the Fred Waring Glee Club (233 performances).

Laffing Room Only was an offspring of the fantastically successful *Hellzapoppin'* and *Sons O' Fun* with which for many years Olsen and Johnson regaled Broadway audiences (*see* SAMMY FAIN). But *Laffing Room Only* lacked much of the spontaneity that made its parents such boisterous entertainment. In *Laffing Room Only* guns popped, sausages fell into the laps of the audience, a live bear paraded down the aisles, and the audience was encouraged to dance and sing songs and come on the stage to compete for prizes. But the over-all impression given by the show was that it was imitating past achievements rather than contributing something vital and fresh. About the best thing about the production was one of the songs, one of the biggest hits Burton Lane had produced up to this time: "Feudin' and Fightin' " (lyrics by Al Dubin). But this song actually became a success a few years after the show closed, when it was introduced over the radio by Dorothy Shay on the Bing Crosby program.

1947   FINIAN'S RAINBOW, a musical play with book by E. Y. Harburg and Fred Saidy. Lyrics by E. Y. Harburg. Produced by Lee Sabinson and William R. Katzell at the 46th Street Theatre on January 10. Staged by Bretaigne Windust. Choreography by Michael Kidd. Cast included Ella Logan, David Wayne, and Donald Richards (725 performances).

This delightful Irish fantasy about a crock of gold and leprechauns is neatly combined with social-conscious conflicts in America involving sharecroppers, labor exploitation, and race hatred. The setting is Rainbow Valley, Missitucky, in southern United States, populated by both whites and Negroes. Finian McLonergan (Albert Sharpe) and his daughter Sharon (Ella Logan) arrive from the mythical Irish town of Glocca Morra. Finian has stolen a pot of gold from the leprechaun, Og (David Wayne), who pursues him; Finian hopes to plant his crock in Fort Knox so that it might sprout into even more gold. However, he settles in Rainbow Valley, where he buys some land from sharecroppers. The Valley suddenly becomes prosperous. Senator Billboard Rawkins, a Negro hater, wants to rob Finian and the Negroes of their land. However, Finian's magic pot has the power to grant three wishes. Finian's first wish is to change the hate-mongering Senator into a Negro evangelist, so that he might know what it means to be colored; the second wish, made by Og, is to bring speech to Susan Mahoney, a beautiful deaf-mute (Anita Alvarez), with whom he is in love, and who up to now has made herself articulate through dancing; the last wish saves Sharon from the Senator's wrath.

The social themes are strongly emphasized. As the play progresses, it makes pointed comment on left-wing socialism, poll tax, anti-Negro legislation, the TVA, sharecropping, the temptations of suddenly-acquired wealth, and so forth. But the love interest is not forgotten. Sharon is in love with Woody Mahoney (Donald Richards), leader of the share-croppers; and the leprechaun, who finds to his confused delight that he is drawn to every girl he sees, is finally transformed into a mortal and can woo Susan.

Burton Lane's remarkable score—one of the best for the Broadway stage in the 1940's—was a principal asset of this musical play. The hit songs were "How Are Things in Glocca Morra?" and "Look to the Rainbow," both gently touched with an Irish flavor and both piquantly sung by Sharon. To Harburg's brilliant lyrics, Lane produced several other attractive numbers: "When the Idle Poor," "The Begat," both choral pieces; and Og's two amusing songs, "When I'm Not Near the Girl I Love" and "Something Sort of Grandish."

JOHN LA TOUCHE, lyricist

John La Touche was born in Richmond, Virginia, on November 13, 1917. He attended the Richmond Academy of Arts and Science where he won a prize in composition. When he was fifteen he came to New York and continued his education at the Riverdale Preparatory School on a scholarship, and at Columbia College. At Columbia he became the first freshman to win the Columbia Award for both prose and poetry; and in his sophomore year he collaborated in the writing of music and lyrics for the annual Varsity Show.

His debut in the professional theater came in 1937 with *Pins and Needles* to which he contributed two numbers. In 1939 *Sing for Your Supper* (a revue produced by the WPA) included a stirring number called "Ballad for Uncle Sam," lyrics by John La Touche and music by Earl Robinson. *Sing for Your Supper* lasted only sixty performances. But the ballad survived the disaster. Renamed "Ballad for Americans" it became outstandingly popular in the 1940's. Revived by Paul Robeson on a radio program, it made such an immediate hit that the network switchboard was jammed for hours with congratulatory calls, and thousands of letters poured in the following day. The ballad was then recorded by three different companies, was bought for motion pictures, was used by Lawrence Tibbett and James Melton (among others) for their concert programs. And it appeared as an inaugural feature of the Republican National Convention in 1939.

With the "Ballad for Americans," John La Touche had his first taste of success as lyricist. With Vernon Duke's *Cabin in the Sky* (1940) he first established his reputation as lyricist for the Broadway stage. He subsequently wrote either the lyrics or book, or both, for several musicals, among them Vernon Duke's *Banjo Eyes,* starring Eddie Cantor (1941) and *The Golden Apple* (1954). His last associations with the musical stage came in 1955, and both were box-office failures: *The Vamp* and Leonard Bernstein's *Candide.*

John La Touche died in Calais, Vermont, on August 7, 1956.

See: LEONARD BERNSTEIN (*Candide*); VERNON DUKE (*Cabin in The Sky, Banjo Eyes*); Appendix I (1954—*The Golden Apple*).

ALAN JAY LERNER, lyricist and librettist. *See* FREDERICK LOEWE and ALAN JAY LERNER

HOWARD LINDSAY, librettist. *See* RUSSEL CROUSE and HOWARD LINDSAY

FRANK LOESSER, composer and lyricist

Frank Loesser was born in New York City on June 29, 1910. His family was musical. His brother, Arthur, became famous as a concert pianist and teacher. Nevertheless, Frank was never given musical instruction—the reason being that at the time Frank, unlike the other members of a highly charged intellectual family, had little sympathy for the classics. When he tried playing the piano (at first only with one finger) it was to pick out the day's popular tunes. Since his family regarded such music contemptuously, they preferred to leave Frank to his own devices. He learned to play the piano by ear; he also managed to acquire an ingratiating personal singing style; and he became adept with a harmonica. What he accomplished in music had to come without benefit of a teacher, and through a hit-and-miss process. To this day, reading music is a difficult chore for him, and most of his music-making is guided more by instincts of sound than training.

Recalling his youth, Loesser has remarked: "In those days I had a rendezvous with failure." Nothing he did, or tried to do, seemed to turn out right. His academic schooling, never distinguished, took place at elementary public schools, the Speyer and Townsend Harris High Schools, and ended abruptly after a single year at the College of the City of New York. He then held one job after another in rapid succession: process server for some lawyers; inspector of a chain of restaurants, testing food; an office boy in a wholesale jewelry house; a waiter and pianist in a Catskill Mountains hotel; reporter for a small paper in New Rochelle; knit-goods editor of a small-town journal; press agent.

While thus floundering about in poorly paid jobs, he tried to write song lyrics. The initial impulse for writing verses came from a favor done for a certain gentleman who needed couplets for each of the guests attending a Lions Club dinner. Loesser wrote these couplets, and they were pretty awful. One of them ran: *"Secretary Albert Vincent, Read the minutes— right this instant."* But the guests at the dinner seemed delighted with his efforts, and the exhilaration of creation had touched Loesser. From then on he spent most of his time writing verses and song lyrics. One of these, a ballad called "Armful of You," was sold to a vaudevillian for fifteen dollars.

He was not yet twenty when he submitted a handful of lyrics to the publisher, Leo Feist, who offered Loesser a job as staff lyricist for 100 dollars a week. During that year Loesser wrote many lyrics to melodies by Joseph Brandfron, but none was considered good enough to publish. Only after Feist had dispensed with Loesser's services was one of his songs published: "I'm in Love with the Memory of You," in 1931. This song is significant because it was Loesser's first publication; also because its composer was a young hopeful named William Schuman, subsequently one of America's most significant serious composers and President of the Juilliard School of Music.

Loesser's first hit came in 1934, "I Wish I Were Twins," music by Joseph Meyer. This success was instrumental in bringing him out to Hollywood to write songs for Grade-B pictures on the Universal lot. When this contract expired, Loesser went to work for Paramount, for whom he completed his first important lyrics. They were "Says My Heart" (music by Burton Lane), "Small Fry" and "Two Sleepy People" (Hoagy Carmichael), and "Jingle, Jangle, Jingle" (Joseph J. Lilley). Other Loesser lyrics were set to music by Arthur Schwartz, Jule Styne, and Jimmy McHugh.

Loesser wrote his first melody as well as the lyrics under the stimulation of World War II—"Praise the Lord and Pass the Ammunition" in 1942. It was a formidable hit, selling over 2,000,000 records and 1,000,000 copies of sheet music before this sales sweep was suddenly arrested by a protest from the clergy against associating the Lord with ammunition. A second war song was even more distinguished, "The Ballad of Rodger Young," written at the request of the Infantry. With these two war hymns Loesser immediately proved himself as gifted in writing melodies as in lyrics, and from then on he wrote both the music and the lyrics for most of his songs.

During World War II Loesser served as private first class in Special Service when he wrote soldier shows packaged and distributed to army camps. He also wrote individual songs for various branches of the service, one of which became the official song of the Infantry, "What Do You Do in the Infantry?" He prepared other songs for the Wacs, Service Forces, Bombardiers, and so forth.

Loesser's first musical-comedy score came after he had become one of Hollywood's topflight lyricists and composers. In 1948 *Where's Charley?* started a Broadway run of 729 performances. While this musical was prospering on Broadway, Loesser kept on writing distinguished songs for the screen, winning an Academy Award in 1949 for "Baby, It's Cold Outside."

Loesser's second musical on Broadway was an even greater triumph than the first, for it was *Guys and Dolls* (1950), one of the most successful musical comedies ever produced. A half dozen years later, with his third musical, *The Most Happy Fella*, Loesser not only wrote music and lyrics but also (for the first time) his own musical-comedy text.

1948   WHERE'S CHARLEY?, a musical comedy with book by George Abbott based on Brandon Thomas' farce, *Charley's Aunt*. Produced by Feuer and Martin in association with Gwen Rickard (Mrs. Ray Bolger) at the St. James Theatre on October 11. Staged by George Abbott. Choreography by George Balanchine. Cast included Ray Bolger, Allyn McLerie, Doretta Morrow, and Byron Palmer (792 performances).

Brandon Thomas' farce, *Charley's Aunt*, had long been a war horse of the professional and amateur theater—actually since it was first produced toward the end of the nineteenth century. As practically everybody must know by now, the setting is Oxford, England. Charley Wykeham (Ray Bolger) impersonates his old maiden aunt from Brazil so that an intimate party for two couples might have a chaperon. Hilarity and broad burlesque are introduced when this "aunt" is madly pursued and courted by an Oxford lawyer, who believes her to be a lady of means. When Charley can discard his disguise he can successfully pursue his quest for Amy Spettigue (Allyn McLerie).

George Abbott's musical-comedy version was a bountiful source of entertainment, even though the sight of a man cavorting in woman's dress and assuming woman's mannerisms was not calculated to amuse a sophisticated audience. One of the main reasons for the success of this musical was Ray Bolger's ingratiating performances as Charley and the "aunt." In a ladies' room, in an athletic love scene with a vigorous man, while fussing around with an affected feminine air—Bolger always succeeded in being amusing without stooping to Varsity-Show vulgarity or offending good taste. His adept tap dancing added still another dimension to his performance. And he had a charm uniquely his in putting over a song, as in "Once in Love with Amy," in which he had the audience participate in singing the chorus.

The main love song was "My Darling," which for several consecutive weeks occupied the leading position on the Hit Parade. "Make a Miracle," in Amy Spettigue's sprightly rendition, proved Loesser's facility with a witty lyric and brisk melody, while "The New Ashmolean Marching Society and Students Conservatory Band" was a vigorous march tune.

1950 GUYS AND DOLLS, a musical comedy with book by Jo Swerling and Abe Burrows based on a story and characters by Damon Runyon. Produced by Feuer and Martin at the 46th Street Theatre on November 24. Staged by George S. Kaufman. Dances and musical numbers staged by Michael Kidd. Cast included Isabel Bigley, Sam Levene, Robert Alda, Vivian Blaine, and Pat Rooney, Sr. (1200 performances).

Guys and Dolls not only belongs with that aristocratic society of musicals that have had a run of over one thousand performances, but it is also one of the very best ever produced. It is wonderful entertainment in which the audience interest is never allowed to relax. It is the model of what an ideal musical comedy should be. Like different parts of a solved jigsaw puzzle, each part is made to fit neatly into the complete picture and is basic to the over-all pattern. George S. Kaufman's staging gave the play much of its tingling air of excitement and its breathless pace: The opening scene, for example, is a pantomime of Broadway life and characters which sets the mood for the entire production. Michael Kidd's dances are exciting, with a genuine masterpiece in a large ballet number using for its theme a crap game. Jo Mielziner's sets were daringly imaginative. The performances of all principals and subordinates were equally effective— not a weak link in the entire chain. Finally, both the melodies and the lyrics of Frank Loesser were remarkable. No wonder then that John Chapman singled out *Guys and Dolls* as the finest play of 1950 because of its "originality and its avoidance of the usual musical comedy patterns."

Described as a "musical fable of Broadway," *Guys and Dolls* is a vibrant, pulsating, and human portrait of the world of Broadway—of big- and little-shot gamblers and Salvation Army proselytizers, of night-club entertainers and a sundry variety of jerks and eccentrics. Each routine, song, dance, bit of humor is germane to the plot and succeeds in giving it additional depth. As Abe Burrows wrote in *Theatre Arts:*

Nothing is in there that doesn't belong. We didn't care about how a single number or scene would go. We didn't concern ourselves with reprising songs for no reason at all. We cared about the whole show and nothing went in unless it fit. . . . Everything fits. That must be what makes it a hit.

The principal source was Damon Runyon's short story, "The Idylls of Sarah Brown," but with characters borrowed from other Runyon tales. (As one of the two adaptors, Abe Burrows here makes his bow as a writer for the Broadway musical-comedy stage.) Two love plots are woven into the fabric. The first involves Sky Masterson (Robert Alda), a high-living, happy-go-lucky sport, with the Salvation Army lass, Sarah Brown (Isabel Bigley). The subsidiary love interest is found in gambler Nathan Detroit (Sam Levene) and the night-club entertainer, Miss Adelaide (Vivian Blaine); they have been engaged for fourteen years but their ever-impending marriage is always frustrated by some crap game or other. When Sarah discovers that the only reason Sky has taken her to Havana is to win a bet, she loses interest in him; but that interest is revived when Sky contrives to save her Mission and at the same time is able to prove that he is really in love with her. The love entanglements, however, are incidental. Much more vital to the play is the picturesque, cynical, hard-boiled universe of Damon Runyon, the strange characters who inhabit it, and the unorthodox forces and impulses that motivate their daily life and philosophy.

The principal love songs are "I'll Know" and "I've Never Been in Love Before," both duets of Sky and Sarah; also Sarah's ballad, "If I Were a Bell." Other songs are rich with the kind of jargon that spices the dialogue of the play and which is the language of Broadway: the opening "Fugue for Tinhorns" ("I've Got the Horse Right Here"), a three-voiced canon sung by three horse players picking out their winners for the day; "Adelaide's Lament," her complaint that her chronic sneezes are only psychosomatic, caused by Nathan Detroit's failure to marry her; and two routines at the "Hot Box" night club, by Adelaide and her girls, "A Bushel and a Peck" and "Take Back Your Mink." (An important Loesser ballad, "Your Eyes Are the Eyes of a Woman in Love," however, was a new song written for the motion-picture adaptation starring Marlon Brando, Frank Sinatra, Jean Simmons, and Vivian Blaine.)

The significance of *Guys and Dolls* as stage entertainment has already been discussed. Its significance at the box office was no less impressive. During its fabulous run it grossed over 12,000,000 dollars.

1956 THE MOST HAPPY FELLA, a musical play, with book by Frank Loesser based on Sidney Howard's 1925 Pulitzer Prize play, *They Knew What*

They Wanted. Produced by Kermit Bloomgarden and Lynn Loesser at the Imperial Theatre on May 3. Staged by Joseph Anthony. Choreography by Dania Krupska. Cast included Robert Weede, Jo Sullivan, Mona Paulee, and Art Lund (678 performances).

Though *The Most Happy Fella* has over thirty basic musical numbers (the program makes no effort to list them) and though most of the play is music rather than spoken dialogue, Loesser refuses to designate the play as an opera. He considers it as an "extended musical comedy"—and with good reason. Its music is steeped in the traditions of Tin Pan Alley and the Broadway stage. There are plenty of excellent show tunes, and some became hits: "Standin' on the Corner," a kind of hillbilly number delivered by a male quartet; "Big D," another choral number paying tribute to the city of Dallas in the style of popular songs of the 1920's; "Happy to Make Your Acquaintance," a warm and genial duet between Tony and Rosabella; the title song; and "Young People."

But the score is much more than just a collection of good musical-comedy songs and routines. It is an expansive and ambitious frame for recitatives, arias, duets, canons, choral numbers, dances, instrumental interludes, parodies, and folk hymns. It includes such sentimental delights as Tony's love song, "My Heart Is So Full of You"; Joe's tender consolation to Rosabella, "Don't Cry"; the waltz, "How Beautiful the Days," which the music critic Harriet Johnson called a "gem of its kind, probably never before equalled on Broadway for subtlety or loveliness of vocal sound"; and two numbers in imitation of Italian folk songs, "Abbondanza" and "Benvenuta." "We're trying to create a form so you can say in music that which might be too emotional for dialogue," explained Don Walker, the orchestrator of the score. "We pass into dialogue only for those developments that are not emotional in content, such as exposition."

The idea to make a musical comedy out of Sidney Howard's play came to Loesser from a playwright friend, Sam Taylor. "I thought he was crazy," Loesser explained. "But when I reread the play I knew he was right." Loesser came to realize that, though a tragedy, Howard's play had a great deal of humor to it, and that such humor could lend itself admirably to musical treatment. It took Loesser four years to complete both his musical-comedy adaptation of the Howard play (for the first time he wrote his own text) and the music.

The basic Howard play remained unchanged. Tony, an aging wine-grower in Napa, California (Robert Weede), falls in love with Rosabella, a young waitress (Jo Sullivan), whom he has met in a San Francisco restaurant. He woos her by mail and sends her, not his own picture, but that of one of his hired hands, Joe (Art Lund). The deception is evident to Rosabella when she appears at Napa for the wedding. In her first pangs of disappointment she has an affair with Joe and becomes pregnant. Tony is heartbroken when he subsequently learns that Rosabella has been unfaithful, but he finally forgives her. Rosabella comes to love Tony for his generosity and humanity.

In his play Howard stressed the growth in maturity of Tony when he recognizes that certain compromises must be made for the happiness of all concerned. But in Loesser's adaptation, greater stress is paid upon the theme of the search of lonely people for companionship and happiness. "Frank Loesser," said Robert Coleman, "has taken an aging play and turned it into a timeless musical."

Though Loesser prefers to call *The Most Happy Fella* a musical comedy instead of an opera, it is nevertheless a play in which much of the emotional, dramatic, and humorous impact comes from the music. Brooks Atkinson emphasized this when he wrote in his review: "He has told everything of vital importance in terms of dramatic music." And in a later article Mr. Atkinson added: "His music drama . . . goes so much deeper into the souls of its leading characters than most Broadway shows and it has such an abundant and virtuoso score in it that it has to be taken on the level of theater."

Besides being a resounding box-office success, *The Most Happy Fella* was selected by the Drama Critics Circle as the best musical of the year.

FREDERICK LOEWE and ALAN JAY LERNER, composer and librettist-lyricist

The son of a tenor famous in Viennese operettas (creator of the role of Prince Danilo in *The Merry Widow*), Frederick ("Fritz") Loewe was early given direction in music. He was born in Vienna on June 10, 1904, and was a prodigy who started playing the piano when he was five, wrote music at seven, when he contributed some numbers for his father's variety skit, and at thirteen became the youngest pianist ever to appear as soloist with the Berlin Symphony Orchestra. He received piano instruction from two of Europe's foremost keyboard masters and scholars—Ferruccio Busoni and Eugène d'Albert—and in composition he was taught by Emil Nikolaus von Reznicek. In 1923 he received one of the most coveted piano awards in Europe, the Hollander Medal.

Both his talent and training were calculated to bring him a career in serious music, but popular music interested him from the beginning. He was only five when he wrote a popular tune for the first time. By the time he was fifteen he was the proud author of an impressive hit, "Katrina," which sold over 1,000,000 copies of sheet music.

He came to the United States in 1924 to begin his American career in music, but found he could make no headway with either serious or popular scores. He decided to quit music for good. For several years he knocked around the country holding down various jobs not usually assumed by musicians. He punched cattle, mined gold, engaged in professional boxing bouts in the bantamweight class, was a riding instructor.

Just before World War II he returned to music, first by playing the piano in a Greenwich Village café, then by composing. In 1938 he managed to get four songs (all in a Viennese style) in a Broadway musical, *Great Lady*, which gave no indication of breaking the jinx that seemed to haunt Loewe's musical career in America; it ran only twenty performances.

A turning point in his career came a few years later through a chance meeting at the Lambs Club with a young librettist-lyricist, Alan Jay Lerner, and their decision to work together.

Alan Jay Lerner was born to wealth, in New York, on August 31, 1918; his parents were proprietors of the prosperous Lerner Shops in New York. Alan received an intensive academic education both in this country and in England, and in 1940 he received his Bachelor of Science degree at Harvard College; while attending Harvard, Lerner wrote sketches and lyrics for two Hasty Pudding Shows.

Attempts to invade the Broadway theater proved as disheartening to Lerner as they had been for Loewe. While biding his time and waiting for opportunity to knock, Lerner wrote scripts for radio programs; in a period of two years he wrote over 500 such scripts.

It was at this point in Lerner's life that he met Loewe at the Lambs Club and they decided to storm the citadels of the theater together. Their first work was a musical written for a Detroit stock company, a chore they completed in about a week. Then came their first Broadway musical, *What's Up?* (1943). Loewe's music, still in a Viennese manner and tempo, was not much more distinguished than Lerner's text, and the play folded after an eight-week run.

Two years after that, Loewe and Lerner reappeared on Broadway with *The Day Before Spring*, a play that hovered delightfully between realism and fantasy and made interesting excursions into the female psyche. The production was interesting for its dream ballets (created by Anthony Tudor) and a musical score that had songs like "The Day Before Spring,"

"You Haven't Changed at All," and "I Love You This Morning," in which Loewe's melodic gift began to acquire an American identity.

Success came in 1947 with *Brigadoon*. And less than a decade later they made stage history with *My Fair Lady*. After *My Fair Lady* they made a swift excursion to Hollywood to write songs for the screen musical, *Gigi*.

Though Lerner's best work for the Broadway stage was done in collaboration with Loewe, he did on occasion work with other composers. In 1948 he wrote book and lyrics for Kurt Weill's *Love Life*. And, without Loewe's partnership, Lerner worked several years in Hollywood writing some outstanding screen musicals, including *An American in Paris*, which won the Academy Award in 1951.

> 1947   BRIGADOON, a musical play with book and lyrics by Alan Jay Lerner. Produced by Cheryl Crawford at the Ziegfeld Theatre on March 13. Staged by Robert Lewis. Choreography by Agnes De Mille. Cast included David Brooks, Marion Bell, and George Keane (581 performances).

The authors called their play "a whimsical musical fantasy." The setting is Brigadoon, a magic village in Scotland, which appears every hundred years out of the Highland mists, only to disappear after a single day. In that one day all the elements of living are confronted: life and death, love and marriage. In present times two American tourists, on a grouse hunt, get lost and stumble upon Brigadoon on a day when a wedding is being celebrated. They are Tommy Albright (David Brooks) and Jeff Douglas (George Keane). They sense that the place has an eerie feeling. The village schoolmaster, Mr. Lundie (William Hansen), relates the village's history. In 1747 a miracle had permitted the village to be preserved from any change by allowing it to disappear, then come to life for a day once a century. If a single native left the place, then Brigadoon would be gone for good; if any visitor arrived, he must be part of Brigadoon's life. During his day in Brigadoon, Tommy falls in love with the charming Scottish lass, Fiona MacLaren (Marion Bell), so much so that he completely forgets the girl he left behind in New York.

Any temptation the authors might have felt to make their play a field day for sentimentality was side-stepped. As Brooks Atkinson wrote:

> The plot works beautifully. Mr. Lerner organized the story. He does not get down to the details of the fairy story until the audience has already been won by the pleasant characters, the exuberant music, and the prim though fiery dances. After that the incantation is complete and easy.

Much of the evocative charm and stage magic evoked by the play was due to Lerner's sensitive writing. Much, too, stemmed from Loewe's music. When *Brigadoon* was revived at the New York City Center on March 27, 1957 (with David Atkinson, Scott McKay, Robert Rounseville, and Virginia Oswald), Richard Watts, Jr., had this to say of Loewe's music:

> I had forgotten . . . what a delightful score Frederick Loewe composed for his and Alan Jay Lerner's fantasy. . . . It came to me as almost a revelation . . . that *Brigadoon* was filled with enchanting melodies.

The most important love song was "Almost Like Being in Love," a big hit in 1947. The song did not have a particularly Scottish identity, but other numbers in the score did: the delightful madrigal "Come to Me, Bend to Me," "The Heather on the Hill," "There but for You Go I," "The Love of My Life," "Waitin' for My Dearie," and "I'll Come Home with Bonnie Jean." But though individual songs were strong in their appeal, the score as a whole was beautifully integrated with the text; it kept the action fluid as the play progressed from speech to song and back again to speech. The spirited and at times deeply moving choreography of Agnes De Mille was also integral to the folk character of the play, and contributory to its over-all fascination.

Brigadoon became the first musical to receive the Drama Critics Circle Award as the best play of the year.

1951   PAINT YOUR WAGON, a musical comedy with book and lyrics by Alan Jay Lerner. Produced by Cheryl Crawford at the Shubert Theatre on November 12. Directed by Daniel Mann. Dances staged by Agnes De Mille. Cast included James Barton, Olga San Juan, and Tony Bavaar (289 performances).

Paint Your Wagon was not a box-office success, nor did it receive the enthusiasm it deserved. But it was a delightful musical in its colorful exploitation of American backgrounds, lore, and geography; a realistic, earthy representation of the old West. "They have eschewed the caricature of routine musical comedy," wrote Walter F. Kerr, "and they have avoided almost entirely the interpolation of random vaudeville."

The setting was northern California in 1853 during the Gold Rush, and the play traces the history of a mining camp from its beginnings through its development into a boom town, down to its disintegration into a ghost town when the lode peters out. (The play, however, ends optimistically: The town is revivified through irrigation and agriculture.) The town itself is named after the central character who founded it, Ben Rumson (James Barton), who tries to fill the varied roles of town sheriff, mayor, judge. His daughter, Jennifer (Olga San Juan), carries on a romance with Julio Valveras (Tony Bavaar), a Mexican of noble birth. For the first half of the play Jennifer is the only female in town, and the atmosphere is bleak with men lonely for women. Then the ladies arrive by stagecoach, infecting the air with exhilaration and bringing to the men a new spurt of ambition and drive.

The play is filled with scenes that provide local color—in a saloon, mine, a miner's cabin, the town square. The action is filled with exciting incidents and episodes—free-for-all saloon fights, cancan dancing, a treasure hunt, and so forth. It has rollicking comedy scenes when Ben buys a wife at auction and then tries to sell her again when he must raise some cash.

The background and atmosphere are enriched through the folk choreography of Agnes De Mille, particularly the exciting dances of James Mitchell and Gemze de Lappe.

The three best songs in Loewe's score were "I Still See Eliza" and "Wandrin' Star," both delivered by Ben Rumson, and Jennifer's ballad, "All for Him." The score also profited from three excellent choral numbers ("There's a Coach Comin' in," "Hand Me Down That Can o' Beans," and "Movin'"), and two sentimental ballads, "I Talk to the Trees," sung and danced by Julio and Jennifer, and Julio's song, "Another Autumn."

1956   MY FAIR LADY, a musical play with book and lyrics by Alan Jay Lerner adapted from Bernard Shaw's comedy, *Pygmalion*. Produced by Herman Levin at the Mark Hellinger Theatre on March 15. Staged by Moss Hart. Choreography and musical numbers staged by Hanya Holm. Cast included Rex Harrison, Julie Andrews, and Stanley Holloway.

This musical play, which certainly seems destined to become a classic of the American theater, took a long time to reach the stage. The original idea of transforming Shaw's *Pygmalion* into a musical first took root with Gabriel Pascal, the motion-picture producer who had already transferred that Shaw comedy to the screen. In 1950, just before Shaw's death, he approached the dramatist with the project of adding songs to *Pygmalion*, and received a favorable reaction. After Shaw's death, Pascal acquired short-term rights for the musical adaptation but was unable to complete negotiations with any Broadway producer, and the venture was stillborn. Several writers had been contacted (including Rodgers and Hammerstein) and they turned down the project. Loewe and Lerner tried their hand at an adaptation in 1952 and also decided it was not for them. The whole plan seemed to have died when Pascal did, in 1954. But late in 1954 Loewe and Lerner tried once again to adapt *Pygmalion*. As Lerner has said:

> We had decided that *Pygmalion* could not be made into a musical because we just didn't know how to enlarge the play into a big musical without hurting the content. But when we went through the play again . . . we had a great surprise. We realized we didn't have to enlarge the plot at all. We just had to add what Shaw had happening offstage.

Now completely convinced of the practicability of their project, they signed Rex Harrison for the starring role of Higgins even before they had completely consummated the difficult and intricate negotiations with the Shaw estate. By July, 1955, all papers were signed. Herman Levin had by then been brought in as producer, and a single backer had been found in the Columbia Broadcasting System, which put up all the money (400,000 dollars).

When finally unfolded at the Mark Hellinger Theatre on March 15, 1956, *My Fair Lady* was received with a delight inspired by few musicals. Brooks Atkinson went all out and called it "one of the best musicals of the century. . . . It gets close to the genius of creation. . . . In taste, intelligence, skill and delight, *My Fair Lady* is the finest musical in years." William Hawkins wrote: "This is a legendary evening. . . . It has everything. *My Fair Lady* takes a grip on your heart, then makes you exult with laughter."

Alan Jay Lerner had enough taste and intelligence in his adaptation to allow as much of Shaw's play as possible to remain. A few additions had to be made—but these, and Lerner's consistently scintillating lyrics, were so Shavian in spirit and style that it is often difficult to tell where Shaw left off and Lerner began. If a new note of humanity, or sentimentality, was introduced into the play to offset Shaw's irony and malice, this was all to the good, as far as the musical theater was concerned; so is the welcome presence of genuine romantic feeling, absent in the Shaw comedy, which brings to the production a radiant glow.

For the most part, the Shaw play never loses its original bite or sting or its penetrating social viewpoints; in the musical, as in the play, there is laughter at false class distinctions and at the so-called "high society" in England.

Except for the end, Shaw's plot remains unaltered. Professor Henry Higgins (Rex Harrison), a distinguished phonetician, meets Eliza Doolittle, an illiterate flower girl (Julie Andrews), daughter of the bibulous and irresponsible but lovable cockney, Alfred P. Doolittle (Stanley Holloway). Spurred on by a bet with Colonel Pickering (Robert Coote), he decides to transform Eliza—in speech, manner, and dress—into a fine lady and pass her off successfully as a duchess. Higgins' transformation of Eliza proves nothing short of magic. At a glamorous social evening at the Embassy, Eliza plays the role of the duchess with complete assurance. The experiment over, Higgins allows Liza to leave his home, but he cannot overcome a feeling of jealousy when she tells him she plans to marry Freddy Eynsford-Hill, a rich man-about-town (John Michael King). In Shaw's play the ending does not clarify whether or not Eliza marries Freddy, though in a preface to one of his later editions he explains that Eliza did, and became proprietress of a flower shop. The musical, however, brings Eliza and Higgins back together in a sentimental closing scene.

Many helped to bring magic to the production of *My Fair Lady:* Oliver Smith with felicitous sets, particularly a black and white background for the "Ascot Gavotte"; Cecil Beaton's costuming in pre-World War I style; Hanya Holm's imaginative staging of songs and dances; masterful direction by Moss Hart, the celebrated "Rain in Spain" episode being merely one example of his inventiveness; remarkable performances by the three principals.

Loewe's music, in its graceful Continental manner and air—especially the "Ascot Gavotte" and "Embassy Waltz"—is beautifully attuned to the atmosphere and background of London in 1912. There are two major song hits and both had become popular on radio, television, and records even before the first curtain went up: "I Could Have Danced All Night," Eliza's expression of exhilaration in her transformation; and Freddy's ballad, "On the Street Where You Live." Touching sentiment is found in both these songs, but also in Professor Higgins' "I've Grown Accustomed to Her Face," with which the play closes. But Loewe's music, at other times, is also touched with a coating of Shavian satire in two of Higgins' patter songs, "Why Can't the English?" and "A Hymn to Him"; and it is also filled with Shavian mockery at middle-class morality in Doolittle's two cockney songs, "With a Little Bit of Luck" and "Get Me to the Church on Time."

My Fair Lady captured more than one-third of the awards in the seventeen categories embraced by the annual Antoinette Perry Awards, equaling a record held previously by *South Pacific* and *Damn Yankees.*

GUSTAV LUDERS, composer

Gustav Luders, composer of delightful operettas and operetta tunes in the early 1900's, was born in Bremen, Germany, on December 13, 1865. He studied music extensively in Europe before coming to the United States in 1888 and settling in Milwaukee. There he conducted orchestras in theaters and beer gardens. Charles K. Harris, composer of "After the Ball," met him in Milwaukee and became so impressed with his talent that he urged Luders to seek out the richer opportunities offered a young musician by a metropolis like Chicago. In Chicago, Luders found employment as conductor in theaters and a permanent post as arranger for the local office of the music publisher, Witmark. One of Luders' chores, in 1896, was an arrangement of one of the most popular rag tunes of that day, Barney Fagan's "My Gal's a Highborn Lady."

> The Witmarks were fond of Gus Luders [recalls Isidore Witmark in his autobiography, *From Ragtime to Swingtime*]. Though high-strung and temperamental, he was a most lovable man, easy to get along with. . . . His music reflected his nature: tuneful, bright, gay. He was a thorough musician, and did all his own scoring.

Luders' first score for the stage came in 1899. It was *Little Robinson Crusoe*, book and lyrics by Harry B. Smith, and starring Eddie Foy. Luders' musicianship led Henry W. Savage, the producer, to commission him to write music for *The Burgomaster*, a comic opera that Savage was planning for Raymond Hitchcock. *The Burgomaster*, produced in Chicago in 1900, was only moderately successful, but it did boast an outstanding song hit (Luders' first) in "The Tale of the Kangaroo." (From this time on, Luders was partial to songs using the word "Tale" in the title; among his best-known songs are "The Tale of the Bumble Bee" and "The Tale of the Turtle Dove.")

The text and lyrics of *The Burgomaster* were by Frank Pixley, editor of the Chicago *Times-Herald*. This play initiated a collaborative arrangement between Pixley and Luders that lasted many years and brought forth a few more operettas—including *The Prince of Pilsen* (1903), their greatest success. Among other Pixley-Luders operettas were: *King Dodo* (1902), *Woodland* (1904)—a fantasy in which all the characters appeared as birds, *The Grand Mogul* (1907), *Marcelle* (1908), and *The Gypsy* (1912).

Pixley was not Luders' only collaborator. On other operettas Luders worked with George Ade, the celebrated columnist and humorist, their best musicals being *The Sho-Gun* (1904) and *The Fair Co-ed* (1909).

The number "13" proved the downfall of Luders. His thirteenth operetta was *Somewhere Else,* produced in 1913. After the opening-night performance Luders was convinced he had another hit, since his friends said the play was as good as *The Prince of Pilsen.* The morning after the opening the critics were annihilating, a fact that so discouraged the producer that he closed down the show after the third performance. Apparently Luders felt his defeat deeply. He died of a heart attack only one day after the show closed.

1902 KING DODO, an operetta with book and lyrics by Frank Pixley. Produced by Henry W. Savage in arrangement with Daniel Frohman at Daly's Theatre on May 12. Cast included Raymond Hitchcock, Margaret McKinney, Greta Risley, and Gertrude Quinlan (64 performances).

In Dodoland, King Dodo (Raymond Hitchcock) seeks youth again, since he wishes to win the love of Angela (Margaret McKinney). Angela, however, is in love with one of the King's soldiers, Piola (Cheridah Simpson). When Piola informs the King that there exists a Fountain of Youth in far-off Spoojuland, the King and his retinue set forth for that land. Spoojuland is ruled by Queen Lili (Greta Risley), who has a weakness for older men. There, King Dodo drinks from the fountain of youth and becomes a young man again. But, unhappily, the King falls in love with Queen Lili, who has no use for him because of his youth. By falling accidentally into a magic spring he becomes an old man again— much to his delight, since he is now being pursued by the Queen. King Dodo renounces his throne in Dodoland and turns it over to Piola, together with his blessings for Piola's marriage with Angela.

Among the brightest songs in a gay score was "The Tale of a Bumble Bee" (one of Luders' best songs), a march called "The Lad Who Leads," and a ballad, "Diana."

1903 THE PRINCE OF PILSEN, an operetta with book and lyrics by Frank Pixley. Produced by Henry W. Savage at the Broadway Theatre on March 17. Staged by George W. Marion. Cast included John W. Ransone, Arthur Donaldson, Lillian Coleman, Anna Lichter, and Albert Paar (143 performances).

The Prince of Pilsen was a far greater success than its initial New York run of 143 performances might suggest. For five consecutive seasons it played to capacity houses on the road, and on three of those seasons it returned to New York for additional runs. It had many revivals throughout the country in the early 1900's: Jess Dandy, who took over the role of Hans Wagner from John Ransone, played the part over 5000 times.

Hans Wagner (John W. Ransone) is a brewer and alderman from Cincinnati, who goes to Europe with his daughter Nellie (Lillian Coleman) to visit his son Tom (Albert Paar), an American Navy man stationed near Nice, France. Upon his arrival in Nice, Hans is mistaken for a Prince who was expected at the hotel. Despite all his protests, Wagner becomes the center of many festivities and is showered with favors. The real Prince, Carl Otto (Arthur Donaldson), arrives, sizes up the situation, and decides that he can have more fun by going about incognito and letting Hans act the part of a Prince. Incognito, the Prince flirts with Nellie; before long they fall in love. Hans Wagner, meanwhile, has an amatory adventure of his own—with a rich American widow, Mrs. Madison Crocker, while Tom is squiring Edith, a girl from Vassar (Anna Lichter). Hans comes into possession of a map of secret fortifications. When it is found on his person he is accused of being a spy. But Carl Otto steps out of his anonymity to straighten out all difficulties and to reveal that he will marry Nellie.

The Prince of Pilsen was Luders' greatest hit and his best score. The music included the duet of Tom and Edith (the hit song), "The Message of the Violet," and a second duet—by Otto, Nellie, and a hidden female chorus—"Pictures in the Smoke." Two stirring choruses—"The Heidelberg Stein Song" and "The Tale of the Seashell"—and an amusing topical song by Hans, "He Didn't Know Exactly What to Do," provided contrast.

1904　THE SHO-GUN, an operetta with book and lyrics by George Ade. Presented by Henry W. Savage at Wallack's Theatre on October 10. Staged by George F. Marion. Cast included Edward Martindel, Georgia Caine, and Charles Evans (125 performances).

Spoofing American ways, manners, and behavior is nothing new for our musical stage. George Ade did it at the turn of the century in *The Sho-Gun*, which he called "a playful treatise upon the gentle arts of promoting and trust-building." *The Sho-Gun* pokes fun at the American go-getter, advertising, politics, big business, and the American love of high-sounding titles.

The setting is an imaginary island, Ka Choo, which lies between Japan and Korea, ruled by the Sho-Gun. William Henry Spangle (Charles Evans), manufacturer of chewing gum, comes to the island. There he hires as lawyer, Hanki-Pank (Thomas C. Leary), the island astrologer, and teaches him the subtleties of American law the better to circumvent that of Ka Choo. By forming trusts and fomenting strikes—and through the far-reaching influence of Hanki-Pank—Spangle becomes the island's new Sho-Gun. Then he marries Omee-Omi (Georgia Caine), the widow of a former Sho-Gun. In office, Spangle wastes no time in reorganizing the island along American ideas, by introducing high-pressure promotion and advertising, together with American political ideas and methods. The islanders do not take kindly to this revolution, and Spangle must finally escape to safety through the help of the U. S. Marines.

The principal songs are: "Little Moozoo May," "I Am Yours Truly," "Flutter Little Bird," and "I'll Live for You."

1909   THE FAIR CO-ED, an operetta with book and lyrics by George Ade. Produced by Charles Dillingham at the Knickerbocker Theatre on February 1. Staged by Fred G. Latham. Dances staged by William Rock. Cast included Elsie Janis and Arthur Stanford (136 performances).

George Ade's humorous nonmusical play, *The College Widow*, which was used for Jerome Kern's musical comedy *Leave It to Jane* (1917), was set in Atwater College, in Atwater, Indiana. The traditional rival of Atwater College was Bringham College. And it is the latter institution that is the background for *The Fair Co-ed*. There Cynthia Bright (Elsie Janis) is the only coed left, and she is adored by the entire faculty and student body. Cynthia's father, just before his death, had ordered her to marry only a Bringham graduate. Cynthia, however, loves Davy Dickerson (Arthur Stanford), who has a difficult time getting through his college courses. Now that he must graduate to win Cynthia, he decides to devote himself more earnestly to his studies. On a lark, Cynthia disguises herself as a naval cadet and goes to a military reception where she is in danger of a hazing and must escape by jumping through the window. Davy finally succeeds in passing his courses and in graduating, and Cynthia now can marry him.

Much of the exuberance of the text came from the abundance of college songs and yells in the production. Luders' leading musical numbers, however, were in a sentimental vein and included "Here in the Starlight," "I'll Dream of That Sweet Co-Ed," and "A Little Girl That's Wise."

JIMMY McHUGH, composer and HAROLD ADAMSON, lyricist

Jimmy McHugh was born in Boston on July 10, 1894. While attending St. John's Preparatory School he studied the piano with his mother. For a while, after his academic schooling ended, he assisted his father, a plumber. Then, eager to get on with a career in music, he turned down a scholarship to the New England Conservatory to work as office boy and rehearsal pianist for the Boston Opera Company. When he reached the conclusion that his future lay in popular, and not serious, music, he found a job in the Boston branch of the Irving Berlin publishing house, serving as song plugger in local theaters and five-and-ten-cent stores. He then came to New York where he wrote "Emaline," his first published song. For seven years after that he wrote songs for revues produced in the Harlem night spot, The Cotton Club; among these efforts was his first hit, "When My Sugar Goes Down the Street" (lyrics by Irving Mills and Gene Austin).

Meeting the young lyricist, Dorothy Fields, in 1928, and deciding to write music for her words, was as much a turning point in his career as it was in hers. It meant McHugh's first Broadway score, and with it his first success in the theater—*Blackbirds of 1928*. This all-Negro revue helped establish the fame of the song-writing team of McHugh and Fields. During the next two years they collaborated on many songs, interpolated in various musicals. Among their own musical comedies the most successful was *Hello Daddy* (1928). They also contributed the songs to two revues that were box-office failures, *International Revue* (1930), which had two fine songs in "On the Sunny Side of the Street" and "Exactly Like You," and *Vanderbilt Revue* (1930), which had "Blue Again."

After 1930 McHugh worked not only with Dorothy Fields but also with several other lyricists. The most significant of these, as far as McHugh's career was concerned, was Harold Adamson.

Adamson was born in Greenville, New Jersey, on December 10, 1906. He attended the New York public schools, the University of Kansas, and Harvard University. While at school he interested himself in theatrical and literary matters. He wrote poetry for various school papers and sketches for school productions. While attending the University of Kansas he completed lyrics for several songs and won some prizes; at Harvard he wrote some fraternity shows and contributed sketches and lyrics to a few Hasty Pudding Shows. During the summers he played in a stock company. He entered upon a professional career as lyricist after leaving Harvard. In 1933 Adamson collaborated with McHugh on three songs for the gala opening of the Radio City Music Hall in New York.

Meanwhile, in 1930, McHugh started writing songs for motion pictures. To lyrics by Dorothy Fields he contributed music for about a dozen films. In 1936 McHugh and Adamson wrote the songs for the motion picture *Banjo on My Knee*. In later pictures McHugh collaborated most frequently with Adamson; but he also wrote music for several other lyricists, including Dorothy Fields, Frank Loesser, Gus Kahn, and Johnny Mercer. Among McHugh's most famous screen songs were: "It's a Most Unusual Day" and "A Lovely Way to Spend the Evening," lyrics by Adamson; "I'm in the Mood for Love" and "The Cuban Love Song," lyrics by Dorothy Fields; "I Wish We Didn't Have to Say Good-night" and "Wouldn't It Be Nice," lyrics by Frank Loesser.

Jimmy McHugh returned to Broadway with songs for *Streets of Paris* (1939)—lyrics, this time by Al Dubin—in which Carmen Miranda was lifted to Broadway fame with the help of McHugh's song, "South American Way." A year after that came another Jimmy McHugh musical, *Keep Off the Grass*, lyrics by Howard Dietz. But McHugh's greatest Broadway success in this second invasion of New York came with *As the Girls Go*, in 1948.

1928   BLACKBIRDS OF 1928, an all-Negro revue, with book and lyrics by Dorothy Fields. Produced by Lew Leslie at the Liberty Theatre on May 9. Staged by Lew Leslie. Cast included Bill Robinson, Adelaide Hall, and Tim Moore (518 performances).

Blackbirds of 1928 was one of the most successful all-Negro revues produced on Broadway—and one performer above all others helped to make this so: "Bojangles" Bill Robinson, here achieving his first Broadway stage success. He did not appear until the second half of the revue. But from the moment he came on the stage to sing and dance in "Doin' the New Low Down," the audience was his. As he shuffled across the stage or tapped up and down a double flight of five steps or beat out the rhythms of a song with his nimble toes, he was a man of rhythm who electrified the theater. "His feet," reported *Time*, "were as quick as a snare drummer's hands."

The cream of the comedy came from Tim Moore—a huge, stout, toothy performer—who did old-fashioned burlesques of a prizefight ("Bear Cat Jones' Last Fight") and a poker game ("Playing According to Hoyle"), and who appeared in a riotous sketch involving a Harlem wedding. The best of the blues singing came from Adelaide Hall, also a new Broadway star. Three of McHugh's best songs, and greatest hits, were assigned to her: "I Can't Give You Anything but Love, Baby" (a duet with Willard MacLean), "Diga, Diga, Doo," and "I Must Have That Man."

1928   HELLO DADDY, a musical comedy with book by Herbert Fields based
on a nonmusical German farce, *The High Cost of Loving*. Lyrics by
Dorothy Fields. Produced by Lew Fields at the Lew Fields Mansfield
Theatre on December 26. Staged by Alexander Leftwich and John Mur-
ray Anderson. Directed by Busby Berkeley. Cast included Lew Fields,
George Hassell, Mary Lawlor, and Allen Kearns (198 performances).

Hello Daddy was based on a play in which Lew Fields had starred on
Broadway a few years earlier. As Henry Block he is one of three middle-
aged respectable men, all members of the local Purity League, who
through the years have been secretly supporting the illegitimate son of a
burlesque queen, each one thinking the son was his. The other two men
are Edward Hauser (George Hassell) and Anthony Bennett (Wilfred
Clark). They finally discover that none of them was the responsible
party. But before they do, Connie Block (Mary Lawlor) and Lawrence
Tucker (Allen Kearns) pursue a legitimate romance.

The scene in which Lew Fields as Henry discovers he is not the father
of the illegitimate son is one of the high comedy moments of the production. Other outstanding comedy scenes are found with Billy Taylor
(Noel Burnham), the nincompoop whose paternity is in so much doubt,
and in the girl he pursues, Betty Hauser (Betty Starbuck). Their song,
"In a Great Big Way," in which they give a funereal description of the
pleasures they are supposed to derive from loving each other, was a show-
stopper. Other outstanding musical numbers included a hot serenade,
a duet by Mary and Lawrence, "I Want Plenty of You," and "Let's Sit
and Talk About Love."

1948   AS THE GIRLS GO, a musical comedy with book by William Roos. Lyrics
by Harold Adamson. Produced by Michael Todd at the Winter Garden
on November 13. Staged by Howard Bay. Dances by Hermes Pan. Cast
included Irene Rich, Bobby Clark, Betty Jane Watson, and Bill Callahan
(420 performances).

What would happen to this country if a woman became President? *As
the Girls Go* tries to supply the answer. Lucille Thompson Wellington
(Irene Rich, making her Broadway debut) is elected the first lady President of the United States. As First Gentleman, her husband, Waldo
(Bobby Clark), must fulfill the social functions previously assumed by
First Ladies. He uses these functions and his high station and authority
at the White House to run after the girls. During these farcical proceedings a more normal and orthodox love interest is consigned to two

charming youngsters, Kathy Robinson (Betty Jane Watson) and Kenny Wellington (Bill Callahan).

The musical opens with best foot forward. Having just been elected, the first lady President expresses gratitude to her voters—not live but on a large screen flashed via NBC-TV newsreel. The opening song, "As the Girls Go," follows, sung by Waldo surrounded by a bevy of beautiful girls. From then on the pace of the comedy is permitted to slacken only to permit the interlude of a tender love song between Kathy and Kenny, "You Say the Nicest Things, Baby," and two sentimental numbers, "Lucky in the Rain" and "Nobody's Heart but Mine." The two best comedy songs were "I've Got the President's Ear" and "It Takes a Woman to Get a Man."

COLE PORTER, composer-lyricist

Cole Porter was born in Peru, Indiana, on June 9, 1893. His grandfather's speculations in West Virginia coal and timber had made him a millionaire, and the Porter family moved in a setting of luxury. Cole's mother, Kate, a cultured woman, saw to it that the boy began his musical training early: the violin when he was six; the piano two years later. She guided him through the task of writing an operetta (words and music) when he was only ten; and when he was eleven arranged for a piano piece, "Bobolink Waltz," to be published by a Chicago firm.

The grandfather wanted Cole to become a lawyer. Cole, consequently, attended the Worcester Academy in Massachusetts, where he was particularly proficient in foreign languages. In 1909 he went to Yale. There his extra-curricular activities included the writing of football songs, two of which became famous ("Yale Bull Dog Song" and "Bingo Eli Yale"). He also sang in and directed the glee club, wrote and helped produce college shows. From Yale, following his graduation in 1913, he went on to Harvard Law School, where he stayed a single year. Having by now decided that his future rested with music, he transferred to the School of Music at Harvard where he collaborated with Lawrason Riggs in writing a musical comedy in the style of Gilbert and Sullivan.

Cole Porter had a musical on Broadway as early as 1916—*See America First*, book by Lawrason Riggs. It closed after only two weeks. Partly out of disappointment, partly in quest of adventure, Porter set off for North Africa to join the French desert troops. A portable piano was tied to his back with the military equipment, and during rest periods he entertained his friends with songs, mostly of his own invention. The French government bestowed on him the Croix de Guerre for helping boost the morale of his fellow soldiers.

As soon as America plunged into World War I, Porter was transferred to Fontainebleau, to the French Officers School. His training ended, he was assigned to teach American soldiers French gunnery.

At this time he acquired a luxurious apartment in Paris and began laying the groundwork for his subsequent reputation as a wealthy playboy of Europe and one of Europe's gracious hosts. Despite his military duties he found time to entertain lavishly, and at these parties he always performed for his guests by singing sexy little songs of his own writing. One of the socialites to come regularly to his apartment became Mrs. Cole Porter after the Armistice; she was Linda Lee Thomas, divorced wife of the publisher of the *Morning Telegraph.*

Just before that marriage Porter paid a brief visit home. While aboard ship he became acquainted with the musical-comedy star and producer, Raymond Hitchcock, whose latest venture was an annual revue, *Hitchy-Koo.* During the Atlantic crossing Porter sang some of his songs to Hitchcock, who commissioned him to write the score for one of the forthcoming editions of his revue. Porter fulfilled the assignment by contributing a dozen numbers to *Hitchy-Koo of 1919.* The best of these was "An Old-Fashioned Garden," which sold well in sheet music and on records.

After his marriage to Linda Lee, Porter set up house on Rue Monsieur in Paris. The ornate, even garish, furnishings were matched only by the splendor of the parties he gave there. For one of these affairs the entire Monte Carlo Ballet performed; on another occasion, at the whim of a moment, all guests were transported by motorcade to the Riviera. Parties were going on all the time; guests sometimes arrived for the evening but stayed on for a week.

In 1923 the Porters rented the Rezzonico Palace in Venice (where Robert Browning died). Gondoliers were hired as footmen, while in front of the palace Porter had built a floating night club capable of accommodating a hundred guests and a Negro jazz band. For some of these gay evenings Elsa Maxwell devised ingenious games, such as a treasure hunt through the canals or unusual masquerade parties at the Lido.

Such happy diversions did not keep Porter from music. He was not only writing all the time—words and music for sophisticated and frequently naughty songs that proved the delight of his friends—he was also doing some serious study, in Paris at the Schola Cantorum, with Vincent d'Indy, one of the most renowned French musicians of the twentieth century.

His second effort to enter the professional Broadway theater took place in 1924, with five songs for *The Greenwich Village Follies,* none of which made an impression. His friends insisted that the kind of songs he wrote best were not commercial, and that when he tried coming to terms with the commercial theater his vivacity and spontaneity were inhibited. Elsa Maxwell put it this way to him: "You are just too good, Cole. Your standards are too high. But one day you will haul the public up to your own level, and then the world will be yours."

Cole Porter's conquest of his public began with his fourth entry into the Broadway theater, with *Paris,* produced by E. Ray Goetz in 1928 to star his wife, Irene Bordoni. There were six Porter songs in this score, three in the slightly risqué and delightfully sophisticated manner he would soon make famous: "Let's Misbehave," "Babes in the Wood," and "Let's Do It." In 1929 came his first Broadway success, with *Fifty Million Frenchmen.* And in 1930 appeared two Cole Porter song classics: "Love for Sale" in the *New Yorkers* and "What Is This Thing Called Love?" in *Wake Up and Dream.*

By 1930 his style, both as composer and lyricist, had crystallized. (Like Irving Berlin, Cole Porter always has written his own lyrics.) In his lyrics he combined the most skillful versification with a debonair manner, sprinkling through his verses sophisticated references to smart names, places, and all kinds of cultural allusions. He also established a definite individuality in his melodies—most of them languorous tunes in the minor mode with broad sweeps of melody against a throbbing background of pulsating and at times primitive rhythms.

Cole Porter has become one of the most distinguished and successful song writers of our generation. He has also been a leader in writing music for the stage. Since 1930 he has been associated with more successful musical comedies than any other composer, with the exception of Richard Rodgers. Most of these were tremendous box-office draws. All of them were generously endowed with wonderful songs that will never be forgotten. For even in those musicals that were failures there were usually one or two songs that are remembered. In *Jubilee* (1935) there was "Begin the Beguine," which passed virtually unnoticed during the run of the play; it came into its own about a decade later when revived on records and over the radio with sensational results. In *Red, Hot and Blue* (1936) there was "It's De-Lovely."

He has also been richly productive in Hollywood, some of his best songs having been written for the screen. Among these are: "I've Got You Under My Skin," "Easy to Love," "In the Still of the Night," "You'd Be

So Nice to Come Home to," "Don't Fence Me in," and "True Love." Porter's best songs of stage and screen (fourteen) formed the backbone of his screen biography, *Night and Day*, in 1946, Cary Grant playing the composer.

Porter's capacity for sustained and concentrated work proves that this man has tough fiber—particularly since, being a wealthy man, he had no economic drive sending him to work. Just how tough his fiber really is was demonstrated after one tragic day in 1937. While riding horseback at the Piping Rock estate of Countess di Zoppola on Long Island, he tried to negotiate a muddy hill. The horse slipped backward and fell on top of him. Porter's legs were so badly crushed, and his nerve tissues so seriously damaged, that at first it was believed he would have to undergo amputation. He had to have over thirty painful operations to save his legs as long as possible. Two of the seven years following this accident had to be spent continually in the hospital; the rest of the time he was prisoner to a wheelchair. He had to take drugs continually to alleviate the pain. Finally, in 1958, amputation of the right leg was found necessary.

Despite his suffering, his theatrical and social activities were pursued stubbornly; nor were his good humor, personal charm, and love of life seriously affected. He continued to travel to far-off places, continued to entertain his friends in the grand manner. And he never stopped working. He wrote the entire score of *Leave It to Me* while bedridden, knowing only agonizing pain. Through all his operations and the mental and physical tortures attending them, the high standard of his writing never deteriorated.

1929   FIFTY MILLION FRENCHMEN, a musical comedy with book by Herbert Fields. Produced by E. Ray Goetz at the Lyric Theatre on November 27. Staged by Monty Woolley. Dances staged by Larry Ceballos. Cast included William Gaxton, Genevieve Tobin, Helen Broderick, and Evelyn Hoey (254 performances).

One year earlier, Porter had written the score for the E. Ray Goetz production of *Paris*. *Fifty Million Frenchmen* was even more Parisian than *Paris*. With seven-league boots it covered the wondrous city on the Seine from the Ritz bar to the Longchamps race track; from the American Express Company on Rue Scribe to Montmartre; from the Claridge Hotel to Les Halles. En route, it gently spoofed American tourists. Helen Broderick, for example, played the part of Violet Hildegarde, a hard-boiled and bored American ever on the lookout for shocking experiences; she sends risqué picture cards back to her relatives at home and buys up copies of *Ulysses* to give as gifts to kids. "Here is a show that will make you homesick for Paris," wrote Robert Littell, "and it's grand fun."

The principal character was Peter Forbes (William Gaxton), a wealthy playboy who at the Ritz Bar meets and falls in love with Looloo Carroll (Genevieve Tobin), fresh from Terre Haute. He is determined to win her love for himself alone, and not for his wealth. Spurred on by a 25,000-dollar bet with a friend, he decides to live in Paris for a month without any funds. He finds a job as a guide, comes upon Looloo who is now being pursued by a Grand Duke picked for her by her ambitious mother. He also becomes a gigolo and an Arabian magician as he undergoes one experience after another in different Parisian settings and backgrounds. In the end he wins his bet, and his girl.

The identity of Cole Porter as lyricist-composer is fully established in the score, which has four songs still favored: "You've Got That Thing" and "You Do Something to Me," breezily sung by Peter Forbes; "You Don't Know Paree"; and "Find Me a Primitive Man," introduced by Evelyn Hoey playing the part of Mary de Vere. Two humorous songs sung by Violet were also above par: "The Tale of an Oyster" and "Where Would You Get Your Coat?"

1932   THE GAY DIVORCE, a musical comedy with book by Dwight Taylor, adapted by Kenneth Webb and Samuel Hoffenstein from an unproduced play by J. Hartley Manners. Produced by Dwight Deere Wiman and Tom Weatherly at the Ethel Barrymore Theatre on November 29. Staged by Howard Lindsay. Cast included Fred Astaire, Luella Gear, Eric Blore, and Claire Luce (248 performances).

The Gay Divorce is a bedroom farce in which Mimi, an actress (Claire Luce), seeks divorce from a dull husband. To get that divorce she goes to an English seaside resort to be compromised by a corespondent. There she meets Guy (Fred Astaire). Guy had seen her briefly two weeks earlier and had fallen in love with her, but Mimi does not recognize him. Guy manages to get the password by which the corespondent is to identify himself to Mimi, and passes himself off as that man. What had been planned as a staged rendezvous becomes the real thing as Guy relentlessly pursues Mimi and finally wins her.

Fred Astaire here made his first musical-comedy appearance without his lifetime partner, his sister Adele. He introduced a song soon recognized as a Porter masterpiece, "Night and Day." "You're in Love" and "I've Got You on My Mind" are effective ballads, and the best humorous numbers are "I Still Love the Red, White and Blue" (delivered at a Communist rally) by Mimi's bosom friend and guide, enacted by Luella Gear and "Mr. and Mrs. Fitch."

1934 ANYTHING GOES, a musical comedy with book by Guy Bolton, P. G. Wodehouse, Howard Lindsay, and Russel Crouse. Produced by Vinton Freedley at the Alvin Theatre on November 21. Staged by Howard Lindsay. Dances by Robert Alton. Cast included Ethel Merman, William Gaxton, Victor Moore, and Bettina Hall (420 performances).

Anything Goes started out as an amusing text by Bolton and Wodehouse about a shipwreck and the effect it has on some screwball characters. But just before it went into production, a major sea disaster took place on September 8, 1934: the *Morro Castle* went up in flames off the coast of New Jersey, costing 134 lives. Shipwrecks, then, no longer seemed like the right material for humor. The authors hurriedly called to Howard Lindsay and Russel Crouse to rewrite their text. The shipwreck idea was completely abandoned. The setting now became a luxury liner crossing the Atlantic, carrying a curious assortment of passengers. One was Public Enemy No. 13 (Victor Moore), renowned for his skill with machine guns, who is fleeing from the law. He comes disguised as Reverend Dr. Moon, clutching under his arm a clarinet case, which conceals a sawed-off machine gun to which he affectionately refers as "my little putt-putt-putt." Another passenger is the rich playboy, Billy Crocker (William Gaxton). He is pursuing his dream girl, Hope Harcourt (Bettina Hall), who in turn is engaged to Sir Evelyn Oakleigh (Leslie Barrie). Since Crocker has come on the boat at the last moment, he has neither a steamship ticket nor a passport, and must sail as a stowaway. He enlists the help of "Reverend Moon" who arranges for him to appear in various disguises: as Nicholas Murray Butler; as a "Pomeranian gentleman" (with hair expropriated from a Pomeranian dog aboard ship); as an American Public Enemy No. 1; as a Chinaman; as a sailor. Finally, among those on board ship is an evangelist-turned-night-club singer, Reno Sweeney (Ethel Merman), who finds Billy Crocker attractive. After multifarious adventures, in which all principals are helplessly involved, Billy Crocker wins the love of Hope. And Public Enemy No. 13—who enjoys a momentary triumph on learning he was graduated into the No. 1 slot—is heartbroken to discover that the FBI is not after him at all, considering him as harmless as a sponge. "I can't understand this administration," he whines in a broken voice.

Anything Goes was Porter's greatest stage success up to then, and his best score. It was a mine of riches. Ethel Merman made unforgettable both "I Get a Kick Out of You" and "Blow, Gabriel, Blow" with her big, vigorous, brassy delivery; and with William Gaxton she helped introduce one of Porter's best-known patter songs, "You're the Top." The other musical highlights were the title song and a take-off on sailor chanteys, "There'll Always Be a Lady Fair."

1938   LEAVE IT TO ME, a musical comedy with book by Bella and Samuel Spewack, based on their own stage comedy, *Clear All Wires*. Produced by Vinton Freedley at the Imperial Theatre on November 9. Staged by Samuel Spewack. Dances by Robert Alton. Cast included William Gaxton, Mary Martin, Victor Moore, Sophie Tucker, and Tamara (307 performances).

Leave It to Me was the first successful spoof of the Soviet Union on the musical stage. The principal character provides the amusement. He is Alonzo P. Goodhue (Victor Moore), the sadly befuddled American Ambassador to the Soviet Union. He has no idea why he was chosen for the job. "Somebody in Washington mustn't like me," he explains. What he does not know is that while he was pitching quoits in his back yard in Topeka, Kansas, his domineering and ambitious wife (Sophie Tucker) had contributed 95,000 dollars to the Party campaign fund—5000 dollars more than a newspaper owner who had aspired to this ambassadorial post—and thus the job became his automatically. Now in Russia with his wife and five beautiful daughters, he can only dream of the time when he can go home again and indulge to his heart's content in double banana splits.

Buckley Joyce Thomas (William Gaxton), a brash young newspaperman, is sent to Moscow by his employer—the same newspaper owner who had been beaten out for the ambassadorial post by Goodhue. Thomas' mission is to get the goods on Goodhue so that he will be recalled. Through the machinations of the young journalist, Goodhue gets into all kinds of trouble, hoping thereby to get home soon, but only to discover to his dismay that things always turned out right. He kicks an arrogant German Ambassador in the stomach and receives a cable of congratulations from Secretary of State Hull. He shoots a Russian diplomat, manages thereby to destroy a notorious Trotzkyite, and to become hero of a two-week celebration in Red Square. Finally he decides to take his job seriously by making a speech on how to stop the world from going into war. He now antagonizes Russia and the American State Department and comes to the end of his diplomatic career. While all this is going on, Buckley Joyce Thomas romances Colette (Tamara) and finds his true love in Dolly Winslow (Mary Martin).

Sophie Tucker, William Gaxton, Tamara, and Victor Moore were hardy veterans of the musical stage. Yet it was not one of these but a complete newcomer who attracted the thunder of the audience: Mary Martin, as Dolly Winslow. Shedding her ermines in a simulated strip tease (in, of all places, a wayside Siberian railroad station), she sang "My Heart Belongs to Daddy." Her innocent, quavering, childlike voice proved a delightful contradiction to the suggestive double-entendres of the lyric. She became at once one of the radiant stars of the American stage. A native of Weatherford, Texas, Mary Martin had made several none too successful appearances in radio and night clubs before *Leave It to Me*. Laurence Schwab heard her sing at the Trocadero in Hollywood and signed her up. When *Leave It to Me* was cast, Schwab loaned her to Vincent Freedley for what had been planned as a minor role. But since there are no such things as minor roles for great performers, Mary Martin made herself the toast of Broadway; her debut was described as one of the most sensational in the history of our theater. And "My Heart Belongs to Daddy" became the hit of the show.

Sophie Tucker, that old "pro," also had a way with a song. As Mrs. Goodhue, she made the most of "I'm Taking the Steps to Russia" (supported by her five daughters), "From U.S.A. to U.S.S.R." (in which her husband, Alonzo, provided an "off to Buffalo" routine), and "Most Gentlemen Don't Like Love." Colette contributed the purple moods in song ballads like "Get Out of Town" and "From Now on," and Buckley Joyce Thomas gave a breezy account of "When It's All Said and Done."

Mary Martin was not the only unknown in the cast of *Leave It to Me* destined to reach heights. There were two others in the cast, although they had to wait for a later date and other productions for recognition. A careful scrutiny of the program reveals that among those who appeared in the chorus were Van Johnson and Gene Kelly.

1939   DU BARRY WAS A LADY, a musical comedy with book by Buddy de Sylva and Herbert Fields. Produced by De Sylva at the 46th Street Theatre on December 6. Staged by Edgar MacGregor. Dances by Robert Alton. Cast included Ethel Merman, Bert Lahr, Ronald Graham, Betty Grable, and Benny Baker (408 performances).

This play takes a long step back into history—to the Petit Trianon in France and the epoch of Louis XIV; and it carries back in time a hapless night-club washroom attendant, Louis Blore (Bert Lahr). Louis works for the Club Petite, where he is in love with its vital entertainer, May Daly (Ethel Merman). When he wins 75,000 dollars in the sweepstakes, he buys the club, hoping thereby to win May's heart. (One of the funniest episodes in the play comes at this point with Louis instructing his successor in the subtleties, refinements, and art of handling a washroom.) But he has a formidable rival in Alex Barton (Ronald Graham), with whom May is in love. In pique he tries to slip Alex a Mickey Finn, but drinks it himself and goes into a deep slumber.

He dreams he is back in the days of Louis XIV, indeed that he is the King himself. His would-be regal attitudes jar incongruously with a Brooklynese jargon and smoke-room smut, as he brings to the role of King a lusty, peasant vitality and an ingenuous informality. "He plays," said Richard Watts, Jr., of Lahr, "with the sort of spluttering, indignant violence and leering impudence that makes him one of the best comedians in the world."

As Louis XIV he is passionately pursuing Mme Du Barry, who looks and acts exactly like May Daly. Just as he is making excellent progress and manages to extract from her a promise to spend the night with him, he is wounded in a most delicate and vulnerable spot by an arrow shot by the half-moronic Dauphin (Benny Baker). The indiscreet involvements of King and mistress in and out of the bedroom make up the bulk of his idyllic dreams.

When Louis wakes up he generously presents Alex with 10,000 dollars so that he can marry May. Since the rest of Louis' money is eaten up by taxes, he must return to the washroom of the Club Petite as attendant.

The best songs were two lustily presented by May—"When Love Beckons" and "Katie Went to Haiti"—and Alex's love ballad, "Do I Love You?". Betty Grable—here making her first stage appearance following her Hollywood successes—is heard in "Ev'ry Day a Holiday" and is seen in several delightful dances, including an old-world gavotte and a gypsy dance.

1940   PANAMA HATTIE, a musical comedy with book by Buddy de Sylva and Herbert Fields. Produced by De Sylva at the 46th Street Theatre on October 30. Staged by Edgar MacGregor. Dances by Robert Alton. Cast included Ethel Merman, Rags Ragland, James Dunn, Betty Hutton, and Arthur Treacher (501 performances).

"Panama Hattie" is Hattie Maloney (Ethel Merman), an entertainer at the Tropical Shore Bar in the Panama Canal Zone. She decides to reform and acquire social polish, since she is in love with Nick Bullett (James Dunn), a Philadelphia socialite serving as a U. S. official. As the story unfolds, she overhears a plot by some spies to blow up the Canal. With the help of three gobs she thwarts the enemy. Then she convinces Nick to bring down his eight-year-old daughter so that they can get better acquainted. The child, Geraldine (Joan Carroll), laughs at Panama Hattie for her rough-and-ready ways and her brusque behavior, but in time a warm attachment develops between them. Hattie and Nick can now get married.

There was a great deal of rowdy, and at times ribald, humor here; a great deal of burlesque, particularly whenever Rags Ragland, as a gob, was on the stage with his buddies (Ragland making his first successful appearance in the legitimate theater after years in the burlesque theater); a good deal of hard-boiled theater. Ethel Merman, supplemented by Betty Hutton as Florry, was loud and brassy and earthy. But some engaging tomfoolery frequently lightened the atmosphere, as in the wacky duet, "You Said It." And there was often a welcome infusion of warmth and sentiment, as when little Geraldine and Hattie sing, "Let's Be Buddies."

Panama Hattie was the first musical in which Ethel Merman occupied the only starring role. Though supported by an excellent cast, she was the dynamo of the production. She was in her finest form, "than which there is none finer," as John Mason Brown put it. "Ethel Merman sweeps triumphantly through *Panama Hattie.* . . . The evening she dominates with all that strident precision which is hers is a happy example of our professional theater when it is functioning at its professional best." Her best songs, besides two already mentioned, were "I've Still Got My Health" and "I'm Throwing a Ball Tonight."

It is not generally known that it was at a performance of *Panama Hattie* that June Allyson made her first important step toward stardom. She was a member of the chorus when, in 1941, she was called upon to substitute for Betty Hutton, stricken with measles. "June Allyson did a perfect job," Ethel Merman recalls. "I'd never seen an understudy take over with such confidence." It was as a result of this performance that Allyson won from George Abbott a starring role in her next stage appearance, *Best Foot Forward.*

1941 LET'S FACE IT, a musical comedy with book by Herbert and Dorothy Fields, based on the stage comedy, *The Cradle Snatchers*. Produced by Vinton Freedley at the Imperial Theatre on October 29. Staged by Edgar MacGregor. Dances and ensembles staged by Charles Walters. Cast included Danny Kaye, Eve Arden, Mary Jane Walsh, and Edith Meiser (547 performances).

The Cradle Snatchers was a Broadway sex comedy in which three ladies decide to avenge themselves on their wandering husbands by taking in young gigolos for the week end. *Let's Face It* borrowed only the bare essentials of the plot, superimposing upon it timely military trimmings. The three women in *Let's Face It* are Nancy Collister (Vivian Vance), Cornelia Abigail Pigeon (Edith Meiser), and Maggie Watson (Eve Arden). Since they reside in Southampton, Long Island—only a stone's throw from Camp Roosevelt—they decide to take on three inductees as young gigolo lovers. One is Jerry Walker, played by Danny Kaye in his first starring role following his recent success in *Lady in the Dark*. The other two are Frankie Burns (Benny Baker) and Eddie Hilliard (Jack Williams). Jerry's adventures in Southampton complicate his own love life, since he is in love with Winnie Potter (Mary Lane Walsh), who in the end is ready to forgive and forget. Frequent allusions to the vicissitudes of an inductee's life give the book topical interest to a 1941 audience concerned with the problems of nation-wide conscription and a war in Europe.

As an army inductee, Kaye delivered a routine that from then on became a staple of his repertory: "Melody in Four F," a tongue-twister relating in double talk the adventures of being conscripted into the army. That song, and another routine entitled "A Modern Fairy Tale," were interpolated into the score for Kaye and are not by Porter but by Sylvia Fine (Mrs. Danny Kaye) in collaboration with Max Liebman. The best Cole Porter song was a ballad, "Everything I Love," presented by Winnie. The lighter numbers included a travesty on rural life, "Farming," "Ace in the Hole," and a saucy duet, "You Irritate Me So."

1943   SOMETHING FOR THE BOYS, a musical comedy with book by Herbert and Dorothy Fields. Produced by Michael Todd at the Alvin Theatre on January 7. Staged by Hassard Short. Book directed by Herbert Fields. Dances by Jack Cole. Cast included Ethel Merman, Paula Laurence, Bill Johnson, and Allen Jenkins (422 performances).

In 1943 America was preoccupied with a global war. Military affairs and characters, which they had injected into *Let's Face It*, continued to dominate the writing and thinking of Herbert and Dorothy Fields. In *Something for the Boys*, the main characters are three cousins, each strangers to the others, located by the Court of Missing Heirs to take over the inheritance of a Texas ranch. They are Blossom Hart, a former chorus girl recently become a defense worker (Ethel Merman), Chiquita Hart, a night-club singer from Kansas City (Paula Laurence), and a New York sidewalk hawker, Harry Hart (Allen Jenkins). They meet for the first time on the Plaza of the Alamo in San Antonio, take an instantaneous dislike to each other, but, for the sake of the inheritance, decide to bury the hatchet. The ranch proves to be a broken-down building near the air base, Keeley Field. An industrious and ambitious girl, Blossom decides to turn the building into a boardinghouse for fliers' wives and to organize a defense plant in some of the lower-story rooms. One of those stationed at Keeley Field is Sergeant Rocky Fulton (Bill Johnson), who falls in love with Blossom. But Rocky is being pursued by Melanie Walker (Frances Mercer), daughter of a Senator. In an effort to break up the budding affair between Blossom and Rocky, and to ruin her rival, Melanie hints to the commanding officer of Keeley Field that Blossom's house is actually a house of ill repute. The commanding officer immediately orders the house off limits for his men. With the world tumbling around her ears, Blossom makes the fantastic discovery that she is a human radio, thanks to the carborundum fillings in her bridgework. Revealing this information to the commanding officer makes her a heroine, since every soldier now can be his own radio. She also saves a plane and its fliers by serving as a radio when the one in the plane breaks down. Winning the interest of the commanding officer, she can now straighten him out about the nature of her establishment. The house is reopened and Blossom and Rocky are reunited.

Ethel Merman's biggest numbers include "Hey, Good Looking," "The Leader of the Big Time Band," "He's a Right Guy," and "Something for the Boys." With Paula Laurence she delivers a comedy song that Brooks Atkinson considered "the funniest moment in a musical show this year"—"By the Mississinewah," in which they appeared as two Indian maids from Indiana. The best sentimental number was "I'm in Love." The score also included a fine patter song in "There's a Happy Land in the Sky" and a take-off on a well-known cowboy song in "When We're Home on the Range."

1944   MEXICAN HAYRIDE, a musical comedy with book by Herbert and Dorothy Fields. Produced by Michael Todd at the Winter Garden on January 28. Staged by Hassard Short. Choreography by Paul Haakon. Cast included June Havoc, Bobby Clark, Wilbur Evans, and George Givot (481 performances).

A Mexican setting, a lady bullfighter from the United States, and an American fugitive from justice are some of the ingredients that make up this appetizing dish. The fugitive is Joe Bascom, alias Humphrey Fish (Bobby Clark); the American lady bullfighter, Montana (June Havoc). In the Plaza de Toros, after her successful tussle with the bull, Montana is about to throw the bull's ear to David Winthrop, American *chargé d'affaires* (Wilbur Evans), a token of her interest in him. But on catching a glimpse of Joe in the stands, she grows so furious that she forgets herself and throws the ear at him. Winning the ear brings Joe the distinction of being "Amigo Americano," which brings with it the adulation of the Mexican people and lovely señoritas. Joe now joins up with the shady speculator, Lombo Campos (George Givot) to form a national lottery. Caught up by Mexican justice they are forced to flee to Xochimilco, where they appear disguised as marachi players, and to Taxco, where they emerge as tortilla vendors. But they are finally captured, and Joe must return to the United States to face trial. At a colorful Mexican fiesta—the most ambitious production number in the play—David and Montana, long separated by misunderstandings and differences, are blissfully reunited.

David's love song to Montana, "I Love You," is the outstanding musical number in the score, and a Cole Porter favorite to this day. Montana sings two amusing ditties, "There Must Be Someone for Me" and "Count Your Blessings," and "Sing to Me, Guitar" is appealing for its Mexican flavor.

1948   KISS ME, KATE, a musical comedy with book by Bella and Samuel Spewack, based on Shakespeare's *The Taming of the Shrew*. Produced by Saint Subber and Lemuel Ayers at the New Century Theatre on December 30. Staged by John C. Wilson. Dances by Hanya Holm. Cast included Alfred Drake, Lisa Kirk, Patricia Morison, and Harold Lang (1077 performances).

As one of a handful of musical comedies to enter the select circle of a thousand performances or more, *Kiss Me, Kate* is one of the outstanding box-office successes of the American theater. It is also an artistic triumph acclaimed not only in this country but also abroad. Presented at the Volksoper on February 14, 1956, it proved the greatest hit in the fifty-eight-year history of that theater. It was subsequently performed with outstanding success throughout Germany, and became the first American musical given in Poland, where it was played two hundred times to sold-out houses.

The springboard for the Spewack text is Shakespeare's comedy about the taming of the shrew Katherine. Fred Graham (Alfred Drake) and Lilli Vanessi (Patricia Morison), though divorced, are the stars of a troupe performing the Shakespeare play. It does not take them long to realize that the flame of their onetime love has not been completely extinguished by the law court. Nevertheless, Fred finds amatory diversion with Lois Lane (Lisa Kirk), who in turn is being pursued by the irresponsible gambler, Bill Calhoun (Harold Lang). The play shifts from present-day Baltimore, where the Shakespeare play is being presented, and the love problems of the principal performers, to the Shakespearean comedy itself, to Padua and the marital distress of Petruchio and Kate. Elizabethan dialogue and Cole Porter sophistication are synchronized in both the dialogue and the lyrics. Eventually the unity of time and place get confused as Lilli, playing the role of the shrew, directs her violent abuse not only against Petruchio but against her ex-husband who is playing that part; and the inevitable reconciliation takes place within an actual performance of *The Taming of the Shrew.*

For Patricia Morison the part of Lilli was her first Broadway starring role; her only previous Broadway appearance had been in 1938 in an inept, ill-fated operetta, *The Two Bouquets,* in which she had also starred with Alfred Drake. After that she played in several minor motion pictures.

The brilliant Spewack book, the felicitous performances of the principals, and Hanya Holm's exciting choreography were some of the elements in this remarkable musical comedy. The Cole Porter score was another significant element, "one of the loveliest and most lyrical yet composed for the contemporary stage," in the opinion of Walter F. Kerr. Porter was at his most sensual in two outstanding love songs, "So in Love Am I" and "Were Thine That Special Face." Tapping his satiric vein, he produced an amusing take-off on the Continental type of operetta waltz melody in "Wunderbar." His sophisticated wit flashed in "I Hate Men," "Too Darn Hot" (which led to an incendiary dance), "Where Is the Life That Late I Led?", "Always True to You," and "Brush Up Your Shakespeare."

1953   CAN-CAN, a musical comedy with book by Abe Burrows. Produced by Feuer and Martin at the Shubert Theatre on May 7. Staged by Abe Burrows. Dances and musical numbers staged by Michael Kidd. Cast included Lilo, Peter Cookson, Hans Conried, Erik Rhodes, and Gwen Verdon (892 performances).

Can-Can was a nostalgic excursion into Bohemian Paris of 1893, a period piece of the Paris of Toulouse-Lautrec, the cancan, and the Moulin Rouge. Paris was evoked in the eye-filling beauty of the scenery and costuming—particularly in Jo Mielziner's opening curtain picture of the city; and in his set atop Paris' rooftops; in some of the brilliant dances—an apache dance, for example, and the cancan that closes the play; in the magnetizing performances of two Broadway newcomers, Lilo and Gwen Verdon.

The story revolves around an investigation of the scandalous dancing seen at a Montmartre café owned by La Mome Pistache (Lilo). An upright judge, Aristide Forestier (Peter Cookson), is dispatched to make an investigation. He succumbs to the temptation of Montmartre night life, and particularly to the winning ways of Pistache. He now uses his legal skill to clear the names of night club and owner. A subsidiary plot involves the amatory complications of a soubrette, Claudine (Gwen Verdon), who is torn between her interest in a Bulgarian sculptor, Boris (Hans Conried), and an art critic, Hilaire (Erik Rhodes). Comic relief comes in the amusing caricature of the sculptor, in an evaluation of his work by the critic, in a brilliant burlesque of a duel atop a Parisian rooftop, in a travesty on an apache dance, and in a comic ballet in the Garden of Eden.

Lilo, imported from Paris for her first American appearance, was a definite winner. The nostalgic and throbbing way she sang "I Love Paris," "C'est Magnifique" and "Allez-Vous-En" did much to create a Parisian atmosphere. But the performer who stopped the show was Gwen Verdon, also new to Broadway. Before *Can-Can* she had made some inauspicious appearances as a dancer in light opera, in a musical that closed out of town, in night clubs, and with the Jack Cole dancers. Her work and personality went unnoticed by all except Michael Kidd, who thought of her when he cast his dances for *Can-Can*. Her dynamic personality, as flaming as her red-tousled hair, won the audience completely. She brought down the house with her wild, uninhibited apache dancing in "The Apaches" and with a strip-tease routine in "The Garden of Eden."

1955   SILK STOCKINGS, a musical comedy with book by George S. Kaufman, Leueen MacGrath, and Abe Burrows, suggested by the motion-picture, *Ninotchka*. Produced by Feuer and Martin at the Imperial Theatre on February 24. Staged by Cy Feuer. Dances and musical numbers staged by Eugene Loring. Cast included Don Ameche, Hildegarde Neff, and Gretchen Wyler (478 performances).

Silk Stockings was Cole Porter's twenty-fifth Broadway score, and during its run his fortieth anniversary as composer for the theater was celebrated. *Silk Stockings* proved a happy event for two happy celebrations, for, as Brooks Atkinson said of it, it was "one of Gotham's memorable shows, on a level with *Guys and Dolls*," and with some of the "wittiest dialogue in years."

In *Silk Stockings*, Cole Porter made his second invasion of the Soviet Union, the first having been in *Leave It to Me*. But the satire cuts deeper in the later play. Americans are still the butt of malicious humor as they had been earlier; particularly devastating in *Silk Stockings* were the portraits of a high-powered artist's agent and a loud and vulgar movie star. But in *Silk Stockings* the main ammunition is reserved for Soviet officialdom (as in the broad caricatures of Soviet agents in Ivanov, Brankov, and Bibinski), for Soviet red tape, and for the tyranny of dictatorship. The commissar of art asks for a copy of "Who's Still Who." When a Soviet agent is informed that the great Soviet composer, Prokofiev, is dead he remarks sadly, "I didn't even know he was arrested." Passing the buck of authority from top to bottom, with each in turn shrugging off the responsibility for decisive action and decisions, becomes an indoor sport. And all this satire is not confined exclusively to the text. There are travesties on Russian songs to which slick, suave Porter lyrics are wedded with delightful incongruity, on pseudo-Russian music in antiphonal choruses combining asides on dialectical materialism with romantic balladry, as in "Siberia" or "Too Bad."

The original source of *Silk Stockings* was *Ninotchka*, a motion picture in which Greta Garbo had starred in 1939. In the musical, as in the movie, Ninotchka is a hard-boiled, frozen-faced Soviet agent (Hildegarde Neff) sent to Paris to bring back to Russia a composer of serious music, Peter Ilyitch Boroff (Philip Sterling), writing music in France for a motion-picture adaptation of *War and Peace*. In Paris, Ninotchka comes into contact with luxury, jazz, freedom, good living—and most seductive of all, the charm and personal attraction of Steve Canfield, an artist's agent (Don Ameche), who represents the composer. She falls in love and begins to waver between her desire to live with Steve in the free world and her sense of duty, which dictates that she return to the Soviet Union. Now it is the mission of three Soviet agents to come to Paris to watch over Ninotchka: Ivanov (Henry Lascoe), Brankov (Leon Belasco), and Bibinski (David Opatoshu). She does return to her native land, but Steve follows her and effects her escape to a world Ninotchka can no longer forget.

The romance of Ninotchka and Steve provides a mellow antidote to the humor and satire. Broad comedy is injected through the antics of Ivanov, Brankov, and Bibinski in Paris. It is also introduced through the character of Janice Dayton (Gretchen Wyler), an exuberant, sexy, noisy Hollywood movie star. Gretchen Wyler was here making her first Broadway appearance, and her voluptuous personality and uninhibited ways won the audience completely—particularly in a hilarious strip-tease number, "Josephine."

The main love song was Steve Canfield's geographical survey of the girl he loves in "All of You." An equally effective ballad, "As on through the Seasons We Sail," was shared by Canfield and Ninotchka, and a great deal of nostalgia for Paris was created with still another duet of Canfield and Ninotchka, "Paris Loves Lovers."

RICHARD RODGERS, composer

I. RODGERS AND HART

Richard Rodgers was born in Hammels Station, near Arverne, Long Island, on June 28, 1902. His father was a physician, his mother an amateur pianist. His first musical experiences came at home from hearing his father sing and his mother play songs from the famous operettas then popular on Broadway. Dick began playing the piano by ear when he was four. He soon received some instruction from an aunt, then from a local teacher. But he disliked scales, exercises, and reading music from the printed page, and before long formal study was abandoned. Henceforth, and for some time to come, he learned music by trial and error, by continually improvising melodies of his own or playing his favorite songs to his own formal accompaniments. He became an expert ear-executant and eventually learned to put down his melodies on paper.

The piano was not his only passion; another was the theater. He saw his first musical when he was only six. Before long he was an inveterate theatergoer. At first he enjoyed the operettas of Victor Herbert and others. Then in 1916 he saw a Jerome Kern musical for the first time—it was *Very Good, Eddie*—and a new world seemed to open up for him. He now lost interest in foreign-made operettas and sought out American musical comedies, particularly those by Kern. He sometimes saw a Kern musical half a dozen times. The vitality and freshness of Kern's music was something of a revelation. "The influence of the hero on such a hero worshiper," he later wrote, "is not easy to calculate."

At the New York public schools he occasionally played the piano at assemblies. At his own graduation ceremonies, at P.S. 166, in 1916, he performed a potpourri of opera melodies that he himself prepared. He also engaged in musical activity at Weingart's summer camp, where he spent several summers from 1914 on. There, in 1916, he wrote his first complete songs, "Campfire Days" and "The Auto Show Girl," the latter a bouncy one-step, which he multigraphed for private distribution.

While attending De Witt Clinton High School, Rodgers became a dedicated lover of good music by attending opera and concert performances. But his musical ambitions never rose above the popular field, and he kept on writing popular songs. In 1917, through his brother Mortimer (now a successful gynecologist) he was asked to write a complete score for an amateur production put on by a boys' club in New York. This show, *One Minute Please,* was presented at the Hotel Plaza on December 29, 1917—Rodgers' debut in writing for the stage. He kept on writing songs for other amateur productions after that.

Up to now he had been writing melodies to lyrics by various friends or relatives. In 1918 he acquired a permanent working partner in Lorenz Hart, who was to be his only lyricist for the next quarter of a century. They met at Hart's house on 119th Street through a mutual friend. At the time Hart was twenty-three, Rodgers was only sixteen. During that first meeting Rodgers was impressed by the older man's wit, sophistication, cultural background and skill at versification—most of all by his trenchant ideas of what a good song should be. Hart recognized Dick's musical gifts immediately. Before the afternoon was over they knew they would henceforth work together. "It was a case of love at first sight," Rodgers recalls. "I acquired in one afternoon a partner, a best friend—and a source of permanent irritation."

Lorenz Hart was born in New York City on May 2, 1895. Except for a brief period at De Witt Clinton High School, his entire elementary and secondary schooling took place in private schools: at Weingart's Institute and the Columbia Grammar School. In 1913, after a European holiday with his family, he entered Columbia College. There, after a single year, he transferred to the school of journalism. While he had always been a brilliant student in literature and languages, and while he did well in all his college subjects, his major interest was the Varsity Show. In 1915 and 1916 he appeared in the Columbia Varsity Shows as a female impersonator, besides writing skits and satirical lyrics.

He left Columbia in 1917 without a degree. For several summers he worked at Brant Lake Camp, a boys' summer camp, putting on shows. His aim was the theater, and for a while he worked for the Shuberts translating German operettas into English, saving his money to produce two plays, both failures. A brilliant intelligence, a fine cultural background that embraced music and opera as well as the theater, and an original and creative thinker, Hart was searching for some avenue of his own in the theater when he first met Richard Rodgers.

Rodgers and Hart began by writing a few songs that, one summer day in 1919, Rodgers brought to Rockaway Beach to play for Lew Fields. Fields liked one particularly, "Any Old Place with You," and placed it into his production of *A Lonely Romeo* on August 16, 1919, where it was sung by Eve Lynn and Alan Hale. This was the official entry of Rodgers and Hart into the professional theater; and this song was also their first to get published.

In the fall of 1919 Rodgers entered Columbia College. During his first year there he worked with Hart on the Varsity Show, *Fly with Me*, produced in the grand ballroom of Hotel Astor on March 24, 1920, Rodgers conducting. This was the first time that the work of a freshman had been taken for one of the Varsity Shows. "Several of the tunes are capital," reported the columnist S. Jay Kaufman in the *Globe*. "They have a really finished touch. . . . We had not heard of Richard Rodgers before. We have a suspicion we shall hear of him again."

Lew Fields liked the Rodgers' music of *Fly with Me* so well that he offered to use some of the numbers in a Broadway production he was projecting. Seven Rodgers and Hart songs appeared in *The Poor Little Ritz Girl*, which opened on July 28, 1920. (Eight other songs in this production were by the veteran, Sigmund Romberg.) Since *The Poor Little Ritz Girl* had a run of 119 performances, the first of the Rodgers and Hart musicals on Broadway was a modest hit. Of Rodgers' music, H. T. Parker, the noted Boston drama and music critic said: "He writes uniformly with a light hand; now and then with neat modulations or pretty turns of ornament; here and there with a clear sensibility to instrumental voices; and once again with a hint of grace and fancy."

It was some time before Rodgers and Hart reappeared successfully on Broadway. Meanwhile they took any assignment that came along, mostly for amateur productions. During this period they acquired a third collaborator—Herbert Fields, son of Lew—who sometimes was the stage director of their amateur shows and sometimes wrote the books for their musical comedies. With Herbert Fields, Rodgers and Hart completed *Winkle Town*, a musical that was never produced. Using the pen name of Herbert Richard Lorenz, they also wrote a Tin Pan Alley comedy, *The Melody Man*, in which Lew Fields starred, presented on May 13, 1924. This last production had only two Rodgers and Hart songs, both of them travesties on Tin Pan Alley. *The Melody Man* was a failure.

Discouragement in the slow progress he was making led Rodgers in 1922 to abandon his song-writing career and return to music study. He spent the next two years at the Institute of Musical Art, and during this

Vandamm Studio

Victor Moore as Vice-President Throttlebottom and
William Gaxton as President Wintergreen in the first
musical to win the Pulitzer Prize, *Of Thee I Sing* (1931)

t to right: Ethel Waters starts a "Heat Wave" in *As Thousands Cheer*
933). Fred and Adele Astaire in *The Band Wagon* (1931), their last ap-
arance as a team. Fred Allen in his first Broadway success, *The Little*
ow (1929). There's *Music in the Air* in the little Bavarian town of Eden-
rff (1932)

A scene from *On Your Toes* (1936). (The two gentlemen in the center are Monty Woolley and Ray Bolger)

Mitzi Green and two young men in *Babes in Arms* (1937)

Vandamm Studio

Gene Kelly is "Bewitched, Bothered, and Bewildered" by Vivienne Segal in *Pal Joey* (1940)

A scene from *Roberta* (1933). The man seated at the piano is a young and still unknown comedian named Bob Hope. Standing near him is young George Murphy. Tamara is standing behind Fay Templeton

Todd Duncan and Ann Brown in *Porgy and Bess* (1935)

left: Todd Duncan, Ethel Waters, and Rex Ingram in *Cabin in the Sky* (1940). *right:* Luther Saxon and Muriel Smith in *Carmen Jones* (1943)

Vandamm Studio

above: Oklahoma! (1943). right:
Carousel (1945)

Vandamm Studio

Vandamm Studio

A scene from Irving Berlin's *This Is the Army* (1942)

Vandamm Studio

Danny Kaye and Eve Arden in *Let's Face It* (1941)

A scene from *Brigadoon* (1947)

Sono Osato as exotic Ivy Smith in *On the Town* (1944)

Ezio Pinza and Mary Martin find an "enchanted evening" in *South Pacific* (1949)

Yul Brynner and Gertrude Lawrence in *The King and I* (1951)

Carol Haney and Marguerite Shaw as employees of the Sleep-Tite pajama factory in *The Pajama Game* (1954)

Stephen Douglass discovers from Gwen Verdon "Whatever Lola Wants," in *Damn Yankees* (1955)

Photo by Talbot

Ethel Merman discovers that "You Can't Get a Man with a Gun" in *Annie Get Your Gun* (1946)

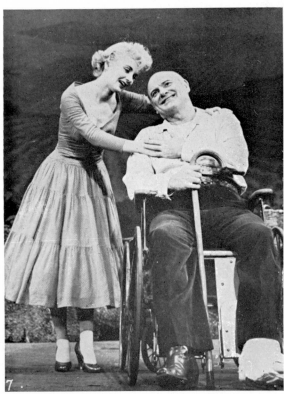

Photo by Arthur Cantor

Jo Sullivan makes Robert Weede *The Most Happy Fella* (1956)

Teen-age street gangs meet at a dance in
West Side Story (1957)

Iggie Wolfington and Robert Preston do a
buck and wing in *The Music Man* (1957)

Photo by Fred Fehl

Friedman-Abeles

Julie Andrews and Rex Harrison in *My Fair Lady* (1957)

period he wrote and helped to put on several shows for the school; and for a few months he served as conductor of Lew Fields' *Snapshots of 1922*, which was then touring the Shubert vaudeville circuit.

After leaving the Institute, Rodgers resumed collaboration with Hart in writing amateur shows. Once again he became discouraged, as neither producers nor publishers seemed interested in what he was doing. This time Rodgers decided to leave music for good and enter business by becoming a salesman for a children's underwear firm. He was about to accept this job when he and Hart were offered the assignment to write the music for *The Garrick Gaieties*, a production put on by several young people connected with the Theatre Guild. The success of *The Garrick Gaieties* in 1925 established the reputation of Rodgers and Hart.

In the same year, 1925, Rodgers and Hart had another successful musical on Broadway—*Dearest Enemy*, for which Herbert Fields wrote the book. During the next half-dozen years Rodgers and Hart wrote the songs for musical comedies, with books by Fields, which not only were major box-office successes but also were responsible for introducing some new techniques and approaches to the writing of musical comedy and which continually tapped fresh and unorthodox materials. These musicals —from *Dearest Enemy* (1925) to *America's Sweetheart* (1931)—made the team of Rodgers, Hart, and Fields a triumvirate that ruled the musical stage for a decade. Several of their shows, however, were failures—but are remembered because they were the point of origin for some unforgettable songs by Rodgers and Hart: "With a Song in My Heart" in *Spring Is Here* (1929); "Ten Cents a Dance" made famous by Ruth Etting in the Ed Wynn extravaganza, *Simple Simon* (1930); "A Ship Without a Sail" in *Heads Up* (1929).

In 1930 Rodgers and Hart went out to Hollywood where for a few years they wrote songs for various motion pictures. They were back on Broadway in 1934, and made their reappearance on the Broadway stage with the Billy Rose circus extravaganza, *Jumbo*. Both Rodgers and Hart now became fired with the ambition of abandoning old formulas and clichés of musical comedy for good by realizing a musical play in which every element would be integral to the play and which would treat unusual themes. With a series of remarkable successes beginning with *On Your Toes* (1937) and ending with *By Jupiter* (1942), they created a veritable revolution in the musical theater.

Hart had never been a disciplined worker, and collaborating with him had always been a serious problem to Rodgers. To his formerly irresponsible ways Hart added, after 1940, a deterioration of health and spirit brought on mostly by alcoholic excesses. After *By Jupiter* he lost the will to work and, eager for a long vacation in Mexico, asked Rodgers to seek out a new collaborator. A proposition from the Theatre Guild—to set Lynn Riggs' folk play *Green Grow the Lilacs* to music—held little interest for Hart. He went off for his Mexican holiday, and Rodgers found a new collaborator in Oscar Hammerstein II.

After Hart's return from Mexico, Rodgers tried to revive his interest in creation by bringing back to Broadway *A Connecticut Yankee*—their success of 1927—for which he and Hart wrote some new songs, including "To Keep My Love Alive." For a while it seemed that Hart was willing to settle down, but after the play tried out in Philadelphia he was off again on a binge that made it necessary to hospitalize him in New York. He disappeared from the theater at the New York première of the revival on November 17, 1943, and was not seen for two days. When found, he was lying unconscious on his hotel bed. He died soon after that at Doctors Hospital, on November 22. Five years after his death the story of his collaboration with Rodgers was told in the motion-picture, *Words and Music*, in which Mickey Rooney played Hart, and Tom Drake, Rodgers.

The partnership of Rodgers and Hart was one of the most fruitful in the entire history of the American musical stage. They wrote twenty-seven musicals in twenty-five years, and for these productions they completed about a thousand songs. The impact of their work on the musical theater, on popular music, and on the song lyric can hardly be overestimated. They changed the destiny of the musical stage by carrying the musical comedy to full maturity. And they enriched popular music through the inventiveness and originality of Rodgers' music and Larry Hart's incomparably brilliant lyrics.

1925-26   *The Garrick Gaieties*

1925 edition, a revue with sketches and additional lyrics by Benjamin Kaye, Louis Sorin, Sam Jaffe, Newman Levy, and Morrie Ryskind, among others. Presented by the Theatre Guild sponsoring the Theatre Guild Junior Players at the Garrick Theatre on May 17. Directed by Philip Loeb. Dances arranged by Herbert Fields. Cast included Sterling Holloway, Romney Brent, June Cochrane, Betty Starbuck, Philip Loeb, Edith Meiser, and Hildegarde Halliday (161 performances).

1926 edition, a revue with sketches by Benjamin Kaye, Newman Levy, Herbert Fields, and Philip Loeb, among others. Presented by the Theatre Guild at the Garrick Theatre on May 10. Staged by Philip Loeb.

Dances and musical numbers staged by Herbert Fields. Cast included Romney Brent, Hildegarde Halliday, Sterling Holloway, Philip Loeb, Edith Meiser, Betty Starbuck, and Lee Strasberg (174 performances).

In the fall of 1924 a group of youngsters associated with the Theatre Guild met from time to time to discuss the possibility of putting on a smart, intimate revue, placing emphasis on satire and parody. These youngsters were supplemented by Benjamin Kaye, a lawyer and a friend of the Richard Rodgers family who liked writing satirical sketches and lyrics. When their planning became serious—and it first became serious when they decided to use such a production to finance two tapestries for a new theater then being built by the Theatre Guild as a permanent home—Kaye brought Rodgers and Hart into the picture to provide the songs for the revue.

The revue, called *The Garrick Gaieties*, was informal and intimate, gay and sophisticated, spirited and youthful. It included parodies of current plays, travesties on a variety of subjects ranging from the New York police to the celebrated diseuse, Ruth Draper. The Rodgers and Hart songs (of which there were seven) were just as bright and fresh. Two became hits: "Manhattan" (still popular), introduced by June Cochrane and Sterling Holloway, and "Sentimental Me," sung by Cochrane, Holloway, James Norris, and Edith Meiser. In addition to these songs there was an American "jazz opera," *The Joy Spreader* (libretto by Hart)—but this was given only during the first two performances.

The critics raved. To Alexander Woollcott it was "bright with the brightness of something new minted"; to Robert Garland, it was the "most civilized show in town"; Gilbert Gabriel described it as a "witty, boisterous, athletic chowchow." The songs of Rodgers and Hart also gathered praise. "They clicked," reported *Variety*, "like a colonel's heels at attention."

The original plan had been to give only two presentations—matinee and evening of Sunday, May 17. But the praises of the critics and the delight of the audience called for a longer run. Four more performances were scheduled in June (all matinees), all of them sellouts. Finally it was put on a regular run, beginning with June 8, and it remained in town twenty-five weeks. *The Garrick Gaieties* not only carried Rodgers and Hart to their first success—a not inconsiderable achievement when we contemplate their subsequent work—but it also made popular the intimate, smart, economically devised revue, a genre that flourished in the Broadway theater for the next decade or so.

The second edition, a year later, once again brought joy and gaiety to the stage. Again there were irreverent parodies of current plays; again gay take-offs and witty sketches (the best being Hildegarde Halliday's impression of Queen Elizabeth and Newman Levy's sketches on George Washington and society ladies). Among the new Rodgers and Hart songs was a new hit, "Mountain Greenery," sung by Bobbie Perkins and Sterling Holloway. In a more ambitious vein was a burlesque of musical comedy, *Rose of Arizona*, in which some of the song styles of the day were parodied.

> Young Rodgers [reported Frank Vreeland] more than fulfilled the promise of yesteryear. . . . In the freshness and spontaneity of his work he is the most auspicious young composer for musical comedy in our midst, and should develop into the Irving Berlin of the future.

1925   DEAREST ENEMY, a musical comedy, with book by Herbert Fields. Presented by George Ford at the Knickerbocker Theatre on September 18. Staged by John Murray Anderson. Dances and ensembles directed by Carl Hemmer. Cast included Helen Ford, Charles Purcell, and Flavia Arcaro (286 performances).

Before *The Garrick Gaieties* established their success, Rodgers and Hart were strolling along Madison Avenue, New York, in the company of Herbert Fields, discussing possible subjects for musical comedies. They lingered momentarily in front of a building on 37th Street that bore the following plaque:

> *Howe, with Clinton, Tryon, and a few others, went to the house of Robert Murray, on Murray Hill, for refreshment and rest. With pleasant conversations and a profusion of cake and wine, the good Whig lady detained the gallant Britons almost two hours. Quite long enough for the bulk of Putnam's division of four thousand men to leave the city and escape to the heights of Harlem by Bloomingdale Road, with the loss of only a few soldiers.*

Hart recognized in this episode from American history the makings of a good musical-comedy plot, and won over his collaborators. Herbert Fields expanded the Murray Hill incident into a full-blown plot. On instructions from George Washington, Mrs. Robert Murray (Flavia Arcaro) detains British officers "by every means at your discretion," as Washington had suggested, long enough to permit the Continental Army to make a strategic withdrawal. A secondary plot involved a romance between the Irish niece of Mrs. Murray, Betsy Burke (Helen Ford), and the redcoat, Captain Sir John Copeland (Charles Purcell).

The story permitted Fields to engage in some discreet pornography, and much of the humor of the play stemmed from such risqué remarks and situations. Betsy Burke makes her first-act entrance protecting her nudity with a barrel: While swimming in Kipp's Bay a dog had stolen her clothing. Double-entendres spiced the dialogue which followed between herself and Captain Henry Tryon (John Seymour). "At first glance," says John, "I thought you were a boy." Betsy replies demurely: "Well, you should have taken a second look." Later on in the play, the Continental ladies learn that British troops are on their way. "Hooray, we are gonna be compromised," they sing, and add philosophically, "war is war."

Notwithstanding this gay and at times impudent text *Dearest Enemy* found few takers among the producers. Not even Herbert's father, Lew, was sympathetic to it, insisting, "the public just won't buy it, for who ever heard of a musical comedy based on American history?" Eventually, an ally was found in the musical-comedy star, Helen Ford, who wanted to play Betsy. Helen Ford interested her husband George, and after that John Murray Anderson. Then it was produced—but only after the first *Garrick Gaieties* had made Rodgers and Hart song writers of consequence.

The handsome production provided the play with some of its attraction. Reginald Marsh designed a striking intermission curtain, a map of old New York. For the play itself such attractive sets and costumes had been designed that, as Alexander Woollcott reported, the play presented an "endlessly lovely picture," which alone was "worth the price of admission."

Rodgers' score was such an ambitious collation of songs, duets, trios, choral numbers (also a delightful gavotte evoking the eighteenth century) that Percy Hammond described the play as a "baby grand opera." The hit song was "Here in My Arms," presented just before the first-act finale by Betsy Burke and Sir John. Another song appealed for its sly wit and sex insinuation, "Old Enough to Love"; and to "Cheerio," Sir John and his officers brought a winning martial spirit.

1926   THE GIRL FRIEND, a musical comedy with book by Herbert Fields. Produced by Lew Fields at the Vanderbilt Theatre on March 17. Production supervised by Lew Fields. Musical numbers arranged and staged by Jack Haskell. Cast included Sam White, Eva Puck, and June Cochrane (409 performances).

When *The Melody Man,* by Rodgers, Hart, and Herbert Fields, was running on Broadway, its authors promised two stars of that show, Sam White and Eva Puck, that they would some day write an intimate musical comedy for them. They kept that promise with *The Girl Friend*. In this play Sam White was cast as a cyclist, Leonard Silver. Silver becomes proficient by training on a wheel attached to a churn on his Long Island dairy farm. Eva Puck was Mollie Farrell, daughter of a professional cyclist, with whom Leonard is in love. An unscrupulous cycling promoter encourages Leonard to enter a fixed six-day race. Despite the devious efforts of corrupt gamblers, Leonard is victorious in the race and wins his girl.

It is not an original or imaginative plot, but it lent distinction through amusing episodes (a burlesque on grand opera, for example, and another on minstrel shows), through some striking dances (particularly by Dorothy Barbour), and through the music of Rodgers. Two songs were of particular merit; both became outstanding hits in 1926. The first was the title song with its rhythmic interest, and the second "Blue Room," its melody of surpassing charm; both were sung by Leonard and Mollie.

As a matter of fact, the two hit songs were largely responsible for making *The Girl Friend* a success. Business at first was slow. But when the two songs gained popularity throughout the country, interest in the play was aroused to a point where it attracted enough customers to warrant a run of over 400 performances; *The Girl Friend* also had a second company on the road.

1926   PEGGY-ANN, a musical comedy with book by Herbert Fields based on *Tillie's Nightmare* by Edgar Smith. Presented by Lew Fields and Lyle D. Andrews at the Vanderbilt Theatre on December 27. Production supervised by Lew Fields. Musical numbers and dances arranged by Seymour Felix. Cast included Helen Ford, Lester Cole, Lulu McConnell, and Betty Starbuck (333 performances).

The dream fantasies of the heroine, Peggy-Ann, provide the startlingly unorthodox material that makes up the plot of this musical play, one of the earliest attempts on the American musical stage to exploit Freudian psychology.

The story itself is not unusual. Peggy-Ann (Helen Ford) is the daughter of a boardinghouse proprietress, Mrs. Frost (Lulu McConnell), in Glens Falls, New York. For three years she is the fiancée of a local boy, Guy Pendleton (Lester Cole). Swallowed in the morass of a humdrum existence, she can find escape only in dreams and fantasies. There she sees herself in New York, the wealthy heroine of many adventures, including a love idyl aboard a yacht, and marriage. Her dreams must finally be crushed by reality, which dictates that she reconcile herself to both Glens Falls and Guy Pendleton.

It is in the treatment of this plot that the musical becomes a daring, and at times a brilliant, adventure. Fantasy becomes inextricably intertwined with reality; the absurd, the impossible, the grotesque acquire plausibility. When Peggy-Ann makes her trip to New York, accompanied by a chorus of girls, the scene shifts from Glens Falls to the metropolis while the girls change from country to city dress. What follows in New York acquires a kind of surrealistic quality, as chaos is projected through undisciplined lighting and disordered dancing; absurdities mount, the confusions grow. Pills become as large as golf balls; fish speak with an English accent; the New York City police wear pink mustaches; race horses are interviewed. At her wedding Peggy-Ann appears only in stepins, and the ceremony calls for the use of a telephone book in place of a Bible. A yacht, in which Peggy-Ann takes a cruise with her lover, becomes the scene of a mutiny when the crew discovers the pair is not married.

The authors were equally bold in their use of musical-comedy techniques. There was no singing or dancing for the first fifteen minutes of the production; and the play ended on a darkened stage with a slow comedy dance. All this meant the shattering of existing musical-comedy procedures—and so did the ballet character of the dancing and the integration of the musical numbers with the action. Though Rodgers' score often caught the strange and nebulous character of the stage action through a considerable amount of atmospheric music, it also had some solid hit songs: "A Tree in the Park" and "Maybe It's Me," both duets of Peggy-Ann and Guy; and "Where's That Rainbow?", by Peggy-Ann. A gay Cuban number, "Havana," was also effective.

1927   A CONNECTICUT YANKEE, a musical comedy with book by Herbert Fields based on Mark Twain's *A Connecticut Yankee in King Arthur's Court.* Presented by Lew Fields and Lyle D. Andrews at the Vanderbilt Theatre on November 3. Production supervised by Lew Fields. Staged by Alexander Leftwich. Dances by Busby Berkeley. Cast included William Gaxton, Constance Carpenter, and June Cochrane (418 performances).

The idea of making Mark Twain's story into a musical comedy occurred to Rodgers, Hart, and Fields several years before they achieved success. In 1921, after seeing a silent movie version of the story, they acquired an option, but at the time were unable to gain a hearing from producers and the option was dropped. Six years later they were in a position to realize their ambition, and they sold Lew Fields on producing the play.

In his text Herbert Fields prefaced the adventures of the Yankee in sixth-century Camelot with a modern-day prologue. Alice Carter (Constance Carpenter) is so enraged at her fiancé, Martin (William Gaxton), who flirts with another girl at a party, that she hits him over the head with a champagne bottle. Martin loses consciousness and lapses into dreams. He finds himself a captive in King Arthur's court, doomed to be burned at the stake. He suddenly remembers that an eclipse of the sun is about due, and by ordering the sun to go black he so endears himself to King Arthur's men that they make him "Sir Boss." Now assuming the management of the kingdom (on a percentage basis), Martin proceeds to introduce the refinements of twentieth-century civilization into Camelot, including telephones, efficiency experts, radio, billboards, and so forth. King Arthur's men get into the spirit of things by beginning to talk in slang ("Methinks yon damsel is a lovely broad").

With gay dialogue and some of the wittiest, breeziest lyrics of Hart's career, A Connecticut Yankee proved "a novel amusement in the best of taste," as Brooks Atkinson said. But according to Alexander Woollcott, "it was Richard Rodgers, with his head full of tunes, who made the most valuable contribution . . . [with] so many fetching songs."

The most "fetching" song, however, was not written directly for this play. It was "My Heart Stood Still," which Alice and Martin introduced in the prologue and repeated in the first act. The idea for the lyric came to Rodgers and Hart in Paris when, in a near-accident in a taxi, one of their girl friends remarked, "my heart stood still." Lyric and melody were written soon afterward in London and introduced in the London revue produced by Charles Cochran in 1927, One Dam Thing After Another (sung by Jessie Matthews and Sonny Hale). At first it did not catch on. One evening, at the Café de Paris in London, the Prince of Wales asked the band to play the song for him. When the bandleader confessed he didn't know it, the Prince whistled the melody and the band picked it up. This incident was widely publicized and helped to make the song popular, indeed such a hit that Rodgers and Hart bought it back from Cochran for 5000 dollars and interpolated it into A Connecticut Yankee.

A second song favorite from the score, "Thou Swell," was almost removed from the production before it reached New York. The reaction to it in Philadelphia had been so frigid that the producers insisted that Rodgers take it out. Rodgers said he would agree, but only if the New

York public proved equally apathetic. New York loved the song, and it stayed in.

Other outstanding numbers were "On a Desert Island with Thee" and "I Feel at Home with You," both perhaps more remarkable for their sprightly, sophisticated lyrics than for the melodies.

A revival of *A Connecticut Yankee,* on November 17, 1943, was the last production on which Rodgers and Hart were destined to collaborate. Hart died only a few days after the show opened in New York. Four songs were added to the revival. One of them (in a rousing rendition by Vivienne Segal as Morgan Le Fay) was "To Keep My Love Alive," in one of Larry Hart's happiest tongue-in-cheek styles—a running commentary by Morgan Le Fay on the ways and means of demolishing her various husbands. The revival of *A Connecticut Yankee* also brought the text up-to-date, giving it greater immediacy with a war-conscious audience of 1943; one of the scenes was laid in a munitions factory, and the two principals wore the uniforms of the United States Navy in the prologue.

1928 PRESENT ARMS, a musical comedy with book by Herbert Fields. Presented by Lew Fields at the Lew Fields Mansfield Theatre on April 26. Production supervised by Lew Fields. Staged by Alexander Leftwich. Musical numbers staged by Busby Berkeley. Cast included Charles King, Flora Le Breton, and Busby Berkeley (155 performances).

Herbert Fields had recently collaborated with Vincent Youmans on a successful musical comedy about the Navy called *Hit the Deck.* Having found the Navy a lucrative source for musical-comedy material, Fields convinced Rodgers and Hart to consider the Marines. Fields now prepared a book with a Hawaiian setting in which Chick Evans (Charles King), a Brooklyn hick serving in Pearl Harbor, as buck private in the Marines, flirts with Lady Delphine (Flora Le Breton), daughter of an English peer. She in turn is being sought after by a German, Ludwig von Richter (Anthony Knilling), who is spending his time in Hawaii raising pineapples. In order to make an impression on Lady Delphine, Chick passes himself off as a Captain. He is discovered and dismissed from the service. He also loses the esteem of Lady Delphine, particularly after she learns he is only a plumber's son. By proving his heroism in a yacht wreck, Chick manages to win Lady Delphine's love.

One of the most effective moments in the production came after the shipwreck scene through some ingenious staging. A raft, floating on the sea, is holding three persons. As it floats, a tropical island is sighted in the distance and, without lowering the curtain, a dense forest appears.

Rodgers' music once again won critical approval. To Brooks Atkinson it was "the most beautiful element in the production." The best songs were "You Took Advantage of Me," introduced as a duet between a tourist and a Marine sergeant, played respectively by Joyce Barbour and Busby Berkeley. " 'You Took Advantage of Me,' " wrote Alison Smith, "will alone keep the music of *Present Arms* echoing over the roof gardens far into another summer"—and it did. "A Kiss for Cinderella," a burlesque of the Cinderella theme, sung by a male quartet, was an amusing episode; and two pseudo-Hawaiian numbers in the last scene contributed local color.

1931   AMERICA'S SWEETHEART, a musical comedy with book by Herbert Fields. Presented by Laurence Schwab and Frank Mandel at the Broadhurst Theatre on February 10. Produced under the supervision of Bobby Connolly. Book directed by Monty Woolley. Cast included Jack Whiting, Harriet Lake (now Ann Sothern), Inez Courtney, and Virginia Bruce (135 performances).

In 1930 Rodgers, Hart, and Herbert Fields went out to Hollywood for the first time to work for the movies. Their contact with the motion-picture industry sparked them into writing a satire on movie stars and Hollywood. Their entire play (except for a brief excursion to the Tennessee hills) was set on the movie lot of Premier Pictures. Two innocents, in love with each other, hitchhike from St. Paul to make their fortune in the movies. The girl, Geraldine March (Harriet Lake) becomes a big star in silent films. Her head turned by the adoration she encounters, she loses all interest in her home-town boy friend, Michael Perry (Jack Whiting), who has been unable to make any headway whatsoever in the movies. But the talkies creates a major upheaval in which Michael Perry suddenly comes to the top of the heap, and Geraldine is unceremoniously dumped to the bottom. More levelheaded than his girl friend, Michael is willing to forgive and forget.

The travesties on the life and mores in Hollywood give the play much of its wit and wisdom; and some of the spice is found in the songs. "Sweet Geraldine" pokes fun at movie magazines in a hillbilly style, appropriately enough sung by the Forman Sisters who hailed from the Tennessee hills. "I Want a Man," a lament of a foreign movie star (Denise Torel played by Jeanne Aubert) is a commentary on the Hollywood sex mania, and "Innocent Chorus Girls of Yesterday," sung by a chorus of movie stars, is a lament on Hollywood "has-beens." "There is a rush about the music and a mocking touch in the lyrics," wrote Brooks Atkinson, "that makes the score more deftly satirical than the production."

The most important song was none of these but a number soon to become one of the theme songs of the depression of the early 1930's: "I've Got Five Dollars," a duet between Geraldine and Michael.

With remarkable appropriateness in a musical about Hollywood, there appeared two young actresses later to become stars in Hollywood. One was Harriet Lake who played the heroine, today better known as Ann Sothern; the other was Virginia Bruce, seen in a minor role as a secretary.

1935 JUMBO, a spectacular musical comedy, with book by Ben Hecht and Charles MacArthur. Presented by Billy Rose at the Hippodrome on November 16. Production staged by John Murray Anderson. Book directed by George Abbott. Equestrian, acrobatic, and aerial ballets staged by Allan K. Foster. Cast included Jimmy Durante, Gloria Grafton, Donald Novis, and Paul Whiteman and his orchestra (233 performances).

The ambition to bring back to the Hippodrome Theatre in New York the kind of breath-taking spectacles for which it had been famous two decades earlier led Billy Rose to devise a production combining the best features of musical comedy, circus, spectacle, and carnival. He procured financial backing from Jock Whitney, tore out the insides of the theater to put the stage right in the middle and make the place look like a circus ring; engaged Ben Hecht and Charles MacArthur to write a text. The play itself was a routined affair, but elastic enough to permit daredevil acts, stunts of all kinds, and the accouterments of the circus (jugglers, trapeze acts, clowns, contortionists, wire-walkers, bears, horseback riders, and so forth). The story centered around the rivalry of two circus proprietors: John A. Considine (Arthur Sinclair) and Matthew Mulligan (W. J. McCarthy). Their feud is intensified when Matt Mulligan, Jr. (Donald Novis), and Mickey Considine (Gloria Grafton) fall in love. Because of his weakness for liquor, Father Considine allows his circus to run down and become bankrupt, and at one point the revenue people are about to confiscate his property. In an effort to save his boss, Considine's press agent, Claudius B. Bowers (Jimmy Durante), solves the financial problems by burning down his employer's residence and collecting the insurance. In the end the family feud is amicably settled and the lovers can get married.

Billy Rose stirred interest in his production and kept that interest alive during the months of rehearsal. Outside the Hippodrome he posted huge signs reading: "Sh-sh-*Jumbo* Rehearsing." He offered to sell a private preview to a distiller. When rehearsals kept dragging on, he advertised in the papers: "I'll be a dirty name if I'll open *Jumbo* before it's ready." Tickets for the opening-night performance were nine times the usual size.

He also went to town in mounting the production. It boasted a thousand animals. Jimmy Durante made his first entrance clinging to the neck of an elephant named Big Rosie, better known as "Jumbo"; Paul Whiteman, on a big white horse. Aerial acrobats did stunts dangling on their toes from a speeding plane; one couple balanced themselves on a plank over an open cage of roaring lions; the clown had bananas thrown into his left pocket while he played the violin.

New York had seen nothing like this since the heyday of the Hippodrome, and loved what it saw. Gilbert Gabriel said it was "chockful of so many thrills, musical, scenic, gymnastic, and humanitarian, it deserves an endowment as an institution." The *Literary Digest* wrote of Billy Rose that he had inherited the mantles of Ziegfeld and Barnum.

For Rodgers and Hart, *Jumbo* meant a return to the Broadway theater after an absence of some four years in Hollywood. Apparently refreshed by his absence from the stage, Rodgers produced a score that included three of the best songs of Rodgers and Hart: "The Most Beautiful Girl in the World," which Matt, Jr., and his girl Mickey sing while riding horseback around the ring; Mickey's lovable ballad, "Little Girl Blue"; and one of Rodgers' most beautiful love songs, "My Romance," a duet of Matt, Jr., and Mickey.

Jumbo was the first play in which George Abbott collaborated with Rodgers and Hart; it was also the first musical production with which Abbott became involved. Since Abbott was henceforth to work so fruitfully in the musical theater—and at times with Rodgers and Hart—his work as stage director is surely not the least of the significant elements in *Jumbo*.

1936 ON YOUR TOES, a musical comedy with book by Rodgers and Hart and George Abbott. Presented by Dwight Deere Wiman at the Imperial Theatre on April 11. Staged by Worthington Miner. Choreography by George Balanchine. Cast included Ray Bolger, Tamara Geva, Doris Carson, Luella Gear, and Monty Woolley (315 performances).

While working in Hollywood in the early 1930's, Rodgers and Hart prepared an outline of a motion-picture script about a vaudeville hoofer involved with the Russian Ballet. They hoped to induce Pandro Berman to buy it for Fred Astaire. The project was turned down. Sometime later, after returning to New York, Rodgers and Hart sold the idea to Shubert for Ray Bolger. Enlisting the aid of George Abbott, Rodgers and Hart whipped together a completed musical-comedy book. But by then Shubert bowed out of the deal and turned the entire project over to Dwight Deere Wiman.

On Your Toes, as the musical was finally titled, drew its background from the world of ballet—a subject comparatively new to American musical comedy. Its hero was Philip Dolan III (Ray Bolger), who, though a son of a vaudeville hoofer, turns to ballet. He only succeeds in making of himself a ridiculous spectacle in a classic work, "Princesse Zenobia." One of his pupils, Frankie Frayne (Doris Carson) creates a ballet in a modern style and tempo which Phil calls to the attention of the noted ballerina, Vera Barnova (Tamara Geva). Largely through her romantic interest in Phil, Vera introduces the ballet with Phil as her dancing partner. This ballet, "Slaughter on Tenth Avenue," becomes a triumph, but by now Phil is convinced he loves Frankie and not Vera.

Since the plot concerned itself with ballet and ballet dancers, *On Your Toes* placed considerable emphasis on the dance, perhaps the earliest musical to do so. It enlisted the services of a noted choreographer, George Balanchine (onetime ballet master of the Diaghilev Ballet and the Ballet Russe de Monte Carlo), the first time he engaged in the American popular theater. Balanchine created two large ballet sequences. The first, "Princesse Zenobia," built around the Scheherazade theme, was intended as a satire on the classic dance traditions. The second, "Slaughter on Tenth Avenue," was a jazz ballet—a satire on gangster stories—and it became the high point of the production. The latter described the flight of a hoofer and his girl from gangsters. They are caught in a Tenth Avenue café, and the girl is shot; but the hoofer is saved by the police. For "Slaughter on Tenth Avenue," Rodgers created his most ambitious orchestral score up to that time, the heart of which was a beautiful lament for strings in the blues style, with a saucy little jazz theme serving as a secondary subject. "Slaughter on Tenth Avenue," with which the plot of *On Your Toes* comes to a climax, always drew thunderous approval from audiences. And when *On Your Toes* was revived on Broadway in 1954, it was this one episode in the play that had not aged at all, but continued to exert an inescapable spell. Richard Watts, Jr., said: "A sizable number of jazz ballets have passed this way since it first appeared, but it still is something of a classic in its field, and the music Mr. Rodgers wrote for it continues to seem one of the major achievements of his career."

Other outstanding songs in the score included the delightful duet of Frankie and Phil, "There's a Small Hotel," and a plangent blues number, "Quiet Night." Two songs were especially interesting for their brilliantly amusing lyrics. One was "The Three B's" (Bach, Beethoven, and Brahms); and the other, "Too Good for the Average Man."

1937   BABES IN ARMS, a musical comedy with book by Rodgers and Hart. Presented by Dwight Deere Wiman at the Shubert Theatre on April 14. Staged by Robert Sinclair. Choreography by George Balanchine. Cast included Mitzi Green, Alfred Drake, Wynn Murray, and Ray Heatherton (289 performances).

Babes in Arms was the first musical for which Rodgers and Hart wrote their own book without outside assistance. The accent of the production was on youth. Two of the principals (Mitzi Green as Billie Smith, and Wynn Murray as Baby Rose) were only sixteen. Most of the others in the cast and chorus were also in their adolescence. Some unknowns in the chorus—or, as it was called in the play, "the gang"—were later destined for fame in the theater; among these were Robert Rounseville and Dan Dailey. Alfred Drake played a lesser role, that of Marshal Blackstone, but made it important; Ray Heatherton was Val Lamar. *Babes in Arms* was, as John Mason Brown reported, "a zestful, tuneful and brilliantly danced affair . . . filled with talented striplings and bubbling over with the freshness and energy of youth."

Children dominated the production; in the story, they were the offspring of touring vaudevillians. Left behind in Eastport, Long Island, by their parents, these children must shift for themselves as best they can. The local sheriff threatens to transfer them to a work camp if their parents do not immediately return to take care of them. Since money is the solution to their problem, they put on their own show which is an artistic success but a financial failure. They are, however, saved from the work camp through the generous ministrations of a transatlantic flier, whose forced landing on their farmyard plunges him into the thick of their difficulties.

Within the framework of this central idea were two self-contained, self-sufficient segments. One was a fanciful ballet, "Peter's Journey," in which Marlene Dietrich, Greta Garbo, and Clark Gable appear as characters. The other was "Lee Calhoun's Follies," the fresh and ebullient amateur show put on by the kids. The conventional musical comedy formula was thus continually "thrust aside," as Robert Coleman noted, "in favor of novelty, surprise, and freshness."

The Rodgers score had four gems, all belonging with the composer's best. The play put its best foot forward by presenting as its first musical number the poignant duet of Billie Smith and Val Lamar, "Where or When?" To Billie Smith was assigned two other Rodgers classics: "My Funny Valentine" and "The Lady Is a Tramp." The vigorous, explosive "Johnny One Note" was introduced by Baby Rose. The score also included two fine duets in "I Wish I Were in Love Again" and "All at Once."

1937   I'D RATHER BE RIGHT, a musical comedy by George S. Kaufman and Moss Hart. Presented by Sam H. Harris at the Alvin Theatre on November 2. Book staged by George S. Kaufman. Choreography by Charles Weidman. Cast included George M. Cohan, Austin Marshall, Joy Hodges, and Florenz Ames (290 performances).

Like *Of Thee I Sing,* the Gershwin Pulitzer Prize musical produced in 1931, *I'd Rather Be Right* is a satire on politics in Washington, D.C. But in the Rodgers and Hart musical, the emphasis is on specific timely issues and actual political luminaries rather than on fictitious characters and episodes. A highly improbable situation sets into motion all ensuing satirical developments. Peggy Jones (Joy Hodges) and Phil Barker (Austin Marshall) find that they cannot get married until he gets a raise; and he won't get that raise unless the national budget is balanced. Phil dreams that he and Peggy meet the President of the United States on a bench in Central Park—the President bearing a striking resemblance to Franklin D. Roosevelt (George M. Cohan). When they confide their troubles to him, the President promises to do all he can to balance the budget. But the political forces inside Washington—and the social and economic forces outside—frustrate his every effort. When, in a fireside chat, he suggests to American women that they give up cosmetics for a year and donate the money to the national budget, they rise in vociferous protest. When an effort is made to use the gold in Fort Knox, there is the threat of a stock-market crash and panic in the business world. The budget goes unbalanced. The President urges the young people to have faith in themselves and their country by getting married anyway. Phil awakens and decides to heed the counsel given him in his dream.

The New Deal and New Dealers are satirized. "What did you do with all the money I gave you last week?" inquires the President peevishly of the Secretary of the Treasury, when the latter comes for more funds. "Three hundred millions *ought* to last a week!" James J. Farley comes to the President seeking an appointment for the chairman of the 4th Assembly District of Seattle as Collector of the Port of New York. When the President suggests that New York already has such a Collector, Farley replies quickly: "But not in Seattle!" The rapidity with which laws are created, the federal-subsidized theater, taxes, Walter Lippmann, the brain trust, labor—these are some of the other subjects laughed at in song and dialogue.

Song is so completely integrated with text that it often cannot be divorced from it without losing something vital. The only exception is "Have You Met Miss Jones?" a first-act duet of Peggy and Phil. The other songs are dependent for relevance upon the action in the play, and the dialogue that precedes it; these include such sprightly items as "A Homogeneous Cabinet," "A Little Bit of Constitutional Fun," "We're Going to Balance the Budget," "Labor Is the Thing," and the President's off-the-cuff confidences, "Off the Record."

Not the least of the attractions of this witty musical was the performance of George M. Cohan as President Roosevelt. It was a performance with dimension and depth, a performance touched with warmth and humanity and wistfulness as well as mockery and gaiety. But to work with Cohan had not been easy. He was starring in a play and singing songs that he had not written. Neither the brittle dialogue nor the spicy songs were the kind with which for many years he had been identified. He took on the role reluctantly, made no effort to conceal the low opinion he had of the Rodgers and Hart songs, and even tried changing some of the lyrics until severely reprimanded after an out-of-town tryout performance.

1938   I MARRIED AN ANGEL, a musical comedy with book by Rodgers and Hart adapted from a play by John Vaszary. Presented by Dwight Deere Wiman at the Shubert Theatre on May 11. Staged by Joshua Logan. Choreography by George Balanchine. Cast included Vera Zorina, Dennis King, Vivienne Segal, Audrey Christie, and Walter Slezak (338 performances).

While working in Hollywood in 1938, Rodgers and Hart became impressed with the possibilities of John Vaszary's play, *I Married an Angel,* for the musical stage. When they learned that M.G.M. owned the rights, they prepared a scenario, hoping to spur that studio into some action. But the studio felt that the scenario was not screen material and stood ready to sell Rodgers and Hart the musical-comedy and screen rights.

I Married an Angel belongs to the world of fantasy in which Rodgers and Hart had long since proved themselves adept. Count Willy Palaffi (Dennis King) is disillusioned with women and vows he will marry only an angel. When an angel (Vera Zorina) flies through the window, he falls in love with her and marries her. But an angel as wife is not quite so ideal an arrangement as the Count had expected. She refuses to tell lies or to deceive anybody, the way most human beings do, and thus manages to involve her husband in all kinds of embarrassment. But the angel finally acquires some of the less desirable traits of humans and the marriage is a success.

As the angel, Vera Zorina achieved her first success in the American musical theater. By profession a ballet dancer, a graduate of the Ballet Russe de Monte Carlo, she had appeared in the London company of *On Your Toes,* and later was starred in the motion-picture adaptation of that play. The original plan had been to cast her in a minor role in *I Married an Angel;* but after Rodgers met her, he wired Wiman, *"Small Part Nothing. Zorina Plays the Angel."* Naturally the ballets of George Balanchine were conceived with her experience and background in mind, the most ambitious being the "Honeymoon Ballet" in the first act.

The stage direction was in the skillful hands of Joshua Logan. This, then, was the first time Logan worked in a Richard Rodgers musical; he would work with Rodgers again in the future, and with epoch-making consequences.

The best songs were the title number, presented by Count Palaffi, and "Spring Is Here," a duet of the Count and the Countess, the latter played by Vivienne Segal. The score included several interesting musical interludes—"The Modiste" in the first act, and "Angel Without Wings" in the second. These interludes, and the ballet music, revealed Rodgers' enlarged canvas; so did the rhythmic dialogue, a successful experiment in which the conversation preceding a song is provided a soft musical background.

Song, dance, comedy, and fantasy combined to make *I Married an Angel* stage magic. Brooks Atkinson called it "one of the best musical comedies of many seasons, an imaginative improvisation with a fully orchestrated score and an extraordinarily beautiful production. Musical comedy has met its masters."

1938 THE BOYS FROM SYRACUSE, a musical comedy with book by George Abbott based on Shakespeare's *A Comedy of Errors.* Presented by George Abbott at the Alvin Theatre on November 23. Directed by George Abbott. Choreography by George Balanchine. Cast included Jimmy Savo, Teddy Hart, Eddie Albert, Ronald Graham, Muriel Angelus, and Marcy Wescott (235 performances).

Ten years before Cole Porter's *Kiss Me, Kate,* Rodgers and Hart discovered that Shakespeare could provide material for musical comedies.

The idea to translate *A Comedy of Errors* into a musical comedy originated with Rodgers. He won over Hart, and together they invited Abbott
to prepare the text. Abbott retained only a single line from Shakespeare:
"The venom clamours of a jealous woman/Poisons more deadly than a
mad dog's tooth." But the setting, plot, and main characters were rec-
ognizably Shakespeare. In ancient Greece, Antipholus of Syracuse (Eddie
Albert) comes to Ephesus with his servant Dromio (Jimmy Savo). There
they are confused with another Antipholus (Ronald Graham) and another Dromio (Teddy Hart). The mistaken identity involves both Antipholuses and both Dromios in all kinds of amusing, irreverent, and at
times bawdy situations, as each one gets involved with the other's wife.

The casting of Jimmy Savo and Teddy Hart as the two Dromios was
one of the delights of the production. Savo and Teddy Hart (the latter
was Larry's brother) looked alike, and both had about them the same
pathetic air and wide-eyed ingenuousness that made them ideal for their
roles. The two Antipholuses were also strong points in a cast that included Burl Ives in a minor role as a tailor's apprentice. (Ives' career
in folk music would come later.) The acting, George Abbott's witty dialogue and brisk direction, Balanchine's imaginative choreography, and
the occasionally plangent and occasionally humorous tunes and lyrics
of Rodgers and Hart all combined to make a field day of Shakespeare.
"I believe," wrote Sidney Whipple, "that *The Boys from Syracuse* will be
regarded as the greatest comedy of its time." To *Life* it was "a fantastically funny and bawdy show in the best musical tradition."

Rodgers was at his best in the lilting waltz, "Falling in Love with
Love," introduced by Muriel Angelis playing Adrianna; in the ballad
"The Shortest Day of the Year," and in "You Have Cast Your Shadow."
Hart was most iridescent in "He and She," "What Can You Do with a
Man?", "Ladies of the Evening," and "This Can't Be Love."

1940 PAL JOEY, a musical comedy with book by John O'Hara based on his
      stories. Presented by George Abbott at the Ethel Barrymore Theatre on
      December 25. Production staged by George Abbott. Dances by Robert
      Alton. Cast included Gene Kelly, June Havoc, Vivienne Segal, and Leila
      Ernst (270 performances).

Rodgers and Hart never lacked courage to do the unusual and the unexpected on the musical stage. They did not lack such courage in bringing
O'Hara's stories about Joey into the Broadway theater. In 1940 a musical
like *Pal Joey* represented iconoclasm. Nobody else would have dared to
populate the stage with such disreputable characters; to point up so

realistically the seamy side of life—blackmail, illicit love affairs, hypoc-
risy, skulduggery, and crass opportunism. This was adult musical theater,
mature in approach and concept.

Pal Joey originated as a series of letters in story form by John O'Hara,
published in *The New Yorker*—Joey being a "heel" who becomes a night-
club operator. O'Hara himself suggested to Rodgers and Hart that they
make these stories into a musical, and the pair was delighted with the
idea. O'Hara wrote his own text. The setting is Chicago's South Side.
Joey Evans (Gene Kelly) is a night-club hoofer, a cheap opportunist
ready to give up the girl he loves, Linda English (Leila Ernst), for a
wealthy, hard-boiled, pleasure-loving matron, Vera Simpson (Vivienne
Segal). Since Vera does not believe in the rewards of virtue, she is ready
to pay hard cash for love, and she sets up Joey in his own swanky night
club. But Joey is not one for constancy. He soon wearies of Vera, begins
looking elsewhere for sexual adventures. Eventually, both Vera and Linda
decide they have had enough of him. Joey, a victim of blackmailers, is
once again broke and alone.

Long before the final plans were crystallized to bring *Pal Joey* to
Broadway, Rodgers and Hart knew who their leading performers would
be. Hart had long since promised Vivienne Segal he would put her in a
play that would do justice to her vital talent, and he knew that the part
of Vera was just right for her. Rodgers had seen Gene Kelly in Saroyan's
The Time of Your Life and recalled that performance when he began
thinking about Joey. Though Rodgers and Hart did not know it at the
time, when they cast June Havoc in the minor role of Gladys they were
also making an act of discovery; for June Havoc, who had never before
appeared on the Broadway stage, was able to use *Pal Joey* as the springboard from which to jump into a rich career on stage and screen.

Pal Joey inspired sharply divided reactions when finally produced.
Some loved it, considered it fresh, original, daring, exciting. In this group
belonged Louis Kronenberger, who thought it was the most unhackneyed
musical he had ever seen. Many others were repelled by its vivid realism.
"If it is possible to make an entertaining musical comedy out of an odious
story, *Pal Joey* is it," wrote Brooks Atkinson. "Although *Pal Joey* is ex-
pertly done, can you draw sweet water from a foul well?" The "nays" had
it. *Pal Joey* did not do too well at the box office; the public simply could
not take to it.

But one decade later *Pal Joey* was revived—on January 3, 1952—with
Harold Lang, Helen Gallagher, Vivienne Segal, and Pat Northrop. It was
now a triumph. The critics were unanimous in their praises. Brooks At-

kinson wrote: "No one is likely to be impervious to the tight organization of the production, the terseness of the writing, the liveliness and versatility of the score, the easy perfection of the lyrics. Brimming over with good music and fast on its toes, it renews confidence in the professionalism of the theatre." Critics Richard Watts, Jr., and Robert Coleman did not hesitate to label it a work of art, a masterpiece. The audience was also enchanted. The play's run of 542 performances was the longest of any musical revival in the history of the American theater. The New York Drama Critics Circle chose it as the best musical of the year; and it received eleven of the sixteen Donaldson Awards, the first time in the then nineyear history of these Awards that one play received so many honors. The original shock may have gone from *Pal Joey* since it was first produced; but the excitement was still there.

The haunting duet of Joey and Linda in the first act, "I Could Write a Book," was the main love song. But possibly the best of all the songs, and one of Hart's most felicitous sets of lyrics, was Vera's lusty and lustful reactions to Joey in "Bewitched, Bothered and Bewildered." "That Terrific Rainbow," in a torrid jazz style, was a third distinctive number. Other distinguished songs—but mostly for Hart's vivacious and suggestive lyrics—were "Zip" (the reflections of a strip-tease artist), "In Our Little Den of Iniquity," and "What Is a Man?," the last an uninhibited expression of Vera's earthy personal philosophy.

1942   BY JUPITER, a musical comedy with book by Rodgers and Hart based on Julian F. Thompson's *The Warrior's Husband*. Presented by Dwight Deere Wiman and Richard Rodgers in association with Richard Kollmar at the Shubert Theatre on June 2. Staged by Joshua Logan. Dances by Robert Alton. Cast included Ray Bolger, Benay Venuta, Vera-Ellen, Ronald Graham, and Constance Moore (427 performances).

By Jupiter was the last of the Rodgers and Hart musicals—the end of an era. It climaxed almost a quarter of a century of stage collaboration by composer and lyricist by becoming the musical having the longest firstrun. Indeed, its impressive total of 427 performances would have been much greater if it had not had to close down at a time when it was still doing capacity business to allow its star, Ray Bolger, to make a secret flight to the South Seas to entertain American troops.

The Warrior's Husband, upon which this musical was based, originated as a one-act play produced in 1921. In 1932 its author, Julian F. Thompson, expanded it into a three-act comedy, and in this vehicle Katharine Hepburn first became a star. The setting is Asia-Minor in mythological times. In Pontus the sexes are reversed. The women, headed by their Queen, Hippolyta (Benay Venuta), are the warriors. The timid men stay at home to primp and cook—and the most timorous of the lot is Hippolyta's husband, Sapiens (Ray Bolger). This power of distaff stems from the girdle of Diana worn by the Queen. As long as she wears it, the women continue to dominate the men. Theseus (Ronald Graham), Hercules (Ralph Dumke), and a band of Greeks invade the island to wrest the girdle from the Queen. They conquer the Amazon women not with their weapons but with their sex wiles. Once the Greeks are victorious over the Amazon women, Sapiens can assume his full authority as King. And the Greek, Theseus, can find love with Antiope (Constance Moore), Hippolyta's sister.

By Jupiter was, in the words of *Variety*, a "lush and lavish musical comedy, extravagant, adult, and betimes amusing." Its rich spice included the condiments of double-entendres and sex implications. The production profited from three excellent songs: "Nobody's Heart Belongs to Me," sung by Antiope; "Careless Rhapsody," a duet of Theseus and Antiope; and a delightful comedy number in "Ev'rything I've Got," a duet of Hippolyta and Sapiens.

II. RODGERS AND HAMMERSTEIN

After almost a quarter of a century of working solely with lyricist Larry Hart, in 1942 Richard Rodgers had to seek out a new collaborator. He found him in Oscar Hammerstein II, a librettist and lyricist who had also enjoyed a rich and productive career in the theater. As collaborators, Rodgers and Hammerstein were destined to reach heights in their respective careers which would even tower above their previous formidable individual achievements. As collaborators they were to open new vistas for the musical theater, to transform musical comedy into a native art. As Cole Porter said, "The most profound change in forty years of musical comedy has been—Rodgers and Hammerstein."

Rodgers was only thirteen when first he met Oscar Hammerstein, then twenty years old. Rodgers' brother, Mortimer—Hammerstein's classmate at Columbia College—took Dick to a performance of *On Your Way*, a Columbia Varsity Show in 1915, in which Hammerstein sang some songs and appeared in a few skits. "I noted with satisfaction," Hammerstein later recalled, "young Richard's respectful awe in the presence of a college junior."

In the fall of 1919, when Rodgers and Hart wrote their first Columbia

Varsity Show, *Fly with Me*, the committee that passed favorably upon them included Hammerstein. In that show most of the lyrics were by Hart, but one was by Hammerstein himself, "Room for One More," which Rodgers set to music. But even this was not the first time Rodgers and Hammerstein worked together. Rodgers had already written melodies for two Hammerstein lyrics—"Can It" and "Weaknesses"—used in an amateur show, *Up Stage and Down*, early in 1919.

But though their paths frequently crossed in the years that followed, Rodgers and Hammerstein did not begin a professional partnership until late in 1942 when Larry Hart decided to go off to Mexico.

With their very first collaboration, *Oklahoma!* Rodgers and Hammerstein ushered in a new era for the musical theater. This beautiful folk play realized fully that for which the earlier Rodgers and Hart musicals had been striving—a synchronization of all the elements of the musical theater into a single and indivisible entity. This concept was further enlarged, developed, and crystallized by succeeding Rodgers and Hammerstein shows, several of which are now classics of the Broadway stage. Brought into association with the poetry and lyricism of Hammerstein's dialogue and verse—and Hammerstein's wisdom and humanity—Rodgers acquired new scope, depth, and dimension in his musical writing, so much so that many of his scores for Hammerstein have the breadth of music dramas.

Rodgers and Hammerstein made significant contributions outside the Broadway theater too. They wrote the songs for the motion picture *State Fair* in 1945, one of which, "It Might as Well Be Spring," won the Academy Award. A decade later they collaborated on their first original musical play for television, *Cinderella*. And without Hammerstein, Rodgers wrote ambitious and artistically significant background music for the documentary film, presented over television, *Victory at Sea*, recipient of numerous honors.

As the first composer of the American musical theater, Richard Rodgers has himself been the recipient of more honors than have been accorded to any other stage composer. In 1949 he received the Columbia University Medal of Excellence; in 1950 the Award of the Hundred Year Association; in 1955 a life membership in the National Institute of Arts and Letters; in 1956 the Alexander Hamilton Award of Columbia College. In 1955 the Library of Congress in Washington, D.C., presented an exhibition of illustrations, photographs, programs, and manuscripts tracing his career in the theater; this was only the second time that a composer of nonclassical music was thus honored, the first being Stephen Foster.

1943   OKLAHOMA!, a musical play with book and lyrics by Oscar Hammerstein
II based on Lynn Riggs' play, *Green Grow the Lilacs*. Presented by the
Theatre Guild at the St. James Theatre on March 31. Directed by
Rouben Mamoulian. Dances by Agnes De Mille. Cast included Alfred
Drake, Joan Roberts, Celeste Holm, Betty Garde, Joan McCracken,
Bambi Linn, Howard da Silva, and Joseph Buloff (2,248 performances).

By 1942 the Theatre Guild of New York had come upon unhappy days.
It had suffered a series of failures which had brought it to the threshold
of insolvency. To extricate themselves from this difficulty, Lawrence
Langner and Theresa Helburn conceived the idea of producing a musical,
their first since Gershwin's *Porgy and Bess*. Helburn had long been convinced that Riggs' folk play, *Green Grow the Lilacs*, produced by the
Guild in 1931, would make a charming musical. She approached Rodgers
and Hart with the idea of making the adaptation. Rodgers was willing,
but Hart was tired and ill and could summon neither the energy nor the
enthusiasm for the project. When Hart left for Mexico for a prolonged
vacation, urging Rodgers to seek out a new collaborator, Rodgers asked
Oscar Hammerstein II to work with him.

By a curious coincidence Hammerstein himself had been interested in
making a musical out of *Green Grow the Lilacs*. He tried to sell the idea
to Jerome Kern but Kern was not enthusiastic. When Hammerstein offered to buy the rights from the Theatre Guild, hoping to find some composer for it, he was informed that Rodgers and Hart were being considered for the adaptation and that the rights were not on the market.

Oscar Hammerstein's play faithfully followed that of Lynn Riggs by
emphasizing the love triangle of Laurey (Joan Roberts), Curly (Alfred
Drake), and Jud Fry (Howard da Silva). The setting is the western Indian country at the turn of the century. Curly and Laurey are in love,
but are at first either aloof, hostile, or uncertain of each other's reactions.
Since she is making no apparent headway with Curly, Laurey responds
to the advances of Jud Fry—a lecherous fellow—accepting an invitation
for a "box-party." There, by outbidding Jud for Laurey's lunch box, which
entitles him to share it with her, Curly openly demonstrates his true feelings for the girl. The love affair now unfolds quickly. At their wedding
Jud appears—a drunk and sinister figure. He attacks Curly with a knife
and in the ensuing brawl falls on his own blade and is killed. Rather than
take Curly to prison on his wedding night, Judge Carnes (Ralph Riggs)
arranges a trial then and there, in which Curly is found innocent. Curly
and Laurey can now go off for their honeymoon in a land soon to be
known as Oklahoma.

A subsidiary love triangle introduces comedy into these otherwise grim developments. This love interest involves Ado Annie (Celeste Holm), a girl who can't say "No," an Oriental peddler, Ali Hakim (Joseph Buloff), and Will Parker (Lee Dixon). Ado's father, Judge Carnes, will not allow her to marry Will Parker until he can raise the seemingly unattainable sum of fifty dollars in cash. Ali Hakim also pursues her. When he discovers that his highly dishonorable intentions are mistaken by the Judge as a marriage proposal to Ado, he is able to elude the disagreeable prospect of marriage by seeing to it that Will gets the fifty dollars.

In discussing the nature of their adaptation, Rodgers and Hammerstein came to an early decision: to abandon old methods. They realized that a play with folk character demanded fresh and original points of view. Consequently, a great deal in their play defied tradition. The play had to open, not with a stage crowded with chorus girls and men, but simply, with a woman churning butter while the hero sings offstage. In fact there were no chorus girls on the stage until midway in the act. In place of formal dances there were American ballets, fully in character with the setting; for this purpose a leading personality of the ballet world, Agnes De Mille, was recruited for the choreography. And not only the dances, but also every bit of music and comedy, had to be germane to the plot. Hammerstein explained:

> Such a course was experimental, amounting almost to a breach of implied contract with a musical-comedy audience. . . . Once we had made the decision everything seemed to work right and we had the inner confidence people feel when they have adopted the direct and honest approach to a problem.

It is now history how virtually everyone connected with the production —except Rodgers—suspected that while *Oklahoma!* might well become an artistic triumph it would surely be a disaster at the box office; how long and painful was the process of gathering the 83,000 dollars needed for production costs. Everything about *Oklahoma!* seemed to smell of failure. It had no stars; it had very little humor; its ballets and extended musical sequences were too high-brow for popular consumption; it had no traditional chorus-girl numbers. It was based on a stage play that had been a failure (with only sixty-four performances); the director, Mamoulian, had had little experience with the musical theater, his only past effort in this direction having been Gershwin's *Porgy and Bess,* a financial deficit to all concerned; the librettist-lyricist, Oscar Hammerstein, came to *Oklahoma!* with a recent distressing succession of flops; and the composer, Rodgers, was here working for the first time in a quarter of a century with a new collaborator.

All the odds, then, seemed to be against *Oklahoma!* being a success. It would have required a fool or a dreamer—or possibly a combination of both—to dare prophesy for it the magnitude of its ultimate triumph. But the accolades of all the critics worked in its behalf. Lewis Nichols called it a "folk opera"; Burns Mantle described it as "different—beautifully different"; Woollcott Gibbs said his "gratitude is practically boundless"; John Anderson described it as "beautiful . . . delightful . . . fresh . . . imaginative." Given such a handsome send-off, *Oklahoma!* went on to create history. Its Broadway run of five years and nine weeks was the longest of any musical production, and its gross of 7,000,000 dollars broke all known box-office records up to that time. After the end of the New York engagement the company went on tour, covering seventy cities in fifty-one weeks. Then there was a national company traveling for ten years, appearing in about 250 cities before an audience estimated at 10,-000,000 and grossing about 20,000,000 dollars. There were companies in Berlin, London, South Africa, Paris, Sweden, Denmark, Australia, and other far-off places. In London it had the longest run of any play in the 287-year history of the Drury Lane Theatre. In all, the original investment of 83,000 dollars yielded a profit of over 5,000,000 dollars; an investor of 1500 dollars received a return of about 50,000 dollars.

Oklahoma! received a special award from the Pulitzer committee; it introduced into the recording industry the practice of putting on records the entire score with the original cast (a million such albums were sold); it was the incubator for stars, many of them unknowns when they first stepped into the play, among whom were Celeste Holm, Shelley Winters, Alfred Drake, Joan McCracken, Bambi Linn, and Howard Keel.

There were thirteen principal numbers in the score. These included Curly's idyllic opening song, "Oh, What a Beautiful Mornin'"; the love duet of Curly and Laurey, "People Will Say We're in Love"; Ado Annie's amusing confessions, "I Cain't Say No" and "All 'Er Nothin'"; Jud Fry's two principal numbers, each revealing facets of his complex personality, "Pore Jud" (a duet with Curly) and "Lonely Room." Other numbers had a distinct folk-song personality: "The Surrey with the Fringe on Top," "Kansas City," "The Farmer and the Cowman," and the title song.

Besides the songs and other self-sufficient numbers, the score also included many little fragments—sometimes slightly altered versions of the aforementioned songs—used as background to the dialogue or as transitions. Six of these quotations make up the ambitious ballet music for the first-act dance sequence, "Laurey Makes Up Her Mind."

1945   CAROUSEL, a musical play with book and lyrics by Oscar Hammerstein
       II, based on Ferenc Molnár's *Liliom* as adapted by Benjamin F. Glazer.
       Produced by the Theatre Guild at the Majestic Theatre on April 19.
       Staged by Rouben Mamoulian. Dances by Agnes De Mille. Cast in-
       cluded Jan Clayton, John Raitt, Christine Johnson, and Jean Darling
       (890 performances).

The plan to make Molnár's *Liliom* into a musical originated with Theresa Helburn of the Theatre Guild. The Guild had successfully produced the Molnár play in 1921. Helburn felt that its Hungarian background, carnival setting and excursions into fantasy made it ideal for musical adaptation. But when she suggested the project to Rodgers and Hammerstein, they were not at first enthusiastic, feeling that the setting of Hungary was not feasible for musical-comedy treatment in the uncertain political climate of 1944-45. Not until Rodgers suggested the transfer of the locale to New England were he and Hammerstein sparked into action. New England provided ensembles germane to the play—fishermen, mill girls; its American background made the subject suitable for the special creative gifts of both the composer and the librettist. After discussing the way the adaptation should be made, Rodgers and Hammerstein completed their first musical number—the now-famous "Soliloquy"—and then, as Rodgers recalls, "we knew we had the play licked." They signed a contract with the Guild.

Some basic changes had to be made in the Molnár play. The title now became *Carousel;* the leading character was changed from Liliom to Billy Bigelow; the time of the play shifted to 1873. Billy Bigelow (John Raitt), a handsome and tough amusement park barker, loses his job when he falls in love with Julie Jordan (Jan Clayton). In the Molnár play Julie becomes Liliom's mistress and bears him a child; in the musical Billy and Julie get married. In both versions Billy remains a rough-and-ready bully, incapable of meeting his wife's material or emotional needs. When, however, he discovers his wife is pregnant, Billy glows with parental pride, is flooded with tenderness for both his wife and unborn child. He must now get money for them. In the attempt he becomes involved in a holdup and commits suicide to elude arrest.

At this point *Liliom* and *Carousel* differ. In that Molnár play Liliom defiantly tells two of Heaven's policemen that he does not regret his actions. For this he is doomed to Purgatory for fifteen years. After that period he must return to earth for a single day to expiate his sins. Liliom appears on earth disguised as a beggar, in his hand a star he has stolen from the heavens, which he is bringing as a gift to his daughter. When she sends him away abruptly, he slaps her face. He is then led away. The play ends on the tragic note of frustration.

But in the musical Billy follows his Purgatory stay with a visit to the Starkeeper in Heaven, who informs him that he can gain admission only after the redemption of his soul. To achieve redemption, Billy is allowed a day on earth. Stealing a star, he returns to earth and tries to present it as a gift to his unhappy, maladjusted daughter. When she turns it down, he slaps her. But the girl feels no hurt, since the slap in given with love and not hate. His tenderness now helps the child overcome her personal misery, and by this one achievement Billy's soul is redeemed. As he witnesses the exercises of her graduation from school, he realizes joyfully that she can enter upon life with head high and singing heart. And his widow knows again what she had always known when Billy was alive: having been married to him had been worth the pain it had cost. The tragedy of Molnár's play becomes dispelled in the musical by love and forgiveness.

Carousel was acclaimed when it reached Broadway. To John Chapman it was "one of the finest musical plays I have ever seen, and I shall remember it always." It received the New York Drama Critics Award as the best musical of the season, and Donaldson Awards in eight categories.

Carousel has lost little of its magic in subsequent Broadway revivals; it has, in short, become a classic. "This is the most glorious of the Rodgers and Hammerstein works," wrote Brooks Atkinson when *Carousel* returned in 1954. "When the highest judge of all hands down the ultimate verdict, it is this column's opinion that *Carousel* will turn out to be the finest of their creations. . . . *Carousel* is a masterpiece that grows in stature through the years." Its status as a classic was again confirmed in 1958 when it was presented and acclaimed at the United States Pavilion at the Brussels World's Fair (a production in which Jan Clayton returned to her original role of Julie).

The love song is the duet of Billy and Julie, "If I Loved You." Other numbers are also unforgettable for their melodic beauty, vitality, and originality: "June Is Bustin' Out All Over"; "You'll Never Walk Alone," with its spiritual overtones; and the expressive and structurally expansive narrative of Billy, "Soliloquy." The symphonic waltz prelude, played under the opening scene as a carousel spins around in an amusement park, reveals new amplitude in Rodgers' writing for the orchestra; and his heightened lyric expressiveness and emotional range is revealed in Julie's poignant expression of devotion to Billy in "What's the Use of Wond'rin?"; in the tender idyl, "When the Children Are Asleep"; and in the rousing choral episodes, "Blow High, Blow Low," and "This Was a Real Nice Clam Bake." In *Carousel* Rodgers is no longer merely a writer of wonderful songs. He is a musical dramatist, capable of bringing operatic dimensions to the popular theater.

1947   ALLEGRO, a musical play with book and lyrics by Oscar Hammerstein II. Produced by the Theatre Guild at the Majestic Theatre on October 10. Stage production supervised by Lawrence Langner and Theresa Helburn. Book, musical numbers, and dances staged by Agnes De Mille. Cast included John Battles, Roberta Jonay, William Ching, and Annamary Dickey (315 performances).

Allegro is one of the most original, one of the most experimental of Rodgers and Hammerstein plays. The plot follows the biography of Dr. Joseph Taylor, Jr. (John Battles), son of a small-town doctor, Joseph Taylor (William Ching). The son is born in 1905 and raised in his home town. He completes his out-of-town education, weathers the depression, and returns home to join his father in the general practice of medicine. But after Joe marries his childhood sweetheart, Jennie Brinker (Roberta Jonay), she becomes an ambitious woman, smothered by the narrowness of life in her home town. She persuades Joe to move on to Chicago. There he acquires a large practice of wealthy neurotics and hypochondriacs, becomes rich, and moves with the social elite. When he learns that Jennie has been unfaithful to him, Joe suddenly realizes how empty his life in Chicago has been. Idealism now conquers over materialism. He returns alone to his small town and his comparatively humble practice, the point at which the play ends.

This story is told not only through action and dialogue but also through song, dance, lights, and colors. The music consists of a few excellent individual numbers like "A Fellow Needs a Girl," a duet of father and mother Taylor; "So Far"; and "The Gentleman Is a Dope." But it is also made up of many orchestral episodes and choral numbers. A kind of Greek chorus is used to comment (sometimes in speech, sometimes in song) on what is taking place. Episodes in Joe's life are treated in large musical designs—for example, Joe's birth and marriage are extended cantatas for solo voices, chorus, and orchestra. Other biographical incidents unfold in ballets—as in Joe's schooldays. One of the most unusual aspects of the Rodgers score is the fact that most of the important songs are assigned to minor characters. Another interesting curiosity is the inclusion of a quotation from the Rodgers and Hart tune, "Mountain Greenery," in the "Freshman Dance Music," to evoke the period of the 1920's. "Yatata Yatata" introduces a note of gaiety by being a delightful take-off on cocktail parties.

Lighting, rather than sets or costumes, became an essential element in the staging. As the action often takes place on a bare stage, not only were lights used to point up an emotion or a state of mind; colors were also thrown on a large backstage screen to emphasize a certain mood.

Allegro was not a box-office success, though the critics liked it considerably. Brooks Atkinson said it had "the lyric rapture of a musical masterpiece." To Robert Coleman it was a "stunning blending of beauty, integrity, imagination, taste and skill." It received three Donaldson awards —for book, lyrics, and musical score.

1949   SOUTH PACIFIC, a musical play with book by Oscar Hammerstein II and Joshua Logan based on James A. Michener's *Tales of the South Pacific*. Produced by Rodgers and Hammerstein in association with Leland Hayward and Joshua Logan at the Majestic Theatre on April 7. Book and musical numbers staged by Joshua Logan. Cast included Mary Martin, Ezio Pinza, William Tabbert, Juanita Hall, and Betta St. John (1,925 performances).

One evening at a dinner party early in 1947, Kenneth MacKenna, story editor of M–G–M, mentioned to Jo Mielziner and Joshua Logan that he had recently read and turned down for his studio a volume of World War II stories by James Michener. MacKenna felt the book might be suitable for stage dramatization and encouraged Logan to consider the project. Logan read the book and immediately decided to bring it to the stage. Since at the time he was co-producer with Leland Hayward of *Mister Roberts*, he interested Hayward in joining him in procuring the stage rights. As they discussed ways and means in which the stories could be adapted for the stage, Logan suggested the necessity of music creating the proper mood and atmosphere. This matter was further explored by Joshua Logan with Richard Rodgers who, in turn, won over the approval of his collaborator, Oscar Hammerstein. The decision was finally reached to have Hammerstein collaborate with Logan in making the stage adaptation and for Rodgers to produce the score. Since Rodgers and Hammerstein had recently agreed to produce their own plays, they acquired the dramatic rights, Logan was engaged as stage director, and Logan and Hayward joined as co-producers. Not long after these complicated negotiations were completed, the faith of all concerned in Michener's book of stories was fully justified when *Tales of the South Pacific* received the Pulitzer Prize in fiction.

In making their adaptation Hammerstein and Logan used only two of the stories from Michener's book. One was "Our Heroine," telling of the love of Emile de Becque, a local planter of French origin, and the American nurse, Nellie Forbush. The other was "Fo' Dolla," describing the romance of the American Marine lieutenant, Joseph Cable, and the native girl, Liat. To consolidate the two stories, an episode of their own invention was introduced—dispatching Cable and De Becque on a hazardous war mission.

In the final version of the text Emile de Becque (Ezio Pinza) is a wealthy middle-aged French planter, settled in the South Pacific long before the outbreak of World War II. As the play opens he is host to Ensign Nellie Forbush (Mary Martin). They soon realize they are in love, and De Becque urges her to marry him. But, somewhat later, Nellie discovers that he was once married to a Polynesian and is the father of two Eurasian children. This fact so disturbs her that she refuses to see him any more. Meanwhile Lieutenant Joseph Cable (William Tabbert) arrives to establish a coast watch on a nearby Japanese-held island. Since De Becque knows this terrain well, Lieutenant Cable tries to induce him to join him on this precarious mission. Unaware that Nellie has renounced him, De Becque refuses to submit to such danger. For the time being Lieutenant Cable finds diversion on the off-limits island of Bali Ha'i, where he meets and falls in love with Liat (Betta St. John), a Tonkinese girl and the daughter of Bloody Mary (Juanita Hall). When De Becque finally discovers that Nellie has left him, he offers his services to Cable. Penetrating the Japanese island they are able to relay back information enabling the American forces to destroy twenty Japanese surface craft and to make a successful invasion of fourteen Japanese-held islands. Lieutenant Cable is killed before the arrival of the Americans, but De Becque is saved. When he returns home he finds Nellie waiting for him. She is feeding and playing with his Eurasian children.

It took courage for the authors to make a middle-aged, gray-haired man the hero of a musical play; and it took courage to cast Ezio Pinza in that role, since the celebrated opera singer had never before appeared on the Broadway stage. But even greater independence of thought and action was required to make the secondary love plot of Cable and Liat a plea for racial tolerance, to write a song on the subject ("You've Got to Be Taught"), and, after having built up a favorable atmosphere for this love affair, to kill Cable. All this iconoclasm paid off. Ezio Pinza became a matinee idol; the secondary love plot brought to the play some of its strength and beauty.

For the part of Nellie Forbush, Rodgers and Hammerstein engaged Mary Martin, already an outstanding star of the musical theater. Between them (separately or together) Martin and Pinza shared the main musical numbers: the leading love song, "Some Enchanted Evening"; "I'm Gonna Wash That Man Right Outa My Hair"; "I'm in Love with a Wonderful Guy"; "A Cockeyed Optimist"; and "This Nearly Was Mine." Other songs reflected the personalities of the characters who sang them: "Bali Ha'i" and "Happy Talk" (Bloody Mary); the tender love duet of Liat and Cable, "Younger than Springtime"; and the amusing lament of the Marines, sailors, and Seabees, "There Is Nothing Like a Dame."

Long before *South Pacific* opened on Broadway, word had begun to circulate that here was a musical to challenge *Oklahoma!* in beauty and originality. *South Pacific* fulfilled all such promises. Not only was it as good as rumor had indicated, it was even better. It was, as Howard Barnes said, a "show of rare enchantment, novel in texture and treatment, rich in dramatic substance, and eloquent in song." Brooks Atkinson described it as "a magnificent musical frame."

South Pacific went on to create stage history, even as *Oklahoma!* had done earlier. It had the second longest run of any musical in Broadway history (only 323 performances less than *Oklahoma!*), was seen in New York by 3,500,000 theatergoers who paid 9,000,000 dollars at the box office. A national company toured several years. The financial returns were astronomic, a profit of 5,000,000 dollars, not counting the revenue from the sale to motion pictures. The sheet music sold over 2,000,000 copies; the long-playing recording of the original cast, over 1,000,000 discs. The name "South Pacific" was licensed for dolls, cosmetics, dresses, lingerie, and so on.

In addition, *South Pacific* absorbed virtually every prize in sight, including the 1950 Pulitzer Prize for drama (the second musical thus honored), the Drama Critics Award as the year's best musical, seven Antoinette Perry and nine Donaldson awards.

1951   THE KING AND I, a musical play with book and lyrics by Oscar Hammerstein II, based on Margaret Landon's novel, *Anna and the King of Siam*. Produced by Rodgers and Hammerstein at the St. James Theatre on March 29. Staged by John van Druten. Choreography by Jerome Robbins. Cast included Gertrude Lawrence, Yul Brynner, Dorothy Sarnoff, and Doretta Morrow (1246 performances).

Before Rodgers and Hammerstein made their musical adaptation of Landon's novel, it had been a successful motion picture, starring Rex Harrison and Irene Dunne, and released in 1946. Gertrude Lawrence was enchanted with this picture, and, seeing herself as Anna, asked her lawyer to convince Rodgers and Hammerstein to make a musical out of it for her. The deal was finally consummated through the office of the William Morris Agency.

It was not an easy adaptation to make. For the librettist it meant preparing a text with "an Eastern sense of dignity and pageantry, and none of this business of girls dressed in Oriental costumes and dancing out onto the stage and singing 'ching-a-ling-a-ling' with their fingers in the air," as Hammerstein himself explained. For Rodgers it meant writing a score with an Oriental flavor. "I never heard the music of the Far East," he said, "and I couldn't write an authentic Far-Eastern melody if my life depended on it." Both Hammerstein and Rodgers solved their respective problems—Hammerstein by not treading on Oriental toes and by treating the potentate and his many wives and children with respect and dignity; Rodgers—by not attempting Oriental music but by creating a score that suggested to him musically what the Far East was like.

Hammerstein did not change the basic structure of the Landon story. Anna Leonowens, an attractive, dignified mid-Victorian lady (Gertrude Lawrence) comes to Siam from England to teach the royal princes and princesses the ways of Western culture. A widow, she has come with her little boy, Louis (Sandy Kennedy), having been promised a house of her own, as well as a salary in English pounds. When she arrives, she discovers that the King (Yul Brynner) has reneged on his promise; she must live in the palace with the royal wives, children, and servants. At first she finds the King overbearing, unreasonable in his dictatorial attitudes, stubborn, childish, and volatile in mood. But Anna is equally dogmatic and intransigent in her own Western thinking and attitudes. The clash between Eastern and Western cultures is thus personified in these two people who, after a while, are drawn to each other. Anna finds that behind the hard surface of the King's despotism is an endearing charm, warmth, and childlike ingenuousness that cannot fail to appeal to a woman who adores children. And the King cannot suppress his admiration for a woman so unlike any he had heretofore known—fiery in her independence, proud, idealistic. The attachment between them, however, is of the mind and spirit, not of the heart. Love is out of the question between two people of such different cultures and social stations. Though Anna's ingenuity saves the King from a difficult political dilemma and allows him to realize a diplomatic coup, he is still adamant about having Anna live in the palace. An impulse on Anna's part to leave Siam for good, however, is throttled when she learns the King is dying. Anna gets her house. After the King's death she decides to stay on in Siam as a teacher of the children she has come to love.

A secondary plot provides the play with its only love interest. Tuptim (Doretta Morrow) and the King's slave, Lun Tha (Larry Douglas) are in love, try to elope, and are separated by death.

Beyond the exotic setting much in the play defied convention. The cast was made up mostly of Orientals, with only four Anglo-Saxon characters, none of whom was American. No love interest involves the two principals (they do not even exchange a single kiss) and one of them dies before the final curtain. Convention was also broken in the way music and dance helped to tell the story. In the opening of the play Anna speaks to the Siamese minister through an interpreter; for a while (that is, until the audience gets used to the idea of hearing English come from the mouths of Siamese) the characters remain silent, and their conversation is assumed by several instruments in the orchestra. Music thus becomes a basic part of the plot, and it is henceforth used to point up some important piece of stage action—in orchestral fragments, as background to the dialogue, as a preface to or interlude after a song, to usher in or dismiss a character. The music itself, while not Oriental at all, is delicately flavored with Oriental idioms and instrumentation. The delightful march of the royal Siamese children is characteristic of such Oriental colorations in melody, harmony, and orchestration; and so are Tuptim's monologue, "My Lord and Master" and the King's effective narrative, "A Puzzlement." Other important musical numbers, however, are more characteristically Rodgers than Oriental in their sensitive lyricism, poignant moods, and at times compelling dramatic thrust. The best are: Anna's duet with her son, "I Whistle a Happy Tune"; Anna's beautiful ballad, "Hello, Young Lovers!", and her delightful exchange with the royal children in "Getting to Know You"; the wistful love duets of Tuptim and Lun Tha, "We Kiss in the Shadow" and "I Have Dreamed"; and Anna's duet with the King, "Shall We Dance?"

Innovation could also be found in the ballet sequences, particularly in "The Small House of Uncle Thomas" (choreography by Jerome Robbins) in which *Uncle Tom's Cabin* is translated in terms of the Siamese dance. The literalness and pictorial beauty of the dance sequences have both an irresistible charm and a delicate humor. For his musical background Rodgers utilizes only percussive effects of woodblock and ancient cymbals to punctuate commentaries by a spoken chorus. The childlike realism of the dance is thus carried over into the music.

There were some important "firsts" in the production of *The King and I*, also a tragic "last." John van Druten, eminent playwright and director, was here making his first attempt at directing a musical production. And Yul Brynner, as the King, stepped quickly from obscurity to fame. Brynner had previously appeared on Broadway in one or two failures and had been directing television plays. He auditioned for Rodgers and Hammerstein at the Hotel Plaza, singing gypsy songs to his own guitar accompaniment while sitting cross-legged on the floor. As soon as they heard him, Rodgers and Hammerstein knew they had found their King.

For Gertrude Lawrence, the part of Anna was both one of her most resplendent performances and, sadly, her last anywhere. While *The King and I* was still running at the St. James Theatre, Gertrude Lawrence died of cancer on September 6, 1952; her role (at her request) was taken over by Constance Carpenter.

When *The King and I* opened on Broadway, the critics found a great deal to delight them—not only the charm and beauty of the action, music, and dance, but also the stunning scenery of Jo Mielziner and the dazzling costuming by Irene Sharaff. The whole production was, as Danton Walker said, "a flowering of all the arts of the theater with moments . . . that are pure genius." Other critics spoke of the authenticity and good taste with which the Orient was recreated, "an East of frank and unashamed romance," as Richard Watts, Jr., wrote, "seen through the eyes of . . . theatrical artists of rare taste and creative power."

1953   ME AND JULIET, a musical comedy with book and lyrics by Oscar Hammerstein II. Presented by Rodgers and Hammerstein at the Majestic Theatre on May 28. Directed by George Abbott. Dances and vocal numbers staged by Robert Alton. Cast included Isabel Bigley, Bill Hayes, and Joan McCracken (358 performances).

In 1952 there took place the highly successful revival of the Rodgers and Hart musical, *Pal Joey*. Preparing that revival awakened in Rodgers a nostalgia for the musical theater of a bygone day. He suggested to Hammerstein that, as a change of pace, they try their hand at "musical comedy" rather than a musical play. Rodgers further outlined an idea he had nursed for some time: a musical comedy that would be set in a theater and would reveal the inner mechanism of a musical show and the people it involves.

Me and Juliet turned out to be a compromise between old ways and new. It was a musical comedy, not far different from the kind Rodgers used to write with Hart. But it also incorporated some of the new ideas, techniques, and approaches he had explored with Hammerstein in integrating plot, music, and dance.

The text was made up of two love themes running contrapuntally. Two timid people of the theater—Jeanie, a chorus girl (Isabel Bigley), and Larry, an assistant manager (Bill Hayes)—are in love, but they are terrorized by an electrician, Bob (Mark Dawson), who is also in love with Jeanie. At one point Bob tries to murder both Jeanie and Larry. A lighter plot involves a dancer, Betty (Joan McCracken), and a stage manager, Mac (Ray Walston). Mac's principle is never to become emotionally involved with anybody working for him. Jeanie and Larry get married secretly in spite of Bob's heavy-handed attempts to break up their romance. And Mac is able to marry Betty and yet remain true to his principles by joining up with another show.

As the story unfolds, the play shifted swiftly from an electrician's bridge to the orchestra pit; from the dressing room to the smoking room; onstage and backstage; into the company manager's office and to a candy counter during intermission; in a back alley outside the theater during an actual performance or audition. What Rodgers and Hammerstein were trying to do was to infect audiences with their own love and enthusiasm for the theater. But as Walter F. Kerr pointed out:

> Like a lot of lovers bent on declaring their passion, the authors strike a point at which they become tongue-tied. They want to say so much, they want to say it burstingly, they want to be sure that no heartfelt endearment is omitted anywhere, that they wind up gasping for breath, and making slightly disconnected sounds.

Individual parts of the play were fascinating, and the action moved so swiftly that interest never lagged. But all the ingredients never quite added up to a single dish.

Rodgers' score in many instances reverted to the styles of a former era, particularly in the hit song, a tango presented as a duet for Larry and Jeanie, "No Other Love." This song was lifted by Rodgers from his own score for the documentary film, *Victory at Sea*. Three vivacious numbers—"Keep It Gay," "We Deserve Each Other," and "It's Me"—were the kind of bright, sophisticated pieces Rodgers used to write so well for Larry Hart's lyrics. On the other hand, an extended narrative about theater audiences, "The Big, Black Giant," delivered by Larry, and an extended sequence about show business called "Intermission Talk" were in the vein more recently tapped by Rodgers and Hammerstein for their musical plays.

1955   PIPE DREAM, a musical play with book and lyrics by Oscar Hammerstein II, based on John Steinbeck's novel, *Sweet Thursday*. Produced by Rodgers and Hammerstein at the Shubert Theatre on November 30. Staged by Harold Clurman. Dances and musical numbers staged by Boris Runanin. Cast included Helen Traubel, William Johnson, and Judy Tyler (246 performances).

The plan to transform Steinbeck's novel, *Sweet Thursday,* into a musical was born in the producing offices of Feuer and Martin, who hoped to interest Frank Loesser in writing the score. When this project fell through, Feuer and Martin turned the idea over to Rodgers and Hammerstein who expressed immediate interest because of the story's unusual setting, and the human and sympathetic treatment it gave to a strange assortment of social misfits.

The love interest is provided by "Doc" (William Johnson), an indigent scientist who studies marine life in his laboratory in Cannery Row, and a vagrant, Suzy (Judy Tyler). Suzy is picked up for breaking into a grocery store where she tries to steal some food. But she is saved from prison when Fauna, a softhearted madame of the local brothel (Helen Traubel), offers her a home. "Doc" and Suzy are attracted to each other but are separated by a quarrel at a masquerade party. They are finally reunited with the unasked-for assistance of Hazel (Mike Kellin), deeply concerned over the Doc's romantic troubles.

But the love complications of Doc and Suzy are only of secondary interest to the misfits who envelop them with their love and unselfish devotion, and who inhabit a sorry place called "The Palace Flophouse." Their concern for Doc and their attachment for Suzy flood the play with heart-warming humanity. They raffle off their house to raise money for a microscope Doc needs badly for his work, then they fix it so that Doc himself is the winner of the raffle. They connive to bring him and Suzy together again by breaking Doc's arm in his sleep; Suzy had previously said that she would come to Doc only if he was in trouble, and with his broken arm he was in need of Suzy's ministrations. These people contribute to the play all of its sentiment and some of its pathos. They also enliven the proceedings with a hilarious episode called "The Bum's Opera" and with several amusing songs, among them "A Lopsided Bus," "The Happiest House on the Block," and Hazel's confession of his mental inadequacy in "Think."

In a more lyrical and sentimental vein are two fine Rodgers songs: Suzy's poignant lament, touched with a kind of radiance Rodgers often brings to his inspiring melodies, "Everybody's Got a Home but Me," and the love duet of Doc and Suzy, "All at Once You Love Her." Doc's ballad, "The Man I used to Be" (supplemented by a dance fantasy by Don Weissmuller), and Fauna's infectious cakewalk, "Sweet Thursday," are also assets.

The casting of Helen Traubel as the madame of a brothel—her bow in musical comedy after a lifetime in the opera house—lacked conviction, and her efforts at earthiness and vigor were at times embarrassing to those who recalled her as Isolde and Brünnhilde. Much more rewarding was the performance of Judy Tyler as Suzy, making a successful Broadway debut and launching what at the time seemed to be the beginning of a rich career. But Judy's life and career came to a tragic ending in 1957 in an automobile accident; by a curious and tragic coincidence, William Johnson's life had also come to a premature end a few months earlier.

SIGMUND ROMBERG, composer

When Sigmund Romberg died in 1951 a dynasty in the American musical theater came to an end. For Romberg was the last in the royal line of operetta composers that had embraced Reginald de Koven, Victor Herbert, Gustave Kerker, Karl Hoschna, and Rudolf Friml, among others. He possessed a Continental charm, an Old World glamour, a touch of magic not often encountered on the American musical stage. Romberg's best scores retain a distinct European flavor, even when the setting of his play is American. Although he was a citizen of America and lived here for almost half a century, his musical roots lay deep in the soil of Vienna where he had spent his most impressionable years.

He was born in the small Hungarian border town of Nazy Kaniza, on July 29, 1887. Soon after Sigmund's birth, the family moved to Belisce where the boy's musical education began on the violin. He was, however, directed not to music but to engineering. He attended the Realschule in Oslek for five years as preparation for engineering study. There his musical interest was kept alive by one of the professors, the director of the school orchestra. When he heard Sigmund play the violin he immediately waived the rules forbidding students to join the orchestra before their fifth year.

While attending another preparatory school, in Szeged, he wrote his first piece of music, a march, which he dedicated to the Grand Duchess.

When she expressed interest in it, the town created an orchestra so that Romberg might conduct it in a public performance. This was his debut as a conductor.

Romberg's next move was to Vienna, to acquire an engineering degree at the Politechnische Hochschule. The greatest German-language operettas could then be seen at the historic Theater-an-der-Wien and other Viennese houses—classics like *Die Fledermaus, The Gypsy Baron,* and *The Merry Widow.* Through one of his friends, Romberg managed to gain access backstage to the Theater-an-der-Wien where he could watch the operettas being rehearsed; for a brief period he even served there as assistant manager.

He now knew that he wanted to desert engineering for music, but his parents were not sympathetic to this plan and offered a compromise. Since military service was then required of all young men, they suggested that Romberg delay a final decision on his future until his military commitment had been met. Romberg joined the 19th Hungarian Infantry Regiment stationed in Vienna and stayed with it a year and a half. Once again he expressed his determination to engage in musical activity, and once again his parents suggested a compromise. They would agree to any decision Sigmund wished to make about his future, if he delayed making that decision for a year and spent the intervening period traveling.

Romberg spent two weeks in London. Then, in his twenty-second year, he came to the United States. The year was 1909. He found a job in a pencil factory for seven dollars a week and spent his free time wandering around New York. Thus he came upon the Café Continental on Second Avenue, where he found employment as café pianist for fifteen dollars a week (plus a percentage of any tips). After a week he found a more desirable post at the Pabst-Harlem Restaurant on 125th Street. He then announced to his parents his intention of staying in America for good, becoming a citizen, and trying to make a success of music.

In 1912, he conducted his own orchestra at Bustanoby's Restaurant, playing salon music mostly of the Viennese variety and usually in his own arrangements. Before long he decided to include in his programs music for dancing—an innovation, since dancing at the time was unknown in restaurants. The novelty took hold. His dance music became such an integral part of Bustanoby's that he performed everyday from noon to 3:00 A.M., earning 150 dollars a week. He also extended his activity by writing music. The publishing house of Joseph W. Stern issued his first three songs: two were one-steps, "Leg of Mutton" and "Some Smoke"; a third was a waltz, "Le Poème." All three became popular with dance orchestras everywhere. Before long, J. J. Shubert came to him with an offer. He had just lost the services of his staff composer, Louis Hirsch, and he wanted Romberg to take over Hirsch's job of preparing the music for Shubert's varied productions.

Romberg's Broadway debut came with a Winter Garden extravaganza, *The Whirl of the World,* starring Eugene and Willie Howard and the Dolly Sisters, and opening on January 10, 1914. He soon became one of Broadway's most prolific composers. Between 1914 and 1917 he wrote 275 numbers for seventeen musicals; fifteen of these productions came within a twenty-two-month period. These shows included Winter Garden extravaganzas, revues, and Romberg's first attempt at writing for America a Continental-type operetta, *The Blue Paradise* (1915). With *Maytime* (1917) and *Blossom Time* (1921), Romberg became one of America's outstanding composers of operettas.

In the early 1930's, Romberg settled in Hollywood, where he worked for motion pictures, sometimes assisting in screen adaptations of his famous operettas, sometimes writing new music for original screen plays. From the latter came one of his most famous ballads, "When I Grow Too Old to Dream" from *The Night Is Young* (1934).

Soon after Pearl Harbor the William Morris Agency prevailed on him to form his own orchestra and tour the country in concerts of "middle-brow music." The first tour, in 1942, was a failure. But subsequent tours proved more favorable, and the fourth, beginning with a performance at Carnegie Hall on September 10, 1943, broke attendance records in several cities. Henceforth, "An Evening with Sigmund Romberg"—as these concerts were billed—was an assured success everywhere. Just before his death Romberg was planning an international tour with his orchestra.

In these concerts the emphasis was not only on Romberg's own songs but also on the ingratiating music of old Vienna, which had always inspired his best creative efforts. Romberg never failed to recognize how strong were his ties to old Vienna. Toward the end of his life he told his wife: "I'm two wars away from my time. My time was pre-World War I. . . . I've got to get away from Vienna. That's all passé."

In line with such thinking he wrote two new Broadway musicals, both thoroughly American. One was outstandingly successful, *Up in Central Park* (1945); the other, *The Girl in Pink Tights,* produced posthumously, was a failure.

But the truth was that he was not at his best in any vein but the

Viennese. He confessed as much to a Baltimore audience when he was making his first appearance conducting his orchestra. In response to an ovation he made a little speech:

I have been told that the music I have lived with for many years now belongs to the past. . . . Perhaps this is so. If so, they are right, and I am wrong. But if some of the lovely music you have listened to tonight, and will listen to again when I've finished this rambling talk, if this music has touched you and made you remember that life was livable once and that it will be again, then I am right, and they are wrong.

Sigmund Romberg died in New York on November 10, 1951. His valedictory to the stage was *The Girl in Pink Tights,* which he did not live to see produced. A few years later his screen biography was released, *Deep in My Heart.*

1914-24 *The Passing Shows*

1914 edition, a revue with book and lyrics by Harold Atteridge. Additional music by Harry Carroll. Presented by the Shuberts at the Winter Garden on June 10. Staged by J. C. Huffman. Dances by Jack Mason. Cast included Marilyn Miller, Jose Collins, Bernard Granville, and Lew Brice (133 performances).

1916 edition, a revue with book and lyrics by Harold Atteridge. Additional music by Otto Motzan. Presented by the Shuberts at the Winter Garden on June 22. Staged by J. C. Huffman and Allen K. Foster. Cast included Ed Wynn, Frances Demarest, Herman Timberg, the Ford Sisters, and Fred Walton (140 performances).

1917 edition, a revue with dialogue and lyrics by Harold Atteridge. Additional music by Otto Motzan. Presented by the Shuberts at the Winter Garden on April 26. Staged by J. C. Huffman. Cast included De Wolf Hopper, Jefferson de Angelis, Johnny Dooley, and Irene Franklin (196 performances).

1918 edition, a revue with book and lyrics by Harold Atteridge. Additional music by Jean Schwartz. Presented by the Shuberts at the Winter Garden on July 25. Staged by J. J. Shubert and J. C. Huffman. Musical numbers and ballets staged by Jack Mason. Cast included Marilyn Miller, Fred and Adele Astaire, Willie and Eugene Howard, Charles Ruggles, and Frank Fay (124 performances).

1919 edition, a revue with book and lyrics by Harold Atteridge. Additional music by Jean Schwartz. Presented by the Shuberts at the Winter

Garden on October 23. Staged by J. C. Huffman. Cast included Charles Winninger, Blanche Ring, James Barton, the Avon Comedy Four, Olga Cook, and Reginald Denny (280 performances).

1923 edition, a revue with book and lyrics by Harold Atteridge. Additional music by Jean Schwartz. Presented by the Shuberts at the Winter Garden on June 14. Staged by J. C. Huffman. Cast included Walter Woolf, George Hassell, George Jessel, and Helen Shipman.

1924 edition, a revue with book and lyrics by Harold Atteridge. Additional music by Jean Schwartz. Presented by the Shuberts at the Winter Garden on September 3. Cast included James Barton, George Hassell, Lulu McConnell, Olga Cook, and Harry McNaughton (93 performances).

Romberg's first association with *The Passing Show* came in 1914 with what undoubtedly was the most lavish, the most eye-catching, the most entertaining, and the most varied edition of these spectacular revues. It set a standard that subsequent editions found hard to match. It signaled the Broadway stage debut of Marilyn Miller, after a career in vaudeville. She appeared as a Dresden doll; she impersonated notable actresses of the day; she sang "Omar Khayyam"; and she danced. And at once she joined the company of Broadway "greats." Bernard Granville and Lew Brice contributed burlesque dancing and brought down the house with a pantomime interlude entitled "The Grape Dance." Jose Collins sang "You're Just a Little Bit Better" and "Dreams of the Past," and appeared as a princess in one of the most sumptuously mounted sketches of the production, a scene in a Persian garden. Another breath-taking stage effect was achieved in the finale with a view of San Francisco from an altitude.

Perhaps as significant in the history of the musical stage as the debut of Marilyn Miller was the emergence of the "modern chorus girl" in the 1914 edition. Cecil Smith tells the story in *Musical Comedy in America:*

Gone forever now were the gigantic chorus ladies with their Amazonian marches and drill. . . . The choral Amazon had been on the way out for some years. But with the *Passing Show of 1914* the metamorphosis was complete. . . . The girls' legs which had been emerging from their tights inch by inch for several seasons, were now presented unadorned and *au naturel.* . . . Skirts were short and arms were bare, and at one point the glittering spangles were dispensed with, revealing bare midriffs on the upper-class New York stage for the first time. The "winsome witches" gave a new and piquant meaning to the runway.

The 1916 edition tried to duplicate the triumph of its predecessor, but not with telling results, though it did have a comedy classic in "A Modern Garage" in which Ed Wynn tried to fix an inner tube with saw and hammer. One of the songs interpolated into this edition was "The Making of a Girl," marking the entrance of George Gershwin into the professional theater.

The 1917 edition boasted two hardy veterans of the musical stage—De Wolf Hopper and Jefferson de Angelis, two outstanding production numbers in "The Wanderer" and "Under the Willow Tree," and an interpolated song that caught the martial spirit of the times and became a hit, "Goodbye Broadway, Hello France!" (words by C. Francis Reisner and Benny Davis, music by Billy Baskette).

In 1918 the production was dominated by the war. There was a skit on War Savings Stamps (chorus girls went down into the aisles to sell the stamps to the audience); a take-off on Salome, in which Salome danced with the head of the Kaiser on a tray; and a reproduction of an aerial raid. The best comedy was contributed by Eugene and Willie Howard in the "Galli-Curci Rag" and in hilarious antics in a Childs' Restaurant.

The outstanding dance numbers in the 1918 edition came from Fred and Adele Astaire who now came into their own for the first time. For many years barred from the Broadway stage because they were under age, Fred and Adele Astaire had for years been hoofing up and down the country in vaudeville theaters. As early as 1906 (when Fred was only seven) the act of Fred and Adele Astaire was billed as "Juvenile Artists Presenting an Electric Musical Toe-Dancing Novelty." They were vaudeville headliners when, in 1917, the Shuberts brought them for the first time into the legitimate theater, in a wartime revue called *Over the Top*, presented at the 44th Street Roof on December 1 (score by Romberg). The entire production had been built around the dynamic personality of its star, Justine Johnson. Yet each time the Astaires went through their suave and sophisticated dance routines the stage was theirs. *Over the Top* was a failure, but the Astaires survived the wreckage. A year later Shubert placed them in the *Passing Show of 1918*, presenting them for the first time as stars.

Romberg's best songs in the 1918 edition were "I Can't Make My Feet Behave" and "My Baby Talking Girl"; better still, however, were two interpolated numbers, both all-time hits, "Smiles" (by J. Will Callahan and Lee G. Roberts) and "I'm Forever Blowing Bubbles" (by Jean Kenbrovin and John W. Kellette).

In 1919, Charles Winninger and Blanche Ring joined in a travesty on

The Jest, Charles Winninger playing Lionel Barrymore with almost incredible similitude, and Blanche strutting around as John Barrymore. Even broader humor appeared in several skits starring the Avon Comedy Four as cooks, physicians, and waiters. Reginald Denny appeared as a genial master of ceremonies; James Barton, making his first Broadway appearance after a career in vaudeville, stock, and repertory companies, scored heavily in specialty dances; and the singing of Blanche Ring was arresting.

The 1923 and 1924 editions of the *Passing Show* were the last. They were substandard productions, and both were failures.

1915   THE BLUE PARADISE, an operetta with book by Edgar Smith based on a Viennese operetta by Leon Stein and Bela Jenbasch. Lyrics by Herbert Reynolds. Additional music by Edmund Eysler. Produced by the Shuberts at the Casino Theatre on August 5. Staged by J. H. Benrimo. Musical numbers and dances staged by Ed Hutchinson. Cast included Vivienne Segal, Cecil Lean, and Cleo Mayfield (356 performances).

"Blue Paradise" is a little Viennese garden restaurant, the principal set of this operetta. Rudolph Stoeger (Cecil Lean) meets his student friends to bid them farewell, since he is off for America to make his career there. He must also part with Mizzi, the flower girl (Vivienne Segal). She knows that their separation is permanent but feigns that it is temporary. In saying good-by the lovers sing a tender song of farewell, a song with which Romberg achieved his first classic in three-quarter time, "Auf Wiedersehen." (This is the only one of the eight numbers Romberg wrote for this score that has survived.)

A quarter of a century later Rudolph, now a wealthy man, returns to Vienna with his fiancée, Gladys (Frances Demarest). In remembrance of things past he revisits the "Blue Paradise," no longer a restaurant but the home of one of his old friends. Rudolph's friends decide to revive the garden of the house into the "Blue Paradise" as Rudolph had once known it, and during this revival Gaby (Cleo Mayfield), daughter of the owner of the house, appears in the same dress Mizzi had worn a quarter of a century earlier, and sings "Auf Wiedersehen." Rudolph then learns that Gaby is the daughter of Mizzi, that Mizzi has married his old-time friend and has become a shrew. Rudolph is now happy to return to America with his fiancée and forget all about Vienna.

As the flower girl Mizzi, Vivienne Segal made her first Broadway stage appearance. Romberg had been searching for a young singing actress to play the lead in his operetta, and his failure to do so almost led him to abandon the project. A voice scout told him of a young student at the Curtis Institute in Philadelphia who might fill the bill. Romberg made a trip to Philadelphia, heard her sing, and exclaimed: "Thank God, you'll do!" In lifting her from the Curtis Institute to the Broadway theater, Romberg was helping create a career that dominated the Broadway musical stage for over thirty years.

1916   ROBINSON CRUSOE, JR., an extravaganza with book and lyrics by Harold Atteridge and Edgar Smith. Additional music by James Hanley. Produced by the Shuberts at the Winter Garden on February 17. Musical numbers staged by J. C. Huffman. Dances by Allen K. Foster. Cast included Al Jolson, Kitty Doner, Claude Flemming, and Mlle Rodriguez (139 performances).

Robinson Crusoe, Jr., set a pattern for the Winter Garden extravaganzas starring Al Jolson which was followed for the next few years and which were completely dominated by his dynamic personality. They would have him fill various colorful roles (usually named Gus) in fantasies that carried him from the present to another age and to far-off exotic places. The plot would generally be diffuse and amorphous, always elastic enough to permit Jolson to seize the limelight and strut his wares.

In *Robinson Crusoe, Jr.*, he first appears as Gus, the chauffeur of Hiram Westbury (Claude Flemming). Weary after permitting a movie company to take film shots of his estate, Hiram falls asleep and dreams he is Robinson Crusoe, dressed in skins. His chauffeur, Gus (Al Jolson), becomes his man Friday. However, they are not confined to any single island. They pass from one exotic scene to another: from a Spanish castle (where Mme Rodriguez performs a virtuoso castanet dance) to a beautifully staged pirate ship, and from there to a forest in which trees come alive and become chorus girls swaying to the lilting rhythm of "My Voodoo Lady." About a half-hour before the ending of the play, background, time, and story are forgotten as Al Jolson takes over—singing (often songs interpolated during the run of the show), ad-libbing, telling stories, clowning. His best comic number was "Where Did Robinson Crusoe Go with Friday on Saturday Night?" and his biggest hit was a Hawaiian song, "Yacka Hula Hickey Dula." (Both these songs were not by Romberg but by E. Ray Goetz, Joe Young, and Pete Wendling.) He also presented "Where the Black-Eyed Susans Grow" (by Dave Radford and Richard Whiting).

1917   MAYTIME, an operetta with book and lyrics by Rida Johnson Young and Cyrus Wood. Produced by the Shuberts at the Shubert Theatre on

August 16. Staged by Edward F. Temple, Allen K. Foster, and J. J. Shubert. Cast included Peggy Wood, Charles Purcell, and William Norris (492 performances).

After the success of *The Blue Paradise*, Romberg determined to devote himself to writing music for the European kind of operetta in preference to the American revues and extravaganzas assigned him by the Shuberts. In 1916 he decided to part company with the Shuberts and try to find projects more suited to his talents. J. J. Shubert urged him to reconsider, promising to try to find for Romberg a book that would lend itself to operetta treatment. Shubert kept his word and early in 1917 turned over to the composer *Maytime*, a European operetta adapted for the American stage by Rida Johnson Young.

Maytime became one of the most successful operettas of the Broadway stage, a triumph that firmly set Romberg's reputation as a composer of operettas. It was such a box-office attraction that within a year a second company opened in a nearby playhouse to accommodate the demand for seats—the first time in the history of our theater that a musical had two productions running simultaneously on Broadway.

Its sentimental plot involved the frustrated love affair of Otillie van Zandt (Peggy Wood) and Richard Wayne (Charles Purcell), carrying them from 1840 to the end of the century. Also involved in the story was a deed to a mansion owned by Richard's father but which he had to turn over to Colonel van Zandt in payment of a long-standing debt. At the old Washington Square home of the Van Zandts, Ottilie and Richard come upon the deed in the garden, blown there through the window of the Colonel's study. They bury it in the garden in a box containing a ring, and while doing so pledge eternal love. Fifteen years later Ottilie is compelled to marry Claude, a distant relative and a gambler. He dies, leaving Ottilie penniless. Richard, still in love with her, buys the mansion when it is put up on auction and deeds it to Ottilie without disclosing that he is the benefactor. At the turn of the century the mansion becomes a dress shop managed by Ottilie's granddaughter. Richard's grandson is in love with the girl, and it is the third generation that finds the happiness that had been denied to the grandparents.

Although Peggy Wood had been appearing on the Broadway musical stage since 1910—when she had appeared in the chorus of *Naughty Marietta*—and had been seen since in various operettas either on the road or as a replacement on Broadway, it was only with the role of Ottilie that she became a musical-comedy star. To her was assigned the hit song of *Maytime*—a number that ran throughout the play as a kind of leitmotif

—the waltz, "Will You Remember?" which she first sang as a duet with Richard. Other popular numbers included a modernized version of a minstrel-show favorite, "Jump Jim Crow," "Dancing Will Keep You Young," and "It's a Windy Day."

1918   SINBAD, a musical comedy with book and lyrics by Harold Atteridge. Additional songs by Al Jolson and others. Presented by the Shuberts at the Winter Garden on February 14. Staged by J. C. Huffman and J. J. Shubert. Cast included Al Jolson, Lawrence d'Orsay, Kitty Doner, Constance Farber, and Forrest Huff (164 performances).

Sinbad, like other Al Jolson extravaganzas, had little rhyme or reason in its plot, but it provided ample room for his contagious personality to unfold. The scene shifts from the North Shore Country Club on Long Island to Sinbad's palace in Bagdad and back again to Long Island. In a series of flashbacks, Inbad, a porter (Al Jolson), finds himself in old Bagdad where he confronts characters out of the *Arabian Nights,* including Sinbad himself (Forrest Huff). He is then carried to "The Perfumed East," "Cabin of the Good Ship Whale," "Grotto of the Valley of the Diamonds," "Island of Eternal Youth," and on a "Raft on the Briny Deep." What transpires is not particularly significant beyond providing a means of introducing elegant sets and stage effects and several routines ranging from a dog act in the opening scene to an exotic Hindu snake dance performed by Roshanara. Significance came when Jolson appeared on the stage. As was customary, he carried the whole show with his infectious singing, ribbing, and ad-libbing.

Though Romberg wrote ten numbers for this Jolson show, the hit songs came from other composers. By now Jolson had established the practice of interpolating during the run of a play any song that struck his fancy without much regard for its relevance. His cogent delivery made them hits, a few were ever after identified with him: "Rock-a-Bye Your Baby with a Dixie Melody," "Hello, Central, Give Me No Man's Land," and "Why Do They All Take the Night Boat to Albany?"—all three by Joe Young, Sam M. Lewis, and Jean Schwartz; "Mammy" by Joe Young, Sam Lewis, and Walter Donaldson; "Chloe" by Buddy de Sylva and Al Jolson; "I'll Say She Does" by Buddy de Sylva, Gus Kahn, and Al Jolson; and "Swanee" by Irving Caesar and George Gershwin. Gershwin had not written "Swanee" for Jolson but for a stage show at the Capitol Theatre in New York, where it failed to attract attention. One day, at a party, Gershwin played the song for Jolson, who was so delighted with it that he decided to introduce it at one of his Sunday evening "concerts" at the

Winter Garden. Soon after that, Jolson interpolated it in *Sinbad*, where the song became so successful that in a year's time it sold over 2,000,000 records and 1,000,000 copies of sheet music—Gershwin's first and greatest hit.

1921   BLOSSOM TIME, an operetta with book and lyrics by Dorothy Donnelly, adapted from a German operetta, *Das drei Mädlerhaus*, based on the life of Franz Schubert. Romberg's music was derived from the works of Schubert. Produced by the Shuberts at the Ambassador Theatre on September 29. Cast included Bertram Peacock, Olga Cook, and Howard Marsh (592 performances).

The Shuberts had acquired the American rights to a celebrated European operetta about Franz Schubert. Feeling that the score was not altogether suited for Americans, the Shuberts asked Romberg to prepare a new one. From the storehouse of Schubert's immortal music, Romberg picked some of the master's most familiar or characteristic melodies and provided new settings within the formal pattern of the American popular song. Thus he wrote the "Song of Love," the hit of the show—a duet of Schober and Mitzi—by adapting the beautiful cello melody from the first movement of the Unfinished Symphony. Other Schubert themes and tunes became the source of such delightful Romberg songs as "Three Little Maids," "Tell Me, Daisy," "Lonely Hearts," "My Springtime Thou Art," and "Serenade."

The plot was a manufactured yarn. The composer (Bertram Peacock), in love with Mitzi (Olga Cook), writes the "Song of Love" as an expression of his tenderness. He asks his best friend, Schober (Howard Marsh), to sing the love song to Mitzi. Mitzi now falls in love with Schober. When he realizes that Schober has won Mitzi and that she will never be his, Schubert writes a symphony and decides to leave it unfinished. At its première Schubert is sick with his last fatal illness; effete and soul-weary, he writes his great religious song, "Ave Maria." It need not be emphasized that none of these incidents jibe with biographical truth.

Blossom Time became one of Romberg's greatest successes. It ran almost two years on Broadway and had four road companies. Since 1921 there has hardly been a period when it has not been revived somewhere in the United States.

1921   BOMBO, a musical extravaganza with dialogue and lyrics by Harold Atteridge. Additional lyrics by Buddy de Sylva, and additional music by other composers. Produced by the Shuberts at the Jolson Theatre on October 6. Staged by J. C. Huffman. Cast included Al Jolson and Janet Adair (219 performances).

"The concoction is not well named" wrote a critic of the New York *Dramatic Mirror*. "It should be called Al Jolson. He's the whole show, which is precisely as it should be." The implication was that the plot made little sense, and the songs and Jolson routines had little relevance within that plot. But it had Jolson singing, joking, and zooming all over the stage like an uncontrolled jet-propelled human missile. The plot had something to do with Christopher Columbus who discovers America with the help of his colored deck hand, Gus (Al Jolson). It involves a bunch of crooks and a seer, and is highlighted by an amusing episode in which Gus barters with the Indians for Manhattan Island. "Give us Brooklyn," Gus tells the Indians, "and I'll give you in exchange a pair of rusty scissors."

Many of the songs Jolson interpolated into *Bombo* during its run became Jolson specialties. They included, "Toot, Toot, Tootsie" by Gus Kahn, Ernie Erdman, and Dan Russo; "California, Here I Come" by Buddy de Sylva, Joseph Meyer, and Al Jolson; "Who Cares?" by Jack Yellen and Milton Ager; "I'm Goin' South" by Abner Silver and Harry Woods; "April Showers" by Buddy de Sylva and Louis Silvers; and "Yoo-Hoo" by Buddy de Sylva and Al Jolson. Though none of the thirteen songs in Romberg's score boasted any hits to match those just mentioned, it had some agreeable items, including the title song, "Oh, Oh Columbus" and "Any Place with You."

1924 THE STUDENT PRINCE, an operetta with book and lyrics by Dorothy Donnelly. Produced by the Shuberts at the Jolson Theatre on December 2. Staged by J. C. Huffman. Cast included Ilse Marvenga, Howard Marsh, George Hassell, and Roberta Beatty (608 performances).

Three years elapsed before Romberg enjoyed another Broadway success like *Blossom Time*. Meanwhile he completed the scores of fourteen Shubert musical comedies and revues. Then the Shuberts called on him to write the music for an American adaptation of a popular European operetta, *Old Heidelberg*, the rights for which they had acquired after prolonged and complicated negotiations.

The setting was old Heidelberg, the German university town; the time, 1860. Prince Karl Franz (Howard Marsh) comes to Heidelberg incognito with his tutor, Dr. Engel (Greek Evans). At "The Golden Apple" inn he meets and falls in love with the waitress, Kathie (Ilse Marvenga). But the romance is doomed when the Prince must return home and ascend the throne. Two years later he returns to Heidelberg to bid a belated farewell to Kathie before marrying Princess Margaret.

The Continental setting and the frustrated love affair of a Prince and a waitress were the stimulants Romberg seemed to need for writing his most ambitious and best score. The Shuberts originally felt his music was "too high-brow" for popular consumption, but Romberg insisted on following his own direction by producing numbers expansive in melodic design and rich in harmonic texture: the love duet of Kathie and the Prince, "Deep in My Heart"; the nostalgic duet of the Prince and Dr. Engel, "Golden Days"; and the Prince's song, "Serenade." In helping cast the play Romberg demanded good voices as well as attractive stage presences; he insisted upon an all-male chorus of forty voices for his ambitious choral numbers, which included his famous "Drinking Song." And he fought against the advice and criticism of several practical show-men who begged him to abandon the sad ending for a happier resolution.

Romberg was permitted to have his way, and with happy results for all concerned. *The Student Prince* played to a capacity house for two years, and had nine different companies touring the country. So large was the sale of the sheet music that Witmark, who published the score and was then in financial difficulties, once again became a major power in Tin Pan Alley.

1926   THE DESERT SONG, an operetta with book and lyrics by Otto Harbach, Oscar Hammerstein II, and Frank Mandel. Produced by Schwab and Mandel at the Casino Theatre on November 30. Book directed by Arthur Hurley. Music numbers staged by Robert Connolly. Cast included Vivienne Segal, Robert Halliday, Eddie Buzzell, and William O'Neal (471 performances).

Originally entitled *My Fair Lady*, this Romberg operetta tried out in Wilmington, Delaware, where it encountered a series of unfortunate accidents that seemed to bode ill for its future. A blown-out fuse threw the performance into total darkness for a few minutes; then one of the ceiling beams collapsed, bringing the scenery down in a crash. In spite of these mishaps the play went over well. By the time the production reached New York, under its new and permanent title, it ran smoothly. The critics praised it for its "pageantry, romance, ringing music, vitality and humor" (in the words of the New York *Sun*). Bide Dudley found it to be an "operetta of much vitality, both in its romantic story and in its music."

During 1925-26 the revolt of the Riffs, under the leadership of Abdel Drim, against the French protectorate in Morocco, was blazed across the front pages of American newspapers. This timely news provided

Harbach, Hammerstein, and Mandel with material for an operetta. In their play the setting is French Morocco, where the bandit chief, the Red Shadow, is secretly in love with Margot Bonvalet (Vivienne Segal). When he learns that she is about to marry the Governor of Morocco, he abducts her and carries her off to the harem of Ali ben Ali. There he tries to win her love, but is coldly rejected since she is in love with Pierre Birabeau (Robert Halliday), the Governor's son. Gallantly the Red Shadow offers to bring Pierre to her, but Margot suddenly realizes that Pierre no longer interests her, that she is more interested in the handsome bandit. The Governor of Morocco, General Birabeau, suddenly appears to rescue Margot. Confronted with the Red Shadow, he attacks him, but the bandit offers no resistance. At the display of weakness the bandit's men are horrified, abandon him, and send him off into exile. But the strange behavior is soon explained. The Red Shadow is none other than Pierre himself. Margot is now in the enviable position of finding that her lover and his most serious rival are really one and the same man.

The principal love song bears the same name as the operetta, but it is perhaps better known today as "Blue Heaven"; it is a duet of Margot and the Red Shadow. Other significant musical items in a rich score include the Red Shadow's beautiful first-act love song, "One Alone," and his second-act "Farewell," both with male chorus; Margot's tender "Romance"; and two stirring numbers for Margot and chorus, "Sabre Song" and "French Marching Song."

1928   THE NEW MOON, a romantic musical comedy with book and lyrics by Oscar Hammerstein II, Frank Mandel, and Laurence Schwab. Produced by Schwab and Mandel at the Imperial Theatre on September 19. Musical numbers staged by Bobby Connolly. Cast included Evelyn Herbert, Robert Halliday, and William O'Neal (509 performances).

The New Moon had the longest run of any Romberg operetta; later on, when it was first bought by the screen, it brought the highest price paid up to then for a Broadway musical. Yet in out-of-town tryouts it gave every indication of being a failure. The audiences were so apathetic that the producers were convinced they had a failure. Extensive revisions then took place with happy consequences. When the play came to New York it was acclaimed. St. John Ervine, then serving as guest critic for the New York *World*, called it "the most charming and fragrant entertainment of its sort that I have seen in a long time."

The text was based on the life of Robert Mission, the French aristocrat. The setting is New Orleans in the late eighteenth century. Robert

(Robert Halliday) is a bondservant to Monsieur Beaunoir, a wealthy New Orleans citizen, and is in love with Beaunoir's daughter, Marianne (Evelyn Herbert). Since he is a political fugitive from the French police, Robert is unable to reveal that he is of noble birth. When Captain Paul Duval arrives from Paris aboard *The New Moon* to apprehend Robert, the latter is taken and shipped back to France for trial. Marianne also manages to get aboard ship. A mutiny breaks out during which the bondservants gain control. They land on a small island off the coast of Florida. Stormy incidents follow between captors and captives until a French ship arrives with the news that France is now a republic. The islanders, with Robert as leader, set up their own government, and Robert finally wins Marianne.

The outstanding love song of the play (and it is one of Romberg's most famous melodies) is Marianne's "Lover, Come Back to Me" (its middle section borrowed from a Tchaikovsky piano piece). Other highly lyrical numbers included the beautiful ballad, "Softly as in a Morning Sunrise"; Marianne's tender "One Kiss"; and a duet of Marianne and Robert, "Wanting You." Robert and a male chorus introduced "Stout-Hearted Men," one of Romberg's most stirring and virile tunes.

1935   MAY WINE, a musical play with book by Frank Mandel, based on *The Happy Alienist*, a novel by Wallace Smith and Erich von Stroheim. Lyrics by Oscar Hammerstein II. Presented by Laurence Schwab at the St. James Theatre on December 5. Book staged by José Rubin. Cast included Walter Slezak, Nancy McCord, and Walter Woolf King (213 performances).

Psychoanalysis is here subjected to musical-comedy treatment. In Vienna the psychiatrist, Professor Johann Volk (Walter Slezak) falls in love with Marie, Baroness von Schlewitz (Nancy McCord). The Baroness, however, loves a poor but high-born gentleman, Baron Kuno Adelhorst (Walter Woolf King). The psychiatrist marries the Baroness, but his assistant soon fills him with doubts about his wife's fidelity. As an escape from his mental torment Professor Volk turns to drink. In a fit of madness he shoots at a figure he believes to be his wife but which is only a dummy. The professor's fears prove completely groundless, and he and his wife are reconciled.

The authors made a notable effort to integrate music and play. Brooks Atkinson noted that "the excrescences and stock appurtenances" of most operettas were here avoided. Mr. Atkinson added: "To some extent they [the authors] have succeeded. . . . But the operetta has certain plodding mannerisms that dull the fine edge of appreciation." Percy Hammond, however, found it to be a "dignified little grand opera" and Gilbert Gabriel felt it was "one of those fragrant and tasty concoctions which, poured in one ear, warms the affections and tickles the humors considerably before it flies out the other."

The two most notable songs were by Marie, "My Darlings" and "Something New Is in My Heart." "A Chanson in the Prater" and "I Built a Dream" were also of melodic interest. Several delightful dance routines by Jack Cole and Alice Dudley added to the charm of the production.

1945   UP IN CENTRAL PARK, a musical comedy with book and lyrics by Herbert and Dorothy Fields. Produced by Michael Todd at the Century Theatre on January 27. Staged by John Kennedy. Dances by Tamiris. Cast included Wilbur Evans, Betty Bruce, and Maureen Cannon (504 performances).

This was the last musical Romberg lived to see produced, and its great success was a source of considerable personal satisfaction. For years before *Up in Central Park* appeared, there had been rumors circulated that Romberg was through as a composer for the stage; that Romberg was incapable of adapting his Continental style of writing to the new demands of the Broadway theater since the mid-1930's. Romberg defied these critics by achieving one of his biggest box-office attractions with a thoroughly American play, a play that in every sense was a musical comedy and not an old-fashioned operetta.

Up in Central Park was set in New York of the 1870's, during the city rule of the Tweed Ring. John Matthews, a reporter for the New York *Times* (Wilbur Evans), investigates the crooked political machine of Boss Tweed, particularly its fraudulent deals connected with the building of Central Park. During these investigations John falls in love with Rosie Moore (Maureen Cannon), daughter of one of Tweed's ward heelers. When Tweed's lieutenant promises to use his influence to further Rosie's career as a singer, she forgets Matthews and marries the politician. Then the Tweed machine collapses and Rosie's husband is killed while escaping from a former mistress. Left on her own, Rosie pursues her musical career. She meets Matthew again in Central Park and their old romance is revived.

Four excellent songs are perfectly attuned to the style and mood of the time and the setting: "Close as Pages in a Book," "Carousel in the Park," "It Doesn't Cost You Anything to Dream," and "April Snow." A powerful contributor to the atmospheric charm and appeal of the play were a delightful ice-skating ballet in a Currier and Ives manner and a Maypole Dance, both creations of Tamiris; and the settings and costumes all patterned after famous Currier and Ives lithographs.

1954   THE GIRL IN THE PINK TIGHTS, a musical comedy with book by Jerome Chodorov and Joseph Fields. Lyrics by Leo Robin. Presented by Shepard Traube in association with Anthony B. Farrell at the Mark Hellinger Theatre on March 5. Production staged by Shepard Traube. Dances and musical numbers by Agnes De Mille. Cast included David Atkinson, Brenda Lewis, and Jeanmaire (115 performances).

This was Romberg's last score and he did not live to see it reach the stage. About a year before the composer's death, Chodorov and Fields discussed with Romberg the idea for a yet-unwritten play: a period piece set in New York immediately after the Civil War and built around the first production of *The Black Crook* (see Appendix I—1866). The composer liked the suggestion, and the collaborators went to work. Romberg completed all his music before his death.

The setting was the New York theatrical district. Clyde Hallam (David Atkinson) has written a play called *Dick the Renegade,* which interests Lotta Leslie, owner of Niblo's Gardens (Brenda Lewis). She stages the play with Hallam and herself in the cast. Nearby, at the Academy of Music, a group of French ballet dancers are about to appear in a large production. Hallam falls in love with its prima ballerina, Lisette Gervais (Jeanmaire). The night before the première of the ballet, the Academy of Music burns down and the ballet company is stranded without a theater. Lotta—in love with the conductor of the ballet company, Maestro Gallo—finds a sponsor for the play. *Dick the Renegade* is now changed from a Western into a musical comedy with French ballets. The show is a success, becomes the first musical comedy in American stage history. Successful, too, are the romances of Hallam and Lisette and Lotta and Maestro Gallo.

Regrettably, Romberg's valedictory to the stage was a dud. The play had a kind of nostalgic charm, but it lacked pace and sustained interest. As Richard Watts, Jr., said: "The narrative plods along with a strange and uncharacteristic lack of imagination and invention, and there are only a few occasions when it lives up to either its own potentialities or the entirely delightful talents of its heroine."

The heroine referred to by Mr. Watts, Jr., was played by Jeanmaire, making her American musical-comedy debut. (She had first appeared here in 1949, in the *Ballets de Paris* and then was seen on the American screen in Danny Kaye's motion picture, *Hans Christian Andersen.*) As Lisette she proved herself to be a "Gallic edition of Mary Martin," in the description of Brooks Atkinson.

Jeanmaire and several delightful dances conceived by Agnes De Mille ("The Ballet Class," "Pas de Deux," and a French bacchanal) were the assets of the production. Romberg's score contained some fetching moments, but it did not rise far above the mediocrity of the text. The best were Clyde's hymn, "Lost in Loveliness"; the duet of Clyde and Lisette, "In Paris and in Love"; and Lisette's song, "Up in the Elevated Railway."

HAROLD ROME, composer-lyricist

Harold Rome was born in Hartford, Connecticut, on May 27, 1908. He received his education in local elementary and secondary schools, at Trinity College in Hartford, and at Yale University. After acquiring his Bachelor of Arts degree at Yale in 1929, he entered Yale Law School. A year later he transferred to the School of Architecture, from which he was graduated in 1934.

Music had always been a major interest. He had studied the piano in boyhood, and while attending college and postgraduate school earned his living by playing in jazz bands. He also wrote special numbers for ballet companies and other groups. At Yale he took courses in music and joined the college orchestra, which toured Europe.

He came to New York in 1934 to find a place for himself as an architect. The depression, then at its peak, made such jobs scarce, particularly for novices. The necessity of earning a living led him to write songs, sometimes only the lyrics, at other times the melodies, occasionally both. Gypsy Rose Lee was effectual in getting one of his lyrics published; and the Ritz Brothers used another of his songs in one of their pictures. Since his income from these tentative efforts exceeded what he earned from architecture, he decided to abandon the latter profession to make his way as a song writer.

He found a job in Green Mansions, an adult summer camp in the Adirondack Mountains in New York, where considerable emphasis was placed on entertainment. This was in the summer of 1935. Green Mansions put on original musical productions with a resident company, and Rome's assignment was to write some of the material and help with the production. He did this work for three summers, and during this period he wrote about a hundred songs, lyrics as well as music.

One of the members of the social staff was Charles Friedman, who had been invited by the International Ladies Garment Workers Union to stage an amateur show with union members. Since a revue was planned, Friedman asked Rome to write some of the songs. That amateur union show was *Pins and Needles,* which made stage history by becoming the most successful Broadway musical production up to that time. It also helped establish Rome as a song writer.

Sponsored as it was by a trade union, *Pins and Needles* had a left-wing slant. Max Gordon now commissioned Rome to write lyrics and music for another political revue, *Sing Out the News* (1938), in which there appeared one of Rome's best political songs, "Franklin D. Roosevelt Jones." *Let Freedom Ring* (1942) was another political and "social-conscious" revue engaging Rome's music, a box-office failure.

In 1942 Rome entered the army. For a while he was stationed at the New York Port of Embarkation, in the Fort Hamilton section of Brooklyn, where he wrote army shows and orientation songs. He also toured the Pacific combat zone. During this army period he completed only a single commercial assignment, the song "Micromania," used in *The Ziegfeld Follies of 1943.*

Mustered out of the army in 1945, Rome completed lyrics and music for a brilliant revue that stayed on Broadway for several years—*Call Me Mister.* Though intended to reflect the experiences and emotions of Americans reverting to civilian life, *Call Me Mister* (like the revues with which Rome had previously been associated) had a pronounced social and political viewpoint. But the political climate was changing rapidly in America, and the left-wing theater was losing its audience. Rome's next revue, *Bless You All* (1950), sought out nonprovocative subjects for humor and sentiment: movie stars from the Deep South; miracle drugs; the Parent-Teacher Association. And the tender songs contributed by Rome—"When," for example, and "You'll Never Know"—were completely devoid of political implications.

Rome then passed on from revue to musical comedy, achieving two successive box-office triumphs—*Wish You Were Here* and *Fanny*—with which he assumed a leading position among contemporary composers for the popular stage. Like Cole Porter and Irving Berlin, Harold Rome always writes his own lyrics.

1937   PINS AND NEEDLES, an amateur political revue with book by Arthur Arent, Marc Blitzstein, Emanuel Eisenberg, and others. Produced by the International Ladies' Garment Workers' Union at the Labor Stage Theatre on November 27. Staged by Charles Friedman. Dances directed by Gluck Sandor. Choreography by Benjamin Zemach. Cast made up of union members (1108 performances).

The aroused political and social consciousness of America during the depression years of the mid-1930's found reflection in this sparkling revue. It discussed labor, the domestic political scene, and the international situation with sprightly sketches, songs, and dances; with sentiment and laughter. Described by the New York *Post* as a "Puckish proletarian romp," *Pins and Needles* was an amateur production by a labor union, and as such identified itself unequivocally with a progressive point of view. This viewpoint was expressed in one of its principal songs, "Sing Me a Song of Social Significance," and in such other numbers as "Big Union for Two," and "It's Better with a Union Man." Capitalism was ridiculed in "Doing the Reactionary." European fascism was scored in "Three Little Angels of Peace Are We." The simple pleasures of the working man were sentimentalized in "Sunday in the Park."

Planned as a week-end diversion for union members and their friends, *Pins and Needles* turned out to be one of the greatest musical successes of all time. The praises of the critics and the delight of audiences soon induced its sponsors to put it on a regular run. It remained at the Princess Theatre (renamed the Labor Stage Theatre) three years. "It clicked so solidly," remarked *Variety,* "that the very people it mocked and ridiculed —the carriage trade—came in droves."

During its long run the name of the revue was changed to *New Pins and Needles* and *Pins and Needles of 1939*—but its basic concept and approach (and much of its material) remained unaltered. New items, however, were continually interpolated to interpret the rapidly changing headlines. After Munich, Prime Minister Chamberlain of England was ridiculed in "Britannia Waives the Rules." After the Soviet-Nazi pact, Stalin was mocked in "The Red Mikado." As mounting national consciousness swept the country, a stirring tribute to the American way of life was introduced in 1940 in "We Sing America."

1946   CALL ME MISTER, a revue with book by Arnold Auerbach and Arnold B. Horwitt. Produced by Melvyn Douglas and Herman Levin at the National Theatre on April 18. Staged by Robert H. Gordon. Dances by John Wray. Cast included Jules Munshin, Betty Garrett, and Lawrence Winters (734 performances).

World War II ended on August 14, 1945. There followed the long and complex problem of mustering Americans out of the armed forces. The problems of readjustment, and nostalgic or humorous recollections of life in uniform, now provided rich material for the musical theater. This material was fully exploited by this brilliant revue that had a two-year run.

The sentiment of the GI's return was effectively highlighted by "Goin' Home Train," poignantly sung by Lawrence Winters, making his Broadway stage debut. Various aspects of army life were mocked in numbers like "Surplus Blues" and "Military Life." But though the emphasis was on the GI, both before and after his separation from the armed forces, political and social consciousness was not forgotten. The revue included a caricature of three reactionary Southern Senators in "The Senators' Song," while a Negro's poignant tribute to the memory of President Roosevelt was given in "The Face on the Dime." The most successful number of the revue—and its biggest song hit—had no relation either to army or to politics. It was a travesty on the craze for South American song and dance—"South America, Take It Away," projected with such devastating effect by Betty Garrett that this one song made her a star.

1952   WISH YOU WERE HERE, a musical comedy with book by Arthur Kober and Joshua Logan based on Kober's Broadway comedy, *Having A Wonderful Time*. Produced by Leland Hayward and Joshua Logan at the Imperial Theatre on June 25. Staged and choreographed by Joshua Logan. Cast included Patricia Marand, Sheila Bond, and Jack Cassidy (598 performances).

This was Rome's first musical comedy, all his earlier associations with the Broadway stage being in revues. *Wish You Were Here* was a musical adaptation of an amusing and at times touching play about adult summer camps and the romances they inspire; and the main love interest of the original production was carried over into the musical. At Camp Karefree, in the Berkshires, Teddy Stern (Patricia Morand) from the Bronx, meets and falls in love with the camp waiter, Chick Miller (Jack Cassidy), for whom she throws over her old beau, Herman Fabricant (Harry Clark). What follows is a warmly appealing and sympathetic account of two young people in love, their problems and their dreams. All this is placed against the setting of a summer camp where the pursuit of happiness and love is relentless and around the clock, stimulated by the ready wisecracks and the indefatigable activity of Itchy, the social director (Sidney Armus), and the untiring quest of females by the camp Romeo, Pinky Harris (Paul Valentine). Verisimilitude is achieved through the first-act finale set: a large permanent swimming pool.

Chick Miller's song, "Wish You Were Here," was a hit and one of

Rome's most successful musical numbers up to that time. The score also included some amusing sidelights on adult camp life, including "Social Director" and "Don José," both presented by Itchy.

1954 FANNY, a musical comedy with book by S. N. Behrman and Joshua Logan, based on a trilogy of plays by Marcel Pagnol. Produced by David Merrick and Joshua Logan at the Majestic Theatre on November 4. Staged by Joshua Logan. Dances staged by Helen Tamiris. Cast included Ezio Pinza, Walter Slezak, William Tabbert, and Florence Henderson (888 performances).

Fanny is a tender and at times singularly moving play set on the water front of Marseilles, France. The heroine, Fanny (Florence Henderson), is deserted by her lover, Marius (William Tabbert), who, though in love with her, must helplessly respond to the call of the sea. Pregnant, Fanny must now marry the middle-aged well-to-do sailmaker, Panisse (Walter Slezak), who has always loved her discreetly but completely. He accepts her as his wife not only without incriminations but even with simple and humble gratitude, and is only too happy to consider her child as his own. When Marius suddenly returns from his voyages, Marius' father, César (Ezio Pinza), convinces him that he must do nothing to break up the harmonious life Fanny and Panisse have built up.

Pagnol flooded his three plays—*Marius, Fanny,* and *César*—with heartwarming humanity and compassion, which S. N. Behrman skillfully carried over into the musical adaptation—up to the point of including the touching death scene of Panisse. (Behrman, long a successful writer of social comedies, was here making his bow as a writer of musical-comedy librettos.) These human qualities were also accentuated by some notable performances: those of Ezio Pinza in his first return to the musical stage since *South Pacific* and (as it turned out) his last as well (he died on May 9, 1957, some months after he had left the cast); Florence Henderson as Fanny; and Walter Slezak as the rich and lovable merchant, but aging philanderer.

Rome's score was one of his most ambitious—penetrating deeply into the heart of the play and its principal characters. Songs like "To My Wife," "Restless Heart," and "Welcome Home" provide fresh insight into the personalities of Panisse, Marius, and César, respectively. Sometimes his background music brought new emotional overtones to a dramatic scene—and his music for the circus, undersea, and wedding ballets had symphonic breadth. Yet, though the artistic horizon of his writing had been extended, Rome had not lost the gift of writing a good tune. There were three: "Fanny," "Love Is a Very Light Thing," and "Never Too Late for Love."

Fanny was the second American musical to be staged in Germany since the end of World War II—in Munich on December 16, 1955, when it received an ovation that demanded over twenty curtain calls.

JERRY ROSS, composer-lyricist. *See* RICHARD ADLER

HARRY RUBY, composer

Harry Ruby was born in New York City on January 27, 1895. He attended the city public schools, commercial high school, then went into business. But business held no interest for him, and music did. Having learned the piano by himself (he received virtually no instruction in any department of music), he found a job as staff pianist with Gus Edwards' publishing establishment in Tin Pan Alley. He remained in Tin Pan Alley several years, working for various publishers as song plugger.

He also toured vaudeville as a pianist for two acts, The Messenger Boys Trio and The Bootblack Trio. While touring the vaudeville circuit he met and befriended another vaudevillian whose extracurricular activities included part ownership in a music-publishing firm and the writing of song lyrics. His name was Bert Kalmar, born in New York City on February 16, 1884. In his tenth year Kalmar ran away from home to join a tent show as child magician. He remained in show business from then on, passing on to vaudeville and burlesque as comedian and singer. While touring vaudeville he managed to organize a small publishing firm in Tin Pan Alley in partnership with another vaudevillian, Harry Puck; and he began writing song lyrics, one of which, "In the Land of Harmony" (music by Ted Snyder), was a minor hit in 1911.

Kalmar induced Ruby to work for him as staff pianist and song plugger in Tin Pan Alley. Then when Kalmar was forced to abandon vaudeville because of a knee injury, he induced Ruby to write the music for his lyrics. Their first song was "He Sits Around," which they wrote for Belle Baker just before America's entry into World War I. In 1917 they wrote "When Those Sweet Hawaiian Babies Roll Their Eyes"; in 1920 "So, Long, Oo Long" and "Timbuctoo"; and in 1921 "My Sunny Tennessee." All four songs were respectable successes. Besides, in 1920, Fanny Brice was bringing down the house at *The Ziegfeld Follies* with their song, "The Vamp from East Broadway."

The year 1923 was decisive in their writing career, for it brought them not only their biggest song hit, "Who's Sorry Now?" but also their first Broadway musical, *Helen of Troy, New York*.

For the next decade they continued writing both individual songs and Broadway scores. Between 1928 and 1941 they worked mainly in Hollywood, where they wrote for various screen productions such song hits as "Three Little Words" and "I Love You So Much." They returned to Broadway in 1941 with *The High Kickers,* a musical starring George Jessel and Sophie Tucker.

Bert Kalmar died in Los Angeles on September 18, 1947. The career of Ruby and Kalmar—and some of their best songs—appeared in the motion picture, *Three Little Words*.

1923   HELEN OF TROY, NEW YORK, a musical comedy with book by George S. Kaufman and Marc Connelly. Lyrics by Bert Kalmar. Produced by Rufus Le Maire at the Selwyn Theatre on June 19. Staged by Bertram Harrison and Bert French. Cast included Helen Ford, Queenie Smith, Tom Lewis, and Paul Frawley (191 performances).

In this, his first musical comedy, George S. Kaufman already demonstrated his gift of satire. The object of his attack was business and advertising; and the Yarrow collar factory in Troy, New York, provided a vulnerable target. This musical spoofs an efficiency expert (enacted by Roy Atwell); a lisping, moronic collar-ad idol (Charles Lawrence); and the head of the collar firm, Mr. Elias Yarrow (Tom Lewis), who can operate an immense establishment but who can never remember the size of his own collar without consulting his memorandum book. Satire was further accented in a Russian-type ballet in which famous trade-marks spring to life.

For this plot Kaufman devised a romance between Helen McGuffey, a stenographer at the Yarrow firm (Helen Ford), and David Williams (Paul Frawley), son of the owner of a rival concern. When Helen is fired, she invents a semi-soft collar that becomes a success and puts David's firm on the map.

Two of the best musical numbers were in a comic vein, a patter song, "I Like a Big Town" and "What Makes a Business Man Tired." In a lyrical and more sentimental vein were "Happy Ending," sung by Helen, and the duet "It Was Meant to Be." The last number was shared by David Williams and Helen McGuffey's sister, Maribel (Queenie Smith). As Maribel, Queenie Smith sang and danced her way to fame in the musical theater.

1926 THE RAMBLERS, a musical comedy with book by Guy Bolton and Bert Kalmar. Lyrics by Bert Kalmar. Produced by Philip Goodman at the Lyric Theatre on September 20. Staged by Philip Goodman. Cast included Clark and McCullough and Marie Saxon (289 performances).

Clark and McCullough who had previously scored successes in various revues, were here appearing in their first full-length musical comedy—and it was written for them with their special talents in mind. Clark was cast as Professor Cunningham, a spiritualistic medium; McCullough, as his servant, Sparrow. They are wandering along the Mexican border when they come upon a movie company filming a picture on location. They begin to mingle freely with the actors and before long become involved in their affairs, even to tracking down the star of the company, Ruth Chester (Marie Saxon), after she has been kidnaped by Black Pedro.

All the equipment by which Clark and McCullough had long since become familiar in revues was carried over into *The Ramblers:* the bouncing cane, trick cigar, painted glasses, raccoon coat, and most of all their own brand of loud, boisterous, burlesque comedy. Besides Clark and McCullough, the big asset of the production was Marie Saxon. She sang the show's hit number "All Alone Monday," and performed an electrifying "aeroplane Charleston dance"—and regularly drew ovations for both achievements. An acrobatic dance performed by Norma Gallo also won favor, as did two additional Ruby songs, "You Smiled at Me" and "Any Little Tune."

1927 FIVE O'CLOCK GIRL, a musical comedy with book by Guy Bolton and Fred Thompson. Lyrics by Bert Kalmar. Produced by Philip Goodman at the 44th Street Theatre on October 10. Staged by Philip Goodman. Dances staged by Jack Haskell. Cast included Mary Eaton, Oscar Shaw, Pert Kelton, and Al Shaw and Sam Lee (280 performances).

The program described this musical as "a fairy tale in modern clothes." The heroine is Patricia Brown (Mary Eaton), who works in a humble cleaning establishment. Each day at teatime she indulges a whim to telephone wealthy Gerald Brooks (Oscar Shaw) and engage him in conversation. Eventually she meets him in person and tries to convince him that she is really a society girl. He, of course, uncovers her true identity and finds that love has made him indifferent to her lowly station. To round out the story his valet, Hudgins (Louis John Bartels), falls in love with one of Patricia's sister-employees at the cleaning establishment—Susan Snow (Pert Kelton).

The comedy of Hudgins—and of a vaudeville team, Al Shaw and Sam Lee, making their Broadway stage debut—and the dancing of Danny Dare were the brightest ornaments of the production. Ruby's best songs were "Thinking of You," "Happy Go Lucky," "Who Did?" and "Up in the Clouds."

1928   GOOD BOY, a musical comedy with book by Otto Harbach, Oscar Hammerstein II, and Henry Myers. Lyrics by Bert Kalmar. Music written collaboratively with Herbert Stothart. Produced by Arthur Hammerstein at the Hammerstein Theatre on September 5. Book staged by Reginald Hammerstein. Dances staged by Busby Berkeley. Cast included Eddie Buzzell, Barbara Newberry, Charles Butterworth, and Helen Kane (253 performances).

Two country bumpkins—Walter Meakin (Eddie Buzzell) and his brother Cicero (Charles Butterworth)—come to the big city from Butlersville, Arkansas. In the city Walter soon forgets the girl he left behind, falls in love with a chorus girl, Betty Summers (Barbara Newberry), and marries her. Barbara manages to get Walter on the stage as a chorus boy. In time she tires of him and he loses her. But he regains her when he makes a fortune by creating a doll.

The ingenious staging provided most of the novelty in a hackneyed story: the realistic reproduction of the sights and sounds of the big city upon the first arrival to New York of the two Arkansas hicks; the effective first-act finale in which a hotel room swings up to reveal Walter and Betty on the balcony, the panorama of New York and Central Park stretching below. (During a visit to Berlin, Oscar Hammerstein II had seen a production of *The Good Soldier Schweik* in which complex and ingenious staging was made possible through the use of treadmills. He made a mental note to experiment some day with these treadmills; and he incorporated them into *Good Boy* with telling effect.)

Otherwise most of the interest in the play lay in the dry, wry humor of Charles Butterworth as Cicero; in the enchanting singing and dancing of Barbara Newberry; and in Helen Kane (the "Boop-de-Boop" Girl), who brought her famous pip-squeak voice and baby talk to the play's foremost song, "I Wanna Be Loved By You." The duet of Walter and Betty, "Some Sweet Someone," and "The Voice of the City" were two other attractive numbers, while "Manhattan Walk" and "Oh, What a Man" profited from the nimble hoofing of Dan Healy.

1928   ANIMAL CRACKERS, a musical comedy with book by George S. Kaufman and Morrie Ryskind. Lyrics by Bert Kalmar. Produced by Sam H. Harris at the 44th Street Theatre on October 23. Cast included the Four Marx Brothers (191 performances).

Animal Crackers was a characteristic Marx Brothers field day. Here they invade and bring chaos to the ritzy Long Island establishment of Mrs. Rittenhouse (Margaret Dumont). Groucho is a famous African explorer, Captain Spalding, dressed appropriately in sun helmet. Harpo is a professor (category unknown), wearing a full-dress suit that insists on falling down to his knees to reveal him in his underwear. Chico, in immigrant attire, is Emanuel Ravelli, and Zeppo is Jamison, Captain Spalding's secretary.

The plot involved a stolen painting, which Chico and Groucho try to retrieve. They find a simple solution: The thief must be in the house. Why not ask everyone there if he is the thief? But, inquires Captain Spalding, what if the thief is not in the house? Then, explains Ravelli, he must be outside the house, and they will go next door and ask everybody there if he is the thief. Still insistent, Captain Spalding inquires: "What if there is no house next door?" "Then," replies Ravelli firmly, "we'll build a house."

So it went—in typical Four Marx Brothers fashion. Groucho spoke "asides" in a style made popular in 1928 by Eugene O'Neill's drama, *Strange Interlude;* he was quick with a pun (to a South American he says, "you go Uruguay and I'll go my way," and to two female suitors he comments, "it's big of me to commit bigamy"). Chico plays a trick piano. Harpo chases the girls, steals everything in sight, and then in a more placid moment plays a sentimental tune on the harp. Zeppo sings the romantic songs, the best being "Watching the Clouds Roll By" and "Who's Been Listening to My Heart?"

The funniest single episode had the four brothers playing the "three Musketeers" ("We're Four of the Three Musketeers," they sing). Groucho becomes King Louis the 57th, frantically trying to make some headway with Mme Du Barry, while he is consistently being interrupted by the three musketeers.

MORRIE RYSKIND, librettist

Morrie Ryskind was born in New York City in 1895, educated in the city public schools and graduated from the Columbia University School of Journalism in 1917. He first became known through his verses published by F.P.A. in his famous newspaper column. His bow in the theater took place with several minor contributions to the first *Garrick Gaieties,* in

1925. He was a comparative novice when George S. Kaufman called on him in 1929 to help revise the text for Gershwin's *Strike Up the Band.* Again as Kaufman's collaborator, he won the Pulitzer Prize in 1932 for Gershwin's *Of Thee I Sing;* also with Kaufman he wrote texts for several other musicals by Gershwin, Irving Berlin, and Harry Ruby. After 1940 Ryskind left Broadway to work for Hollywood, where since then he has established permanent residence and to which he has confined his creative activity.

See: IRVING BERLIN (*Louisiana Purchase*); GEORGE GERSHWIN (*Strike Up the Band, Of Thee I Sing, Let 'Em Eat Cake*); HARRY RUBY (*Animal Crackers*).

ARTHUR SCHWARTZ, composer, and HOWARD DIETZ, lyricist

Arthur Schwartz was born in Brooklyn, New York, on November 25, 1900. His father, a lawyer, allowed his oldest son to specialize in music; but for Arthur he had other plans. Though Arthur early revealed an unmistakable gift for music by playing the harmonica skillfully and by making up his own tunes, Father Schwartz wanted him to follow in his own footsteps by becoming a lawyer. A formal musical education, then, was denied Arthur; and all the musical instruction he ever received was a term in harmony at New York University.

His academic education took place in Brooklyn public schools, at Boys High School, also in Brooklyn, and at New York University and Columbia University. At N.Y.U., from which he received his Bachelor of Arts degree in 1920, he was known for the marches and songs he wrote for the college football games. At the time his main interest was not music but books and the theater. He specialized in literature and the contemporary drama, continuing these and relevant studies at Columbia University, from which he received a Master's degree in 1921. For a while he contemplated a literary career, having done some writing for the college paper. But he bowed to parental guidance by taking up law at Columbia, supporting himself during this period by teaching English in a New York high school.

He was admitted to the bar in 1924. For four years he practiced law, and did well at it. But in 1928 he suddenly decided to abandon law for the theater—this decision reached after some minor successes with some of his songs. In 1923 he had contributed a number called "Alibi Baby" to the W. C. Fields musical, *Poppy.* A year later another song, "All Lanes Must Reach a Turning," was used in the Jerome Kern musical, *Dear Sir.*

After that came "Baltimore, Md., You're the Only Doctor for Me," in the 1925 edition of *The Grand Street Follies*. He also had ghosted a few songs for an ill-fated musical production that never reached Broadway, had doctored the score for still another musical to open and close out of town, and contributed a few special numbers to several vaudeville acts.

Some measure of encouragement came his way in 1925 from George Gershwin to whom he humbly submitted a number of songs for appraisal. Gershwin listened patiently and told Schwartz he liked them. "I found his reaction the warmest, most encouraging I had yet received," Schwartz later recalled.

He also received heartening praise from a close friend, then working in the advertising business, but whose extra-curricular activities included the writing of song lyrics. The friend's name was Howard Dietz.

Howard Dietz was born in New York City on September 8, 1896. He first attended Townsend Harris Hall, then Columbia College, where he was a fellow student of Lorenz Hart and Oscar Hammerstein II. He contributed verses and humorous pieces to college magazines and newspaper columns while attending Columbia, and even won a prize of 500 dollars for writing copy for an advertisement. Upon being graduated from Columbia he entered the advertising field and—after a stint in the navy during World War I—became a successful advertising executive. But he still liked writing verses. Having become a friend of Arthur Schwartz, whom he admired greatly and encouraged in his music, Dietz soon began writing lyrics for Schwartz' music. Dietz' first published lyric was the already-mentioned "Alibi Baby," with which Dietz also made his stage bow. In 1924 he wrote the lyrics for Kern's musical *Dear Sir*, and consequently also for the Arthur Schwartz song that was interpolated in that score. Three years after that, Dietz collaborated with Morrie Ryskind in writing book and lyrics for an intimate revue, *Merry-Go-Round*.

In 1928 Dietz suggested to Schwartz that they team up on a permanent basis and devote themselves completely to the business of writing songs and getting them performed. Since this idea jibed with Schwartz' own desires, Schwartz decided to leave law and enter the ranks of professional composers. At the same time Dietz left the advertising business.

Their first important collaboration was also their first box-office triumph, *The Little Show*, in 1929. The collaboration of Schwartz and Dietz continued for many years after that, resulting in several outstanding Broadway successes, and a few failures. Among the failures was an interesting experiment in musical play-writing, *Revenge with Music* (1934), which contained such remarkable Schwartz songs as "You and the Night and the Music" and "If There Is Someone Lovelier than You."

It was quite some time before Schwartz was able to duplicate in musical comedy the success he had won with his revues. When he finally did so, it was without Dietz' collaboration—with *A Tree Grows in Brooklyn* (1951). But on several occasions before that, Schwartz had worked with collaborators other than Dietz. *Stars in Your Eyes* (1939) had a book by J. P. McEvoy and lyrics by Dorothy Fields; *Park Avenue* (1946) had a book by George S. Kaufman and Nunnally Johnson and lyrics by Ira Gershwin.

From 1941 on, Arthur Schwartz was active in Hollywood, first as composer for motion-picture musicals, then as a producer. He returned to the Broadway stage in 1951 with *A Tree Grows in Brooklyn,* and again in 1954 with *By the Beautiful Sea.*

Howard Dietz' later history covers a long and rich association with Metro-Goldwyn-Mayer, from 1927 to 1957 as publicity director, then vice-president in charge of advertising, publicity, and exploitation. Since 1957 he has been a consultant for that company.

1929-30   *The Little Shows*

THE LITTLE SHOW, an intimate revue with book and lyrics mainly by Howard Dietz. Additional songs by Kay Swift, Ralph Rainger, and others. Produced by William A. Brady, Jr., and Dwight Deere Wiman in association with Tom Weatherly on April 30, 1929. Staged by Dwight Deere Wiman. Dances staged by Danny Dare. Cast included Fred Allen, Clifton Webb, Libby Holman, John McCauley, and Romney Brent (321 performances).

THE SECOND LITTLE SHOW, an intimate revue assembled by Dwight Deere Wiman. Book and lyrics by Howard Dietz. Produced by William A. Brady, Jr., Dwight Deere Wiman and Tom Weatherly at the Royale Theatre on September 2, 1930. Staged by Dwight Deere Wiman, Dave Gould, and Monty Woolley. Cast included Al Trahan, Jay C. Flippen, and Gloria Grafton (63 performances).

In the early and middle 1920's, *The Grand Street Follies* and *The Garrick Gaieties* introduced a new approach and format to the revue. Simplicity and economy replaced elaborateness of setting and costuming and the large casts found in such revues as *The Ziegfeld Follies* and the George White's *Scandals;* satire and parody were given preference over formal skits and sketches; sophistication and an adult intelligence were introduced into song, lyric, and dance. *The Little Show* became one of the most successful of these intimate revues, and it helped induce a vogue for this kind of entertainment on Broadway.

The Little Show developed out of informal Sunday-evening entertainments put on at the Selwyn Theatre by James B. Pond and Tom Weatherly. With the principal musical numbers supplied by Schwartz and most of the book and lyrics by Dietz, *The Little Show* was made into slick entertainment from opening to final curtain. And it helped to lift several unknown performers to recognition in the theater. One of them was Libby Holman. As an unknown chorus girl in *Merry-Go-Round* (1927) she was allowed to sing a featured number, Gorney's "Hogan Alley." A year later she was given a leading role in the Vincent Youmans' operetta, *Rainbow* (a box-office flop), in which she sang "I Want a Man." But in *The Little Show* she finally came into her own as a striking new torch singer, with her sultry, plangent renditions of blues songs.

Another newcomer was Fred Allen, onetime vaudeville juggler and ventriloquist, whose previous appearance on the Broadway stage, in *Polly* (1928), had done little to advance his career. In *The Little Show* he stopped the performance nightly with his dead-pan deliveries of wry monologues in a slow, rasping voice; from 1932 on, and for almost two decades, he would be one of the most brilliant comedians over the radio.

Romney Brent (by no means an unknown in the theater when he first appeared in *The Little Show*) here tapped a new vein for himself by becoming a sophisticated comedian, particularly in a wry number singing a hymn of praise to Hammacher, Schlemmer, a business establishment in New York. Clifton Webb had long been a stage celebrity; but in *The Little Show* he reached new heights in his debonair and suave delivery of "I Guess I'll Have to Change My Plan," and in his sleek dance performance in "Moanin' Low."

"I Guess I'll Have to Change My Plan" was one of Schwartz' best numbers. Two others were appealing: "I've Made a Habit of You" and "Little Old New York." But the most successful songs in *The Little Show* were not by Schwartz. "Moanin' Low" was by Ralph Rainger (a pianist in the orchestra pit), lyrics by Dietz. "Can't We Be Friends?" was by Kay Swift and Paul James, the latter a pseudonym for James Warburg, Kay's husband at the time. And both these numbers profited immeasurably from the unforgettable performance of Libby Holman.

The revue was studded with bright, sparkling sketches. One of the best was by George S. Kaufman, "The Still Alarm," in which some imperturbable firemen continue to play cards peacefully while the bells clang all around them announcing a hotel fire nearby. A second sketch satirized advertisements designed to develop hidden personal charms and powers.

There were two more *Little Shows,* but neither managed to catch the verve and spontaneity of the original product, and both did poorly. *The Second Little Show* (1930)—book and lyrics by Howard Dietz, and most of the music by Schwartz—starred Jay C. Flippen, Gloria Grafton, and Al Trahan. It had an endearing little musical number by Herman Hupfeld, "Sing Something Simple." *The Third Little Show* (1931)—book and lyrics by Dietz, but the music by various composers—starred Beatrice Lillie. A top attraction of this revue was Lillie's performance of Noel Coward's "Mad Dogs and Englishmen." A feature of the original score was Herman Hupfeld's, "When Yuba Plays the Rumba on the Tuba."

1930   THREE'S A CROWD, an intimate revue, with book and lyrics by Howard Dietz. Additional songs by Johnny Green, Vernon Duke, Burton Lane, and others. Produced by Max Gordon at the Selwyn Theatre on October 15. Staged by Hassard Short. Dances staged by Albertina Rasch. Cast included Fred Allen, Libby Holman, Clifton Webb, and Tamara Geva, with Fred MacMurray in a minor role (272 performances).

One of the reasons why the two successors to the first *Little Show* had been failures was that they departed from the informal, intimate pattern of the original production. And the reason why *Three's a Crowd* was a success was that it returned to that pattern. It also brought back the stars of the first *Little Show*—Clifton Webb, Libby Holman, and Fred Allen. Their songs, routines, and dances had all the spice and savor of the dishes they had originally concocted in *The Little Show.* Libby Holman had two new blues melodies to add to her permanent repertory: Schwartz' "Something to Remember You By" and Johnny Green's "Body and Soul." Fred Allen had a new selection of drawling monologues and Clifton Webb's aristocratic air and subtle sense of timing again personalized his songs and dances. Arthur Pollock wrote: *"Three's a Crowd* has beauty and grace without effort, and a high polish and a civilized sophistication and a little good, clean-cut gentlemanly dirt unmarred by vulgarity and exhibitionism." Characteristic of the "gentlemanly dirt" is a bathroom sketch in which a young lady intrudes upon a young man taking a bath. They are strangers—but then the lady accidentally stumbles near the bathtub, catches a glimpse of the young man's anatomy, and suddenly recognizes him as an old-time acquaintance.

1931   THE BAND WAGON, a revue with book and lyrics by George S. Kaufman
and Howard Dietz. Produced by Max Gordon at the New Amsterdam
Theatre on June 3. Staged by Hassard Short. Dances staged by Albertina Rasch. Cast included Fred and Adele Astaire, Frank Morgan,
Helen Broderick, Philip Loeb, and Tilly Losch (260 performances).

In many ways *The Band Wagon* was the best of the Schwartz-Dietz
revues. As Brooks Atkinson said of it: "After *The Band Wagon* it will
be difficult for the old time musical show to hold up its head." It had
sparkling sketches by George S. Kaufman. In one of these, "The Pride
of the Claghornes," a travesty on the Southland, Frank Morgan (appearing for the first time in a musical) was seen as a Southern colonel.
In another, Helen Broderick proved she could maintain a matronly dignity while shopping for undignified bathroom appliances. *The Band
Wagon* had glamour, beauty, and charm, as well as gaiety and satire. It
had the incomparable dancing of Fred and Adele Astaire—the last time
they appeared as a team. It had one of Schwartz' greatest songs, "Dancing
in the Dark" (subsequently used as the title of one of the two motion
pictures adapted from this revue); and with it were two other charming Schwartz songs, "New Sun in the Sky" and "I Love Louisa." Interesting too—from the point of view of stage technique—was the fact that
The Band Wagon was one of the first Broadway musicals to use a revolving stage; in fact, it had two. The revolving stage was used with
extraordinary effect in the first-act finale, featuring the dancing of the
Astaires and the song "I Love Louisa."

1948   INSIDE U.S.A., a revue with book by Arnold Auerbach, Moss Hart, and
Arnold B. Horwitt. Lyrics by Howard Dietz. Produced by Arthur
Schwartz at the Century Theatre on April 30. Dances and musical num-
bers staged by Helen Tamiris. Cast included Beatrice Lillie, Jack Haley,
Valerie Bettis, and Herb Shriner (337 performances).

Early in the revue, Herb Shriner appeared with a copy of John Gunther's
Inside U.S.A. under his arm. This is the only connection between this
production and the Gunther book from which it borrowed the title. Perhaps a better title would have been *Inside Comedy,* for comedy was the
keynote. Beatrice Lillie appeared as a mermaid; in a Moss Hart sketch
as a fussy, annoying maid whose antics drove a Broadway star mad just
before an opening-night performance; in a travesty, "Song to Forget,"
in which she was pursued by suitors who included Tchaikovsky, Chopin,
and Liszt. Jack Haley was seen in a Miami Beach hotel, to which he came

for a sadly needed rest, only to become involved with a trick bed; and in a swank night club where he gave waiters valuable instruction on how best to harass waiters. Herb Shriner, making his debut on the Broadway stage, carried off the rest of the comedy with his Hoosier monologues, and there was a fine topical satirical number sung by two Indians, "We Won't Take It Back."

Other departments were also strong. Valerie Bettis starred in two effective ballet sequences, "Tiger Lily" and "Haunted Heart," the latter with a San Francisco background. The score's best numbers were "Haunted Heart" and the duet "Rhode Island Is Famous for You."

1951   A TREE GROWS IN BROOKLYN, a musical comedy with book by Betty Smith and George Abbott based on Betty Smith's novel of the same name. Lyrics by Dorothy Fields. Produced by George Abbott in association with Robert Fryer at the Alvin Theatre on April 19. Staged by George Abbott. Choreography by Herbert Ross. Cast included Shirley Booth, Johnny Johnston, Marcia Van Dyke, and Dody Heath (270 performances).

It cannot be said that the musical-comedy adaptation caught all the nostalgic charm and heart-warming sentiment of the novel from which it was derived. But when Shirley Booth was on the stage as Cissie, it did possess an endearing quality. The basic story-thread was retained, though with slightly changed emphasis. Where the main interest in the novel had been largely focused on little Francie and on the tragic love and life of Katie and Johnny Nolan, the musical concentrated on the amoral, rowdy character of Cissie, the children's aunt, a part built up for clowning and hilarity but against a deep undercurrent of tragedy.

Otherwise the musical, like the novel, concerned itself with the vicissitudes of the Nolan family in the Williamsburg section of Brooklyn at the turn of the century. Johnny Nolan (Johnny Johnston) is a singing waiter who finds refuge from a world he cannot understand in dreams and drink. His hard-working wife, Katie (Marcia Van Dyke), keeps the family together with her good sense and industry and makes every effort to keep her children—Francie and Neeley—from succumbing to their father's daydreams. The family circle is rounded out by Cissie (Shirley Booth).

The atmospheric settings by Jo Mielziner helped to establish the mood and setting of the play. So did the songs, the best of which were two sung by Cissie, "He Had Refinement" and "Love Is the Reason," and one by Johnny, "I'll Buy You a Star."

1954   BY THE BEAUTIFUL SEA, a musical comedy with book by Herbert and Dorothy Fields. Lyrics by Dorothy Fields. Produced by Robert Fryer and Lawrence Carr at the Majestic Theatre on April 8. Production staged by Marshall Jamison. Choreography by Helen Tamiris. Cast included Shirley Booth and Wilbur Evans (270 performances).

Nostalgia and sentiment, combined with the performance of Shirley Booth, were the redeeming features of *By the Beautiful Sea*. Once again, as in *A Tree Grows in Brooklyn*, the setting is Brooklyn, at the turn of the century. Shirley Booth appeared as Lottie Gibson, a vaudeville trouper who has invested her savings in a boardinghouse in Coney Island, "By the Beautiful Sea." Her clientele is mostly show people. During one of her tours through the vaudeville circuit, she falls in love with Dennis Emery (Wilbur Evans), a Shakespeare actor. When Emery is booked to appear in the Brighton Theatre, Lottie prevails on him to stay at her boardinghouse. Their romance develops against the background of Coney Island attractions: Steeplechase, the scenic railway, the Tunnel of Love. Emery's divorced wife and daughter are also boarders at "By the Beautiful Sea." The child does her best to break up the romance of Lottie and Dennis. With the cooperation of some of the boarders, Lottie succeeds in winning the affection of the child and in getting her man.

On the credit side of the ledger was Helen Tamiris' choreography, particularly a devastating take-off on a moving-picture machine in a penny arcade. The best musical numbers were Dennis' songs "Alone Too Long" and "More Love than Your Love" and Lottie's number, "I'd Rather Wake Up By Myself."

JEAN SCHWARTZ, composer and WILLIAM JEROME, lyricist

Jean Schwartz was born in Budapest, Hungary, on November 4, 1878. His sister (a pupil of Liszt) gave him his first piano lessons. When Jean was in his early teens, his family settled on New York's East Side. In the next few years he held various jobs: as office boy in a cigar factory, night cashier in a Turkish bath, pianist in a Coney Island band, pianist in the first sheet-music department installed in a department store—that of Siegal-Cooper—and pianist and song plugger for the Tin Pan Alley firm of Shapiro-Bernstein. Before the century ended he published an instrumental number, *Dusky Dudes Cakewalk*.

In 1901 he was hired as an onstage pianist in the Weber and Fields burlesque, *Hoity-Toity*. One of his songs was interpolated into that production, "When Mr. Shakespeare Comes to Town," an important event in Schwartz' career since it marked not only his entrance into the Broadway theater but also the beginning of a ten-year collaboration with the lyricist William Jerome.

In 1901 Jerome was already a professional, successful lyricist. Thirteen years Schwartz' senior, William Jerome was born in Cornwall-on-the-Hudson, New York, on September 30, 1865. For a while he thought of becoming a lawyer, and began to study law. But in his eighteenth year he ran away from home and joined a minstrel troupe which played at Tony Pastor's Music Hall and other leading theaters. Then he went on to writing song lyrics, a few becoming popular, including "A Little Bunch of Whiskers on His Chin," "The Same Old Mother Loves Me," and "My Pearl Is a Bowery Girl," all published before 1895 with music by Andrew Mack. It is more than probable that William Jerome was also the lyricist, and possibly even the composer, of that 1890 classic, "Sweet Rosie O'Grady." The authorship is attributed to the popular entertainer Maude Nugent, who made the song famous. But since Maude Nugent was the wife of William Jerome, and since Maude had never before or since written a successful song, it is not without good reason to believe that her husband had had more than a share in its writing.

Jerome, then, was a song writer of some rank and esteem in Tin Pan Alley when he joined Schwartz in 1901 to write "When Mr. Shakespeare Comes to Town." A few more hits came from them immediately after that: "Rip Van Winkle Was a Lucky Man" in 1901, "Mister Dooley" in 1902, and the sensational "Bedelia" in 1903, the last made famous by Blanche Ring. They also wrote special numbers for such outstanding performers as Eddie Foy ("I'm Tired" and "The Wild Rose"). In 1904 they wrote all the words and music for their initial Broadway stage success, *Piff, Paff, Pouf*, following it in 1905 with songs for *The Ham Tree*, starring McIntyre and Heath. After that came a few more song hits—"Chinatown, My Chinatown" and "The Hat My Father Wore on St. Patrick's Day"—and appearances on the vaudeville circuits, singing and playing their songs.

Their partnership was over by 1914. Jerome went on to write lyrics for other composers, and with no diminution in his popularity: "Row, Row, Row" (James Monaco), "Get Out and Get Under the Moon" (Larry Shay), and "That Old Irish Mother of Mine" (Harry von Tilzer). He also made a success of song publishing, being the head of the firm that issued

George M. Cohan's "Over There." Jerome died in New York City on June 25, 1932.

With other lyricists, Jean Schwartz was equally productive. He wrote scores for many Broadway musicals including several editions of *The Passing Show* and *Artists and Models*. Subsequently Schwartz became identified with Al Jolson (for whom he wrote the score for the Winter Garden extravaganza, *The Honeymoon Express,* in 1913) by preparing for him two songs that became Jolson favorites and were interpolated into *Sinbad* (1918): "Rock-a-bye Your Baby with a Dixie Melody" and "Hello Central, Give Me No Man's Land." Among his later song hits were Ben Bernie's theme song, "Au Revoir, Pleasant Dreams," and "Trust in Me" which in 1937 enjoyed a high rating on the Hit Parade.

Jean Schwartz died in Los Angeles on November 30, 1956.

1904 PIFF, PAFF, POUF, a musical comedy with book by Stanislaus Stange. Lyrics by William Jerome. Produced by F. C. Whitney at the Casino Theatre on April 2. Staged by Gerard Coventry. Cast included Joseph Miron, Alice Fischer, Eddie Foy, and Mabel Hollins (264 performances).

August Melon (Joseph Miron) can inherit his share of the fortune left him by his deceased wife only if each of his four daughters gets married successfully according to their ages. Since August is bent on marrying the widow, Mrs. Lillian Montague (Alice Fischer), he is determined to see his daughters marry quickly. But three of them have eccentric ideas on the kind of husbands they want. One wants a man who has never been kissed; another, a man who is the paragon of virtue; the third, a man who has posed for a patent-medicine ad. The fourth daughter is not capricious at all, but being the youngest she cannot marry until the others do. After numerous amusing trials, the three girls find their men in Poufle, Piffle, and Paffle; and the fourth selects Dick Daily, a newspaper reporter.

Eddie Foy appeared as Peter Poufle, a "Scarecrow" character similar to the one in which he had achieved a triumph a year earlier in *The Wizard of Oz,* as a replacement for Fred Stone who created the role. His song, "The Ghost That Never Walked," was one reason for the success of *Piff, Paff, Pouf.* Other Schwartz tunes included a ballad, "Good Night, My Own True Love," and a lilting melody, "Love, Love, Love." "The Radium Dance" was an outstanding production number in which chorus girls appeared on a darkened stage, their phosphorescent costumes gleaming in the darkness.

1913-21   *The Passing Shows*

> 1913 edition, a revue with book and lyrics by Harold Atteridge. Additional music by Al W. Brown. Produced by the Shuberts at the Winter Garden on July 24. Staged by Ned Wayburn. Cast included Charles and Mollie King, Bessie Clayton, Charlotte Greenwood, and Wellington Cross (116 performances).

> 1921 edition, a revue with book mostly by Harold Atteridge. Lyrics by Harold Atteridge. Produced by the Shuberts at the Winter Garden on December 29, 1920. Staged by J. C. Huffman. Cast included Willie and Eugene Howard, Marie Dressler, Janet Adair, and Harry Watson (200 performances).

For other editions of The Passing Show *see* LOUIS HIRSCH *and* SIGMUND ROMBERG.

The Passing Show had been instituted in 1912 by the Shuberts as a lush revue to rival *The Ziegfeld Follies* (see LOUIS HIRSCH). For its second edition the Shuberts engaged Jean Schwartz for the score. Unlike most revues this had a slight thread of a plot to bind the production into a single package. Peg o' My Heart (Mollie King) comes to the United States to be taught the turkey trot under the direction of Mrs. Potiphar (May Boley) and Joseph Asche Kayton (Herbert Corthill). In America, Peg falls in love with Broadway Jones (Charles King). Other characters were borrowed from various Broadway productions of that period: *Within the Law, Oh, Oh, Delphine!, Peg o' My Heart*, and *Broadway Jones*.

Two highlights of this edition were a big production number reviving the cakewalk, and a striking scene in which the huge staircase of the Capitol in Washington, D.C., leads a bevy of beautiful chorus girls to heaven. Bessie Clayton delivered some effective dances; and there were in addition a striking "Silhouette Dance," performed by Wellington Cross and Lois Josephine, and Ned Wayburn's conception of the tango and turkey trot. The comedy included allusions to the political events of the day and an irreverent burlesque of President Wilson. Schwartz' best songs were "If You Don't Love Me Why Do You Hang Around?", "I'm Looking for a Sweetheart," and "My Cinderella Girl." Some of these numbers profited from the beautiful baritone voice of John Charles Thomas (later famous in concert hall and opera house), making here his Broadway stage debut.

The 1921 edition was notable mostly for burlesques of current plays. Willie Howard did a take-off of Frank Bacon in *Lightnin'*, and Marie Dressler appeared in a travesty on the mystery play, *The Bat*. One of the best comedy routines was a skit, "Spanish Love," starring Marie Dressler as a much sought-after señorita; and one of the best dance numbers was an exotic number performed by Cleveland Bronner. The Schwartz score included "In Little Old New York," "When There's No One to Love," "Let's Have a Rattling Good Time," and "Charm School."

1923 ARTISTS AND MODELS, a revue with book and lyrics by Harold Atteridge. Produced by the Shuberts at the Shubert Theatre on August 20. Staged by Harry Wagstaff Gribble and Francis Weldon. Cast included Frank Fay, Grace Hamilton, Harry Kelly, and Bob Nelson (312 performances).

For later editions of Artists and Models *see* J. FRED COOTS *and* SIGMUND ROMBERG.

This revue was evolved from an intimate show staged by the Illustrators Society of New York, in which many eminent artists participated, including James Montgomery Flagg, Rube Goldberg, H. T. Webster, and Harry Hirschfield. Presented by the Shuberts as an annual revue, the first edition appearing in 1923, it changed character to glorify female nudity and place emphasis on spectacle. One of the scenes set the tone for the whole production: an artist's studio in which the models parade with a minimum of dress. The best comedy was found in a satire on Somerset Maugham's *Rain,* starring Harry Kelly; in a satirical skit on drama critics; and in a travesty on presidential cabinet meetings. A dynamic South Sea Island dance was performed by Kyra. Schwartz' songs included "Music of Love" and "Somehow."

A. BALDWIN SLOANE, composer

A. Baldwin Sloane was born in Baltimore, Maryland, on August 28, 1872, where he attended the public schools, received his musical training from private teachers, and helped found the Baltimore Paint and Powder Club, which produced some of his earliest operettas. He came to New York in the early 1890's, where he became a prominent song writer, his first hits including "While Strolling Down the Forest" and "When You Ain't Got No Money, Well You Needn't Come Around," the latter made famous by May Irwin. Edward E. Rice, the producer, became interested in him and arranged for the first Broadway productions of Sloane's musicals. These early Sloane productions are all forgotten, but a few songs have survived: "My Tiger Lily" in *Aunt Hannah* (1900), "There's a Little Street in Heaven Called Broadway" in *The Belle of Broadway* (1902), and "What's the Matter with the Moon Tonight?" in *The Mocking Bird* (1902).

Sloane's first Broadway success came with the sensational *The Wizard of Oz* (1903), in which Sloane collaborated with Paul Tietjens in preparing the music. It was some time before Sloane realized another stage success of such magnitude. Meanwhile, in 1909, one of his biggest song hits appeared in a musical called *Tillie's Nightmare,* starring Marie Dressler; the hit was one of the leading sentimental ballads of the 1890's, "Heaven Will Protect the Working Girl." (In 1927 Herbert Fields adapted *Tillie's Nightmare* for the Rodgers and Hart musical, *Peggy Ann.*) *Tillie's Nightmare* had a secondary Sloane hit in "Life Is Only What You Make It, After All."

Sloane's first Broadway success after *The Wizard of Oz* was *The Summer Widowers* (1910). After that, and up to the time of his death, Sloane continued writing music for the Broadway stage. His last production was *China Rose* (1921), a failure. Sloane died in Red Bank, New Jersey, on February 21, 1926.

1903   THE WIZARD OF OZ, a musical fantasy with book and lyrics by L. Frank Baum, adapted from Baum's novel of the same name. Additional music by Paul Tietjens. Produced by Fred R. Hamlin at the Majestic Theatre on January 21. Staged by Julian Mitchell. Cast included Fred Stone, David Montgomery, Grace Kimball, and Bessie Wynn (293 performances).

With this musical fantasy a new theater opened in New York, the Majestic. This was certainly an auspicious beginning for a theater, since few productions of the early 1900's were so handsomely acclaimed and so widely imitated. Made up of a series of unforgettable stage pictures, numerous specialties and production numbers, and lavish sets and costumes—and touched with the storybook magic of a child's world of fantasy—*The Wizard of Oz* completely won the hearts of young and old.

Dorothy Dale (Anna Laughlin) and her pet cow, Imogene, are lifted by a cyclone from their Kansas farm and carried into the fairy garden, Oz. Her Kansas homestead crashes from the sky to kill the cruel witch who has ruled the Munchkins, inhabitants of Oz, and set them free from her spell. The good witch of Oz, in gratitude, presents Dorothy with a ring capable of fulfilling two wishes. Dorothy wastes the first wish on a triviality, but with the second she brings to life Scarecrow (Fred Stone). The Scarecrow has lost his brains, and the only one able to restore them is the Wizard of Oz. Dorothy accompanies the Scarecrow in the search for the Wizard, and they are soon joined by Tim Woodman (David C. Montgomery) who seeks his heart, which had been taken away from him when he fell in love with Cynthia. After numerous vicissitudes and adventures, they manage to find the Wizard (Bobby Gaylor) who magnanimously returns the Scarecrow's brains and Tim Woodman's heart.

As the Scarecrow and Tim Woodman, Fred Stone and David Montgomery became Broadway stage stars, though they had been around the theater a long time. Stone had appeared as a boy actor in Kansas in 1884 when he was eleven, and two years after that he became a member of a traveling circus. In 1895 he started an acting partnership with David Montgomery that lasted twenty-two years. For several years they appeared in vaudeville both in the United States and in England before scoring personal triumphs in *The Wizard of Oz*. Much of the gaiety, humor, and burlesque of that production came from their shenanigans. The enchantment came from some of the spectacular staging—a cyclone scene with which the play opened; a poppy field with chorus girls in large hats representing poppies; the lavish courtyard of the Wizard's palace.

Some of the best songs in this Sloane-Tietjens score were by Sloane: "Niccolo's Piccolo" and "The Medley of Nations." But the two biggest song hits to come from *The Wizard of Oz* were interpolated after the musical opened, and were by other composers. The first was "Sammy" by James O'Dea and Edward Hutchinson, the other, "Hurrah for Baffin's Bay," by Vincent Bryan and Charles Zimmerman. Harold Arlen's popular Academy Award song, "Over the Rainbow"—with which Judy Garland will always be identified—was written for the motion-picture adaptation of *The Wizard of Oz*, released in 1939.

1910 THE SUMMER WIDOWERS, a musical extravaganza, with book and lyrics by Glen MacDonough. Produced by Lew Fields at the Broadway Theatre on June 4. Staged by Ned Wayburn. Cast included Lew Fields, Irene Franklin, Ada Lewis, Ada Dovey, Willis P. Sweatnam, and Vernon Castle (140 performances).

The Summer Widowers was described in the program as a "musical panorama." It was vaudeville entertainment rather than musical comedy, consisting more of self-sufficient sequences than of an integrated plot. It had scenes in Atlantic City (an opening episode on the boardwalk; a closing number realistically reproducing girls bathing in the surf); an extended sketch set in a delicatessen store of which Lew Fields was proprietor; an apartment-house scene presenting a cross-section of a typical New York apartment with its tenants; a roof-garden act in which dancing routines and acrobatic specialties were given.

Lew Fields provided the principal comedy with his familiar German-Jewish dialect. Other leading performers included Willis P. Sweatnam, a Negro comedian appearing as a janitor; Ada Lewis as a flirtatious widow; Irene Franklin as an eccentric detective; and an eight-year-old girl named Helen Hayes who had made her stage debut two years earlier in *Old Dutch,* a Victor Herbert musical starring Lew Fields. Sloane's major songs were "On the Boardwalk," "I'd Like to Furnish a Flat for You," and "Those Were the Happy Days."

1911   THE HEN PECKS, a musical extravaganza, with book by Glen Mac-Donough. Lyrics by E. Ray Goetz. Produced by Lew Fields at the Broadway Theatre on February 4. Staged by Ned Wayburn. Cast included Lew Fields, Laurence Wheat, Vernon Castle, Gertrude Quinlan, Blossom Seeley, and Ethel Johnson (137 performances).

Once again, as in *The Summer Widowers,* the program described this entertainment as a "musical panorama," and once again emphasis was placed on individual sequences. But *The Hen Pecks* had a slight plot to create unity. The entire Peck family make a trip to New York from their farm in Cranberry Grove. Son Henderson and his bride Verbena have come to make New York their permanent home; Father Peck (Lew Fields) is running away from a termagant wife, Henrietta, who pursues him. Each of the Peck daughters has her own reason for coming: Henoria (Gertrude Quinlan) because she is being pursued by Zowie (Vernon Castle), Henolia (Ethel Johnson) because she has eloped with the real-estate promoter, Ayer Castle (Laurence Wheat), and Henelia (Blossom Seeley) to become a Broadway chorus girl.

The production opened well—with a farcical enactment of life on a farm at sunrise. But most of the appeal of *The Hen Pecks* was visual, particularly in its effective display of colors: in a sunrise scene; in the garish splashes of vivid colors in a series of pageants; in the bright yellows, blacks, purples, lavenders, and violets of the costumes.

Sloane's best songs were "Little Italy," "June," "White Light Alley," and "It's a Skirt." One of the numbers was a Jerome Kern interpolation, "The Manicure Girl."

1918   LADIES FIRST, a musical comedy with book and lyrics by Harry B. Smith, based on Charles Hoyt's *A Contented Woman.* Produced by H. H. Frazee at the Broadhurst Theatre on October 24. Staged by Frank

Smithson. Cast included Nora Bayes, William Kent, Irving Fisher, and Clarence Nordstrom (164 performances).

Ladies' First was Nora Bayes' show—which meant that everything about it was intended to set off her talent. The slim plot concerned the suffragette movement with Nora Bayes playing Betty Burt, and William Kent appearing in a comical role as Uncle Tody. But the story was just a framework on which to display Miss Bayes effectively. Midway the plot was completely forgotten to allow her to give a recital of her song specialties. One of these was an early George Gershwin song, "Some Wonderful Sort of Someone." When *Ladies First* went on tour, George Gershwin served as her piano accompanist in this song sequence; and during this tour the first song George Gershwin wrote in collaboration with his brother, Ira, was introduced by Bayes, "The Real American Folk Song." Another interpolation was "Just Like a Gypsy" by Seymour B. Simons and Nora Bayes. One of the Bayes' most successful numbers in the actual show was "Spanish," a satire on the country that contributed to America outlandish dances, the flu, and Columbus. Other popular Sloane songs were "What Could Be Sweeter than You?" and "What Men Can Do."

1919-20   *The Greenwich Village Follies*

1919 edition, a revue with book by Philip Bartholomae. Lyrics by Arthur Swanstrom and J. Murray Anderson. Produced by The Bohemians at the Greenwich Village Theatre on July 15. Staged by J. Murray Anderson. Cast included Bessie McCoy, Ted Lewis and his band, and Harry Delf (232 performances).

1920 edition, a revue with book by Thomas J. Gray. Lyrics by Arthur Swanstrom and J. Murray Anderson. Produced by the Shuberts at the Greenwich Village Theatre on August 30. Cast included Frank Crumit, Jay Brennan, Bert Savoy, Howard Marsh, and Harriet Gimble (192 performances).

For other editions of The Greenwich Village Follies *see* LOUIS HIRSCH.

The 1919 edition of *The Greenwich Village Follies* was the first of an annual series of revues that appeared up to 1925 and was revived a last time in 1928. The 1919 and 1920 editions lived up to their name by being presented in Greenwich Village and by evoking the spirit of—and occasionally satirizing—the Village. The 1919 edition had one of Sloane's major song hits, "I Want a Daddy Who Will Rock Me to Sleep." Bessie

McCoy scored with "I'm the Hostess of a Bum Cabaret" and "Message of the Cameo" and with a marionette dance; Jane Carroll presented "My Little Javanese" effectively. James Watts was one of the principal comedians, seen in various female impersonations and in a satire on ballet. Ada Forman appeared in several Oriental dances.

The 1920 edition was prominent for "Just Sweet Sixteen," beautifully sung by Howard Marsh and a bevy of sweet innocents. This edition had two impressive production numbers: "The Birthday Cake," with chorus girls dressed like birthday candles and dancing on an elaborately decorated table; and a cabaret scene with Russian costumes, folk songs, and dances.

Moving uptown in 1921, *The Greenwich Village Follies* became even bigger and more lavish—a competitor for *The Ziegfeld Follies* and George White's *Scandals*. For the 1922 and 1923 editions see LOUIS HIRSCH. The score in 1924 was the work of Cole Porter, and in 1925 Hassard Short succeeded John Murray Anderson as stage director.

HARRY B. SMITH, librettist-lyricist

Harry Bache Smith was one of the most prolific writers of operetta and musical-comedy texts the American stage has known. He is believed to have written the books for over 300 musical plays; there were times when he had from six to ten shows running simultaneously.

He was born in Buffalo, New York, on December 28, 1860. Before turning to the theater he had been a newspaperman, working as reporter and later music critic for the Chicago *Daily News,* then as drama critic for the Chicago *Tribune.* To both these newspapers he used to contribute a daily column made up of verses, quips, and humorous comments; and while holding down his newspaper jobs he also wrote articles on music and literature for outstanding magazines.

His initiation into musical comedy came with the texts for *Rosita* and *Amarylis,* two failures. In 1887 he entered into collaboration with Reginald de Koven, with whom he wrote *The Begum* (1887), an attempt to imitate *The Mikado* of Gilbert and Sullivan. This, too, was a failure, and so was *Don Quixote,* which followed in 1889. But with their third effort, the comic opera, *Robin Hood* (1890), Smith and De Koven achieved a triumph. After that they produced a string of comic operas and musical comedies, many of which were successes.

Even more fruitful was Smith's collaboration with Victor Herbert, begun in 1895 with *The Wizard of the Nile* and continuing for two decades. They wrote about a dozen operettas, among them some of Herbert's most popular musicals.

Irving Berlin, Ludwig Englander, Raymond Hubbell, Gustave Kerker, Jerome Kern, Sigmund Romberg, and A. Baldwin Sloane were some other composers with whom Smith worked successfully.

Smith died in Atlantic City, New Jersey, on January 2, 1936.

See: IRVING BERLIN (*Watch Your Step*); REGINALD DE KOVEN (*Robin Hood, Rob Roy, The Highwayman*); LUDWIG ENGLANDER (*The Casino Girl, The Strollers*); VICTOR HERBERT (*The Wizard of the Nile, The Serenade, The Fortune Teller, Sweethearts*); RAYMOND HUBBELL (*The Ziegfeld Follies of 1912*); JEROME KERN (*The Girl from Utah*); A. BALDWIN SLOANE (*Ladies First*); Appendix I (1906—*The Parisian Model*; 1907—*The Ziegfeld Follies*).

DAVE STAMPER, composer

The name of David (Dave) Stamper is inevitably associated with that of Florenz Ziegfeld. For almost twenty years he contributed songs to the *Follies* and the Ziegfeld *Midnight Frolics*. Though occasionally other Broadway musicals used his music, Stamper will always be known as a "Ziegfeld composer." And it is perhaps no coincidence or accident that with Ziegfeld's death, Dave Stamper's career as a successful stage song writer came to an end.

He was born in New York City on November 10, 1883, and attended the city public schools. He learned the piano by himself. When he was seventeen, he left school for good and found a job as pianist in a Coney Island dance hall. From there he progressed to Tin Pan Alley to work as song plugger and staff pianist for various publishers. When he was twenty, he toured the vaudeville circuits as piano accompanist, working for four years with Nora Bayes.

While pursuing his own career as popular pianist, Stamper was writing songs, his first effort being "In the Cool of the Evening." His first song to appear in a *Ziegfeld Follies* was "Daddy Has a Sweetheart and Mother Is Her Name," in the 1912 edition, lyrics by Gene Buck, henceforth Stamper's most frequent collaborator. From then on hardly a season of the *Follies* passed without at least one Stamper song in it. He had three in the 1913 edition; in 1914 he shared responsibility for most of the score with Raymond Hubbell, and in 1915 with Louis A. Hirsch. Among his most prominent songs in later editions of the *Follies* were "Sweet Sixteen" and "Tulip Time" (1919); "Plymouth Rock," "Come Back to Our Alley," and "Raggedy Ann" (1921); "My Rambler Rose" and " 'Neath the South Sea Moon," both written with Hirsch (1922); "Some Sweet Day," again with Hirsch (1923).

The last *Follies* produced by Ziegfeld was in 1931, and it was with this production—to which he contributed "Broadway Reverie" and "Bring on the Follies Girl"—that Stamper made his last major appearance on Broadway.

Of Stamper's scores for other Broadway productions, two were successes and are discussed below.

See: IRVING BERLIN (*The Ziegfeld Follies*); LOUIS A. HIRSCH (*The Ziegfeld Follies*); RAYMOND HUBBELL (*The Ziegfeld Follies*).

1927 TAKE THE AIR, a musical comedy with book by Anne Caldwell. Lyrics by Gene Buck. Presented by Gene Buck at the Waldorf Theatre on November 22. Staged by Alexander Leftwich and Gene Buck. Dances arranged by Ralph Reader. Cast included Will Mahoney, Kitty O'Connor, Dorothy Dilley, and Trini (206 performances).

Take the Air was the first musical comedy starring Will Mahoney (he had previously appeared only in revues), and he dominated the production. In his eccentric dancing he fell all over his tangled legs; his gift at travesty revealed itself in a take-off on a ventriloquist and on a prima donna delivering a curtain speech. He mimed and mugged and mimicked his way through a complicated plot that featured him as Happy Hokum, a Broadway hoofer stranded in Texas near an air base. With the help of Señorita Carmela Cortez (Trini), a visitor from Spain, he manages to foil a smuggling plot, and in the process wins the heart of Lillian Bond (Dorothy Dilley), daughter of a Long Island banker. The play ends as Hokum makes off in a plane for the Long Island estate of Lillian's father, to ask him for her hand.

Kitty O'Connor's throbbing, low-register singing of "We'll Have a New Home in the Morning" was a musical high spot; another was the song, "All I Want Is a Lullaby."

1927 THE LOVELY LADY, a musical comedy with book by Gladys Unger and Cyrus Wood based on *Déjeuner de soleil*. Lyrics by Cyrus Wood. Additional music by Harold Levey. Produced by the Shuberts at the Sam H. Harris Theatre on December 29. Staged by J. C. Huffman. Dances by Dave Bennett. Chester Hale Dances arranged by Mr. Hale. Cast included Edna Leedom, Guy Robertson, Frank Greene, Doris Pattson, and Jack Sheehan (164 performances).

The "lovely lady" is Folly Watteau (Edna Leedom), a rich, spoiled American girl on the loose in Paris. She falls in love with a svelte but penniless nobleman, Count Paul de Morlaix (Guy Robertson), and is being pursued by an English nincompoop, Lord Islington (Frank Greene). She finally gets the man she loves.

A dance-studded production was highlighted by the spirited jazz number, "At the Barbecue," starring Eloise Bennett. A melodious score included the title song and "Make Believe You're Happy," both presented by Count Paul de Morlaix, together with "Lingerie," "Boy Friends," and "Ain't Love Grand."

JOHN STROMBERG, composer

Though he wrote a popular-song hit before becoming the official conductor and composer of the Weber and Fields burlesques, Stromberg's six-year career as an important composer for the Broadway stage was devoted exclusively to his activity at the Weber and Fields Music Hall.

John ("Honey") Stromberg was born in 1853 and received his musical apprenticeship in Tin Pan Alley where he worked as arranger for the publishing house of Witmark. The success of his song, "My Best Girl's a Corker," in 1895, drew the interest of Weber and Fields. Since they were about to open their own theater in New York featuring their burlesques, they invited Stromberg to be their composer and conductor. Thus Stromberg wrote the score for *The Art of Maryland*, with which Weber and Fields opened their Music Hall in 1896. During the next six years he wrote the scores for ten Weber and Fields productions (conducting nine of them). He amassed a fortune and invested most of his money in a quixotic real-estate development in Freeport, Long Island—a residential community to be called Stromberg Park with streets named after stars from the various Weber and Fields productions. This venture was a failure.

He was working on the score for the Weber and Fields burlesque, *Twirly-Whirly*, when he was found dead in his New York apartment in July, 1902. It was generally agreed that he had committed suicide. In his pocket was the manuscript of his last song, and probably his greatest hit, "Come Down, Ma Evenin' Star," written for Lillian Russell. When *Twirly-Whirly* opened two months after Stromberg's death (a new conductor in the pit for the first time in six years), Lillian Russell introduced the song, breaking down before she could finish it. It has remained the one with which Lillian Russell has ever since been identified.

1896-1903   *The Weber and Fields Burlesques*

1896   THE ART OF MARYLAND, book and lyrics by Joseph Herbert. Presented
     by Weber and Fields at the Music Hall on September 5. Cast included
     Weber and Fields, Lottie Gilson, Sam Bernard, John T. Kelly, and the
     Beaumont Sisters.

Joe Weber and Lew Fields inaugurated their acting partnerships as boys
on New York's East Side in 1877, when they formed an Irish song, dance,
and comedy act that appeared in variety theaters and at Duffy's Pavilion
in Coney Island. In 1884 they were hired for Ada Richmond's burlesque
shows at Miner's Bowery Theatre. It was there that they evolved their
own personal brand of broad and rowdy humor and horseplay, and created their caricatures of Dutchmen for which they later became famous.
Fields was the tall and thin partner; Weber, short and fat. Both spoke
in a thick German-English dialect and indulged in all kinds of rough-
and-tumble shenanigans.

With a loan of 1500 dollars from Fields' brother-in-law added to their
own capital (300 dollars), Weber and Fields acquired in 1895 a theater
just off Broadway and Twenty-Ninth Street, henceforth known as the
Weber and Fields Music Hall. It opened in September, 1896, with *The
Art of Maryland.* For a while Weber and Fields had to supplement their
activity in New York by taking their troupe on extensive road trips in
order to make ends meet. But their burlesques caught on and became
a vogue in New York. By 1898 they were operating such a financially
successful venture that they could afford to pay their stars some of the
highest salaries in the trade.

Like the burlesques of Harrigan and Hart, those of Weber and Fields
followed a pattern. The first half of each production consisted of broad
satires on nonmusical plays of current New York interest. *The Art of
Maryland* was a travesty on *The Heart of Maryland* in which Mrs. Leslie
Carter had recently starred in New York. In later burlesques their hilarity
and satire ran riot in travesties on *The Geisha,* William Gillette's *Secret
Service,* J. M. Barrie's *The Little Minister, Cyrano de Bergerac, Barbara
Frietchie,* and so forth.

The second half of each Weber and Fields production was a variety
show with various leading performers offering their song-and/or-dance
specialties, either singly or in groups. After the travesty on *The Heart
of Maryland*—in their initial production—Weber and Fields introduced
their famous pool-table skit; Lottie Gilson, "The Little Magnet," sang

songs; a novelty was provided by something called an Animatograph, described as "a new kind of motion picture." In 1899, with the *Whirl-i-Gig*, the variety half was eliminated permanently to give the stage entirely over to the travesty and to the performances of the many stars now crowding the Music Hall stage.

From out of the Weber and Fields burlesques came some of the foremost stars of the New York stage of the 1890's and early 1900's—in many cases their first important step toward greatness. David Warfield made his first appearance in New York as a Jewish comedian, and Fay Templeton made her Weber and Fields debut in *Hurly-Burly* (1898); Lillian Russell made her bow under Weber and Fields star in *Whirl-i-Gig* (1899); De Wolf Hopper appeared for the first time with the company in *Fiddle-Dee-Dee* (1900), and William Collier and Louise Allen in *Twirly-Whirly* (1902). Among others whose names would brighten the Broadway theater for years to come, seen in Weber and Fields burlesques were Marie Dressler, Charles Ross, Peter F. Dailey, Julian Mitchell, Henry E. Dixey, Louis Mann, May Robson, Bessie Clayton, Cecilia Loftus, Carter de Haven, and the McCoy Sisters.

And not only great stars were born in the Weber and Fields Music Hall, but also great songs, all of them by Stromberg. In *Whirl-i-Gig*, Peter F. Dailey sang "Dinah" (sometimes known as "Kiss Me Honey, Do"). In her Music Hall debut, in the same production, Lillian Russell introduced one of her favorite numbers, "When Chloe Sings a Song." That score also included "Say You Love Me, Sue." The music for *Fiddle-Dee-Dee* included "Ma Blushin' Rose," "Come Back, My Honey Boy, to Me," and "Tell Us, Pretty Ladies." "How I Love My Lu," appeared in *Pousse Café* (1897), and in *Twirly-Whirly*, Lillian Russell sang "Come Down, Ma Evenin' Star"—a score that also included "Dream On, Dream of Me."

Stromberg's premature death in 1902 left the score for *Twirly-Whirly* unfinished; the remaining numbers were done by William T. Francis who succeeded Stromberg as conductor. William T. Francis also wrote the score for *Whoop-Dee-Do* (1903) with which the partnership of Weber and Fields ended after a quarter of a century.

After 1904 Weber and Fields went their separate ways in producing and acting in musicals. In 1912 they were temporarily reunited in *Hokey-Pokey*, score by A. Baldwin Sloane, a valiant attempt to revive the brilliance and abandon of the old Weber and Fields plays. The overture consisted of all the John Stromberg favorites; the production included a travesty in the old Weber and Fields style; and the cast included such old Music Hall favorites as Fay Templeton, Lillian Russell, and Bessie

Clayton. *Hokey-Pokey* did only moderately well—it was apparent that the day of the Weber and Fields burlesque was over.

The only other time Weber and Fields were on the same platform was in 1932 when they were honored by the theater world on the occasion of the golden jubilee of their partnership. Lew Fields died in 1941; his partner, Weber, followed him a year later.

JULE STYNE, composer and SAMMY CAHN, lyricist

Jule Styne was born in London, England, on December 31, 1905. He was only eight when his family settled in Chicago. Since both parents were musical they recognized his talent and saw to it that he received a thorough training on the piano. Jule made such progress that he appeared as a child prodigy with the Detroit and Chicago Symphony orchestras. A scholarship then brought him to the Chicago Musical College when he was thirteen. There he specialized in piano while receiving a thorough grounding in harmony, theory, and composition.

Renouncing all thoughts of a career in serious music, Styne organized his own dance band in 1931 which performed in various Chicago hotels and clubs. For this group he made up all the arrangements, and Chicago soon sat up and took notice of his original harmonizations and unusual tone colorations. Even Hollywood was impressed. Styne was hired to do arrangements and write background music for several films. He also filled a job as vocal coach for 20th Century-Fox, where he worked with Alice Faye, Linda Darnell, and Shirley Temple, among others.

His musical activities in Hollywood would probably have excluded the writing of songs if he had not met and become a friend of Sammy Cahn, a young lyricist, to whose lyrics he soon started writing melodies. Cahn—who was born in New York City on June 18, 1913—was already the proud author of several successful lyrics, including an English adaptation of the Yiddish song, "Bei Mir Bist du Schön," which the Andrew Sisters popularized in 1938 and which (by reciprocity) popularized the Andrew Sisters. Cahn followed up this initial victory with another adaptation of a Yiddish song, "Joseph, Joseph," once again introduced by the Andrew Sisters. In 1942 Cahn came out to Hollywood. Soon after his arrival there he interested Styne in working with him.

Their first song was a winner, "I've Heard That Song Before," which Frank Sinatra introduced in a movie short. This new partnership continued reaping a harvest. Their songs appeared in many important motion pictures, and some of them were hits. Only a few of these need be mentioned: "It's Been a Long, Long Time," "Let It Snow!", "I'll Walk Alone" (one of the outstanding ballads of World War II), "There Goes That Song Again," "Give Me Five Minutes More," "I Love an Old-Fashioned Song," and "I've Never Forgotten." In 1954 they won an Academy Award with "Three Coins in a Fountain."

Still with Cahn as his lyricist, Styne first invaded the Broadway theater in 1947 with a smash success, *High Button Shoes*. While Styne and Cahn continued working together after that in Hollywood, Styne's career on Broadway was pursued with the cooperation of other lyricists.

1947   HIGH BUTTON SHOES, a musical comedy with book by Stephen Longstreet based on his own novel. Lyrics by Sammy Cahn. Produced by Monte Proser and Joseph Kipness at the Century Theatre on October 9. Staged by George Abbott. Choreography by Jerome Robbins. Cast included Phil Silvers, Nanette Fabray, Jack McCauley, and Joey Faye (727 performances).

High Button Shoes was a peppery mixture of burlesque, vaudeville, and musical comedy—with a generous dash of nostalgia.

In the year 1913 a couple of swindlers—Harrison Floy (Phil Silvers) and Mr. Pontdue (Joey Faye)—arrive in New Brunswick, New Jersey, home of Rutgers University. They sell underwater real estate, try fixing the Rutgers-Princeton game, reach for an easy buck through any dishonest method that two conniving minds can concoct.

To the role of a con man Phil Silvers brought much of the bounce, rowdy humor, and boisterousness he had formerly injected for so many years in burlesque theaters. Singlehanded, he tries to annihilate a whole football squad; he delivers a speech to a lady bird-watcher society; he does a burlesque fight scene with a football player; and with equal vigor and élan he delivers, "You're My Girl" and does impersonations in "Can't You Just See Yourself in Love with Me?"

Nostalgia was evoked by the 1913 setting, with its amusing recollections of the feminine fashions of that day, the perverse behavior of a Model-T Ford, and in the escapades of Keystone Cops and Mack Sennett Bathing Beauties of silent-film days recreated in a hiliarious ballet conceived by Jerome Robbins ("a masterpiece of controlled pandemonium," in the words of *Time* magazine).

Styne's score had many songs to remember: the duets, "Papa, Won't "You Dance with Me?" and "I Still Get Jealous," and the specialty number, "Security." Nanette Fabray—who played in a comparatively minor role—participated in all three numbers, and through her singing, dancing, and miming proved herself a major performer. "Can't You Just See Yourself in Love with Me?" and "Get Away for a Day in the Country" were two other attractive Styne numbers.

1949   GENTLEMEN PREFER BLONDES, a musical comedy with book by Anita Loos and Joseph Fields based on the novel and Broadway stage comedy of the same name by Anita Loos. Lyrics by Leo Robin. Produced by Herman Levin and Oliver Smith at the Ziegfeld Theatre on December 8. Staged by John C. Wilson. Cast included Carol Channing, Yvonne Adair, and Jack McCauley (740 performances).

The 1924 American Olympic team is sailing to France aboard the French liner, *Ile de France*. The principal action of this musical carries two dizzy American flappers—Dorothy Shaw (Yvonne Adair) and Lorelei Lee (Carol Channing)—and an American sugar daddy, Gus Esmond (Jack McCauley), aboard ship to France. They come to Paris—to the Ritz and the Pré Catalan restaurant in the Bois de Boulogne—and finally return home to celebrate at the Central Park Casino.

Like *High Button Shoes*, *Gentlemen Prefer Blondes* was lively stage entertainment. Its greatest strength lay in the sharp lines with which an entire era was drawn—the raucous, jazz-mad, iconoclastic 1920's. The musical comedy may have lacked some of the split-second timing of dialogue and exciting pace of the action found in the nonmusical stage play that preceded it. But it did succeed in bringing to life again an era symbolized by the heroine, Lorelei Lee. With her shrill, baby voice and Dixie accent, this provocative blonde became a symbol of the roaring 1920's, her personal philosophy succinctly summed up in her two main songs, "A Little Girl from Little Rock" (delivered with appropriate grinds and bumps) and "Diamonds Are a Girl's Best Friend." As Lorelei Lee— and in these two songs—Carol Channing proved what one year earlier she had merely suggested in the revue *Lend an Ear:*—that here was a new, shining musical-comedy star.

"Mamie Is Mimi," a hot American novelty number presented in a Paris night spot, and the finale, "Keeping Cool with Coolidge," maintained the 1920's frenetic spirit. But the score also produced gentler moments of sentiment in "You Say You Care" and "Just a Kiss Apart."

1951   TWO ON THE AISLE, a revue with sketches and lyrics by Betty Comden and Adolph Green, Nat Hiken, and William Friedberg. Presented by Arthur Lesser at the Mark Hellinger Theatre on July 19. Entire production directed by Abe Burrows. Musical numbers staged by Ted Cappy. Cast included Bert Lahr, Dolores Gray, Elliott Reid, and Colette Marchand (281 performances).

Three sketches involving Bert Lahr, and two songs sung by Dolores Gray, were the high spots of this revue. One of the sketches, "Space Brigade," had Bert Lahr playing Captain Universe in a farcical satire on such television serials as "Captain Video"; a second sketch was a Wagnerian travesty, "At the Met," which cast Bert Lahr as Siegfried and Dolores Gray as Brünnhilde; and the third sketch has become a Bert Lahr classic, "Schneider's Miracle," with Bert Lahr as a street-cleaner in Central Park proud of his achievements in gathering refuse and faced with disaster when a competitive go-getter street-cleaner proves more diligent than he. The two outstanding songs were "If You Hadn't, But You Did" (particularly memorable for its sparkling lyrics) and "Give a Little, Get a Little Love."

1956   BELLS ARE RINGING, a musical comedy with book and lyrics by Betty Comden and Adolph Green. Produced by the Theatre Guild at the Shubert Theatre on November 29. Production directed and dances and musical numbers staged by Jerome Robbins. Cast included Judy Holliday, Sydney Chaplin, Eddie Lawrence.

The ringing bells are those of "Susanswerphone," a telephone-answering service in Manhattan. One of its operators is Ella Peterson (Judy Holliday), a girl who puts on lipstick before answering the phone, whose somewhat scatterbrain conversation is punctuated with high squeaks and nervous laughs, and who insists upon meddling in the private affairs of her clients. When she discovers that playwright Jeff Moss (Sydney Chaplin) has trouble writing his play and is getting into trouble with his producer, she boldly invades his apartment and gets involved in his life until he writes the play and has it produced. When she learns that the dentist, Dr. Kitchell (Bernie West), wants to write songs and that a would-be Marlon Brando wants to be an actor (Frank Aletter as Blake Barton), she manages to get them to realize their ambitions. While performing these benefactions she falls in love with, and succeeds in winning, Jeff.

If Ella's "Fix-it" complex is not enough to complicate the activities of Susanswerphone, the place is haunted by the police who suspect it of being involved in some vice racket. Actually, the place is used by a bookie taking bets on horse races—the front being a recording company, with names and numbers of symphonies, opus numbers, and their composers serving as the code for horse, track, race, and so forth.

Bells Are Ringing became a box-office triumph—the recipient of accolades from all the critics—mainly because of Judy Holliday's performance, her first appearance in a musical comedy. Brooks Atkinson said of her: "She sings, dances, clowns—and also carries on her shoulders one of the most antiquated plots of the season."

For Judy Holliday this appearance marked a reunion with Betty Comden and Adolph Green, authors of book and lyrics—for in 1938 all three had appeared in a night-club act called "The Revuers," for which Comden and Green wrote all the material. Since that time the gift of Betty Comden and Adolph Green for sophisticated lyrics, nimble dialogue, and vitriolic satire have developed prodigiously. Some of the best numbers in *Bells Are Ringing* were dressed in bright, amusing, and satirical lyrics: "It's a Simple Little System," a *Schnitzelbank* based on *The Racing Form;* "Drop That Name," a devastating take-off on the practice of name-dropping at swank parties; and a "going-home song" to end all such songs, "I'm Goin' Home," with which the play comes to a rousing finale. Styne's songs were attractive in a more mellow mood too, the best being Jeff's two ballads, "Long Before I Knew You" and "Just in Time." And a bit of homey philosophy on better human relations was introduced in song by Ella Peterson, in the subway scene, with "Hello, Hello There!" That subway scene had one of Jerome Robbins' happy choreographic creations, a whirling fandango. Equally effective were several amusing parodies of night-club routines.

HARRY TIERNEY, composer

Harry Tierney was born in Perth Amboy, New Jersey, on May 21, 1895. He came from a musical household, his mother being an excellent pianist and his father a trumpet player in symphony orchestras. Harry received his first instruction in music from his mother. After being graduated from the Perth Amboy High School, he continued his musical education at the Virgil Music School in New York where he received training in piano, theory, and counterpoint.

Tierney made no secret of the fact that his preference in music lay in the popular field. He wrote popular songs even while pursuing his studies in more serious branches of music and while touring the country as concert pianist. When his studies were completed, he went to England in 1915, where he worked as staff composer for a London music publisher, had three songs published, and received two commissions to write music for the stage.

He was back in the United States in 1916, when he found employment in Tin Pan Alley. His songs were now being interpolated into current

Broadway productions, and several became hits. "M-i-s-s-i-s-s-i-p-p-i" was introduced by Frances White in Ziegfeld's 1916 *Midnight Frolics;* "It's a Cute Little Way of My Own," by Anna Held in *Follow Me* (1917); "On Atlantic Beach" and "Everything Is Hunky Dory Down in Honky Tonky Town" in the Hippodrome in 1918. Other songs were heard in Ziegfeld and George M. Cohan productions in 1919.

The year 1919 also marked Tierney's first complete stage score in New York. Since that production was *Irene,* it lifted him to fame. He now became one of Ziegfeld's favored composers. Ziegfeld assigned to him several of his pet stage projects—*Kid Boots* (1923) and *Rio Rita* (1927)—besides introducing other Tierney songs in various editions of the *Follies.*

In 1929 Tierney went to Hollywood to help in the screen adaptation of *Rio Rita.* Otherwise his stay there was not particularly fruitful. Contracted to write music for two new screen musicals, he was a victim of a new directive then issued by the New York bankers to cut down on the filming of musical productions. Back on Broadway, he found himself haunted by the same bad luck that had oppressed him in California—and it spelled doom to his career. One of his musicals, an operetta about Omar Khayyam, never reached production. Another operetta (his last stage score), with Beau Brummel as hero, was played in St. Louis in 1933 but never reached Broadway.

1919   IRENE, a musical comedy with book by James Montgomery. Lyrics by Joseph McCarthy. Produced by Joseph McCarthy at the Vanderbilt Theatre on November 18. Cast included Edith Day, Walter Regan, and Bobbie Watson (670 performances).

Irene made stage history by having the longest run of any musical on Broadway up to that time—surpassing by thirteen performances the record achieved a quarter of a century earlier by *A Trip to Chinatown.* Besides this long New York run, the play enjoyed seventeen road companies.

Its charm lay in its escapist Cinderella story. Irene O'Dare (Edith Day), a poor girl who lives in the slums on Ninth Avenue, New York, is a shop girl who must make a delivery to the home of wealthy Donald Marshall (Walter Regan). Donald becomes interested in her and, to advance her career, finds her a job as model at the modiste establishment of Mme Lucy. At a party on Long Island, Irene sings, dances, and wears the shop's beautiful clothing—winning the hearts of all those present. Through her beauty and charm, Irene helps bring success to Mme Lucy's shop. She also wins the love of Donald, who now must overcome the prejudice of Mrs. O'Dare to rich young men before he can marry Irene.

In this play we find one of the most popular American waltzes of all time—"Alice Blue Gown," enchantingly sung by Irene. To this day it is Tierney's best-known song. The score also included the delightful title song and "Castle of Dreams," the latter borrowing its main melody from Chopin's "Minute Waltz."

1922   UP SHE GOES, a musical comedy with book by Frank Craven based on his own comedy, *Too Many Cooks*. Lyrics by Joseph McCarthy. Produced by William A. Brady at the Playhouse on November 6. Staged by Frank Craven and Bert French. Cast included Donald Brian and Gloria Foy (256 performances).

Albert Bennett (Donald Brian) and Alice Cook (Gloria Foy) are planning to get married. Albert is having a bungalow built in Pleasantville, New York, for that happy day. But the Cook family, which numbers ten members, insists on making so many suggestions about the construction of the house that they finally succeed in embroiling the lovers in a fight that separates them. They are reconciled when Alice comes to the bungalow to get a look at it, and while there confronts Albert.

This sweet and sentimental play had a score to match, its leading numbers including Albert's song, "Lady Luck, Smile on Me," and the duets of Albert and Alice, "Journey's End" and "Let's Kiss and Make Up."

1923   KID BOOTS, a musical comedy with book by William Anthony McGuire and Otto Harbach. Lyrics by Joseph McCarthy. Produced by Florenz Ziegfeld at the Earl Carroll Theatre on December 31. Cast included Eddie Cantor, Mary Eaton, Jobyna Howland, and George Olsen and his orchestra (198 performances).

The play was a showcase for the dynamic, restless, pop-eyed comedian who was its star: Eddie Cantor, cast as Kid Boots, caddie master of the swank Everglades Golf Club in Palm Beach, Florida. For a side-line he gives golf lessons (with crooked balls so that his clients might be convinced of their need for more instruction); he is also a bootlegger and general nosybody. Nobody has the nerve to fire him, since he has something on every member of the club. But his heart is in the right place, and he manages to straighten out the love life of Polly Pendleton (Mary Eaton) and Tom Sterling (Harry Fender)—even while one of his crooked balls costs Tom the match in a golf tournament.

In some of the major comedy scenes Eddie Cantor is handsomely supported by, and is the helpless victim of, Jobyna Howland, appearing as Dr. Josephine Fitch, the club physical director. When she gives him an electrical treatment in an electric bath, she almost shocks him to death; and she handles him mercilessly on an osteopath table during a vigorous treatment.

Eddie Cantor's most famous song was an interpolation—"Dinah" by Sam M. Lewis and Joe Young and Harry Akst, introduced by Kid Boots in the finale of the play; from then on it was one of Cantor's song favorites. Another rousing number was part of the regular score, "Keep Your Eye on the Ball." The love songs were entrusted either to Polly or Tom or both: "If Your Heart's in the Game" and "Someone Loves You, After All."

1927   RIO RITA, a musical comedy with book and lyrics by Guy Bolton and Fred Thompson. Produced by Florenz Ziegfeld at the Ziegfeld Theatre on February 2. Staged by John Harwood. Cast included Ethelind Terry, J. Harold Murray, Bert Wheeler, Robert Woolsey, and Ada May (494 performances).

On February 2, 1927, Ziegfeld opened his new palatial theater on Sixth Avenue—the Ziegfeld. And as befitted the occasion, he put on one of his most lavish productions. The Mexican setting of *Rio Rita* gave scenic designer Joseph Urban and costume designer John Harkrider an opportunity to express some of their most colorful and exotic designs; and the production was endowed with handsome ballets and spectacles, the best of which was called "Black and White."

The play itself seemed only a convenience for the handsome scenes and costumes. Jim, a Texas Ranger captain (J. Harold Murray), is hunting along the Rio Grande for a notorious Mexican bandit. After crossing into Mexico he falls in love with Rio Rita (Ethelind Terry). Their love affair is complicated by the fact that Rio Rita is loved by General Estaban, and also by the suspicion that the bandit is her brother. This dual interference is disposed of. The right bandit is finally found and he is not Rio Rita's brother, and General Estaban yields to his rival. Comic relief was contributed by Wheeler and Woolsey, the latter outstanding in the role of Ed Lovett, a smart-aleck lawyer. Sentiment came from three songs: the title number, a duet of Jim and Rio Rita; "The Ranger's Song"; and "Following the Sun Around."

KURT WEILL, composer

Kurt Weill was born in Dessau, Germany, on March 2, 1900. As a child, Kurt was given musical instruction by his parents. In 1918 he continued his musical education at the Berlin High School of Music, and in 1921 studied privately with one of Europe's most scholarly musicians and esoteric musical thinkers, Ferruccio Busoni. Weill's training, then, was a comprehensive preparation for a career in serious music, a career launched early in the 1920's with several orchestral and chamber-music works.

Though much of the music he wrote at the time was in the advanced techniques and ideas of the *avant-garde* in German music, Weill was no ivory-tower musician. While still a student he earned his living playing popular tunes in a German beer hall. Other jobs—coach and conductor in various small theaters—taught him something of the way a theater functions, and what makes an appeal to an audience.

In Germany in the 1920's there came into vogue a cultural movement called "contemporary art" (*Zeitkunst*). Composers marching under this banner produced "functional music" (*Gebrauchsmusik*), attuned to the times through the assimilation of popular techniques and idioms and through adapting this music for such popular media as radio, cinema, the school, and so forth. Since Weill had always been interested in popular music and since he was a devotee of the stage, he soon came to write operas that became outstanding examples of *Zeitkunst*. Within the formal framework of the opera Weill produced music-hall songs and ballads, current dances like the tango and the shimmy, and idioms like the "blues" and American jazz. Beginning with his first opera and continuing with each successive work, Weill used these popular ideas more and more boldly and made them more and more essential to his over-all texture. "I want to reach the real people, a more representative public than any opera house attracts," he said at the time. "I write for today. I don't care about writing for posterity."

His first opera was *The Protagonist*, written in 1924 to a surrealistic text by Georg Kaiser, and produced in Dresden in 1926. Here Weill's interpolation of popular musical elements was still cautious; but the juxtaposition of popular and serious ideas created enough of a shock for one eminent critic, Oskar Bie, to remark that "all the philosophical theories of teacher Busoni have been swept aside by the reality of Kurt Weill's score."

Weill next wrote *The Royal Palace*, a work typically *Zeitkunst* in its interpolation of actual motion pictures within the play, and in the free mixture of drama and pantomime. It was also *Zeitkunst* in the music's increasing interest in the grammar of American jazz.

Weill's third opera, *The Czar Has Himself Photographed*, shows greater boldness in introducing jazz and popular songs within the operatic texture; in fact, one German critic did not hesitate to designate it a "jazz opera." The intelligentsia might lament that Weill had strayed from the classical fold and was "decadent"; but the rank and file in Germany liked the opera so well that the work played in eighty theaters to meet the tremendous box-office demand.

By the time Weill started writing his next opera—a one-act sketch, *Mahagonny*—he had a clear idea of the kind of work he wanted to produce. *Mahagonny* was his first work for the theater in a new form of his own invention, called "song-play." The formal arias and ensemble numbers of traditional opera were now entirely displaced by popular songs; and the operatic vocabulary made way for the argot of the people.

The text of *Mahagonny* was by Bertholt Brecht. When Weill and Brecht next collaborated they created their most famous work, and one of the most provocative stage musicals of the twentieth century—*The Three-Penny Opera* (*Die Dreigroschenoper*) (1928). Brecht here revised and adapted the historic *Beggar's Opera* of John Gay and transformed it into a bitter, scathing indictment of life and manners in twentieth-century Germany. Weill's music was now completely in the style and ritual of the popular musical theater. It was filled with engaging airs, ballads, tunes, duets, trios. Each number was basic to the play, serving either as a character study or to point up some situation or provide a commentary on what was happening. *The Three-Penny Opera* had about 4000 performances in over 120 different theaters in Germany in a single year. It has since become a stage classic, frequently revived in all parts of the world, and on several occasions adapted for the screen. An off-Broadway revival at the Theatre de Lys on March 10, 1954—with text modernized and revised by Marc Blitzstein, but with the Weill score left intact—resulted in the longest run ever achieved by an off-Broadway production, over 1000 performances.

The star of the original Berlin production of *The Three-Penny Opera* was a young singer and diseuse named Lotta Lenya Blaumauer, who appeared as Jenny. In 1938 Lotta Lenya became Kurt Weill's wife. She would appear as Jenny in several later revivals of *The Three-Penny Opera*, including the sensational 1954 off-Broadway production.

For their next presentation Weill and Brecht expanded their one-act sketch, *Mahagonny*, into a three-act opera renamed *The Rise and Fall of Mahagonny*. This was one of the most controversial musical works given in Germany between the two world wars. Weill's musical treatment was not only in the popular style of his earlier operas but even in the vein of Tin Pan Alley. Some of his lyrics were in English (at times gibberish English), and it is for this reason that the hit song had the English title of "Alabamy Song," one of the biggest song successes in Germany in the early 1930's.

Weill's last opera in Germany was *The Lake of Silver.* It gave every promise of approximating the triumph of *The Three-Penny Opera.* Eleven theaters in as many different cities arranged for a simultaneous première, on February 18, 1933. A long run seemed indicated. But on February 19 the Reichstag in Berlin was set aflame by the Nazis, Weill realized that *Der Tag* had come, and he fled with his wife to Paris.

In Paris, Weill wrote music for several productions that proved failures. Nursing his wounds, he welcomed an offer to come to America. Max Reinhardt had been engaged to stage and direct a pageant of Jewish history by Franz Werfel, *The Eternal Road.* In this production Reinhardt sought to make "a perfect fusion of speech and music," and envisioned the music as the unifying thread within the play. He wanted Weill to write that music. Weill arrived in the United States in 1935. Even then he knew he was coming here for good, for no sooner did he arrive when he began studying the English language, applied for citizenship, and did some research in American popular music and the American musical theater.

The Eternal Road hit one snag after another, suffering numerous delays and postponements; it was not produced until 1937. Consequently, when Weill made his bow in the American theater, it was with a play far different from a religious spectacle. That play was *Johnny Johnson,* a fable about World War I by Paul Green, produced by the Group Theatre in 1936.

The two scores for *The Eternal Road* and *Johnny Johnson,* each so different from the other yet each so remarkably effective within its own context, gave proof of Weill's versatility and pronounced gift in writing for the stage. Though neither production was good box office, Weill became a composer greatly in demand. He was called to Hollywood to write music for several films; he was commissioned to write background music for a spectacle at the New York World's Fair; he was engaged to prepare the score for a Broadway musical that turned out to be his first American success, *Knickerbocker Holiday* (1938).

After *Knickerbocker Holiday,* Weill was invited to become a member of equal status in the newly formed Playwrights Company, which included Maxwell Anderson, Elmer Rice, and Robert E. Sherwood. Their first production requiring music was Moss Hart's *Lady in the Dark*

(1941). This, and its immediate successor, *One Touch of Venus* (1943), placed Weill among the leaders of those writing music for the stage.

Firebrand of Florence (1945) was an unhappy attempt to dress Edwin Justus Mayer's risqué Broadway comedy about Benvenuto Cellini with music and dances. Weill's subsequent music for Broadway acquired operatic dimensions. He now collaborated in three productions whose artistic value has always been appreciated, but none of which enjoyed financial success: *Street Scene* (1947), *Love Life* (1948), and *Lost in the Stars* (1949). The circle of Weill's artistic career had now closed. He had begun his career in Germany by making opera into popular music; he now succeeded making popular music into opera. Indeed, Weill's last work for the stage actually was an opera, an American folk opera, *Down in the Valley*, introduced at Indiana University on July 15, 1948, and since then become a staple in the repertory of many amateur, semi-professional, and professional opera companies. *Down in the Valley* was excellent theater, but it also made for excellent listening. To the end of his life Weill succeeded in being popular in the serious theater, and serious in the popular theater.

He died in New York City on April 3, 1950. A few years after his death, in commenting on the happy revival of *The Three-Penny Opera*, Brooks Atkinson wrote: "Everyone agrees that Mr. Weill was one of the finest composers we have had in the last twenty-five years, and there is reason to think he was the best."

1936 JOHNNY JOHNSON, a "legend" with book and lyrics by Paul Green. Produced by the Group Theatre at the 44th Street Theatre on November 19. Staged by Lee Strasberg. Cast included Russell Collins, Art Smith, Morris Carnovsky, and Phoebe Brand, with John Garfield, Elia Kazan, and Lee J. Cobb in minor roles (68 performances).

The program described *Johnny Johnson* as a "fable." But it was also, as Richard Watts, Jr., noted, "a medley of caricature, satire, musical comedy, melodrama, social polemic and parable." The story traced the decaying idealism of soldier Johnny Johnson (Russell Collins). He goes to war against Germany during World War I because he is engaged in a personal crusade to end all wars. Johnny is honest, direct, naïve. In one way or another he continually embarrasses his superior officers and almost succeeds in bringing about world peace by feeding laughing gas to generals. But in the end he loses the girl he loves, Minny Belle (Phoebe Brand), is confined to an insane asylum, and becomes the disenchanted idealist seeing a world prepare itself for another war. "The world has slapped him with its ultimate indignity," explained Brooks Atkinson. "It can no longer find room for a completely honest man, for it has surrendered to the charlatans, opportunists, and rogues who are the captains and kings of destruction."

Johnny Johnson was weakest on the soap box, in its repeated tirades against war; it was strongest when it used propaganda as the starting point for sentiment and comedy. Several of the comedy scenes were so good that Mr. Watts was repeatedly reminded of "the quality of Charlie Chaplin's greatest comedy, *Shoulder Arms.*" One such scene showed Johnny taking a military psychological test and completely confusing his examiners; another involved Johnny in the manual-of-arms; and a third pitted him against a psychiatrist, who gives voice to a delightfully satirical song about his profession, "They All Take Up Psychiatry."

Songs, musical incidents, and background musical episodes were intended as integral to the story development. The score neatly assimilated many elements of American popular music—including Tin Pan Alley tunes, sentimental stage ballads, cowboy songs. Two songs stood out prominently: "To Love You and to Leave You" and "Oh Heart of Love."

Johnny Johnson enjoyed a brief revival in New York, in an off-Broadway production, on October 21, 1956.

1938   KNICKERBOCKER HOLIDAY, a musical comedy with book and lyrics by Maxwell Anderson. Produced by the Playwrights Company at the Ethel Barrymore Theatre on October 19, 1938. Staged by Joshua Logan. Dances by Carl Randall and Edwin Denby. Cast included Walter Huston, Ray Middleton, Jeanne Madden, and Clarence Nordstrom (168 performances).

One of America's leading playwrights, Maxwell Anderson, here turned for the first time to the musical-comedy stage. He tore a leaf from Washington Irving's *Father Knickerbocker's History of New York.* The setting of New Amsterdam, in 1647, enabled Anderson to point up some of the political problems and misadventures of America in 1938. Peter Stuyvesant (Walter Huston), the peg-legged Governor General, is a dictator who sets up a semi-fascist, semi-New Deal state, which antagonizes the good Dutch people, ever resentful of confining orders and systems. He is surrounded by scurrilous councilmen who exploit the people for their own benefit and who, in the end, are exploited by the even more scurrilous Governor. Since a political allegory is not the stuff of which effective musical comedies are generally made, there is also a minor love plot. Tina Tienhoven (Jeanne Madden), compelled to marry Stuyvesant, loves and is loved by Brom Broeck (Clarence Nordstrom), a young man incapable of taking orders from ruthless politicians. Washington Irving (Ray Middleton) is himself a character in the play, sitting outside the proscenium, writing down his history as the play's action progresses.

Despite its love interest the play would have bogged down in the morass of political and social thinking but for two happy factors. One was Walter Huston's earthy, infectious portrait of Stuyvesant; the other Weill's score, the most tuneful he had written for the American stage up to this point. Weill's best number was the now-famous "September Song," delivered by Stuyvesant in a nasal, half-recitative style. Weill wrote this song with Huston's nonsinging style in mind, and song and singer became one. "It is the composer Weill with his delightful music and actor Huston, gaily spinning about on his peg leg, who provide the holiday," reported Brooks Atkinson. Several other Weill songs and sequences—though much less familiar than "September Song"—added brightness and charm to the play. Among these were "The Dance of the Aborigines," "Young People Think About Love," and "The Dirge for a Soldier."

1941 LADY IN THE DARK, a musical play with book by Moss Hart. Lyrics by Ira Gershwin. Produced by Sam H. Harris at the Alvin Theatre on January 23. Staged by Hassard Short and Moss Hart. Choreography by Albertina Rasch. Cast included Gertrude Lawrence, Victor Mature, Danny Kaye, and Bert Lytell (388 performances).

The idea for this play came to Moss Hart from his own experiences with psychoanalytic treatment. Since psychoanalysis was still an uncultivated field in the theater in 1941, Hart seized on the subject.

Hart recognized that his play would require dream sequences, and with an equally sure instinct he felt that music was indispensable in pointing up such sequences and intensifying their moods. (*Lady in the Dark*, however, was not the first musical to use dream sequences; Rodgers and Hart had done this a decade earlier in *Peggy-Ann*.)

In *Lady in the Dark*, Hart leads his heroine—Liza Elliott, editor of *Allure* (Gertrude Lawrence)—through the tortuous labyrinth of an analysis and carries her to its final happy resolution. On the verge of a breakdown, Liza decides to visit a psychoanalyst. From then on the scenes move deftly back and forth from Liza's office at *Allure* to that of the psychoanalyst. And as significant episodes from Liza's life or from her dreams are brought to the surface at the psychoanalyst's office, the scene dissolves into a dream sequence. In one dream sequence she is the glamorous enchantress to whom all pay homage; in another she attends a wedding ceremony as the bride of her real-life beloved, Kendall Nesbitt (Bert Lytell), a ceremony that turns to horror. In a third a picture layout she is planning for her journal comes vividly to life, and she is brought to task by a circus ringmaster for being unable to make up her mind about major decisions. In the fourth she is once again a child, her father's "ugly duckling," only too well aware of her plainness. The analytical treatment finally enables Liza to understand that it was the consciousness of her plainness that made her flee from womanhood. Now she knows that it is the advertising manager of *Allure* who is the man of her life, even though up to now she has been in constant conflict with him.

A consummate writing technique was required to keep the play moving fluidly from the reality of Liza's actual business and love life, to the confused world of her subconscious; from her everyday problems and frustrations to the nebulous world of her dreams and the misty memories of her past. Hart possessed that skill. But he also profited from one of the most remarkable virtuoso performances of our contemporary musical stage, that of Gertrude Lawrence. Long a star, Gertrude Lawrence helped make the production the vital and unforgettable experience it proved to be. But *Lady in the Dark* was not only the showcase for an established star; it also helped create a star of its own in Danny Kaye. During the writing of *Lady in the Dark* Moss Hart saw Kaye in a night-club act in which the young comedian made his first entry to Broadway by way of an adult camp in Pennsylvania. The impact on Hart of Kaye's versatility, and his unique delivery of comedy numbers, was such that Hart decided to write into the play the part of Russell Paxton for Kaye. When with his athletic tongue Kaye spluttered in rapid succession the names of Russian composers of past and present ("Tchaikovsky") he immediately came into his own on the Broadway stage.

Weill's music also made a fruitful contribution to the success of the play. His atmospheric music was so perfectly attuned to the dream situations that it seemed to be an inextricable part of them; and the theme song, "My Ship," was beautifully suited for such dream sequences through its hauntingly individual melodic structure. Weill's score also consisted of some outstanding individual numbers: "Saga of Jenny," "The Princess of Pure Delight," "One Life to Live," and "Oh Fabulous One in Your Ivory Tower." Yet even these numbers, good as they were in themselves—and appealing though they remain outside their context—are so much a part of the dramatic pattern that *Lady in the Dark* must be considered a "play with music" (as Moss Hart designated it) rather than a musical comedy.

1943 ONE TOUCH OF VENUS, a musical comedy with book by S. J. Perelman and Ogden Nash, suggested by F. Anstey's *The Tinted Venus*. Lyrics by Ogden Nash. Produced by Cheryl Crawford, in conjunction with John Wildberg, at the Imperial Theatre on October 7. Staged by Elia Kazan. Choreography by Agnes De Mille. Cast included Kenny Baker, Mary Martin, John Boles, and Paula Laurence (567 performances).

One Touch of Venus was a formal musical comedy, as opposed to *Lady in the Dark*, a play with music. A lovelorn barber, Rodney Hatch (Kenny Baker), visits the Whitelaw Savory Foundation of Modern Art. There he casually puts the engagement ring he had bought for his girl friend, Gloria (Ruth Bond), on the finger of a statue of Venus, imported into this country by the wealthy art collector, Whitelaw Savory (John Boles). Venus (Mary Martin) comes to life, falls in love with Rodney, and meekly follows him wherever he goes: to Radio City, a bus terminal, a barber shop, and a hotel room. The play is concerned principally with the often madcap adventures of Rodney and Venus in modern Manhattan; one of these escapades provides the excuse for a ballet starring Sono Osato, "Forty Minutes for Lunch." When Gloria disappears mysteriously, Rodney is accused of having murdered her and is incarcerated in the Tombs. But Gloria finally shows up again, becomes reconciled with Rodney, and Venus returns to her formerly inanimate existence as a work of art.

The principal songs were assigned to Rodney and Venus: "Speak Low," "How Much Do I Love You?", "That's Him," and "I'm a Stranger Here Myself." Paula Laurence, who plays the part of Whitelaw's acidulous secretary, has an amusing number in "Very, Very, Very." The principal comedy in the play comes from her performance, and that of Teddy Hart as a private detective.

1947 STREET SCENE, a folk play with music, with book by Elmer Rice based on his 1929 Pulitzer Prize play of the same name. Lyrics by Langston Hughes. Produced by Dwight Deere Wiman and the Playwrights Company at the Adelphi Theatre on January 9. Staged by Charles Friedman. Dances by Anna Sokolow. Cast included Norman Cordon, Anne Jeffreys, Hope Emerson, Polyna Stoska, and Brian Sullivan (148 performances).

Street Scene is a folk drama in which the music brings new dimensions to a compelling stage play. The elemental passions, frustrated ideals, tortured hopes, and poetic dreams that seize and activate the lives of a group of people in a New York City tenement make for realism; and realism rarely profits from musical adaptation. Yet in *Street Scene* the febrile atmosphere and the mounting tragedy gain in momentum, power, and intensity through Weill's evocative background music. Rosamond Gilder said in *Theatre Arts:*

> Kurt Weill turned *Street Scene* into a symphony of the city with its strands of love and yearning and violence woven into the pattern of daily drudgery. His music reflects the hot night, the chatter and gossiping housewives, the sound of children at play, the ebb and flow of anonymous existence.

While Weill's score had several numbers to haunt the memory—principally "Lonely House," "Somehow I Never Could Believe," "A Boy like You," and "We'll All Go Away Together"—it is no single number that gives the play its emotional urge, but the integrated musical texture.

Street Scene may be described as a white man's *Porgy and Bess*—a slice of everyday life carved from the New York City slums in the same way that *Porgy and Bess* portrayed Negro life in Catfish Row in Charleston, South Carolina. Mrs. Anna Maurrant (Polyna Stoska), hungry for love, which her husband, Frank (Norman Cordon), denies her, is carrying on an affair with the milkman. Love also complicates the life of their daughter, Rose (Anne Jeffreys), and her neighbor, the college student Sam Kaplan (Brian Sullivan). Sam is only too willing to give up his studies to marry Rose, but she is reluctant to have him make this sacrifice. When Frank Maurrant returns home unexpectedly one day to find his wife with the milkman, he shoots them and is led off by the police. This tragedy convinces Rose that she must not destroy Sam's life by marrying him before he has made his way in the world. She flees with her younger brother to find a new life elsewhere.

1948   LOVE LIFE, a musical comedy with book and lyrics by Alan Jay Lerner. Produced by Cheryl Crawford at the 46th Street Theatre on October 7. Staged by Elia Kazan. Dances by Michael Kidd. Cast included Ray Middleton and Nanette Fabray (252 performances).

The provocatively unusual text of *Love Life* carries Sam and Susan Cooper (Ray Middleton and Nanette Fabray) through a marriage that lasts from 1791 to 1948. Sam and Susan never grow a day older. But the marriage does—withered and desiccated and finally destroyed by greed and crass materialism.

Love Life is not only a study of marriage and a side glance at social mores. It is also a cavalcade of America from 1791 on. The story of America is told intriguingly through vaudeville acts, madrigal singers, crooners, magicians, vocal quartets. But the over-all idea is more striking than its execution; individual sequences are more arresting than the play as a whole. This is also true of Weill's music, which is better for its parts than as a unified whole. One of his most famous songs appears here: "Green-Up Time." Other notable Weill numbers are: "Mr. Right," "Here I'll Stay," "I Remember It Well," "I'm Your Man," and "Woman's Club Blues."

1949   LOST IN THE STARS, a musical tragedy with book and lyrics by Maxwell Anderson, based on Alan Paton's novel, *Cry, the Beloved Country*. Produced by the Playwrights Company at the Music Box Theatre on October 30. Staged by Rouben Mamoulian. Cast included Todd Duncan, Inez Matthews, Sheila Guyse, and Herbert Coleman (273 performances).

Lost in the Stars is stirring dramatic art, and like the novel from which it was derived, touching in its compassion and humanity and inspiring in its promise of a better life of tolerance and human understanding. Absalom (Julian Mayfield), son of the humble Negro parson, Reverend Stephen Kumalo (Todd Duncan), leaves his native South African town of Ndotsheni for Johannesburg. There he falls in love with Irina (Inez Matthews), who becomes pregnant. To gain money quickly for Irina, Absalom becomes involved in a robbery during which he kills a white man. He confesses everything at the trial and is sentenced to be hanged. Just before the execution Jarvis, father of the murdered man, visits Stephen Kumalo and is touched by the way the old man is broken with grief, and moved by his dignity and integrity. Tragedy now unites white man and black in a mutual bond of sympathy and understanding.

As in *Street Scene*, music endows a human, and at times a profound, play with deeper overtones. Perhaps never before or since has the popular American stage boasted such moving choral music. Weill uses the chorus as the Greek dramatists did, to provide commentary: In the dirge, "Cry the Beloved Country," a lament for Absalom's lost childhood; in "Fear," a penetrating psychological commentary on that emotion; in "Bird of Passage," a deeply religious statement about the life of man. The solo melodies (one is reluctant to refer to them as songs, so fluidly do they rise and then ebb back again into the dramatic situation) are equally expressive. They bring up the immeasurable sorrow of Stephen Kumalo when he realizes that his son is a murderer ("O Tixo, Tixo" and "Lost in the Stars"). They help define character vividly, that of the entertainer Linda, for example, in "Who'll Buy?" and that of Irina in "Trouble Man." So germane is Weill's music to the play, and so integral to the over-all context, that one can readily understand the tendency of a serious music critic like Olin Downes to consider it an American opera; and, indeed, it was presented as an opera by the New York City Opera during its 1958 Spring season.

RICHARD A. WHITING, composer

Richard A. Whiting was born in Peoria, Illinois, on November 12, 1891. Both his parents were musical, but neither gave him any formal instruction. What he learned about the piano and harmony he acquired for himself. Even while attending Harvard Military School in Los Angeles he began writing popular songs. After his graduation he found employment as office manager of the Detroit branch of Remick. Remick published his first song in 1913. Two years later Whiting wrote "It's Tulip Time in Holland," which sold 1,500,000 copies of sheet music. "Mammy's Little Coal Black Rose" in 1916 and "Where the Black-Eyed Susans Grow" in 1917 were also hits, the latter interpolated by Al Jolson in *Robinson Crusoe, Jr.* In 1918 came one of the great ballads of World War I in Whiting's " 'Til We Meet Again," which amassed the formidable sale of 5,000,000 copies.

In 1919 Whiting came to New York where his first stage assignment was to write music for a postwar revue, *Toot Sweet.* In the same year he was also engaged by George White to produce a score for the first edition of the *Scandals.*

Between 1920 and 1931 Whiting did no writing for the Broadway theater, but in Tin Pan Alley his stature kept growing all the time by virtue of such resounding song hits as "Japanese Sandman," "Ain't We Got Fun," and "Sleepy Time Gal."

In 1929 he went out to Hollywood where during the next decade his songs appeared in over two dozen screen musicals. Among his most popular screen songs were two written for and made famous by Maurice Chevalier, "Louise" and "One Hour with You." Others included "Beyond the Blue Horizon," "Too Marvelous for Words," and "When Did You Leave Heaven?"

When Whiting returned to Broadway in 1931 it was with a failure, *Free for All,* which lasted only fifteen performances. But one year later he had a major success in *Take a Chance,* his valedictory to Broadway. From

1932 on Whiting's writing was confined to Hollywood, where he died on February 10, 1938.

1919 SCANDALS, a revue with book and lyrics by George White and Arthur Jackson. Produced by George White at the Liberty Theatre on June 2, 1919. Staged by George White. Cast included George White, Ann Pennington, Lou Holtz, and Yvette Rugel (128 performances).

For other editions of the Scandals *see* DE SYLVA, BROWN *and* HENDERSON, *and* GEORGE GERSHWIN.

This was the first edition of an annual revue planned, written and produced by George White as a competitor to *The Ziegfeld Follies.* This was George White's bow as a producer; up to 1919 he had been a successful dancer in leading musical comedies and revues, including the *Passing Show* of 1914 and *The Ziegfeld Follies* of 1915.

He did not spare expense in making his production as lavish as possible; the emphasis was on huge production numbers, gorgeous sets and costumes, and elaborate dance numbers. The dances, ranging from ballet to the shimmy, highlighted performances by George White himself, and by Ann Pennington, acknowledged queen of the shimmy.

This new revue was a veritable feast for the eye. What it lacked most of all was fresh comedy, whose main representatives were Lou Holtz (in his debut on the Broadway stage) and a blackface team by the name of Bennett and Richards. "When there was so much money to be spent," lamented Arthur Hornblow in *Theatre Magazine,* "Mr. White might have set aside a few dollars for a good scenario writer."

Nevertheless the *Scandals* proved at once a formidable rival to the *Follies,* and nobody recognized this more quickly than Ziegfeld himself. Immediately after the opening of the *Scandals,* Ziegfeld tried to remove a serious competitor by offering George White and Ann Pennington 3000 dollars a week to appear in the *Follies.* White's reply was immediate. He was ready to offer 7000 dollars a week for Ziegfeld and his wife, Billie Burke, to appear in the *Scandals.*

The *Scandals* continued to appear on Broadway up to 1939 (with intermissions in 1927, 1930, 1932, 1934, and between 1936 and 1938). Beginning with the 1921 edition its name was officially changed to George White's *Scandals,* and after the fourth edition George White no longer appeared in the cast.

1932 TAKE A CHANCE, a musical comedy with book by Buddy de Sylva and Laurence Schwab. Additional dialogue by Sid Silvers. Additional music

by Herb Nacio Brown and Vincent Youmans. Produced by Laurence
Schwab and Buddy de Sylva at the Apollo Theatre on November 26.
Musical numbers staged by Bobby Connolly. Book directed by Edgar
MacGregor. Cast included Ethel Merman, Jack Haley, Jack Whiting,
and June Knight (243 performances).

Kenneth Raleigh (Jack Whiting) is a rich young man from Harvard who
got a taste of show business there with the Hasty Pudding Shows. He
decides to go professional by putting on a Broadway musical. Two confidence men—Duke Stanley (Jack Haley) and Louie Webb (Sid Silvers)
—are trying to promote the stage career of Toni Ray (June Knight).
They become involved with Kenneth who, in turn, becomes involved
with Toni. Much of the interest of *Take a Chance* comes from backstage
glimpses into the trials and tribulations of producing a musical show.
Much of its comedy came from the mad antics of Sid Silvers (formerly
the stooge of Phil Baker) and Jack Haley—especially in the scene where,
recuperating from a hang-over, they inexplicably find themselves in the
same bed. And most of the dynamic singing came from Ethel Merman,
appearing as Wanda Brill, and bringing the house down with "Eadie Was
a Lady," "I've Got Religion," and "Rise 'n Shine" (the last by Vincent
Youman's); and with Jack Haley in "You're an Old Smoothie."

P. G. WODEHOUSE, lyricist

Though P. G. Wodehouse is most famous for his whimsical novels and
stories—particularly those involving Psmith and Jeeves as characters—
he has also been a significant writer for the popular Broadway musical
stage. As a lyricist he has been a pioneer in bringing a skillful technique
at versification and an adult sophistication to song verses, thereby setting
the stage for writers like Lorenz Hart, Ira Gershwin, and Cole Porter.

Pelham Grenville Wodehouse ("Plum" to his friends) was born in
Guildford, Surrey, England, on October 15, 1881. He was educated at
Dulwich College with the hope of becoming a banker. After completing
his schooling he did make an attempt at banking but after two years was
firmly told by his employer that his talent lay elsewhere. Wodehouse
agreed eagerly, for by then he was already earning money by his pen. He
found several jobs where his writing ability could be used advanta-
geously. In 1902 he started writing lyrics to music by Jerome Kern for
songs appearing on the London stage during the next few years; their
first hit was a topical song called "Mr. Chamberlain" (Mr. Chamberlain
being a noted politician of the time, the father of Neville).

From 1903 to 1909 Wodehouse filled a post as columnist for the London *Globe*. During this period he also started writing stories about a bright young fellow named Psmith. Wodehouse's first novel about him, *Psmith in the City* (1910), made him famous.

Wodehouse had paid two visits to the United States before arriving in 1915 for a somewhat more permanent settlement. He sold some stories to *The Saturday Evening Post* and worked as a drama critic for *Vanity Fair*. In the latter capacity he attended the opening-night performance of the Kern musical *Very Good, Eddie* where his onetime London friendship with the composer was revived. Kern introduced Wodehouse to Guy Bolton, his collaborator, and suggested that the three of them join forces in writing musicals. "Wodehouse was so overcome," noted Bolton in his diary, "that he couldn't answer for a minute, then grabbed my hand and stammered out thanks." Wodehouse reported a somewhat different story in his own diary. "Bolton . . . offered partnership. Tried to hold back and weigh suggestion, but his eagerness was so pathetic that I consented." Thus it came about that Wodehouse joined Bolton and Kern in writing the celebrated Princess Theatre Shows, for which this triumvirate became famous in the 1910's.

P. G. Wodehouse has written either libretto or lyrics for almost two dozen musicals by Kern, Gershwin, Caryll, Friml, and Hirsch, among others.

After World War II, Wodehouse established permanent residence in the United States, at Remsenburg, Long Island.

See: RUDOLF FRIML (*The Three Musketeers*); GEORGE GERSHWIN (*Oh Kay, Rosalie*); JEROME KERN (The Princess Theatre Shows—*Oh Boy; Oh Lady, Lady. Leave It to Jane*).

ROBERT WRIGHT and GEORGE (CHET) FORREST, composers-lyricists

Robert Wright and George Forrest have been collaborators in the writing of both music and lyrics. Their careers have followed parallel lines. Wright is the older, born in Daytona Beach, Florida, on September 25, 1914; Forrest came less than a year later, in Brooklyn, New York, July 31, 1915. Both attended the Miami (Florida) High School and the University of Miami. Both achieved their first successes in Hollywood where, in a writing partnership, they produced special material for stage and night-club revues, and contributed songs for a number of screen musicals, including *Maytime, Firefly,* and *Sweethearts*. For *Firefly* they wrote the lyrics of "Donkey Serenade" (music by Friml and Stothart); for *Sweethearts* they created the lyrics and music of a hit song, "Pretty as a Picture."

Their career on Broadway has alternated between formidable successes and equally formidable failures. Success came first, with *The Song of Norway* (1944). *Gypsy Lady* (1946)—an operetta whose score was made up of Victor Herbert favorites—was a dud. Then came another box-office smash in *Kismet* (1953). But in 1957 *Carefree Heart* (text derived from the "Doctor" comedies of Molière) expired out of town.

1944   SONG OF NORWAY, an operetta with book by Milton Lazarus based on a play by Homer Curran. Lyrics by Wright and Forrest. Music by Wright and Forrest adapted from the works of Edvard Grieg. Produced by Edwin Lester at the Imperial Theatre on August 21. Staged by Charles K. Freeman. Choreography by George Balanchine. Cast included Lawrence Brooks, Irra Petina, Helena Bliss, and Sig Arno (860 performances).

The story is supposedly the life of Edvard Grieg (Lawrence Brooks), with accent on his love affair with and marriage to Nina Hagerup (Helena Bliss). In the beginning of the operetta Grieg is a humble, unknown, and struggling composer whose genius is recognized only by one of his cronies. Then Grieg achieves world fame and wealth through his Piano Concerto (some of the music of which appears in the operetta without alteration). But he is not happy. Now he is embroiled in misunderstandings with Nina, the lady he loves; her parents oppose his marriage to their daughter because they suspect him of having a mistress, in the prima donna Louisa Giovanni (Irra Petina). Time and again he is so distressed by his personal problems that he threatens to give up composition for good. But his problems find a happy resolution, and he marries Nina.

The hit song, "Strange Music," was a popular-song adaptation of Grieg's "Wedding Day in Troldhaugen," from his *Lyric Pieces* for piano. The love song, "I Love You," was a popularization of Grieg's *Lied*, "Ich liebe Dich," which he actually did write to Nina. Other Wright-Forrest songs came from the Violin Sonata in G major, *Peer Gynt Suite*, and various songs and piano pieces. Grieg's music was also used as the background for a sumptuously mounted ballet, "Song of Norway," starring Alexandra Danilova and Frederic Franklin of the Ballet Russe de Monte Carlo.

1953   KISMET, a musical extravaganza, with book by Charles Lederer and Luther Davis based on the play of the same name by Edward Knoblock.

Lyrics by Wright and Forrest. Music adapted by Wright and Forrest from the works of Borodin. Produced by Charles Lederer at the Ziegfeld Theatre on December 3. Staged by Albert Marre. Choreography by Jack Cole. Cast included Alfred Drake, Doretta Morrow, and Joan Diener (583 performances).

The program described this extravaganza as "a musical Arabian night," and it comes from the Broadway play in which Otis Skinner starred. The public poet of ancient Bagdad, Hajj (Alfred Drake), comes to town with his beautiful daughter, Marsinah (Doretta Morrow). Marsinah is married to the Wazir of Police, but her father has other plans for her, namely to have her marry the handsome young Caliph (Richard Kiley). He achieves this by drowning the Wazir in a fountain. He also manages to elope to an oasis with an attractive widow, and to compete successfully in the writing of verses with Omar the tentmaker (Philip Coolidge).

The lavish sets and costumes found their match in the rich Oriental colors of Borodin's music, beautifully adapted for popular consumption. The score boasted two hits. "Stranger in Paradise," a duet of Marsinah and the young Caliph, came from one of the Polovtsian Dances from *Prince Igor*. Marsinah's ballad, "This Is My Beloved," is derived from the atmospheric Nocturne of the Quartet in D major. Two numbers by Hajj— "Fate" and "The Olive Tree"—and the background music for the ceremonial of the Caliph's Diwan and the presentation of the Princesses were also of special musical interest.

VINCENT YOUMANS, composer

Vincent Youmans was born in New York City on September 27, 1898. His father was a famous hatter, whose stores on lower and upper Broadway in the early 1900's helped dictate the prevailing hat fashions for both men and ladies. Financially comfortable, the Youmans family moved from New York City to Westchester when Vincent was a child. He started taking piano lessons when he was four, but his parents had no intention of encouraging him to become a professional musician. They hoped to direct him into science, and for this purpose he was placed in private schools in Mamaroneck and Rye, New York. When engineering was finally decided upon, Youmans was enrolled in the Sheffield Scientific School at Yale University. But even before he started attending the classes there he firmly vetoed the idea of engineering and chose finance instead. In the summer of 1916 he found a job as clerk in a Wall Street brokerage house.

During World War I, Youmans enlisted in the Navy. He was assigned to the entertainment unit at the Coast Lakes Training Station, where he helped produce musicals for the navy. Occasionally he wrote music for these presentations. John Philip Sousa, then leading navy as well as army bands, liked one of his pieces and played it; other navy bands followed suit until it became known to sailors everywhere. Ten years later this same piece became even more popular as "Hallelujah" in *Hit the Deck*.

By the time the war ended, Youmans had crystallized his thinking about his future and had come to the conclusion that he wanted to write popular songs. He went to Tin Pan Alley and found a job as staff pianist for the publishing house of Harms. One of his duties was to help Victor Herbert rehearse singers. "I got something in less than a year that money couldn't buy," he recalled some years later. Working with Herbert taught him a great deal about techniques and approaches in writing a popular tune. In 1918 one of Youmans' songs appeared in a Broadway musical, *From Piccadilly to Broadway* ("Who's Who with You"). Three years later Youmans completed an entire stage score in collaboration with Paul Lannin, *Two Little Girls in Blue,* a success.

During the next four years Youmans was associated with several stage productions. Two of these (both in 1923) were in collaboration with Oscar Hammerstein II, then still green at the business of writing lyrics or working with musical-comedy books. One of these two musicals was a failure. But the other, *Wildflower,* was a decided hit. *No, No, Nanette,* a year later, was an even greater success and put Youmans among the foremost writers of stage music of his day. Youmans' fourth major musical came to Broadway two years after that, *Hit the Deck*.

Between 1927 and 1933 Youmans was represented on Broadway with a disconcerting succession of box-office failures. But he did not have to be ashamed of two of these, since each in its own way represented a courageous effort on Youmans' part to bring a fresh, new approach to the musical theater: *Rainbow* (1928) and *Through the Years* (1932). The latter was Brian Hooker's adaptation of a sentimental play by Jane Cowl long popular on stage and screen, now acquiring new radiance through Youmans' songs. Two of them have become famous: the title song, the composer's own favorite, and "Drums in My Heart."

Individual songs rather than the productions for which they were intended brought significance to several Youmans' musicals. *Great Day* (1929) had "More than You Know" and "Without a Song"; *Smiles* (1930) might have had one of Youmans' classics, "Time on My Hands," if its star, Marilyn Miller, had not objected to it and forced its removal from that play (it was used as an independent song). *Take a Chance* (1932), a score written with Richard E. Whiting, had another Youmans' delight in "Rise 'n Shine" in the style of a revivalist hymn (*see* RICHARD WHITING).

Youmans' music for *Take a Chance* was his last contribution to Broadway. In 1933 he went out to Hollywood to write an original score for the Fred Astaire-Ginger Rogers musical, *Flying Down to Rio*, a score that had "Carioca" and "Orchids in the Moonlight."

The intensity with which Youmans had always lived and worked finally undermined his sensitive health. A victim of tuberculosis, he had to quit work late in 1933 and withdraw to a Colorado sanitarium. The long period of quiet and rest induced introspection and re-evaluation. He began speaking of deserting popular music and devoting himself to more serious endeavors, possibly an opera or a symphony. An improvement in his health enabled him to go to New Orleans, where for a while he immersed himself in music study.

The symphony remained only random sketches; the opera, only vague dreams. Late in 1943 Youmans decided to channel his ambitions through the artery of the musical theater. He planned a new kind of musical production—the Vincent Youmans Ballet Revue, embracing classic and modern dance, beautiful costuming and scenery, interludes for puppets; the score would be derived from classics by Rimsky-Korsakov, Ravel, and others, with a few special new numbers by Ernest Lecuona. Financed by Doris Duke, he planned this production along spacious lines. Opening in Baltimore on January 27, 1944, it was coldly received. It limped on to Boston where it expired—collapsing under the dead weight of its own pretentious aims.

This was Youmans' farewell to the theater. His health broke down again. He entered Doctors Hospital in New York early in 1945, and a year later was back again in a Colorado sanitarium, from which he was not destined to emerge alive. He died on April 5, 1946.

1922   TWO LITTLE GIRLS IN BLUE, a musical comedy with book by Fred Jackson. Lyrics by Arthur Francis (pseudonymn for Ira Gershwin). Music written in collaboration with Paul Lannin. Produced by A. L. Erlanger at the Cohan Theatre on May 3. Staged by Ned Wayburn. Cast included the Fairbanks Twins, Oscar Shaw, and Fred Santley (226 performances).

The Sartoris twins, Dolly and Polly (the Fairbanks Twins), have to go to India to claim an inheritance. Since they have only the price for a single steamship ticket, they try to fool the ship's captain by taking turns in the dining room, on the deck, in the ballroom, and in the stateroom. They

manage well enough until each meets the young man of her heart's desire
—Robert Barker (Oscar Shaw) and Jerry Lloyd (Fred Santley). The two
men, not knowing they are involved with twins, get confused in their
pursuit now of one girl, and now of another, until the two girls can
finally disclose that they are really different people. From then on their
love affairs can achieve a happy resolution.

Two Little Girls in Blue was Youmans' entry into the Broadway theater
with a full score—even if written collaboratively. And it also marked the
first musical for which young Ira Gershwin was engaged to write all the
lyrics; this was two years before he entered into a permanent working
arrangement with his brother George. The Youmans-Gershwin score had
two delightful songs—the title number and "Oh Me, Oh My, Oh You."

1923   WILDFLOWER, a musical comedy with book and lyrics by Otto Harbach
and Oscar Hammerstein II. Music written in collaboration with Herbert
Stothart. Presented by Arthur Hammerstein at the Casino Theatre on
February 7. Book staged by Oscar Eagle. Dances and ensembles by
David Bennett. Cast included Edith Day, Guy Robertson, and Evelyn
Cavanaugh (477 performances).

Wildflower is a charming play, rich with atmospheric interest and enlivened by a delightful characterization—that of the fiery, hot-tempered
little peasant maid, Nina Benedetto (Edith Day). The death of a distant
uncle brings her a rich legacy, but only if she can control her temper and
act like a lady for a period of six months. Failing to fulfill this provision
meant that Nina must let the fortune pass on to her detestable cousin,
Bianca (Evelyn Cavanaugh)—a thought so distasteful to Nina that she
finds the discipline to carry out the demands of the legacy, even to the
point of temporarily deserting her lover, Guido (Guy Robertson).

The New York *World* described *Wildflower* as "a musical comedy of
delightful manner and really gorgeous melodies," adding that "these song
numbers not only are prepared with taste and understanding, but they
seem a most essential part in the make-up of the whole. . . . Its music
and tempo are extraordinary." The two main songs are still remembered:
the title number introduced by Guido, and "Bambalina," first presented by
Nina and an ensemble.

1925   NO, NO, NANETTE, a musical comedy with book by Otto Harbach and
Frank Mandel. Lyrics by Irving Caesar and Otto Harbach. Produced by
H. H. Frazee at the Globe Theatre on September 16. Staged by H. H.
Frazee. Cast included Mary Lawlor, Charles Winninger, Beatrice Lee,
Wellington Cross, and Edna Whistler (321 performances).

The triumph of *No, No, Nanette* was practically global. It had a brief tryout in Chicago in 1924, then opened in London on March 11, 1925, to achieve the then-unprecedented run for Chicago of 665 performances. After a long stay on Broadway, seventeen companies played it in Europe, South America, New Zealand, the Philippines, and China. It brought in a profit of over 2,000,000 dollars.

No, No, Nanette was a disarming escapade. The central figure is Billy Early (Wellington Cross), wealthy publisher of Bibles, who has an irresistible weakness for helping pretty young girls in trouble. His protective wing spreads generously over three winsome creatures: Betty from Boston (Beatrice Lee), Flora from Frisco (Edna Whistler), and Winnie from Washington (Mary Lawlor). This trio has no difficulty in getting Billy to open up for them both his heart and his purse. Complications ensue when a jealous wife gets wind of Billy's involvements; but a wily lawyer, Jimmy Smith (Charles Winninger), manages to extricate Billy from a difficult situation to everyone's satisfaction.

It was in the deft handling of this material that the play won its distinction. Comic episodes were so generously sprinkled throughout that the merriment never relaxed. Another strong point was the Youmans score, his best up to then. A deceptive simplicity and a remarkable economy of means concealed the skill with which the two main songs were fashioned: "Tea for Two" and "I Want to Be Happy." The title song was a third sprightly number.

1927 HIT THE DECK, a musical comedy with book by Herbert Fields based on *Shore Leave,* a play by Hubert Osborne. Lyrics by Leo Robin and Clifford Grey. Produced by Lew Fields and Vincent Youmans at the Belasco Theatre on April 25. Staged by Lew Fields and Alexander Leftwich. Dances arranged by Seymour Felix. Cast included Louise Groody, Charles King, and Stella Mayhew (352 performances).

Loulou (Louise Groody) is the proprietress of a coffee shop in Newport, Rhode Island, frequented by sailors. She falls in love with one of them— Bilge (Charles King). When Bilge sails for distant ports, Loulou—now an heiress—follows him around the world, hoping to convince him to marry her. She finally catches up with him, but he seems reluctant to marry a wealthy woman. Loulou saves the situation by signing away her fortune—to their first-born child.

Youmans, doubling as composer and co-producer, contributed two song classics. One was "Hallelujah," a rousing sailor's chorus he had written a decade earlier when he himself had been a sailor; the other, "Sometimes

I'm Happy," a duet of Loulou and Bilge. As Alan Dale wrote of Youmans' music, the "melodies will be radioed and gramophoned and whistled and pianoed and pianolad, and even jazzed until you'll cry for
mercy. . . . If 'Sometimes I'm Happy' isn't sung all over the world until
sometimes you'll be unhappy, I'll eat my own chapeau." The melody of
"Sometimes I'm Happy" was used by Youmans for an earlier song, and in
another musical. As "Come On and Pet Me" it appeared in *A Night Out*
and was published, but it did not make much of an impression. Then
Irving Caesar wrote new lyrics for the Youmans melody, called it "Sometimes I'm Happy," and the new version was brought to *Hit the Deck*,
where it scored heavily.

1928   RAINBOW, a romantic musical play, with book by Laurence Stallings
and Oscar Hammerstein II. Presented by Philip Goodman at the Gallo
Theatre on November 21. Book staged by Oscar Hammerstein II. Musical numbers staged by Busby Berkeley. Cast included Brian Donlevy,
Allan Prior, Charles Ruggles, Louise Brown, and Libby Holman (29
performances).

Someday *Rainbow* will be revived. Perhaps then Broadway will finally
recognize how far in advance of its time it was in 1928. Here was a play
whose adjustment of spoken text and music—and vice-versa—was almost
operatic, whose atmosphere, local color, and dramatic truth were all in
the best traditions of the legitimate theater. Here was a romantic play
almost in the folk style later made popular by Rodgers and Hammerstein. Had *Rainbow* come in the 1940's, it would surely have enjoyed a
far greater audience response than it received in 1928, when it could not
survive a single month.

Many critics, however, recognized its originality and beauty—even if
they failed to convince audiences. Howard Barnes described it as "a
prodigal, bright-hued entertainment . . . with absorbing melodramatic
overtones which burst through the thin veil of a graceful score and pretty
dances." To Robert Littell "the best of *Rainbow* is wonderfully good and
also brand new . . . so gorgeously different in its high spots that the
weaker spots don't matter." Gilbert Gabriel regarded it as "a stirring
treat . . . a lusty, happy, often handsome show, picturesque . . . and
somehow full of . . . simple and effective fervor."

The play was set mostly in California, the time the era of the 1849 gold
rush. Harry Stanton (Allan Prior), a young scout at Fort Independence,
kills Major Davolo (Rupert Lucas) in self-defense. Escaping from prison,
he sets out for the West and settles in California where the fever for gold

prospecting was then at its height. He meets and falls in love with Virginia Brown (Louise Brown) and wins her against the colorful background of the gold-rush days in California.

Despite strong performances of the principals, two minor stars stole the limelight. As Nasty Howell, the muleteer, Charles Ruggles scored a personal triumph singing "The Bride Was Dressed in White," in the style of the period. And when she sang "I Want a Man," the then-unknown Libby Holman—appearing as Lotta—for the first time gave full measure to her ample talent as a singer of ballads and torch songs. Some of the choral numbers (such as "On the Golden Trail" with which the play opens and closes) and the dances had an American folk character that at the time was something vital and fresh and new for the American stage.

APPENDIXES

SOME OTHER OUTSTANDING MUSICAL
PRODUCTIONS: 1866-1958*

MILTON AGER and OWEN MURPHY (*Rain or Shine*—1928)
HARRY ARCHER (*Little Jessie James*—1928)
ANTHONY BAFUNNO (*Somebody's Sweetheart*—1918)
JERRY BOCK, LARRY HOLOFCENER, and GEORGE WEISS (*Mr. Wonderful*—1956)
PHIL CHARIG (*Follow the Girls*—1944)
WALTER DONALDSON (*Whoopee*—1928)
WILLIAM WALLACE FURST (*The Isle of Champagne*—1892)
PERCY GAUNT (*A Trip to Chinatown*—1893)
CHARLES GAYNOR (*Lend an Ear*—1948)
LEWIS E. GENSLER (*Queen High*—1926)
JEAN GILBERT & ALFRED GOODMAN (*Lady in Ermine*—1922)
ALBERT HAGUE (*Plain and Fancy*—1955)
JAMES T. HANLEY (*Honeymoon Lane*—1927)
MAX HOFFMAN (*A Parisian Model*—1906)
VICTOR JACOBI and FRITZ KREISLER (*Apple Blossoms*—1919)
TOM JOHNSTONE (*I'll Say She Is*—1924)
STEPHEN JONES and ARTHUR SAMUELS (*Poppy*—1923)
HAROLD KARR (*Happy Hunting*—1956)
MAURICE LEVI (The Rogers Brothers Vaudeville Farces—1899)
RICHARD LEWINE (*Make Mine Manhattan*—1948)
JAY LIVINGSTON and RAY EVANS (*Oh, Captain!*—1958)
HUGH MARTIN (*Best Foot Forward*—1941)
JOHNNY MERCER (*Top Banana*—1951)
BOB MERRILL (*New Girl in Town*—1957)
JEROME MOROSS (*Golden Apple*—1954)
WOOLSON MORSE (*Wang*—1891)
GIUSEPPE OPERTI (*The Black Crook*—1866)

* *Note:* Significant musical productions by composers other than those discussed in the main section of this book will be found below in chronological order. These musicals are by the following composers:

HAROLD ORLOB (*Listen Lester*—1918)
GENE DE PAUL (*Li'l Abner*—1956)
A. REIFF (*Humpty Dumpty*—1868)
EDWARD E. RICE (*Adonis*—1884; *Evangeline*—1874)
CARLO SANDERS (*Tangerine*—1921)
NOBLE SISSLE and EUBIE BLAKE (*Shuffle Along*—1921)
WILLARD SPENCER (*The Little Tycoon*—1887; *Princess Bonnie*—1895)
JOHN PHILIP SOUSA (*El Capitan*—1896)
HERBERT STOTHART (*Tickle Me*—1920)
KAY SWIFT (*Fine and Dandy*—1930)
ALBERT VON TILZER (*The Gingham Girl*—1922)
MEREDITH WILLSON (*The Music Man*—1957)
ED WYNN (*The Perfect Fool*—1921)
EFREM ZIMBALIST (*Honeydew*—1920)

1866   THE BLACK CROOK, a musical extravaganza with book by Charles M. Barras. Music mostly by Giuseppe Operti (mostly adaptations). Produced by William Wheatley and Henry C. Jarrett at Niblo's Gardens on September 12 (474 performances).

The Black Crook has often been called the first American musical comedy. It was the first major success of our musical theater; it was the first musical in which undraped females, suggestive dances, and sex insinuations in song were prominently exploited.

The production was largely the result of chance. In the 1860's Henry C. Jarrett and Harry Palmer imported from France a troupe of ballet dancers and some expensive stage sets. They planned to put on a French ballet at the Academy of Music in New York. Before this production could be realized, the Academy burned down. The only other place Jarrett and Palmer could put on their show was at Niblo's Gardens, and they entered into negotiations with William Wheatley, its proprietor. It so happened that during this period Wheatley had acquired the rights to a melodrama by Charles M. Barras called *The Black Crook*. He consummated a deal with Jarrett and Palmer whereby they would join forces in producing *The Black Crook* at Niblo's Gardens, with the imported ballet troupe and sets.

Once this deal was set, Wheatley began planning his production along most elaborate designs. He rebuilt his stage to permit trap doors everywhere, to accommodate the elaborate settings he had in mind and to house the complex machinery necessary to create the remarkable stage effects he was planning. He outfitted the girls of the ballet in expensive, usually transparent, silks and laces. He built up an enormous cast. By the time the curtain went up he had spent the then-unprecedented sum of 50,000 dollars.

The play itself was merely an excuse for presenting a continual succession of spectacles, ballets, transformations, enchantments. Hertzog, the Black Crook, makes a pact with the devil to deliver a human soul each year, just before midnight on New Year's Eve. Endowed by the devil with supernatural powers, Hertzog selects for his victim, Rudolph, a painter then imprisoned by Count Wolfenstein. Hertzog manages Rudolph's release from his cell, then leads him on a quest for hidden gold. En route, Rudolph saves the life of a dove, which in reality is a fairy queen. She discloses to Rudolph Hertzog's evil design, and thus Rudolph is saved. Hertzog is led away by the devil for failing to fulfill his bargain, and Rudolph finds not only freedom but also his beloved, Amina.

For five and a half hours audiences were held spellbound not only by the play itself, which was often confusing, but by the fantastic stage effects, mammoth production numbers, opulent ballets, and the sensual display of female beauty. Among the stage effects were a hurricane in the Harz Mountains, a demon ritual, a "grand ballet of gems," a carnival, a masquerade, a pageant. The closing scene depicted fairies on silver couches, and angels in gilded chariots, ascending and descending "amid a silver rain."

Never before had New York seen anything on its stage to equal such splendors. But stage spectacle was not the only attraction to entice audiences into Niblo's Gardens. Another lure was the "sinful entertainment" provided by the girls in pink tights in suggestive dance numbers. "The police should arrest all engaged in such a violation of public decency," bellowed James Gordon Bennett in an editorial in the *Herald*. From a platform the Reverend Charles B. Smythe denounced the "immodest dress of the girls" who appeared "with thin gauze-like material allowing the form of the figure to be discernible." He went on to say: "The attitudes were exceedingly indelicate. . . . When a danseuse is assisted by a danseur, the attitudes assumed by both in conjunction suggest to the imagination scenes which one may read, describing the ancient heathen orgies."

The Black Crook, then, became the thing to see—even if respectable women had to wear heavy veils to conceal their identity. Many came not once but several times, as new and ever greater stage spectacles were interpolated. (In 1867 a baby ballet of several hundred infants was introduced!) The run of 474 performances proved the most profitable for an American theater impresario up to that time. The show earned a profit of over 1,000,000 dollars in its initial run, and this figure was swelled considerably in succeeding years through frequent revivals.

Two of its musical numbers became popular. One was the "March of the Amazons" by Operti. The other was the song, "You Naughty, Naughty Men" (by T. Kennick and G. Bicknell), which Milly Cavendish sang provocatively to the men in the audience from the front of the stage.

The circumstances surrounding the first production of *The Black Crook* were borrowed and embellished upon for the Sigmund Romberg musical comedy, *The Girl in Pink Tights*.

1868   HUMPTY DUMPTY, an extravaganza, with book mostly by George L. Fox. Music by A. Reiff (mostly adaptations). Produced by George L. Fox at the Olympic Theatre on March 10. Cast included G. L. Fox, F. Lacy, C. K. Fox, and Emily Rigl (483 performances).

Humpty Dumpty was an attempt to imitate the attractions of *The Black Crook*. Like its predecessor, *Humpty Dumpty* featured transformation scenes, spells, and rituals. The elaborate ballets were more than a casual reminder of those in *The Black Crook*, since one of these used babies headed by a five-year-old première danseuse, and another starred Rita Sangalli, a graduate of the earlier extravaganza. The huge stage held not only enormous forces including dancers, circus acts, a bicycle act by two tots, and even a roller-skating routine (the last said to be the first of its kind on the American stage); it also included sumptuous sets displaying a subterranean fairy grotto, a moonlit skating pond featuring champion skaters Carrie A. Moore and John Engle, a dell of ferns, a Neapolitan market place, and so forth.

But in one important respect this extravaganza differed from *The Black Crook*. It was the frame for the remarkable pantomime art of its producer-star, George L. Fox. As an unidentified critic of that day said of him:

> He was not content to please merely by being knocked down numerous times and jumping over tables and through windows. His muteness and passivity were infinitely more ludicrous than the bustling antics of other clowns, as also was his affectation of ignorant simplicity and credulous innocence.

Like *The Black Crook, Humpty Dumpty* enjoyed many revivals through the years. Its star, George L. Fox, appeared in it 1128 times.

1874   EVANGELINE, an American extravaganza, with book by Edward E. Rice and J. Cheever Goodwin. Lyrics by J. Cheever Goodwin. Music by

E. E. Rice. Produced by Goodwin and Rice at Niblo's Gardens on July 27. Cast included Ione Burke, W. H. Crane, and J. W. Thoman (two weeks).

Evangeline has historical importance for the American theater for several reasons. A travesty on Longfellow's poem of the same name, it was one of the most successful examples of "burlesque," a genre of American musical theater long popular. (The term "burlesque" is here used in its original meaning as travesty or parody or caricature, rather than in its later connotation.) It was also with this extravaganza that the term "musical comedy" was used for the first time. In speaking of *Evangeline*, Rice said he hoped it would "foster a taste for musical comedy relieved of the characteristic and objectionable features of opéra-bouffe." Finally, *Evangeline* was one of the earliest musicals in which the entire score was written directly for its production, rather than comprising adaptations and interpolations. Rice's score embraced a waltz, march, topical songs, comedy numbers, ballads, duets, trios, and choral numbers.

Though intended as a burlesque on Longfellow, there was little in the play to identify it with the poem. Most of the locales were far removed from Nova Scotia, as far as Arizona and Africa. Evangeline became, as Rice said of her, " a creature of impulse pursued through love's impatient prompting by Gabriel, and with a view to audacious contingencies—by a whale."

A trick cow (one man in front, the other in the rear) performing an eccentric dance and staggering all over the stage was a main attraction; another was a spouting whale; a third was a silent character called "The Lone Fisherman" (played in New York by J. W. Thoman) who seemed to have no relation to anything taking place but who floated in and out at will with half-serious, half-comic routines. To add further to the oddities, the leading male role of Gabriel was played by a woman in tights, while one of the lady characters was played by George K. Fortesque.

Evangeline had a long and sustained success—though it is not possible to compute its run. It played only two weeks at first, not because it lacked an audience but because it was used to fill in a lull in the Niblo's Garden season and had to depart to make room for another previously scheduled production. But in the years that followed, it returned to New York frequently and deserves to be placed in the hit class of *The Black Crook* and *Humpty Dumpty*.

1879 THE BROOK, a farce, with book and lyrics by Nate Salsbury. The music consisted of adaptations. Produced by Nate Salsbury in New York on

May 12. Cast included the Five Salsbury Troubadours and Nellie Mc-
Henry (six weeks).

This was one of the first American musical comedies to attempt some
kind of integration between plot and musical routines. Topical materials
and a vaudeville show were logically interpolated into a workable, even
if naïve, plot described in the program as "depicting the pleasures of a
jolly pic-nic." The principal characters, the Five Salsbury Troubadours,
appear as members of a theatrical troupe who go on a boat trip for a
picnic. During the picnic everything that can go wrong does go wrong; a
basket supposed to contain watermelons actually yields theatrical costumes. The performers accept this bad situation gracefully, don the costumes, and perform songs, dances, and specialty numbers. Then they return home.

Besides its tentative efforts at integration, *The Brook* was also note-
worthy for its naturalism of setting, characterization, and humorous episodes. As Nate Salsbury explained in describing his play as "a novelty,"
his aim was "the natural reproduction of the jollity and funny mishaps
that attend the usual pic-nic excursion." One of the critics of the play
pointed up Salsbury's success by saying: "*The Brook* appeals to the natural impulses of everybody, and all Nature is held up to the mirror."

Nate Salsbury, who toured with *The Brook* for many years, took it to
London, where it became the first American musical production given in
the British Isles.

1884 ADONIS, a burlesque-extravaganza, with book and lyrics by William
      Gill and Henry E. Dixey. Music by Edward E. Rice. Produced by
      William Gill at the Bijou Theatre on September 4. Cast was headed by
      Henry E. Dixey (603 performances).

Adonis was Henry E. Dixey's show. Within the context of a play burlesquing the theme of Pygmalion and Galatea, Henry E. Dixey was given opportunities to dance, sing, be funny, and look handsome. He did all these
so admirably that he instantly became a matinee idol and kept the limelight on himself not only during the play's tryout in Chicago and through
its long run in New York but also for many years in tours in the United
States and London. In all, Dixey made over 1000 appearances. People
kept coming to see *Adonis* over and over—largely because new dialogue
and songs of topical interest were continually being introduced. As the
New York *Dramatic Mirror* reported at the time, *Adonis* was "an institution to be regularly patronized like the El railways or the Eden Musée."

1887 THE LITTLE TYCOON, a comic opera with book, lyrics, and music by Willard Spencer. Produced at the Standard Theatre in New York on March 29. Cast included R. E. Graham, Carrie M. Dietrich, and Joseph Mealy.

Since it had no foreign derivation and since its authorship is exclusively American, *The Little Tycoon* is sometimes spoken of as the first American comic opera. It opened not in New York but in Philadelphia, where it enjoyed a run of five hundred performances before coming to New York's Standard Theatre.

Aboard an oceanliner bound for the United States, General Knickerbocker (R. E. Graham) is eager to make a favorable match for his daughter, Violet (Carrie M. Dietrich), and chooses for her Lord Dolphin, one of the passengers. But Violet loves Alvin, an American. Back in America, Alvin comes to the Newport estate of General Knickerbocker, where he is ejected unceremoniously. But when he returns disguised as the Great Tycoon of Japan he is welcomed with pomp and ceremony. He is now able to win the General's consent to his marriage with Violet, who acquires from Alvin the honorary title of "the little tycoon."

The leading musical numbers were the title song, "On the Sea," "Doomed Am I to Marry a Lord," "Love Comes Like a Summer Night," and "Sad Heart of Mine."

1891 WANG, a comic opera with book by J. Cheever Goodwin. Music by Woolson Morse. Produced at the Broadway Theatre on May 4. Cast included De Wolf Hopper and Della Fox (151 performances).

Wang was described by its authors as an "operatic burletta." The "operatic" half of this description referred to its debt to Gilbert and Sullivan's *Mikado,* in which the star of *Wang*—De Wolf Hopper—had enjoyed outstanding success in the 1880's. The "burletta" part justified the appearance of the female star, Della Fox, in tights—in the male role of Mataya. Comic opera or "burletta," *Wang* was one of the most popular extravaganzas of the period, justifying its advertising slogan, "*Wang* goes with a bang!" After a successful stay in New York the company went on a nation-wide tour, traveling in elegant George Wagner Palace Cars—a trip that was described in a pamphlet entitled "De Wolf Hopper's Wagner Tour."

Much of the popularity of *Wang* was due to the comical portrayal of the title role by De Wolf Hopper. Wang is the Regent of Siam, beset by financial problems, partly through his own extravagance (one of his indulgences is the purchase of a sacred elephant) and largely because his empire is poverty-stricken. Uncle and guardian of Mataya, Wang learns that Mataya's dead father had left a fortune to the boy in the custody of the widow of the late French consul. To gain this fortune Wang marries the widow and assumes parental control over her large retinue of daughters, one of whom falls in love with Mataya. When the treasure chest is brought to Wang it proves to be empty. But Wang's despair is soon dissipated when he learns where the treasure actually is concealed. Mataya, eager only to marry the girl he loves, turns over the fortune to Wang and renounces his right to the throne.

The Woolson Morse score was nondescript, best in some Oriental-type marches (Wang's first entrance on an elephant, and the Wedding and Coronation Marches), in Wang's amusing topical song, "The Man with the Elephant," and in the ballads, "A Pretty Girl" and "Ask the Man in the Moon."

1892   THE ISLE OF CHAMPAGNE, a comic opera with book by Charles A. Byrne and Louis Harrison. Music by William Wallace Furst. Produced at the Manhattan Opera House on December 5. Cast included Thomas Q. Seabrook, Walter Allen, Eugene O'Rourke, and Eliva Crox.

The Isle of Champagne is a happy kingdom where the only known beverages are wine and champagne. It is ruled by King Pommery Sec'nd (Thomas Q. Seabrook), with Appollinaris Frappé as an unscrupulous Prime Minister (Walter Allen) who has robbed the King of both power and wealth. A schooner from New Bedford is blown toward the island with a cargo of water—a beverage hitherto unknown to the Isle of Champagne. To replenish his empty coffers, the King decrees water to be a beverage superior to wine and champagne; and to gain possession of the water he must marry the owner of the schooner, the New England spinster, Abigail Peck. Water becomes a luxury, and the King becomes rich. The most pleasing numbers in Furst's score were "Fly Sweet Bird," "There's a Land in the Shimmery Silver Moon," and a topical song called "Old King Mumm Could Make Things Hum."

1893   A TRIP TO CHINATOWN, a musical farce, with book by Charles Hoyt. Music by Percy Gaunt, with interpolated numbers. Produced by Charles Hoyt at the Madison Square Theatre on August 7. Cast included J. Aldrich Libby and Loie Fuller (650 performances).

A *Trip to Chinatown* toured for over a year before finally settling down at the Madison Square Theatre for the longest run achieved up to then by any stage production in New York. Taking his cue from Harrigan and

Hart, Charles Hoyt filled his play with recognizable American types and realistic everyday scenes. His plot was a convenience to bring these scenes and characters together, consisting primarily of the adventures of two couples, slumming in San Francisco's Chinatown, who try to avoid each other but who finally meet in the same restaurant. What gave the play its main appeal, apart from the characterizations, were the numerous satirical allusions to topical subjects such as women's suffrage and the temperance crusade. But the adornments of the musical stage—dance and song—were not slighted either. Loie Fuller enchanted audiences with a butterfly dance in which she used her skirt as the wings of a butterfly. And some of Percy Gaunt's songs were among the most popular in America in the 1890's. Indeed, *A Trip to Chinatown* was the first musical production to learn what a bountiful source of revenue could be derived from sheet-music publication. Three of Gaunt's songs sold hundreds of thousands of copies of sheet music, and the first of these songs named here is an American classic: "The Bowery," "Reuben, Reuben," and "Push the Clouds Away."

During the run of the play new songs were continually interpolated. One of these was among the most successful sentimental ballads of the 1890's—Charles K. Harris' "After the Ball." When J. Aldrich Libby introduced it in this play, "for a full minute the audience remained quiet," Harris later recalled in his autobiography, "and then broke loose with applause. . . . The entire audience arose and, standing, wildly applauded for fully five minutes." A few days later the Boston music shop, Oliver Ditson, sent Harris an order for 75,000 copies of the sheet music, setting into motion a sale throughout the country that eventually reached the 5,000,000 mark.

1895   PRINCESS BONNIE, a comic opera with book, lyrics, and music by Willard Spencer. Produced at the Broadway Theatre on September 2. Staged by Richard Barker. Cast included Fred Lennox, Jr., William M. Armstrong, George O'Donnell, and Hilda Clark (40 performances).

The figure of forty performances credited to *Princess Bonnie* is highly deceptive. The comic opera had a run of 1039 performances in Philadelphia before it came to New York; and after its brief initial New York run it remained a favorite for a long time through periodic revivals and extended road tours. *Princess Bonnie* was undoubtedly one of the most successful American comic operas produced before 1900.

Its heroine, Bonnie (Hilda Clark), had been rescued from a shipwreck by Captain Tarpaulin (George O'Donnell), a Maine lighthouse-keeper who has raised her. She falls in love with Roy Stirling (Will M. Armstrong), but their romance is shattered when a Spanish admiral comes to claim her as his niece and proves she is really a princess. He carries her back to Spain, where she is followed by both the Captain and Roy. They save her from an impending disagreeable marriage, and Princess Bonnie finds happiness with Roy.

1896   EL CAPITAN, a comic opera with book by Charles Klein. Lyrics by Tom Frost and J. P. Sousa. Music by John Philip Sousa. Produced at the Broadway Theatre on April 20. Staged by H. A. Cripps. Cast included De Wolf Hopper, Edna Wallace Hopper, John Parr, and Alfred Klein (112 performances).

El Capitan has several points of interest. It was one of the earliest American comic operas; its score was by America's celebrated march king; of Sousa's ten comic operas this was the most successful; and, finally, a male chorus of the second act became one of Sousa's famous marches, also entitled "El Capitan."

The setting is sixteenth-century Peru, and the story centers around the political struggles of its Viceroy, Don Errico Medniga (De Wolf Hopper). A weak ruler, the Viceroy transacts all his business through his Chamberlain, Pozzo (Alfred Klein). When threatened by overthrow, the Viceroy assumes the identity of the bandit, El Capitan (who is actually dead, although this fact is known only to the Viceroy). As El Capitan, the Viceroy comes upon the conspirators, wins them over, and becomes a leader in the conspiracy against himself. He also wins the love of Estrelda (Edna Wallace Hopper). After the revelation that El Capitan and the Viceroy are one, the latter must give up Estrelda since he is a married man, and Estrelda must find solace with the soldier with whom she had previously been in love.

Besides the second-act male chorus, "Behold El Capitan," which subsequently became a famous Sousa march, the score included a topical song in "A Typical Tune of Zanzibar" and a lyrical duet in "Sweetheart, I'm Waiting."

1899-1904 *The Rogers Brothers Vaudeville Farces*

1899   THE ROGERS BROTHERS IN WALL STREET, a vaudeville farce with book by John J. McNally. Lyrics by J. Cheever Goodwin. Music by Maurice Levi. Produced at the Victoria Theatre on September 18. Cast included Max and Gus Rogers, Ada Lewis, and Georgia Caine (108 performances).

Max and Gus Rogers—the former a comedian, the latter a straight man —were an acting partnership like that of Weber and Fields. In a series of vaudeville farces presented from 1899 on, they imitated not only the dialect and low comedy of Weber and Fields but even the kind of burlesque then being presented at the Music Hall. In later productions the Rogers Brothers carried their burlesques, horseplay, and rowdy humor into Central Park, Washington, D.C., Harvard University, Paris, Ireland, London, Panama. Until 1904 all their music was written by Maurice Levi, who was also the conductor. Beginning with *The Rogers Brothers in Paris* (1904), their music was by Max Hoffman. Levi's most popular songs from these productions included: "The Belle of Murray Hill" from *The Rogers Brothers in Wall Street;* "When Reuben Comes to Town," from *The Rogers Brothers in Central Park* (1901); "The Girl of Greater New York" from *The Rogers Brothers in Washington* (1901); and "Troubles of Reuben and the Maid" from *The Rogers Brothers in Harvard* (1902).

1906 A PARISIAN MODEL, a musical comedy with book and lyrics by Harry B. Smith. Music by Max Hoffman. Additional songs by Will D. Cobb and Gus Edwards. Produced by Frank McKee at the Broadway Theatre on November 27. Directed by Florenz Ziegfeld. Staged by Julian Mitchell. Cast included Anna Held, Henry Leoni, and Truly Shattuck (179 performances).

A Parisian Model was one of the most luxurious frames created by Florenz Ziegfeld for his wife, Anna Held; and as Anna, a model in a dress establishment, Anna Held scored one of the outstanding personal triumphs of her career. She had made her American debut a decade earlier in a revival of Charles Hoyt's *A Parlour Match,* presented by Florenz Ziegfeld in his initial venture as producer on September 21, 1896. When she sang "Won't You Come and Play with Me?" with a piquant French accent, while rolling her eyes, she instantly became a beloved of New York theatergoers. A year later she married Ziegfeld, who presented her in the next few years in a series of musicals built around her winning personality. These appearances—and the publicity about her baths in milk—made her one of the most glamorous singing and dancing stars on Broadway in the early 1900's. *A Parisian Model* was the best of these plays. Once again she rolled her eyes roguishly; in a saucy, captivating French accent sang provocative songs like "I Just Can't Make My Eyes Behave" (by Will D. Cobb and Gus Edwards); wore in one scene six alluring gowns while a chorus of girls chanted "A Gown for Each Hour of the Day"; with Gertrude Hoffmann danced a sexy number imported from Paris which shocked some of the critics.

Ziegfeld surrounded Anna Held with some of the most beautiful girls he had thus far brought before the footlights. They appeared in an eye-filling "pony ballet"; and they sang "I'd Like to See a Little More of You" (by Cobb and Edwards) while undressing—a trick stage effect making them appear completely nude.

A *Parisian Model* had all this—and a story too. Anna falls heir to a fortune and has her portrait painted by Julien de Marsay (Henry Leoni), with whom she falls in love. She must compete for his love with Violette (Truly Shattuck), over whom she is finally victorious. Comedy scenes featured Charles Bigelow as Silas Goldfinch, an American trying desperately to spend some of his money, and who is forced to appear throughout the play in various disguises—as Paderewski, a Mexican, and an old woman.

1907-1943   *The Ziegfeld Follies*

1907   THE ZIEGFELD FOLLIES, a revue with book and lyrics by Harry B. Smith, and others. Music by various composers. Produced by Florenz Ziegfeld at the Jardin de Paris (roof of the New York Theatre) on July 8. Principals directed by Herbert Gresham. Ensemble numbers staged by Julian Mitchell, Jose Smith, and John O'Neil. Cast included Grace La Rue, Emma Carus, Harry Watson, Jr., and Helen Broderick (70 performances).

This was the first edition of the revue that became an institution on Broadway glorifying the American girl. The production cost was 13,000 dollars—with a weekly expense of 3800 dollars in salaries and overhead (approximately one tenth of the amount a *Follies* would cost Ziegfeld in another decade). The strong accent that Ziegfeld henceforth would place on female pulchritude was already evident with the decorative presence of fifty of the so-called "Anna Held Girls." The future partiality of Ziegfeld for elaborate sets, costumes, and production numbers was already broadly suggested in several scenes, including one providing a kind of motion-picture effect in showing girls swimming in the water. Mlle Dazie performed a provocative Salome dance; Helen Broderick revealed her flair for comedy in several amusing skits. Among the songs were Jean Schwartz' "Handle Me with Care," Gus Edwards' "Bye, Bye Dear Old Broadway," and E. Ray Goetz' "Come and Float Me, Freddie Dear." "Mr. Ziegfeld," reported one critic, "has given New York the best mélange of mirth, music, and pretty young girls that has been seen here in many summers."

He would continue to provide such a mélange—and with ever-increasing abundance, up to 1931 (with the exception of 1926, 1928, and 1929 when there were no *Follies* produced). In 1908 and 1909 most of the score for each edition was the contribution of Maurice Levi, though interpolated songs were also used. In 1908 the unknown Nora Bayes, who was earning seventy-five dollars a week, made a sensational *Follies* debut, singing "You Will Have to Sing an Irish Song" and a song she wrote with her husband, Jack Norworth, and which henceforth would serve as her musical trade-mark, "Shine On, Harvest Moon." A unifying theme provided integration to the 1908 *Follies*, the history of civilization from the Garden of Eden to New York of 1908.

In 1909 Sophie Tucker, already famous as a "red hot momma," came for the first time to the *Follies*. So did Lillian Lorraine, first seen in a sea of soap bubbles singing "Nothing but a Bubble" and later cruising in a flying machine, scattering flowers on the audience while singing, "Up, Up, Up in My Aeroplane." Harry Kelly provided the comedy highlight with a remarkable impersonation of Teddy Roosevelt in the jungle, while an additional comedy asset was Nora Bayes' characterization of a prima donna.

Many of the later editions of the *Follies* are discussed in the composers' section: 1911-14, 1917 (RAYMOND HUBBELL); 1915-17, 1918 (LOUIS A. HIRSCH); 1919, 1927 (IRVING BERLIN).

Of the other editions of the *Follies* a few salient events are of particular interest.

Fanny Brice, a novice from an obscure burlesque house, made her *Follies* debut in 1910, sang "Goodbye, Becky Cohen," and was a triumph. Bert Williams, already famous in musical comedy was also a Ziegfeld star in 1910, singing "Nobody" and "Late Hours." In 1920 Fanny Brice appeared as an East Broadway vampire and was featured in an automobile skit with W. C. Fields, while Van and Schenck scored a major success with their song, "All She'd Say was Uh Hum." Here, too, Ray Dooley was seen in her famous baby-carriage act, and Jack Donahue, a newcomer, brought down the house with his eccentric dancing. The excellent score in 1920 included Irving Berlin's "Girl of My Dreams" and "Syncopated Vamp" and Victor Herbert's "The Love Boat."

In 1921 Fanny Brice, still a comedienne without equal in singing a song like "Second Hand Rose," turned from laughter to tears with her unforgettable rendition of "My Man," a French song that stirred audiences particularly since they associated it with Fanny Brice's own turbulent and tragic personal life with her husband, the gangster, Nick Arnstein.

Jack Whiting, formerly a private secretary and an amateur actor, seized the limelight in the 1922 edition with his ingratiating singing and dancing. He would hold that limelight in the Broadway theater for many years more. In 1927 Ruth Etting stepped from oblivion to the heights. And almost as if in reminder of the past glories of the *Follies,* she returned in 1931 (the last *Follies* produced by Ziegfeld) to revive the old Nora Bayes hit, "Shine On, Harvest Moon."

Ziegfeld died in 1932. Since his death there have been four editions of his *Follies.* That in 1943 had the longest run of any *Follies*—553 performances. Produced by the Shuberts at the Winter Garden on April 1, 1943 (lyrics by Jack Yellen, music by Ray Henderson), the *Follies* starred Milton Berle, and Ilona Massey made her first Broadway appearance. Berle was all over the stage most of the time. He appeared as the proprietor of a lunch counter arguing with his customer; as a butcher guarded by tommy guns as he deposits a steak in the safe (this was the war year of 1943); as Noel Coward in a parody of *Private Lives* presented in the style of *Hellzapoppin'.* He was continually intruding into other acts and at times engaged in informal conversations with the audience. Berle's follies dominated those of Ziegfeld that year, but there were other diversions. Ilona Massey nostalgically recalled the first *Follies,* of 1907, in "Thirty Five Summers Ago" and presented the production's best ballad in "Love Songs Are Made at Night." Jack Cole appeared in two outstanding dance sequences, "Hindu Serenade" and "The Wedding of the Solid Sender." And Dean Murphy was a winner in his impersonations of Bette Davis, President and Mrs. Franklin D. Roosevelt, Katharine Hepburn, and Wendell Willkie.

1918   LISTEN LESTER, a musical comedy with book and lyrics by Harry L. Cort and George T. Stoddard. Music by Harold Orlob. Produced by John Cort at the Knickerbocker Theatre on December 23. Cast included Johnny Dooley, Ada Lewis, Clifton Webb, Hansford Wilson, and Eddie Garvie (272 performances).

Colonel Rufus Dodge (Eddie Garvie) has written indiscreet letters to Arbutus Quilty (Gertrude Vanderbilt). Since he is now in love with Tillie Mumm (Ada Lewis), he must recover and destroy them. Two allies help him get his letters back: William Penn, Jr. (Johnny Dooley), and Lester Lite (Hansford Wilson). During the quest for the letters Jack Griffith (Clifton Webb) pursues and wins Mary Dodge (Ada Mae Weeks); and when the quest is successful, the Colonel successfully woos Tillie.

The hit song was a ballad called "Waiting for You." But the main attraction of *Listen Lester* was not so much the music as the dancing, which was virtually continuous throughout the production.

1918   SOMEBODY'S SWEETHEART, a musical comedy with book and lyrics by Alonzo Price. Music by Anthony Bafunno. Produced by Arthur Hammerstein at the Central Park Theatre on December 23. Cast included Nonette, William Kent, and Louise Allen (224 performances).

In Seville, Spain, Harry Edwards (Walter Scanlan) is about to be married to Helen (Eva Fallon), daughter of the U. S. Consul. The natives of Seville arrange a festival in his honor at which the seductive gypsy violinist, Zaida (Nonette), is principal performer. Harry's shady past included an affair with Zaida. To avoid embarrassment at the party, Harry arranges for his friend, Sam Benton (William Kent), to occupy Zaida's time and interest when she is not performing. Since Sam is in love with the bride's sister, he must do some tall explaining before his sweetheart realizes that his attentions to Zaida are innocent.

The score has several delightful melodies, the best being "Spain Girl of My Heart," "Then I'll Marry You," "It Gets Them All," and "In the Old-Fashioned Way" (the last two by Arthur Hammerstein and Herbert Stothart). A great deal of the appeal of this musical came from the dancing of Louise Allen and the comedy of William Kent.

1919   APPLE BLOSSOMS, an operetta with book and lyrics by William Le Baron based on Dumas' *A Marriage of Convenience*. Music by Victor Jacobi and Fritz Kreisler. Produced by Charles Dillingham at the Globe Theatre on October 7. Cast included Wilda Bennett, John Charles Thomas, and Fred and Adele Astaire (256 performances).

"A musical comedy of supreme elegance and old-time musical dignity," as the New York *American* described it, *Apple Blossoms* had much more than a distinguished musical score to recommend it. It boasted gay comedy with Percival Knight playing an amiable philanderer, Roy Atwell a philosophic valet, and Florence Shirley a flirtatious widow. It also enjoyed the dancing of Fred and Adele Astaire, whose dance routine in the finale ballroom scene was always thunderously acclaimed.

The plot concerned itself principally with a marriage of convenience by Nancy (Wilda Bennett) and Philip Campbell (John Charles Thomas) to unite the fortunes of the two families. Since the hearts of Nancy and Philip belong elsewhere, they decide to pursue their love interests freely and for a while they enjoy their philandering ways. But they soon grow weary of their extracurricular love affairs—and, besides, they have fallen in love with each other. They are now happy to accept their own marriage.

Fritz Kreisler, who wrote half the score, is the world-famous violin virtuoso. The same Viennese charm, grace, and freshness that Kreisler brought to his celebrated violin pieces are found in his melodies for this operetta. The opening number, "Who Can Tell?" is a lilting Viennese waltz sung by Nancy. Nancy also presents another infectious Kreisler tune, "Star of Love." It is perhaps to be expected that one of the big musical numbers involves the violin: the duet, "Second Violin," utilizes a background of chorus girls playing violins in pantomime. Victor Jacobi's best numbers were "Little Girls, Good-Bye," sung by Philip, and "You Are Free," a duet by Nancy and Philip.

1920   TICKLE ME, a musical comedy with book and lyrics by Otto Harbach, Oscar Hammerstein II, and Frank Mandel. Music by Herbert Stothart. Produced by Arthur Hammerstein at the Selwyn Theatre on August 17. Dances and ensembles by Bert French. Staged by William Collier. Cast included Frank Tinney, Louise Allen, and Marguerite Zander (207 performances).

Herbert Stothart has been a distinguished composer both for the Broadway musical stage and in Hollywood. As far as his Broadway career is concerned, his best work was done in collaboration with other composers, as was the case in *Rose Marie* and *Wildflower*, in which he worked with Rudolf Friml and Vincent Youmans respectively. *Tickle Me* was one of the less frequent instances in which he successfully wrote a complete score without outside assistance. (A half-year earlier he had also written a complete stage score—*Always You*, in which Oscar Hammerstein II made his bow as musical-comedy librettist and lyricist; but *Always You* had been a failure.)

Tickle Me was a production conceived for and dominated by Frank Tinney, who appeared as himself. He is seen as a man-of-all-trades in a movie studio where he writes a scenario that is accepted and hailed as a masterpiece. When the "angel" arrives to finance the film production, he calls in Tinney for a conference. Spurred on by his love of travel, Tinney suggests location shots in Tibet. The company, headed by the star Mary Fairbanks (Louise Allen) and accompanied by Tinney, make for Tibet where they confront innumerable complications and where Tinney is given frequent opportunity to engage in all kinds of ad-libs, songs, dances, buffoonery, and eccentric whirligigs. "Frank Tinney," reported the New York *Globe*, "had never before been so entertaining. . . . *Tickle Me* is a joyous, romping absurdity." The principal songs in a score which the *Globe* described as "uniformly excellent" were: "If a Wish Could Make It So," "We've Got Something," and "Until You Say Goodbye."

1920 HONEYDEW, an operetta with book and lyrics by Joseph Herbert. Music by Efrem Zimbalist. Produced by Joe Weber at the Casino Theatre on September 6. Staged by Hassard Short. Cast included Ethelind Terry, Hal Forde, and Mlle Marguerite (231 performances).

Efrem Zimbalist was undoubtedly stimulated to invade the popular musical theater by his colleague, Fritz Kreisler, who one year earlier had achieved success on the musical-comedy stage with his delightful score for *Apple Blossoms*. Himself a world-famous violin virtuoso, Zimbalist flooded his operetta with a wealth of lovable tunes, topped by "Oh, How I Long for Someone," "The Morals of a Sailorman" (which had the flavor of a Gilbert and Sullivan song), "Drop Me a Line," and "Believe Me, Beloved."

Honeydew was a satire on a musician—Henry Honeydew (Hal Forde) —an eccentric who spent his time writing cantatas about insects. His father-in-law, head of an exterminating business, takes one of his ditties, "The June Bug," and gives it as a premium with one of his products. "The June Bug" becomes a hit, and Honeydew is finally a successful composer.

The Spanish dancing of Mlle Marguerite was a strong point of the production. A beautiful pantomime was enacted in a Chinese interlude in which the figures on a tea-service set—a maid and a mandarin—come to life. In the leading feminine role of Muriel, Ethelind Terry was making her first major Broadway musical-comedy appearance and was scoring her first personal success.

1921 SHUFFLE ALONG, an all-Negro revue with book by Miller and Lyle. Lyrics and music by Noble Sissle and Eubie Blake. Produced by the Nikko Company at the 63rd Street Music Hall on May 23. Cast included Noble Sissle and Florence Mills (504 performances).

Shuffle Along, which began its career in Harlem before settling down for a long run on 63rd Street, was the first highly successful all-Negro revue. Whirlwind dancing and spectacular choral singing were the strong suits in a production that was vital and energetic from first to final curtain. A slender plot held the whole thing together: A mayoralty race in Jim Town between Steven Jackson (F. E. Miller) and Sam Peck (Aubrey Lyle). The hit song was "I'm Just Wild About Harry," with other appealing numbers including the title song, "Bandana Days" and "Love Will Find a Way."

1921   TANGERINE, a musical comedy with book by Philip Bartholmae and Guy Bolton. Lyrics by Howard Johnston. Music by Carlo Sanders. Produced by Carle Carleton at the Casino Theatre on August 9. Staged by George Marion and Bert French. Cast included Julia Sanderson, Shirley Dalton, and Frank Crumit (337 performances).

Fred Allen (Joseph Herbert, Jr.), Jack Floyd (Harry Puck), and Lee Loring (Jack Kearns) are confined to Ludlow Street Jail for failing to pay alimony. Their friend, Dick Owens (Frank Crumit), arranges for their release and suggests that they go off to a South Sea island where man is king and women do his bidding. The three Americans set forth for this island. There they luxuriate at home while their women do all the work. But they soon get tired of this arrangement and are only too happy to return home—and to their ex-wives. Romantic interest is confined to Dick Owens and Shirley Dalton, the latter played by Julia Sanderson to whom the hit song of the play is assigned, "Sweet Lady" (lyrics by Howard Johnson, music by Frank Crumit and David Zoob).

1921   THE PERFECT FOOL, a revue with book, lyrics, and music by Ed Wynn. Presented by A. L. Erlanger at the George M. Cohan Theatre on November 7. Directed by B. C. Whitney. Staged by Julian Mitchell. Cast included Ed Wynn, Janet Velie, and Guy Robertson (256 performances).

Of the seventeen scenes, Ed Wynn expropriated seven. He appeared in his various bizarre costumes and hats, introduced some of his newer inventions—including a typewriterlike machine for eating corn on a cob, a non-eye-destroying spoon for iced tea, and a shield to prevent a knife from cutting the mouth. In his first curtain routine Ed Wynn explained that his show had some kind of a plot: A young fellow and a girl get married, and three months later he gets stuck on another girl. But the plot is forgotten even before it is allowed to develop to make room for Ed Wynn's clowning, routines, and rambling and aimless monologues. When he was off the stage, it was able to present several beautiful production numbers: a dueling dance, with rapiers, by chorus girls; a huge typewriter in which the key-bars are girls' legs. Janet Velie and Guy Robertson either shared or joined in the leading songs: "Girls, Pretty Girls," "She Loves Me, She Loves Me Not," "Days of Romance," and "My Garden of Perfume."

1922 THE GINGHAM GIRL, a musical comedy with book by Daniel Kussell. Lyrics by Neville Fleeson. Music by Albert von Tilzer. Produced by Schwab and Kussell at the Earl Carroll Theatre on August 28. Cast included Eddie Buzzell and Helen Ford (422 performances).

John Cousins (Eddie Buzzell) and Mary Thompson (Helen Ford) are natives of Crossville Corners, New Hampshire. Besides being in love, both are fired with ambition to get ahead in the world. John comes to New York, where he becomes a success, assumes the attitudes of a city slicker, and has various amatory adventures in Greenwich Village. Mary follows him to the city and is disheartened to see how her beau has changed. She sets herself up in the cookie business and becomes prosperous. Finally John comes to his senses and realizes that Mary is the girl he loves. The eccentric dancing of Helen Coyne and Henri French, and the song, "As Long as I Have You," were two attractions helping to make *The Gingham Girl* an outstanding hit.

1922 LADY IN ERMINE, a musical comedy with book by Frederick Lonsdale and Cyrus Wood based on a London musical, *The Lady of the Rose,* by Rudolph Schanzer and Ernest Welisch. Lyrics by Harry Graham and Cyrus Wood. Music by Jean Gilbert and Alfred Goodman. Produced by the Shuberts at the Ambassador Theatre on October 2. Staged by Charles Sinclair and Allan K. Foster. Cast included Wilda Bennett, Walter Woolf, and Harry Fender (232 performances).

During the Napoleonic invasion of Italy, Count Adrian Beltrami (Harry Fender) and his sister Mariana (Wilda Bennett) occupy a castle that is forced to quarter a French regiment, headed by Colonel Belovar (Walter Woolf). The Colonel thinks Adrian and Mariana are husband and wife. Since he is determined to make love to Mariana, he frames up a charge accusing Adrian of being a spy, and offers to save his life only if Mariana is ready to surrender to him. Mariana accepts the bargain, then tells the Colonel about a "lady in ermine," whose picture hangs on the wall and who had triumphed over a similar predicament some centuries earlier. While awaiting his tryst with Mariana, the Colonel gets drunk. Suddenly "the lady in ermine" descends from the picture frame and invites him to dance with her. By the time Mariana comes to pay her debt to the Colonel, "the lady in ermine" has returned to the picture and the Colonel, now convinced that he loves Mariana, finds he cannot take advantage of her.

As Colonel Belovar, Walter Woolf made a successful debut on the Broadway stage. He presented two of the best songs in the score, "Land o' Mine" and "Mariana," the latter a duet with Mariana. But the most popular song from *Lady in Ermine* was an interpolation—"When Hearts Are Young," by Sigmund Romberg, presented by Wilda Bennett.

1922-1929   *The Grand Street Follies*

1922   THE GRAND STREET FOLLIES, a revue with book assembled by Agnes Morgan. Music arranged by Lily Hyland. Produced at the Neighborhood Playhouse. Cast included Albert Carroll and Aline McMahon (148 performances).

This was the parent of the intimate revue that flourished on Broadway in the 1920's, 1930's, and early 1940's with productions like *The Garrick Gaieties, The Little Show,* and *Pins and Needles.* Entered into with a spirit of levity—the program described the first edition as a "low-brow show for high-grade morons"—"its creators emphasized wit and satire. The first edition mocked at Walt Whitman's poetry and at stars of stage, ballet, and opera (Elsie Janis, Pavlova, Irene Castle, Chaliapin, and so forth); and it ridiculed current dances. Albert Carroll immediately revealed himself a master of caricature and mimicry, equally adept in male and female impersonations—perhaps best in "The Royal Damn Fandango" in which he impersonated a lady with a fan.

In 1923 Albert Carroll was supplemented by Dorothy Sands. Both in this and in all succeeding editions they dominated the production with their devastating take-offs on outstanding personalities of the world of the theater, ballet, and opera.

In 1924 Aline Bernstein became principal costume and scenic designer. In 1927 the production moved uptown to the Little Theatre, and in 1928 and 1929 it played at the Booth Theatre.

Among the high spots of *The Grand Street Follies* through the years were the caricatures by Albert Carroll of John Barrymore, Ethel Barrymore, Emily Stevens, and other stars of the Broadway stage; Dorothy Sands' varied impersonations, such as that of a Town Hall recitalist; satirical sketches like "The Wild Duck of the 18th Century" (as Ibsen would have written the play if he had lived a century earlier), "The South Sea Islands According to Broadway," "The Siege of Troy, as Produced by David Belasco," "Caesar's Invasion of Britain" (with lyrics by Noel Coward). The Ziegfeld girl was lampooned in "Glory, Glory, Glory," and a delightful impression of the Four Marx Brothers featured Albert Carroll as Harpo.

Among the leading performers, besides those already mentioned, were

Marc Loebell, Paula Trueman, Jessica Dragonette, Joanna Roos, and James Cagney (Cagney appeared as a tap dancer in 1928). Among those who wrote the music for the various editions were Dan Walker, Max Ewing, Arthur Schwartz, and Randall Thompson.

1923   LITTLE JESSIE JAMES, a musical farce with book and lyrics by Harlan Thompson. Music by Harry Archer. Produced by L. Lawrence Weber at the Longacre Theatre on August 15. Cast included Nan Halperin, Allen Kearns, and Miriam Hopkins (453 performances).

As the heroine, Jessie Jamieson, Nan Halperin here makes her bow on the Broadway musical stage. And as Juliet, Miriam Hopkins finds her first important musical-comedy role; she had previously been seen in a minor dancing part in *The Music Box Revue* of 1921.

Jessie Jamieson is a flapper from Kansas who meets Tommy Tinker (Allen Kearns) in his apartment. With her open, staring eyes and baby voice she wins him away from his girl friend, Juliet (Miriam Hopkins).

A major song hit sprang from this Archer score: "I Love You," sung repeatedly throughout the play. Jessie Jamieson presents two other fetching musical numbers, "My Home Town in Kansas" and "From Broadway to Main Street." The production also boasted a seductive octet of chorus girls that reminded some critics of the Floradora sextet of another era, and a Paul Whiteman orchestral combination called The James Boys.

1923   POPPY, a musical comedy with book and lyrics by Dorothy Donnelly. Music by Stephen Jones and Arthur Samuels. Produced by Philip Goodman at the Apollo Theatre on September 3. Staged by Julian Alfred and Dorothy Donnelly. Cast included W. C. Fields, Madge Kennedy, Luella Gear, and Robert Woolsey (328 performances).

W. C. Fields here appeared as Professor Eustace McGargle, a con man who is the foster father of Poppy (Madge Kennedy). The time is 1874. During their trips in which the Professor earns a dishonest "buck" as gambler and medicine man—and Poppy assists him as a fortuneteller— they arrive at Meadowbrook, Connecticut, Poppy's home town and scene of a county fair. There Poppy meets and falls in love with the wealthy William van Wyck (Alan Edwards). Learning of an unclaimed inheritance, the Professor presents Poppy as the lost heiress, but Poppy balks at the idea of entering into such a swindle. But it turns out that Poppy is really the heiress, a development that brings about a happy culmination to her love affair with William.

The hit song was "Mary," lyrics by Irving Caesar. Another song was

"Alibi Baby," lyrics by Howard Dietz and music by Arthur Schwartz, the first time one of their songs appeared in a Broadway musical.

1924   I'LL SAY SHE IS, a revue with book and lyrics by Will B. Johnstone. Music by Tom Johnstone. Produced by James B. Beury at the Casino Theatre on May 19. Staged by Eugene Sanger and Vaughan Godfrey. Cast included the Four Marx Brothers.

This was the first appearance on the Broadway stage of the Four Marx Brothers after years spent in vaudeville. The book was made up mainly of material they had previously used in their vaudeville acts, including such sketches as "Home Again," "Mr. Green's Reception," and "On the Mezzanine." The identities of Groucho, Harpo, Chico, and Zeppo—which they would henceforth assume in all their musical comedies and motion pictures—were now established; so were their individual routines and mannerisms. Their madcap antics inspired such accolades from Alexander Woollcott, Ben Hecht, and other New York sophisticates that not only did *I'll Say She Is* become a hit, but from this point on the Four Marx Brothers were a vogue. Among the songs were "Only You," "I'm Saving for a Rainy Day," and "Give Me a Thrill."

1926   QUEEN HIGH, a musical comedy with book and lyrics by Buddy De Sylva and Laurence Schwab. Music by Lewis E. Gensler, with additional songs by Arthur Schwartz and Ralph Rainger. Produced by Laurence Schwab at the Ambassador Theatre on September 8. Staged by Edgar McGregor and Sammy Lee. Cast included Charles Ruggles, Frank McIntyre, Luella Gear, and Mary Lawlor (378 performances).

T. Boggs Johns (Charles Ruggles) and George Nettleton (Frank McIntyre) are partners in a garter and novelty business. Embroiled in squabbles, they decide to play a game of poker—the winner to become the boss the loser to act as his butler. Nettleton wins, and the comedy that follows results from Johns' efforts to serve as a butler. The romantic interest is centered on their two offspring, Richard Johns and Polly Nettleton, played by Clarence Nordstrom and Mary Lawlor; Gaile Beverly scored a personal hit in the part of an amorous housemaid whose activity is extracurricular, divided between loving and dancing. The principal songs were "You'll Never Know" and "Cross Your Heart."

1926   HONEYMOON LANE, a musical comedy with book and lyrics by Eddie Dowling. Music by James T. Hanley. Produced by A. L. Erlanger at the Knickerbocker Theatre on September 20. Staged by Edgar MacGregor. Dances by Bobby Connolly. Cast included Eddie Dowling, Pauline Mason, and Kate Smith (364 performances).

Honeymoon Lane is a street in Canningville, Pennsylvania, where Tim Murphy (Eddie Dowling) buys a cottage as a home for his future bride, Mary Brown (Pauline Mason). They both work in the same pickle factory where the boss' son turns Mary's head until she wants to go to New York to become a stage star. Simplehearted Tim is horrified to learn of the adventures that beset Mary in the big city. But the whole New York excursion turns out to be merely one of Tim's dreams. The final scene finds them embracing in their cottage on Honeymoon Lane.

Before the show reached New York, the producer sent out releases prophesying that an unknown comedienne and singer, Kate Smith, about to make her first Broadway appearance, would steal the limelight. The critics agreed with him when they saw her in the role of Tiny Little. "As a dancer and blues singer," reported the New York *Times*, "she proved unusually adept, and stop the show she did last night."

The hit song was presented by Tim, "The Little White House at the End of Honeymoon Lane" (lyrics by Irving Caesar). "Dreams for Sale" also proved a strong favorite.

1928 RAIN OR SHINE, a musical comedy with book by James Gleason and Maurice Marks. Lyrics by Jack Yellen. Music by Milton Ager and Owen Murphy. Produced by A. L. Jones and Morris Green at the George M. Cohan Theatre on February 9. Staged by Alexander Leftwich. Cast included Joe Cook, Tom Howard, and Janet Velie (356 performances).

Time magazine said: "It is a wretched show. But for those who like Joe Cook it is heavenly." For Joe Cook was the whole show. He is Smiley Johnson, proprietor of a bankrupt circus. When the troupe goes on strike, Smiley takes over and does the performance himself. He juggles twenty Indian clubs; balances himself on a wire and shoots out rows of lighted candles; balances himself atop a twelve-foot pole swinging hoops on his heels; walks a huge ball up a steep incline; whirls with his foot a pole with a man dangling at each end; catches lighted matches in his mouth. He also sings, dances, and tells long, disconnected stories, many of them without endings. And he fills the stage with a mammoth crazy Rube Goldberg-like contraption.

Additional comedy was provided by the dry, brittle humor of Smiley's partner, Amos K. Shrewsberry (Tom Howard). The love interest involved Jack Wayne (Warren Hull) and Mary Wheeler (Nancy Welford), owner of the Wheeler Circus.

The principal musical numbers were the title song, "So Would I," "Falling Star," and "Forever and Ever."

1928   WHOOPEE, a musical comedy with book by William Anthony McGuire based on Owen Davis' Broadway comedy, *The Nervous Wreck*. Lyrics by Gus Kahn. Music by Walter Donaldson. Produced by Florenz Ziegfeld at the New Amsterdam Theatre on December 4. Staged by William Anthony McGuire and Seymour Felix. Cast included Eddie Cantor, Ruth Etting, and Tamara Geva (379 performances).

Henry Williams, a hypochondriac (Eddie Cantor), leaves for California to recover his health, accompanied by a valiseful of pills. Out West, at the Bar M Ranch at Mission Rest, Henry gets involved with a girl and Indians. Wanenis, believed to be a half-breed (Paul Gregory), and Sally Morgan (Frances Upton) are in love. When she is compelled to marry the local sheriff, Bob Wells (Jack Rutherford), she tries to elude this disaster by inducing Henry to elope with her. They are pursued by the sheriff to an Indian reservation where it is discovered that Wanenis is no Indian at all. Henry loses the girl, and so does the sheriff.

The music included two all-time Eddie Cantor favorites: "Makin' Whoopee," made up of half a dozen amusing verses of topical interest, and "My Baby Just Cares for Me." Also in the score were found "Love Me or Leave Me," sung and made famous by Ruth Etting (and subsequently used as the title of her screen biography), and "I'm Bringing a Red, Red Rose."

While *Whoopee* had a successful Broadway run of a year, it would have lasted longer, since even the last performances played to crowded theaters. What happened was that Ziegfeld went broke and had to sell the movie rights to Samuel Goldwyn; he also had to close down the show to allow Eddie Cantor to act as consultant for and star in the movie adaptation (Cantor's first appearance on the screen).

1930   FINE AND DANDY, a musical comedy with book by Donald Ogden Stewart. Lyrics by Paul James. Music by Kay Swift. Produced by Morris Gest and Lewis E. Gensler at the Erlanger Theatre on September 23. Staged by Dave Gould, Morris Green, Frank McCoy, and Tom Nip. Cast included Joe Cook, Alice Boulden, and Nell O'Day (255 performances).

As in *Rain or Shine* (1928), Joe Cook monopolized *Fine and Dandy* and single-handedly made it "not just a good show," in the words of John Mason Brown, "but a grand and glorious one." As Joe Squibb, the benevolent general manager of Fordyce Drop Forge and Tool Factory, he flirts with the widow-owner of the factory, is engaged to lovely Nancy Ellis (Alice Boulden), and ultimately reveals himself to be married and the father of four children. Also as Joe Squibb he lights a bearded man's whiskers, impersonates four German acrobats, plays the saxophone and uke-lele, turns handsprings, plays golf with a shovel, eats lunch from a lunch-box the size of an automobile crate, examines the insurance doctor come to examine him, creates a gadget that can puncture balloons while cracking nuts and another for inflating paper bags so that when punctured they can make a resounding noise.

An adagio dance by Nell O'Day nightly received an ovation. The most popular song from the score was the title number, a duet by Joe and Nancy. Nancy also presented a second distinguished number, "Can This Be Love?"

1936 THE SHOW IS ON, a revue with sketches by David Freedman and Moss Hart. Lyrics and music by numerous writers and composers. Presented by the Shuberts at the Winter Garden on December 25. Entire production conceived, staged, and designed by Vincente Minnelli. Choreography by Harry Losee. Cast included Beatrice Lillie, Bert Lahr, and Reginald Gardiner (237 performances).

Three routines—one each by each of the three principals—alone would have made *The Show Is On* outstanding. Beatrice Lillie sitting on a moon, swings out into the audience distributing garters while singing a satirical version of a Tin Pan Alley ballad, Herman Hupfeld's "Buy Yourself a Balloon." Bert Lahr delivers a number since become a staple in his repertory, "Song of the Woodman," by Harburg and Arlen. And Reginald Gardiner (in his first Broadway appearance) presented a devastating impersonation of a prima-donna conductor (probably Stokowski) leading his orchestra.

But there were other high spots. Lillie mimicked Josephine Baker, appeared as an amorous French actress, proved herself a first-night nuisance, and served as the garrulous ticket saleslady at the Theatre "Geeld." Bert Lahr was a much-harassed taxpayer being examined by the internal revenue department, spoofed jazz in "Woof," and appeared as a Republican working in the home of Democrats in a travesty on *Tovarisch* and the plight of Republicans in 1936. Together, Lillie and Lahr did a burlesque on burlesque—Lillie as a strip-tease artist ogled by the putty-nosed Lahr. And Reginald Gardiner starred in a Moss Hart sketch lampooning John Gielgud in *Hamlet*.

Among the best songs were George and Ira Gershwin's "By Strauss" and Hoagy Carmichael's sentimental, "Little Old Lady" (lyrics by Stanley Adams), both presented by Mitzi Mayfair. The best dance number was the "Casanova Ballet," starring Paul Haakon.

1941   BEST FOOT FORWARD, with book by John Cecil Holm. Lyrics by Hugh
       Martin. Music by Ralph Blane. Produced by George Abbott at the Ethel
       Barrymore Theatre on October 1, 1941. Staged by George Abbott.
       Dances directed by Gene Kelly. Cast included Rosemary Lane, Nancy
       Walker, June Allyson, and Gil Stratton, Jr. (326 performances).

Best Foot Forward was a young people's frolic. The principals were
comparative youngsters—two of them, Nancy Walker and June Allyson,
at the beginning of lustrous careers. The whole production was charged
with youthful energy and vitality that reminded many playgoers of the
Rodgers and Hart carnival of youth, *Babes in Arms* (1937). (It is interesting to point out that though his name does not appear on the billing,
Richard Rodgers was one of the producers of *Best Foot Forward*.)

The setting is Winsocki School near Philadelphia. On a lark, young
Bud Hooper (Gil Stratton, Jr.) sends an invitation to the Hollywood star,
Gale Joy (Rosemary Lane), to be his "date" at the Junior Prom. In Hollywood, Gale's press agent, Marty May (Jack Haggerty) recognizes the
publicity value of having Gale attend a school prom with a teen-ager
and urges her to accept the invitation. Gale's arrival at Winsocki creates a
sensation. Bud ditches his own girl, Helen (Maureen Cannon), to take
Gale to the prom. At the dance, in a fit of jealousy, Helen tears the sash
from Gale's gown. Realizing they can get valuable souvenirs of a movie
queen, the other young people proceed to tear off her clothes until she is
stripped down to bare essentials. A scandal ensues at the school, with
Bud in danger of being expelled. But the difficulties are straightened out
when Gale returns to Hollywood and Bud and Helen are reconciled.

The leading musical number was the semi-satirical football song,
"Buckle Down, Winsocki." June Allyson scored with "Who Do You Think
I Am?" Nancy Walker with "Just a Little Joint with a Juke Box," and
Rosemary Lane with "That's How I Love the Blues." Two other songs
were of interest: "Shady Lady Bird" and "Everytime."

1942   STAR AND GARTER, a revue, with book, lyrics, and music by various
       writers and composers. Produced by Michael Todd at the Music Box
       Theatre on June 24. Staged by Hassard Short. Dances directed by Al
       White, Jr. Cast included Bobby Clark, Gypsy Rose Lee, Georgia
       Sothern, and Professor Lamberti (609 performances).

Michael Todd attempted to make a lady out of burlesque by bringing it
into the dignified setting of the legitimate Broadway theater. But the lady
is still a tramp. The main attractions of burlesque are to be found in *Star
and Garter*: strip-tease acts, grinds and bumps, undraped females, songs

and skits filled with double-entendres, slapstick. Georgia Sothern did a hot strip-tease routine. Gypsy Rose Lee did a sedate and leisurely one; she also lamented on how hard it was to do a strip tease to classical music. Bobby Clark appeared as a roué from Pennsylvania, a judge at a murder trial who busies himself by throwing spitballs, a lover caught redhanded by an irate husband in "That Merry Wife of Windsor." Also in the tradition of burlesque was an amusing routine by Professor Lamberti (a seedy-looking musician), who plays the xylophone and is delighted with the joy and loud enthusiasm of his audience; what he does not know is that a luscious wench is standing behind him doing a strip tease. Professor Lamberti's act and several other skits were interpolated from other, earlier musical productions. So were some of the best songs—including Irving Berlin's "The Girl on the Police Gazette" (serving as the music for a first-act finale production number) and Harold Arlen's "Blues in the Night."

1944   FOLLOW THE GIRLS, a musical comedy with book by Guy Bolton and Eddie Davis. Additional dialogue by Fred Thompson. Lyrics by Dan Shapiro and Milton Pascal. Music by Phil Charig. Produced by Dave Wolper in association with Albert Borde at the Century Theatre on April 8. Staged by Harry Delmar. Dances by Catherine Littlefield. Cast included Gertrude Niesen, Jackie Gleason, and Irina Baronova (882 performances).

Long before 1944, Gertrude Niesen had proved she could sing a sultry song with extraordinary effect. In *Follow the Girls* she showed that she was not only a singer but an outstanding comedienne as well. She was cast as Bubbles La Marr, a strip-tease burlesque queen, who has given up the stage to devote herself to her duties in "Spotlight," a serviceman's canteen. Goofy Gale (Jackie Gleason) is madly in love with her. Since he has been rejected by the army, he cannot gain access to the "Spotlight." By stealing a uniform from a British sailor he finally is able to get into the canteen, only to discover that he has a serious rival for Bubbles in a petty naval officer. At the canteen the dancer Anna Viskinova (Irina Baranova) performs a beautiful adagio dance for the boys, hoping thereby to catch the interest of a theatrical booking agent.

Gertrude Niesen was a sensation in the bawdy comedy song, "I Wanna Get Married." "Where Are You?"—a romantic ballad, sung by Frank Parker, throughout the play—and "Today Will Be Yesterday Tomorrow" were also winning to the ear.

Jackie Gleason as the fat, lovelorn Goofy supplied most of the comedy —and proved a winner in what thus far was his best comedy role in the theater. Brooks Atkinson remarked prophetically: "Some day when he gets the words, he will be wonderful, instead of just very good."

1948   MAKE MINE MANHATTAN, an intimate revue with sketches and lyrics by Arnold Horwitt. Music by Richard Lewine. Produced by Joseph Hyman at the Broadhurst Theatre on January 15. Staged by Hassard Short. Choreography by Lee Sherman. Cast included Sid Caesar, David Burns, Jack Kilty, Kyle MacDonnell, and Sheila Bond (429 performances).

Variety described *Make Mine Manhattan* as "a crowded entertainment of bubbling youth." Perhaps its greatest significance lay in the fact that it introduced Sid Caesar as one of the supreme comics of our time. In his very first sketch, a satire on the U.N., Caesar betrayed his extraordinary gift for caricature by assuming the identities of various U.N. delegates. In later sketches he appears as a dentist, in a remarkable travesty on the Rodgers and Hammerstein musical play, *Allegro;* he narrates the trials and tribulations of a penny gum machine that grows up to be a quarter slot machine; appears as a customer trying to buy a fountain pen; does a take-off on critics and Hollywood producers. In the last two routines he was ably assisted by David Burns.

Make Mine Manhattan also featured a beautiful song-and-dance fantasy, "Phil the Fiddler"; an effective production number following a cabbie, milkman, street-cleaner, newsboy on their daily rounds, "Noises in the Street"; a fine romantic song in "I Don't Know His Name," presented by Jack Kilty and Kyle MacDonnell in a rooftop scene; and a good jitterbug number by Sheila Bond and Danny Daniels.

1948   LEND AN EAR, an intimate revue with sketches, lyrics, and music by Charles Gaynor. Additional sketches by Joseph Styne and Will Glickman. Produced by William Katzell, Franklin Gilbert, and William Eythe at the National Theatre on December 16. Directed by Hal Gerson. Staged by Gower Champion. Cast included Carol Channing, William Eythe, and Yvonne Adair (460 performances).

Lend an Ear spent several years in tryouts outside New York before it finally settled at the National Theatre for a long run. It proved to be bright, vivacious, fresh entertainment. Carol Channing and Yvonne Adair were two unknowns in the cast who were swept to recognition. Channing was particularly effective in a satirical sketch on grand opera. "The Gladiola Girl," the first-act finale, was a brilliant lampoon of a 1925 road-company musical—a pioneer in laughing at the dress, habits, mores, and indiscretions of the roaring 1920's. (This sequence was used several times on television some years later, including an "Omnibus" program in 1958.) Another outstanding sketch satirized psychiatrists and psychiatry. The songs passed the gamut from the witty and satirical to the romantic and sentimental. The best were: "Neurotic You and Psychopathic Me," "Three Little Queens of the Silver Screen," "When Someone You Love Loves You," "Where Is the She for Me?" and "I'm Not in Love."

1951   TOP BANANA, a musical comedy with book by Hy Kraft. Lyrics and music by Johnny Mercer. Produced by Paula Stone and Mike Sloane at the Winter Garden on November 1. Staged by Jack Donahue. Dances by Ron Fletcher. Cast included Phil Silvers, Joey and Herbie Faye, Rose Marie, and Jack Albertson (350 performances).

In 1951 Milton Berle was "top banana" of the television industry, "Mr. Television." The character of Jerry Biffle (Phil Silvers), comic star of the Blendo Soap Program, may not have been Berle, but there was little doubt that the writers had Berle in mind when they created him. The febrile, frenetic, even hysterical activity surrounding the preparation of a weekly television program is largely of Jerry's making. For he is loud, brash, bossy, a dynamo of energy. He must always be in motion, always functioning at top speed, always occupying the center of attention. Surrounded by a retinue of gag writers, cronies, and other hangers-on, he is a man convinced of the infallibility of his judgment and genius, a man so in love with himself that he continually blows kisses to his image in the mirror.

A slim plot unfolds as the sponsor insists that Jerry's TV program needs love interest to gain a larger public. Jerry brings Sally Peters (Judy Lynn) into his show, gets the idea that he is in love with her, then is ready to help her elope with the singer, Cliff Lane (Lindy Doherty), when he discovers that Cliff is the man she really loves.

The play was charged with the electricity of Phil Silvers' performance as a TV comic. Two episodes in which he was involved had particular impact. In one Jerry and his cronies sing the title song, which inspires Jerry to reminisce on his old days in burlesque—the gags, the slapstick, the color and atmosphere of burlesque entertainment. In another Jerry gets tangled up with Walter Dare Wahl's old vaudeville routine, a hectic elopement scene.

Rose Marie, as Betty Dillon, discharged the main comedy songs zestfully. The best were a duet with Jerry, "A Word a Day," filled with choice malapropisms; "I Fought Every Step of the Way," describing romance in terms of a prizefight; and "Sans Souci." "Only if You're in Love" was the love duet of Sally and Cliff.

1952   NEW FACES OF 1952, a revue, with book, lyrics, and music by various
       writers. Produced by Leonard Sillman at the Royale Theatre on May 16.
       Staged by John Murray Anderson. Musical and dance numbers staged
       by Richard Barstow. Sketches directed by John Beal. Cast included
       Eartha Kitt, Alice Ghostley, Ronny Graham, and June Carroll (365
       performances).

This was the most successful edition of a revue produced intermittently
since 1934. The first edition—produced by Charles Dillingham and assembled by Leonard Sillman—attempted to revive the spontaneity and
brilliance of the first *Garrick Gaieties* by tapping exclusively the resources
of young, unknown, fresh writers and performers. Consequently, the title
New Faces is singularly appropriate. Beginning with the second edition
in 1936, Leonard Sillman has served as producer—and as the discoverer of
new talent. In its various editions *New Faces* has proved luckier in un-
covering new talent among performers than writers. The first edition introduced Imogene Coca and Henry Fonda; the second, Van Johnson; the
1956 edition, the impersonator, T. C. Jones. The major discovery in *New
Faces of 1952* was Eartha Kitt. Singing "Bal Petit Bal" and "Monotonous,"
she became one of the most exciting and provocative new singers to appear on Broadway in some years. Another find was Alice Ghostley,
a fresh, new comedienne—outstanding in sketches like "Time for Two,"
"Of Fathers and Sons," and "The Great American Opera."

1954   THE GOLDEN APPLE, a musical play with book and lyrics by John La
       Touche. Music by Jerome Moross. Produced by the Phoenix Theatre
       at the Phoenix Theatre on March 11, and at the Alvin Theatre on April
       20. Staged by Norman Lloyd. Choreography by Hanya Holm. Cast in-
       cluded Kaye Ballard, Stephen Douglass, and Jonathan Lucas (125 per-
       formances).

The Golden Apple was written with the aid of a Guggenheim Fellowship
several years before it was produced. In all that time it was turned down
by several producers who insisted that it was too unorthodox to have
public appeal. When finally presented, it was so successful in an off-
Broadway production that five weeks later it was transferred to Broadway. To John McClain it was "easily the most satisfactory and original
song and dance effort of the past several seasons, and in my opinion can
be classed as an American Gilbert and Sullivan." Robert Coleman called
it "a magnificent achievement . . . a sensational success . . . quite the
most original and imaginative work of its kind to blaze across the theatrical horizon in many a moon." It received the Drama Critics Award as
the best musical of the year.

Sung throughout, *The Golden Apple* is a satire that transfers the Homeric legend of Helen and Ulysses to an American town, Angel's Roost, in the state of Washington, at the turn of the present century. Ulysses is an American soldier (Stephen Douglass) returning home from the Spanish-American War; Penelope (Priscilla Gillette) is his wife; Helen (Kaye Ballard), a farmer's daughter who falls in love with a traveling salesman, Paris (Jonathan Lucas). Paris and Helen run off to the big city. For ten years Ulysses goes in search of Helen to save her from Paris. In the city, Ulysses succumbs to its temptations, enjoying the allurements of Siren and Circe, among others. He bests Paris in a boxing match, then finally returns home to his patient, long-waiting Penelope, happy to spend with her the rest of his years.

The story is told briskly in song, lyrics, pantomime, and some beautiful dances conceived by Hanya Holm; of the last, the most memorable was a hilarious travesty called "By Goona Goona Lagoon." The best of the comedy songs was "The Judgment of Paris," while those in a more sober and sentimental vein included "Lazy Afternoon" (followed by an attractive dance by Jonathan Lucas), the musical high point of the play, and "My Love Is on the Way."

1955 PLAIN AND FANCY, a musical comedy with book by Joseph Stein and William Glickman, suggested by an original play by Marion Weaver. Lyrics by Arnold B. Horwitt. Music by Albert Hague. Produced by Richard Kollmar and James W. Gardiner in association with Yvette Schumer at the Mark Hellinger Theatre on January 27. Directed by Morton da Costa. Dances and musical numbers staged by Helen Tamiris. Cast included Richard Derr, Shirl Conway, Stefan Schnabel, and David Daniels (461 performances).

The authors found their characters and setting with the Amish sect, which inhabits parts of Pennsylvania and which has clung tenaciously to its time-honored customs, speech, dress, and morality. The specific setting is the town of Bird in Hand, in Lancaster County. During a motor trip two city folk—Ruth Winters (Shirl Conway) and Dan King (Richard Derr)—invade the cloistered life of the Amish. They find the people and their way of life quaint and primitive. The first act is dedicated to presenting these good and happy people and their benevolent way of life; it has the simple and at times eloquent character of a folk tale. The central characters are Papa Yoder (Stefan Schnabel), a stern Amish parent, and his attractive daughter, Katie (Gloria Marlowe), who is in love with a man to whom Yoder objects, Peter Reber (David Daniels). Two musical highlights in this act give a poignant picture of these people. The first is Katie Yoder's song, "It Wonders Me"; the second, by Papa Yoder and chorus, speaks of the Amish philosophy of life, "Plain We Live."

As the two city people become a part of the Amish community and learn to love it, *Plain and Fancy* abandons its folk character and uses the Amish background and characters merely as material for musical-comedy routines. Here we find an attractive carnival ballet and the hit song of the show, "Young and Foolish," presented by Peter Reber.

1956 MR. WONDERFUL, a musical comedy with book by Joseph Stein and Will Glickman. Lyrics and music by Jerry Bock, Larry Holofcener, and George Weiss. Produced by Jule Styne and George Gilbert, in association with Lester Osterman, Jr., at the Broadway Theatre on March 22. Production conceived by Jule Styne. Staged by Jack Donohue. Cast included Sammy Davis, Jr., Jack Carter, Olga James, and Chita Rivera (383 performances).

Mr. Wonderful brought Sammy Davis, Jr.—the brilliant and versatile night-club star, dynamo of the Mastin Trio—into the Broadway theater. In writing a musical for Sammy Davis, the authors had to find a place for Sammy's famous night-club routines. They solved the problem simply— by interpolating a night-club scene into the second act, having the musicians clamber up to the stage from the pit and Sammy and the two other members of his trio do their act. Sammy sings, dances, plays the drums, does impersonations—and with all his restless energy—and as far as *Mr. Wonderful* is concerned, *this* is the show. The frail plot that preceded it was merely a necessary preliminary. In Union City, New Jersey, Charlie Welch (Sammy Davis, Jr.) is an ingratiating song-and-dance man. His girl friend, Ethel Pearson (Olga James), and his friend, Fred Campbell (Jack Carter), want him to aspire to Broadway success, but Charlie is diffident about leaving Union City. He is finally convinced to make a try, and the second-act night-club scene establishes him as a star.

Sammy Davis, Jr. provides all the momentum needed to keep the play moving to its breath-taking night-club finale. Such comedy as is found in the play appears with Fred Campbell, and his wife, Lil (Pat Marshall), especially in a scene set in Miami. Ethel's beautiful ballad, "Mr. Wonderful," became the show's big song hit, with Charlie's number, "Too Close for Comfort," crowding it for honors. A duet by Fred and Lil Campbell, "Without You I'm Nothing," was also melodically appealing.

1956 LI'L ABNER, a musical comedy with book by Norman Panama and Melvin Frank based on characters created by Al Capp. Lyrics by Johnny

Mercer. Music by Gene de Paul. Produced by Norman Panama, Melvin Frank and Michael Kidd at the St. James Theatre on November 15. Direction and choreography by Michael Kidd. Cast included Edith Adams, Peter Palmer, Stubby Kaye, and Tina Louise (693 performances).

Li'l Abner carries the grotesque characters of Dogpatch, in Al Capp's famous cartoon strip, into the theater. The principals, of course, are Daisy Mae (Edith Adams), who is bent on catching the recalcitrant bachelor, Li'l Abner (Peter Palmer); in the final scene Abner drinks a potion that makes him want to marry Daisy Mae. Others in Dogpatch include Appassionata von Climax (Tina Louise), Daisy Mae's rival for Li'l Abner during the Sadie Hawkins sweepstakes in which the women go racing after the men; Mammy Yokum (Charlotte Rae), with her delusions of grandeur, and her Pappy (Joe E. Marks); and the industrialist General Bullmoose, the politician Senator Phogbound, Marryin' Sam, Evil Eye Fleagle who "gives the whammies," and so forth. These good and kind people, so sound of body and mind, help to point up the follies of civilization on the periphery of their own fantastic world. And the satire that Capp always permits to intrude into his comic strip also penetrates the musical, which finds occasion to mock big business, our atom policy and security program, and can find comfort in the scientific discovery of a formula capable of producing healthy people by depriving them of their minds.

Brooks Atkinson pointed up the fact that "ballet is a more suitable medium for comic-strip theatricalization than the complex form of the musical stage. . . . Motion is a better medium than words for animating this sort of drawing." And it is in the dances, conceived by Michael Kidd, that *Li'l Abner* has exceptional interest. One of these comes just before the end of the first act, during the Sadie Hawkins Day helter-skelter chase of the women after the men. "All that happens," explains Brooks Atkinson, "is that the girls leg it after the boys at top speed. But Mr. Kidd is the man who can see comic-strip humor in this primitive rite by varying the speed, by introducing low-comedy antics and by giving *Li'l Abner* its most exuberant scene."

The comedy songs were the best, especially "Jubilation T. Cornpone," with which Marryin' Sam (Stubby Kaye) stopped the show. In a broader satirical vein were "The Country's in the Very Best of Hands," "Oh, Happy Day," and "Progress Is the Root of All Evil"; and the sentimental duet of Abner and Daisy Mae, "Namely You," and Abner's homey ditty, "If I Had My Druthers," were more in character with the warm and gentle people who inhabit Dogpatch.

1956   HAPPY HUNTING, a musical comedy with book by Howard Lindsay and Russel Crouse. Lyrics by Matt Dubey. Music by Harold Karr. Presented by Jo Mielziner at the Majestic Theatre on December 6. Staged by Abe Burrows. Dances and musical numbers staged by Alex Romero and Bob Herget. Cast included Ethel Merman, Fernando Lamas, Virginia Gibson, and Gordon Polk (408 performances).

Happy Hunting had an old-fashioned kind of musical-comedy content with stereotyped book, routine situations, and more or less humdrum dialogue. But it counted heavily on its star, Ethel Merman—and it was the star who carried the show on her shoulders to success. Returning to the Broadway stage after a six-year absence, Ethel Merman belted out songs and lines with all her old verve and vigor, and made them sound much better than they really were. Whether she had a confidential chat with a horse, or went to bed wearing all her jewels to avoid being robbed, or questioned with bewilderment, "Is his name Grace *too?*" when she heard Prince Rainier being referred to as "His Grace"—she was her inimitable robust self, a boon to a sagging book.

> The thing about Merman is that she doesn't need comedy because she just naturally drips comedy the way some trees drip maple syrup [reported Walter Kerr]. Lines? Who needs lines? Her tone is funny, her attitude . . . is funny, her simple presence in the neighborhood is humor itself. . . . A glorious creature, capable of saying "What the hell!" in twenty different inflections and making celestial melody out of all of them.

Ethel Merman appears as Liz Livingstone, a rich Philadelphian who resents the fact that she has not been invited to Monaco to attend the wedding of Grace Kelly and Prince Rainier. She is determined to arrange a festive wedding for her own daughter, Beth (Virginia Gibson), which will outdo the Monaco ceremony. However, when she finds and buys for her daughter a Spanish grandee, the Duke of Granada (Fernando Lamas), she falls in love with the man herself. This hardly poses a problem to Beth, since she is in love with a Philadelphia lawyer, Sanford Stewart, Jr. (Gordon Polk).

The duet of mother and daughter, "Mutual Admiration Society," became a hit with disc jockeys and on juke boxes even before *Happy Hunting* reached Broadway. The mother delivered two more effective musical numbers in the title song and "Mr. Livingstone." During the run of the show Ethel Merman interpolated several new songs into the production, two of them by Kay Thompson, "I'm Old Enough to Know Better" and "Just a Moment Ago."

1957 NEW GIRL IN TOWN, a musical play, with book by George Abbott based on Eugene O'Neill's 1922 Pulitzer Prize play, *Anna Christie*. Lyrics and music by Bob Merrill. Presented by Frederick Brisson, Robert E. Griffith, and Harold S. Prince at the 46th Street Theatre on May 14. Staged by George Abbott. Dances and musical numbers staged by Bob Fosse. Cast included Gwen Verdon, Thelma Ritter, Cameron Prud'homme, and George Wallace (432 performances).

In fashioning a musical play out of Eugene O'Neill's famous play *Anna Christie*, George Abbott made only minor alterations, none in the basic plot. In the musical, as in the play, Anna Christie (Gwen Verdon) remains a prostitute from the Midwest who, recovering from tuberculosis, returns to New York to find shelter with her father, Chris (Cameron Prud'homme), whom she has not seen in twenty years. The father, of course, knows nothing of his daughter's sordid past and welcomes her tenderly, determined to be a worthy father to a wonderful daughter. In New York, Anna falls in love with Mat (George Wallace), an Irish seaman. Anna's past becomes known to Mat, who denounces her and then goes off to sea to forget her. But he returns and, convinced that love has purified Anna, is ready to forget and forgive.

One of the changes in the adaptation came in shifting the time of the play from 1921 to 1900 because, as Abbott explained, "clothes were prettier then." *New Girl in Town*, then, becomes a decorative period piece, bright and colorful with costumes, sets, and dances of the period. At times it is a nostalgic backward look into the era of 1900, and at times it burlesques that era. The play loses no time in setting forth its purpose. It opens with a rousing routine called "Roll Yer Socks Up," set against a picturesque water-front backdrop in which sailors and girls do a fandango. Later in the play a picturesque ballroom ballet is once again evocative of the early 1900's.

Another important change came through bolstering and building up the role of Marthy—Chris' middle-aged and blowzy mistress and companion. As played by Thelma Ritter, in her first appearance in the musical theater, the character of Marthy is one of the brightest ornaments of the production. Indeed, Thelma Ritter would undoubtedly have stolen the show from the rest of the performers if Gwen Verdon, as Anna, did not prove so sensational. In *Can-Can* and *Damn Yankees*, Gwen Verdon had proved that she is an exciting dancer. In *New Girl in Town* she is given ample opportunities to demonstrate that talent, particularly in a ballet that reveals her disgust at men's carnal appetite for sex. But in portraying Anna she also proves herself to be an outstanding actress. As Brooks Atkinson wrote:

> She gives a complete characterization from the slut to the woman—common in manner, but full of pride, disillusioned, but willing to believe, a woman of silence and mysteries. It would be an affecting job on any stage. Amid the familiar diversions of a Broadway musical jamboree, it is sobering and admirable.

With *New Girl in Town*, a new composer appears on the Broadway scene—young Bob Merrill, a man who proved himself as apt with a bright and catchy lyric as with a pleasing melody. His gift for affecting lyricism was revealed most forcefully in the beautiful ballad, "Sunshine Girl," which became a hit song. Other pleasing tunes included a lilting waltz, "Ven I Valse"; a tender duet of Anna and Mat, "Did You Close Your Eyes?"; Mat's song, "Look at 'Er"; and two poignant songs of Anna, "It's Good to Be Alive" and "If That Was Love." Merrill's strength with lyrics is found in Marthy's amusing ditty, "Flings," about the rewards two older people can find in love ("Flings is wonderful things—but they gotta be flung by the young"). And his fine gift for writing atmospheric music was displayed in effective background music for several scenes between Chris and Marthy.

1957   THE MUSIC MAN, a musical comedy with book, lyrics, and music by Meredith Willson, based on a story by Meredith Willson and Franklin Lacey. Presented by Kermit Bloomgarden with Herbert Greene, in association with Frank Productions, Inc., at the Majestic Theatre on December 19. Staged by Morton da Costa. Choreography by Oona White. Cast included Robert Preston, Barbara Cook, and David Burns.

Unlike most outstandingly successful musicals, *The Music Man* slipped in rather unobtrusively and quietly to Broadway. Few in that first-night audience had any reason to suspect that something special was being presented. They were, then, caught completely by surprise by the irresistible charm of a play that wore its heart so openly on its sleeve, and sought to woo and win its audience with sentiment that often turned to sentimentality, with comedy that sometimes became corn, with nostalgia for an American past that was more old-fashioned than homey, and for excitement which sometimes was mere razzle-dazzle.

> Not in recent memory [said *Variety*] has a Broadway audience been so spectacularly carried away. Something happened in that theater on opening

night which was without precedent: In the touching finale, the audience broke out spontaneously into applause to the even rhythm of the music. Nothing like it has ever been seen on Broadway.

The Music Man did not delay longer than the rise of the first curtain to cast its spell on the audience. The opening scene was a moving railroad coach, in which the dialogue of a traveling salesman and the music were beautifully integrated with the bouncy rhythm of the moving train. The infectious mood thus established is not dissipated until the equally fresh and exciting final scene.

The "music man" is a swindler named Harold Hill (Robert Preston), who goes from town to town selling the idea of forming a local boys' band. He says he is ready to train it if the town buys from him all the necessary equipment. However, since Hill cannot read a note of music and knows nothing about training a band, he absconds with the money as soon as he has made the sale. He comes to the town of River City, Iowa, where his easy spiel wins the townsfolk. But when their suspicions are momentarily aroused, he overcomes the incredulity of a committee sent to investigate his credentials by inducing them to form a barbershop quartet. The mountebank, however, is foiled by two unforeseen developments. He falls in love with the local librarian-piano teacher, Marian Paroo (Barbara Cook)—the only one who really knows he is a con man but is willing to ignore this unsavory fact because she loves him. The other development is the contagious spirit generated in the town for song and dance which even infects our charlatan. He has a change of heart and falls in line with the rest of the town. In the final scene the boys appear in full regalia with their instruments to sound the first sour notes of their band music.

Every element in the production was beautifully coordinated to create a consistent picture of life in a small American town in 1912. The staging of Morton da Costa had a keen eye for detail. The costumes of Raoul Pene du Bois and the settings of Howard Bay were evocative of the Midwest of yesteryear. The choreography of Oona White had a folksy character, to the point of including a soft-shoe dance. The performance of principals and supporting cast was completely in tune with story and background. For Robert Preston, a stage veteran, the role of music man was his first invasion of the musical theater.

It took his current vehicle [said Robert Coleman] to bring home . . . just how versatile our boy really is. He paces the piece dynamically, acts ingratiatingly, sings as if he'd been doing it all his life, and offers steps that would score on the cards of dance judges. A triumphant performance in a triumphant musical!

Meredith Willson's music (which made no pretense at subtlety) is tuneful, gay, sentimental, rousing as the occasion demanded. The touching ballad, "Goodnight, My Someone," is perhaps the best of the numbers. But "Seventy Six Trombones," "Shipoopi," "Lida Rose," and "Gary, Indiana," also delighted the ear.

1958   OH, CAPTAIN! a musical comedy with book by Al Morgan and José Ferrer based on the motion picture *The Captain's Paradise*. Lyrics and music by Jay Livingston and Ray Evans. Produced by Howard Merrill and the Theatre Corporation of America at the Alvin Theatre on February 4. Staged by José Ferrer. Dances and musical numbers staged by James Starbuck. Cast included Tony Randall, Abbe Lane, Susan Johnson, and Jacquelyn McKeever (192 performances).

Alec Coppel's original screenplay—upon which *Oh, Captain!* was based—was rich with subtle details, nuances, and innuendos, which made *The Captain's Paradise*, starring Alec Guinness, a motion picture of irresistible charm and wit. *Oh, Captain!* however, made no pretense at being subtle. All its attractions were on the surface. As Robert Coleman reported, this is "no musical-comedy classic . . . merely a gold-mine of frolic, fun and beautiful babes."

The basic concept (if not the delightful essentials) of the motion picture was retained, though with a shift in locale. Captain St. James (Tony Randall) is the captain of a freighter making regular five-day trips across the Channel from England to France. Since his free time is divided between these two countries he has a woman both in London and in Paris. In London she is the staid, somewhat timid, but always proper Mrs. St. James (Jacquelyn McKeever). In France she is the torrid, sexy Parisian strip-tease cabaret artist, Bobo (Abbe Lane). With each of his women our captain assumes a different identity. With his wife in London he is the stuffy homebody; with Bobo, in Paris, he is the irrepressible cut-up. What the musical comedy only suggests—but what the motion picture emphasized so amusingly—was that each of these women not only secretly aspired to be but eventually even openly became the exact opposite of what she was. Thus, in his search for abandoned pleasures in Paris with Bobo, the captain found to his consternation that all she really wanted was to become a respectable homemaker; and in his pursuit of the simpler and more wholesome pleasures of domesticity, he discovered that his prim little wife really wished to cut capers. In the musical the wife wins a trip to Paris, where she uncovers the double life of her husband. She then proceeds to give him a lesson on what gay living really is like.

Of the three principals only Tony Randall is a veteran of the stage. But this is his first musical, and it is an auspicious debut. He sings with such contagious élan and vitality that it is easy to forget he is no singer; he dances with complete aplomb—even to the point of invading ballet, with Alexandria Danilova as his partner, in a hilarious dance sequence that stops the show; and he is completely at ease in his dual, sharply contrasted impersonations. (Actually he is forced to reveal a third facet of his personality when, aboard his ship, he is the ruthless martinet.) "He acts the triple-threat role," says Robert Coleman, "so persuasively as to make you forget that Alec Guinness did it for the film. Terrific is the word for Tony."

Both female principals proved to be star material. Jacquelyn McKeever was a former schoolteacher; Abbe Lane is the famous sultry songstress of the Xavier Cugat orchestra, and in private life is Mrs. Cugat.

For the song writers, Jay Livingston and Ray Evans, *Oh, Captain!* represents their debut on the Broadway stage. But this team is no novice by any means. Over a period of many years Livingston and Evans have been writing outstanding scores for motion pictures; on two occasions they won Academy Awards ("Whatever Will Be, Will Be" and "Mona Lisa"). For Bobo they wrote such arresting torrid numbers as "Femininity," "You Don't Know Him," and "Double Standard." For Susan Johnson—playing Mae, a night-club singer from Kentucky—they wrote the equally effective "Give It All You Got," "Love Is Hell," and "Montmartre in the Morning." Two other songs were particularly appealing: "Surprise" and "All the Time."

2

A CHRONOLOGY OF THE AMERICAN
MUSICAL THEATER *

1866   *The Black Crook (Operti)*
1868   *Humpty Dumpty (A. Reiff)*
1874   *Evangeline (E. E. Rice)*
1879   *The Brook (adapted music)*
      The Mulligan Guard Ball, and other Harrigan and Hart burlesques (David Braham)
1884   Adonis (E. E. Rice)
1887   *The Little Tycoon (Willard Spencer)*
1890   Castles in the Air (Gustave Kerker)
      Robin Hood (Reginald de Koven)
1891   *Wang (Woolson Morse)*
1892   *The Isle of Champagne (William Wallace Furst)*
1893   *A Trip to Chinatown (Percy Gaunt)*
1894   The Passing Show of 1894 (Ludwig Englander)
      Rob Roy (Reginald de Koven)
1895   *Princess Bonnie (Willard Spencer)*
      The Wizard of the Nile (Victor Herbert)
1896   The Art of Maryland, and other Weber and Fields burlesques (John Stromberg)
      El Capitan (John Philip Sousa)
1897   The Belle of New York (Gustave Kerker)
      The Highwayman (Reginald de Koven)
      The Serenade (Victor Herbert)
1898   The Fortune Teller (Victor Herbert)
1899   *The Rogers Brothers in Wall Street, and other Rogers Brothers Vaudeville-Farces (Maurice Levi)*
1900   The Belle of Bohemia (Ludwig Englander)

* *Note:* Only musicals discussed either in the main body of the book or in Appendix 1 are listed below.

    Musicals that are italicized will be found in Appendix 1. All others appear in the main body of the book under the biography of the composer named in parentheses.

The Casino Girl (Ludwig Englander)
1901 The Strollers (Ludwig Englander)
1902 A Chinese Honeymoon (Gustave Kerker)
      King Dodo (Gustav Luders)
1903 Babes in Toyland (Victor Herbert)
      The Prince of Pilsen (Gustav Luders)
      The Runaways (Raymond Hubbell)
      The Wizard of Oz (A. Baldwin Sloane)
1904 It Happened in Nordland (Victor Herbert)
      Little Johnny Jones (George M. Cohan)
      Piff, Paff, Pouf (Jean Schwartz)
      The Shogun (Gustav Luders)
1905 Fantana (Raymond Hubbell)
      Mlle Modiste (Victor Herbert)
      The Rich Mr. Hoggenheimer (Ludwig Englander)
      A Society Circus, and other Hippodrome extravaganzas (Manuel Klein)
1906 Forty-Five Minutes from Broadway (George M. Cohan)
      George Washington, Jr. (George M. Cohan)
      The Red Mill (Victor Herbert)
      A Parisian Model (Max Hoffman)
1907 *The Ziegfeld Follies* of 1907, *and other Follies editions* (*various composers*)
1908 The Three Twins (Karl Hoschna)
1909 The Fair Co-ed (Gustav Luders)
1910 Madame Sherry (Karl Hoschna)
      Naughty Marietta (Victor Herbert)
      The Social Whirl (Gustave Kerker)
      The Summer Widowers (A. Baldwin Sloane)
1911 The Hen Pecks (A. Baldwin Sloane)
      The Little Millionaire (George M. Cohan)
      The Pink Lady (Ivan Caryll)
      Vera Violetta (Louis Hirsch)
      The Ziegfeld Follies of 1911 (Raymond Hubbell)
1912 The Firefly (Rudolf Friml)
      Oh, Oh, Delphine! (Ivan Caryll)
      The Passing Show of 1912 (Louis Hirsch)
      The Wall St. Girl (Karl Hoschna)
      The Ziegfeld Follies of 1912 (Raymond Hubbell)
1913 High-Jinks (Rudolf Friml)
      The Passing Show of 1913 (Jean Schwartz)
      Sweethearts (Victor Herbert)
      The Ziegfeld Follies of 1913 (Raymond Hubbell)
1914 Chin-Chin (Ivan Caryll)
      The Girl from Utah (Jerome Kern)
      Hello Broadway (George M. Cohan)
      The Passing Show of 1914 (Sigmund Romberg)
      Watch Your Step (Irving Berlin)

The Ziegfeld Follies of 1914 (Raymond Hubbell)

1915 The Blue Paradise (Sigmund Romberg)
Hip-Hip-Hooray (Raymond Hubbell)
Nobody Home (Jerome Kern)
Very Good Eddie (Jerome Kern)
The Ziegfeld Follies of 1915 (Louis Hirsch)

1916 The Passing Show of 1916 (Sigmund Romberg)
Robinson Crusoe, Jr. (Sigmund Romberg)
The Ziegfeld Follies of 1916 (Louis Hirsch)

1917 Going Up (Louis Hirsch)
Leave It to Jane (Jerome Kern)
Maytime (Sigmund Romberg)
Oh Boy! (Jerome Kern)
The Passing Show of 1917 (Sigmund Romberg)
The Ziegfeld Follies of 1917 (Raymond Hubbell)

1918 Ladies First (A. Baldwin Sloane)
Listen Lester (Harold Orlob)
Oh, Lady, Lady (Jerome Kern)
The Passing Show of 1918 (Sigmund Romberg)
Sinbad (Sigmund Romberg)
Somebody's Sweetheart (Anthony Bafunno)
Sometime (Rudolf Friml)
Yip, Yip, Yaphank (Irving Berlin)
The Ziegfeld Follies of 1918 (Louis Hirsch)

1919 *Apple Blossoms (Victor Jacobi and Fritz Kreisler)*
The Greenwich Village Follies of 1919 (A. Baldwin Sloane)
George White's Scandals of 1919 (Richard Whiting)
Irene (Harry Tierney)
La, La, Lucille (George Gershwin)
The Passing Show of 1919 (Sigmund Romberg)
The Ziegfeld Follies of 1919 (Irving Berlin)

1920 George White's Scandals of 1920 (George Gershwin)
The Greenwich Village Follies of 1920 (A. Baldwin Sloane)
Honeydew (Efrem Zimbalist)
Mary (Louis Hirsch)
Sally (Jerome Kern)
Tickle Me (Herbert Stothart)
The Ziegfeld Follies of 1920 (Irving Berlin).

1921 Blossom Time (Sigmund Romberg)
Bombo (Sigmund Romberg)
George White's Scandals of 1921 (George Gershwin)
Good Morning, Dearie (Jerome Kern)
The Music Box Revue (Irving Berlin)
The Passing Show of 1921 (Jean Schwartz)
The Perfect Fool (Ed Wynn)
Shuffle Along (Noble Sissle and Eubie Blake)
Tangerine (Carlo Sanders)

1922   George White's Scandals of 1922 (George Gershwin)
       The Gingham Girl (Albert von Tilzer)
       The Grand Street Follies, and later editions (various composers)
       The Greenwich Village Follies of 1922 (Louis Hirsch)
       Lady in Ermine (Jean Gilbert and Alfred Goodman)
       The Music Box Revue of 1922 (Irving Berlin)
       Sally, Irene and Mary (J. Fred Coots)
       Two Little Girls in Blue (Vincent Youmans)
       Up She Goes (Harry Tierney)
       The Ziegfeld Follies of 1922 (Louis Hirsch)
1923   Artists and Models of 1923 (Jean Schwartz)
       George White's Scandals of 1923 (George Gershwin)
       The Greenwich Village Follies of 1923 (Louis Hirsch)
       Helen of Troy, New York (Harry Ruby)
       Kid Boots (Harry Tierney)
       Little Jessie James (Harry Archer)
       The Music Box Revue of 1923 (Irving Berlin)
       The Passing Show of 1923 (Sigmund Romberg)
       Poppy (Stephen Jones and Arthur Samuels)
       Stepping Stones (Jerome Kern)
       Wildflower (Vincent Youmans)
1924   Artists and Models of 1924 (J. Fred Coots)
       George White's Scandals of 1924 (George Gershwin)
       I'll Say She Is (Tom Johnstone)
       Lady Be Good (George Gershwin)
       The Music Box Revue of 1924 (Irving Berlin)
       The Passing Show of 1924 (Sigmund Romberg)
       Rose Marie (Rudolf Friml)
       The Student Prince (Sigmund Romberg)
1925   Artists and Models of 1925 (J. Fred Coots)
       Cocoanuts (Irving Berlin)
       Dearest Enemy (Richard Rodgers—Rodgers and Hart)
       Garrick Gaieties (Richard Rodgers—Rodgers and Hart)
       George White's Scandals of 1925 (De Sylva, Brown, and Henderson)
       No, No, Nanette (Vincent Youmans)
       Sally (Jerome Kern)
       A Song of the Flame (George Gershwin)
       The Vagabond King (Rudolf Friml)
1926   Criss Cross (Jerome Kern)
       The Desert Song (Sigmund Romberg)
       The Garrick Gaieties of 1926 (Richard Rodgers—Rodgers and Hart)
       George White's Scandals of 1926 (De Sylva, Brown, and Henderson)
       The Girl Friend (Richard Rodgers—Rodgers and Hart)
       Honeymoon Lane (James T. Hanley)
       A Night in Paris (J. Fred Coots)
       Oh Kay! (George Gershwin)
       Peggy-Ann (Richard Rodgers—Rodgers and Hart)

Queen High (*Lewis E. Gensler*)
The Ramblers (Harry Ruby)
1927   A Connecticut Yankee (Richard Rodgers—Rodgers and Hart)
Five O'clock Girl (Harry Ruby)
Funny Face (George Gershwin)
Good News (De Sylva, Brown, and Henderson)
Hit the Deck (Vincent Youmans)
Lovely Lady (Dave Stamper)
Rio Rita (Harry Tierney)
Show Boat (Jerome Kern)
Take the Air (Dave Stamper)
The Ziegfeld Follies of 1927 (Irving Berlin)
1928   Animal Crackers (Harry Ruby)
Blackbirds of 1928 (Jimmy McHugh)
George White's Scandals of 1928 (De Sylva, Brown, and Henderson)
Good Boy (Harry Ruby)
Hello Daddy (Jimmy McHugh)
Hold Everything (De Sylva, Brown, and Henderson)
The New Moon (Sigmund Romberg)
Present Arms (Richard Rodgers—Rodgers and Hart)
Rain or Shine (Milton Ager and Owen Murphy)
Rainbow (Vincent Youmans)
Rosalie (George Gershwin)
The Three Musketeers (Rudolf Friml)
Whoopee (Walter Donaldson)
1929   Fifty Million Frenchmen (Cole Porter)
Follow Through (De Sylva, Brown, and Henderson)
The Little Show (Arthur Schwartz)
Show Girl (George Gershwin)
Sketch Book of 1929 (Jay Gorney)
Sons O' Guns (J. Fred Coots)
Strike Up the Band (George Gershwin)
Sweet Adeline (Jerome Kern)
1930   The Earl Carroll Vanities (Jay Gorney)
Fine and Dandy (Kay Swift)
Flying High (De Sylva, Brown, and Henderson)
The Second Little Show (Arthur Schwartz)
Three's a Crowd (Arthur Schwartz)
1931   America's Sweetheart (Richard Rodgers—Rodgers and Hart)
The Band Wagon (Arthur Schwartz)
The Cat and the Fiddle (Jerome Kern)
Of Thee I Sing (George Gershwin)
1932   Face the Music (Irving Berlin)
The Gay Divorce (Cole Porter)
Music in the Air (Jerome Kern)
Take a Chance (Richard Whiting)
Walk a Little Faster (Vernon Duke)

1933   As Thousands Cheer (Irving Berlin)
       Let 'Em Eat Cake (George Gershwin)
       Roberta (Jerome Kern)
1934   Anything Goes (Cole Porter)
1935   Jumbo (Richard Rodgers—Rodgers and Hart)
       May Wine (Sigmund Romberg)
       Porgy and Bess (George Gershwin)
1936   Johnny Johnson (Kurt Weill)
       On Your Toes (Richard Rodgers—Rodgers and Hart)
       The Show Is On (various composers)
1937   Babes in Arms (Richard Rodgers—Rodgers and Hart)
       Hooray for What? (Harold Arlen)
       I'd Rather Be Right (Richard Rodgers—Rodgers and Hart)
       Pins and Needles (Harold Rome)
1938   The Boys from Syracuse (Richard Rodgers—Rodgers and Hart)
       The Cradle Will Rock (Marc Blitzstein)
       Hellzapoppin' (Sammy Fain)
       I Married an Angel (Richard Rodgers—Rodgers and Hart)
       Knickerbocker Holiday (Kurt Weill)
       Leave It to Me (Cole Porter)
1939   Du Barry Was a Lady (Cole Porter)
1940   Cabin in the Sky (Vernon Duke)
       Hold On to Your Hats (Burton Lane)
       Louisiana Purchase (Irving Berlin)
       Meet the People (Jay Gorney)
       Pal Joey (Richard Rodgers—Rodgers and Hart)
       Panama Hattie (Cole Porter)
1941   Banjo Eyes (Vernon Duke)
       Best Foot Forward (Ralph Blane)
       Let's Face It (Cole Porter)
       Sons O' Fun (Sammy Fain)
1942   By Jupiter (Richard Rodgers—Rodgers and Hart)
       Star and Garter (various composers and writers)
       This Is the Army (Irving Berlin)
1943   Carmen Jones (Oscar Hammerstein II)
       Oklahoma! (Richard Rodgers—Rodgers and Hammerstein)
       One Touch of Venus (Kurt Weill)
       Something for the Boys (Cole Porter)
       The Ziegfeld Follies of 1943 (Ray Henderson, discussed with Follies
          of 1907)
1944   The Bloomer Girl (Harold Arlen)
       Follow the Girls (Phil Charig)
       Laffing Room Only (Burton Lane)
       Mexican Hayride (Cole Porter)
       On the Town (Leonard Bernstein)
       Song of Norway (Wright and Forrest)
1945   Carousel (Richard Rodgers—Rodgers and Hammerstein)

Up in Central Park (Sigmund Romberg)
1946   Annie Get Your Gun (Irving Berlin)
Call Me Mister (Harold Rome)
St. Louis Woman (Harold Arlen)
1947   Allegro (Richard Rodgers—Rodgers and Hammerstein)
Brigadoon (Frederick Loewe)
Finian's Rainbow (Burton Lane)
High Button Shoes (Jule Styne)
Street Scene (Kurt Weill)
1948   As the Girls Go (Jimmy McHugh)
Inside U.S.A. (Arthur Schwartz)
Kiss Me, Kate (Cole Porter)
Lend an Ear (*Charles Gaynor*)
Make Mine Manhattan (*Richard Lewine*)
Where's Charley? (Frank Loesser)
1949   Gentlemen Prefer Blondes (Jule Styne)
Lost in the Stars (Kurt Weill)
Miss Liberty (Irving Berlin)
Regina (Marc Blitzstein)
South Pacific (Richard Rodgers—Rodgers and Hammerstein)
1950   Call Me Madam (Irving Berlin)
Guys and Dolls (Frank Loesser)
1951   The King and I (Richard Rodgers—Rodgers and Hammerstein)
Paint Your Wagon (Frederick Loewe)
Top Banana (*Johnny Mercer*)
A Tree Grows in Brooklyn (Arthur Schwartz)
Two on the Aisle (Jule Styne)
1952   *New Faces of 1952* (various composers)
Wish You Were Here (Harold Rome)
1953   Can-Can (Cole Porter)
Kismet (Wright and Forrest)
Me and Juliet (Richard Rodgers—Rodgers and Hammerstein)
Wonderful Town (Leonard Bernstein)
1954   By the Beautiful Sea (Arthur Schwartz)
Fanny (Harold Rome)
The Girl in Pink Tights (Sigmund Romberg)
The Golden Apple (*Jerome Moross*)
House of Flowers (Harold Arlen)
The Pajama Game (Richard Adler)
1955   Damn Yankees (Richard Adler)
Pipe Dream (Richard Rodgers—Rodgers and Hammerstein)
Plain and Fancy (*Albert Hague*)
Silk Stockings (Cole Porter)
1956   Bells Are Ringing (Jule Styne)
Candide (Leonard Bernstein)
Happy Hunting (*Harold Karr*)
Li'l Abner (*Gene de Paul*)

The Most Happy Fella (Frank Loesser)
Mr. Wonderful (Block, Holofcener and Weiss)
My Fair Lady (Frederick Loewe)
1957 Jamaica (Harold Arlen)
The Music Man (Meredith Willson)
New Girl in Town (Bob Merrill)
West Side Story (Leonard Bernstein)
1958 *Oh, Captain! (Jay Livingston and Ray Evans)*

3

SOME OUTSTANDING SONGS OF THE AMERICAN MUSICAL THEATER * (AND THE PRODUCTIONS IN WHICH THEY WERE INTRODUCED)

"A Bushel and a Peck," introduced by Vivian Blaine in *Guys and Dolls* (Frank Loesser).

"A Fellow Needs a Girl," in *Allegro* (Richard Rodgers—II. Rodgers and Hammerstein).

"After the Ball," by Percy Gaunt, in *A Trip to Chinatown* (Appendix I—1893).

"Ah, Sweet Mystery of Life," introduced by Emma Trentini in *The Fortune Teller* (Victor Herbert).

"Alice Blue Gown," introduced by Edith Day in *Irene* (Harry Tierney).

"All Alone," introduced by Grace Moore in *The Music Box Revue* of 1924. (Irving Berlin).

"All of You," introduced by Don Ameche in *Silk Stockings* (Cole Porter).

"Almost Like Being in Love," in *Brigadoon* (Frederick Loewe and Alan Jay Lerner).

"Always True to You in My Fashion," in *Kiss Me, Kate* (Cole Porter).

"April in Paris," introduced by Evelyn Hoey in *Walk a Little Faster* (Cole Porter).

"April Showers," by Buddy de Sylva and Louis Silvers, introduced by Al Jolson in *Bombo* (Sigmund Romberg).

"A Puzzlement," introduced by Yul Brynner in *The King and I* (Richard Rodgers—II. Rodgers and Hammerstein).

"Auf Wiedersehen," introduced by Vivienne Segal and Cecil Lean in *The Blue Paradise* (Sigmund Romberg).

"Bambalina," introduced by Edith Day in *Wildflower* (Vincent Youmans).

"The Best Things in Life Are Free," in *Good News* (De Sylva, Brown, and Henderson).

* *Note:* Outstanding songs introduced in productions not discussed either in the main section nor in Appendix 1 are not listed below.

"Bewitched," introduced by Vivienne Segal in *Pal Joey* (Richard Rodgers—
I. Rodgers and Hart).

"Big D," in *The Most Happy Fella* (Frank Loesser).

"Bill," introduced by Helen Morgan in *Show Boat* (Jerome Kern).

"Birth of the Blues," in George White's *Scandals* of 1926 (De Sylva, Brown
Henderson).

"Black Bottom," introduced by Ann Pennington, in George White's *Scandals*
of 1926 (De Sylva, Brown, and Henderson).

"Blow, Gabriel, Blow," introduced by Ethel Merman in *Anything Goes* (Cole
Porter).

"Blue Heaven." See *Desert Song*.

"Blue Room," introduced by Eva Puck and Sam White in *The Girl Friend*
(Richard Rodgers—I. Rodgers and Hart).

"Body and Soul," introduced by Libby Holman in *Three's a Crowd* (Arthur
Schwartz).

"The Bowery," by Percy Gaunt, in *A Trip to Chinatown* (Appendix I—1893).

"Buckle Down, Winsocki," in *Best Foot Forward* (Appendix I—1941).

"But Not for Me," introduced by Ginger Rogers in *Girl Crazy* (George Gershwin).

"Button Up Your Overcoat," introduced by Jack Haley and Zelma O'Neal in
Follow Through (De Sylva, Brown, and Henderson).

"California, Here I Come," by Buddy de Sylva and Joseph Meyer, introduced
by Al Jolson in *Bombo* (Sigmund Romberg).

"Can't Help Lovin' That Man," introduced by Norma Terris in *Show Boat*
(Jerome Kern).

"Can't We Be Friends?" by Paul James and Kay Swift, introduced by Libby
Holman, in *The Little Show* (Arthur Schwartz).

"Carousel in the Park," in *Up in Central Park* (Sigmund Romberg).

"C'est Magnifique," introduced by Lilo in *Can-Can* (Cole Porter).

"Clap Yo' Hands," in *Oh Kay!* (George Gershwin).

"Close as Pages in a Book," in *Up in Central Park* (Sigmund Romberg).

"Cocoanut Sweet," introduced by Lena Horne in *Jamaica* (Harold Arlen).

"Come Down Ma' Evenin' Star," introduced by Lillian Russell in *Twirly-
Whirly* (John Stromberg).

"Come to Me, Bend to Me," in *Brigadoon* (Frederick Loewe and Alan Jay
Lerner).

"Cuddle Up a Little Closer," introduced by Bessie McCoy in *The Three Twins*
(Karl Hoschna).

"Dancing in the Dark," in *The Band Wagon* (Arthur Schwartz).

"Deep in My Heart," introduced by Ilse Marvenga and Howard Marsh in
The Student Prince (Sigmund Romberg).

"Desert Song" (Blue Heaven), introduced by Vivienne Segal and Robert
Halliday in *The Desert Song* (Sigmund Romberg).

"Diga, Diga, Doo," introduced by Adelaide Hall in *Blackbirds of 1928* (Jimmy
McHugh).

"Dinah," by Harry Akst, introduced by Eddie Cantor in *Kid Boots* (Harry
Tierney).

"Dinah" (Kiss Me Honey, Do), by Peter F. Dailey, in *Whirl-i-Gig* (John Stromberg).

"Do, Do, Do," introduced by Gertrude Lawrence in *Oh Kay!* (George Gershwin).

"Eadie Was a Lady," introduced by Ethel Merman in *Take a Chance* (Richard Whiting).

"Easter Parade," introduced by Marilyn Miller and Clifton Webb in *As Thousands Cheer* (Irving Berlin).

"Embraceable You," introduced by Ginger Rogers in *Girl Crazy* (George Gershwin).

"Everybody's Got a Home but Me," introduced by Judy Tyler in *Pipe Dream* (Richard Rodgers—II. Rodgers and Hammerstein).

"Everybody Step," introduced by the Brox Sisters in the *Music Box Revue* of 1921 (Irving Berlin).

"Every Little Movement Has a Meaning All Its Own," in *Madame Sherry* (Karl Hoschna).

"Falling in Love with Love," in *The Boys from Syracuse* (Richard Rodgers—I. Rodgers and Hart).

"Fascinating Rhythm," introduced by Fred and Adele Astaire in *Lady Be Good* (George Gershwin).

"Feudin' and Fightin'," in *Laffing Room Only* (Burton Lane).

"Georgette," by Lew Brown and Ray Henderson, in *The Greenwich Village Follies of 1922* (Raymond Hubbell).

"Giannina Mia," introduced by Emma Trentini in *The Firefly* (Rudolf Friml).

"Give My Regards to Broadway," introduced by George M. Cohan in *Little Johnny Jones* (George M. Cohan).

"Golden Days," introduced by Howard Marsh in *The Student Prince* (Sigmund Romberg).

"Good News," introduced by Zelma O'Neal in *Good News* (De Sylva, Brown, and Henderson).

"Green-Up Time," in *Love Life* (Kurt Weill).

"Gypsy Love Song" (Slumber On, My Little Gypsy Sweetheart), introduced by Eugene Cowles in *The Fortune Teller* (Victor Herbert).

"Hallelujah," in *Hit the Deck* (Vincent Youmans).

"Hello Central, Give Me No Man's Land," introduced by Al Jolson in *Sinbad* (Sigmund Romberg).

"Hello, Frisco, Hello," in *The Ziegfeld Follies* of 1915 (Louis Hirsch).

"Hello, Young Lovers," introduced by Gertrude Lawrence in *The King and I* (Richard Rodgers—II. Rodgers and Hammerstein).

"Here in My Arms," introduced by Helen Ford and Charles Purcell in *Dearest Enemy* (Richard Rodgers—I. Rodgers and Hart).

"Hernando's Hideaway," introduced by Carol Haney and John Raitt in *The Pajama Game* (Richard Adler and Jerry Ross).

"Hey, There," introduced by Janis Paige and John Raitt in *The Pajama Game* (Richard Adler and Jerry Ross).

"How Are Things in Glocca Morra?" introduced by Ella Logan in *Finian's Rainbow* (Burton Lane).

"I Can't Give You Anything but Love, Baby," in *Blackbirds of 1928* (Jimmy McHugh).

"I Could Have Danced All Night," introduced by Julie Andrews in *My Fair Lady* (Frederick Loewe and Alan Jay Lerner).

"I Could Write a Book," introduced by Gene Kelly and Leila Ernst in *Pal Joey* (Richard Rodgers—I. Rodgers and Hart).

"I Get a Kick Out of You," introduced by Ethel Merman in *Anything Goes* (Cole Porter).

"I Got Plenty of Nuttin'," introduced by Todd Duncan and Anne Brown in *Porgy and Bess* (George Gershwin).

"I Guess I'll Have to Change My Plan," introduced by Clifton Webb in *The Little Show* (Arthur Schwartz).

"I Just Can't Make My Eyes Behave," introduced by Anna Held in *A Parisian Model* (Appendix I—1906).

"If I Loved You," introduced by Jan Clayton and John Raitt in *Carousel* (Richard Rodgers—II. Rodgers and Hammerstein).

"I'll Build a Stairway to Paradise," in George White's *Scandals* of 1922 (George Gershwin).

"I'll Say She Does," by Buddy de Sylva, Gus Kahn, and Al Jolson, introduced by Al Jolson in *Sinbad* (Sigmund Romberg).

"I'm the Belle of New York," introduced by Edna May in *The Belle of New York* (Gustave Kerker).

"I'm Falling in Love with Someone," introduced by Orville Harrold in *The Fortune Teller* (Victor Herbert).

"I'm Forever Blowing Bubbles," by Jean Kenbrovin and John La Kellette in *The Passing Show* of 1918 (Sigmund Romberg).

"I'm Goin' South," by Abner Silver and Harry Woods, introduced by Al Jolson in *Bombo* (Sigmund Romberg).

"I'm Just Wild About Harry," in *Shuffle Along* (Appendix I—1921).

"I'm in Love with a Wonderful Guy," introduced by Mary Martin in *South Pacific* (Richard Rodgers—II. Rodgers and Hammerstein).

"I Love Paris," introduced by Lilo in *Can-Can* (Cole Porter).

"I Love You," in *Little Jessie James* (Appendix I—1923).

"I Love You," introduced by June Havoc in *Mexican Hayride* (Cole Porter).

"Indian Love Call," introduced by Mary Ellis and Dennis King in *Rose Marie* (Rudolf Friml).

"The Isle of Our Dreams," in *The Red Mill* (Victor Herbert).

"It Ain't Necessarily So," introduced by John W. Bubbles in *Porgy and Bess* (George Gershwin).

"Italian Street Song," introduced by Emma Trentini in *The Fortune Teller* (Victor Herbert).

"I've Got a Crush on You," in *Strike Up the Band* (George Gershwin).

"I've Got Five Dollars," introduced by Jack Whiting and Harriet Lake (Ann Sothern) in *America's Sweetheart* (Richard Rodgers—I. Rodgers and Hart).

"I've Got Rhythm," introduced by Ethel Merman in *Girl Crazy* (George Gershwin).

"I've Never Been in Love Before," introduced by Robert Alda and Isabel Bigley in *Guys and Dolls* (Frank Loesser).

"I've Told Every Little Star," introduced by Walter Slezak and Katherine Carrington in *Music in the Air* (Jerome Kern).

"I Want to Be Happy," in *No, No, Nanette* (Vincent Youmans).

"Jubilation T. Cornpone," introduced by Stubby Kaye in *Li'l Abner* (Appendix I—1956).

"June Is Bustin' Out All Over," in *Carousel* (Richard Rodgers—II. Rodgers and Hammerstein).

"Just in Time," introduced by Sydney Chaplin in *Bells Are Ringing* (Jule Styne).

"Ka-lu-a," in *Good Morning, Dearie* (Jerome Kern).

"Katie from Haiti," introduced by Ethel Merman in *Du Barry Was a Lady* (Cole Porter).

"Kiss Me Again," introduced by Fritzi Scheff in *Mlle Modiste* (Victor Herbert).

"Kiss Me Honey, Do." See *Dinah*.

"The Lady Is a Tramp," introduced by Mitzi Green in *Babes in Arms* (Richard Rodgers—I. Rodgers and Hart).

"Lady of the Evening," introduced by John Steele in *The Music Box Revue* of 1922 (Irving Berlin).

"Liza," introduced by Ruby Keeler in *Show Girl* (George Gershwin).

"Long Before I Knew You," introduced by Sydney Chaplin in *Bells Are Ringing* (Jule Styne).

"Look for the Silver Lining," introduced by Marilyn Miller and Irving Fisher in *Sally* (Jerome Kern).

"Look to the Rainbow," introduced by Ella Logan in *Finian's Rainbow* (Burton Lane).

"Love Me or Leave Me," introduced by Ruth Etting in *Whoopee* (Appendix I —1928).

"Love Nest," introduced by Jack McGowan in *Mary* (Louis Hirsch).

"Lover, Come Back to Me," introduced by Evelyn Herbert in *The New Moon* (Sigmund Romberg).

"Makin' Whoopee," introduced by Eddie Cantor in *Whoopee* (Appendix I— 1928).

"Mammy," by Joe Young, Sam M. Lewis and Walter Donaldson, introduced by Al Jolson in *Sinbad* (Sigmund Romberg).

"Mandy," introduced by Marilyn Miller in *The Ziegfeld Follies* of 1919 (Irving Berlin), originally in *Yip, Yip Yaphank* (Irving Berlin).

"Manhattan," introduced by June Cochrane and Sterling Holloway in *The Garrick Gaieties* of 1925 (Richard Rodgers—I. Rodgers and Hart).

"March of the Toys," in *Babes in Toyland* (Victor Herbert).

"Mary's a Grand Old Name," introduced by Donald Brian in *Forty-Five Minutes from Broadway* (George M. Cohan).

"Melody in 4-F," by Sylvia Fine and Max Liebman, introduced by Danny Kaye in *Let's Face It* (Cole Porter).

"The Message of the Violet," in *The Prince of Pilsen* (Gustav Luders).

"Mine," introduced by William Gaxton in *Of Thee I Sing* (George Gershwin).

"Moanin' Low," introduced by Libby Holman in *The Little Show* (Arthur Schwartz).

"Moonbeams," in *The Red Mill* (Victor Herbert).

"The Most Beautiful Girl in the World," in *Jumbo* (Richard Rodgers—I. Rodgers and Hart).

"Mr. Wonderful," in *Mr. Wonderful* (Appendix I—1956).

"Mutual Admiration Society," introduced by Ethel Merman and Virginia Gibson in *Happy Hunting* (Appendix I—1956).

"My Baby Just Cares for Me," introduced by Eddie Cantor in *Whoopee* (Appendix I—1928).

"My Beautiful Lady," introduced by Hazel Dawn in *The Pink Lady* (Ivan Caryll).

"My Darling," in *Where's Charley?* (Frank Loesser).

"My Funny Valentine," introduced by Mitzi Green in *Babes in Arms* (Richard Rodgers—I. Rodgers and Hart).

"My Heart Belongs to Daddy," introduced by Mary Martin in *Leave It to Me* (Cole Porter).

"My Man," by Maurice Yvain, adapted by Channing Pollock, introduced by Fanny Brice in the *Ziegfeld Follies* of 1921 (Appendix I—1907).

"My Romance," in *Jumbo* (Richard Rodgers—I. Rodgers and Hart).

"My Ship," introduced by Gertrude Lawrence in *Lady in the Dark* (Kurt Weill).

"Night and Day," introduced by Fred Astaire in *The Gay Divorce* (Cole Porter).

"The Night Was Made for Love," in *The Cat and the Fiddle* (Jerome Kern).

"No Other Love," introduced by Bill Hayes and Isabel Bigley in *Me and Juliet* (Richard Rodgers—II. Rodgers and Hammerstein).

"Of Thee I Sing," introduced by William Gaxton and Lois Moran in *Of Thee I Sing* (George Gershwin).

"Oh, How I Hate to Get Up in the Morning," introduced by Irving Berlin in *Yip, Yip, Yaphank* (Irving Berlin).

"Ohio," introduced by Rosalind Russell and Edith Adams in *Wonderful Town* (Leonard Bernstein).

"Oh, Lady Be Good," introduced by Walter Catlett in *Lady Be Good* (George Gershwin).

"Oh, Promise Me," introduced by Jesse Bartlett Davis in *Robin Hood* (Reginald De Koven).

"Oh, What a Beautiful Mornin'," introduced by Alfred Drake in *Oklahoma!* (Richard Rodgers—II. Rodgers and Hammerstein).

"Ol' Man River," introduced by Jules Bledsoe in *Show Boat* (Jerome Kern).

"Once in Love With Amy," introduced by Ray Bolger in *Where's Charley?* (Frank Loesser).

"One Alone," introduced by Robert Halliday in *The Desert Song* (Sigmund Romberg).

"One Kiss," introduced by Evelyn Herbert in *The New Moon* (Sigmund Romberg).

"Only a Rose," in *The Vagabond King* (Rudolf Friml).

"On the Street Where You Live," in *My Fair Lady* (Frederick Loewe and Alan Jay Lerner).

"Pack Up Your Sins," introduced by the McCarthy Sisters in *The Music Box Revue* of 1924 (Irving Berlin).

"People Will Say We're in Love," introduced by Alfred Drake and Joan Roberts in *Oklahoma!* (Richard Rodgers—II. Rodgers and Hammerstein).

"A Pretty Girl Is Like a Melody," in *The Ziegfeld Follies* of 1919 (Irving Berlin).

"Reuben, Reuben," by Percy Gaunt, in *A Trip to Chinatown* (Appendix I—1893).

"Rio Rita," introduced by Ethelind Terry and J. Harold Murray in *Rio Rita* (Harry Tierney).

"Rise 'n Shine," by Vincent Youmans, introduced by Ethel Merman in *Take a Chance* (Richard Whiting).

"Rock-a-bye Your Baby With a Dixie Melody," by Joe Young, Sam M. Lewis, and Jean Schwartz, introduced by Al Jolson in *Sinbad* (Sigmund Romberg).

"Rose Marie," introduced by Dennis King and Arthur Deagon in *Rose Marie* (Rudolf Friml).

"Row, Row, Row," introduced by Lillian Lorraine in *The Ziegfeld Follies* of 1912 (Raymond Hubbell).

"Saga of Jenny," introduced by Gertrude Lawrence in *Lady in the Dark* (Kurt Weill).

"Sam and Delilah," introduced by Ethel Merman in *Girl Crazy* (George Gershwin).

"Say It With Music," introduced by Wilda Bennett and Paul Frawley in *The Music Box Revue* of 1921 (Irving Berlin).

"Second Hand Rose," by Grant Clarke and James F. Hanley, introduced by Fanny Brice in *The Ziegfeld Follies* of 1921 (Appendix I—1907).

"September Song," introduced by Walter Huston in *Knickerbocker Holiday* (Kurt Weill).

"Serenade," introduced by Howard Marsh in *The Student Prince* (Sigmund Romberg).

"She Didn't Say Yes," introduced by Bettina Hall in *The Cat and the Fiddle* (Jerome Kern).

"Shine On, Harvest Moon," introduced by Nora Bayes in *The Ziegfeld Follies* of 1908 (Appendix I—1907).

"Show Business," in *Annie Get Your Gun* (Irving Berlin).

"Sing Something Simple," by Herman Hupfeld, in *The Second Little Show* (Arthur Schwartz).

"Siren's Song," introduced by Edith Hallor in *Leave It to Jane* (Jerome Kern).

"Slumber On, My Little Gypsy Sweetheart," see *Gypsy Love Song*.

"Smiles," by J. Will Callahan and Lee M. Roberts, in *The Passing Show* of 1918 (Sigmund Romberg).

"Smoke Gets in Your Eyes," introduced by Tamara in *Roberta* (Jerome Kern).

"Soft Lights and Sweet Music," in *Face the Music* (Irving Berlin).

"Softly as in a Morning Sunrise," in *The New Moon* (Sigmund Romberg).

"So in Love Am I," in *Kiss Me, Kate* (Cole Porter).

"Soliloquy," introduced by John Raitt in *Carousel* (Richard Rodgers—II. Rodgers and Hammerstein).

"So Long, Mary," introduced by Donald Brian in *Forty-Five Minutes from Broadway* (George M. Cohan).

"Some Enchanted Evening," introduced by Ezio Pinza in *South Pacific* (Richard Rodgers—II. Rodgers and Hammerstein).

"Someone to Watch Over Me," introduced by Gertrude Lawrence in *Oh Kay!* (George Gershwin).

"Something to Remember You By," introduced by Libby Holman in *Three's a Crowd* (Arthur Schwartz).

"Sometimes I'm Happy," introduced by Louise Groody and Charles King in *Hit the Deck* (Vincent Youmans).

"The Song Is You," introduced by Tullio Carminati in *Music in the Air* (Jerome Kern).

"Song of Love," in *Blossom Time* (Sigmund Romberg).

"Song of the Vagabonds," in *The Vagabond King* (Rudolf Friml).

"Song of the Woodman," by E. Y. Harburg and Harold Arlen, introduced by Bert Lahr in *The Show Is On* (Appendix I—1936).

"Soon," introduced by Margaret Schillings in *Strike Up the Band* (George Gershwin).

"South America, Take It Away," introduced by Betty Garrett in *Call Me Mister* (Harold Rome).

"Spring Is Here," introduced by Vivienne Segal and Dennis King in *I Married an Angel* (Richard Rodgers—I. Rodgers and Hart).

"Standin' on the Corner," in *The Most Happy Fella* (Frank Loesser).

"Stout-Hearted Men," in *The New Moon* (Sigmund Romberg).

"Strange Music," in *The Song of Norway* (Robert Wright and George Forrest).

"Stranger in Paradise," in *Kismet* (Robert Wright and George Forrest).

"Strike Up the Band," in *Strike Up the Band* (George Gershwin).

"Summertime," introduced by Abbe Mitchell in *Porgy and Bess* (George Gershwin).

"Sunshine Girl," in *New Girl in Town* (Appendix I—1957).

"Swanee," by Irving Caesar and George Gershwin, introduced by Al Jolson in *Sinbad* (Sigmund Romberg).

"Sweethearts," introduced by Christine McDonald in *Sweethearts* (Victor Herbert).

"Sweet Lady," by Howard Johnson, Frank Crumit, and David Zoob, introduced by Julia Sanderson in *Tangerine* (Appendix I—1921).

"'S Wonderful," introduced by Allen Kearns and Adele Astaire in *Funny Face* (George Gershwin).

"Take It Slow, Joe," introduced by Lena Horne in *Jamaica* (Harold Arlen).

"Tammany," by Vincent Bryan and Gus Edwards in *Fantana* (Raymond Hubbell).

"Tchaikovsky," introduced by Danny Kaye in *Lady in the Dark* (Kurt Weill).

"Tea for Two," in *No, No, Nanette* (Vincent Youmans).

"There's a Small Hotel," introduced by Ray Bolger and Doris Carson in *On Your Toes* (Richard Rodgers—I. Rodgers and Hart).

"They Didn't Believe Me," introduced by Julia Sanderson in *The Girl from Utah* (Jerome Kern).

"This Is My Beloved," introduced by Doretta Morrow in *Kismet* (Robert Wright and George Forrest).

"Tickle Toe," introduced by Edith Day in *Going Up* (Louis Hirsch).

"Till the Clouds Roll By," in *Oh Boy!* (Jerome Kern).

"To Keep My Love Alive," introduced by Vivienne Segal in *Pal Joey,* 1943 revival (Richard Rodgers—I. Rodgers and Hart).

"Too Close for Comfort," introduced by Sammy Davis, Jr., in *Mr. Wonderful* (Appendix I—1956).

"Toot, Toot, Tootsie," by Gus Kahn, Ernie Friedman and Dan Russo, introduced by Al Jolson in *Bombo* (Sigmund Romberg).

"The Touch of Your Hand," in *Roberta* (Jerome Kern).

"Toyland," in *Babes in Toyland* (Victor Herbert).

"The Vamp from East Broadway," by Bert Kalmar and Harry Ruby, introduced by Fanny Brice in *The Ziegfeld Follies* of 1920 (Appendix I—1907).

"Varsity Drag," introduced by Zelma O'Neal in *Good News* (De Sylva, Brown, and Henderson).

"Waltz Huquette," in *The Vagabond King* (Rudolf Friml).

"I Wanna Be Loved by You," introduced by Helen Kane in *Good Boy* (Harry Ruby).

"Wanting You," introduced by Robert Halliday in *The Desert Song* (Sigmund Romberg).

"Whatever Lola Wants," introduced by Gwen Verdon in *Damn Yankees* (Richard Adler and Jerry Ross).

"What'll I Do?" introduced by Grace Moore in *The Music Box Revue* of 1923 (Irving Berlin).

"When Chloe Sings a Song," introduced by Lillian Russell in *Whirl-i-gig* (John Stromberg).

"When Hearts Are Young," by Sigmund Romberg, introduced by Wilda Bennett in *Lady in Ermine* (Appendix I—1922).

"When a Maid Comes Knocking at Your Heart," introduced by Emma Trentini in *The Firefly* (Rudolf Friml).

"Where or When?" introduced by Mitzi Green and Ray Heatherton in *Babes in Arms* (Richard Rodgers—I. Rodgers and Hart).

"Who?" introduced by Marilyn Miller and Paul Frawley in *Sunny* (Jerome Kern).

"Why Do I Love You?" in *Show Boat* (Jerome Kern).

"Wildflower," introduced by Guy Robertson in *Wildflower* (Vincent Youmans).

"Will You Remember?" introduced by Peggy Wood and Charles Purcell in *Maytime* (Sigmund Romberg).

"Wish You Were Here," introduced by Jack Cassidy in *Wish You Were Here* (Arthur Schwartz).

"Yacka Hula, Hickey Doola," by E. Ray Goetz, Jose Young, and Pete Wendling, introduced by Al Jolson in *Robinson Crusoe, Jr.* (Sigmund Romberg).

"Yankee Doodle Dandy," introduced by George M. Cohan in *Little Johnny Jones* (George M. Cohan).

"Yama-Yama Man," introduced by Bessie McCoy in *The Three Twins* (Karl Hoschna).

"Yesterday," in *Roberta* (Jerome Kern).

"You Do Something to Me," introduced by William Gaxton in *Fifty Million Frenchmen* (Cole Porter).

"You'll Never Walk Alone," introduced by Christine Johnson in *Carousel* (Richard Rodgers—II. Rodgers and Hammerstein).

"Young and Foolish," introduced by Gloria Marlowe and David Daniels in *Plain and Fancy* (Appendix I—1955).

"You're the Cream in My Coffee," introduced by Jack Whiting in *Hold Everything* (De Sylva, Brown, and Henderson).

"You're a Grand Old Flag," introduced by George M. Cohan in *George Washington, Jr.* (George M. Cohan).

"You're Here and I'm Here," introduced by Julia Sanderson in *The Girl from Utah* (Jerome Kern).

"You're Just in Love," introduced by Ethel Merman and Russell Nype in *Call Me Madam* (Irving Berlin).

"You're an Old Smoothie," introduced by Ethel Merman and Jack Haley in *Take a Chance* (Richard Whiting).

"You're the Top," introduced by Ethel Merman and William Gaxton in *Anything Goes* (Cole Porter).

"You Took Advantage of Me," in *Present Arms* (Richard Rodgers—I. Rodgers and Hart).

INDEX